-CIRCULATING

The Films of the Seventies

The Films of the Seventies

A Filmography of American, British and Canadian Films 1970–1979

MARC SIGOLOFF

McFarland & Company, Inc., Publishers
Jefferson, N.C., & London

*For my Mother and Father
and Tiger*

Library of Congress Cataloging in Publication Data

Sigoloff, Marc.
Films of the seventies.

Includes index.
1. Moving-pictures—Dictionaries. I. Title.
II. Title: Films of the 70s.
PN1993.45.S53 1984   791.43'75   83-42887

ISBN 0-89950-095-1

Manufactured in the United States of America

McFarland   Box 611   Jefferson NC 28640

Table of Contents

Introduction

The purpose of *The Films of the Seventies: A Filmography of American, British and Canadian Films 1970–1979* is to present an overview of the decade, concentrating on mainstream filmmaking. Some exploitation films such as sex-oriented and low-budget independent ones, and also animated films and documentaries, are excluded because they are out of the mainstream and serve no purpose here.

Many exploitation films are included, however, because they have either broken through their origins or were early works by filmmakers who have themselves achieved major status.

For the Anglo-American cinema, the 1970's seems to be a most misunderstood and maligned of decades. The critical consensus during this period seems to have been that each successive year was the worst since the beginning of time. While perhaps movies had, in some cases, reached new lows, it is the compiler's contention that they had in fact achieved new highs, with such masterpieces as *Barry Lyndon*, *Apocalypse Now*, *A Clockwork Orange*, *The Godfather* films, *Taxi Driver* and *The Deer Hunter*.

Cinema is an art form, but few people in Hollywood realized it until recent years. While there were a few gems among the rubble in Hollywood's so-called Golden Age, most movies tended toward pretentiousness and superficiality and were populated by caricatures rather than characters.

This was not the case in Europe. Since its inception the cinema of Europe had put Hollywood to shame. Suddenly there was a reversal in the 1970's. Europe fell on hard times and Hollywood had finally arrived. Change tends to generate adverse reactions, particularly when it occurs suddenly, and this shift toward art ironically antagonized the American critical establishment. What was acceptable from European directors was not from Americans.

It is time to begin to set the record straight of the American cinema's most fascinating and productive decade to date. Because of the many connections, not least that of language, among Britain, Canada and the United States in the making of movies, the output of all three is included.

Explanation of Listings

Ratings

***** superb
**** excellent
*** good
** mediocre
* poor

Abbreviations

Art   art director
Assoc associate
Chor choreographer
Cin cinematographer
Cos costume designer
Des production designer
Dir director
Ed editor
Exec executive
Min minutes running time
Mus composer
Prod producer
Scr screenwriter
Sp special effects
UN uncredited

Awards

A   Academy Award
AN Academy Award Nomination
NS National Society of Film Critics Award
NY New York Film Critics Award
G Golden Globe Award
GMC Golden Globe Award–Musical or Comedy
LA Los Angeles Film Critics Award
BFA British Academy Award

D   Directors Guild Award
W   Writers Guild Award
CF   Cannes Film Festival Award
BF   Berlin Film Festival Award

Following the cast and credits of each film are the Motion Picture Association of America (MPAA) rating of G, PG (previously GP and M), R or X, and the domestic (U.S. and Canada) box-office rentals, which is the box-office gross minus the theatres' expenses and share. Only those with a rental figure of at least $4 million are acknowledged, as per the source, *Variety*. All figures are as of January 1982, and are rounded off to the nearest $5,000.

Each film listing includes a brief summary of major plot details and characters and an evaluation of its virtues or flaws. Naturally an in-depth analysis of this many films is impossible in a single volume.

The Films, Alphabetically

1 **The Abdication** (1974) * Britain, Warner Bros., 103 min. *Dir* Anthony Harvey, *Scr* Ruth Wolff based on her play, *Cin* Geoffrey Unsworth, *Ed* John Bloom, *Des* Terry Marsh, *Art* Alan Tomkins, *Cos* Farani, Peter J. Hall, *Mus* Nino Rota, *Prod* James Cresson, Robert Fryer, *Assoc Prod* William Hill.

Cast: Peter Finch, *Azzolino,* Liv Ullman, *Queen Christina,* Cyral Cusack, *Oxenstierna,* Paul Rogers, *Altieri,* Graham Crowden, *Barberini,* Michael Dunn, *The Dwarf,* Kathleen Byron, *Queen Mother,* Lewis Flander, *Dominic,* Harold Goldblatt, *Pinamonti,* Tony Steedman, *Carranza,* Noel Trevarthen, *Ginetti,* Richard Cornish, *Charles,* James Faulkner, *Magnus,* Ania Marson, *Ebba,* Franz Drago, *Birgito,* Suzanne Huddart, *Young Christina,* Debbie Nicholson, *Young Ebba,* Edward Underdown, *Christina's Father.* PG.

Boring historical drama about the abdication of Queen Christina of Sweden in 1654. Drama probably is the wrong term to use to describe *The Abdication,* as very little occurs other than Christina's contemplation of the less than earth-shattering question whether to convert to Catholicism and abdicate the throne. This may have succeeded as a play, but on screen it becomes very boring.

2 **The Abominable Dr. Phibes** (1971) *** Britain, American International, 93 min. *Dir* Robert Fuest, *Scr* William Goldstein, James Whiton, *Cin* Norman Warwick, *Ed* Tristam Cones, *Des* Brian Eatwell, *Art* Bernard Reeves, *Cos* Elsa Fennell, *Mus* Basil Kirchin, *Prod* Ronald S. Dunas, Louis M. Heyward, *Exec Prod* Samuel Z. Arkoff, James H. Nicholson.

Cast: Vincent Price, *Dr. Anton Phibes,* Joseph Cotten, *Dr. Vesalius,* Hugh Griffith, *Rabbi,* Terry-Thomas, *Dr. Longstreet,* Virginia North, *Vulnavia,* Audrey Woods, *Goldsmith,* Susan Travers, *Nurse Allan,* Alex Scott, *Dr. Hargreaves,* Edward Burnham, *Dr. Dunwoody,* Peter Gilmore, *Dr. Kitaj,* Peter Jeffrey, *Inspector Trout,* Maurice Kaufman, *Dr. Whitcombe,* Norman Jones, *Sgt. Schenley,* John Cater, *Waverly,* Derek Godfrey, *Crow,* Sean Bury, *Lem Vesalius,* Walter Horsbrugh, *Ross,* Barbara Keogh, *Mrs. Frawley,* David Hutcheson, *Dr. Hedgepath,* Caroline Munro, *Victoria Phibes.* PG.

Campy horror thriller starring Vincent Price as a disfigured madman, who goes on a bizarre murder spree to seek revenge for the death of his wife. The film's highlights are the several ingenious murders, which are executed with a sense of humor. Price gives a wonderfully hammy performance, in one of his finest horror roles. The success of this film prompted a sequel, *Dr. Phibes Rises Again,* which was similar to the first and every bit its equal.

3 **Aces High** (1977) *** Britain, Cinema Shares, 114 min. *Dir* Jack Gold, *Scr* Howard Barker, based on play *Journey's End* by R.C. Sheriff, *Cin* Peter Allwork, *Ed* Anne Coates, *Mus* Richard Hartley, *Prod* S. Benjamin Fisz.

Cast: Malcolm McDowell, *Gresham*, Christopher Plummer, *Sinclair*, Simon Ward, *Crawford*, Peter Firth, *Croft*, John Gielgud, *Headmaster*, Trevor Howard, *Lt. Col. Silkin*, Richard Johnson, *Col. Lyle*, Ray Milland, *Brigadier Whale*, David Wood, *Thompson*, David Daker, *Bennett*, Elliot Cooper, *Wade*, Pascale Christophe, *Croft's Girl Friend*, Jeanne Patou, *Chanteuse*. PG.

Average anti-war drama centering on a group of British WWI aerial combat pilots. Being based on a stage play, *Aces High* relies more on talk than on action, although there are some fine aerial scenes. The excellent British cast is headed by Malcolm McDowell as the cynical squadron leader and Peter Firth as the new member of the group. This was filmed previously as *Journey's End* (1930).

4 **Across 110th Street** (1972) **** United Artists, 102 min. *Dir* Barry Shear, *Scr* Luther Davis, based on novel by Wally Ferris, *Cin* Jack Priestley, *Ed* Bryon "Buzz" Brandt, *Art* Perry Watkins, *Cos* Joe Fretwell, *Mus* J.J. Johnson, *Songs* Bobby Womack, *Prod* Fouad Said, Ralph Serpe, *Exec Prod* Anthony Quinn, Barry Shear, *Assoc Prod* Richard Stenta.

Cast: Anthony Quinn, *Capt. Mattelli*, Yaphet Kotto, *Lt. Pope*, Anthony Franciosa, *Nick D'Salvio*, Paul Benjamin, *Jim Harris*, Ed Bernard, *Joe Logart*, Richard Ward, *Doc Johnson*, Norma Donaldson, *Gloria Roberts*, Antonio Fargas, *Henry J. Jackson*, Gilbert Lewis, *Shevvy*, Marlene Warfield, *Mrs. Jackson*, Nat Polen, *Lt. Reilly*, Tim O'Connor, *Lt. Hatnett*. R.

Extremely violent, but excellent, crime thriller about three men who stupidly rob the Mafia. The suspense is riveting as the police attempt to find the crooks before the Mafia does. *Across 110th Street* is different from many of the "blaxploitation" films of the early 1970's. While it does acknowledge racism, it is not itself racist; many of these other films had what was known as a "get whitey" theme. This film has more balance in its attitude, and for this reason rises above the others.

5 **Act of the Heart** (1970) ** Canada, Universal, 103 min. *Dir* Paul Almond, *Scr* Paul Almond, *Cin* Jean Boffety, *Ed* James D. Mitchell, *Art* Anne Pritchard, *Mus* Harry Freedman, *Prod* Paul Almond, Presented by Jennings Lang.

Cast: Genevieve Bujold, *Martha Hayes*, Donald Sutherland, *Father Michael Ferrier*, Monique Leyrac, *Johane Foss*, Bill Mitchell, *Russell Foss*, Suzanne Langlois, *Housekeeper*, Sharon Acker, *Adele*, Ratch Wallace, *Diedrich*, Jean Duceppe, *Parks Commissioner*, Gilles Vigneault, *Coach Ti-Jo*, Eric House, *Choirmaster*. PG.

Strange drama about a religious farm girl (Genevieve Bujold), who goes to Montreal to earn money for her parents. She is chosen to sing in a choir by an Augustinian monk (Donald Sutherland). Their relationship leads to a love affair which causes her to have a breakdown. *Act of The Heart* is a well-made and well-acted story, but it stretches credibility at times, particularly in the tragic ending.

6 **Adam at 6 A.M.** (1970) *** National General, 100 min. *Dir* Robert Scheerer, *Scr* Stephen and Elinor Karpf, *Cin* Charles Rosher, *Ed* Jack

McSweeney, *Art* Dale Hennessey, *Cos* Joanne Haas, Ray Summers, *Prod* Robert Christiansen, Rick Rosenberg, *Exec Prod* Robert E. Relyea.

Cast: Michael Douglas, *Adam Gaines*, Lee Purcell, *Jerri Jo Hopper*, Joe Don Baker, *Harvey Gavin*, Grayson Hall, *Inez Treadley*, Charles Aidman, *Mr. Hopper*, Marge Redmond, *Cleo*, Louise Latham, *Mrs. Hopper*, Carolyn Conwell, *Mavis*, Dana Elcar, *Van*, Meg Foster, *Joyce*, Richard Derr, *Roger Gaines*, Ann Gwynn, *Mrs. Gaines*, Ned Wertheimer, *Dr. Peters*, Ed Call, *Orville*, David Sullivan, *Leroy*, Butch Youngblood, *Elwood*, Bud Trone, *Ray*, Jim Lantz, *Strawboss*, Pat Randall, *Pearlie*, Jo Ella Defenbaugh, *Marylist*, Sharon Marshall, *Rosalie*. PG.

Fine drama about a liberal college professor who travels to Missouri for an aunt's funeral. Being disillusioned with the superficial people from back home he decides to go out into the real world. He gets a job with a power company road crew, only to learn that these so-called real people can be just as false as those he left in California. Michael Douglas is excellent in one of his few starring roles.

7 **The Adventure of Sherlock Holmes' Smarter Brother** (1975) ** 20th Century–Fox, 91 min. *Dir* Gene Wilder, *Scr* Gene Wilder, *Cin* Gerry Fisher, *Ed* Jim Clark, *Des* Terry Marsh, *Cos* Ruth Myers, *Mus* John Morris, *Chor* Alan Johnson, *Prod* Richard A. Roth.

Cast: Gene Wilder, *Sigerson Holmes*, Madeline Kahn, *Jenny*, Marty Feldman, *Orville Sacker*, Dom DeLuise, *Gambetti*, Leo McKern, *Moriarty*, Roy Kinnear, *Moriarty's Aide*, John LeMeasurier, *Lord Redcliff*, Douglas Wilmer, *Sherlock Holmes*, Thorley Walters, *Dr. Watson*, George Silver, *Bruner*, Susan Field, *Queen Victoria*, PG. $9,400,000

Disappointing spoof of Sherlock Holmes. Gene Wilder was the first graduate of the Mel Brooks school of comedy and proved that he could be just as sophomoric as his mentor. What could have been a classy and witty comedy is little more than a low "Three Stooges" style comedy. There are some laughs, but children will likely appreciate this more than adults.

8 **The Adventurers** (1970) * Paramount, 171 min. *Dir* Lewis Gilbert, *Scr* Lewis Gilbert, Michael Hastings, based on novel by Harold Robbins, *Cin* Claude Renoir, *Ed* Anne V. Coates, *Des* Tony Masters, *Art* Aurelio Crugnola, John Hoesli, Jack Maxsted, Harry Pottle, *Cos* Ronald Paterson, *Mus* Antonio Carlos Jobim, *Prod* Lewis Gilbert, Presented by Joseph E. Levine.

Cast: Bekim Fehmiu, *Dax Xenos*, Charles Aznavour, *Marcel Campion*, Alan Badel, *Rojo*, Candice Bergen, *Sue Ann Daley*, Thommy Berggren, *Sergei Nikovitch*, Delia Boccardo, *Caroline de Coyne*, Ernest Borgnine, *Fat Cat*, Rossano Brazzi, *Baron de Coyne*, Olivia de Havilland, *Deborah Hadley*, Anna Moffo, *Dania Leonardi*, Leigh Taylor-Young, *Amparo*, Christian Roberts, *Robert*, Yorgo Voyagis, *El Lobo*, Fernando Rey, *Jaime Xenos*, John Ireland, *Mr. Hadley*, Jorge Martinez de Hoyos, *El Condor*, Sydney Tafler, *Col. Gutierrez*. PG. $7,750,000

Dull film adaptation of the Harold Robbins bestseller set in a fictional South American country plagued by revolutions. *The Adventurers* is just another big, overproduced, overlong and overeverything cinematic soap opera. Robbins' potboiler novels have never been translated into intelligent films and this one is certainly no exception. The large all-star cast has been completely wasted on this travesty.

9 **Agatha** (1979) ******* Britain, Warner Bros., 98 min. *Dir* Michael Apted, *Scr* Arthur Hopcraft, Kathleen Tynan, based on the story by Kathleen Tynan, *Cin* Vittorio Storaro, *Ed* Jim Clark, *Des* Shirley Russell, *Art* Sim Holland, *Mus* Johnny Mandel, *Prod* Jarvis Astaire, Gavrick Losey.

Cast: Vanessa Redgrave, *Agatha Christie*, Dustin Hoffman (NS), *Wally Stanton*, Timothy Dalton, *Archie Christie*, Helen Morse, *Evelyn*, Celia Gregory, *Nancy Neele*, Tony Britton, *William Collins*, Timothy West, *Kenwood*, Alan Badel, *Lord Brackenbury*. PG.

A fictional account of the real-life disappearance of mystery novelist Agatha Christie for eleven days in 1926. Those looking for a good mystery will be greatly disappointed as it fails on this point. The Christie-style twist ending seems extraneous to the main action and proves to be anti-climactic. Where *Agatha* does succeed, somewhat, is as a love story, particulary due to the performances of Redgrave and Hoffman.

10 **Airport** (1970) (AN) ****** Universal, 137 min. *Dir* George Seaton, *Dir (Additional Sequences)*, Henry Hathaway, *Scr* George Seaton (AN), based on novel by Arthur Hailey, *Cin* Ernest Laszlo (AN), *Ed* Stuart Gilmore (AN), *Art* Preston Ames, Alexander Golitzen (AN), *Cos* Edith Head (AN), *Mus* Alfred Newman (AN), *Prod* Ross Hunter, *Assoc Prod* Jacque Mapes.

Cast: Burt Lancaster, *Mel Bakersfield*, Dean Martin, *Vernon Demerest*, Jean Seberg, *Tanya Livingston*, Jacqueline Bisset, *Gwen Meighen*, George Kennedy, *Patroni*, Helen Hayes (A), *Ada Quonsett*, Van Heflin, *D.O. Guerrero*, Maureen Stapleton (AN,G), *Inez Guerrero*, Barry Nelson, *Lt. Anson Harris*, Dana Wynter, *Cindy*, Lloyd Nolan, *Harry Standish*, Barbara Hale, *Sarah*, Gary Collins, *Cy Jordan*, John Findlater, *Peter Coakley*, Jessie Royce Landis, *Mrs. Harriet DuBarry Mossman*, Larry Gates, *Commissioner Ackerman*, Peter Turgeon, *Marcus Rathbone*, Whit Bissell, *Mr. Davidson*, Virginia Grey, *Mrs. Schultz*, Eileen Wesson, *Judy*, Paul Picerni, *Dr. Compagno*, Robert Patten, *Capt. Benson*, Clark Howat, *Bert Weatherby*, Lew Brown, *Reynolds*, Ilana Dowding, *Roberta Bakersfield*, Lisa Garritson, *Libby Bakersfield*, Jim Nolan, *Father Lonigan*. G. $45,300,000

Silly disaster film focusing on the goings-on at a large airport and the numerous people involved. This "Grand Hotel" of the sky is nothing more than a dull soap opera that is completely blown out of proportion. The success of *Airport* not only prompted three even sillier sequels, *Airport 1975*, *Airport '77* and *The Concorde–Airport '79*, but it spawned an entire unintelligent genre.

11 **Airport 1975** (1974) ****** Universal, 107 min. *Dir* Jack Smight, *Scr* Don Ingalls, inspired by film *Airport* and based upon novel by Arthur Hailey, *Cin* Philip Lathrop, *Ed* J. Terry Williams, *Art* George C. Webb, *Cos* Edith Head, *Mus* John Cacavas, *Song* R. Burton, Helen Reddy, performed by Helen Reddy, *Prod* William Frye, *Exec Prod* Jennings Lang.

Cast: Charlton Heston, *Murdock*, Karen Black, *Nancy*, George Kennedy, *Patroni*, Efrem Zimbalist, Jr., *Stacy*, Gloria Swanson, *Herself*, Susan Clark, *Mrs. Patroni*, Helen Reddy, *Sister Ruth*, Linda Blair, *Janice*, Dana Andrews, *Scott Freeman*, Roy Thinnes, *Urias*, Sid Caesar, *Barney*, Myrna Loy, *Mrs. Devaney*, Ed Nelson, *Maj. Alexander*, Nancy Olson, *Mrs. Abbott*, Larry Storch, *Purcell*, Martha Scott, *Sister Beatrice*, Jerry Stiller, *Sam*, Norman Fell, *Bill*,

Conrad Janis, *Arnie*, Beverly Garland, *Mrs. Scott Freeman*, Augusta Summerland, *Winnie*, Guy Stockwell, *Col. Moss*, Erik Estrada, *Julio*, Kip Niven, *Lt. Thatcher*, Charles White, *Fat Man*, Brian Morrison, *Joseph*, Amy Farrell, *Amy*, Irene Tsu, *Carol*, Ken Sansom, *Gary*, Alan Fudge, *Danton*, Christopher Norris, *Bette*, Austin Stoker, *Air Force Sergeant*, John Lupton, *Oringer*, Gene Dynarski, *First Friend*, Aldine King, *Aldine*, Sharon Gless, *Sharon*, Laurette Spang, Arlene. PG. $25,805,000.

See *Airport.*

12 **Airport '77** (1977) * Universal, 113 min. *Dir* Jerry Jameson, *Scr* Michael Scheff, David Spector, inspired by film *Airport* and based on novel by Arthur Hailey, *Cin* Philip Lathrop, *Ed* Robert Watts, J. Terry Williams, *Des* George C. Webb (AN), *Cos* Edith Head, Burton Miller (AN), *Mus* John Cacavas, *Prod* William Frye, *Exec Prod* Jennings Lang.

Cast: Jack Lemmon, *Don Gallagher*, Lee Grant, *Karen Wallace*, Brenda Vaccaro, *Eve Clayton*, Joseph Cotten, *Nicholas St. Downs III*, Olivia DeHavilland, *Emily Livingston*, Darren McGavin, *Stan Buchek*, Christopher Lee, *Martin Wallace*, Robert Foxworth, *Chambers*, Robert Hooks, *Eddie*, Monte Markham, *Banker*, Kathleen Quinlan, *Julie*, Gil Gerard, *Frank Powers*, James Booth, *Ralph Crawford*, Monica Lewis, *Anne*, Maidie Norman, *Dorothy*, Pamela Bellwood, *Lisa*, Arlene Golonka, *Mrs. Jane Stern*, James Stewart, *Philip Stevens*, Tom Sullivan, *Steve*, M. Emmett Walsh, *Dr. Williams*, Michael Richardson, *Walker*, Michael Pataki, *Wilson*, George Furth, *Gerald Lucas*. PG. $16,200,000.

See *Airport.*

13 **Alex & the Gypsy** (1976) *** 20th Century–Fox, 99 min. *Dir* John Korty, *Scr* Lawrence B. Marcus, based on novella *The Bailbondsman* by Stanley Elkin, *Cin* Bill Butler, *Ed* Donn Cambern, *Des* Bill Malley, *Mus* Henry Mancini, *Prod* Richard Shepard.

Cast: Jack Lemmon, *Alexander Main*, Genevieve Bujold, *Maritza*, James Woods, *Crainpool*, Gino Ardito, *The Golfer*, Robert Emhardt, *Judge*, Joseph X. Flaherty, *Morgan*, Todd Martin, *Roy Blake*, Victor Pinhiero, *Sanders*. R.

One of the oddest love stories ever made. Jack Lemmon, in one of his strangest roles, portrays Alex, a perfectly loathsome bailbondsman, who has a relationship with one of his clients, a young Gypsy woman. Stylistically, *Alex & the Gypsy* resembles the gritty black comedies of the late 1960's and early 1970's, but Korty and the performances of Lemmon, Bujold and Woods make it seem fresh.

14 **Alex in Wonderland** (1970) *** MGM, 109 min. *Dir* Paul Mazursky, *Scr* Paul Mazursky, Larry Tucker, *Cin* Laszlo Kovacs, *Ed* Stuart H. Pappe, *Des* Pato Guzman, *Mus* Tom O'Horgan, *Prod* Larry Tucker.

Cast: Donald Sutherland, *Alex*, Ellen Burstyn, *Beth*, Meg Mazursky, *Amy*, Glenna Sergent, *Nancy*, Viola Spolin, *Mother*, Federico Fellini, Jeanne Moreau, *Themselves*, André Philippe, *André*, Michael Lerner, *Leo*, Joan Delaney, *Jane*, Neil Burstyn, *Norman*, Leon Frederick, *Lewis*, Carol O'Leary, *Marlene*, Paul Mazursky, *Hal Stern*, Moss Mabry, *Mr. Wayne*. R.

Fine autobiographical comedy drama about a young hot-shot director, who is unable to come up with a worthy follow-up to his debut film, which was a big hit. This film has been described as a poor man's *8½*; it certainly suffers by comparison to Fellini's classic; but it does stand on its own as a good indictment of contemporary Hollywood. *Alex in Wonderland* apparently had been loosely based on Paul Mazursky's own experiences as a director, after debuting with the hit film *Bob & Carol & Ted & Alice*.

15 **Alice Doesn't Live Here Anymore** (1974) (BFA) ******** Warner Bros., 113 min. *Dir* Martin Scorsese, *Scr* Robert Getchell (AN, BFA), *Cin* Kent L. Wakeman, *Ed* Marcia Lucas, *Des* Toby Carr Rafelson, *Prod* Audry Maas, David Susskind, *Assoc Prod* Sandra Weintraub.

   Cast: Ellen Burstyn (A, BFA), *Alice Hyatt*, Alfred Lutter, *Tommy*, Kris Kristofferson, *David*, Billy "Green" Bush, *Donald*, Diane Ladd (AN, BFA), *Flo*, Lelia Goldoni, *Bea*, Lane Bradbury, *Rita*, Vic Tayback, *Mel*, Jodie Foster, *Audry*, Harvey Keitel, *Ben*, Valerie Curtin, *Vera*, Murray Moston, *Jacobs*, Harry Northup, *Bartender*, Mia Bendixson, *Alice Age 8*, Ola Moore, *Old Woman*, Martin Brinton, *Lenny*, Dean Casper, *Chicken*. PG. $7,900,000

   Martin Scorsese's first excursion into mainstream Hollywood. Although he proved that he could make "their" films as good as anyone else, it is certainly a considerable waste of Scorsese's unique talents. Something of a *cause célèbre* for women, following in the wake of an almost totally male-dominated American cinema, *Alice* is an episodic road film that, through a blend of comedy and drama, explores the unusual relationship of a recently widowed mother and her slightly obnoxious teenage son. Some of Scorsese's bleak realism and intensity does manage to occasionally sneak through, and as is commonplace in his films, the performances are uniformly excellent.

16 **Alice, Sweet Alice** (1978) ******* Allied Artists, 108 min. *Dir* Alfred Sole, *Scr* Rosemary Ritvo, Alfred Sole, *Cin* John Friberg, Chuck Hall, Edward Salier, *Mus* Stephen Lawrence, *Prod* Richard K. Rosenberg.

   Cast: Paula Sheppard, *Alice*, Brooke Shields, *Karen*, Linda Miller, *Catherine*, Jane Lowry, *Aunt Annie*, Alphonso DeNoble, *Alphonso*, Rudolph Willrich, *Father Tom*, Mildred Clinton, *Mrs. Tredoni*, Niles McMaster, *Dom Spages*, Michael Hardstark, *Detective*, Gary Allen, *Uncle*, Tom Signorelli, *Brenner*, Louisa Horton, *Psychiatrist*, Antonino Rocco, *Funeral Attendant*, Lillian Roth, *Pathologist*. R.

   Above average murder thriller about a young girl who may or may not be a killer. *Alice, Sweet Alice* is not just another low-budget shocker, although it has been exploited as such. Alfred Sole has an excellent visual style and has been influenced by both Alfred Hitchcock and Roman Polanski. Other titles: *Communion* (its original) and *Holy Terror*.

17 **Alien** (1979) ********* 20th Century–Fox, 125 min. *Dir* Ridley Scott, *Scr* Dan O'Bannon, Ronald Shusett, David Giler (UN), Walter Hill (UN), *Cin* Derek Vanlint, *Ed* Terry Rawlings, *Des* Michael Seymour (AN, BFA), *Art* Les Dilley, Roger Christian (AN), *Sp* Brian Johnson, Nick Alider (A), *Cos* John Mollo, *Mus* Jerry Goldsmith, *Prod* Gordon Carroll, David Giler, Walter Hill, *Exec Prod* Ronald Shusett.

   Cast: Sigourney Weaver, *Ripley*, Tom Skerritt, *Dallas*, Veronica Cartwright, *Lambert*, Harry Dean Stanton, *Brett*, Yaphet Kotto, *Parker*, Ian Holm, *Ash*, John Hurt, *Kane*. R. $39,845,000

   A brilliantly powerful science-fiction horror thriller about an alien creature, mistakenly brought aboard a space freighter, which subsequently eliminates the members of the crew. *Alien* is essentially a haunted house thriller set in outer space, as the space ship *Nostromo* resembles a mysterious castle with towering spires and dark narrow corridors. The characters come alive as realistic human beings rather than like the cardboard characters that grace most SF films, and the special effects are so realistic that they almost go unnoticed. Ridley Scott directs with such precision that *Alien* retains its intensity for its entire two hour length.

18 The All-American Boy (1973) ** Warner Bros., 118 min. *Dir* Charles Eastman, *Scr* Charles Eastman, *Cin* Philip Lathrop, *Ed* Christopher Holmes, *Art* Carey O'Dell, *Prod* Saul J. Krugman, Joseph T. Naar.

Cast: Jon Voight, *Vic Bealer*, Carol Androsky, *Rodine*, Anne Archer, *Drenna Valentine*, Gene Borkan, *Rockoff*, Ron Burns, *Larkin*, Rosalind Cash, *Poppy*, Jeanne Cooper, *Nola Bealer*, Peggy Cowles, *Bett Van Daumee*, Leigh French, *Lovette*, Ned Glass, *Arty*, Bob Hastings, *Ariel Van Daumee*, Kathy Mahoney, *Shereen Bealer*, Art Metrano, *Jay David Swooze*, Jaye P. Morgan, *Magda*, Harry Northup, *Parker*, Nancie Phillips, *Connie Swooze*, Jeff Thompson, *High Valentine*. R.

A somewhat pretentious drama about a down-and-out boxer. As an indictment of society's losers *The All-American Boy* has some interest, but unfortunately everyone is a loser. Because Eastman's approach is too one-sided, he fails to completely bring the characters to life. In comparison, Billy Wilder seems an idealist. Warner Bros., knowing they had an uncommercial film on their hands, kept this film on the shelf for a few years.

19 All That Jazz (1979) (AN) ***** Columbia/20th Century–Fox, 123 min. *Dir* Bob Fosse (AN), *Scr* Robert Alan Aurthur, Bob Fosse (AN), *Cin* Giuseppe Rotunno (AN, BFA), *Ed* Alan Heim (A, BFA), *Des* Philip Rosenberg (A), *Art* Tony Walton (A), *Cos* Albert Wolsky (A), *Mus Adaptation* Ralph Burns (A), *Chor* Bob Fosse, *Prod* Robert Alan Aurthur, *Exec Prod* Daniel Melnick, *Assoc Prod* Wolfgang Gattes, Kenneth Utt.

Cast: Roy Scheider (AN), *Joe Gideon*, Jessica Lange, *Angelique*, Ann Reinking, *Kate Jagger*, Leland Palmer, *Audrey Paris*, Cliff Gorman, *Davis Newman*, Ben Vereen, *O'Connor Flood*, Erzsebet Foldi, *Michelle*, Deborah Geffner, *Victoria*, Michael Tolan, *Dr. Ballinger*, Max Wright, *Joshua Penn*, William LeMassena, *Jonesy Hecht*, Chris Chase, *Leslie Perry*, Kathryn Doby, *Kathryn*, Anthony Holland, *Paul Dann*, Robert Hitt, *Ted Christopher*, David Margulies, *Larry Goldie*, Sue Paul, *Stacy*, Keith Gordon, *Young Joe Gideon*, Frankie Man, *Comic*, Alan Heim, *Eddie*, John Lithgow, *Lucas Sergeant*, Sloane Shelton, *Mother*, Ben Masters, *Dr. Garry*. R. $20,000,000

Brilliant dramatic musical about an obsessive and self-destructive choreographer and director. *All That Jazz* is a semi-autobiographical film of Bob Fosse's near fatal heart attack, and what led up to it. Joe Gideon, Fosse's alter ego, drives himself too hard by preparing a Broadway musical (*Chicago?*), while completing the editing on a movie (*Lenny?*). Fosse alternates between fantasy and reality, much in the manner of Fellini, but *All That Jazz* is not a copy of *8½* as some critics have suggested. This is Fosse's greatest achievement, and one of the few true masterpieces of the generally inane biography genre.

20 **All the President's Men** (1976) (AN, NS, NY, NB) ***** Warner Bros., 138 min. Dir Alan J. Pakula (AN, NY, NB), Scr William Goldman (A, W), based on book by Carl Bernstein and Bob Woodward, Cin Gordon Willis, Ed Robert L. Wolfe (AN), Des George Jenkins (A), Mus David Shire, Prod Walter Coblenz, Assoc Prod Jon Boorstin, Michael Britton.

Cast: Dustin Hoffman, Carl Bernstein, Robert Redford, Bob Woodward, Jack Warden, Harry Rosenfeld, Martin Balsam, Howard Simons, Hal Holbrook, Deep Throat, Jason Robards (A, NS, NY, NB), Ben Bradlee, Jane Alexander (AN), Bookkeeper. Meredith Baxter, Debbie Sloan, Ned Beatty, Dardis, Stephen Collins, Hugh Sloan, Jr., Penny Fuller, Sally Aiken, John Mc-Martin, Foreign Editor, Robert Walden, Donald Segretti, Frank Wills, Himself, F. Murray Abraham, Arresting Officer #1, David Arkin, Bachinski, Henry Calvert, Barker, Dominic Chianese, Martinez, Bryan E. Clark, Arguing Attorney, Nicholas Costa, Markham, Lindsay Ann Crouse, Kay Eddy, Valerie Curtin, Miss Millard, Cara Duff-MacCormick, Tammy Ulrich. PG. $30,000,000

By far the best film to date based on the Watergate scandal. Rather than boring the audience with a drawing room drama of politicians discussing their crimes, All the President's Men sets its focus on Woodward and Bernstein, the two Washington Post reporters who uncovered the scandal. This is essentially a detective story. Robert Redford who made this film through his production company, deserves much credit for its success, as he oversaw the details of the filming and opted for reality and truth, rather than sinking to the level of a star vehicle. Future generations may find All the President's Men difficult to comprehend, as it dispenses with exposition that would have bored an audience who lived through the scandal.

21 **An Almost Perfect Affair** (1979) *** Paramount, 93 min. Dir Michael Ritchie, Scr Walter Bernstein, Don Peterson, Story Don Peterson, Michael Ritchie, Cin Henri Decae, Ed Richard A. Harris, Art Willy Holt, Cos Tanine Autre, Valentino, Mus Georges Delerue, Prod Terry Carr.

Cast: Keith Carradine, Hal, Monica Vitti, Maria, Raf Vallone, Freddie, Christian De Sica, Carlo, Dick Anthony Williams, Jackson, Henri Garcin, Lt. Montand, Anna Maria Horsford, Amy Zon. PG.

Comedy love story set at the Cannes Film Festival. Keith Carradine stars as a young filmmaker who tries to get his recently completed film into the festival. He runs into problems with customs, but the wife (Monica Vitti) of a producer helps him out, and they subsequently have an affair. An Almost Perfect Affair succeeds more as a satire of the industry than as a romance.

22 **Almost Summer** (1978) ** Universal, 88 min. Dir Martin Davidson, Scr Judith Berg, Sandra Berg, Martin Davidson, Marc Reid Rubel, Cin Stevan Larner, Ed Lynzee Klingman, Art William M. Hiney, Cos Sandra Davidson, Mus Ron Altbach, Charles Lloyd, Title Song Brian Wilson, Prod Rob Cohen, Exec Prod Steve Tisch, Assoc Prod Anthony R. Clark.

Cast: John Friedrich, Darryl, Bruno Kirby, Bobby, Lee Purcell, Christine, Didi Conn, Donna, Thomas Carter, Dean, Tim Matheson, Kevin, Petronia Paley, Nicole, David Wilson, Duane, Sherry Hursey, Lori, Harvey Lewis, Stanley, Karen Lamm, Felicia, Judith Nugent-Hart, Susie, Denise Denise, Gwen, Catherine Lee Smith, Bonnie, John Kirby, Larry, Allen G. Norman, Scratch, Byron Stewart, Scottie, Merie Earle, Mrs. Jenkins, Bill Bogert, Albrecht, Kris Mersky, Miss Margulies. PG.

Average teen comedy about a high school student election, in which a con artist masterminds a campaign to elect a shy and quiet student as president of the student body. *Almost Summer* is farcical in style and resembles the beach movies of the 1960's, but the performances by an almost entirely young cast are far better than those in other films of this type.

23 Aloha, Bobby and Rose (1975)   **   Columbia, 88 min. *Dir* Floyd Mutrux, *Scr* Floyd Mutrux, *Cin* William A. Fraker, *Ed* Danford B. Greene, *Prod* Fouad Said, *Exec Prod* Edward J. Rosen.

Cast: Paul Le Mat, *Bobby*, Diane Hull, *Rose*, Tim McIntire, *Buford*, Leigh French, *Donna Sue*, Noble Willingham, *Uncle Charlie*, Martine Bartlett, *Rose's Mother*, Robert Carradine, *Moxey*. PG. $6,000,000

Typical young couple on-the-run drama. A mechanic (Paul Le Mat) falls for a car wash worker (Dianne Hull), and the two accidently become involved in a shooting at a liquor store. From then on *Aloha, Bobby and Rose* becomes another chase film, with the obligatory tragic conclusion. Floyd Mutrux tries to push the story with his flashy direction, but the material is not strong enough.

24 Alpha Beta (1976)   ***   Britain, Cine III, 70 min. *Dir* Anthony Page, *Scr* E.A. Whitehead, based on his play, *Cin* Charles Stewart, *Ed* Tom Priestley, *Prod* Timothy Burrill.

Cast: Albert Finney, *Frank Elliot*, Rachel Roberts, *Nora Elliot*. PG.

Powerful drama of the disintegration of an English working-class marriage, which is highlighted by the excellent performances of the two leads, Albert Finney and Rachel Roberts, repeating their stage roles. *Alpha Beta* is essentially a filmed play rather than a true movie, and is divided into three separate acts, each representing a different stage of the breakdown of the marriage.

"American Film Theatre": Series of films based on plays, originally sold only on subscription basis. The resulting films are hardly cinematic, and are likely of more interest to theatre-goers than to fans of the cinema. Plays, by nature, do not translate well to film, particularly when they are left untouched as they are here. A few do succeed, however, due to some fine acting and writing, particularly *In Celebration, Butley, The Man in the Glass Booth* and *The Homecoming*.

25 American Graffiti (1973) (AN, GMC)   ****   Universal, 110 min. *Dir* George Lucas (AN), *Scr* Willard Huyck, Gloria Katz, George Lucas (AN, NS, NY), *Cin* Jan D'Alquen, Ron Eveslage, *Ed* Verna Fields, Marcia Lucas (AN), *Art* Dennis Clark, *Cos* Aggie Guerard Rodgers, *Chor* Toni Basil, *Prod* Francis Coppola, *Co-Prod* Gary Kurtz.

Cast: Richard Dreyfuss, *Curt*, Ron Howard, *Steve*, Paul LeMat, *John*, Charlie Martin Smith, *Terry*, Cindy Williams, *Laurie*, Candy Clark (AN), *Debbie*, Mackenzie Phillips, *Carol*, Wolfman Jack, *Disc Jockey*, Harrison Ford, *Bob*, Bo Hopkins, *Joe*, Manuel Padilla, Jr., *Carlos*, Beau Gentry, *Ants*, Kathy Quinlan, *Peg*, Joe Spano, *Vic*, Suzanne Somers, *Blonde in T-Bird*, Debralee Scott, *Falfa's Girl*. PG. $55,885,000

Excellent comedy focusing on several youths in a small California town in 1962, and how they spend their final day of summer vacation. *American Graffiti* is a plotless kaleidoscope detailing their many adventures. There have been numerous nostalgic films about growing up, but none have the substance, wit and charm of this film, and the large ensemble cast is superb.

26 **American Hot Wax** (1978) *** Paramount, 91 min. *Dir* Floyd Mutrux, *Scr* John Kaye, *Cin* William A. Fraker, *Ed* Ronald J. Fagan, Melvin Shapiro, *Art* Elayne Barbara Ceder, *Prod* Art Linson.

Cast: Tim McIntire, *Alan Freed*, Fran Drescher, *Sheryl*, Jay Leno, *Mookie*, Laraine Newman, *Teenage Louise*, Al Chalk, Sam Harkness, Arnold Mc-Culler, Carl Earl Weaver, *The Chesterfields*, Jeff Altman, *Lennie Ritchfield*, Moosie Drier, *Artie Moress*, John Lehne, *District Attorney*, Kenny Vane, *Prof. La Plano*, Chuck Berry, Screamin' Jay Hawkins, Jerry Lee Lewis, *Themselves*. PG. $5,530,000

Well-made celebration of the spirit of rock 'n' roll during the 1950's. *American Hot Wax* is purported to be the story of famed disc jockey Alan Freed, but it only covers the events surrounding one of Freed's most important rock concerts. Tim McIntyre is superb as Freed, but this story takes a backseat to the music, comedy and energy, nicely balanced by director Floyd Mutrux.

27 **Americathon** (1979) ** United Artists, 85 min. *Dir* Neil Israel, *Scr* Neil Israel, Michael Mislove, Monica Johnson, *Adaptation*. Phillip Proctor, Peter Bergman, based on their play, *Cin* Gerald Hirschfeld, *Ed* John C. Howard, *Des* Mark L. Fabus, Stan Jolley, *Cos* Daniel Paredes, *Chor* Jaime Rogers, *Mus* Earl Brown, Jr., Elvis Costello, Reggie Knighton, Alan Parsons, David Pomeranz, Jim Steinman, *Prod* Joe Roth, *Exec Prod* Edward Rosen, *Assoc Prod* David Nichols.

Cast: Peter Riegert, *Eric*, Harvey Korman, *Monty*, Fred Willard, *Vanderhoof*, John Ritter, *Chet Roosevelt*, Nancy Morgan, *Lucy*, Richard Schaal, *Jerry*, Zane Buzby, *Mouling*, Chief Dan George, *Sam*, Tommy Lasorda, *Announcer*, Jay Leno, *Larry*, Peter Marshall, *Himself*, Meat Loaf, *Oklahoma Roy*, Howard Hesseman, *Kip*, Geno Andrews, *Chris*, Robert Beer, *David Eisenhower*, Terry McGovern, *Danny*, Nellie Bellflower, *VP Advertising*, Jimmy Weldon, *VP Research*, David Opatoshu, Allan Arbus, *Hebrabs*. PG.

Lame and fragmented futuristic comedy set in the year 1998, when America is bankrupt. The government holds a telethon, known as the "Americathon," to raise money to pay off the country's debt before a rich business man forecloses. This was intended to be a satire of America's economic problems through a projection of where it may lead, but this point is made early in the film; from then on it is nothing but dumb jokes.

28 **The Amityville Horror** (1979) ** American International, 126 min. *Dir* Stuart Rosenberg, *Scr* Sandor Stern, based on book by Jay Anson, *Cin* Fred J. Koenekamp, *Ed* Robert Brown, *Art* Jim Swados, *Mus* Lalo Schifrin (AN), *Prod*. Elliot Geisinger, Ronald Saland, *Exec Prod* Samuel Z. Arkoff.

Cast: James Brolin, *George Lutz*, Margot Kidder, *Kathleen Lutz*, Rod Steiger, *Father Delaney*, Don Stroud, *Father Bolen*, Murray Hamilton, *Father Ryan*, John Larch, *Father Nuncio*, Natasha Ryan, *Amy*, K.C. Martel, *Greg*, Meeno Peluce, *Matt*, Michael Sacks, *Jeff*, Helen Shaver, *Carolyn*, Amy Wright, *Jackie*, Val Avery, *Sgt. Gionfriddo*, Irene Dailey, *Aunt Helen*, Marc Vahanian, *Jimmy*, Elsa Raven, *Mrs. Townsend*, Ellen Saland, *Bride*, Ed Barth, *Agucci*. R. $35,000,000

Average haunted house thriller that was blown out of proportion due to the purported "truth" of the story. Whether *The Amityville Horror* is a true story or not is irrelevant, because it is just as dumb and illogical as any fiction films of the genre. This was American International's biggest film, but, ironically, it appeared just prior to the company's demise.

29 **The Amsterdam Kill** (1977) ** Columbia, 89 min. *Dir* Robert Clouse, *Scr* Robert Clouse, Gregory Teifer, *Story* Gregory Teifer, *Cin* Alan Hume, *Ed* Gina Brown, Allan Holzman, *Art* John Blezard, K.S. Chen, *Mus* Hal Schaefer, *Prod* Andre Morgan, *Exec Prod* Raymond Chow.

Cast: Robert Mitchum, *Quinlan*, Bradford Dillman, *Odums*, Richard Egan, *Ridgeway*, Leslie Nielson, *Knight*, Keye Luke, *Chung Wei*, George Cheung, *Jimmy Wong*, Chan Sing, *Assassin*. R.

Dull action thriller of international intrigue. In one of his lesser roles, Robert Mitchum stars as a former narcotics cop who comes out of retirement to investigate a drug smuggling ring, because a former colleague may or may not be involved. There isn't much to recommend in this television style movie, particularly the numerous action sequences, which are too bland to perk up the dull story.

30 **...And Justice for All** (1979) *** Columbia, 120 min. *Dir* Norman Jewison, *Scr* Valerie Curtin, Barry Levinson (AN), *Cin* Victor J. Kemper, *Ed* John F. Burnett, *Des* Richard MacDonald, *Art* Peter Samish, *Cos* Ruth Myers, *Mus* Dave Grusin, *Prod* Norman Jewison, Patrick Palmer, *Exec. Prod* Joe Wizan.

Cast: Al Pacino (AN), *Arthur Kirkland*, Jack Warden, *Judge Rayford*, John Forsythe, *Judge Fleming*, Lee Strasberg, *Grandpa Sam*, Jeffrey Tambor, *Jay Porter*, Christine Lahti, *Gail Packer*, Sam Levene, *Arnie*, Robert Christian, *Ralph Agee*, Thomas Waites, *Jeff McCullaugh*, Larry Bruggman, *Warren Fresnell*, Craig T. Nelson, *Frank Bowers*, Dominic Chianese, *Carl Travers*, Victor Arnold, *Leo Fauci*, Vincent Beck, *Officer Leary*, Michael Gorrin, *Elderly Man*, Baxter Harris, *Larry*, Joe Morton, *Prison Doctor*, Alan North, *Deputy Sheriff*, Charles Siebert, *Assistant D.A. Keene*. R. $14,600,000

Disappointing indictment of America's legal system, with a superb performance by Al Pacino as a lawyer who tries to take on the system. *And Justice for All* had enormous potential to be a powerful and socially relevant film, but it is flawed by an overloaded script that attempts far more than it can handle. Every minor legal error results in a great tragedy, and this one-sidedness mars its credibility.

31 **The Anderson Tapes** (1971) *** Columbia, 98 min. *Dir* Sidney Lumet, *Scr* Frank R. Pierson, based on novel by Lawrence Sanders, *Cin* Arthur J. Ornitz, *Ed* Joanne Burke, *Des* Benjamin J. Kassackrow, *Art* Philip Rosenberg, *Cos* Gene Coffin, *Mus* Quincy Jones, *Prod* Robert M. Weitman.

Cast: Sean Connery, *Duke Anderson*, Dyan Cannon, *Ingrid Everleigh*, Martin Balsam, *Tommy Haskins*, Ralph Meeker, *Capt. Delaney*, Alan King, *Pat Angelo*, Christopher Walken, *The Kid*, Val Avery, *Socks Parelli*, Dick Williams, *Spencer*, Garrett Morris, *Everson*, Stan Gottlieb, *Pop*, Paul Benjamin, *Jimmy*, Anthony Holland, *Psychologist*, Conrad Bain, *Dr. Rubicoff*, Richard B. Shull, *Werner*, Margaret Hamilton, *Miss Kaler*, Judith Lowry, *Mrs. Hathaway*, Max Showalter, *Bingham*, Janet Ward, *Mrs. Bingham*, Scott Jacoby, *Jerry Bingham*. PG. $5,000,000

Above-average caper thriller about a group of ex-cons, led by Sean Connery, who rob an apartment building. Since leaving prison Connery is under constant surveillance and all the plans of the robbery are taped. The taping is nothing more than a gimmick and really adds little to the story. Ironically *The Anderson Tapes*, a perfect Watergate Era film, was made prior to the break-in.

32 **The Andromeda Strain** (1971) ** Universal, 130 min. *Dir* Robert Wise, *Scr* Nelson Gidding, based on novel by Michael Crichton, *Cin* Richard H. Kline, *Ed* Stuart Gilmore, John W. Holmes, *Des* Boris Levin, *Art* William Tuntke, *Cos* Helen Colvig, *Sp* James Shourt, Douglas Trumbull, *Mus* Gil Melle, *Prod* Robert Wise.

Cast: Arthur Hill, *Dr. Jeremy Stone*, David Wayne *Dr. Charles Dutton*, James Olson, *Dr. Mark Hall*, Kate Reid, *Dr. Ruth Leavitt*, Paula Kelly, *Karen Anson*, George Mitchell, *Jackson*, Ramone Bieri, *Maj. Manchek*, Kermit Murdock, *Dr. Robertson*, Richard O'Brien, *Grimes*, Peter Hobbs, *Gen. Sparks.* G.

Dull science-fact thriller set almost entirely in an underground installation where a group of scientists attempt to analyze a deadly virus, from a crashed satellite, that has wiped out a small Western town. *The Andromeda Strain* is far too clinical and drags along up until the climactic race to save the installation from destruction, but that is just too little, too late.

33 **The Angel Levine** (1970) *** United Artists, 104 min. *Dir* Jan Kader, *Scr* Bill Gunn, Ronald Ribman, *Story* Bernard Malamud, *Cin* Richard Kratina, *Ed* Carl Lerner, *Des* George Jenkins, *Cos* Domingo Rodriguez, *Mus* Xdenek Liska, *Prod* Chiz Schultz.

Cast: Zero Mostel, *Moris Mishkin*, Harry Belafonte, *Alexander Levine*, Ida Kaminska, *Fanny Mishkin*, Milo O'Shea, *Dr. Arnold Berg*, Gloria Foster, *Sally*, Barbara Ann Teer, *Welfare Lady*, Eli Wallach, *Store Clerk*, Anne Jackson, *Lady in the Store.* PG.

Interesting but sentimental story of an old Jewish man (Zero Mostel), who loses his faith after being plagued by family and financial problems. He is visited by a black angel (Harry Belafonte), who tries to save the man's faith. *The Angel Levine* is to some extent a ghetto version of *It's A Wonderful Life*, but hardly in the same class as that Frank Capra classic.

34 **Annie Hall** (1977) (A, NY, NS, BFA) ***** United Artists, 93 min. *Dir* Woody Allen (A, NY, BFA, D), *Scr* Woody Allen, Marshall Brickman (A, NY, NS, BFA, LA, W), *Cin* Gordon Willis, *Ed* Wendy Greene Bricmont, Ralph Rosenblum (BFA), *Prod* Charles H. Joffe, *Exec Prod* Robert Greenhut, *Assoc Prod* Fred T. Gallo.

Cast: Woody Allen (AN), *Alvy Singer*, Diane Keaton (A, NS, NY, NB, BFA, GMC), *Annie Hall*, Tony Roberts, *Rob*, Carol Kane, *Allison*, Paul Simon, *Tony Lacey*, Colleen Dewhurst, *Mom Hall*, Janet Margolin, *Robin*, Shelley Duvall, *Pam*, Christopher Walken, *Duane Hall*, Donald Symington, *Dad Hall*, Helen Ludlam, *Granny Hall*, Mordecai Lawner, *Alvy's Dad*, Joan Newman, *Alvy's Mom*, Jonathan Munk, *Alvy at 9*, Ruth Volner, *Alvy's Aunt*, Martin Rosenblatt, *Alvy's Uncle*, Hy Ansel, *Joey Nichols*, Rashel Novikoff, *Aunt Tessie*, Marshall McLuhan, *Himself.* PG. $18,095,000

Woody Allen's semi-autobiographical account of his real-life relationship with Diane Keaton raised him from the level of a superior comic filmmaker to that of a great cinematic artist, on a par with Charles Chaplin and Buster Keaton. Allen dispenses with his previous use of slapstick humor and anachronisms that filled his earlier comedies and sticks more closely to reality as he examines human beings and their relationships. One should not assume that Allen has lost his sense of humor, because his brilliant verbal wit, the only comedic device Allen really needs, makes *Annie Hall* one of his funniest films. *Annie Hall* is the only film made by a comic performer to win the Academy Award for Best Picture.

35 **Another Man, Another Chance** (1977) ******** U.S./France, United Artists, 129 min. *Dir* Claude Lelouch, *Scr* Claude Lelouch, *Cin* Stanley Cortez, Jacques Lefrancois, *Ed* George Klotz, Fabien Tordjmann, *Des* Robert Clatworthy, *Mus* Frances Lai, *Prod* Georges Dancigers, Alexandre Mnouchkine.

Cast: James Caan, *David Williams*, Genevieve Bujold, *Jeanne Leroy*, Francis Huster, *Francis Leroy*, Jennifer Warren, *Mary*, Susan Tyrell, *Debbie/Alice*, Rossie Harris, *Simon*, Linda Lee Lyons, *Sarah*, Diana Douglas, *Mary's Mother*, Fred Stuthman, *Mary's Father*, Bernard Behrens, *Springfield*, Oliver Clark, *Evans*, William Bartman, *Telegrapher*, Burton Gilliam, *Sheriff Murphy*, Richard Farnsworth, *Stagecoach Driver*, Walter Barnes, *Foster*, Walter Scott, *Bill*. PG.

Wonderful, but unusual, western love story. This western version of *A Man and A Woman* parallels the separate stories of the characters portrayed by James Caan and Genevieve Bujold, which eventually merge into one single story. This structure is rather unique and sets it apart from other films. This is one of Lelouch's finest films, but it was unfairly overlooked by critics at the time of its release.

36 **Apocalypse Now** (1979) (AN, CF) ********* United Artists, 146 min. *Dir* Francis Coppola (AN, BFA), *Scr* Francis Coppola, John Milius (AN), based on novel *Heart of Darkness* by Joseph Conrad, *Narration* written by Michael Herr, *Cin* Vittorio Storaro (A), *Ed* Richard Marks (AN), *Des* Dean Tavoularis (AN), *Art* Angelo Graham (AN), *Mus* Carmine Coppola, *Prod* Francis Coppola, *Co-Prod* Gray Frederickson, Tom Sternberg.

Cast: Martin Sheen, *Capt. Willard*, Marlon Brando, *Col. Kurtz*, Robert Duvall (AN, BFA,G), *Lt. Col. Kilgore*, Frederic Forrest (NS), *Chef*, Albert Hall, *Chief*, Sam Bottoms, *Lance*, Larry Fishburne, *Clean*, Dennis Hopper, *Photo Journalist*, G.D. Spradlin, *General*, Harrison Ford, *Colonel*, Scott Glenn, *Civilian*, Bill Graham, *Agent*, Cyndi Wood, Colleen Camp, Linda Carpenter, *Playmates*. R. $37,270,000

How does any director top an achievement of the calibre of the two *Godfather* films? Despite his naysayers, Francis Coppola did, with this film. *Apocalypse Now* is not only the ultimate war film, but is one of the all time screen masterpieces. Using the Vietnam War as merely a setting, Coppola examines war in general and explores the nature of violence as inherently part of man; his darker side. While even the toughest of critics lauded most of his film, the final third left most people confused; many labeled it as muddled self-indulgence. In this section Coppola brilliantly visualizes the deep recesses of a schizophrenic mind, in which Col. Kurtz is the darker side of Capt. Willard.

37 The Apple Dumpling Gang (1975) ** Buena Vista, 100 min. *Dir* Norman Tokar, *Scr* Don Tait, based on novel by Jack M. Bickham, *Cin* Frank Phillips, *Ed* Ray de Leuw, *Art* John B. Mansbridge, Walter Tyler, *Cos* Shelby Anderson, *Mus* Buddy Baker, *Title Song* Shane Tatum, *Prod* Bill Anderson, A Walt Disney Production.

Cast: Bill Bixby, *Russel Donavan*, Susan Clark, *Magnolia Dusty Clydesdale*, Don Knotts, *Theodore Ogelvie*, Tim Conway, *Amos*, David Wayne, *Col. T.T. Clydesdale*, Slim Pickens, *Frank Stillwell*, Harry Morgan, *Homer McCoy*, John McGiver, *Leonard Sharpe*, Don Knight, *John Wintle*, Clay O'Brien, *Bobby Bradley*, Brad Savage, *Clovis Bradley*, Stacy Manning, *Celia Bradley*, Dennis Fimple, *Rudy Hooks*, Pepe Callahan, *Clemons*, Iris Adrian, *Poker Polly*, Fran Ryan, *Mrs. Stockley*. G. $16,500,000.

A somewhat typical Disney comedy western that is filled with their usual doses of childish slapstick. *The Apple Dumpling Gang* rises above most due to the presence of Don Knotts and Tim Conway, a juvenile version of Abbott and Costello, in their first screen teaming. Proving to be the film's most interesting characters, Knotts and Conway were brought back to star in the sequel (next entry), which was no better or worse than the first.

38 The Apple Dumpling Gang Rides Again (1979) ** Buena Vista, 88 min. *Dir* Vincent McEveety, *Scr* Don Tait, based on characters created by Jack M. Bickham, *Cin* Frank Phillips, *Ed* Gordon D. Brenner, *Art* John B. Mansbridge, Frank T. Smith, *Cos* Mary Dye, Chuck Keehne, *Mus* Buddy Baker, *Prod* Ron Miller, *Co-Prod* Tom Leetch, A Walt Disney Production.

Cast: Tim Conway, *Amos*, Don Knotts, *Theodore*, Tim Matheson, *Private Jeff Reid*, Kenneth Mars, *Marshall*, Elyssa Davalos, *Millie*, Jack Elam, *Big Mac*, Robert Pine, *Lt. Ravencroft*, Harry Morgan, *Maj. Gaskill*, Ruth Buzzi, *Tough Kate*, Audrey Totter, *Martha*. G. $9,425,000. See *The Apple Dumpling Gang*.

39 The Apprenticeship of Duddy Kravitz (1974) **** Canada, Paramount, 121 min. *Dir* Ted Kotcheff, *Scr* Mordecai Richler (AN), based on his novel, *Adaptation*. Lionel Chetwynd (AN), *Cin* Brian West, *Ed* Thom Noble, *Des* Anne Pritchard, *Prod* John Kemeny, *Exec Prod* Gerald Schneider, *Assoc Prod* Don Duprey.

Cast: Richard Dreyfuss, *Duddy*, Micheline Lanctot, *Yvette*, Jack Warden, *Max*, Randy Quaid, *Virgil*, Joseph Wiseman, *Uncle Benjy*, Denholm Elliot, *Friar*, Henry Ramer, *Dingleman*, Joe Silver, *Farber*, Zvee Scooler, *Grandfather*, Robert Goodier, *Calder*, Allan Rosenthal, *Lennie*, Barry Baldaro, *Paddy*, Allan Magicovsky, *Irwin*, Barry Pascal, *Bernie Farber*, Susan Friedman, *Linda*. PG.

Excellent picaresque character study of an ambitious Jewish youth growing up in Montreal, Canada, during the 1940's. Richard Dreyfuss' superb performance in the title role highlights *The Apprenticeship of Duddy Dravitz* as he convincingly portrays the character from his teens through young adulthood. Although not a financial blockbuster in the U.S., this was a breakthrough film for the Canadian film industry by bringing it prominence outside its borders.

40 Ash Wednesday (1973) * Paramount, 99 min. *Dir* Larry Peerce, *Scr* Jean Claude Tramont, *Cin* Ennio Guarnieri, *Ed* Marion Rothman, *Art* Philip Abramson, *Mus* Maurice Jarre, *Prod* Dominick Dunne.

Cast: Elizabeth Taylor, *Barbara Sawyer*, Henry Fonda, *Mark Sawyer*, Helmut Berger, *Erich*, Keith Baxter, *David*, Maurice Teynac, *Dr. Lambert*, Margaret Blye, *Kate Sawyer*, Monique Van Vooren, *German Woman*. R.

Dismal soap opera style film about a woman, Elizabeth Taylor, who undergoes a facelift to look younger. This is hardly an entertaining subject for a film, and the filmmakers succeed in making it far worse than one could have expected. The operation scenes are simply repulsive, but this may attract fans of *Friday the 13th* and other gruesome slasher films.

41 **The Assassination of Trotsky** (1972) ** Britain/France/Italy, Cinerama, 103 min. *Dir* Joseph Losey, *Scr* Nicholas Mosley, *Cin* Pasquel De Santis, *Ed* Reggie Beck, *Des* Richard MacDonald, *Art* Arrigo Equini, *Prod* Joseph Losey, Norman Priggen, *Exec Prod* Josef Shaftel.

Cast: Richard Burton, *Leon Trotsky*, Alain Delon, *Frank Jackson*, Romy Schneider, *Gita*, Valentina Cortese, *Natasha Trotsky*, Enrico Maria Salerno, *Salazar*, Luigi Vannucchi, *Ruiz*, Duilio Del Prete, *Felipe*, Jean Desailly, *Alfred Rosmer*, Simone Valere, *Marguerite Rosmer*, Carlos Miranda, *Sheldon Harte*, Peter Chatel, *Otto*, Mike Forrest, *Jim*, Marco Lucantoni, *Seva*, Claudio Brook, *Roberto*, Hunt Powers, *Lou*, Gianni Lofredo, *Sam*, Pierangelo Civera, *Pedro*. R.

Fair historical drama based on the murder of famed Russian revolutionary leader, Leon Trotsky (Richard Burton) during his exile in Mexico. Although not a great film, *The Assassination of Trotsky* is not as bad as its reputation would indicate, and Losey uses the story as a springboard for his own brand of psychological drama. Much more was expected, though, because of all the talent involved.

42 **Assault on Precinct 13** (1976) **** Turtle Releasing Org., 91 min. *Dir* John Carpenter, *Scr* John Carpenter, *Cin* Douglas Knapp, *Ed* John T. Chance, *Art* Tommy Wallace, *Mus* John Carpenter, *Prod* J.S. Kaplan, *Exec Prod* Joseph Kaufman.

Cast: Austin Stoker, *Bishop*, Darwin Joston, *Wilson*, Laurie Zimmer, *Leigh*, Martin West, *Lawson*, Tony Burton, *Wells*, Charles Cyphers, *Starker*, Nancy Loomis, *Julie*, Peter Bruni, *Ice Cream Man*, John J. Fox, *Warden*, Kim Richards, *Kathy*. R.

Excellent low-budget thriller about youth gangs attacking a soon to be closed police station, where a man takes refuge after killing one gang member. John Carpenter loosely based this story on Howard Hawk's *Rio Bravo*, but with the cold-bloodedness and facelessness of the gangs *Assault on Precinct 13* also resembles *Night of the Living Dead*. Carpenter directed this thriller with complete precision and never slows the film down with unnecessary exposition. Surprisingly, after failing in this country, *Assault on Precinct 13* caused a sensation in England.

43 **At Long Last Love** (1975) * 20th Century–Fox, 118 min. *Dir* Peter Bogdanovich, *Scr* Peter Bogdanovich, *Cin* Laszlo Kovacs, *Ed* Douglas Robertson, *Des* Gene Allen, *Art* John Lloyd, *Cos* Bobbie Mannix, *Mus* Cole Porter, *Chor* Rita Abrams, Albert Lantieri, *Prod* Peter Bogdanovich, *Assoc. Prod* Frank Marshall.

Cast: Burt Reynolds, *Michael Oliver Pritchard III*, Cybill Shepherd, *Brooke Carter*, Madeline Kahn, *Kitty O'Kelly*, Duilio Del Prete, *Johnny*

Spanish, Eileen Brennan, *Elizabeth*, John Hillerman, *Rodney James*, Mildred Natwick, *Mabel Pritchard*, Quinn Redeker, *Phillip*. G.

It is difficult to imagine how a filmmaker as talented as Peter Bogdanovich could have made a film as inept as this musical. Was he serious? Absolutely nothing seems to work, and no film in recent memory has been more consistently miscast. On the other hand *At Long Last Love* should become a cult classic as one of the great guilty pleasures of the cinema.

44 At the Earth's Core (1976) ** Britain, American International, 89 min. *Dir* Kevin Connor, *Scr* Milton Subotsky, based on novel by Edgar Rice Burroughs, *Cin* Alan Hume, *Ed* John Ireland, Barry Peters, *Des* Maurice Carter, *Art* Bert Davey, *Mus* Mike Vickers, *Prod* John Dark, *Exec Prod* Harry N. Blum, Presented by Samuel Z. Arkoff.

Cast: Doug McClure, *David*, Peter Cushing, *Dr. Perry*, Caroline Munro, *Dia*, Cy Grant, *Pa*, Godfrey James, *Ghak*, Sean Lynch, *Hooja*. PG. See *The Land that Time Forgot*.

45 Audrey Rose (1977) ** United Artists, 113 min. *Dir* Robert Wise, *Scr* Frank De Felitta, based on his novel, *Cin* Victor J. Kemper, *Ed* Carl Kress, *Des* Harry Horner, *Cos* Dorothy Jeakins, *Mus* Michael Small, *Prod* Frank De Felitta, Joe Wizan.

Cast: Marsha Mason, *Janice Templeton*, Anthony Hopkins, *Elliot Hoover*, John Beck, *Bill Templeton*, Susan Swift, *Ivy Templeton*, Norman Lloyd, *Dr. Steven Lipscomb*, John Hillerman, *Scott Velie*, Robert Walden, *Brice Mack*, Philip Sterling, *Judge Langley*, Ivy Jones, *Mary Lou Sides*, Stephen Pearlman, *Russ Rothman*. PG.

A mediocre thriller about reincarnation that seems to contain almost no thrills. A strange man annoys a couple claiming that their daughter is actually a reincarnation of his daughter. That is the basic premise and most of the plot of this overlong film. Subtlety is quite often considered a virtue in thrillers, but when this is taken too far, the results are simply dull.

46 Avalanche (1978) ** New World, 91 min. *Dir* Corey Allen, *Scr* Corey Allen, Claude Pola, *Story* Frances Doel, *Cin* Pierre William Glenn, *Ed* Larry Bock, Stuart Schoolnik, *Des* Sharon Compton, *Art* Phillip Thomas, *Mus* William Kraft, *Prod* Roger Corman, *Exec Prod* Paul Rapp.

Cast: Rock Hudson, *David Shelby*, Mia Farrow, *Caroline Brace*, Robert Forster, *Nick Throne*, Jeanette Nolan, *Florence Shelby*, Rick Moses, *Bruce Scott*, Steve Franken, *Henry McDade*, Barry Primus, *Mark Elliot*, Cathy Paine, *Tina Elliot*, Jerry Douglas, *Phil Prentiss*, Tony Carbone, *Leo The Coach*, Peggy Browne, *Annette Rivers*, Pat Egan, *Cathy Jordan*, Joby Baker, *TV Director*, X Brands, *Marty Brenner*, Cindy Luedke, *Susan Maxwell*, John Cathey, *Ed the Pilot*, Angelo Lamonea, *Bruce's Coach*. PG. $4,000,000.

Although merely a Roger Corman cheapie, *Avalanche* possesses more wit and intelligence than many of the big-budgeted Hollywood disaster films. The premise of a giant avalanche covering a ski resort at least contains some logic. Where it does fail is in its inferior special effects. Shots of snow are obviously superimposed over those of buildings. Afficionados of this genre will be disappointed in the low production values, but this film should be of interest to followers of Corman's career.

47 Avalanche Express (1979) * 20th Century–Fox, 88 min. *Dir* Mark Robson, *Scr* Abraham Polonsky, based on novel by Colin Forbes, *Cin* Jack Cardiff, *Ed* Garth Craven, *Des* Fred Tuch, *Cos* Mickey Shirard, *Mus* Allyn Ferguson, *Prod* Mark Robson, *Assoc Prod* Lynn Guthrie.

Cast: Robert Shaw, *Marenkov*, Lee Marvin, *Wargrave*, Linda Evans, *Elsa Lang*, Maximilian Schell, *Bunin*, Mike Connors, *Haller*, Joe Namath, *Leroy*, Horst Buchholz, *Scholten*, Davis Hess, *Geiger*, Arthur Brauss, *Neckerman*, Kristine Nel, *Helga Mann*, Sylva Langover, *Olga*. PG.

Dismal action thriller that mixes a cold war spy drama with a disaster film plot, neither of which have one shred of intelligence. It is difficult to believe a writer of the calibre of Abraham Polonsky could have written such a dull script. Some of the blame for the poor results must go to the untimely deaths of Mark Robson and Robert Shaw, but not all of it, since *Avalanche Express* is a disaster in every sense of the word.

48 Avanti (1972) *** United Artists, 143 min. *Dir* Billy Wilder, *Scr* I.A.L. Diamond, Billy Wilder, based on play by Samuel Taylor, *Cin* Luigi Kuveiller, *Ed* Ralph E. Winters, *Art* Ferdinando Scarfiotti, *Prod* Billy Wilder.

Cast: Jack Lemmon, *Wendell Armbruster*, Juliet Mills, *Pamela Piggott*, Clive Revill, *Carlo Carlucci*, Edward Andrews, *J.J. Blodgett*, Gianfranco Barra, *Bruno*, Franco Angrisano, *Arnold Trotta*, Pippa Franco, *Mattarazzo*, Franco Acampora, *Armando Trotta*, Giselda Castrini, *Anna*. R.

This overlong, but nevertheless enjoyable, Billy Wilder sex farce is at least as good as several of his better known and somewhat overrated comedies of the past. Lemmon goes to Italy to claim the body of his father, who has died during one of his yearly visits, where he meets Juliet Mills the daughter of the woman who died with Lemmon's father. The rest is rather predictable, but the script and the performances almost make it seem fresh.

49 B.S. I Love You (1971) ** 20th Century–Fox, 99 min. *Dir* Steven Hillard Stern, *Scr* Steven Hillard Stern, *Cin* David Dans, *Ed* Melvin Shapiro, *Art* Ernest Fegte, *Cos* Forrest T. Butler, *Mus* Jimmy Dale, Mark Shekter, *Prod* Arthur M. Broidy, *Exec Prod* Steve Broidy, *Assoc Prod* Hurley A. Graffius.

Cast: Peter Kastner, *Paul Bongard*, Joanna Cameron, *Marilyn/Michele*, Louise Sorel, *Ruth*, Gary Burghoff, *Ted*, Richard B. Shull, *Mr. Harris*, Joanna Barnes, *Jane Ink*, John Gerstad, *Paul's Father*, Mary Lou Mellace, *Car Rental Girl*, Jeanne Sorel, *Paul's Mother*, Joe Kottler, *Cab Driver*, Tom Ruisinger, *Travel Agent*, Frank Orsatti, *Manuel*, Barry Woloski, *Hippie*. R.

Poor imitation of *The Graduate* starring Peter Kastner as a young employee in an advertising agency, who has an affair with his boss (Joanna Barnes) who also happens to be his fiancée's mother. Kastner is basically repeating the schlemiel role he played in *You're a Big Boy Now*, a similar, but superior film. *B.S. I Love You* has all the wit and intelligence its title suggests.

50 Baby Blue Marine (1976) *** Columbia, 90 min. *Dir* John Hancock, *Scr* Stanford Whitmore, *Cin* Laszlo Kovacs, *Ed* Marion Rothman, *Des* Walter Scott Herndon, *Mus* Fred Karlin, *Prod* Aaron Spelling, Leonard Goldberg, *Assoc Prod* Robert LaVigne.

Cast: Jan-Michael Vincent, *Marion*, Glynnis O'Connor, *Rose*, Katherine Helmond, *Mrs. Hudkins*, Dana Elcar, *Sheriff Wenzel*, Bert Remsen, *Mr. Hudkins*, B. Kirby, Jr., *Pop Mosley*, Richard Gere, *Marine Raider*, Art Lund,

Mr. Elmore, Michael Conrad, *Drill Instructor*, Allan Miller, *Capt. Bittman*, Michael LeClair, *Barney Hudkins*, Will Seltzer, *Pat Phelps*, Kenneth Tobey, *Buick Driver*. PG.

Appealing, but somewhat sentimental story of a youth who, after washing out of the Marines, is mistaken for a war hero in a small Colorado town during WWII. *Baby Blue Marine* is a good portrait of the times, and nicely examines hero worship and the attitudes of Americans toward those who fail. Michael Vincent, in one of his better roles, is excellent as the youth who is too ashamed to admit the truth.

51 **The Baby Maker** (1970) * National General, 109 min. *Dir* James Bridges, *Scr* James Bridges, *Cin* Charles Rosher, Jr., *Ed* Walter Thompson, *Des* Francis M. Noden, *Art* Mort Rabinowitz, *Mus* Fred Karlin (AN), *Lyrics* Tylwyth Kymry (AN), *Prod* Richard Goldstone, A Robert Wise Production.

Cast: Barbara Hershey, *Tish Gray*, Collin Wilcox-Horne, *Suzanne Wilcox*, Sam Groom, *Jay Wilcox*, Scott Glenn, *Ted Jacks*, Jeannie Berlin, *Charlotte*, Lili Valenty, *Mrs. Culnick*, Helena Kallianiotes, *Helena*, Robert Pickett, *Dr. Sims*, Paul Linke, *Sam*, Phillis Coates, *Tish's Mother*, Madge Kennedy, *Tish's Grandmother*, Ray Hemphill, *George*, Brenda Sykes, *Frances*, Michael Geoffrey Horne, *Jimmy*. R.

Strange drama about a hippie girl (Barbara Hershey), who agrees to become pregnant for a childless couple (Sam Groom, Collin Wilcox-Horne). This offbeat idea had potential because of its daring, but James Bridges bogs *The Baby Maker* down with a dull soap opera plot. The girl moves in with the couple and later her boyfriend interferes, all with predictable results. Bridges has done far better work in his later films.

52 **Bad Company** (1972) **** Paramount, 91 min. *Dir* Robert Benton, *Scr* Robert Benton, David Newman, *Cin* Gordon Willis, *Ed* Ron Kalish, Ralph Rosenblum, *Des* Paul Sylbert, *Art* Robert Gundlach, *Mus* Harvey Schmidt, *Prod* Stanley R. Jaffe.

Cast: Jeff Bridges, *Jake Rumsey*, Barry Brown, *Drew Dixon*, Jim Davis, *Marchal*, David Huddleston, *Big Joe*, John Savage, *Loney*, Jerry Houser, *Simms*, Damon Cofer, *Jim Bob Logan*, Joshua Hill Lewis, *Boog Bookin*, Geoffrey Lewis, Raymond Guth, Ed Lauter, John Quade, *Big Joe's Gang*, Jean Allison, Ned Wertimer, *Dixon's Parents*, Charles Tyner, *Farmer*. PG.

Excellent comedy-drama about a group of young drifters in the old West. Of the several youth-oriented westerns to emerge during this period, *Bad Company* is by far the best. The theme of growing up quickly in the real world is a bit unusual for this genre, but it works well here. Noted screenwriter Robert Benton (*Bonnie and Clyde*) made a fine directorial debut, but unfortunately was forced to wait several years for his second.

53 **The Bad News Bears** (1976) *** Paramount, 102 min. *Dir* Michael Ritchie, *Scr* Bill Lancaster (W), *Cin* John A. Alonzo, *Ed* Richard A. Harris, *Des* Polly Platt, *Mus* Jerry Fielding, *Prod* Stanley R. Jaffe.

Cast: Walter Matthau, *Morris Buttermaker*, Tatum O'Neal, *Manda Whurlitzer*, Vic Morrow, *Roy Turner*, Joyce Van Patten, *Cleveland*, Ben Piazza, *Councilman Whitewood*, Jackie Earle Haley, *Kelly Leak*, Alfred Lutter, *Ogilvie*, Brandon Cruz, *Joey Turner*, Chris Barnes, *Tanner Boyle*, Erin Blunt, *Ahmed Abdul Rahim*, Gary Lee Cavagnaro, *Engelberg*, Quinn Smith, *Timmy*

Lupus, Scott Firestone, *Regi Tower*, David Pollock, *Rudi Stein*, David Stambaugh, *Toby Whitwood*, Brett Marx, *Jimmy Feldman*, Jamie Escobedo, *José Aguilar*, George Gonzales, *Miguel Aguilar*, Timothy Blake, *Mrs. Lupus*, Bill Sorrells, *Mr. Tower*, Shari Summers, *Mrs. Turner*, Joe Brooks, *Umpire*, George Wyner, *White Sox Manager*. PG. $24,890,000.

Surprisingly good comedy about a down-and-out former minor league baseball player who is hired to coach the worst team in the little league. *The Bad News Bears* received much criticism for its honest and realistic portrayal of young boys. The boys continually use four-letter words and resort to cheating and physical violence to win. This is no Disney film by any means. The plot may be a bit too predictable, but this is still one of the finest films made about children. Unfortunately the same cannot be said about the two sequels, *The Bad News Bears in Breaking Training* and *The Bad News Bears Go To Japan* which followed the same course as the first, but without its wit and intelligence.

54 The Bad News Bears in Breaking Training (1977) ** Paramount, 99 min. *Dir* Michael Pressman, *Scr* Paul Brickman, based on characters created by Bill Lancaster, *Cin* Fred J. Koenekamp, *Ed* John W. Wheeler, *Art* Steve Berger, *Cos* Jack Martell, *Mus* Craig Safan, *Song Lyrics* Norman Gimbel, *Prod* Leonard Goldberg.

Cast: William Devane, *Mike Leak*, Clifton James, *Sy Orlansky*, Jackie Earle Haley, *Kelly Leak*, Jimmy Baio, *Carmen Ronzonni*, Chris Barnes, *Tannar Boyle*, Erin Blunt, *Ahmad Abdul Rahim*, Jaime Escobedo, *Jose Aguilar*, George Gonzales, *Miguel Aguilar*, Alfred Lutter, *Ogilvie*, Brett Marx, *Jimmie Feldman*, David Pollock, *Rudi Stein*, Quinn Smith, *Timmy Lupus*, David Stambaugh, *Toby Whitewood*, Jeffrey Louis Starr, *Mike Engelberg*, Fred Stuthman, *Caretaker*, Dolph Sweet, *Coach Manning*, Lane Smith, *Officer Mackie*, Pat Corley, *Coach Morrie Slaytor*. PG $15,050,00. See *The Bad News Bears*.

55 Badge 373 (1973) ** Paramount, 116 min. *Dir* Howard W. Koch, *Scr* Pete Hamill, *Cin* Arthur J. Ornitz, *Ed* John Woodcock, *Art* Philip Rosenberg, *Prod* Howard W. Koch.

Cast: Robert Duvall, *Eddie Ryan*, Verna Bloom, *Mareen*, Henry Darrow, *Sweet William*, Eddie Egan, *Scanlon*, Filipe Luciano, *Ruben*, Tina Cristiani, *Mrs. Caputo*, Marina Dwell, *Rita Garcia*, Chico Martinez, *Frankie Diaz*, Jose Duval, *Ferrer*, Louis Cosentino, *Gigi Caputo*, Luis Avalos, *Chico*, Nubia Olivero, *Mrs. Diaz*, Sam Schact, *Assistant D.A.*, Edward F. Carey, *Commissioner*, John Marriot, *Superintendent*, Pete Hamill, *Reporter*. R.

Although not really a sequel to *The French Connection*, *Badge 373* is based on the exploits of the same New York cop, Eddie Egan. This film is, in no way, in the same class with that cop classic. It attemps to add a skimpy plot to its episodic structure and fails with both. Duvall is excellent as the cop, but *Badge 373* never really gets off the ground.

56 Badlands (1974) ***** Warner Bros., 95 min. *Dir* Terrence Malick, *Scr* Terrence Malick, *Cin* Tak Fujimoto, Steven Larner, Brian Probyn, *Ed* Robert Estrin, *Art* Jack Fisk, *Mus* George Tipton, *Prod* Terrence Malick, *Exec Prod* Edward R. Pressman, *Assoc Prod* Lou Stroller.

Cast: Martin Sheen, *Kit*, Sissy Spacek, *Holly*, Warren Oates, *Holly's Father*, Ramon Bieri, *Cato*, Alan Vint, *Deputy*, Gary Littlejohn, *Sheriff*, John Carter, *Rich Man*, Bryan Montgomery, *Boy*, Gail Threlkeld, *Girl*, Charles Fitzpatrick, *Clerk*, Howard Ragsdale, *Boss*, John Womack, Jr., *Trooper on Plane*, Dona Baldwin, *Maid*, Ben Bravo, *Gas Station Attendant*, Terrence Malick, *Salesman*. PG.

Terrence Malick made a brilliantly audacious directorial debut with this eccentric black comedy loosely based on the real-life exploits of killers Charles Starkweather and Carol Fugate in the 1950's. Unlike other nostalgia films about that decade the point of view of *Badlands* is very bleak, perhaps the title is a reference to the decade itself. The entire mood of this film is very odd as both the performances and dialogue are very nonchalant and almost thrown away as if unimportant. *Badlands* is about boredom, but it is not boring.

57 **The Ballad of Cable Hogue** (1970) **** Warner Bros., 121 min. *Dir* Sam Peckinpah, *Scr* John Crawford, Edward Penny, *Cin* Lucien Ballard, *Ed* Lou Lombardo, Frank Santillo, *Art* Leroy Coleman, *Cos* Robert Fletcher, *Mus* Jerry Goldsmith, *Songs* Richard Gillis, Jerry Goldsmith, Sung by Richard Gillis, *Prod* Sam Peckinpah, *Co-Prod* William Faralla, *Exec Prod* Phil Feldman, *Assoc Prod* Gordon Dawson.

Cast: Jason Robards, *Cable Hogue*, Stella Stevens, *Hildy*, David Warner, *Joshua*, Strother Martin, *Bowen*, Slim Pickens, *Ben*, L.Q. Jones, *Taggert*, Peter Whitney, *Cushing*, R.G. Armstrong, *Quittner*, Gene Evans, *Clete*, William Mims, *Jensen*, Kathleen Freeman, *Mrs. Jensen*, Susan O'Connell, *Claudia*, Vaughn Taylor, *Powell*, Felix Nelson, *William*. R.

Unusual western comedy drama about a prospector who is abandoned in the desert and establishes his own personal oasis. Jason Robards is excellent as the man who tries to live out his life as a hermit to escape the modernization of society. *The Ballad of Cable Hogue* is Sam Peckinpah's wonderful tribute to the old West and a metaphor for its death.

58 **Bananas** (1971) *** United Artists, 81 min. *Dir* Woody Allen, *Scr* Woody Allen, Mickey Rose, *Cin* Andrew M. Costikyan, *Ed* Ron Kalish, *Des* Ed Wittstein, *Mus* Marvin Hamlisch, *Prod* Jack Grossberg, *Exec Prod* Charles H. Joffe, *Assoc Prod* Ralph Rosenblum.

Cast: Woody Allen, *Fielding Mellish*, Louise Lasser, *Nancy*, Carlos Montalban, *Gen. Vargas*, Natividad Abascal, *Yolanda*, Jacobo Marales, *Esposito*, Miguel Suarez, *Luis*, David Ortiz, *Sanchez*, Rene Enriquez, *Diaz*, Jack Axelrod, *Arroyo*, Howard Cosell, Roger Grimsby, Don Dunphy, *Themselves*, Charlotte Rae, *Mrs. Mellish*, Stanley Ackerman, *Dr. Mellish*, Dan Frazer, *Priest*, Martha Greenhouse, *Dr. Feigen*, Axel Anderson, *Tortured Man*, Tigre Perez, *Perez*, Baron De Beer, *British Ambassador*, Arthur Hughes, *Judge*, John Braden, *Prosecutor*, Dorthi Fox, *J. Edgar Hoover*. PG.

Hilarious, but sloppily made Woody Allen comedy. *Bananas*, a satire of South American revolutions and revolutionaries, mixes Allen's usual brilliant verbal humor with slapstick comedy, sight gags and anachronisms. This was made before Allen had refined his directorial skills and it shows. The structure is not very tight and everything seems to have been thrown together. Despite all this *Bananas* does contain some of the funniest sequences ever put on film.

59 **Bang the Drum Slowly** (1973) *** Paramount, 98 min. *Dir* John Hancock, *Scr* Mark Harris, based on his novel, *Cin* Richard Shore, *Ed* Richard Marks, *Des* Robert Gundlach, *Mus* Stephen Lawrence, *Prod* Maurice and Lois Rosenfield.

Cast: Michael Moriarty, *Henry Wiggen*, Robert DeNiro (NY), *Bruce Pearson*, Vincent Gardenia (AN), *Dutch Schnell*, Phil Foster, *Joe Jaros*, Ann Wedgeworth, *Katie*, Patrick McVey, *Mr. Pearson*, Heather MacRae, *Holly Wiggen*, Selma Diamond, *Tootsie*, Barbara Babcock, Maurice Rosenfield, *Team Owners*, Andy Jarrell, *Ugly Jones*, Marshall Efron, *Bradley Lord*, Barton Heyman, *Red Traphagen*, Donny Burks, *Perry*, Hector Elias, *Diego*, Tom Signorelli, *Goose Williams*, Jim Donahue, *Canada Smith*, Nicolas Surovy, *Aleck Olson*, Danny Aiello, *Horse*, Hector Troy, *George*, Tony Major, *Jonah*, Alan Manaon, *Dr. Loftus*, Ernesto Gonzales, *Dr. Chambers*. PG.

Above-average baseball film about the friendship of two professional baseball players, the star pitcher (Michael Moriarty) and a mediocre catcher (Robert DeNiro), who is dying of Hodgkin's Disease. *Bang the Drum Slowly* is more of a character study, which focuses on the two player's relationship, than a sports film, and it avoids the drippy sentimentality that plagues other fatal disease films.

60 **Bank Shot** (1974) *** United Artists, 100 min. *Dir* Gower Champion, *Scr* Wendell Mayes, based on novel by Donald E. Westlake, *Cin* Harry Stradling, Jr., *Ed.* David Bretherton, *Art* Albert Brenner, *Mus* John Morris, *Prod* Hal Lander, Bobby Roberts.

Cast: George C. Scott, *Walter Ballantine*, Joanna Cassidy, *El*, Sorrell Booke, *Al. G. Karp*, G. Wood, *FBI Agent Constable*, Clifton James, *Frank "Bulldog" Streiger*, Robert Balaban, *Victor Karp*, Bibi Osterwald, *Mums*, Frank McRae, *Herman X*, Don Calfa, *Stosh Gornick*, Harvey Evans, *Irving*, Hank Stohl, *Johnson*, Liam Dunn, *Painter*, Jack Riley, *Jackson*, Pat Zurica, *Man in Privy*, Harvey J. Goldenberg, Jamie Reidy, *Policemen*. PG.

Above average bank heist comedy with a strange twist, the robbers steal the entire bank which is temporarily housed in a trailer. George C. Scott is excellent in an offbeat role, that brings his generally bigger than life screen persona down to a much lower level, as the leader of a gang of burglars who pull off this unlikely robbery. *Bank Shot* is silly at times, but it does succeed on this level.

61 **The Barefoot Executive** (1971) ** Buena Vista, 96 min. *Dir* Robert Butler, *Scr* Joseph L. McEveety, based on story by Stewart C. Billett, Lila Garrett, Bernie Kahn, *Cin* Charles F. Wheeler, *Ed* Robert Stafford, *Art* Ed Graves, John B. Mansbridge, *Cos* Chuck Keehne, Emily Sundby, *Mus* Robert F. Brunner, *Prod* Bill Anderson, A Walt Disney Production.

Cast: Kurt Russell, *Steve Post*, Joe Flynn, *Francis X. Wilbranks*, Harry Morgan, *E.J. Crampton*, Wally Cox, *Mertons*, Heather North, *Jennifer Scott*, Alan Hewitt, *Farnsworth*, Hayden Rorke, *Clifford*, John Ritter, *Roger*, Jack Bender, *Tom*, Tom Anfinsen, *Dr. Schmidt*. G.

Standard Disney comedy that spoofs television networks. Kurt Russell discovers a chimpanzee, who has the uncanny ability to pick hit television shows and uses this to become vice-president of the company. Disney took a potentially good idea for a comedy, but instead of using this idea to its full advantage they ruined it, as usual, with a series of slapstick sight gags.

62 **Barry Lyndon** (1975) (AN, NB) ***** Britain, Warner Bros., 185 min.
Dir Stanley Kubrick (AN, NB, BFA), *Scr* Stanley Kubrick (AN), based on novel
by William Makepeace Thackerey, *Cin* John Alcott (A, NS, BFA), *Ed* Tony
Lawson, *Des* Ken Adam (A), *Art* Roy Walker (A), *Cos* Milena Canonero,
Ulla-Britt Soderland (A), *Mus Adaptation* Leonard Rosenman (A), *Chor*
Geraldine Stephenson, *Prod* Stanley Kubrick.

   Cast: Ryan O'Neal, *Barry Lyndon*, Marisa Berenson, *Lady Lyndon*, Partick Magee, *The Chevalier*, Hardy Kruger, *Capt. Potzdorf*, Steven Berkoff,
Lord Ludd, Gay Hamilton, *Nora*, Marie Kean, *Barry's Mother*, Diana Koerner,
German Girl, Murray Melvin, *Rev. Runt*, Frank Middlemass, *Sir Charles Lyndon*, Andre Morell, *Lord Wendover*, Arthur O'Sullivan, *Highwayman*, Godfrey Quigley, *Capt. Grogan*, Leonard Rossiter, *Capt. Quin*, Philip Stone,
Graham, Leon Vitali, *Lord Bullingdon*, David Morley, *Brian*, Michael Hordern, *Narrator*. PG. $9,200,000.

   The single greatest achievement in cinema history. *Barry Lyndon* is a
masterful period adventure starring Ryan O'Neal as an 18th century Irish
rogue, whose great goal in life is to gain a title. Stanley Kubrick creates a
mood and tone of almost unobtainable brilliance and miraculously maintains
it for the film's entire three hours. Re-creating a past time on film is relatively
simple, but this film literally vaults the viewer back into time. *Barry Lyndon* is
as near to perfection as any film can be, and mere words cannot do it justice.

63 **Battle for the Planet of the Apes** (1973) * 20th Century–Fox, 86 min.
Dir J. Lee Thompson, *Scr* John William Corrington, Joyce Hooper
Corrington, *Story* Paul Dehn, based on characters created by Pierre Boulle,
Cin Richard H. Kline, *Ed* John C. Horger, Ala L. Jaggs, *Art* Dale Hennesy, *Mus*
Leonard Rosenman, *Prod* Arthur P. Jacobs, *Assoc Prod* Frank Capra, Jr.

   Cast: Roddy McDowell, *Caesar*, Claude Akins, *Aldo*, John Huston,
Lawgiver, Natalie Trundy, *Lisa*, Severn Darden, *Kolp*, Lew Ayres, *Mandemus*,
Paul Williams, *Virgil*, Austin Stoker, *MacDonald*, Noah Keen, *Teacher*,
Richard Eastham, *Mutant Captain*, France Nuyen, *Alma*, Paul Stevens, *Men-
dez*, Heather Lowe, *Doctor*, Bobby Porter, *Cornelius*, Michael Stearns, *Jake*,
Cal Wilson, *Soldier*, Pat Cardi, *Young Chimp*, John Landis, *Jake's Friend*, An-
dy Knight, *Mutant on Motorcycle*. G. $4,000,000. See *Beneath the Planet of
the Apes*.

64 **Battlestar Gallactica** (1979) ** Universal, 120 min. *Dir* Richard A.
Colla, *Scr* Glen A. Larson, *Cin* Ben Coleman, *Ed* Robert L. Kimble, Leon Or-
tiz-Gil, Larry Strong, *Art* John E. Chilberg II, *Cos* Jean-Pierre Dorleac, *Sp*
Apogee Inc., *Mus* Stu Phillips, *Prod* John Dykstra, *Exec Prod* Glen A. Larson,
Assoc Prod Winrich Kolbe, *Supervising Prod* Leslie Stevens.

   Cast: Richard Hatch, *Capt. Apollo*, Dirk Benedict, *Lt. Starbuck*, Lorne
Greene, *Commander Adama*, Ray Milland, *Uri*, Lew Ayres, *Adar*, Jane
Seymour, *Serina*, Wilfrid Hyde-White, *Anton*, John Colicos, *Count Baltar*,
Laurette Spang, *Cassiopea*, John Fink, *Dr. Page*, Terry Carter, *Col. Tighe*,
Herb Jefferson, Jr., *Lt. Boone*, Maren Jensen, *Athena*, Tony Swartz, *Lt. Jolly*,
Noah Hathaway, *Boxey*, Ed Begley, Jr., *Ensign Greenbean*, Rick Springfield,
Lt. Zac, Randi Oakes, *Young Woman*. PG. $7,100,000.

   Nothing more than a re-edited version of the television pilot film of the
failed series, with the addition of the gimmick Sensurround. Putting this

television production on the big screen only accentuates its inferiority to other science fiction adventures, such as *Star Wars*. There are no real ideas or characterizations, and the plot seems like a rehash of other television dramas transposed to an outer space setting.

65 The Bawdy Adventures of Tom Jones (1976) * Britain, Universal, 94 min. *Dir* Cliff Owen, *Scr* Jeremy Lloyd, based on musical play *Tom Jones* by Dan MacPherson with music and lyrics by Paul Holden, from novel *Tom Jones* by Henry Fielding, *Cin* Douglas Slocombe, *Ed* Bill Blunden, *Art* Jack Shampan, *Cos* Beatrice Dawson, *Mus* Ron Grainer, *Songs* Paul Holden, David Matthews and Michael Guilgud, Annie and Christopher Gunning, *Prod* Robert Sadoff.

Cast: Nicky Henson, *Tom Jones*, Trevor Howard, *Squire Western*, Terry-Thomas, *Mr. Square*, Arthur Lowe, *Dr. Thwackum*, Georgia Brown, *Jenny Jones (Mrs. Waters)*, Joan Collins, *Black Bess*, William Mervyn, *Squire Alworthy*, Murray Melvin, *Blifil*, Madeline Smith, *Sophia*, Geraldine McEwan, *Lady Bellaston*, Jeremy Lloyd, *Lord Fellemar*, Janie Greenspun, *Daisy*, Michael Bates, *Madman*, Hilda Fenemore, *Mrs. Belcher*, Patricia MacPherson, *Molly Seagram*, Isabel Dean, *Bridget*, James Hayter, *Briggs*, Frank Thornton, *Whitlow*, Gladys Henson, *Mrs. Wilkins*, Joan Cooper, *Nellie*, Maxine Casson, *Prudence*, Judy Buxton, *Lizzie*. R.

Trashy period musical comedy about the amorous adventures of a young English rogue living in the 18th century. This was based on the stage show *Tom Jones*, which was inspired by the classic comedy of the 1960's. *The Bawdy Adventures of Tom Jones* pales miserably in comparison to the brilliance of the original film and Nicky Henson is a poor imitation of Albert Finney.

66 Baxter (1973) ** Britain, National General, 105 min. *Dir* Lionel Jeffries, *Scr* Reginald Rose, based on novel *The Boy Who Could Make Himself Disappear* by Kim Platt, *Cin* Geoffrey Unsworth, *Ed* Teddy Darvas, *Art* Anthony Pratt, *Mus* Michael J. Lewis, *Prod* Arthur Lewis, *Exec Prod* Howard G. Barnes, John L. Hargreaves.

Cast: Patricia Neal, *Dr. Clemm*, Jean-Pierre Cassel, *Roger Tunnell*, Britt Ekland, *Chris Bentley*, Lynn Carlin, *Mrs. Baxter*, Scott Jacoby, *Roger Baxter*, Sally Thomsett, *Nemo*, Paul Eddington, *Mr. Rawling*, Paul Maxwell, *Mr. Baxter*, Ian Thomson, *Dr. Walsh*, Ronald Leigh-Hunt, *Mr. Fishie*, Frances Bennett, *Mrs. Newman*, George Tovey, *George*. PG.

Sentimental drama about a young boy (Scott Jacoby) with a speech impediment, who also has to cope with the divorce of his parents (Lynn Carlin, Paul Maxwell). Patricia Neal also stars as a speech therapist, who tries to correct his impediment. This is merely the beginning of his problems, and *Baxter* really piles it on. The film does go overboard, but it is saved by some fine performances.

67 Bedknobs and Broomsticks (1971) ** Buena Vista, 117 min. *Dir (Animation)* Ward Kimbell, *Scr* Don Da Gradi, Bill Walsh, based on novel by Mary Norton, *Cin* Frank Phillips, *Ed* Cotton Warburton, *Art* Peter Ellenshaw, John B. Mansbridge (AN), *Cos* Bill Thomas (AN), *Sp* Danny Lee, Eustace Lycett, Alan Maley (A), *Mus* Richard M. Sherman, Robert B. Sherman (AN), *Mus Adaptation*, Irwin Kostal (AN), *Song*, "The Age of Not Believing," *Mus* Richard M. Sherman, Robert B. Sherman (AN), *Prod* Bill Walsh, A Walt Disney Production.

Cast: Angela Lansbury, *Eglantine Price*, David Tomlinson, *Emelius Browne*, Roddy McDowell, *Mr. Jelk*, Sam Jaffe, *Book Dealer*, John Ericson, *Col. Heller*, Bruce Forsyth, *Swinburne*, Cindy O'Callaghan, *Carrie*, Roy Snart, *Paul*, Ian Weighill, *Charlie*, Tessie O'Shea, *Mrs. Hobday*, Arthur E. Gould-Porter, *Capt. Greer*, Ben Wrigley, *Portobello Road Workman*, Reginald Owen, *Gen. Teagler*, Cyril Delevanti, *Elderly Farmer*, Rick Traeger, Manfred Lating, *German Sergeants*, John Orchard, *Vendor*, Robert Holt, *Voice of Codfish*, Lennie Weinrib, *Voices of Secretary Bird & Lion*, Dal McKennon, *Voice of Bear*. G. $11,400,000.

Unusual Disney musical fantasy starring Angela Lansbury as a 20th century witch, who uses magic to battle Nazis. *Bedknobs and Broomsticks* blends live action with animation, much like Disney's earlier blockbuster *Mary Poppins*, but not with the same results. The animation sequences are well-done, as is usually the case with Disney, but the storyline is weak and the songs are unmemorable.

68 **The Beguiled** (1971) *** Universal, 109 min. *Dir* Don Siegel, *Scr* Grimes Grice, John B. Sherry (pseudonyms for Irene Kamp, Albert Maltz, Claude Traverse), based on novel by Thomas Cullinan, *Cin* Bruce Surtees, *Ed* Carl Pingitore, *Des* Ted Haworth, *Art* Alexander Golitzen, *Cos* Helen Colvig, *Prod* Don Siegel, *Assoc Prod* Claude Traverse.

Cast: Clint Eastwood, *Corp. John McBurney*, Geraldine Page, *Martha Farnsworth*, Elizabeth Hartman, *Edwina Dabney*, Jo Ann Harris, *Carol*, Darleen Carr, *Doris*, Mae Mercer, *Hallie*, Pamelyn Ferdin, *Amy*, Melody Thomas, *Abigail*, Peggy Drier, *Lizzie*, Pattye Mattick, *Janie*, Patrick Culliton, *Miles*, George Dunn, *Jepson*. R.

Offbeat Clint Eastwood Civil War vehicle about a wounded Union soldier who is taken to a Confederate girl's school to recuperate. *The Beguiled* is more interesting than most Eastwood films as the emphasis is more on mood and character than action, and it could be described as a gothic horror film. This was Eastwood's only failure at the box-office during the 1970's.

69 **Being There** (1979) ***** United Artists, 130 min. *Dir* Hal Ashby, *Scr* Jerzy Kosinski (W), based on his novel, *Cin* Caleb Deschanel (NS), *Ed* Don Zimmerman, *Des* Michael Haller, *Art* James Schoppe, *Cos* May Routh, *Mus* John Mandel, *Prod* Andrew Braunsberg, *Exec Prod* Jack Schwartzman, *Assoc Prod* Charles Mulvehill.

Cast: Peter Sellers (AN, NB, GMC), *Chance*, Shirley MacLaine, *Eve Rand*, Melvyn Douglas (A, NY, LA, G), *Benjamin Rand*, Jack Warden, *President "Bobby"*, Richard Dysart, *Dr. Robert Allenby*, Richard Basehart, *Vladimir Skrapinov*, Ruth Attaway, *Louise*, Dave Clennon, *Thomas Franklin*, Fran Brill, *Sally Hayes*, Denise DuBarry, *Johanna Franklin*, James Noble, *Presidential Advisor*, Alice Hirson, *First Lady*, Donald Jacob, *David*, Ernest M. McClure, *Jeffrey*, Kenneth Patterson, *Perkins*, Richard Venture, *Wilson*, Arthur Grundy, *Arthur*, W.C. "Mutt" Burton, *Lewis*. PG. $10,805,000

Brilliant black comedy about a simpleton who becomes a national celebrity. Peter Sellers is superb as a gardener who after years of isolation is thrust out into the world and is taken into the home of a wealthy industrialist, brilliantly played by Melvyn Douglas. There he meets many high officials, including the President of the U.S., all of whom misinterpret his simplistic comments about gardening to be perceptive metaphors. The humor and mood is kept at a very low-key throughout, and the pace is slow and deliberate, but *Being There* is never boring and retains interest for the entire two hours. Most of all as Chance, Sellers creates one of the most unique and memorable of all screen characters.

70 **The Bell Jar** (1979) * Avco Embassy, 112 min. *Dir* Larry Peerce, *Scr* Marjorie Kellogg, based on novel by Sylvia Plath, *Cin* Gerald Hirschfeld, *Ed* Marvin Wallowitz, *Des* John Robert Lloyd, *Cos* Donald Brooks, *Mus* Gerald Fried, *Prod* Jerrold Brandt, Jr., Michael Todd, Jr., *Exec Prod* Robert A. Goldston.

Cast: Marilyn Hassett, *Esther*, Julie Harris, *Mrs. Greenwood*, Anne Jackson, *Dr. Nolan*, Barbara Barrie, *Jay Cee*, Robert Klein, *Lenny*, Donna Mitchell, *Joan*, Mary Louise Weller, *Doreen*, Scott McKay, *Gilling*, Jameson Parker, *Buddy*, Thaao Penghlis, *Marco*, Meg Mundy, *Bea Ramsey*, Elizabeth Hubbard, *Vikki St. John*, Carol Monferdini, *Hilda*, Debbie McLeod, *Betsy*, Karen Howard, *Toni La Bouchere*, Margaret Hall, *Jane McLode*. R.

Pretentious psychological drama about a female student with a "mother problem" modeled on Sylvia Plath. *The Bell Jar* purports to be a serious study of mental illness, but the filmmakers have turned it into a Harold Robbins style potboiler. The dialogue is poor and sometimes quite ridiculous, and Marilyn Hassett is not a strong enough actress to handle the more difficult breakdown scenes. This film is a loser on all counts.

71 **Ben** (1972) * Cinerama, 95 min. *Dir* Phil Karlson, *Scr* Gilbert A. Ralston, based on characters created by Stephen Gilbert, *Cin* Russell Metty, *Ed* Harry Gerstad, *Art* Rolland M. Brooks, *Cos* Ray Harp, Mina Mittelman, *Mus* Walter Scharf, *Song* "Ben," *Mus* Walter Scharf (AN, G), *Lyrics* Don Black (AN, G), sung by Michael Jackson, *Prod* Mort Briskin, *Exec Prod* Charles A. Pratt, *Assoc Prod* Joel Briskin.

Cast: Lee H. Montgomery, *Danny Garrison*, Joseph Campanella, *Cliff Kirtland*, Arthur O'Connell, *Billy Hatfield*, Rosemary Murphy, *Beth Garrison*, Meredith Baxter, *Eve Garrison*, Kaz Garas, *Joe Greer*, Paul Carr, *Kelly*, Richard Van Vleet, *Reade*, Kenneth Tobey, *Engineer*, James Luisi, *Ed*, Lee Paul, *Carey*, Norman Alden, *Policeman*, Scott Garrett, *Henry Gray*, Arlen Stuart, *Mrs. Gray*, Richard Drasin, *George*. PG. See *Willard*.

72 **Beneath the Planet of the Apes** (1970) ** 20th Century–Fox, 98 min. *Dir* Ted Post, *Scr* Paul Dehn, *Story* Mort Abrahams, Paul Dehn, based on character created by Pierre Boulle, *Cin.* Milton Krasner, *Ed* Marion Rothman, *Art* William Creber, Jack Martin Smith, *Cos* Morton Haack, *Mus* Leonard Rosenman, *Prod* Arthur P. Jacobs, *Assoc Prod* Mort Abrahams.

Cast: Charlton Heston, *Taylor*, James Franciscus, *Brent*, Kim Hunter, *Zira*, Maurice Evans, *Dr. Zaius*, Linda Harrison, *Nova*, Paul Richards, *Mendez*, Victor Buono, *Fat Man*, James Gregory, *Ursus*, Jeff Corey, *Caspay*, Natalie Trundy, *Albina*, Thomas Gomez, *Minister*, David Watson, *Cornelius*, Don Pedro Colley, *Negro*, Tod Andrews, *Skipper*, Gregory Sierra, *Verger*, Eldon Burke, *Gorilla Sergeant*, Lou Wagner, *Lucius*. G. $8,600,000.

In 1968 an unusually good science fiction drama, titled *The Planet of the Apes*, was released. The success of this film prompted a series, with four sequels, in an attempt to complete the cycle by explaining how the Earth became the "monkey planet." Unfortunately none of these sequels, *Beneath the Planet of the Apes*, *Escape from the Planet of the Apes*, *Conquest of the Planet of the Apes*, and *Battle for the Planet of the Apes*, equal their predecessor, with the final installment little more than a shoddy mess.

73 **Benji** (1974) *** Mulberry Square, 85 min. *Dir* Joe Camp, *Scr* Joe Camp, *Cin* Don Reddy, *Ed* Leon Smith, *Des* Harland Wright, *Mus* Euel Box, *Prod* Joe Camp.

Cast: Higgens, *Benji*, Patsy Garrett, *Mary*, Allen Fiuzat, *Paul*, Cynthia Smith, *Cindy*, Peter Breck, *Dr. Chapman*, Frances Bavier, *Lady with Cat*, Terry Carter, *Tuttle*, Edgar Buchanon, *Bill*, Tom Lester, *Riley*, Christopher Connelly, *Henry*, Deborah Walley, *Linda*, Mark Slade, *Mitch*, Herb Vigran, *Samuels*, Larry Swartz, *Floyd*, J.D. Young, *2nd Policeman*, Edwin Hearne, *Harvey*, Katie Hearne, *Mrs. Harvey*, Don Puckett, *Plainclothesman*, Ed De Latte, *Bob*, Victor Raider-Wexler, *Payton*, Charles Starkey, *Custodian*, Ben Vaughn, *Man*. G. $12,000,000.

Above-average family film about a little dog who saves two children from kidnappers and is subsequently adopted by the children's family. The dog is the real star of the film and he surprisingly proves to be a good actor, thanks to excellent training by Frank Inn. *Benji* does not have much of a plot, as the film just follows the dog's adventures. A sequel *For the Love of Benji* followed, in which the dog becomes involved in international intrigue.

74 **The Betsy** (1978) ** Allied Artists, 120 min. *Dir* Daniel Petrie, *Scr* William Bast, Walter Bernstein, based on novel by Harold Robbins, *Cin* Mario Tosi, *Ed* Rita Roland, *Des* Herman A. Blumenthal, *Cos* Dorothy Jeakins, *Mus* John Barry, *Prod* Robert R. Weston, *Assoc Prod* Jack Grossberg, Presented by Emanuel L. Wolf.

Cast: Laurence Olivier *Loren Hardeman, Sr.*, Robert Duvall, *Loren Hardeman III*, Katharine Ross, *Salley Hardeman*, Tommy Lee Jones, *Angelo Perino*, Jane Alexander, *Alicia Hardeman*, Lesley-Anne Down, *Lady Bobby Ayres*, Joseph Wiseman, *Jake Weinstein*, Kathleen Beller, *Betsy Hardeman*, Edward Herrmann, *Dan Weyman*, Paul Rudd, *Loren Hardeman, Jr.*, Roy Poole, *Duncan*, Richard Venture, *Mark Sampson*, Titos Vandis, *Angelo Luigi Perino*, Clifford David, *Joe Warren*, Inga Swenson, *Mrs. Craddock*, Whitney Blake, *Elizabeth Hardeman*, Carol Williard, *Roxanne*, Read Morgan, *Donald*, Charlie Fields, *Loren III (As a Boy)*. R. $7,850,000.

Above average soap opera about a rich auto manufacturing family, and their cutthroat deals in business and also in their private lives. This is nothing more than the usual trash from Harold Robbins, but it rises above most due to its fine cast, particularly Laurence Olivier as the cantankerous patriarch. "The Betsy" of the title is a new car, reminiscent of the Edsel, named after Olivier's great-granddaughter.

75 **Between the Lines** (1977) **** Midwest, 101 min. *Dir* Joan Micklin Silver, *Scr* Fred Barron, *Story* Fred Barron, David M. Helpern, Jr., *Cin* Kenneth Van Sickle, *Ed* John Carter, *Des* Stuart Wurtzel, *Cos* Patrizia Von Brandenstein, *Prod* Raphael D. Silver.

Cast: John Heard, *Harry*, Lindsay Crouse, *Abbie*, Jeff Goldblum, *Max*, Jill Eikenberry, *Lynn*, Bruno Kirby, *David*, Gwen Welles, *Laura*, Stephen Collins,

Michael, Lewis J. Stadlen, *Stanley*, Michael J. Pollard, *Hawker*, Lane Smith, *Roy*, Marilu Henner, *Danielle*, Jon Korkes, *Frank*, Joe Morton, *Ahmed*, Susan Haskins, *Sarah*, Ray Barry, *Herbert Fisk*, Douglas Kenney, *Doug Henkel*. R.

A wonderful comedy-drama about an underground Boston newspaper. The threadbare plot involves the takeover of paper by a conglomerate, but this is secondary to the theme of the loss of the idealism of the 1960's in the 1970's. The Altmanesque episodic structure serves the film well, with many wonderful and some hysterically funny vignettes, and the performances of the ensemble cast are uniformly brilliant.

76 Beyond the Poseidon Adventure (1979) * Warner Bros., 122 min. *Dir* Irwin Allen, *Scr* Nelson Gidding, based on novel by Paul Gallico, *Cin* Joseph Biroc, *Ed* Bill Brame, *Des* Preston Ames, *Cos* Paul Zastupnevich, *Mus* Jerry Fielding, *Prod* Irwin Allen, *Assoc Prod* Al Gail.

Cast: Michael Caine, *Mike Turner*, Sally Field, *Celeste Whitman*, Telly Savalas, *Capt. Svevo Stefan*, Peter Boyle, *Frank Mazzetti*, Jack Warden, *Harold Meredith*, Shirley Knight, *Hannah Meredith*, Shirley Jones, *Gina Rowe*, Karl Malden, *Wilber*, Slim Pickens, *Tex*, Veronica Hamel, *Suzanne*, Angela Cartwright, *Theresa Mazzetti*, Mark Harmon, *Larry Simpson*, Paul Picerni, *Kurt*, Patrick Culliton, *Doyle*, Dean Ferrandini, *Castorp*. PG. See *The Poseidon Adventure*.

77 The Big Bus (1976) ** Paramount, 88 min. *Dir* James Frawley, *Scr* Lawrence J. Cohen, Fred Freeman, *Cin* Harry Stradling, Jr., *Ed* Edward Warschilka, *Mus* Joel Schiller, *Prod* Lawrence J. Cohen, Fred Freeman, *Exec Prod* Michael and Julia Phillips.

Cast: Joseph Bologna, *Dan Torrance*, Stockard Channing, *Kitty Baxter*, John Beck, *Shoulders O'Brien*, Rene Auberjonois, *Father Kudos*, Ned Beatty, *Shorty Scotty*, Bob Dishy, *Dr. Kurtz*, Jose Ferrer, *Ironman*, Ruth Gordon, *Old Lady*, Harold Gould, *Prof. Baxter*, Larry Hagman, *Parking Lot Doctor*, Sally Kellerman, *Sybil Crane*, Richard Mulligan, *Claude Crane*, Lynn Redgrave, *Camille Levy*, Richard B. Shull, *Emery Bush*, Stuart Margolin, *Alex*, Howard Hesseman, *Scotty's Aide Jack*, Mary Wilcox, *Mary Jane Beth Sue*, Walter Brooke, *Mr. Ames*, Vic Tayback, *Goldie*, Murphy Dunne, *Tommy Joyce*, James Jeter, *Bus Bartender*, Raymond Guth, Miriam Byre-Nethery, Dennis Kort, *Farm Family*. PG.

Average spoof of disaster films and all their clichés and stereotypes. A group of the strangest passengers imaginable take a cross country trip on the world's first nuclear powered bus. This offbeat premise had potential, but unfortunately *The Big Bus* does not have enough good ideas to sustain itself. The large cast tries its best, but far too much of the humor is sophomoric and ridiculous.

78 The Big Fix (1978) *** Universal, 108 min. *Dir* Jeremy Paul Kagan, *Scr* Roger L. Simon, based on his novel, *Cin* Frank Stanley, *Ed* Patrick Kennedy, *Des* Robert F. Boyle, *Art* Raymond Brandt, *Cos* Edith Head, *Mus* Bill Conti, *Prod* Carl Borack, Richard Dreyfuss.

Cast: Richard Dreyfuss, *Moses Wine*, Susan Anspach, *Lila*, Bonnie Bedelia, *Suzanne*, John Lithgow, *Sam Sebastion*, Ofelia Medina, *Alora*, Nicolas Coster, *Spitzler*, F. Murray Abraham, *Eppis*, Fritz Weaver, *Oscar Procari Sr.*, Jorge Cervera, Jr., *Jorge*, Michael Hershewe, *Jacob*, Rita Karin,

Aunt Sonya, Ron Rifkin, *Randy*, Larry Bishop, *Wilson*, Andrew Bloch, *Michael Linker*, Sidney Clute, *Mr. Johnson*, John Cunningham, *Hawthorne*, Frank Doubleday, *Jonah's Partner*, Joyce Easton, *Woman in Mercedes*, Martin Garner, *Bittleman*, Danny Gellis, *Simon*, William Glover, *Commentator*, Kathryn Grody, *Wendy Linker*, Murray MacLeod, *Perry*. PG. $5,935,000.

Well-made detective thriller starring Richard Dreyfuss as Moses Wine, 1960's radical turned private detective in the 1970's, who becomes involved in the search for a missing Abbie Hoffman–type radical and an assassination plot. *The Big Fix* is slightly overlong and is not as taut as a detective thriller should be, but it compensates for this with some genuine ideas involving the changes undergone since the 1960's and the loss of those ideals. Moses Wine could have been the basis for a good series of films, had *The Big Fix* succeeded at the box-office.

79 **Big Jake** (1971) ** National General, 110 min. *Dir* George Sherman, *Scr* Harry Julian Fink, R.M. Fink, *Cin* William Clothier, *Ed* Harry Gerstad, *Art* Carl Anderson, *Cos* Luster Bayless, *Mus* Elmer Bernstein, *Prod* Michael Wayne.

Cast: John Wayne, *Jacob (Jake) McCandles*, Richard Boone, *John Fain*, Maureen O'Hara, *Martha McCandles*, Patrick Wayne, *James McCandles*, Chris Mitchum, *Michael McCandles*, Bobby Vinton, *Jeff McCandles*, Bruce Cabot, *Sam Sharpnose*, Glenn Corbett, *O'Brien*, Harry Carey, Jr., *Pop Dawson*, John Doucette, *Buck Dugan*, Jim Davis, *Head of Lynching Party*, John Agar, *Bert Ryan*. PG. $7,500,000.

Dull western comedy-drama with John Wayne searching for his kidnapped grandson. *Big Jake* is a feeble attempt to combine a traditional John Wayne western with a more fashionable youth-oriented spoof. Unfortunately neither style works, and the mixture is truly bad. The plot is slightly reminiscent of one of Wayne's best films, *The Searchers*.

80 **The Big Sleep** (1978) * Britain, United Artists, 99 min. *Dir* Michael Winner, *Scr* Michael Winner, based on novel by Raymond Chandler, *Cin* Robert Paynter, *Ed* Freddie Wilson, *Des* Harry Pottle, *Art* John Graysmark, *Cos* Ron Beck, *Mus* Jerry Fielding, *Prod* Elliot Kastner, Michael Winner.

Cast: Robert Mitchum, *Philip Marlowe*, Sarah Miles, *Charlotte Sternwood*, Richard Boone, *Lash Canino*, Candy Clark, *Camilla Sternwood*, Joan Collins, *Agnes Lozelle*, Edward Fox, *Joe Brody*, John Mills, *Inspector Carson*, James Stewart, *Gen. Sternwood*, Oliver Reed, *Eddie Mars*, Harry Andrews, *Butter Norris*, Colin Blakely, *Harry Jones*, Richard Todd, *Barker*, Diana Quick, *Mona Grant*, James Donald, *Inspecter Gregory*, John Justin, *Arthur Geiger*, Simon Turner, *Karl Lundgren*. R. See *Farewell My Lovely*.

81 **Big Wednesday** (1978) **** Warner Bros., 126 min. *Dir* John Milius, *Scr* Dennis Aaberg, John Milius, *Cin* Bruce Surtees, *Ed* Tim O'Meara, Robert L. Wolfe, *Des* Charles Rosen, *Art* Dean Mitzner, *Mus* Basil Poledouris, *Prod* Buzz Feitshans.

Cast: Jan-Michael Vincent, *Matt*, William Katt, *Jack*, Gary Busey, *Leroy*, Patti D'Arbanville, *Sally*, Lee Purcell, *Peggy*, Sam Melville, *Bear*. PG.

Unusual comedy-drama about three surfing buddies, spanning the years 1962–1974. *Big Wednesday* may be the ultimate proof that a good film can be made on any subject, if done properly. This is nothing like the dimwitted beach musical-comedies of the 1960's, by any means. Surfing is merely a part of the lives of the three youths as the film examines their friendship through the years, and how they are affected by the changes around them. John Milius injects this with his usual brand of heroism and in the climax the three prepare for the surf as if they were preparing for battle.

82 **Billy Jack** (1971) * Warner Bros., 112 min. *Dir* T.C. Frank (pseudonym for Tom Laughlin), *Scr* Frank and Teresa Christina, *Cin* Fred Koenekamp, *Ed* Larry Heath, Marion Rothman, *Mus* Mundell Lowe, *Prod* Mary Rose Solti, *Assoc Prod* Earl D. Elliot, Ed Haldeman.

Cast: Tom Laughlin, *Billy Jack*, Delores Taylor, *Jean Roberts*, Clark Howat, *Sheriff Cole*, Bert Freed, *Stuart Posner*, Julie Webb, *Barbara*, Ken Tobey, *Deputy*, Victor Izay, *Doctor*, Debbie Schock, *Kit*, Stan Rice, *Martin*, Teresa Kelly, *Carol*, Katy Moffat, *Maria*, Susan Foster, *Cindy*, Paul Bruce, *Councilman*, Lynn Baker, *Sarah*, Susan Sosa, *Sunshine*, David Roga, *Bernard*, Gwen Smith, *Angela*, John McClure, *Dinosaur*, Cissie Colpitts, *Miss Eyelashes*, Richard Stahl, *Council Chairman*, Allan Meyerson, *O.K. Corrales*, PG. $32,500,000.

Hypocritical vengeance drama that exploits the feelings and attitudes of youths of the late 1960's and early 1970's. Beneath the liberal surface of *Billy Jack* is a film with a fascist viewpoint. All those who disagree are evil and must be dealt with properly. Billy Jack is a halfbreed Indian who protects the "freedom school," a home for runaway youths, from unfriendly outsiders. Everything is completely black and white; the villains are all bad and the residents of the "freedom school" are all good. There is not one real moment in the film. *The Trial of Billy Jack* has all the flaws of its predecessor multiplied tenfold and may rank as one of the single greatest abominations in cinema history.

83 **The Bingo Long Traveling All-Stars and Motor Kings** (1976) **** Universal, 110 min. *Dir* John Badham, *Scr* Hal Barwood, Mathew Robbins, based on novel by William Brashler, *Cin* Bill Butler, *Ed* David Rawlins, *Des* Lawrence G. Paull, *Cos* Bernard Johnson, *Mus* William Goldstein, *Songs* performed by Thelma Houston, *Prod* Rob Cohen, *Exec Prod* Michael Chinich, Janet Hubbard, Bennett Tramer.

Cast: Billy Dee Williams, *Bingo*, James Earl Jones, *Leon*, Richard Pryor, *Charlie Snow*, Rico Dawson, *Willie Lee*, Sam "Birmingham" Brison, *Louis*, Jophery Brown, *Champ Chambers*, Leon Wagner, *Fat Sam*, Tony Burton, *Isaac*, John McCurry, *Walter Murchman*, Stan Shaw, *Esquire Joe Calloway*, DeWayne Jessie, *Rainbow*, Ted Ross, *Sallie Potter*, Mabel King, *Bertha*, Sam Laws, *Henry*, Alvin Childress, *Horace*, Ken Foree, *Honey*, Carl Gordon, *Mack*, Ahna Capri, *Prostitute*, Joel Fluellen, *Mr. Holland*, Sarina C. Grant, *Pearline*. PG. $5,340,000.

Excellent period comedy about a black barnstorming baseball team during the 1930's, before blacks were accepted into the major leagues. Unlike many black oriented films this is not a racist film, as the team is also exploited by other blacks, the owners of the Negro National League. Refusing to succumb to this pressure, the team goes independent. John Badham, in his first feature, creates a wonderful 1930's atmosphere, but the true highlight is the ensemble acting by the large cast, from the leads down to the minor roles.

84 **Bite the Bullet** (1975) ** Columbia, 131 min. *Dir* Richard Brooks, *Scr* Richard Brooks, *Cin* Harry Stradling, Jr., *Ed* George Granville, *Art* Robert Boyle, *Mus* Alex North, *Prod* Richard Brooks.

Cast: Gene Hackman, *Sam Clayton*, Candice Bergen, *Miss Jones*, James Coburn, *Luke Matthews*, Ben Johnson, *"Mister"*, Ian Bannen, *Norfolk*, Jan-Michael Vincent, *Carlo*, Mario Arteaga, *Mexican*, Robert Donner, *Reporter*, Robert Hoy, *Lee Christie*, Paul Stewart, *J.B. Parker*, Jean Willes, *Rosie*, John McLiam, *Gebhardt*, Dabney Coleman, *Jack Parker*, Jerry Gatlin, *Woodchopper*, Sally Kirkland, *Honey*, Walter Scott, Jr., *Steve*. PG. $5,000,000.

Pretentious western about a 600-mile horse race. *Bite the Bullet* just wanders without having enough interesting ideas or situations to fill its more than two hour length. The characters are too shallow and too broadly played to come alive. This had the promise of being a great epic western, but it does not even come close. In reality, *Bite the Bullet* is little more than a period version of those cross country auto race films.

85 **Bittersweet Love** (1976) * Avco Embassy, 90 min. *Dir* David Miller, *Scr* D.A. Kellogg, Adrian Morrall, *Cin* Stephen Katz, *Ed* Bill Butler, *Art* Vince Cresciman, *Mus* Ken Wannberg, *Prod* Joel B. Michaels, Gene Slott, Joseph Zappala.

Cast: Scott Hylands, *Michael*, Meredith Baxter-Birney, *Patricia*, Lana Turner, *Claire*, Robert Lansing, *Howard*, Celeste Holm, *Marian*, Robert Alda, *Ben*, Gail Strickland, *Roz*, Richard Masur, *Alex*, Denise De Mirjian, *Nurse Morrison*, John Friedrich, *Josh*, Amanda Gavin, *Judy*, Jerome Guardino, *Psychiatrist*. PG.

A truly dismal love story with a gimmicky "shock" twist that was intended to add contemporary relevance to a basically old fashioned film. The gimmick of incest is hardly that shocking and adds nothing of value to the film. This type of soap-operatic trash went out in the early 1960's and belongs on television rather than the theatres.

86 **The Black Bird** (1975) *** Columbia, 98 min. *Dir* David Giler, *Scr* David Giler, *Story* Gordon Colter, Don M. Mankiewicz, *Cin* Philip Lathrop, *Ed* Margaret Booth, Lou Lombardo, Walter Thompson, *Des* Harry Horner, *Mus* Jerry Fielding, *Prod* Michael Levee, Lou Lombardo, *Exec Prod* George Segal.

Cast: George Segal, *Sam Spade Jr.*, Stephane Audran, *Anna Kemidon*, Lionel Stander, *Immelman*, Lee Patrick, *Effie*, Elisha Cook, Jr., *Wilmer*, Felix Silla, *Litvak*, Signe Hasso, *Dr. Crippen*, John Abbott, *Du Quai*, Connie Kreski, *Decoy Girl*, Harry Kenoi, Titus Napoleon, *Hawaiian Thugs*, Howard Jeffrey, *Kerkorian*, Richard B. Shull, *Prizer*, Ken Swafford, *McGregor*. PG.

An unusual spoof of detective films, *The Black Bird* is actually a sequel to *The Maltese Falcon* (1941); the title is merely a reference to the same object. This time the search is led by Sam Spade, Jr., the son of the late great detective. The premise may seem silly, but the film does succeed in its own oddball manner. One interesting note is that Lee Patrick and Elisha Cook, Jr., reprise their roles from the original film.

87 **Black Caesar** (1973) * American International, 92 min. *Dir* Larry Cohen, *Scr* Larry Cohen, *Cin* Fenton Hamilton, *Ed* George Folsey, Jr., *Mus* James Brown, *Prod* Larry Cohen, *Co-Prod* Janelle Cohen, *Exec Prod* Peter Sebiston, *Assoc Prod* James P. Dixon.

Cast: Fred Williamson, *Tommy*, D'Urville Martin, *Rev. Rufus*, Julius W. Harris, *Gibbs*, Don Pedro Colley, *Crawdaddy*, Gloria Hendry, *Helen*, Art Lund, *McKinney*, Val Avery, *Cardoza*, Minnie Gentry, *Mama Gibbs*, Phillip Roye, *Joe*, William Wellman, Jr., *Alfred*, James Dixon, *Bryant*, Myrna Hansen, *Virginia*, Patrick McAllister, *Grossfield*, Cecil Alonzo, *Motor*, Allen Bailey, *Sport*, Omer Jeffrey, *Tommy as Boy*, Michael Jeffrey, *Joe as Boy*. R.

Low-grade gangster film with Fred Williamson ruthlessly rising to the top of the heap in the Harlem underworld. *Black Caesar* could have at least been acceptable had it received stronger and more stylish direction, but it appears to have been thrown together with little care. The sequel *Hell Up in Harlem* has Fred Williamson killing everyone who gets in his way, while trying to clean up Harlem. This was made with the same amount of care as the first.

88 **Black Christmas** (1974) ** Canada, Ambassador, 93 min. *Dir* Bob Clark, *Scr* Roy Moore, *Cin* Reg Morris, *Ed* Stan Cole, *Art* Karen Bromley, *Mus* Carl Zittrer, *Prod* Bob Clark, *Co-Prod* Gerry Arbeid, *Exec Prod* Findlay Quinn.

Cast: Olivia Hussey, *Jess*, Keir Dullea, *Peter*, Margot Kidder, *Barb*, Andrea Martin, *Phyl*, John Saxon, *Lt. Fuller*, Marian Waldman, *Mrs. Mac*, Art Hindle, *Chris*, Lynne Griffin, *Clare*, James Edmonds, *Harrison*. R.

Fair murder thriller about a psychotic killer who makes obscene phone calls and murders the girls in a university sorority. *Black Christmas* is too dull for a thriller and has a forced surprise ending, which does not make much sense. Margot Kidder steals the film as a foul-mouthed student. Other titles, *Silent Night, Holy Night* and *Stranger in the House*.

89 **The Black Hole** (1979) *** Buena Vista, 97 min. *Dir* Gary Nelson, *Scr* Gerry Day, Jeb Rosebrook, *Story* Bob Barbash, Richard Landau, Jeb Rosebrook, *Cin* Frank Phillips (AN), *Ed* Greg McLaughlin, *Des* Peter Ellenshaw, *Art* Robert T. McCall, John B. Mansbridge, Al Roelofs, *Sp* Art Cruickshank, Harrison Ellenshaw, Peter Ellenshaw, Joe Hale, Danny Lee, Eustace Lycette (AN), *Cos* Bill Thomas, *Mus* John Barry, *Prod* Ron Miller, A Walt Disney Production.

Cast: Maximilian Schell, *Dr. Hans Reinhardt*, Anthony Perkins, *Dr. Alex Durant*, Robert Forster, *Capt. Dan Holland*, Joseph Bottoms, *Lt. Charles Pizer*, Yvette Mimieux, *Dr. Kate McCrae*, Ernest Borgnine, *Harry Booth*, Tommy McLoughlin, *Capt. Starr*. PG. $25,400,000.

Above average science fiction film with some excellent special effects. This was Disney's grand attempt to change their image with more adult oriented films. *The Black Hole* failed to do this because with all its expensive hardware and more adult ideas it still looks and sounds like a Disney film. Strong drama was never Disney's forte, and this film strains to correct this; the characters are wooden and the dialogue is weak. Disney does deserve credit for having the nerve to visualize something unknown to man. Whatever a black hole is really like, it is doubtful that it will look like *Fantasia*.

90 **The Black Stallion** (1979) **** United Artists, 118 min. *Dir* Carroll Ballard, *Scr* Melissa Mathison, Jeanne Rosenberg, William D. Wittliff, based on novel by Walter Farley, *Cin* Caleb Deschanel (NS, LA), *Ed* Robert Dalva (AN), *Art* Aurelio Crugnola, Earl Preston, *Mus* Carmine Coppola (G, LA), *Prod* Fred Roos, Tom Sternberg, *Exec Prod* Francis Coppola.

Cast: Kelly Reno, *Alec Ramsey*, Mickey Rooney (AN), *Henry Dailey*, Teri

Garr, *Alec's Mother*, Clarence Muse, *Snoe*, Hoyt Axton, *Alec's Father*, Michael Higgens, *Neville*, Ed McNamara, *Jake*, Dogmi Larbi, *Arab*, John Burton, John Buchanon, *Jockeys*, Kristen Vigard, *Becky*, Fausto Tozzi, *Rescue Captain*. G. $15,765,000.

One of the best and most beautiful animal films ever made. A boy befriends an Arabian stallion that saved him from a shipwreck, and with the help of an old horse trainer (Mickey Rooney) turns him into a great race horse. *The Black Stallion* is one of a very small number of family films that is not insulting to adults. Carroll Ballard tells his story with some of the most breathtaking images ever put on film.

91 **Black Sunday** (1977) *** Paramount, 143 min. *Dir* John Frankenheimer, *Scr* Ernest Lehman, Ivan Moffat, Kenneth Ross, based on novel by Thomas Harris, *Cin* John A. Alonzo, *Ed* Tom Rolf, *Art* Walter Tyler, *Cos* Ray Summers, *Mus* John Williams, *Prod* Robert Evans, *Exec Prod*, Robert L. Rosen.

Cast: Robert Shaw, *Kabakov*, Bruce Dern, *Lander*, Marthe Keller, *Dahlia*, Fritz Weaver, *Corley*, Steven Keats, *Moshevsky*, Bekim Fehmiu, *Fasil*, Michael V. Gazzo, *Muzi*, William Daniels, *Pugh*, Walter Gotell, *Col. Riaf*, Victor Campos, *Nageeb*, Walter Brooke, *Fowler*, James Jeter, *Watchman*, Clyde Kusatsu, *Freighter Captain*, Tom McFadden, *Farley*, Robert Patten, *Vickers*, Than Wyenn, *Israeli Ambassador*, Pat Summerall, Joseph Robbie, Robert Wussler, Tom Brookshier, *Themselves*. R. $14,200,000.

Above-average Hitchcockian-style thriller, that falls short of its potential. Arab terrorists plot to blow up the Goodyear Blimp at the Super Bowl, and thus killing all the spectators. There are numerous great and exciting scenes, and *Black Sunday* retains its suspense despite the obviousness of its outcome, but it is far too long for its own good. *Black Sunday* has been mistakenly compared to *Two-Minute Warning*, which is also set at a football stadium, but their plotlines could not be more dissimilar.

92 **The Black Windmill** (1974) *** Britain, Universal, 106 min. *Dir* Don Siegel, *Scr* Leigh Vance, based on book *Seven Days to A Killing* by Clive Egleton, *Cin* Outsama Rawi, *Ed* Anthony Gibbs, *Art* Peter Murton, *Cos* Anthony Mendleson, *Mus* Roy Budd, *Prod* Don Siegel, *Exec Prod* Richard D. Zanuck, David Brown, *Assoc Prod* Scott Hale.

Cast: Michael Caine, *Maj. John Tarrant*, Joseph O'Conor, *Sir Edward Julyan*, Donald Pleasence, *Cedric Harper*, John Vernon, *McKee*, Janet Suzman, *Alex Tarrant*, Delphine Seyrig, *Ceil Burrows*, Joss Ackland, *Chief Superintendent Wray*, Clive Revill, *Alf Chesterman*, Edward Hardwicke, *Mike McCarthy*, Catherine Schell, *Lady Julyan*, Hermione Baddely, *Hetty*, David Daker, *Thickset M.I. 5 Man*, Denis Quilley, *Bateson*, Paul Moss, *David Tarrant*, Mark Praid, *James Stroud*, George Cooper, *Pincus*, Derek Newark, *Monitoring Policeman*, John Rhys-Davies, *Special Policeman*, Brenda Cowling, *Pleasant Secretary*, Preston Lockwood, *Ilkeston*. PG.

Well-made espionage thriller starring Michael Caine as a British agent, who investigates the kidnapping of his son by a group out to disgrace him. Unlike most films of its genre, *The Black Windmill* is not bogged down with endless dialogue and a hopelessly confusing plot. Under Don Siegel's expert direction, the film moves briskly to its exciting climax.

93 **Blacula** (1972) *** American International, 92 min. *Dir* William Crain, *Scr* Raymond Koenig, Joan Torres, *Cin* John Stevens, *Ed* Allan Jacobs, *Art* Walter Herndon, *Mus* Gene Page, *Songs* Wally Holmes, *Prod* Joseph T. Naar, *Exec Prod* Samuel Z. Arkoff.

Cast: William Marshall, *Blacula*, Vonetta McGee, *Tina*, Denise Nicholas, *Michelle*, Thalmus Rasulala, *Gordon*, Charles Macaulay, *Dracula*, Emily Yancy, *Nancy*, Lance Taylor, Sr., *Swenson*, Ted Harris, *Bobby*, Rick Metzler, *Billy*, Jitu Cumbuka, *Skillet*, Logan Field, *Barnes*, Ketty Lester, *Juanita*, Elisha Cook, *Sam*, Eric Patterson, *Real Estate Agent*. PG.

Surprisingly good black version of Dracula. An 18th century African prince is bitten by Count Dracula himself and appears 200 years later in contemporary Los Angeles to wreak the usual havoc. William Marshall is excellent as the title creature, and although *Blacula* contains some genuine scares, throughout, it does not take itself too seriously and contains a few good laughs, too.

94 **Blazing Saddles** (1974) ** Warner Bros., 93 min. *Dir* Mel Brooks, *Scr* Andrew Bergman, Mel Brooks, Richard Pryor, Norman Steinberg, Alan Uger (W), *Story* Andrew Bergman, *Cin* Joseph Biroc, *Ed* Danford Greene, John C. Howard (AN), *Des* Peter Wooley, *Cos* N. Novarese, *Mus* John Morris, *Title Song* Mel Brooks, John Morris (AN), sung by Frankie Laine, *Chor* Alan Johnson, *Prod* Michael Hertzberg.

Cast: Cleavon Little, *Bart*, Gene Wilder, *Jim*, Harvey Korman, *Hedley Lamarr*, Madeline Kahn (AN), *Lili Von Shtupp*, Slim Pickens, *Taggart*, David Huddleston, *Olson Johnson*, Liam Dunn, *Rev. Johnson*, Alex Karras, *Mongo*, John Hillerman, *Howard Johnson*, George Furth, *Van Johnson*, Claude E. Starrett, Jr., *Gabby Johnson*, Mel Brooks, *Gov. Lepetomane/Indian Chief*, Carol Arthur, *Harriet Johnson*, Charles McGregor, *Charlie*, Robyn Hilton, *Miss Stein*, Dom DeLuise, *Buddy Bizarre*, Richard Collier, *Dr. Sam Johnson*, Don Megowan, *Gum Chewer*, Karl Lukas, *Cut Throat #1*, Burton Gilliam, *Lyle*, Count Basie, *Himself*. R. $45,200,000.

Sophomoric comedy western that depends entirely on anachronisms and vulgarisms rather than wit. This total hit-and-miss joke machine has some good moments, but they are very few. The jokes depend too much on surprise and for this reason *Blazing Saddles* tends to fall apart after repeated viewings. Brooks' career soared due to this film, but it is in no way his best work.

95 **Bless the Beasts and Children** (1971) * Columbia, 106 min. *Dir* Stanley Kramer, *Scr* Mac Benoff, based on novel by Glendon Swarthout, *Cin* Michel Hugo, *Ed* William A. Lyon, *Art* Lyle Wheeler, *Cos* Seth Banks, *Mus* Perry Botkin, Jr., Barry DeVorzon, *Song* "Bless the Beasts and Children," *Mus* Perry Botkin, Jr., Barry DeVorzon (AN), *Prod* Stanley Kramer, *Assoc Prod* George Glass.

Cast: Bill Mumy, *Teft*, Barry Robins, *Cotton*, Miles Chapin, *Shecker*, Darel Glaser, *Goodenow*, Bob Kramer, *Lally 1*, Marc Vahanian, *Lally 2*, Jesse White, *Sid Shecker*, Ken Swofford, *Wheaties*, Dave Ketchum, *Camp Director*, Elaine Devry, *Cotton's Mother*, Wayne Sutherlin, Bruce Glover, *Hustlers*, William Bramley, *Mr. Goodenow*, Vanessa Brown, *Mrs. Goodenow*, Charles H. Gray, *Capt. Cotton*, Vincent Van Lynn, *Mr. Teft*, June C. Ellis, *Mom*, Frank Farmer, *Doctor*, Jess Smart, *Young Shooter*. PG.

Another in the seemingly endless line of Stanley Kramer message films and probably his worst. A group of six boys from an Arizona boys school, who are deemed outcasts by the rest of the boys, witness the killing of buffalo at a government preserve and plan to set those still alive free. As usual Kramer's message is honorable, but his method of delivering it is questionable.

96 Bloodbrothers (1978) *** Warner Bros., 116 min. *Dir* Robert Mulligan, *Scr* Walter Newman (AN), based on novel by Richard Price, *Cin* Robert Surtees, *Ed* Shelly Kahn, *Des* Gene Callahan, *Mus* Elmer Bernstein, *Prod* Stephen Friedman.

Cast: Richard Gere, *Stony DeCoco*, Paul Sorvino, *Chubby DeCoco*, Tony Lo Bianco, *Tommy DeCoco*, Lelia Goldoni, *Marie*, Yvonne Wilder, *Phyllis*, Kenneth McMillan, *Banion*, Floyd Levine, *Dr. Harris*, Marilu Henner, *Annette*, Michael Hershewe, *Albert*, Kristine DeBell, *Cheri*, Pamela Myers, *Mrs. Pitts*, Gloria LeRoy, *Sylvia*, Bruce French, *Paulie*, Peter Sacangelo, *Malfie*, Kim Milford, *Butler*, Robert Englund, *Mott*, Raymond Singer, *Jackie*, Lila Teigh, *Jackie's Mother*, Eddie Jones, *Blackie*, Danny Aiello, *Artie*. R.

An overwrought, even extremely hyped-up drama about an Italian-American family, *Bloodbrothers* is surprisingly effective due in part to its excellent cast. Mulligan charges every scene with such high voltage that he never allows the viewer time to breathe. The theme of family bonds is nothing new, but it does seem somewhat fresh in *Bloodbrothers* because of the film's enormous energy.

97 Bloodline (1979) * Paramount, 116 min. *Dir* Terence Young, *Scr* Laird Koenig, based on novel by Sidney Sheldon, *Cin* Freddie Young, *Ed* Bud Molin, *Des* Ted Haworth, *Cos* Enrico Sabbatini, *Mus* Ennio Morricone, *Prod* Sidney Beckerman, David V. Picker, *Assoc Prod* Richard McWhorter.

Cast: Audrey Hepburn, *Elizabeth Roffe*, Ben Gazzara, *Rhys Williams*, James Mason, *Sir Alec Nichols*, Claudia Mori, *Donatella*, Irene Papas, *Simonetta Palazzi*, Michelle Phillips, *Vivian Nichols*, Maurice Ronet, *Charles Martin*, Romy Schneider, *Helen Martin*, Omar Sharif, *Ivo Palazzi*, Beatrice Straight, *Kate Erling*, Gert Frobe, *Inspector Hornung*, Wolfgang Priess, *Julius Prager*, Marcel Bozzuffi, *Man in Black*, Pinkas Braun, *Dr. Wal*, Wulf Kessler, *Young Sam Roffe*, Maurice Colbourne, *Jon Swinton*, Guy Rolfe, *Tod Michaels*, Dietlinde Turban, *Terenia*, Walter Kohut, *Krauss*, Donald Symington, *Henley*. R. $5,365,000.

Terrible soap opera potboiler about a woman whose life is threatened after inheriting a large pharmaceutical company. This Harold Robbins style trash fails terribly as a murder mystery, because it is impossible to care anything about the shallow characters. *Bloodline's* one bright spot is the delightful, comedic performance of Omar Sharif, who steals what few scenes he has.

98 Bloody Mama (1970) ** American International, 90 min. *Dir* Roger Corman, *Scr* Robert Thom, *Story* Don Peters, Robert Thom, *Con* John A. Alonzo, *Ed.* Eve Newman, *Cos* Thomas Costich, *Mus* Don Randi, *Prod* Roger Corman, *Co-Prod* Norman T. Herman, *Exec Prod* Samuel Z. Arkoff, James H. Nicholson.

Cast: Shelley Winters, *Kate "Ma" Barker*, Pat Hingle, *Sam Pendlebury*, Don Stroud, *Herman Barker*, Diane Varsi, *Mona Gibson*, Bruce Dern, *Kevin Dirkman*, Clint Kimbrough, *Arthur Barker*, Robert Walden, *Fred Barker*, Robert DeNiro, *Lloyd Barker*, Alex Nicol, *George Barker*, Michael Fox, *Dr. Roth*, Scatman Crothers, *Moses*, Stacy Harris, *Agent McClellan*, Pamela Dunlap, *Rembrandt*. R.

Disappointing fictionalized account of notorious 20th century outlaw gang, Ma Barker and her sons. Shelley Winters is properly overbearing as Ma Barker, but *Bloody Mama* is far trashier than it needed to be. Rather than developing the characters to appear as well-rounded realistic human beings as in *Bonnie and Clyde*, the Barker gang comes off as a nothing more than a group of retarded maniacs. This is unfortunate, because this could have been a fine film had Roger Corman had more confidence in his subject.

99 The Blue Bird (1976) * U.S./U.S.S.R., 20th Century–Fox, 100 min. *Dir* George Cukor, *Scr* Alfred Hayes, Hugh Whitemore, based on play by Maurice Maeterlinck, *Cin* Ionas Gritzus, Freddie Young, *Ed* Stanford C. Allen, Tatyanna Shapiro, Ernest Walter, *Des* Brian Wildsmith, *Art* Valery Urkevich, *Mus* Irwin Kostel, Lionel Newman, *Lyrics* Tony Harrison, *Prod* Paul Maslansky, *Co-Prod* Paul Radin, Lee Savin, *Exec Prod* Edward Lewis.

Cast: Elizabeth Taylor, *Mother/Maternal Love/Witch/Light*, Jane Fonda, *Night*, Ava Gardner, *Luxury*, Cicely Tyson, *Cat*, Robert Morley, *Father Time*, Harry Andrews, *Oak*, Todd Lookinland, *Tyltyl*, Patsy Kensit, *Myltyl*, Will Geer, *Grandfather*, Mona Washbourne, *Grandmother*, George Cole, *Dog*, Richard Pearson, *Bread*, Nadia Pavlova, *Blue Bird*, George Vitzen, *Sugar*, Margareta Terechova, *Milk*, Oleg Popov, *Fat Laughter*, Leonid Nevedomsky, *Father*, Valentina Ganilae Ganibalova, *Water*, Yevgeny Scherbakov, *Fire*, Pheona McLellen, *Sick Girl*, and the Leningrad Kirov Ballet. G.

Dismal children's fantasy film about two children and their search for the blue bird of happiness. *The Blue Bird* is a feeble attempt at creating a children's classic on par with *The Wizard of OZ*. The entire cast seems uncomfortable in their roles and this unfortunate circumstance prevents any chance for believability. This is a candidate for worst film ever made by a major director.

100 Blue Collar (1978) ***** Universal, 110 min. *Dir* Paul Schrader, *Scr* Leonard Schrader, Paul Schrader, *Source Material* Sydney A. Glass, *Cin* Bobby Byrne, *Ed* Tom Rolf, *Des* Lawrence G. Paull, *Cos* Ron Dawson, Alice Rush, *Mus* Jack Nitzsche, *Prod* Don Guest, *Exec Prod* Robin French, *Assoc Prod* David Nichols.

Cast: Richard Pryor, *Zeke*, Harvey Keitel, *Jerry*, Yaphet Kotto, *Smokey*, Ed Begley, Jr., *Bobby Joe*, Harry Bellaver, *Eddie Johnson*, George Memmoli, *Jenkins*, Lucy Saroyan, *Arlene Bartowski*, Lane Smith, *Clarence Hill*, Cliff DeYoung, *John Burrows*, Borah Silver, *Dogshit Miller*, Chip Fields, *Caroline Brown*, Harry Northup, *Hank*, Leonard Gaines, *IRS Man*, Milton Seltzer, *Sumabitch*, Sammy Warren, *Barney*, Jimmy Martinez, *Charlie T. Hernandez*, Jerry Dahlmann, *Superintendent*, Denny Arnold, *Unshaven Thug*, Rock Riddle, *Blonde Thug*, Stacey Baldwin, *Debby Bartowski*, Steve Butts, *Bob Bartowski*. R.

Superb caper comedy focusing on three auto workers (Richard Pryor, Harvey Keitel, Yaphet Kotto), who are exploited by both their bosses and their union. To get revenge they break into the safe belonging to their union. There have been few films dealing with unions and *Blue Collar* is the first to have the daring to attack the system itself. Screenwriter Paul Schrader made one of cinema's finest directorial debuts, perfectly blending intelligence, humor and social commentary, to create a classic crime film.

101 **Blume in Love** (1973) ******** Warner Bros., 115 min. *Dir* Paul Mazursky, *Scr* Paul Mazursky, *Cin* Bruce Surtees, *Ed* Don Cambern, *Des* Pato Guzman, *Prod* Paul Mazursky, *Assoc Prod* Tony Ray.

Cast: George Segal, *Blume,* Susan Anspach, *Nina,* Kris Kristofferson, *Elmo,* Marsha Mason, *Arlene,* Shelley Winters, *Mrs. Cramer,* Donald F. Muhich, *Analyst,* Paul Mazursky, *Blume's Partner,* Erin O'Reilly, *Cindy,* Annazette Chase, *Gloria,* Shelley Morrison, *Mrs. Greco,* Mary Jackson, *Louise,* Ed Peck, *Ed Goober.*

Excellent comedy about a divorced man who falls in love with his ex-wife. *Blume in Love* approaches the same subject as Mazursky's later film *An Unmarried Woman,* but examines it from the man's point of view. *Blume* may be more farcical than the other film, but it is no less serious in the examination of the anxieties of going through divorce. Mazursky seems to have been influenced by the Italian cinema, and this film is reminiscent of Italian sex farces, and there is also a satire of *Death in Venice* in the Venice sequence. Largely ignored at the time of its release, *Blume* has proven to be one of Mazursky's finest films.

102 **Boardwalk** (1979) ****** Atlantic Releasing Corp., 98 min. *Dir* Stephen Verona, *Scr* Leigh Chapman, Stephen Verona, *Cin* Billy Williams, *Ed* Thom Noble, *Des* Glenda Ganis, *Cos* Betsy Jones, *Prod* George Willoughby, *Exec Prod* Gerry Herrod.

Cast: Lee Strasberg, *David Rosen,* Ruth Gordon, *Becky Rosen,* Janet Leigh, *Florence,* Michael Ayr, *Peter,* Joe Silver, *Leo,* Eli Mintz, *Mr. Friedman,* Eddie Barth, *Eli,* Merwin Goldsmith, *Charlie,* Kim Delgado, *Strut,* Forbesy Russell, *Marilyn.* Not Rated.

Confused drama centering on an old Jewish couple and the problems they face in contemporary society. *Boardwalk* wanders aimlessly from one idea to another, throwing in everything from a Hare Krishna to a ruthless street gang, which appears and disappears more as a plot convenience than a thematic device. Stephen Verona fails to develop any of his ideas and the couple's truly serious problems are unrelated to the decaying society.

103 **The Boatniks** (1970) ******* Buena Vista, 100 min. *Dir* Norman Tokar, *Scr* Arthur Julian, based on story by Marty Roth, *Cin* William Snyder, *Ed* Cotton Warburton, *Art* Hilyard Brown, John B. Mansbridge, *Cos* Chuck Keehne, Emily Sundby, *Mus* Robert F. Brunner, *Prod* Ron Miller, *Assoc Prod* Tom Leetch, A Walt Disney Production.

Cast: Robert Morse, *Ensign Garland,* Stefanie Powers, *Kate,* Phil Silvers, *Harry Simmons,* Norman Fell, *Max,* Mickey Shaughnessy, *Charlie,* Wally Cox, *Jason,* Don Ameche, *Cmdr. Taylor,* Joey Forman, *Lt. Jordan,* Vito Scotti, *Pepe Galindo,* Tom Lowell, *Wagner,* Bob Hastings, *Chief Walsh,* Sammy Jackson, *Garlotti,* Joe E. Ross, *Nutty Sailor,* Judy Jordon, *Tina,* Al Lewis, *Bert,*

Midori, *Chiyoko Kuni*, Kelly Thordsen, *Motorcycle Cop*, Gil Lamb, *Mr. Mitchell*. G. $9,150,000.

Above-average Disney slapstick comedy starring Robert Morse as a misfit Coast Guard officer, who attempts to capture three equally incompetent jewel thieves (Phil Silvers, Norman Fell, Mickey Shaughnessy). *The Boatniks* features many hilarious sight gags and slapstick chases, and a wonderful gallery of kooks. This is one of Disney's best films.

104 Bobby Deerfield (1977) ** Columbia, 124 min. *Dir* Sydney Pollack, *Scr* Alvin Sargent, based on novel *Heaven Has No Favorites* by Erich Maria Remarque, *Cin* Henri Decae, *Ed* Fredric Steinkamp, *Des* Stephen Grimes, *Art* Mark Frederix, *Mus* Dave Grusin, *Prod* Sydney Pollack, *Exec Prod* John Foreman.

Cast: Al Pacino, *Bobby*, Marthe Keller, *Lillian*, Anny Duperey, *Lydia*, Walter McGinn, *The Brother*, Romolo Valli, *Uncle Luigi*, Stephan Meldegg, *Karl Holtzmann*, Jaime Sanchez, *Delvecchio*, Norm Nielson, *The Magician*, Mickey Knox, Dorothy James, *Tourists*, Giudo Alberti, *Priest in the Garden*, Monique Lejeune, *Catherine Modave*, Steve Gadler, *Bertrand Modave*. PG. $9,000,000.

Pretentious love story involving a race car driver (Al Pacino) and his affair with an aristocratic woman (Marthe Keller), who is dying of some disease. *Bobby Deerfield* is paced so slow that it becomes tedious. On the surface it resembles European art films from such masters as Michelangelo Antonioni and Alain Resnais, but without their aesthetic genius. Sydney Pollack, normally a fine director, has the dubious distinction of extracting a dull performance from Al Pacino.

105 Born to Win (1971) *** United Artists, 83 min. *Dir* Ivan Passer, *Scr* David Scott Milton, *Cin* Richard Kratina, Jack Priestley, *Ed* Ralph Rosenblum, *Art* Murray Stern, *Cos* Albert Wolsky, *Mus* William S. Fisher, *Prod* Philip Langner, *Exec Prod* Jerry Tokofsky, *Assoc Prod* Renata Stoia.

Cast: George Segal, *J*, Paula Prentiss, *Veronica*, Karen Black, *Parm*, Jay Fletcher, *Billy Dynamite*, Hector Elizondo, *The Geek*, Marcia Jean Kurtz, *Marlene*, Irving Selbst, *Stanley*, Ed Madsen, *Detective*, Sylvia Sims, *Restaurant Cashier*, Robert DeNiro, *Danny*, Andy Robinson, *Killer*. R.

Unusual black comedy about drug addiction. George Segal stars as an ex-hairdresser, who turns to crime to support his expensive heroin habit. *Born to Win* is one of the most intelligent and perceptive films on the suject, but its true highlight is Segal's outstanding performance. This was Czechoslovakian director Ivan Passer's first American film, and like his fellow countryman Milos Forman, he shows an unusually fine sense of American culture.

106 Boulevard Nights (1979) *** Warner Bros., 102 min. *Dir* Michael Pressman, *Scr* Desmond Nakano, *Cin* John Bailey, *Ed* Richard Halsey, *Des* Jackson DeGovia, *Mus* Lalo Schifrin, *Prod* Bill Benenson, *Exec Prod* Tony Bill.

Cast: Richard Yniguez, *Raymond Avila*, Danny De La Paz, *Chuco Avila*, Marta Du Bois, *Shady Landeros*, James Victor, *Gil Moreno*, Betty Carvalho, *Mrs. Avila*, Carmen Zapato, *Mrs. Landeros*, Victor Millan, *Mr. Landeros*, Gary Cervantes, *Big Happy*, Roberto Corarrubias, *Toby*, Garret Pearson, *Ernie*, Jerado Carmona, *Wolf*, Jesse Arogon, *Casper*. R.

Above average character study of two Mexican-American brothers and their involvement with street gangs. *Boulevard Nights* has been unfairly compared that infamous street gang epic, *The Warriors*, because of the similarity in their subject matter. The approach to the subject of the two films is entirely different, though. This film places less emphasis on action, although there are some violent scenes, and focuses more on the people and why they resort to violence.

107 **Bound for Glory** (1976) (AN) ***** United Artists, 147 min. *Dir* Hal Ashby, *Scr* Robert Getchell (AN), based on autobiography by Woody Guthrie, *Cin* Haskell Wesler (A, NS, LA), *Ed* Pembroke J. Herring, Robert Jones (AN), *Des* Michael Haller, *Art* James H. Spencer, William Sully, *Mus Adaptation* Leonard Rosenman (A), *Prod* Robert F. Blumofe, Harold Leventhal.

Cast: David Carridine (NB), *Woody Guthrie*, Ronny Cox, *Ozark Bule*, Melinda Dillon, *Mary Guthrie/Memphis Sue*, Gail Strickland, *Pauline*, John Lehne, *Locke*, Ji-Tu Cumbuka, *Slim Snedeger*, Randy Quaid, *Luther Johnson*, Elizabeth Macy, *Liz Johnson*, Allan Miller, *Agent*. PG.

Superb biography of noted folk singer Woody Guthrie. Unlike most biographies of entertainers, *Bound for Glory* does not make the fatal error of attempting to cover a lifetime. Instead, only the period 1936–1940 is covered, giving the filmmakers the opportunity to bring out Guthrie's character, rather than skimming over pointless career highlights. *Bound for Glory* is also a film about the Depression, as seen through the eyes of the politically active Guthrie. This is the finest film yet made on that period in American history, lacking the phony melodramatics of *The Grapes of Wrath*.

108 **Boxcar Bertha** (1972) *** American International, 92 min. *Dir* Martin Scorsese, *Scr* John William Corrington, Joyce H. Corrington, based on book *Sister of the Road* by Boxcar Bertha Thompson as told to Ben L. Reitman, *Cin* John Stephens, *Ed* Buzz Feitshans, *Cos* Bob Modes, *Mus* Gib Gilbeau, Thad Maxwell, *Prod* Roger Corman, *Assoc Prod* Julie Corman, Presented by James H. Nicholson.

Cast: Barbara Hershey, *Boxcar Bertha*, David Carradine, *Big Bill Shelley*, Barry Primus, *Rake Brown*, Bernie Casey, *Von Morton*, John Carradine, *H. Buckram Sartoris*, Victor Argo, David R. Osterhout, *The McIvers*, Ann Morell, *Tillie Stone*, Grahame Pratt, *Emeric Pressburger*, Chicken Holleman, *M. Powell*, Marianne Dole, *Mrs. Mailler*, Harry Northup, *Harvey Saunders*, Joe Reynolds, *Joe Dreft*. R.

Fine period crime thriller, set during the Depression, starring Barbara Hershey and David Carradine as a pair of union organizers in Arkansas who mistakenly take on the railroads. *Boxcar Bertha* is loosely based on fact, but *Bonnie and Clyde* seems to be a bigger inspiration. Martin Scorsese did a fine job of directing in this early film, which showed the promise of the major talent he later became.

109 **A Boy and His Dog** (1975) *** LG Jaf, 89 min. *Dir* L.Q. Jones *Scr* L.Q. Jones, based on novella by Harlan Ellison, *Cin* John Arthur Morrill, *Ed* Scott Conrad, *Des* Ray Boyle, *Mus* Tim McIntire, *Prod* Alvy Moore.

Cast: Don Johnson, *Vic*, Susanne Benton, *Quilla June*, Jason Robards, *Mr. Craddock*, Ron Feinberg, *Fellini*, Tim McIntire, *Voice of Blood*, Charles

McGraw, *Preacher*, Alvy Moore, Helene Winston, *Committee Members*, Tiger, *Blood*. R.

Billed as "a rather kinky tale of survival," this is hardly a kiddie film as its title suggests. *A Boy and His Dog* is a strange adult science-fiction tale of a young drifter and his telepathic dog, Blood, surviving on a post-apocalyptic Earth. Through his power, Blood can find food and women for his master and also warn him of approaching danger. Character actor L.Q. Jones proves to be a surprisingly good writer and director.

110 **The Boy Friend** (1971) ******** Britain, MGM, 110 min. *Dir* Ken Russell (NB), *Scr* Ken Russell, based on musical play by Sandy Wilson *Cin* David Watkin, *Ed* Michael Bradsell, *Art* Simon Holland, *Cos* Shirley Russell, *Mus Dir* Peter Maxwell Davies, *Chor* Christopher Gable, Terry Gilbert, Gilliam Gregory, *Prod* Ken Russell, *Assoc Prod* Harry Benn.

Cast: Twiggy, *Polly Browne*, Christopher Gable, *Tony Brockhurst*, Barbara Windsor, *Hortense*, Moyra Fraser, *Madame Dubonnet/Mrs. Parkhill*, Max Adrian, *Lord Brockhurst/Max Mandeville*, Catherine Wilmer, *Lady Brockhurst/Catherine*, Vladek Sheybal, *DeThrill*, Ann Jameson, *Mrs. Peter*, Peter Greenwell, *The Pianist*, Antonia Ellis, *Maisie*, Caryl Little, *Dulcie*, Georgina Hale, *Fay*, Sally Bryant, *Nancy*, Tommy Tune, *Tommy*, Murray Melvin, *Alphonse*, Graham Armitage, *Michael*, Brian Murphy, *Peter*. G.

Wonderful homage to the Hollywood musicals of the 1930's. Without compromising or toning down his unusual outlandish and sometimes bombastic style, Ken Russell has beautifully and accurately captured the spirit of the musicals of that era, with choreography that rivals that of Busby Berkeley. Even the plot is reminiscent, with an assistant stage manager (Twiggy) who gets her big break when the star is injured.

111 **The Boys from Brazil** (1978) ******* 20th Century–Fox, 124 min. *Dir* Franklin Schaffner, *Scr* Heywood Gould, based on novel by Ira Levin, *Cin* Henri Decae, *Ed* Robert E. Swink (AN), *Des* Gil Parrondo, *Art* Peter Lamont, *Cos* Anthony Mendleson, *Mus* Jerry Goldsmith (AN), *Prod* Martin Richards, *Exec Prod* Robert Fryer.

Cast: Gregory Peck, *Dr. Joseph Mengele*, Laurence Olivier (An, NB), *Ezra Lieberman*, James Mason, *Edward Seibert*, Lilli Palmer, *Esther Lieberman*, Uta Hagen, *Frieda Maloney*, Steven Guttenberg, *Barry Kohler*, Denholm Elliot, *Sidney Beynon*, Rosemary Harris, *Mrs. Doring*, John Dehner, *Henry Wheelock*, John Rubinstein, *David Bennett*, Anne Meara, *Mrs. Curry*, Jeremy Black, *Jack Curry/Simon Harrington/Erich Doring/Bobby Wheelock*, David Hurst, *Strasser*, Bruno Ganz, *Prof Bruckner*, Walter Gotell, *Mundt*, Michael Gough, *Harrington*, Wolfgang Priess, *Lofquist*. R. $10,165,000.

Okay semi-science-fiction thriller about a mad Nazi doctor Joseph Mengele (Gregory Peck), who plots to produce clones of Hitler in hopes of taking over the world. *The Boys from Brazil* is basically a cat-and-mouse thriller as Mengele is being pursued throughout by a Jewish Nazi hunter (Laurence Olivier). The plot is a little weak to sustain the film for two hours, but Schaffner's stylish direction almost compensates, and the performances are excellent, particularly those of Peck, in his first truly villainous role, and Olivier.

112 **The Boys in Company C** (1978) *** Columbia, 125 min. *Dir* Sidney J. Furie, *Scr* Sidney J. Furie, Rich Natkin, *Cin* Godfrey A. Godar, *Ed* James Benson, Michael Berman, Allan Pattillo, Frank J. Urioste, *Des* Robert Lang, *Art* Laida Perez, *Mus* Jaime Mendoza-Nava, *Song* "Here I Am" by Craig Wasson, *Prod* Andrew Morgan, *Exec Prod* Raymond Chow, *Assoc Prod* Dennis Juban.

Cast: Stan Shaw, *Tyrone Washington*, Andrew Stevens, *Billy Ray Pike*, James Canning, *Alvin Foster*, Michael Lembeck, *Vinnie Fazio*, Craig Wasson, *Dave Bisbee*, Scott Hylands, *Capt. Collins*, James Whitmore, Jr., *Lt. Archer*, Noble Willingham, *Sgt. Curry*, Lee Ermey, *Sgt Loyce*, Santos Morales, *Sgt Aquilla*, Drew Michaels, *Capt. Metcalfe*. R. $4,150,000.

Minor but exciting film about the Vietnam War. Comparisons with *Apocalypse Now* and *The Deer Hunter* are slightly unfair because of the difference in intentions and ambitions. Whereas those two films were about much more than war, *The Boys in Company C* is merely a well made straight action drama with the simple theme, war is hell; basically an updating of war movies of the past. This is the best film Sidney J. Furie has directed to date.

The Boys in the Band (1970) *** National General, 120 min. *Dir* William Friedkin, *Scr* Mart Crowley, based on his play, *Cin* Arthur J. Ornitz, *Ed* Jerry Greenberg, Carl Lerner, *Des* John Robert Lloyd, *Cos* Robert LaVine, *Prod* Mart Crowley, *Exec Prod* Dominick Dunne, Robert Jiras, *Assoc Prod* Ken Utt.

Cast: Frederick Combs, *Donald*, Leonard Frey, *Harold*, Cliff Gorman, *Emory*, Reuben Greene, *Bernard*, Robert LaTourneaux, *Cowboy*, Laurence Luckinbill, *Hank*, Kenneth Nelson, *Michael*, Keith Prentice, *Larry*, Peter White, *Alan*. R.

Sensitive film centering on a gathering of a group of male homosexuals for a birthday party, and the complications that arise with the surprise arrival of a heterosexual. *The Boys in the Band* is one of the first films on that subject and does not exploit it, nor does it stereotype homosexuals. Unfortunately the film is too stagey, looking too much like a filmed play.

114 **Brannigan** (1975) ** Britain, United Artists, 111 min. *Dir* Douglas Hickox, *Scr* Michael Butler, William P. McGivern, William Norton, Christopher Trumbo, *Story* Michael Butler, Christopher Trumbo, *Cin* Gerry Fisher, *Ed* Malcolm Cooke, *Art* Ted Marshall, *Cos* Emma Porteous, *Mus* Dominic Frontiere, *Prod* Arthur Gardner, Jules Levy, *Exec Prod* Michael Wayne.

Cast: John Wayne, *Jim Brannigan*, Richard Attenborough, *Commander Swann*, Judy Geeson, *Jennifer Thatcher*, Mel Ferrer, *Mel Fields*, John Vernon, *Larkin*, Donald Pilon, *Gorman*, John Stride, *Traven*, James Booth, *Charlie*, Del Hanney, *Drexel*, Lesley-Ann Down, *Luana*, Barry Dennen, *Julian*, Anthony Booth, *Freddy*, Brian Glover, *Jimmy The Bet*, Ralph Meeker, *Capt. Moretti*, Jack Watson, *Carter*, Arthur Batanides, *Angell*, Stewart Bevan, *Alex*, Kathryn Leigh Scott, *Miss Allen*, Don Henderson, *Geef*. PG.

Take a plot of a typical John Wayne western and set it in contemporary London and the result will look like *Brannigan*. Wayne wreaks havoc in London as a Chicago policeman sent to bring back an escaped criminal. These tired old plots killed off the western, and they do not work any better with a change of genre. The filmmakers even threw in an innocuous bar fight scene.

115 **Brass Target** (1978) ** United Artists, 111 min. *Dir* John Hough, *Scr* Alvin Boretz, based on novel *The Algonquin Project* by Frederick Nolan, *Cin* Tony Imi, *Ed* David Lane, *Des* Rolf Zehetbauer, *Cos* Monika Bauert, *Mus.* Laurence Rosenthal, *Prod* Arthur Lewis, *Exec Prod* Berle Adams.

Cast: Sophia Loren, *Mara*, John Cassavetes, *Maj. Joe DeLucca*, George Kennedy, *Gen. George S. Patton Jr.*, Robert Vaughn, *Col. Donald Rogers*, Patrick McGoohan, *Col. Mike McCauley*, Bruce Davison, *Col. Robert Dawson*, Edward Herrman, *Col. Walter Gilchrist*, Max von Sydow, *Shelley/Webber*, Ed Bishop, *Col. Elton F. Stewart*, Lee Montague, *Lucky Luciano*. PG.

Dull WWII drama that speculates that General George S. Patton was assassinated because he was held responsible for a gold robbery perpetrated by some of his subordinates–rather than being killed in an auto accident. George Kennedy is okay as Patton, but his performance totally pales when compared to that of George C. Scott. It is unimportant whether the theory is believable, because even if it were a documented fact *Brass Target* would still be a bland film.

116 **Breakheart Pass** (1976) *** United Artists, 95 min. *Dir* Tom Gries, *Scr* Alistair MacLean, based on his novel, *Cin* Lucien Ballard, *Ed* Buzz Brandt, *Mus* Jerry Goldsmith, *Prod* Jerry Gershwin, *Exec Prod* Elliot Kastner.

Cast: Charles Bronson, *John Deakin*, Ben Johnson, *Nathan Pearce*, Richard Crenna, *Richard Fairchild*, Jill Ireland, *Marcia*, Charles Durning, *Frank O'Brien*, Ed Lauter, *Maj. Clarement*, David Huddleston, *Dr. Molyneux*, Roy Jenson, *Danlon*, Casey Tibbs, *Jackson*, Archie Moore, *Carlos*. PG.

Above average action western set almost entirely aboard a train, with Charles Bronson as an undercover agent searching for gun runners. *Breakheart Pass* is sort of a *Murder on the Orient Express* in the old west, with many plot twists and surprises that complicate Bronson's investigation. The script is far more intelligent than most Bronson films and does not sacrifice the usual amount of action.

117 **Breaking Away** (1979) (AN, NS, GMC) ***** 20th Century-Fox, 100 min. *Dir* Peter Yates (AN), *Scr* Steve Tesich (A, NS, NY, NB, W), *Cin* Matthew F. Leonetti, *Ed* Cynthia Scheider, *Art* Partizia von Brandenstein, *Cos* Betsy Cox, *Mus* Patrick Williams (AN), *Prod* Peter Yates, *Assoc Prod* Art Levinson.

Cast: Dennis Christopher, *Dave Stohler*, Dennis Quaid, *Mike*, Daniel Stern, *Cyril*, Jackie Earle Haley, *Moocher*, Barbara Barrie (AN), *Mrs. Stohler*, Paul Dooley (NB), *Mr. Stohler*, Robyn Douglas, *Katherine*, Hart Bochner, *Rod*, Amy Wright, *Nancy*, Peter Maloney, *Doctor*, John Ashton, *Mike's Brother*, Lisa Shure, *French Girl*, Jennifer K. Mickel, *Girl*, P.J. Soles, *Suzy*. PG. $9,875,000.

A wonderful and intelligent comedy of life in a midwest college town and the rivalry between the townspeople and the students. *Breaking Away* combines elements from *American Graffiti* and Rocky and is surprisingly better than both. This film is something of a shock coming from Peter Yates who, in the past, has concentrated mainly on straight action thrillers. *Breaking Away* possesses the qualities Yates' earlier films lacked; character; depth and emotion. Underneath this light comedy is a very serious and cynical theme of the rejection of various ethnic groups who helped build this nation, but later were shamefully treated as outsiders.

118 **Breakout** (1975) *** Columbia, 96 min. *Dir* Tom Gries, *Scr* Elliot Baker, Howard B. Kreitsek, Marc Norman, based on novel by Eliot Asinof, Warren Hinckle, William Turner, *Cin* Lucien Ballard, *Ed* Bud Isaacs, *Art* Ira Bates, *Mus* Jerry Goldsmith, *Prod* Robert Chartoff, Irwin Winkler, *Exec Prod* Ron Buck.

Cast: Charles Bronson, *Nick*, Robert Duvall, *Jay*, Jill Ireland, *Ann*, John Huston, *Harris*, Randy Quaid, *Hawk*, Sheree North, *Myrna*, Alejandro Rey, *Sanchez*, Paul Mantee, *Cable*, Roy Jenson, *Spencer*, Alan Vint, *Pilot*, Jorge Moreno, *Soza*. PG. $7,500,000.

One of the better and more offbeat Charles Bronson vehicles. Bronson is fine as a klutzy helicopter pilot who is hired by a woman to break her husband (Robert Duvall), who was framed for a murder, out of a Mexican prison. *Breakout* contains more humor than most Bronson films, without sacrificing the obligatory action, and he seems to be satirizing his own macho image.

119 **Breezy** (1973) ** Universal, 108 min. *Dir* Clint Eastwood, *Scr* Jo Heims, *Cin* Frank Stanley, *Ed* Ferris Webster, *Art* Alexander Golitzen, *Mus* Michel Legrand, *Title Song* Michel Legrand, Alan and Marilyn Bergman, *Prod* Robert Daley, *Exec Prod* Jennings Lang.

Cast: William Holden, *Frank Harmon*, Kay Lenz, *Breezy*, Roger C. Carmel, *Bob Henderson*, Marj Dusay, *Betty*, Joan Hotchkis, *Paula*, Jamie Smith Jackson, *Marcy*, Norman Bartold, *Man in Car*, Lynn Borden, *Overnight Date*, Shelley Morrison, *Nancy*, Dennis Olivieri, *Bruno*, Eugene Peterson, *Charlie*, Lew Brown, *Police Officer*, Richard Bull, *Doctor*, Johnnie Collins III, *Norman*. R.

Fair love story about an older divorced man (William Holden), and a young hippie girl (Kay Lenz). At first she is an annoyance to him, but his attitudes soon change, and they begin to have an affair. *Breezy* attempts to be a relevant film by contrasting the different sides of the generation gap; unfortunately the film offers no new ideas and the underlying story is unexceptional.

120 **Brewster McCloud** (1970) *** MGM, 105 min. *Dir* Robert Altman, *Scr* Doran William Cannon, Brian McKay (UN), *Cin* Lumar Boren, Jordan Cronenweth, *Ed* Lou Lombardo, *Art* Preston Ames, George W. Davis, *Mus* Gene Page, *Prod* Lou Adler.

Cast: Bud Cort, *Brewster McCloud*, Sally Kellerman, *Louise*, Michael Murphy, *Frank Shaft*, William Windom, *Sheriff Weeks*, Shelley Duvall, *Suzanne*, Rene Auberjonois, *Lecturer*, Stacy Keach, *Abraham Wright*, John Schuck, *Policeman Johnson*, Margaret Hamilton, *Daphne Heap*, Jennifer Salt, *Hope*, Corey Fischer, *Policeman Hines*, G. Wood, *Police Capt. Crandell*, Bert Remsen, *Policeman Breen*, Angelin Johnson, *Breen's Wife*, William Baldwin, *Week's Aide*. R.

Surrealistic comedy that nearly defies description. The threadbare plot centers on a young lunatic (Bud Cort), who builds a pair of wings in hope to fly around the Houston Astrodome like a bird. He is but one of the many weird characters that fill this episodic film. *Brewster McCloud* is hardly one of Robert Altman's best films, but his wonderful anarchic style raises this above most other such films that were prevalent in the early part of the decade.

121 **A Bridge Too Far** (1977) *** Britain, United Artists, 176 min. *Dir* Richard Attenborough, *Scr* William Goldman, based on book by Cornelius Ryan, *Cin* Geoffrey Unsworth (BFA), *Ed* Anthony Gibbs, *Des* Terry Marsh, *Art* Stuart Craig, Roy Stannard, *Cos* Anthony Mendleson, *Mus* John Addison (BFA), *Prod* Joseph E. Levine, Richard P. Levine, *Co-Prod* Michael Stanley-Evans, *Assoc Prod* John Palmer.

    Cast: Dirk Bogarde, *Lt. Gen. Frederick "Boy" Browning,* James Caan, *Staff Sgt. Eddie Dohun,* Michael Caine, *Lt. Col. Joe Vandeleur,* Sean Connery, *Maj. Gen. Robert Urguhart,* Edward Fox (NS, BFA), *Lt. Gen. Brian Horrocks,* Elliot Gould, *Col. Bobby Stout,* Gene Hackman, *Maj. Gen. Stanislaw Sosobowski,* Anthony Hopkins, *Lt. Col. John Frost,* Hardy Kruger, *Gen. Karl Ludwig,* Laurence Olivier, *Dr. Spaander,* Ryan O'Neal, *Brig. Gen. James M. Gavin,* Robert Redford, *Maj. Julian Cook,* Maximilian Schell, *Lt. Gen. Wilhelm Bittrich,* Liv Ullman, *Kate ter Horst,* Arthur Hill, *Tough Colonel.* PG. $21,000,000.

    Compared to other multi-million war spectaculars, *A Bridge Too Far* is a relatively intelligent movie. Much of the enormous budget was wasted on one of the most impressive cast of stars ever assembled, but their presence actually adds little to the film, other than marquee value. For such a large production, the film, surprisingly, holds together very well, and Richard Attenborough deserves the lion's share of the credit for just pulling the whole thing off.

122 **Bring Me the Head of Alfredo Garcia** (1974) **** United Artists, 112 min. *Dir* Sam Peckinpah, *Scr* Gordon Dawson, Sam Peckinpah, *Story* Frank Kowalski, Sam Peckinpah, *Cin* Alex Phillips, Jr., *Ed* Dennis E. Dolan, Sergio Ortega, Robbe Roberts, *Mus* Jerry Fielding, *Prod* Martin Baum, *Exec Prod* Helmut Dantine, *Assoc Prod.* Gordon Dawson.

    Cast: Warren Oates, *Bennie,* Isela Vega, *Elita,* Gig Young, *Quill,* Robert Webber, *Sappensly,* Helmut Dantine, *Max,* Emilio Fernandez, *El Jefe,* Kris Kristofferson, *Raco,* Chano Urueta, *One-armed Bartender,* Jorge Russek, *Cueto.* R.

    Underrated Sam Peckinpah thriller with a self-explanatory title. A wealthy Mexican puts a price on the head of the man who impregnated his daughter. Warren Oates is excellent as a Bogart type expatriate, who joins in the search. This was labeled as a runaway production by Hollywood unions, because westerns can be filmed just as easily in the U.S. As Peckinpah insisted during production, *Bring Me The Head of Alfredo Garcia* is not a western, but a comtemporary film set in Mexico.

123 **The Brink's Job** (1978) **** Universal, 118 min. *Dir* William Friedkin, *Scr* Walon Green, based on book *Big Stick Up at Brink's* by Noel Behn, *Cin* Norman Leigh, *Ed* Bud Smith, *Des* Dean Tavoularis (AN), *Art* Angelo Graham (AN), *Cos* Ruth Morley, *Mus* Richard Rodney Bennett, *Prod* Ralph Serpe.

    Cast: Peter Falk, *Tony Pino,* Peter Boyle, *Joe McGinnis,* Allen Goorwitz, *Vinnie Costa,* Warren Oates, *"Specs" O'Keefe,* Gena Rowlands, *Mary Pino,* Paul Sorvino, *Jazz Maffie,* Sheldon Leonard, *J. Edgar Hoover,* Gerard Murphy, *Sandy Richardson,* Kevin O'Connor, *Stanley "Guss" Gusciora,* Claudia Peluso, *Gladys,* Patrick Hines, *H.H. Rightmire,* Malachy McCourt, *Mutt Murphy,* Walter Klavun, *Daniels,* Randy Jurgensen, John Brandon, Earl Hindman, John Farrel, *F.B.I. Agents.* PG. $6,935,000.

Excellent burlesque style comedy based on the real-life "crime of the century," the famed Brinks robbery in Boston in the 1950's. *The Brink's Job* disappointed many who expected a straight crime thriller from William Friedkin in the style of his earlier film, *The French Connection*. The nature of this particular robbery almost requires a comic treatment, due to ridiculous ease of the actual heist. The acting is splendid and *The Brink's Job* is a gold mine for character actors.

124 **The Brood** (1979) * Canada, New World, 91 min. *Dir* David Cronenberg, *Scr* David Cronenberg, *Cin* Mark Irwin, *Ed* Allan Collins, *Art* Carol Spier, *Prod* Claude Heroux, *Exec Prod* Pierre David, Victor Solnicki.

Cast: Oliver Reed, *Dr. Raglan*, Samantha Eggar, *Nola*, Art Hindle, *Frank*, Cindy Hinds, *Candice*, Nuala Fitzgerald, *Juliana*, Henry Beckman, *Barton*, Susan Hogan, *Ruth*, Michael McGhee, *Inspector*, Gary McKeehan, *Mike*, Bob Silverman, *Jan*, Joseph Shaw, *Dr. Desborough*, Felix Silla, *Child*, Larry Solway, *Resnikoff*, Rainer Schwartz, *Birkin*, Nicholas Campbell, *Chris*. R.

Grim horror film with Oliver Reed as the head of a bizarre psychiatric institute, where he is conducting sick experiments, and one of his patients (Eggar) gives birth to killer babies. When it is not ghastly, *The Brood* is extremely dull. For some unknown reason David Cronenberg gained a reputation as an exceptional director of horror films because of this trash.

125 **Brother John** (1971) ** Columbia, 94 min. *Dir* James Goldstone, *Scr* Ernest Kinoy, *Cin* Gerald Perry, *Ed* Edward A. Biery, *Art* Al Brenner, *Cos* Guy Verhille, *Mus* Quincy Jones, *Song* "Children of The Summer" *Mus* Quincy Jones, *Lyrics* Ernie Sheldon, *Prod* Joel Glickman, *Exec Prod* Sidney Poitier.

Cast: Sidney Poitier, *John Kane*, Will Geer, *Doc Thomas*, Bradford Dillman, *Lloyd Thomas*, Beverly Todd, *Louise MacGill*, Ramon Bieri, *Orly Ball*, Warren J. Kemmerling, *George*, Lincoln Kilpatrick, *Charley Gray*, P. Jay Sidney, *Rev. MacGill*, Richard Ward, *Frank*, Paul Winfield, *Henry Birkardt*, Zara Cully, *Miss Nettie*, Michael Bell, *Cleve*, Howard Rice, *Jimmy*, Darlene Rice, *Marsha*, Harry Davis, *Turnkey*, Lynn Hamilton, *Sarah*, Gene Tyburn, *Calvin*, E.A. Nicholson, *Perry*, Bill Crane, *Bill Jones*, Richard Bay, *Lab Deputy*, John Hancock, *Henry's Friend*, Lynne Arden, *Nurse*, William Houze, *Motel Owner*, Maye Henderson, L. Smith, *Neighbors*. PG.

Unusual fantasy drama starring Sidney Poitier as an angel, who returns to his hometown in Alabama to check up on the progress of its citizens, but unfortunately he finds only hatred and turmoil. *Brother John* has a good premise for a socially relevant film about contemporary society, but it is filled with the same clichés and stereotypes that plague many Southern melodramas.

126 **Buck and the Preacher** (1972) ** Columbia, 102 min. *Dir* Sidney Poitier, *Scr* Ernest Kinoy, *Story* Ernest Kinoy, Drake Walker, *Cin* Alex Philips, Jr., *Ed* Pembroke J. Herring, *Des* Sydney Z. Litwak, *Cos* Guy Verhille, *Mus* Benny Carter, *Prod* Joel Glickman, *Assoc Prod* Herb Wallerstein.

Cast: Sidney Poitier, *Buck*, Harry Belafonte, *Preacher*, Ruby Dee, *Ruth*, Cameron Mitchell, *Deshay*, Denny Miller, *Floyd*, Nita Talbot, *Madam Esther*, John Kelly, *Sheriff*, Tony Brubaker, *Headman*, Bobby Johnson, *Man who is Shot*, James McEachin, *Kingston*, Clarence Muse, *Cudjo*, Lynn Hamilton, *Sarah*, Doug Johnson, *Sam*, Errol John, *Joshua*, Ken Menard, *Little Henry*, Pamela Jones, *Delilah*, Drake Walker, *Elder*, Dennis Hines, *Little Toby*, Fred

Waugh, *Mizoo*, Bill Shannon, *Tom*, Phil Adams, *Frank*, Walter Scott, *Earl*, John Howard, *George*. PG.

Standard western comedy drama that teams Sidney Poitier as an ex-Union Army cavalryman, who leads a group of former slaves out West, and Harry Belafonte as a shady preacher. On the surface *Buck and the Preacher* is a socially conscious film, but underneath it is just an ordinary western, with a clichéd story and sterotypical characters.

127 Buck Rogers in the 25th Century (1979)   ****** Universal, 89 min. *Dir* Daniel Haller, *Scr* Glen A. Larson, Leslie Stevens, *Cin* Frank Beascoechea, *Ed* John J. Dumas, *Art* Paul Peters, *Cos* Jean-Pierre Dorleac, *Mus* Stu Phillips, *Chor* Miriam Nelson, *Prod* Richard Coffey, *Exec Prod* Glen A. Larson, *Assoc Prod* Andrew Mirisch, David Phinney, *Supervising Prod* Leslie Stevens.

Cast Gil Gerard, *Buck Rogers*, Pamela Hensley, *Princess Ardala*, Erin Gray, *Wilma Deering*, Henry Silva, *Kane*, Tim O'Connor, *Dr. Huer*, Joseph Wiseman, *Draco*, Duke Butler, *Tigerman*, Felix Silla, *Twiki*, Mel Blanc, *Voice of Twiki*. PG. $12,010,000.

Average science-fiction adventure based on comic strip character. Originally made for television *Buck Rogers in the 25th Century* was released to theatres to capitalize on the science-fiction craze, but this juvenile space opera is no *Star Wars* and should have stayed on television. Despite the more advanced special-effects this is not much better than the old serial with Buster Crabbe.

128 The Buddy Holly Story (1978)   ******* Columbia, 113 min. *Dir* Steve Rash, *Scr* Robert Gittler, *Story* Fred Bauer, Steve Rash, *Cin* Steven Larner, *Ed* David Blewitt, *Des* John Schiller, *Mus* adaptation by Joe Renzetti (A), *Prod* Fred Bauer, *Exec Prod* Edward H. Cohen, *Co-Exec Prod* Fred T. Kuehnert, *Assoc Prod* Frances Avrut-Baur.

Cast: Gary Busey (AN, NS), *Buddy Holly*, Don Stroud, *Jessie*, Charles Martin Smith, *Ray Bob*, Bill Jordan, *Riley Randolph*, Maria Richwine, *Maria Elena Holly*, Conrad Janis, *Ross Turner*, Albert Popwell, *Eddie Foster*, Amy Johnston, *Jenny Lou*, Jim Beach, *Mr. Wilson*, John F. Goff, *T.J.*, Fred Travalena, *Madman Mancuso*, Dick O'Neil, *Sol Zuckerman*, Stymie Beard, *Luther*, M.G. Kelly, *M.C. (Buffalo)*, Paul Mooney, *Sam Cooke*, Arch Johnson, *Mr. Holly*, Neva Patterson, *Mrs. Holly*. PG. $5,900,000.

Excellent and surprisingly restrained biography of the legendary rock singer, which is not the usual trashy and sensationalized Hollywood film biography. *The Buddy Holly Story* seems very honest and real as Holly comes to life as a real human being through the film's heavy concentration on his private life, rather than barraging the viewer with unnecessary details of his music career. The film's real highlight, though, is Gary Busey's brilliant performance, in which he also did his own singing.

129 Buffalo Bill and the Indians, or Sitting Bull's History Lesson (1976) ********* United Artists, 120 min. *Dir* Robert Altman, *Scr* Robert Altman, Alan Rudolph, based on play *Indians* by Arthur Kopit, *Cin* Paul Lohmann, *Ed* Peter Appleton, Dennis Hill, *Des* Tony Masters, *Cos* Anthony Powell, *Mus* Richard Baskin, *Prod* Robert Altman, *Exec Prod* David Susskind.

Cast: Paul Newman, *Buffalo Bill*, Joel Grey, *Nate Salsbury*, Kevin McCarthy, *Maj. John Burke*, Allan Nicholls, *Col Prentiss Ingraham*, Harvey Keitel, *Ed*

Goodman, Mike Kaplan, *Jules Keen*, Bert Remsen, *Crutch*, Burt Lancaster, *Ned Buntline*, Geraldine Chaplin, *Annie Oakley*, John Considine, *Frank Butler*, Frank Kaquitts, *Chief Sitting Bull*, Will Sampson, *Interpreter*, Denver Pyle, *Indian Agent McLaughlin*, Pat McCormick, *Grover Cleveland*, Shelley Duvall, *Mrs. Cleveland*, Evelyn Lear, *Nina Cavalini*, Bonnie Leaders, *Margaret*, Noelle Rogers, *Lucille DuCharmes*, Fred N. Larsen, *King of the Cowboys*, Jerri & Joy Duce, *Trick Riders*, Humphrey Gratz, *Old Soldier*. PG.

Excellent western comedy-drama focusing on Buffalo Bill Cody, superbly played by Paul Newman, and his famous Wild West Show. The film tears away the legend of Buffalo Bill and portrays him as he really was, a liar, a phony and a braggart. *Buffalo Bill and the Indians* is a very complex western, mixing numerous ideas and themes including the treatment of Indians and the hypocrisy of history, and it is a metaphor for both show business and America. This is Robert Altman's most brilliant film.

130 **Bug** (1975) ** Paramount, 99 min. *Dir* Jeannot Szwarc, *Scr* William Castle, Thomas Page, based on novel *The Hephaestus Plague* by Thomas Page, *Cin* Michel Hugo, *Ed* Allan Jacobs, *Art* Jack Martin Smith, *Cos* Guy Verhile, *Mus* Charles Fox, *Prod* William Castle.

Cast: Bradford Dillman, *James*, Joanna Miles, *Carrie*, Richard Gilliland, *Gerald*, Jamie Smith Jackson, *Norma*, Alan Fudge, *Mark*, Jesse Vint, *Tom*, Patty McCormack, *Sylvia*, Brendon Dillon, *Charlie*, Fred Downs, *Henry*, James Greene, *Rev. Kern*, Jim Poyner, *Kenny*, Sam Jarvis, *Taxi Driver*, Brad Stevens, *Guard*. PG.

Silly horror film about a group of mutated cockroaches that rise to the surface following an earthquake and wreak fiery havoc on a farm community. Bradford Dillman stars as a scientist, who tries to communicate with these super bugs after they attack his wife (Joanna Miles). Most of the action occurs during the first part of the film, while *Bug* climaxes with talk.

131 **Bugsy Malone** (1976) *** Britain, 93 min. *Dir* Alan Parker, *Scr* Alan Parker (BFA), *Cin* Peter Biziou, Michael Seresin, *Ed* Gerry Hambling, *Des* Geoffrey Kirkland (BFA) *Art* Malcolm Middleton, *Mus* Paul Williams (AN), *Chor* Gillian Gregory, *Prod* Alan Marshall, *Exec Prod* David Puttnam, A Robert Stigwood Presentation.

Cast: Scott Baio, *Bugsy Malone*, Florrie Dugger, *Blousey*, Jodie Foster (BFA), *Tallulah*, John Cassisi, *Fat Sam*, Martin Lev, *Dandy Dan*, Paul Murphy, *LeRoy Smith*, Sheridan Russell, *Knuckles*, Albin Jenkins, *Fizzy*, Paul Chirelstein, *Smolsky*, Andrew Paul, *O'Dreary*, Davidson Knight, *Cagey Joe*, Michael Jackson, *Razmataz*, Jeffrey Stevens, *Louis*, Peter Holder, *Ritzy*, Donald Waugh, *Snake Eyes*, Michael Kirby, *Angelo*, Jon Zebrowski, *Shoulders*, Jorge Valdez, *Bronx Charlie*, John Lee, *Benny Lee*, Ron Meleleu, *Doodle*, Paul Besterman, *Yonkers*. G.

Ironically this musical spoof of Hollywood gangster films, cast entirely with children, is as real as some of those "classics" of the thirties, i.e. *Little Caesar* and *Public Enemy*. In those films and others the actors resembled children playing "cops and robbers" rather than life-like human beings. Alan Parker made an interesting directorial debut with this film oddity, which was intended to be merely an attention getter. *Bugsy Malone* was overlooked in the U.S., but received ecstatic praise in England, Parker's native country.

132 **Burnt Offerings** (1976) ** United Artists, 116 min. *Dir* Dan Curtis, *Scr* Dan Curtis, William F. Nolan, based on novel by Robert Marasco, *Cin* Stevan Larner, Jacques Marquette, *Ed* Dennis Virkler, *Des* Eugene Lourie, *Mus* Robert Cobert, *Prod* Dan Curtis, *Assoc Prod* Robert Singer.

Cast: Karen Black, *Marian*, Oliver Reed, *Ben*, Burgess Meredith, *Brother*, Eileen Heckart, *Roz*, Lee Montgomery, *David*, Dub Taylor, *Walker*, Bette Davis, *Aunt Elizabeth*, Anthony James, *Chauffeur*, Orin Cannon, *Minister*, James T. Myers, *Dr. Ross*, Todd Turquand, *Young Ben*, Joseph Riley, *Ben's Father*. PG.

Standard horror film about an average family that rents a house for the summer, which just happens to be haunted. The house begins to possess the father (Oliver Reed) and he begins to act strangely and even tries to kill his son. *Burnt Offerings* is somewhat similar to *The Shining* in plot, but it does not have Stanley Kubrick's breathtaking style to heighten the story.

133 **Buster and Billie** (1974) ** Columbia, 100 min. *Dir* Daniel Petrie, *Scr* Ron Turbeville, *Story* Ron Baren, Ron Turbeville, *Cin* Mario Tosi, *Ed* Michael Kahn, *Mus* Al DeLory, *Prod* Ron Silverman, *Exec Prod* Ted Mann.

Cast: Jan-Michael Vincent, *Buster Lane*, Joan Goodfellow, *Billie*, Pamela Sue Martin, *Margie Hooks*, Clifton James, *Jake*, Robert Englund, *Whitney*, Jessie Lee Fulton, *Mrs. Lane*, L.B. Joiner, *Mr. Lane*, Dell C. Payne, *Warren*. R. $4,000,000.

Fair period film set in Georgia in 1948. Jan-Michael Vincent stars as a youth who, in feeling frustrated by his girlfriend, visits the local tramp (Joan Goodfellow). She is not what everyone thinks she is and is only trying to be accepted. Predictably Vincent falls for her. *Buster and Billie* could have been a sensitive film but it forces in the obligatory violent ending stemming from a rape.

134 **Busting** (1974) *** United Artists, 92 min. *Dir* Peter Hyams, *Scr* Peter Hyams, *Cin* Earl Rath, *Ed* James Mitchell, *Mus* Billy Goldenberg, *Prod* Robert Chartoff, Irwin Winkler.

Cast: Elliot Gould, *Michael Keneely*, Robert Blake, *Patrick Farrel*, Allen Garfield (Goorwitz), *Carl Rizzo*, Antonio Fargas, *Stephen*, Michael Lerner, *Marvin*, Sid Haig, *Rizzo's Bouncer*, Ivor Francis, *Judge Simpson*, John Lawrence, *Sgt. Kenflick*, Cornelia Sharp, *Jackie*, William Sylvester, *Weldman*, Logan Ramsey, *Dr. Berman*, Richard X. Slattery, *Desk Sergeant*. R.

Well-done police thriller about two irreverent vice cops, who break all the rules in pursuing a gangster. Elliot Gould and Robert Blake are well paired as the cops. *Busting* is similar in plot to *Freebie and the Bean*, released later the same summer, but it is less spectacular and more of a gritty street film. The main flaw is that the film's most exciting sequence, a chase through an urban supermarket, comes too early.

135 **Butch and Sundance: The Early Days** (1979) **** 20th Century–Fox, 110 min. *Dir* Richard Lester, *Scr* Allan Burns, *Cin* Laszlo Kovacs, *Ed* Anthony Gibbs, George Trirogoff, *Des* Brian Eatwell, *Art* Jack DeGovia, *Cos* William Thiess (AN), *Mus* Patrick Williams, *Prod* Steven Bach, Gabriel Katzka, *Assoc Prod* Jack B. Bernstein.

Cast: William Katt, *Sundance Kid*, Tom Berenger, *Butch Cassidy*, Jeff Corey, *Ray Bledsoe*, John Schuck, *Harvey Logan*, Michael C. Gwynne, *Mike*

Cassidy, Peter Weller, *Joe LeFors,* Brian Dennehy, *O.C. Hanks,* Christopher Lloyd, *Bill Carver,* Jill Eikenberry, *Mary,* Arthur Hill, *Wyoming Governor,* Vincent Schiavelli, Patrick Egan, *Guards,* Noble Willingham, *Capt. Prewitt,* Sherril Lynn Katzman, *Annie,* Elya Buskin, *Bookkeeper,* Peter Brocco, *Old Robber,* Liam Russell, *Banker,* Carol Ann Williams, *Lily,* Charles Knapp, *Telegrapher,* Jane Austin, *Daisy Mullen,* Paul Price, *Skinner,* Hugh Gillan, *Cyrus Antoon,* Will Hare, *Conductor.* PG.

Excellent prequel to the western classic *Butch Cassidy and the Sundance Kid. Butch and Sundance: The Early Days* traces the lives of the famed outlaws from their meeting through their growing friendship and partnership. Tom Berenger and William Katt are good young counterparts for Newman and Redford, although they lack the charisma of the originals. *Butch and Sundance* could have easily failed had it not been for Richard Lester's superb comic direction.

136 Butley (1974) **** Britain, American Film Theatre, 129 min. *Dir* Harold Pinter, *Scr* Simon Gray, based on his play, *Cin* Gerry Fisher, *Ed* Malcolm Cooke, *Art* Carmen Dillon, *Prod* Ely A. Landau, *Exec Prod* Otto Plaschkes.

Cast: Alan Bates, *Ben Butley,* Jessica Tandy, *Edna Shaft,* Richard O'Callaghan, *Joey Keyston,* Susan Engel, *Anne Butley,* Michael Byrne, *Reg Nuttall,* Georgina Hale, *Miss Heasman,* Simon Rouse, *Mr. Gardner,* John Savident, *James,* Oliver Maguire, *Train Passenger,* Colin Haigh, Darien Angadi, *Male Students,* Susan Woodridge, Lindsay Ingram, Patti Love, Belinda Low, *Female Students.* R. See *American Film Theatre.*

137 Butterflies Are Free (1972) *** Columbia, 109 min. *Dir* Milton Katselas, *Scr* Leonard Gershe, based on his play, *Cin* Charles B. Lang (AN), *Ed* David Blewitt, *Des* Robert Clatworthy, *Cos* Moss Mabry, *Mus* Bob Alcivar, *Prod* M.J. Frankovich.

Cast: Goldie Hawn, *Jill,* Edward Albert, *Don* Eileen Heckart (A), *Mrs. Baker,* Paul Michael Glaser, *Ralph,* Mike Warren, *Roy.* PG. $6,770,000.

Funny and touching comedy about the relationship between a slightly kooky actress and her next door neighbor, a young blind man, which is complicated by his domineering mother. The filmmakers have done a fine job of adapting the play to the screen without expanding its setting. The performances of the three leads are all excellent, which is essential for this type of film to maintain interest.

138 Cabaret (1972) (AN, NB, BFA, GMC) **** Allied Artists, 124 min. *Dir* Bob Fosse (A, NB, BFA), *Scr* Jay Presson Allen (AN, W), based on play by Joe Masteroff, play *I Am a Camera* by John Van Druten and writings of Christopher Isherwood, *Cin* Geoffrey Unsworth (A, BFA); *Ed* David Bretherton (A), *Des* Rolf Zehetbauer (A, BFA), *Art* Jurgen Kiebach (A), *Cos* Charlotte Flemming, *Mus* John Kander, *Lyrics* Fred Ebb, *Adaptation* Ralph Burns (A), *Chor* Bob Fosse, *Prod* Cy Feuer, *Assoc Prod* Harold Nebenzal.

Cast: Liza Minnelli (A, BFA, GMC), *Sally Bowles,* Michael York, *Brian Roberts,* Helmut Griem, *Maximilian von Heune,* Joel Grey (A, NS, NB, G), *Master of Ceremonies,* Fritz Wepper, *Fritz Wendel,* Marisa Berenson (NB), *Natalia Landauer,* Elizabeth Neumann-Viertel, *Fraulein Schneider,* Sigrid Von Richthofen, *Fraulein Maur,* Helen Vita, *Fraulein Kost,* Gerd Vespermann,

Bobby, Ralf Wolter, *Herr Ludwig*, George Hartman, *Willi*, Ricky Renee, *Elke*, Estrongo Nachama, *Cantor*. PG. $20,250,000.

Excellent musical set in pre-war Nazi Germany. *Cabaret* was, in its own way, a daring film; the first major American musical aimed at a strictly adult audience. Because of this it lacks the standard moronic dialogue and unbearably sugarcoated characters. This innovativeness led to some overpraise by many critics, because although *Cabaret* towers above most films of its genre it is in no way a masterpiece. Liza Minnelli and Joel Grey are fine in their roles, but hardly deserved Oscars.

139 **Cahill, United States Marshal** (1973) ** Warner Bros., 103 min. *Dir* Andrew V. McLaglen, *Scr* Harry Julian Fink, Rita M. Fink, *Story* Barney Slater, *Cin* Joseph Biroc, *Ed* Robert L. Simpson, *Des* Walter Simonds, *Mus* Elmer Bernstein, *Prod* Michael Wayne.

Cast: John Wayne, *Cahill*, George Kennedy, *Fraser*, Gary Grimes, *Danny Cahill*, Neville Brand, *Lightfoot*, Clay O'Brien, *Billy Joe Cahill*, Marie Windsor, *Mrs. Green*, Morgan Paull, *Struther*, Dan Vadis, *Brownie*, Royal Dano, *Mac-Donald*, Scott Walker, *Ben Tildy*, Denver Pyle, *Denver*, Jackie Coogan, *Charlie Smith*, Rayford Barnes, *Pee Wee Simser*, Dan Kemp, *Joe Meehan*, Harry Carey, Jr., *Hank*, Walter Barnes, *Sheriff Grady*, Paul Fix, *Old Man*, Pepper Martin, *Hard Case*. PG. ¢4,100,000.

Another tired John Wayne western that attempts to throw in youth themes. Wayne stars as a U.S. marshal whose sons become involved in crime. As in the case of most of his later films *Cahill, United States Marshal* is too preachy for its own good. This is not Wayne's worst film by any means, but it's a long way from his best.

140 **California Dreaming** (1979) ** American International, 92 min. *Dir* John Hancock, *Scr* Ned Wynn, *Cin* Bobby Byrne, *Ed* Herb Dow, Roy Peterson, *Des* Bill Hiney, *Mus* Fred Karlin, *Prod* Christian Whittaker, *Exec Prod* Louis S. Arkoff.

Cast: Glynnis O'Connor, *Corky*, Seymour Cassell, *Duke*, Dorothy Tristan, *Fay*, Dennis Christopher, *T.T.*, John Calvin, *Rick*, Tanya Roberts, *Stephanie*, Jimmy Van Patten, *Mike*, Todd Susman, *Jordy*, Alice Playten, *Corrine*, Ned Wynn, *Earl*, John Fain, *Tenner*, Marshall Efron, *Ruben*. R.

Fair updating of the beach movies of the 1960's to the mores of the late 1970's. Dennis Christopher is good as a country bumpkin from the Midwest who is completely out of place on a California beach, but who tries desperately to fit in. *California Dreaming* is considerably raunchier than those earlier films, and is not quite as silly.

141 **California Split** (1974) ***** Paramount, 108 min. *Dir* Robert Altman, *Scr* Joseph Walsh, *Cin* Paul Lohmann, *Ed* Lou Lombardo, *Art* Leon Ericksen, *Mus* Phyllis Shotwell, *Prod* Robert Altman, Joseph Walsh, *Exec Prod* Aaron Spelling, Leonard Goldberg, *Assoc Prod* Robert Eggenweiler.

Cast: George Segal, *Bill Denny*, Elliott Gould, *Charlie Walters*, Ann Prentiss, *Barbara Miller*, Gwen Welles, *Susan Peters*, Edward Walsh, *Lew*, Joseph Walsh, *Sparkie*, Bert Remsen, *"Helen Brown"*, Barbara London, *Lady on the Bus*, Barbara Ruick, *Reno Barmaid*, Jay Fletcher, *Robber*, Jeff Goldblum, *Lloyd Harris*, Barbara Colby, *Receptionist*. R. $5,000,000.

Superb comedy character study featuring superb performances by

George Segal and Elliott Gould as a pair of compulsive gamblers; it focuses on these people and their motives rather than the games, themselves. In fact Altman properly leaves out the rules and details of the games, which slow down many gambling films. There is also no misguided attempt to put all gamblers in the same category, as these two particular gamblers are very different. They may each also represent two sides of a split personality; the film's title, which is the name of a poker game, also indicates that possibility. *California Split* is very complex for a comedy and is one of Altman's finest films.

142 **California Suite** (1978) ** Columbia, 103 min. *Dir* Herbert Ross, *Scr* Neil Simon (AN), based on his play, *Cin* David M. Walsh, *Ed* Michael A. Stevenson, *Des* Albert Brenner (AN), *Cos* Patricia Norris, Ann Roth, *Mus* Claude Bolling, *Prod* Ray Stark, *Assoc Prod* Ronald L. Schwary.

Cast: Alan Alda, *Bill Warren*, Michael Caine, *Sidney Cochran*, Bill Cosby, *Dr. Willis Panama*, Jane Fonda, *Hannah Warren*, Walter Matthau, *Marvin Michaels*, Elaine May, *Millie Michaels*, Richard Pryor, *Dr. Chauncy Gump*, Maggie Smith (A, G), *Diana Barrie*, Gloria Gifford, *Lola Gump*, Sheila Frazier, *Bettina Panama*, Herbert Edelman, *Harry Michaels*, Denise Galik, *Bunny*. PG. $29,200,000.

A West Coast version of Neil Simon's *Plaza Suite*, *California Suite* is a group of vignettes strung together by their location in the same hotel. The four vignettes herein point out Simon's strengths and weaknesses as a writer. He is good at verbal humor as evidenced by the Smith/Caine segment, but when he attempts seriousness (Alda/Fonda segment) or slapstick (Cosby/Pryor segment) the results are strained and sometimes embarrassing. The Matthau/May segment succeeds due almost entirely to Walter Matthau's brilliant comedic performance.

143 **Cancel My Reservation** (1972) * Warner Bros., 99 min. *Dir* Paul Bogart, *Scr* Robert Fisher, Arthur Marx, based on novel *Broken Gun* by Louis L'Amour, *Cin*, Russell L. Metty, *Ed* Michael A. Hoey, *Art* Rolland M. Brooks, *Mus* Dominic Frontiere, *Prod* Gordon Oliver, *Exec Prod* Bob Hope.

Cast: Bob Hope, *Dan Bartlett*, Eva Marie Saint, *Sheila Bartlett*, Ralph Bellamy, *John Ed*, Forrest Tucker, *Reese*, Anne Archer, *Crazy*, Keenan Wynn, *Sheriff Riley*, Henry Darrow, *Joe Little Cloud*, Doodles Weaver, *Cactus*, Betty Carr, *Mary Little Cloud*, Herb Vigran, *Snagby*, Pat Morita, *Yamamoto*, Gordon Oliver, *Mr. Sparker*, Buster Shaefer, *Doc Morton*, Chief Dan George, *Old Bear*. G.

Typically dimwitted Bob Hope comedy about a talk show host who becomes involved in a murder. This comedy is so terrible that one would assume that a top comedian like Hope would know better, but a quick survey of his past films should kill this notion. His major status as a comedian has never really been based on his film career, anyway, but at least his earliest films had some laughs.

144 **The Candidate** (1972) *** Warner Bros., 109 min. *Dir* Michael Ritchie, *Scr* Jeremy Larner (A, W), *Cin* Victor J. Kemper, *Ed* Robert Estrin, Richard A. Harris, *Des* Gene Callahan, *Cos* Patricia Norris, *Mus* John Rubinstein, David Colloff, *Prod* Walter Coblenz, *Assoc Prod* Nelson Rising.

Cast: Robert Redford, *Bill McKay*, Peter Boyle, *Lucas*, Don Porter, *Jar-*

man, Allen Garfield (Goorwitz) *Klein*, Karen Carlson, *Nancy*, Quinn Redeker, *Jenkin*, Morgan Upton, *Henderson*, Melvyn Douglas, *John J. Mc-Kay*, Michael Lerner, *Corliss*, Kenneth Tobey, *Starkey*, Chris Prey, *David*, Joe Miksak, *Neal Atkinson*, Jenny Sullivan, *Lynn*, Tom Dahlgren, *Pilot*, Gerald Hiken, *Station Master*, Leslie Allen, *Mabel*, Jason Goodrow, *Boy in Commercial*, Robert DeAnda, *Jaime*, Robert Goldsby, *Fleischer*, Michael Barnicle, *Wilson*, Lois Foraker, *Large Girl*, David Moody, *Watts Heckler*, George Meyer, *Man in Urinal*, Dudley Knight, *Magazine Editor*. PG.

Realistic, but slightly overrated political satire with Robert Redford as a candidate for the U.S. Senate who is chosen to run because he is sure to lose. The filmmakers stayed so close to reality–they had worked in real political campaigns, themselves–they they failed to make *The Candidate* a very interesting film. This is unfortunate, because this could have been a truly great film.

145 **Candleshoe** (1977) ** Buena Vista, 101 min. *Dir* Norman Tokar, *Scr* Rosemary Anne Sisson, David Swift, Based on novel *Christmas at Candleshoe* by Michael Innes, *Cin* Paul Beeson, *Ed* Peter Boita, *Art* Albert Witherick, *Cos* Julie Harris, *Mus* Ron Goodwin, *Prod* Ron Miller, *Assoc Prod* Hugh Attwooll, A Walt Disney Production.

Cast: David Niven, *Priory*, Helen Hayes, *Lady St. Edmund*, Jodie Foster, *Casey*, Leo McKern, *Bundage*, Vivian Pickles, *Grimsworthy*, Veronica Quilligan, *Cluny*, Ian Sharock, *Peter*, Sarah Tamakuni, *Anna*, David Samuels, *Bobby*, John Alderson, *Jenkins*, Mildred Shay, *Mrs. McCress*, Sydney Bromley, *Mr. Thresher*, Michael Segal, *Train Guard*, G. $7,225,000.

Standard Disney comedy about three con artists (Jodie Foster, Leo McKern, Vivian Pickles), who try to cheat an old woman (Helen Hayes) out of some coins hidden by her husband in an estate known as "Candleshoe." Foster pretends to be Hayes' granddaughter in order to find the coins, but she runs into opposition from David Niven. *Candleshoe* is like many films from Disney, pleasant, but somewhat dull.

146 **Cannonball** (1976) ** New World, 93 min. *Dir* Paul Bartel, *Scr* Paul Bartel, Donald C. Simpson, *Cin* Tak Fujimoto, *Ed* Morton Tubor, *Art* Michael Levesque, *Mus* David A. Axelrod, *Prod* Samuel W. Gelfman, *Exec Prod* Gustave Berne, Run Run Shaw, *Assoc Prod* Peter Cornberg.

Cast: David Carradine, *Coy "Cannonball" Buckman*, Bill McKinney, *Cade*, Veronica Hamel, *Linda*, Gerri Graham, *Perman*, Robert Carradine, *Jim* Belinda Balaski, *Maryann*, Judy Canova, *Sharma*, Carl Gottlieb, *Terry*, Mary Woronov, *Sandy*, Aron Kincaid, *David*, James Keach, Dick Miller, Louisa Moritz, Allan Arkush, Paul Bartel, Roger Corman, Joe Dante, Jonathan Kaplan, Martin Scorsese, Sylvester Stallone. PG.

A non-science-fiction follow-up to Paul Bartel's own *Death Race 2000*. *Cannonball*, also about a cross-country road race, lacks the offbeat satirical wit of the first film. Most of the attempted humor is unfortunately derived from an endless series of car crashes. The most interesting aspects are the numerous cameos, many of whom are from Roger Corman's extensive stable of talent.

147 **Capone** (1975) ** 20th Century–Fox, 101 min. *Dir* Steve Carver, *Scr* Howard Browne, *Cin* Vilis Lapenieks, *Ed* Richard Meyer, *Art* Ward Preston, *Mus* David Grisman, *Prod* Roger Corman.

Cast: Ben Gazzara, *Al Capone*, Susan Blakely, *Iris Crawford*, Harry Guardino, *Johnny Torrio*, John Cassavetes, *Frankie Yale*, Sylvester Stallone, *Frank Nitti*, Peter Maloney, *Jake Guzik*, Frank Campanella, *Big Jim Colosimo*, John Chandler, *Hymie Weiss*, John Orchard, *Dion O'Banion*, Mario Gallo, *Aiello*, Russ Marin, *Stenson*, George Chandler, *Prosecutor*. R.

Fair film biography of notorious gangster, Al Capone, following his rise to power and his eventual downfall. *Capone* seems to be an attempt at seriousness, but it seldom rises above the level of an exploitation film, laced with sex and violence. Ben Gazzara is good as Capone, but his stuffed cheeks are merely a copy of Marlon Brando in *The Godfather*. Some of the action sequences, further, are in fact stock footage from *The St. Valentine's Day Massacre*.

148 **Capricorn One** (1978) *** Warner Bros., 127 min. *Dir* Peter Hyams, *Scr* Peter Hyams, *Cin* Bill Butler, *Ed* James Mitchell, *Des* Albert Brenner, *Art* David M. Haber, *Cos* Patricia Norris, *Mus* Jerry Goldsmith, *Prod* Paul N. Lazarus III, *Assoc Prod* Michael Rachmil.

Cast: Elliot Gould, *Robert Caulfield*, James Brolin, *Charles Brubaker*, Brenda Vaccaro, *Kay Brubaker*, Sam Waterston, *Peter Willis*, O.J. Simpson, *John Walker*, Hal Holbrook, *Dr. James Kelloway*, David Huddleston, *Hollis Peaker*, David Doyle, *Walter Loughlin*, Denise Nicholas, *Betty Walker*, Robert Walden, *Elliot Whittier*, Lee Bryant, *Sharon Willis*, Alan Fudge, *Capsule Communicator*, Karen Black, *Judy Drinkwater*, Telly Savalas, *Albain*. PG. $12,000,000.

Interesting science-fact drama about a fake landing on Mars perpetrated by the American government, which subsequently tries to eliminate the three astronauts to prevent them from talking. *Capricorn One* is sort of a science-fiction version of Watergate. The film is a little too long, but it climaxes with an exciting chase sequence which is worth the wait.

149 **The Car** (1977) * Universal, 95 min. *Dir* Elliot Silverstein, *Scr* Michael Butler, Lane Slate, Dennis Shryack, *Story* Michael Butler, Dennis Shryack, *Cin* Gerald Hirschfeld, *Ed* Michael McCroskey, *Art* Loyd S. Papez, *Mus* Leonard Rosenman, *Prod* Marvin Birdt, Elliot Silverstein.

Cast: James Brolin, *Wade Parent*, Kathleen Lloyd, *Lauren*, John Marley, *Everett*, R.G. Armstrong, *Amos*, John Rubenstein, *John Morris*, Elizabeth Thompson, *Margie*, Roy Jensen, *Ray Mott*, Kim Richards, *Lynn Marie*, Kyle Richards, *Debbie*, Ronny Cox, *Luke*, Henry O'Brien, *Chas*, Eddie Little Sky, *Denson*, Lee McLaughlin, *Marvin Fats*, Margaret Willey, *Navajo Woman*, Read Morgan, *Mac Gruder*, Ernie Orsatti, *Dalton*, Joshua Davis, *Jimmy*, Geraldine Keams, *Donna*. PG.

Inane occult thriller concerning a car that is possessed by the devil. If the premise sounds ridiculous, *The Car* more than lives up to its promise. This mysterious black vehicle terrorizes a small western town and spends most of the time running over its citizens. If this was intended to scare an audience then the filmmakers were certainly misguided.

150 **Car Wash** (1976) ** Universal, 97 min. *Dir* Michael Schultz, *Scr* Joel Schumacher, *Cin* Frank Stanley, *Ed* Christopher Holmes, *Art* Robert Clatworthy, *Cos* Daniel Paredes, *Mus* Norman Whitfield, *songs* performed by Rose Royce, *Prod* Art Linson, Gary Stromberg, *Assoc Prod* Don Phillips.

Cast: Franklyn Ajaye, *T.C.*, Sully Boyar, *Mr. B.*, Richard Brestoff, *Irwin*, George Carlin, *Taxi Driver*, Prof. Irwin Corey, *Mad Bomber*, Ivan Dixon, *Lonnie*, Bill Duke, *Duane*, Antonio Fargas, *Lindy*, Michael Fennell, *Calvin*, Arthur French, *Charlie*, Darrow Igus, *Floyd*, Leonard Jackson, *Earl*, DeWayne Jessie, *Lloyd*, Lauren Jones, *Hooks*, Jack Kehoe, *Scruggs*, Henry Kingi, *Goody*, Melanie Mayron, *Marsha*, Garrett Morris, *Slide*, Clarence Muse, *Snapper*, Leon Pinkney, *Justin*, Pointer Sisters, *Wilson Sisters*, Richard Pryor, *Daddy Rich*. PG. $9,000,000.

An unsuccessful attempt at a M*A*S*H-style comedy about a day in-the-life of a large car wash. This plotless comedy lacks the intelligence and wit of the aforementioned film. The humor is forced and sometimes ridiculous, and not even cameos by comedians Richard Pryor, George Carlin and Prof. Irwin Corey can do much to save it.

151 **The Carey Treatment** (1972) ** MGM, 101 min. *Dir* Blake Edwards, *Scr* James P. Bonner (pseudonym for John D.F. Black, Harriet Frank Jr., Irving Ravetch), based on novel *A Case of Need* by Jeffrey Hudson (pseudonym for Michael Crichton), *Cin* Frank Stanley, *Ed* Ralph E. Winters, *Art* Alfred Sweeney, *Cos* Jack Bear, *Mus* Roy Budd, *Prod* William Belasco, *Assoc Prod* Barry Mendelson.

Cast: James Coburn, *Peter Carey*, Jennifer O'Neill, *Georgia Hightower*, Pat Hingle, *Capt. Pearson*, Skye Aubrey, *Angela Holder*, Elizabeth Allen, *Evelyn Randall*, John Fink, *Murphy*, Dan O'Herlihy, *J.D. Randall*, James Hong, *David Tao*, Alex Dreier, *Joshua Randall*, Michael Blodgett, *Roger Hudson*, Regis Toomey, *Sanderson*, Steve Carlson, *Walding*, Rosemary Edelman, *Janet Tao*, Jennifer Edwards, *Lydia Barrett*, John Hillerman, *Jenkins*, Robert Mandan, *Dr. Barr*. PG.

Dull hospital thriller about a doctor who turns to sleuthing to solve a murder mystery. Part of its failure probably can be attributed to the supposed butchering of the film by MGM prior to its release, which prompted Blake Edwards to publicly disowning it. On the other hand, Edwards, a highly respected comedy director, seems to strain himself with dramatic films.

152 **Carnal Knowledge** (1971) *** Avco Embassy, 97 min. *Dir* Mike Nichols, *Scr* Jules Feiffer, *Cin* Giuseppe Rotunno, *Ed* Sam O'Steen, *Des* Richard Sylbert, *Art* Robert Luthardt, *Cos* Anthea Sylbert, *Prod* Mike Nichols, *Exec Prod* Joseph E. Levine.

Cast: Jack Nicholson, *Jonathan*, Candice Bergen, *Susan*, Arthur Garfunkel, *Sandy*, Ann-Margret (*AN, G*), *Bobbie*, Rita Moreno, *Louise*, Cynthia O'Neal, *Cindy*, Carol Kane, *Jennifer*. R.

Interesting comedy-drama that examines American sexual mores and attitudes. The film follows two friends (Jack Nicholson, Art Garfunkel) from college in the 1940's where they both fall in love with the same girl (Candice Bergen), to middle-age in the 1960's. Ann-Margret gives a fine performance, in her first dramatic role, as Nicholson's girlfriend, but it is Nicholson's brilliant performance that is the film's highlight. Although *Carnal Knowledge* has a perceptive and witty script, the film is disjointed and does not live up to its potential.

153 **Carrie** (1976) **** United Artists, 97 min. *Dir* Brian De Palma, *Scr* Lawrence D. Cohen, based on novel by Stephen King, *Cin* Mario Tosi, *Ed*

Paul Hirsch, *Art* Jack Fisk, William Kenny, *Cos* Rosanna Norton, *Mus* Pino Donaggio, *Prod* Paul Monash, *Assoc Prod* Louis Stroller.

Cast: Sissy Spacek (AN, NS), *Carrie*, Piper Laurie (AN), *Margaret White*, Amy Irving, *Sue Snell*, William Katt, *Tommy Ross*, Nancy Allen, *Chris Hargenson*, Betty Buckley, *Miss Collins*, John Travolta, *Billy Nolan*, P.J. Soles, *Norma Watson*, Sydney Lassick, *Mr. Fromm*, Stefan Gierash, *Mr. Morton*, Priscilla Pointer, *Mrs. Snell*, Michael Talbot, *Freddy*, Doug Cox, *The Beak*, Harry Gold, *George*, Noelle North, *Frieda*, Cindy Daly, *Cora*, Dierdre Berthron, *Thonda*, Anson Downs, *Ernest*, Rory Stevens, *Kenny*, Edie McClurg, *Helen*, Cameron De Palma, *Boy on Bicycle*. R. $15,000,000.

Excellent horror film starring Sissy Spacek as a lonely girl with telekinetic powers, who wreaks havoc on her prom. Unlike most horror films Carrie has some interesting ideas and themes, including the danger of repression, and rather than being another film about good vs. evil, this one's central theme is science vs. religion. *Carrie* resorts to science to explain her power, while her fanatic mother (Piper Laurie) turns to religion, and the two ideas eventually clash. Much has been made of De Palma's influence by Alfred Hitchcock, but in *Carrie* there seems to be more of an influence by Luis Bunuel.

154 **Casey's Shadow** (1978) *** Columbia, 116 min. *Dir* Martin Ritt, *Scr* Carol Sobieski, based on short story *Ruidoso* by John McPhee, *Cin* John A. Alonzo, *Ed* Sidney Levin, *Des* Robert Luthardt, *Cos* Moss Mabry, *Mus* Patrick Williams, *Prod* Ray Stark, *Exec Prod* Michael Levee.

Cast: Walter Matthau, *Lloyd Bourdell*, Alexis Smith, *Sarah Blue*, Robert Webber, *Mike Marsh*, Murray Hamilton, *Tom Patterson*, Andrew A. Rubin, *Buddy Bourdell*, Stephen Burns, *Randy Bourdell*, Susan Myers, *Kelly Marsh*, Michael Hershewe, *Casey Bourdell*, Harry Caesar, *Calvin Lebec* Joel Fluellen, *Jimmy Judson*, Whit Bissell, *Dr. Williamson*, Jimmy Halty, *Donovan*, William Pitt, *Dr. Pitt*, Dean Turpitt, *Dean*, Sanders Delhomme, *Old Cajun*, Richard Thompson, *Lenny*, PG. $4,300,000.

Interesting family film about a horse trainer who will do anything to train a winning horse, while at the same time trying to raise three sons by himself. The story may sound like it came from a Disney film, but *Casey's Shadow* is told with more honesty and realism. The film is slightly overlong, but Walter Matthau, as usual, turns in an excellent performance.

155 **The Cassandra Crossing** (1977) ** Avco Embassy, 125 min. *Dir* George Cosmatos, *Scr* George Cosmatos, Robert Katz, Tom Mankiewicz, *Cin* Ennio Guarnieri, *Ed* Francois Bonnot, Roberto Silvi, *Art* Aurelio Crugnola, *Cos* Adriana Berselli, *Prod* Carlo Ponti, *Exec Prod* Giancarlo Pettini, Presented by Sir Lew Grade and Carlo Ponti.

Cast: Sophia Loren, *Jennifer*, Richard Harris, *Chamberlain*, Ava Gardner, *Nicole*, Burt Lancaster, *Mackenzie*, Martin Sheen, *Navarro*, Ingrid Thulin, *Elena*, Lee Strasberg, *Kaplan*, John Phillip Law, *Stack*, Ann Turkel, *Susan*, O.J. Simpson, *Father Haley*, Lionel Stander, *Conductor*, Raymond Lovelock, *Tom*, Alida Valli, *Mrs. Chadwick*, Lou Castell, *Swede (Driver)*, Stefano Patrizi, *Attendant*, Carlo DeMejo, *Patient*, Fausta Avelli, *Katherine*. R. $4,185,000.

Another in a seemingly endless series of dull international thrillers that substitute major stars in place of an intelligent script. American audiences tired of these films years ago, but audiences overseas continue to support them. *The Cassandra Crossing* is slightly better than most, due to a few well-paced action sequences, but the idea of terrorists inadvertently contaminating a trainload of people is not really an appealing subject for a movie.

156 **The Cat from Outer Space** (1978) *** Buena Vista, 103 min. *Dir* Norman Tokar, *Scr* Ted Key, *Cin* Charles F. Wheeler, *Ed* Cotton Warburton, *Art* Preston Ames, John B. Mansbridge, *Mus* Lalo Schifrin, *Prod* Ron Miller, *Co-Prod* Norman Tokar, *Assoc Prod* Jan Williams, A Walt Disney Production.

Cast: Ken Berry, *Frank*, Sandy Duncan, *Liz*, Harry Morgan, *Gen. Stilton*, Roddy McDowell, *Mr. Stallwood*, McLean Stevenson, *Link*, Jesse White, *Earnest Ernie*, Alan Young, *Dr. Wenger*, Hans Conreid, *Dr. Heffel*, Ronnie Schell, *Sgt. Duffy*, James Hampton, *Capt. Anderson*, Howard T. Platt, *Col. Woodruff*, William Prince, *Mr. Olympus*. G. $8,465,000.

Enjoyable Disney comedy about an extraterrestrial cat that is forced to land on Earth to repair its spaceship. The cat has special powers, for which its collar is the source, and Earthlings fight over the collar and exploit the cat for gambling purposes. Disney's venture into science-fiction is well made, but it is hardly in the same class with *Star Wars* and others.

157 **Catch-22** (1970) **** Paramount, 122 min. *Dir* Mike Nichols, *Scr* Buck Henry, based on novel by Joseph Heller, *Cin* David Watkin, *Ed* Sam O'Steen, *Des* Richard Sylbert, *Cos* Ernest Adler, Lambert Marks, *Prod* John Calley, Martin Ransohoff, *Assoc Prod* Clive Reed.

Cast: Alan Arkin, *Capt. Yossarian*, Martin Balsam, *Col. Cathcart*, Richard Benjamin, *Maj. Danby*, Art Garfunkel, *Capt. Nately*, Jack Gilford, *Dr. Daneeka*, Bob Newhart, *Maj. Major*, Anthony Perkins, *Chaplain Tappman*, Paula Prentiss, *Nurse Duckett*, Martin Sheen, *Lt. Dobbs*, Jon Voight, *Milo Minderbinder*, Orson Welles, *Gen Dreedle*, Seth Allen, *Hungry Joe*, Robert Balaban, *Capt. Orr*, Susanne Benton, *Gen. Dreedle's WAC*, Peter Bonerz, *Capt. McWatt*, Norman Fell, *Sgt. Towser*, Charles Grodin, *Aardvark*, Buck Henry, *Lt. Col. Korn*, Austin Pendleton, *Col. Moodus*, Gina Rovere, *Nately's Whore*, Olympia Carlisli, *Luciana*, Marcel Dalio, *Old Man*, Eva Maltagliati, *Old Woman*, Liam Dunn, *Father*, Elizabeth Wilson, *Mother*, Richard Libertini, *Brother*, Jon Korkes, *Snowden*. R. $12,250,000.

Bizarre anti-war black comedy starring Alan Arkin as a WWII bombardier stationed in Italy, who pretends to be insane in order to be grounded from bombing missions. The collaboration of Mike Nichols and Buck Henry is superb, brilliantly matching surrealistic images with sharp satire to create one of the finest war films ever made. Unfortunately in the second half, the surrealism becomes too dominant and it overshadows the satire.

158 **The Champ** (1979) ** United Artists, 121 min. *Dir* Franco Zeffirelli, *Scr* Walter Newman, based on story by Francis Marion, *Cin* Fred J. Koenekamp, *Ed* Michael J. Sheridan, *Des.* Herman A. Blumenthal, *Cos* Theoni V. Aldredge, *Mus* Dave Grusin (AN), *Prod* Dyson Lovell.

Cast: Jon Voight, *Billy*, Ricky Schroder, *T.J.*, Faye Dunaway, *Annie*, Jack Warden, *Jackie*, Arthur Hill, *Mike*, Strother Martin, *Riley*, Joan Blondell, *Dolly Kenyon*, Mary Jo Catlett, *Josie*, Elisha Cook, *George*, Stefan Gierasch, *Charlie Goodman*, Allan Miller, *Whitey*, Joe Tornatore, *Hesh*, Shirlee Kong, *Donna Mae*, Jeff Blum, *Jeffie*, Dana Elcar, *Hoffmaster*, Randall Cobb, *Bowers*,

Christoff St. John, *Sonny*, Gina Gallego, *Cuban Girl*, Jody Wilson, *Mrs. Riley*, Reginal M. Toussaint, *Groom*, Bob Gordon, *TV Reporter*, Gene Picchi, *Dolly's Trainer*, Anne Logan, *Horse Owner*, Bill Baldwin, *Race Track Announcer*. PG. $12,600,000.

Overly sentimental story of a has-been boxer and his relationship with his young son, whom he must fight for in a custody battle with his ex-wife. *The Champ* is a remake of the Wallace Beery film of the same title and the new version is not any worse than the original, which has not held up well over the years. Both seem to be nothing more than excuses to wrench tears from the audience and Ricky Schroder, as the son, cries more than any child star since Margaret O'Brien.

159 **Chapter Two** (1979) ** Columbia, 124 min. *Dir* Robert Moore, *Scr* Neil Simon, *Cin* David M. Walsh, *Ed* Margaret Booth, Michael A. Stevenson, *Des* Gene Callahan, *Art* Pete Smith, *Cos* Vicki Sanchez, *Mus* Marvin Hamlisch, *Lyrics* Carol Bayer Sagar, *Prod* Ray Stark, *Exec Prod* Roger M. Rothstein, *Assoc Prod* Margaret Booth.

Cast: James Caan, *George Schneider*, Marsha Mason (AN), *Jennie MacLaine*, Joseph Bologna, *Leo Schneider*, Valerie Harper, *Faye Medwick*, Alan Fudge, *Leo Michaels*, Judy Farrell, *Gwen Michaels*, Debra Mooney, *Marilyn*. PG. $15,250,000.

Pretentious Neil Simon comedy-drama loosely based on his real-life marriage to actress Marsha Mason. James Caan and Mason, basically portraying herself, try their best with Simon's heavy-handed script, which contains overly cute and totally unreal dialogue that strains for laughs. Simon has overreached himself in recent years, and it has never been more apparent than in this film.

160 **Charley Varrick** (1973) *** Universal, 111 min. *Dir* Don Siegel, *Scr* Dean Riesner, Howard Rodman, based on novel *The Looters*, by John Reese, *Cin* Michael Butler, *Ed* Frank Morriss, *Art* Fernando Carrere, *Cos* Helen Colvig, *Mus* Lalo Schifrin, *Prod* Don Siegel, *Exec Prod* Jennings Lang.

Cast: Walter Matthau (BFA), *Charley Varrick*, Joe Don Baker, *Molly*, Felicia Farr, *Sybil Fort*, Andy Robinson, *Harman Sullivan*, John Vernon, *Maynard Boyle*, Sheree North, *Jewell Everett*, Norman Fell, *Mr. Garfinkle*, Benson Fong, *Honest John*, Woodrow Parfrey, *Howard Young*, William Schallert, *Sheriff Bill Horton*, Jacqueline Scott, *Nadine Varrick*, Marjorie Bennett, *Mrs. Taff*, Rudy Diaz, *Rudy Sanchez*, Colby Chester, *Steele*, Charlie Briggs, *Highway Deputy*, Priscilla Garcia, *Miss Ambar*, Scott Hale, *Mr. Scott*, Charles Matthau, *Boy*, Hope Summers, *Miss Vesta*, Monica Lewis, *Beverly*, Don Siegel, *Murph*. PG.

In a nice change of pace Walter Matthau stars as a small-time crook who gets in over his head. He and his partner rob a bank that just happens to contain Mafia money. *Charley Varrick* is an expert cat-and-mouse thriller, as the two are pursued by a sadistic hit man (Joe Don Baker). Matthau proves, in this film more than any other, that he can do more than comedy.

161 **The Cheap Detective** (1978) ** Columbia, 92 min. *Dir* Robert Moore, *Scr* Neil Simon, *Cin* John A. Alonzo, *Ed* Sidney Levin, Michael A. Stevenson, *Des* Robert Luthardt, *Art* Phillip Bennett, *Cos* Theoni V. Aldredge, *Mus* Patrick Williams, *Prod* Ray Stark, *Assoc Prod* Margaret Booth.

Cast: Peter Falk, *Lou Peckinpaugh*, Ann-Margret, *Jezebel Dezire*, Eileen Brennan, *Betty DeBoop*, Sid Caesar, *Ezra Dezire*, Stockard Channing, *Bess*, James Coco, *Marcel*, Dom DeLuise, *Pepe Damascus*, Louise Fletcher, *Marlene DuChard*, John Houseman, *Jasper Blubber*, Madeline Kahn, *Mrs. Montenegro*, Fernando Lamas, *Paul DuChard*, Marsha Mason, *Georgia Merkle*, Phil Silvers, *Happy*, Abe Vigoda, *Sgt. Rizzuto*, Paul Williams, *Boy*, Nicol Williamson, *Col. Schissel*, Emory Bass, *Butler*, Carmine Caridi, *Sgt. Crosseti*, James Cromwell, *Schell*, Scatman Crothers, *Tinker*, David Ogden Stiers, *Captain*, Vic Tayback, *Lt. DiMaggio*, Carole Wells, *Hat Check Girl*. PG. $19,500,000.

Mediocre follow-up to Neil Simon's other detective spoof *Murder by Death*. The *Cheap Detective* concentrates on one detective, rather than a half-dozen as in the earlier film, and satirizes several Humphrey Bogart films. Peter Falk, again, does an excellent job mimicking Bogart, a reprisal from *Murder by Death*, but he is hindered by a poor script, which contains too few laughs. Bogart fans may derive some pleasure, though, guessing the source of each joke.

162 **The Cheyenne Social Club** (1970) *** National General, 103 min. *Dir* Gene Kelly, *Scr* James Lee Barrett, *Cin* William Clothier, *Ed* Adrienne Fazan, *Des* Gene Allen, *Cos* Yvonne Wood, *Mus* Walter Scharf, *Prod* Gene Kelly, *Exec Prod* James Lee Barrett.

Cast: James Stewart, *John O'Hanlan*, Henry Fonda, *Harley Sullivan*, Shirley Jones, *Jenny*, Sue Ane Langdon, *Opal Ann*, Elaine Devry, *Pauline*, Robert Middleton, *Barkeep (Great Plains)*, Arch Johnson, *Marshal Anderson*, Dabbs Greer, *Willowby*, Jackie Russell, *Carrie Virginia*, Jackie Joseph, *Annie Jo*, Sharon DeBord, *Sara Jean*, Richard Collier, *Nathan Potter*, Charles Tyner, *Charlie Bannister*, Jean Willes, *Alice*, Robert J. Wilke, *Corey Bannister*, Carl Reindel, *Pete Dodge*, J. Pat O'Malley, *Dr. Foy*, Jason Wingreen, *Dr. Carter*, John Dehner, *Clay Carroll*, Hal Baylor, *Barkeep (Lady of Egypt)*. PG. $5,250,000.

Pleasant western comedy highlighted by the teaming of James Stewart and Henry Fonda. Stewart inherits a small town brothel, not realizing the true nature of the establishment, and Fonda goes along for the ride. The *Cheyenne Social Club* is hardly daring and is so light it looks like a television film, but Stewart and Fonda play so well together it does not really matter.

163 **Child's Play** (1972) ** Paramount, 100 min. *Dir* Sidney Lumet, *Scr* Leon Prochnik, based on play by Robert Marasco, *Cin* Gerald Hirschfeld, *Ed* Joanne Burke, Edward Warschilka, *Des* Philip Rosenberg, *Mus* Michael Small, *Prod* David Merrick.

Cast: James Mason, *Jerome Malley*, Robert Preston, *Joseph Dobbs*, Beau Bridges, *Paul Reis*, Ronald Weyand, *Father Mozian*, Charles White, *Father Griffin*, David Rounds, *Father Penny*, Kate Harrington, *Mrs. Carter*, Jamie Alexander, *Sheppard*, Brian Chapin, *O'Donnell*, Bryant Frazer, *Jennings*, Mark Hall Haefeli, *Wilson*, Tom Leopold, *Shea*, Julius Lo Iacono, *McArdie*, Christopher Man, *Travis*, Paul O'Keefe, *Banks*, Robert D. Randall, *Medley*, Robbie Reed, *Class President*. PG.

Dull thriller set in a boy's boarding school. One of the teachers (James Mason) believes there is a conspiracy and the students, led by another teacher (Robert Preston) are out to get him. *Child's Play* is based on a stage play and it shows. There is very little action and far too much emphasis on dialogue. Lumet does set up a proper claustrophobic mood, but the ending is disappointing and anti-climactic.

164 The China Syndrome (1979) *** Columbia, 122 min. *Dir* James Bridges, *Scr* James Bridges, T.S. Cook, Mike Gray (AN, W), *Cin* James Crabe, *Ed* David Rawlins, *Des* George Jenkins (AN), *Song* "Some Where In Between" by Stephen Bishop, *Prod* Michael Douglas, *Exec Prod* Bruce Gilbert, *Assoc Prod* James Nelson, *Assistant Prod* Penny McCarthy, Jack Smith Jr.

Cast: Jane Fonda (AN, BFA), *Kimberly Wells*, Jack Lemmon (AN, BFA, CF), *Jack Godell*, Michael Douglas, *Richard Adams*, Scott Brady, *Herman DeYoung*, James Hampton, *Bill Gibson*, Peter Donat, *Don Jacovich*, Wilford Brimley, *Ted Spindler*, Richard Herd, *Evan McCormack*, Daniel Valdez, *Hector Salas*, Stan Bohran, *Pete Martin*, James Karen, *Mac Churchill*, Michael Alaimo, *Greg Minor*, Donald Hotton, *Dr. Lowell*, Khalilah Ali, *Marge*, Paul Larson, *D.B. Royce*, Ron Lombard, *Barney*, Tom Eure, *Tommy*, Nick Pellegrino, *Borden*, Daniel Lewk, *Donny*, Allan Chinn, *Holt*. PG. $26,075,000.

Well-made, but overrated thriller about an accident at a nuclear power plant and the subsequent cover-up by the authorities. *The China Syndrome* tries too hard to be both a message film and an exciting suspense film, but it strains a bit to achieve both. Jack Lemmon steals the film with one of his best performances as a man torn between his loyalty to his company and his conscience. The release of *The China Syndrome* was one of the most perfectly timed in history, as it opened just prior to the real nuclear accident at Three Mile Island.

165 Chinatown (1974) (AN, G) ***** Paramount, 131 min. *Dir* Roman Polanski (AN, BFA, G), *Scr* Robert Towne (A, BFA, W), *Cin* John A. Alonzo (AN), *Ed* Sam O'Steen (AN), *Des* Richard Sylbert (AN), Gage Resh, Robert Resh, *Art* W. Stewart Campbell (AN), *Cos* Anthea Sylbert (AN), *Mus* Jerry Goldsmith (AN), *Prod* Robert Evans, *Assoc Prod* C.O. Erickson.

Cast: Jack Nicholson (AN, NS, NY, BFA, G), *J.J. Gittes*, Faye Dunaway (AN), *Evelyn Mulwray*, John Huston, *Noah Cross*, Perry Lopez, *Escobar*, John Hillerman, *Yelburton*, Darrell Zwerling, *Hollis Mulwray*, Diane Ladd, *Ida Sessions*, Roy Jenson, *Mulvihill*, Roman Polanski, *Man with Knife*, Dick Bakalyan, *Loach*, Joe Mantell, *Walsh*, Bruce Glover, *Duffy*, Nandu Hinds, *Sophie*, James O'Reare, *Lawyer*, James Hong, *Evelyn's Butler*, Beulah Quo, *Maid*, Jerry Fujikawa, *Gardener*, Roy Roberts, *Mayor Bagby*, Noble Willingham, Elliot Montgomery, *Councilmen*, Rance Howard, *Irate Farmer*, Burt Young, *Curly*. R. $12,400,000.

The finest achievement in the detective genre to date. Polanski's masterpiece set in Los Angeles in the 1930's, centers on private eye J.J. Gittes who inadvertantly becomes involved in a murder. Through his investigation, he uncovers a water conspiracy during a major drought. The drought serves as a metaphor for sexual and emotional repression, which leads to violence and perversion, normal elements in Polanski's films. J.J. Gittes is a classic screen detective and *Chinatown* proves that it is unnecessary to continually exhume the detectives of the past.

166 **Chisum** (1970) *** Warner Bros., 111 min. *Dir* Andrew V. McLaglen, *Scr* Andrew J. Fenady, *Cin* William H. Clothier, *Ed* Robert Simpson, *Art* Carl Anderson, *Cos* Luster Bayless, Michael Harte, *Mus* Dominic Frontiere, *Song*, "Ballad of John Chisum," *Mus* Andrew J. Fenady, Dominic Frontiere, *Prod* Andrew J. Fenady, *Exec Prod* Michael Wayne.

Cast: John Wayne, *John Chisum*, Forrest Tucker, *Lawrence Murphy*, Christopher George, *Dan Nodeen*, Ben Johnson, *James Pepper*, Glenn Corbett, *Pat Garrett*, Bruce Cabot, *Sheriff Brady*, Andrew Prine, *Alex McSween*, Patric Knowles, *Tunstall*, Richard Jaeckel, *Evans*, Lynda Day George, *Sue McSween*, John Agar, *Patton*, Lloyd Battista, *Neemo*, Robert Donner, *Morton*, Ray Teal, *Justice Wilson*, Edward Faulkner, *Dolan*, Pedro Armandariz, Jr., *Ben*, Christopher Mitchum, *O'Folliard*, Geoffrey Deuel, *Billy the Kid*, Glenn Langan, *Dudley*, Alan Baxter, *Gov. Axtell*. G. $6,000,000.

Above average John Wayne western. Wayne is a rancher, who tries to prevent an evil landowner (Forrest Tucker) from illegally foreclosing the mortgages on all the nearby ranches in order to gain control of the entire area. Most of Wayne's latter day westerns are nothing more than tired old vehicles, but this one is entertaining enough to rise slightly above most of the others.

167 **The Choirboys** (1977) *** Universal, 119 min. *Dir* Robert Aldrich, *Scr* Christopher Knopf, based on novel by Joseph Wambaugh, *Cin* Joseph Biroc, *Ed* William Martin, Irving Rosenblum, Maury Winetrobe, *Des* Bill Kenney, *Mus* Frank DeVol, *Prod* Merv Adelson, Lee Rich, *Exec Prod* Mario Bregni, Pietro Bregni, Mark Damon.

Cast: Charles Durning, *Whalen*, Louis Gossett, Jr., *Motts*, Perry King, *Slate*, Clyde Kusatsu, *Tanaguchi*, Stephen Macht, *Van Moot*, Tim McIntire, *Roscoe Rules*, Randy Quaid, *Proust*, Chuck Sacci, *Sartino*, Don Stroud, *Lyles*, James Woods, *Bloomguard*, Burt Young, *Scuzzi*, Robert Webber, *Riggs*, Jeanie Bell, *Fanny*, Blair Brown, *Mrs. Lyles*, Michele Carey, *Ora Lee Tingle*, Charles Haid, *Yanov*, Joe Kapp, *Hod Carrier*, Barbara Rhodes, *Hadley*, Jim Davis, *Capt. Drobeck*, Phyllis Davis, *Foxy Gina*, Jack DeLeon, *Luther Quigley*, George Di Cenzo, *Lt. Grimsley*, David Spielberg, *Lt. Finque*, Vic Tayback, *Pete Zooney*, Michael Wills, *Blaney*, Susan Batson, *Sabrina*, Claire Brennon, *Carolina Moon*. R. $7,630,000.

Well-made, but unflattering portrait of contemporary uniformed policeman. The structure is episodic as *The Choirboys* follows the irreverent exploits of a group of Los Angeles cops on and off-duty, which at times seem like episodes from *M*A*S*H* or *Animal House*. Robert Aldrich's treatment received enormous adverse reaction from nearly everyone, including Wambaugh, who disowned the film. The film actually is an enjoyable black comedy and should not have been taken that seriously.

168 **Cinderella Liberty** (1973) *** 20th Century–Fox, 117 min. *Dir* Mark Rydell, *Scr* Darryl Ponicson, based on his novel, *Cin* Vilmos Zsigmond, *Ed* Donn Cambern, *Des* Leon Ericksen, *Cos* Rita Riggs, *Mus* John Williams (AN), *Song*, "Nice to be Around." John Williams, Paul Williams (AN), *Prod* Mark Rydell.

Cast: James Caan, *John Baggs, Jr.*, Marsha Mason (AN, G), *Maggie Paul*, Kirk Calloway, *Doug*, Eli Wallach, *Forshay*, Burt Young, *Master at Arms*, Allyn Ann McLerie, *Miss Watkins*, Dabney Coleman, *Executive Officer*, Fred Sadoff,

Dr. Osgood, Allan Arbus, *Drunken Sailor,* Jon Korkes, *Dental Corpsman,* Don Calfa, *Lewis,* Paul Jackson, *Sam,* David Proval, *Sailor #1,* Ted D'Arms, *Cook,* Sally Kirkland, *Fleet Chick.* R. $4,005,000.

Average love story starring James Caan as a sailor, who falls for a prostitute (Marsha Mason). Mason's life is a shambles; she has a black son and she is pregnant by someone else. Caan feels a sense of responsibility to her and tries to help her, despite her outward hostility. *Cinderella Liberty* tries to be realistic, but that is only on the surface. Underneath it is just another overly sentimental film that aims for the tear ducts.

169 **Cisco Pike** (1972) ** Columbia, 94 min. *Dir* Bill L. Norton, *Scr* Bill L. Norton, *Cin* Vilis Lapenieks, *Ed* Robert C. Jones, *Art* Alfred Sweeney, *Mus* Kris Kristofferson, *Prod* Gerald Ayres, *Assoc Prod* Herbert Wallerstein.

Cast: Kris Kristofferson, *Cisco Pike,* Karen Black, *Sue,* Gene Hackman, *Holland,* Harry Dean Stanton, *Jesse,* Viva, *Merna,* Joy Bang, *Lynn,* Roscoe Lee Browne, *Music Store Owner,* Chuy Franco, *Mexican,* Severn Darden, *Lawyer,* Herb Weil, *Customer,* Antonio Fargas, *Buffalo,* Douglas Sahm, *Rex,* Don Sturdy, *Recording Engineer,* Allan Arbus, *Sim,* Frank Hotchkiss, *Motorcycle Officer,* Hugh Romney, *Reed,* James Oliver, *Narc,* Nawana Davis, *Mouse,* Timothy Near, *Waitress,* Lorna Thayer, *Swimmer,* William Taylor, *Jack.* R.

Fair crime thriller starring Kris Kristofferson as a rock star, who vows to go straight after his release from prison, for dealing in drugs. He is harassed by a crooked cop (Gene Hackman), who forces Kristofferson into a drug deal. Kristofferson makes a fine acting debut, but the film is slightly flat, lacking a needed bit of tension and excitement.

170 **Class of '44** (1973) ** Warner Bros., 95 min. *Dir* Paul Bogart, *Scr* Herman Raucher, *Cin* Andrew Laszlo, *Ed* Michael A. Hoey, *Des* Ben Edwards, *Mus* David Shire, *Prod* Paul Bogart, *Exec Prod* Harry Keller.

Cast: Gary Grimes, *Hermie,* Jerry Houser, *Oscy,* Oliver Conant, *Benjie,* William Atherton, *Fraternity President,* Sam Bottoms, *Marty,* Deborah Winters, *Julie,* Joe Ponazecki, *Professor,* Murray Westgate, *Principal,* Marion Waldman, *Grade Advisor,* Mary Long, *Valedictorian,* Marcia Diamond, *Mrs. Gilhuly,* Jeffrey Cohen, *Editor,* Susan Marcus, *Assistant Editor,* Lamar Criss, *First Proctor,* Michael A. Hoey, *Second Proctor,* Dan McDonald, *Father,* Jan Campbell, *Mother.* PG. $7,000,000.

See *Summer of '42.*

171 **Claudine** (1974) *** 20th Century–Fox, 92 min. *Dir* John Beery, *Scr* Tina and Lester Pine, *Cin* Gayne Rescher, *Ed* Luis San Andres, *Des* Ted Haworth, *Art* Ben Kasazkow, *Cos* Bernard Johnson, *Mus* Curtis Mayfield, performed by Gladys Knight and the Pips, *Prod* Hannah Weinstein, *Exec Prod* J. Lloyd Grant.

Cast: Diahann Carroll (AN), *Claudine,* James Earl Jones, *Roop,* Lawrence-Hilton-Jacobs, *Charles,* Tamu, *Charlene,* David Kruger, *Paul,* Yvette Curtis, *Patrice,* Eric Jones, *Francis,* Socorro Stephens, *Lurlene,* Adam Wade, *Owen,* Harrison Avery, *Minister,* Mordecai Lawner, *Process Server,* Terry Alexander, *Teddy,* Carolyn Adams, *Dance Teacher,* Bob Scarantino, Bill Bressant, *Cops,* Elisa Loti, *Miss Kabak,* Roxie Roker, *Mrs. Winston,* Stefan Gierasch, *Sanitation Foreman.* PG.

Above average black family film about a garbage collector (James Earl Jones), who has an affair with a woman on welfare (Diahann Carroll), who has six children. *Claudine* touches on several social issues, including the unfairness of the welfare system, but it treats them superficially. This is a likable comedy, that was a welcome relief from the blaxtoitation films of the time, highlighted by the superb performances of the two leads.

172 **Cleopatra Jones** (1973) * Warner Bros., 89 min. *Dir* Jack Starrett, *Scr* Max Julien, Sheldon Keller, *Story* Max Julien, *Cin* David Walsh, *Ed* Allan Jacobs, *Art* Peter Wooley, *Mus* Carl Brandt, J.J. Johnson, Brad Shapiro, *Title Theme* Joe Simon, *Prod* William Tennant, *Co-Prod* Max Julien.

Cast: Tamara Dobson, *Cleopatra Jones*, Bernie Casey, *Reuben*, Shelley Winters, *Mommy*, Brenda Sykes, *Tiffany*, Antonio Fargas, *Doodlebug*, Bill McKinney, *Purdy*, Dan Frazer, *Crawford*, Stafford Morgan, *Kert*, Mike Warren, *Andy*, Albert Popwell, Caro Kenyatta, *Johnson Boys*, Esther Rolle, *Mrs. Johnson*, Paul Koslo, Joseph A. Tornatore, *Mommy's Hoods*, Hedley Mattingly, *Chauffeur*, George Reynolds, Theodore Wilson, *Doodlebug's Hoods*, Christopher Joy, *Snake*, Keith Hamilton, *Maxwell*, Angela Gibbs, *Annie* John Garwood, *Lieutenant*, John Alderman, *Mommy's Assistant*. PG.

Standard blaxtoitation film with a plot that seems to have been lifted directly from a comic book. Tamara Dobson stars in the title role as an Amazon-like government agent who battles drug dealers, led by the evil Mommy (Shelley Winters). In the equally dimwitted sequel *Cleopatra Jones and the Casino of Gold*, Jones' adversary is "The Dragon Lady" played by Stella Stevens.

173 **Cleopatra Jones and the Casino of Gold** (1975) * Warner Bros. 96 min. *Dir* Chuck Bail, *Scr* William Tennant, based on characters created by Max Julien, *Cin* Alan Hume, *Ed* Willy Kemplen, *Art* Johnson Tsao, *Mus* Dominic Frontiere, *Prod* William Tennant.

Cast: Tamara Dobson, *Cleopatra Jones*, Stella Stevens, *Dragon Lady*, Tanny, *Mi Ling*, Norman Fell, *Stanley*, Albert Popwell, *Matthew*, Caro Kenyatta, *Melvin*, Chan Sen, *Soo*, Christopher Hunt, *Mendez*, Lin Chen Chi, *Madalyna*, Liu Loke Hua, *Tony*, Eddy Donno, *Morgan*, Bobby Canavarro, *Lin Ma Chen*, Mui Kwok Sing, *Benny*, John Cheng, *David*. R. See *Cleopatra Jones*.

174 **A Clockwork Orange** (1971) (AN, NY) ***** Britain, Warner Bros., 135 min. *Dir* Stanley Kubrick (AN, NY), *Scr* Stanley Kubrick (AN), based on novel by Anthony Burgess, *Cin* John Alcott, *Ed* Bill Butler (AN), *Des* John Barry, *Art* Russell Hagg, Peter Shields, *Cos* Milena Canonero, *Prod* Stanley Kubrick, *Exec Prod* Si Litvinoff, Max L. Raab, *Assoc Prod* Bernard Williams.

Cast: Malcolm McDowell, *Alex*, Patrick Magee, *Mr. Alexander*, Michael Bates, *Chief Guard*, Warren Clarke, *Dim*, John Clive, *Stage Actor*, Adrienne Corri, *Mrs. Alexander*, Carl Duering, *Dr. Brodsky*, Paul Farrell, *Tramp*, Clive Francis, *Lodger*, Michael Gover, *Prison Governor*, Miriam Karlin, *Catlady*, James Marcus, *Georgie*, Aubrey Morris, *Deltoid*, Godfrey Quigley, *Prison Chaplin*, Sheila Raynor, *Mum*, Madge Ryan, *Dr. Barnom*, John Savident, *Conspirator*, Anthony Sharpe, *Minister of the Interior*, Philip Stone, *Dad*, Pauline Taylor, *Psychiatrist*, Margaret Tyzack, *Conspirator*. X. (Re-rated as R). $16,000,000.

Brilliant science-fiction, black comedy set in the near future, in which hoodlum gangs prowl the streets at night raping and pillaging. Malcolm Mc-Dowell stars as the leader of one of these gangs, who is imprisoned for murder and becomes a guinea pig in an experiment that conditions him to be revolted by violence. Stanley Kubrick superbly combines violence and satire in this controversial film about freedom of choice at all costs. The pacing is incredible, as its 135 minute running time plays like 90. McDowell gives a magnificent performance, and somehow imbues his sadistic character with charm. A Clockwork Orange is a towering achievement that nearly obliterates every other film in its genre, including Kubrick's earlier classic 2001: A Space Odyssey, and must rank as one of the great masterpieces of the cinema.

175 **Close Encounters of the Third Kind** (1977) ***** Columbia, 135 min. Dir Steven Spielberg (AN), Scr Steven Spielberg, Cin Vilmos Zsigmond (A), Cin (Additional Sequences) John A. Alonzo, William A. Fraker, Laszlo Kovacs, Douglas Slocombe, Dave Stewart, Robert Hall, Don Jarel, Dennis Muren, Ed Michael Kahn (AN), Des Joe Alves (AN), Art Dan Lomino (AN), Cos Jim Linn, Sp Roy Arbogast Gregory Jein, Douglas Trumbull, Matthew Yuricich, Richard Yuricich (AN), Mus John Williams (AN), Prod Julia and Michael Phillips.

Cast: Richard Dreyfuss, Roy Neary, Francois Truffaut, Claude Lacombe, Teri Garr, Ronnie, Melinda Dillon (AN), Jilian Guiler, Cary Guffey, Barry Guiler, Bob Balaban, Interpreter Laughlin, J. Patrick McNamara, Project Leader, Warren Kemmerling, Wild Bill, Roberts Blossom, Farmer, Philip Dodds, Jean Claude, Shawn Bishop, Adrienne Campbell, Justin Dreyfuss, Neary Children, Lance Henricksen, Robert, Merrill Connally, Team Leader, George Dicenzo, Maj. Benchley. PG. $77,000,000/Special Addition. $5,710,000.

One of the most spectacular and visually opulent science-fiction films ever made. Steven Spielberg's vision of man's first encounter with alien life is inspired by the science fiction films of the 1950's, but with the feeling of hope and optimism, rather than that of hostility and pessimism. Spielberg has populated his film with human beings, instead of cartoon characters that usually inhabit science fiction films. The special effects cannot be faulted and never in any way appear to be miniatures. In 1980 a revamped version with newly shot footage, unused old footage and re-edited scenes, known as the Special Edition, was released surprisingly with even better results.

176 **Cockfighter** (1974) *** New World, 85 min. Dir Monte Hellman, Scr Charles Willeford, based on his novel, Cin Nestor Almendros, Ed Lewis Teague, Mus Michael Franks, Prod Roger Corman, Co-Prod Samuel Gelfman.

Cast: Warren Oates, Frank, Richard B. Shull, Omar, Harry Dean Stanton, Jack, Ed Begley, Jr., Tom, Laurie Bird, Dody, Troy Donahue, Randall, Warren Finnerty, Sanders, Robert Earl Jones, Buford, Patricia Pearcy, Mary Elizabeth, Millie Perkins, Frances, Steve Railsback, Junior, Tom Sprately, Milam, Charles Willeford, Ed, Pete Munro, Packard, Kermit Echols, Fred, Ed Smith, Whipple, Jimmy Williams, Buddy, John Trotter, Hanson, Lois Zeitlin, Lucille, Joe Bently, Peach, A.B. Greeson, Pete, Bob Earl Hannah, Deputy, Sara Rickman, Martha, Meg Brush, Mary's Mother, Oliver Coleman, Senator,

Donnie Fritts, *Gangleader*, Bobby Dunn, Kim Bernard, *Gamblers*, Ank Carleton, *Capt. Mack*, Billy Abbott, *Referee*. R.

Unusual drama about the illegal sport of cockfighting and one of its participants who, after losing vows silence and refuses to speak until he again wins. Warren Oates is surprisingly effective as this man, having to convey his feelings and emotions without the aid of dialogue. *Cockfighter* is the best film to date by noted director Monte Hellman, whose talents have been virtually ignored by the major American studios.

177 **Cold Turkey** (1971) *** United Artists, 102 min. *Dir* Norman Lear, *Scr* Norman Lear, *Story* William Price Fox, Jr., Norman Lear, based on unpublished material by Margaret and Neil Rau, *Cin* Charles F. Wheeler, *Ed* John C. Horger, *Art* Arch Bacon, *Cos* Rita Riggs, *Mus* Randy Newman, *Prod* Norman Lear, *Exec Prod* Bud Yorkin.

Cast: Dick Van Dyke, *Rev. Clayton Brooks*, Pippa Scott, *Natalie Brooks*, Tom Poston, *Mr. Stopworth*, Edward Everett Horton, *Hiram Grayson*, Bob Elliott and Ray Goulding, *TV Commentators*, Bob Newhart, *Merwin Wren*, Vincent Gardenia, *Mayor Wappler*, Barnard Hughes, *Dr. Procter*, Graham Jarvis, *Amos Bush*, Jean Stapleton, *Mrs. Wappler*, Barbara Cason, *Letitia*, Judith Lowry, *Odie*, Sudie Bond, *Cissy*, Helen Page Camp, *Mrs. Watson*, Paul Benedict, *Zen Buddhist*, Simon Scott, *Mr. Kandiss*, Raymond Kark, *Homer Watson*, Peggy Rea, *Mrs. Procter*, Woodrow Parfrey, *Tobacco Executive*, George Mann, *Bishop Manley*, Charles Pinney, *Col. Galloway*, M. Emmet Walsh, *Art* Gloria LeRoy, *Hooker*, Eric Boles, *Dennis*, Jack Grimes, *TV Stage Manager*, Walter Sande, *Tobacco Executive*, Harvey Jason, *Hypnotist*. PG. $4,975,000.

Surprisingly good comedy set in a small Midwestern town, in which the entire populace must give up smoking for 30 days, in order to win a large sum of money from a tobacco company. *Cold Turkey* rises above its situation comedy style plot, due to its witty and perceptive examination of the mores and attitudes of small town America.

178 **Coma** (1978) ** United Artists, 113 min. *Dir* Michael Crichton, *Scr* Michael Crichton, based on novel by Robin Cook, *Cin* Gerald Hirschfeld, Victor J. Kemper, *Ed* David Bretherton, *Des* Albert Brenner, *Cos* Yvonne Kubis, Eddie Marks, *Mus* Jerry Goldsmith, *Prod* Martin Erlichman.

Cast: Genevieve Bujold, *Dr. Susan Wheeler*, Michael Douglas, *Dr. Mark Bellows*, Elizabeth Ashley, *Mrs. Emerson*, Rip Torn, *Dr. George*, Richard Widmark, *Dr. Harris*, Lois Chiles, *Nancy Greenly*, Harry Rhodes, *Dr. Morelind*, Gary Barton, *Computer Technician*, Frank Downing, *Kelly*, Richard Doyle, *Jim*, Alan Haufrect, *Dr. Marcus*, Lance Le Gault, *Vince*, Michael MacRae, *Cheif Resident*, Betty McGuire, *Nurse*, Tom Selleck, *Murphy*, Charles Siebert, *Dr. Goodman*, William Wintersole, *Lab Technician*. PG. $14,600,000.

Dull hospital thriller in which a female doctor uncovers a medical conspiracy where patients are deliberately put into comas and their organs sold on the black market. This is not as gruesome as it may sound. Casting a woman as the protagonist is a welcome change of pace, and Bujold is excellent in the role, but *Coma* tends nevertheless to be too sterile and unemotional.

179 **Come Back Charleston Blue** (1972) *** Warner Bros., 100 min. *Dir* Mark Warren, *Scr* Peggy Elliot, Bontche Schweig, based on novel *The Heat's On* by Chester Himes, *Cin* Dick Kratina, *Ed* George Bowers, Gerald Greenberg, *Des* Robert Gundlach, *Art* Perry Watkins, *Cos* Anna Hill Johnstone, *Mus* Donny Hathaway, *Prod* Samuel Goldwyn, Jr., *Assoc Prod* Al Fann.

Cast: Godfrey Cambridge, *Gravedigger Jones*, Raymond St. Jacques, *Coffin Ed Jones*, Peter DeAnda, *Joe*, Janelle Allen, *Carol*, Maxwell Glanville, *Casper*, Minnie Gentry, *Her Majesty*, Dick Sabol, *Jarema*, Leonardo Cimino, *Frank Mago*, Percy Rodrigues, *Bryce*, Toney Brealond, *Drag Queen*, Tim Pelt, *Earl J.*, Darryl Knibb, *Douglas*, Marcia McBroom, *Girl Barber*, Adam Wade, *Benjy*, Joseph Ray, *Bubba*, Theodore Wilson, *Cemetery Guard*, Dorothi Fox, *Streetwalker*. PG. See *Cotton Comes to Harlem*.

180 **Comes a Horseman** (1978) *** United Artists, 118 min. *Dir* Alan J. Pakula, *Scr* Dennis Lynton Clark, *Cin* Gordon Willis, *Ed* Marion Rothman, *Des* George Jenkins, *Cos* Luster Bayless, *Mus* Michael Small, *Prod* Gene Kirkwood, Dan Paulson, *Exec Prod* Robert Chartoff, Irwin Winkler, *Assoc Prod* Ronald Caan.

Cast: James Caan, *Frank*, Jane Fonda (LA), *Ella*, Jason Robards, *Ewing*, George Grizzard, *Neil Atkinson*, Richard Farnsworth (AN, NS, NB), *Dodger*, Jim Davis, *Julie Blocker*, Mark Harmon, *Billy Joe Meynert*, Macon McCalman, *Hoverton*, Basil Hoffman, *George Bascomb*, James Kline, *Ralph Cole*, James Keach, *Kroegh*, Clifford A. Pellow, *Cattle Buyer*. PG $4,185,000.

Disappointing contemporary Western set right after WWII. An independent rancher (Jane Fonda) hires a cowboy (James Caan) to help protect her ranch from takeover by a wealthy landowner (Jason Robards). This same story has been told before and it is not particularly fresh here. Overshadowing the entire film, are the magnificent landscapes, beautifully photographed by Gordon Willis, which nearly dwarf the actors.

181 **Coming Home** (1978) (AN, LA) **** United Artists, 126 min. *Dir* Hal Ashby (AN), *Scr* Robert C. Jones, Waldo Salt, based on story by Nancy Dowd (A, W), *Cin* Haskell Wexler, *Ed* Don Zimmerman (AN), *Des* Mike Haller, *Cos* Mike Hoffman, Jennifer Parson, Ann Roth Silvio Scarano, *Prod* Jerome Hellman.

Cast: Jane Fonda (A, LA, G), *Sally Hyde*, Jon Voight (A, NY, NB, LA, G, CF), *Luke Martin*, Bruce Dern (AN), *Capt. Bob Hyde*, Penelope Milford (AN), *Viola Munson*, Robert Ginty, *Sgt. Dink Mobley*, Robert Carradine, *Bill Munson*. R. $13,400,000.

Excellent, but slightly overlong Vietnam War film. *Coming Home* is to that war what *The Best Years of Our Lives* was to World War II, as it examines the problems facing returning veterans. *Coming Home* succeeds far better as a love story than as an indictment of the war, which has been done better in other films. The relationship between a lonely woman, whose husband is overseas, and a paraplegic, wounded in the war, is beautifully and tastefully handled and with a surprisingly wonderful sense of humor.

182 **The Computer Wore Tennis Shoes** (1970) *** Buena Vista, 90 min. *Dir* Robert Butler, *Scr* Joseph L. McEveety, *Cin* Frank Phillips, *Ed* Cotton Warburton, *Art* John B. Mansbridge, *Cos* Chuck Keehne, Emily Sundby, *Mus* Robert F. Brunner, *Prod* Bill Anderson, *Assoc Prod* Joseph L. McEveety, A Walt Disney Production.

Cast: Kurt Russell, *Dexter*, Cesar Romero, *A.J. Arno*, Joe Flynn, *Dean Higgens*, William Schallert, *Prof. Quigley*, Alan Hewitt, *Dean Collingsgood*, Richard Bakalyan, *Chillie Walsh*, Debbie Paine, *Annie*, Frank Webb, *Pete*, Michael McGreevey, *Schuyler*, Jon Provost, *Bradley*, Frank Walker, *Henry*, Alexander Clarke, *Myles*, Bing Russell, *Angelo*, Pat Harrington, *Moderator*, Fabian Dean, *Little Mac*, Fritz Feld, *Sigmund Van Dyke*, Pete Renoudet, *Lt. Hannah*, Hillyard Anderson, *J. Reedy*. G. $6,000,000.

Fine Disney slapstick comedy starring Kurt Russell as a college student, who accidently has a computer fused into his brain and is subsequently pursued by gangsters. The success of this film led to two similar follow-ups also starring Russell, In *Now You See Him, Now You Don't* he discovers a formula that turns him invisible and in *The Strongest Man in the World* he discovers a formula that gives him great strength. These films may be repetitious, but they are among Disney's better comedies.

183 **The Concorde–Airport '79** (1979)   *   Universal, 123 min. *Dir* David Lowell Rich, *Scr* Eric Roth, *Story* Jennings Lang, inspired by the film *Airport* and based on novel by Arthur Hailey, *Cin* Philip Lathrop, *Ed* Dorothy Spencer, *Des* Henry Bumstead, *Cos* Burton Miller, *Mus* Lalo Schifrin, *Prod* Jennings Lang.

Cast: Alain Delon, *Metrand*, Susan Blakely, *Maggie*, Robert Wagner, *Kevin*, Sylvia Kristel, *Isabelle*, George Kennedy, *Patroni*, Eddie Albert, *Eli*, Bibi Anderson, *Francine*, Charo, *Margarita*, John Davidson, *Robert Palmer*, Andrea Marcovicci, *Alicia*, Martha Raye, *Loretta*, Cicely Tyson, *Elaine*, Jimmie Walker, *Boisie*, David Warner, *O'Neill*, Mercedes McCambridge, *Nelli*, Avery Schreiber, *Coach Markov*, Sybil Danning, *Amy*, Monica Lewis, *Gretchen*, Nicolas Coster, *Dr. Stone*, Robin Gammell, *William Halpern*. PG. $8,910,000. See *Airport*.

184 **Conduct Unbecoming** (1975)   ***   Britain, Allied Artists, 107 min. *Dir* Michael Anderson, *Scr* Robert Enders, *Cin* Bob Huke, *Ed* John Glen, *Art* Ted Testor, *Cos* Joan Bridge, Elizabeth Haffenden, *Mus* Stanley Myers, *Prod* Michael Deeley, Barry Spikings, *Co-Prod* Andrew Donally.

Cast: Michael York, *Second Lt. Arthur Drake*, Richard Attenborough, *Maj. Lionel Roach*, Trevor Howard, *Col. Benjamin Strang*, Stacy Keach, *Capt. Rupert Harper*, Christopher Plummer, *Maj. Alastair Wimbourne*, Susannah York, *Mrs. Marjorie Scarlett*, James Faulkner, *Second Lt. Edward Millington*, Michael Culver, *Second Lt. Richard Fothergill*, James Donald, *Regimental Doctor*, Rafiq Anwar, *Pradad Singh*, Helen Cherry, *Mem Strang*, Michael Fleming, *Lt. Frank Hart*, David Robb, *Second Lt. Winters*, David Purcell, *Second Lt. Boulton*, Andrew Lodge, *Second Lt. Hutton*, David Neville, *Second Lt. Truly*, Persis Khambatta, *Mrs. Bandanai*, Michael Byrne, *Second Lt. Toby Strang*. PG.

Interesting but flawed military drama about a young lieutenant, who is put on trial for supposedly molesting the widow of an officer. *Conduct Unbecoming* unsuccessfully tries to turn the story into a mystery and the poorly conceived surprise ending almost destroys the entire mood. This is certainly not in the same class as *Paths of Glory*, the classic of the genre. The real asset, through, is the extraordinary British cast.

185 **Conrack** (1974) ******* 20th Century–Fox, 107 min. *Dir* Martin Ritt, *Scr* Harriet Frank, Jr., Irving Ravetch, based on book *The Water Is Wide* by Pat Conroy, *Cin* John Alonzo, *Ed* Frank Bracht, *Des* Walter Scott Herndon, *Mus* John Williams, *Prod* Harriet Frank, Jr., Martin Ritt, *Assoc Prod* Richard Kobritz.

Cast: Jon Voight, *Pat Conroy*, Paul Winfield, *Mad Billy*, Hume Cronyn, *Skeffington*, Madge Sinclair, *Mrs. Scott*, Tina Andrews, *Mary*, Antonio Fargas, *Quickfellow*, Ruth Attaway, *Edna*, James O'Reare, *Little Man*. PG.

Interesting story, based on fact, about a white teacher (Jon Voight) who goes to a South Carolina island to teach a group of underprivileged black children. The story is very predictable; he runs into opposition at first, but gradually wins them over. Voight is excellent in the lead, but *Conrack* is too sweet and sentimental for its own good.

186 **Conquest of the Planet of the Apes** (1972) ****** 20th Century–Fox, 87 min. *Dir* J. Lee Thompson, *Scr* Paul Dehn, based on characters created by Pierre Boulle, *Cin* Bruce Surtees, *Ed* Marjorie Fowler, Allan Jaggs, *Art* Philip Jeffries, *Mus* Tom Scott, *Prod* Arthur P. Jacobs, *Assoc Prod* Frank Capra, Jr.

Cast: Roddy McDowell, *Caesar*, Don Murray, *Breck*, Ricardo Montalban, *Armando*, Natalie Trundy, *Lisa*, Hari Rhodes, *MacDonald*, Severn Darden, *Kolp*, Lou Wagner, *Busboy*, John Randolph, *Commission Chairman*, Asa Maynor, *Mrs. Riley*, H.M. Wynant, *Hoskyne*, David Chow, *Aldo*, Buck Kartalian, *Frank (Gorilla)*, John Dennis, *Policeman*, Gordon Jump, *Auctioneer*, Dick Spangler, *Announcer*, Joyce Haber, *Zelda*, Hector Soucy, *Ape with Chain*, Paul Comi, *Second Policeman*. PG. $4,500,000. See *Beneath the Planet of the Apes*.

187 **The Conversation** (AN, NB, CF) (1974) ********* Paramount, 113 min. *Dir* Francis Coppola (NS, NB), *Scr* Francis Coppola (AN), *Des* Dean Tavoularis, *Ed* Richard Chew, Walter Murch (BFA), *Mus* David Shire, *Prod* Francis Coppola, *Co-Prod* Fred Roos.

Cast: Gene Hackman (NB), *Harry Caul*, John Cazale, *Stan*, Allen Garfield (Goorwitz), *Bernie Moran*, Frederick Forrest, *Mark*, Cindy Williams, *Ann*, Michael Higgins, *Paul*, Elizabeth MacRae, *Meredith*, Teri Garr, *Amy*, Harrison Ford, *Martin Stett*, Mark Wheeler, *Receptionist*, Robert Shields, *The Mime*, Phoebe Alexander, *Lurleen*, Robert Duvall, *The Director*. PG.

Brilliant thriller that is to sound recording what *Blow Up* was to photography. Harry Caul is a surveillance expert, who is hired to record a conversation between a young man and woman. Through repeated listenings he finds a clue to a murder plot. Coppola handles this plot expertly, which includes a nice twist ending, but he has far more on his mind than just a mere murder story. The film's many themes include paranoia and a citizen's right to privacy. Coppola made a wise choice in following *The Godfather* with this small film, rather than immediately attempting to top his blockbuster.

188 **Convoy** (1978) ****** United Artists, 110 min. *Dir* Sam Peckinpah, *Scr* B.W.L. Norton, based on song by C.W. McCall, *Cin* Harry Stradling, Jr., *Ed* Graeme Clifford, Garth Craven, John Wright, *Des* Fernando Carrere, *Art* Francis Lombardo, Jr., Dennis Washington, *Cos* Carol James, Kent James, *Mus* Chip Davis, *Song Lyrics* Bill Fries, *Prod* Robert M. Sherman, *Exec Prod* Michael Deeley, Barry Spikings.

Cast: Kris Kristofferson, *Rubber Duck*, Ali MacGraw, *Melissa*, Ernest Borgnine, *Lyle Wallace*, Burt Young, *Pig Pen*, Madge Sinclair, *Widow Woman*, Franklyn Ajaye, *Spider Mike*, Brian Davies, *Chuck Arnoldi*, Seymour Cassel, *Gov. Haskins*, Cassie Yates, *Violet*, Walter Kelley, *Hamilton*. PG. $9,525,000.

Silly trucking film based on the hit song by C.W. McCall about an unstoppable convoy of trucks. There seems to be little motivation for the formation of this convoy, which was spawned by the rivalry between a trucker (Kris Kristofferson) and a corrupt sheriff (Ernest Borgine), other than an excuse for a series of chases and crashes. *Convoy* is less violent than most of Peckinpah's other films and also less interesting.

189 **Cooley High** (1975) *** American International, 107 min. *Dir* Michael Schultz, *Scr* Eric Monte, *Cin* Paul Vom Brack, *Ed* Christopher Holmes, *Art* William B. Fosser, *Mus* Freddie Perren, *Prod* Steve Krantz, *Exec Prod* Samuel Z. Arkoff.

Cast: Glynn Turman, *Preach*, Lawrence-Hilton Jacobs, *Cochise*, Garrett Morris, *Mason*, Cynthia Davis, *Brenda*, Corin Rogers, *Pooter*, Maurice Leon Havis, *Willie*, Joseph Carter Wilson, *Tyrone*, Sherman Smith, *Stone*, Norman Gibson, *Robert*, Maurice Marshall, *Damon*, Steven Williams, *Jimmy*, Jackie Taylor, *Johnny Mae*, Christine Jones, *Sandra*, Lynn Caridine, *Dorothy*. PG.

Well-made comedy-drama focusing on black high school students living in the projects in Chicago. *Cooley High* has been compared to *American Graffiti* due to its episodic structure, but that is where the similarities end.The film focuses on two youths (Glynn Turman, Lawrence-Hilton Jacobs) and their experiences in and out of school, with tragic results. Unfortunately, a sloppy structure mars what is an honest and realistic portrayal of black youths.

190 **Cops and Robbers** (1973) ** United Artists, 89 min. *Dir* Aram Avakian, *Scr* Donald E. Westlake, *Cin* David Quaid, *Ed* Barry Malkin, *Art* Gene Rudolf, *Cos* John Boyt, *Mus* Michel Legrand, *Prod* Elliot Kastner.

Cast: Cliff Gorman, *Tom*, Joe Bologna, *Joe*, Dick Ward, *Paul Jones*, Shepperd Strudwick, *Eastpoole*, Ellen Holly, *Secretary*, John Ryan, *Patsy*, Nino Ruggeri, *Bandell*, Gayle Gorman, *Mary*, Lucy Martin, *Grace*, Joe Spinnell, *Marty*. PG.

Mild caper comedy with a slight twist, the crooks are two uniformed policemen. The screenplay is by novelist Donald Westlake, who wrote *The Hot Rock*, but this film is not as funny or as briskly paced as the other film. Gorman and Bologna give fine performances as the two cops and film editor Aram Avakian does a fine job as director, but the main problem lies in the script which contains too few memorable moments.

191 **Corvette Summer** (1978) *** United Artists, 105 min. *Dir* Matthew Robbins, *Scr* Hal Barwood, Matthew Robbins, *Cin* Frank Stanley, *Ed* Amy Jones, *Art* James Schoppe, *Cos* Aggie Guerard Rodgers, *Mus* Craig Safan, *Prod* Hal Barwood.

Cast: Mark Hamill, *Ken Dantley*, Annie Potts, *Vanessa*, Eugene Roche, *Ed McGrath*, Kim Milford, *Wayne Lowry*, Richard McKenzie, *Principal*, William Bryant, *Police P.R.*, Philip Bruns, *Gil*, Danny Bonaduce, *Kootz*, Jane A. Johnston, *Mrs. Dantley*, Albert Insinnia, *Ricci*, Isaac Ruiz, Jr., *Tico*, Stanley Kamel,

Con Man, Jason Ronard, *Tony*, Brion James, *Jeff*. PG. $6,500,000.

Simple but enjoyable tale of a teenager (Mark Hamill), who goes in pursuit of his stolen Corvette. Along the way he meets a kooky young prostitute, wonderfully played by Annie Potts, who goes along for the ride and eventually becomes his love interest. The title *Corvette Summer* gives the impression of being just another dumb teen comedy, but this film rises above that with its witty and very funny script.

192 **Cotton Comes to Harlem** (1970) *** United Artists, 97 min. *Dir* Ossie Davis, *Scr* Ossie Davis, Arnold Perl, based on novel by Chester Himes, *Cin* Gerald Hirschfeld, *Ed* John Carter, Robert Q. Lovett, *Art* Manny Gerard, *Cos* Anna Hill Johnstone, *Mus* Galt MacDermot, *Prod* Samuel Goldwyn, Jr.

Cast: Godfrey Cambridge, *Grave Digger Jones*, Raymond St. Jacques, *Coffin Ed Johnson*, Calvin Lockhart, *Rev. Deke O'Malley*, Judy Pace, *Iris*, Redd Foxx, *Uncle Budd*, John Anderson, *Bryce*, Emily Yancy, *Mabel*, J.D. Cannon, *Calhoun*, Mabel Robinson, *Billie*, Dick Sabol, *Jarema*, Theodore Wilson, *Barry*, Eugene Roche, *Anderson*, Maxwell Glanville, *Casper*, Van Kirksey, *Early Riser*, Cleavon Little, *Lo Boy*, Helen Martin, *Church Sister*, Arnold Williams, *Hi Jinks*. R. $5,125,000.

Unusual comedy-drama about two unorthodox plain clothes policemen, who investigate a suspicious preacher and his "Back-to-Africa" campaign. Godfrey Cambridge and Raymond St. Jacques are excellent as the two cops. *Cotton Comes to Harlem* is better than most films of its type, due to its sense of humor, and its success led to a huge wave of black-oriented films, including a superior sequel *Come Back, Charleston Blue*, which reteamed Cambridge and St. Jacques.

193 **The Cowboys** (1972) ** Warner Bros., 128 min. *Dir* Mark Rydell, *Scr* Harriet Frank, Jr., William Dale Jennings, Irving Ravetch, based on novel by William Dale Jennings, *Cin* Robert Surtees, *Ed* Robert Swink, *Des* Philip Jeffries, *Cos* Anthea Sylbert, *Mus* John Williams, *Prod* Mark Rydell, *Assoc Prod* Tim Zinnemann.

Cast: John Wayne, *Will Anderson*, Roscoe Lee Browne, *Jebediah Nightlinger*, Bruce Dern, *Long Hair*, Colleen Dewhurst, *Kate*, Slim Pickens, *Anse*, Lonny Chapman, *Preacher*, Charles Tyner, *Jenkins*, A. Martinez, *Cimarron*, Alfred Barker, Jr., *Singing Fats*, Nicolas Beauvy, *Four Eyes*, Steve Benedict, *Steve*, Robert Carradine, *Slim Honeycutt*, Norman Howell, Jr., *Weedy*, Stephen Hudis, *Charlie Schwartz*, Sean Kelly, *Stuttering Bob*, Clay O'Brien, *Hardy Fimps*, Sam O'Brien, *Jimmy Phillips*, Mike Pyeatt, *Homer Weems*, Sarah Cunningham, *Annie Anderson*, Allyn Ann McLerie, *Ellen Price*, Matt Clark, *Smiley*. PG. $7,500,000.

Fair youth-oriented western starring John Wayne as a cattleman, who hires eleven young boys, after his regular help quits, to work on his roundup. Wayne is killed and the boys become killers to avenge his death. This is the most popular of Wayne's several youth-oriented westerns, but it is in no way superior to the others. *The Cowboys* is overlong and dull.

194 **Crazy Joe** (1974) ** Columbia, 100 min. *Dir* Carlo Lizzani, *Scr* Lewis John Carlino, based on story by Nicholas Gage, *Cin* Aldo Tonti, *Ed* Peter Zinner, *Art* Robert Gundlach, *Mus* Gian Carlo Caramello, *Exec Prod* Nino E. Krisman, A Dino De Laurentiis Presentation.

Cast: Peter Boyle, *Crazy Joe*, Paula Prentiss, *Anne*, Fred Williamson, *Willy*, Charles Cioffi, *Coletti*, Rip Torn, *Richie*, Luther Adler, *Falco*, Fausto Tozzi, *Frank*, Franco Lantieri, *Nunzio*, Eli Wallach, *Don Vittorio*, Louis Guss, *Magliocco*, Carmine Caridi, *Jelly*, Henry Winkler, *Mannie*, Gabrielle Torrei, *Cheech*, Guido Leontini, *Angelo*, Sam Coppola, *Chick*, Mario Erpichini, *Danny*, Adam Wade, *J.D.*, Timothy Holley, *Lou*, Ralph Wilcox, *Sam*, Peter Savage, *DeMarco*, Herve Villechaize, *Samson*, Robert Riesel, Dan Resin, *F.B.I. Agents*, Nella Dina, *Mrs. Falco. R.*

Typical violent gangster melodrama. Peter Boyle is okay as New York gangster Crazy Joe Gallo, but this film is nothing more than an excuse for violence rather than a biography of a human being. This is one of several screen biographies of gangsters that were released in the wake of the success of *The Godfather* and not one even made an earnest effort to be as serious and intelligent as their inspiration.

195 Crazy Mama (1975) *** New World, 80 min. *Dir* Jonathon Demme, *Scr* Robert Thom, *Story* Francis Doel, *Cin* Bruce Logan, *Ed* Allan Holzman, Lewis Teague, *Art* Peter Jamison, *Cos* Joe McAnelly, *Prod* Julie Corman, *Assoc Prod* Peter Cornberg.

Cast: Cloris Leachman, *Melba*, Stuart Whitman, *Jim Bob*, Ann Southern, *Sheba*, Jim Backus, *Albertson*, Donny Most, *Shawn*, Linda Purl, *Cheryl*, Bryan Englund, *Snake*, Merie Earle, *Bertha*, Sally Kirkland, *Ella Mae*, Clint Kimbrough, *Daniel*, Dick Miller, *Wilbur Janeway*, Carmen Argenziano, *Supermarket Manager*, Harry Northup, *F.B.I Man*, Ralph James, *Sheriff (1932)*, Dinah Englund, *Melba (1932)*, Trish Sterling, *Sheba (1932)*. PG.

One of the best of the *Bonnie and Clyde* type gangster films. Set mostly in the 1950's, *Crazy Mama* centers on yet another outlaw clan, this time headed by Cloris Leachman. There is the usual abundance of action and eccentric humor, that one expects from Roger Corman's company, but *Crazy Mama* rises above most of the rest due to Jonathon Demme's expert direction. Demme showed great promise in this early film of his career, which he more than delivered in subsequent films.

196 The Crazy World of Julius Vrooder (1974) ** 20th Century–Fox, 98 min. *Dir* Arthur Hiller, *Scr* Daryl Henry, *Cin* David M. Walsh, *Ed* Robert C. Jones, *Art* Hilyard Brown, *Mus* Bob Alcivar, *Prod* Arthur Hiller, Edward Rissien, *Exec Prod* Hugh M. Hefner, *Assoc. Prod* Daryl Henry, Peter V. Herald.

Cast: Timothy Bottoms, *Julius Vrooder*, Barbara Seagull, *Zanni*, Lawrence Pressman, *Dr. Passki*, Albert Salmi, *Splint*, Richard A. Dysart, *Father*, Dena Dietrich, *Mother*, Debralee Scott, *Sister*, Lou Frizzell, *Fowler*, Jack Murdock, *Millard*, Michael Ivan Cristofer, *Allessini*, DeWayne Jessie, *Rodali*, Ron Glass, *Quintus*, Barbara Douglas, *Roberta*, Andrew Duncan, *Chaplain*, Jack Colvin, *Sergeant*, Jarion Monroe, *Mosby*, George Marshall, *Corky*. PG.

Dull comedy about a crazy Vietnam vet (Timothy Bottoms) who is confined to a hospital and builds a small hideaway under a nearby highway off-ramp. *The Crazy World of Julius Vrooder* throws in a dull love story involving Bottoms and a sympathetic nurse (Barbara Seagull). One good point is the film also contains crazies from WWI and WWII, rather than blaming only one war.

197 Crime and Passion (1976) *** U.S./Germany, American International, 92 min. *Dir* Ivan Passer, *Scr* Jesse Lasky, Jr., Pat Silver, based on novel *An Ace Up Your Sleeve* by James Hadley Chase, *Cin* Denis C. Lewiston, *Ed* Bernard Gribble, John Jympson, *Art* Herta Pischinger, *Cos* Yvonne Blake, *Mus* Van Gelis Papathanassiou, *Prod* Robert L. Abrams, *Exec Prod* Barney Bernard.

Cast: Omar Sharif, *Andre*, Karen Black, *Susan*, Joseph Bottoms, *Larry*, Bernhard Wicki, *Rolf*, Heinz Ehrenfreund, *Henkel*, Elma Karlowa, *Masseuse*, Volker Prechtel, *Innkeeper*, Erich Padalewski, *Car Salesman*, Robert Abrams, *Mr. Blatt*, Franz Muxeneder, *Priest*, Margarete Soper, *Sylvia*. R.

Unusual comedy-drama starring Omar Sharif as an investment counsellor, who gets into trouble with his bad speculative investments and is marked for murder by a vengeful tycoon (Bernhard Wicki). Sharif convinces his girlfriend (Karen Black) to marry Wicki to get him out of trouble, but to no avail. The storyline is little weak, and it tends to wander, but Sharif gives a surprisingly good deadpan comic performance. Other title, *Ace up Your Sleeve*.

198 Cromwell (1970) ** Britain, Columbia, 139 min. *Dir* Ken Hughes, *Scr* Ken Huges, *Cin* Geoffrey Unsworth, *Ed* Bill Lenny, *Des* John Stoll, *Art* Herbert Westbrook, *Cos* Nino Novarese (A), *Mus* Frank Cordell (AN), *Prod* Irving Allen, *Assoc Prod* Andrew Donally.

Cast: Richard Harris, *Oliver Cromwell*, Alec Guinness, *King Charles I*, Robert Morley, *Earl of Manchester*, Dorothy Tutin, *Queen Henrietta Maria*, Frank Finlay, *John Carter*, Timothy Dalton, *Prince Rupert*, Patrick Wymark, *Earl of Stafford*, Patrick Magee, *Hugh Peters*, Nigel Stock, *Sir Edward Hyde*, Charles Gray, *Lord Essex*, Michael Jayston, *Henry Ireton*, Richard Cornish, *Oliver Cromwell II*, Anna Cropper, *Ruth Carter*, Michael Goodliffe, *Solicitor General*, Jack Gwillim, *Gen. Byron*, Basil Henson, *Hacker*, Patrick Holt, *Capt. Lunsford*, Stratford Johns, *Pres. Bradshaw*, Geoffrey Keen, *John Pym*, Anthony May, *Richard Cromwell*, Ian McCulloch, *John Hampden*, Patrick O'Connell, *John Lilburne*, John Paul, *Gen. Digby*, Bryan Pringle, *Trooper Hawkins*, Llewelyn Rees, *The Speaker*, Robin Stewart, *Prince of Wales*, Adreevan Gysegham, *Archbishop Rinucinni*, Zena Walker, *Mrs. Cromwell*. G.

Dull historical drama about the English Civil War during the 17th century. *Cromwell* is visually impressive with magnificent sets and costumes, and spectacular battle scenes. Unfortunately, so much time and money was spent on the visual aspect of the film, things such as character and historical accuracy were completely ignored. Alec Guinness gives the best performance as Charles I, the villainous king of England.

199 Cross of Iron (1977) ***** Britain/Germany, Avco Embassy, 133 min. *Dir* Sam Peckinpah, *Scr* Herbert Asmodi, Julius J. Epstein, based on novel *The Cross of Iron* by Willi Heinrich, *Cin* John Coquillon, *Ed* Mike Ellis, Tony Lawson, *Des* Ted Haworth, Brian Ackland Snow, *Mus* Ernest Gold, *Prod* Wolf C. Hartwig.

Cast: James Coburn, *Steiner*, Maximilian Schell, *Stransky*, James Mason, *Brandt*, David Warner, *Kiesel*, Klaus Lowitsch, *Kruger*, Vadim Glowna, *Kern*, Roger Fritz, *Triebig*, Dieter Schidor, *Anselm*, Burkhardt Driest, *Maag*, Fred Stillkraut, *Schnurrbart*, Michael Nowka, *Dietz*, Veronique Vendell, *Marga*, Arthur Brauss, *Zoll*, Senta Berger, *Eva*, Slavco Stimac, *Mikael*. R.

Absolutely brilliant WWII drama, which ironically appeared after the subject had become stale. Sam Peckinpah, in his finest film to date, examines the perversity of war through a renegade group of German soldiers, that resembles in some ways the "wild bunch," on the Russian front. Peckinpah's main targets are the unnaturalness of male camaraderie, that is generally celebrated in similar films, and the gross effect of war on children. The battle scenes are breathtakingly heightened by montage sequences that rival the best of Eisenstein.

200 Crossed Swords (1978) ******* Warner Bros., 113 min. *Dir* Richard Fleischer, *Scr* Berta Dominguez, George MacDonald Fraser, Pierre Spengler, based on novel *The Prince and the Pauper* by Mark Twain, *Cin* Jack Cardiff, *Ed* Ernest Walter, *Des* Tony Pratt, *Cos* Judy Moorcroft, *Mus* Maurice Jarre, *Chor* Sally Gilpin, *Prod* Pierre Spengler, *Exec Prod* Ilya Salkind.

Cast: Oliver Reed, *Miles Hendon*, Racquel Welch, *Lady Edith*, Mark Lester, *Edward/Tom*, Ernest Borgnine, *John Canty*, George C. Scott, *Ruffler*, Rex Harrison, *Duke of Norfold*, David Hemmings, *Hugh Hendon*, Harry Andrews, *Hertford*,Julian Orchard, *St. John*, Murray Melvin, *Prince's Dresser*, Graham Stark, *Jester*, Sybil Danning, *Mother Canty*, Lalla Ward, *Princess Elizabeth*, Felicity Dean, *Lady Jane*, Charlton Heston, *Henry VIII*. PG.

Well-made adaptation of Mark Twain's classic *The Prince and the Pauper*. The filmmakers apparently wanted to disguise the true storyline by changing the title to *Crossed Swords*, but it appears to be inspired more by Richard Lester's *The Three Musketeers* than its source novel. Richard Fleischer does a fine job with this period comedy, but he lacks the rapier wit and the comic timing of Lester.

201 Cuba (1979) ********* United Artists, 122 min. *Dir* Richard Lester, *Scr* Charles Wood, *Cin* David Watkin, *Ed* John Victor Smith, *Des* Shirley Russell, *Art* Denis Gordon Orr, *Cos* Shirley Russell, *Mus* Patrick Williams; *Prod* Arlene Sellers, Alex Winitsky, *Exec Prod* Denis O'Dell.

Cast: Sean Connery, *Robert Dapes*, Brooke Adams, *Alexandra Pulido*, Jack Weston, *Gutman*, Hector Elizondo, *Ramirez*, Denholm Elliot, *Skinner*, Martin Balsam, *Gen. Bello*, Chris Sarandon, *Juan Pulido*, Alejandro Rey, *Faustino*, Lonette McKee, *Therese*, Danny De La Paz, *Julio*, Louisa Moritz, *Miss Wonderly*, Dave King, *Press Agent*, Walter Gotell, *Don Pulido*, Earl Cameron, *Col. Rosell Y Leyva*, Pauline Peart, *Delores*, Anna Nicholas, *Maria*, David Rappaport, *Jesus*, Tony Matthews, *Corillo*, Leticia Garrado, *Cecilia*, John Morton, *Gary*, Anthony Pullen Shaw, *Spencer*, Stefan Kalipha, *Ramon*. R.

Brilliant satirical comedy set in Cuba during the final days of the Batista regime. Sean Connery is excellent as a British mercenary who is hired to train Batista's troops to battle Castro's revolutionaries. *Cuba* was labeled a Socialist film, because all its criticism was directed at Batista with Castro seemingly unscathed, but this misses the film's point. The new revolution of Castro is paralleled to the old revolution of Batista, meaning despite the difference in politics things will not really change. *Cuba* is filled with intrigue and romance, much like *Casablanca*, but it is not stale or pretentious like that earlier film. Richard Lester excels at period satirical comedy and this film ranks with his best.

202 **The Culpepper Cattle Company** (1972) *** 20th Century–Fox, 92 min. *Dir* Dick Richards, *Scr* Eric Bercovici, Gregory Prentiss, *Story* Dick Richards, *Cin* Lawrence Edward Williams, Ralph Woolsey, *Ed* John F. Burnett, *Art* Carl Anderson, Jack Martin Smith, *Cos* Ted Parvin, *Mus* Jerry Goldsmith, Tom Scott, *Prod* Paul A. Helmick, *Assoc Prod* Jerry Bruckheimer.

Cast: Gary Grimes, *Ben Mockridge*, Billy "Green" Bush, *Frank Culpepper*, Luke Askew, *Luke*, Bo Hopkins, *Dixie Brick*, Geoffrey Lewis, *Russ*, Wayne Sutherlin, *Missoula*, John McLiam, *Thornton Pierce*, Matt Clark, *Pete*, Raymond Guth, *Cook*, Anthony James, *Nathaniel*, Charlie Martin Smith, *Tim Slater*, Larry Finley, *Mr. Slater*, Bob Morgan, *Old John*, Jan Burrell, *Mrs. Mockridge*, Hal Needham, *Burgess*, Jerry Gatlin, *Wallop*, Bob Orrison, *Rutter*, Walter Scott, *Print*, Royal Dano, *Cattle Rustler*. PG.

Typical youth-oriented western about growing up in the days directly following the Civil War. Gary Grimes is good as a youth who joins up with a cattle drive as a cook's assistant, and in the process becomes a man. *The Culpepper Cattle Company* concentrates heavily on details and authenticity and is visually impressive, but unfortunately this same attention was not paid to the story.

203 **Daisy Miller** (1974) ** Paramount, 91 min. *Dir* Peter Bogdanovich, *Scr* Frederic Raphael, based on story by Henry James, *Cin* Albert Spagnoli, *Ed* Verna Fields, *Art* Ferdinando Scarfiotti, *Cos* John Furness, *Prod* Peter Bogdanovich, *Assoc Prod* Frank Marshall.

Cast: Cybill Shepherd, *Annie P. "Daisy" Miller*, Barry Brown, *Frederick Winterbourne*, Cloris Leachman, *Mrs. Ezra B. Miller*, Mildred Natwick, *Mrs. Costello*, Eileen Brennan, *Mrs. Walker*, Duilio Del Prete, *Giovanelli*, James McMurtry, *Randolph C. Miller*, Nicholas Jones, *Charles*, George Morfogen, *Eugenio*, Jean Pascal Bongard, *Hotel Receptionist in Vevey*, Albert Messmer, *Tutor*, Jacques Guhl, Hubert Geoldlin, *Polish Boys*, David Bush, *Man at Chillon*, Henry Hubinet, *Chillon Guide*, Maurizio Lucci, *Miniaturist*, Tom Felleghy, *Mrs. Walker's Butler*, Luigi Gabellone, *Punch and Judy*. G.

Dull adaptation of Henry James' story of a young American woman living in Europe in the late nineteenth century. Cybill Shepherd is completely miscast in the title role and her narrow acting range throws the entire film off. With a stronger actress in the part, *Daisy Miller* might have succeeded. After a string of successes this was Bogdanovich's first failure, from which he never fully recovered.

204 **Damien–Omen II** (1978) ** 20th Century–Fox, 110 min. *Dir* Don Taylor, *Scr* Michael Hodges, Stanley Mann, *Story* Harvey Bernhard, based on characters created by David Seltzer, *Cin* Bill Butler, *Ed* Robert Brown, Jr. *Des* Fred Harpman, Philip M. Jefferies, *Mus* Jerry Goldsmith, *Prod* Harvey Bernhard, *Co-Prod* Charles Orme, *Assoc Prod* Joseph "Pepi" Lenzi.

Cast: William Holden, *Richard Thorn*, Lee Grant, *Ann Thorn*, Jonathan Scott-Taylor, *Damien Thorn*, Robert Foxworth, *Paul Buher*, Nicholas Pryor, *Charles Warren*, Lew Ayres, *Bill Atherton*, Sylvia Sidney, *Aunt Marion*, Lance Henriksen, *Sgt. Neff*, Elizabeth Shepherd, *Joan Hart*, Lucas Donat, *Mark Thorn*, Allan Arbus, *Pasarian*, Fritz Ford, *Murray*, Meshach Taylor, *Dr. Kane*, John J. Newcombe, *Teddy*, John Charles Burns, *Butler*, Paul Cook, *Colonel*, Diane Daniels, *Jane*, Robert E. Ingham, *Teacher*, William B. Fosser, *Minister*,

Corney Morgan, *Greenhouse Technician*, Russell P. Delia, *Truck Driver*, Judith Dowd, *Maid*. R. $13,630,000. See *The Omen*.

205 **Damnation Alley** (1977) ** 20th Century–Fox, 95 min. *Dir* Jack Smight, *Scr* Lucas Heller, Alan Sharp, based on novel by Roger Zelanzny, *Cin* Harry Stradling, Jr., *Ed* Frank J. Urioste, *Des* Preston Ames, *Art* William Cruse, *Mus* Jerry Goldsmith, *Prod* Paul Maslansky, Jerome M. Zeitman, *Exec Prod* Bobby Roberts, Hal Landers.

    Cast: Jan-Michael Vincent, *Tanner*, George Peppard, *Denton*, Dominique Sanda, *Janice*, Paul Winfield, *Keegan*, Jackie Earle Haley, *Billy*, Kip Niven, *Perry*. PG. $5,030,000.

    Boring science-fiction thriller set some time after a nuclear holocaust. A group of survivors journey across the wasteland of the United States in tank-line vehicles in search of living people. This search comprises most of *Damnation Alley*, in which the group encounters several unexciting dangers. Other than the specially built vehicles, the special effects are artificial and unconvincing.

206 **Dark Star** (1974) *** Jack H. Harris Enterprises, 83 min. *Dir* John Carpenter, *Scr* Dan O'Bannon, John Carpenter, *Cin* Douglas Knapp, *Ed* Dan O'Bannon, *Des* Dan O'Bannon, *Prod* John Carpenter, *Exec Prod* Jack H. Harris.

    Cast: Brian Narelle, *Doolittle*, Andreijah Pahich, *Talby*, Carl Kuniholm, *Boiler*, Dan O'Bannon, *Pinback*. G.

    Sophomoric, but occasionally clever spoof of science-fiction films set entirely aboard a space-ship containing a somewhat irreverent crew of weirdos and a pet alien that resembles a bean bag chair. *Dark Star* is an extremely low-budget film and it shows in the special-effects and production values, along with a group of obviously non-professional actors. This is most notable as John Carpenter's debut film.

207 **Darling Lili** (1970) *** Paramount, 136 min. *Dir* Blake Edwards, *Scr* William Peter Blatty, Blake Edwards, *Cin* Russell Harlan, *Ed* Peter Zinner, *Des* Fernando Carrere, *Cos* Jack Bear, Donald Brooks (AN), *Mus* Henry Mancini (AN), *Lyrics* Johnny Mercer (AN), *song* "Whistling Away the Dark," *Mus* Henry Mancini (AN, G), *Lyrics* Johnny Mercer (AN, G), *Prod* Blake Edwards, *Exec Prod* Owen Crump, *Assoc Prod* Ken Wales.

    Cast: Julie Andrews, *Lili Smith*, Rock Hudson, *Maj. William Larrabee*, Jeremy Kemp, *Kurt von Ruger*, Lance Percival, *Lt. Carstairs (T.C.) Twombley-Crouch*, Jacques Marin, *Maj. Duvalle*, Michael Witney, *Lt. George Youngblood Carson*, Andre Maranne, *Lt. Liggett*, Bernard Kay, *Bedford*, Doreen Keogh, *Emma*, Gloria Paul, *Suzette*, Carl Duering, *Kessler*, Vernon Dobtcheff, *Kraus*, A.E. Gould-Porter, *Sgt. Wells*, Louis Mercier, Laurie Main, *French Generals*, Ingo Mogendorf, *Baron von Richthofen*, Niall MacGinnis, *von Hindenberg*, Mimi Monti, *Chanteuse*. G.

    Fine musical comedy set during WWI. Julie Andrews stars as a popular British singer, who becomes a spy for Germany. She is to befriend an American officer (Rock Hudson) in order to gain secret information, and her mission is complicated when the two fall in love. *Darling Lili* is better than most romantic comedies of its time, due to its avoidance of unnecessary cuteness.

208 **Dawn of the Dead** (1979) ***** United Film Distribution, 125 min. *Dir* George Romero, *Scr* George Romero, *Cin* Michael Gornick, *Ed* George Romero, *Mus* The Goblins with Dario Argento, *Prod* Richard P. Rubinstein, *Assistant Prod* Donna Siegel.

Cast: David Emge, *Stephen*, Ken Foree, *Peter*, Scott Reiniger, *Roger*, Gaylen Ross, *Francine*. Not Rated.

Brilliant sequel to *Night of the Living Dead* that is actually superior to its predecessor. In the first film the living dead begin to rise and in *Dawn of the Dead* they have nearly taken over, forcing a group of four people to take refuge in a deserted shopping mall. Not needing unnecessary exposition the film opens with the world plunged into total chaos, allowing the viewer two full hours of riveting horror. In a surprise change in style, Romero has substituted comedy for scares. Achieving true laughs in a film this shocking is a considerable achievement. The violence is so extreme that *Dawn of the Dead* would have received an X rating. Not wanting his film associated with sex films, Romero released it without a rating.

209 **A Day in the Death of Joe Egg** (1972) *** Britain, Columbia, 106 min. *Dir* Peter Medak, *Scr* Peter Nichols, based on his play, *Cin* Ken Hodges, *Ed* Ray Lovejoy, *Art* Ted Tester, *Mus* Marcus Dods, *Prod* David Deutsch.

Cast: Alan Bates, *Bri*, Janet Suzman, *Sheila*, Peter Bowles, *Freddie*, Sheila Gish, *Pam*, Joan Hickson, *Grace*, Elizabeth Robillard, *Jo*, Murray Melvin, *Doctor*, Fanny Carby, *Nun*, Constance Chapman, *Moonrocket Lady*, Elizabeth Tyrell, *Midwife*. R.

Unusual comedy-drama focusing on an English couple (Alan Bates, Janet Suzman) and how they deal with the situation of having a spastic daughter. Rather than revelling in pity they brave the problem with a sense of humor, and eventually plan a mercy killing. This film is certainly not for all tastes, but although slightly flawed by staginess, it is well-made and well-acted.

210 **The Day of the Dolphin** (1973) ** Avco Embassy, 104 min. *Dir* Mike Nichols, *Scr* Buck Henry, based on novel by Robert Merle, *Cin* William A. Fraker, *Ed* Sam O'Steen, *Des* Richard Sylbert, *Art* Angelo Graham, *Cos* Anthea Sylbert, *Mus* Georges Delerue, *Prod* Robert E. Relyea, *Exec Prod* Joseph E. Levine, *Assoc Prod* Dick Birkmayer.

Cast: George C. Scott, *Dr. Jake Terrell*, Trish Van Devere, *Maggie Terrell*, Paul Sorvino, *Mahoney*, Fritz Weaver, *Harold DeMilo*, Jon Korkes, *David*, Edward Herrmann, *Mike*, Leslie Charleson, *Maryanne*, John David Carson, *Larry*, Victoria Racimo, *Lana*, John Dehner, *Wallingford*, Severn Darden, *Schwinn*, William Roerick, *Dunhill*, Elizabeth Wilson, *Mrs. Rome*, Pat Englund, Julie Follansbee, Brooke Haywood, Florence Stanley, *Women at Club*, Willie Meyers, *Stone*, Phyllis Davis, *Secretary*. PG.

Dull assassination thriller involving dolphins trained by terrorists to carry bombs to the intended target. *The Day of the Dolphin* mostly centers on George C. Scott's relationship with his dolphins, which eventually even talk to him. This is either science-fiction or comedy, but which one is not quite certain. With direction by Mike Nichols and script by Buck Henry, who also did the dolphin's voices, the latter may be possible, but it is difficult to tell.

211 **The Day of the Jackal** (1973) **** Britain/France, Universal, 142 min. *Dir* Fred Zinnemann, *Scr* Kenneth Ross, based on novel by Frederick Forsyth,

Cin Jean Tournier, *Ed* Ralph Kemplen (AN, BFA), *Des* Ernest Archer, Willy Holt, *Cos* Joan Bridge, Rosine Delamare, Elizabeth Haffenden, *Mus* Georges Delerue, *Prod* John Woolf, *Co-Prod* Julien Derode, David Deutsch.

Cast: Edward Fox, *"The Jackal"*, Terence Alexander, *Lloyd*, Michel Auclair, *Col. Rolland*, Alan Badel, *The Minister*, Tony Britton, *Inspector Thomas*, Denis Carey, *Casson*, Adrien Cayla-Legrand, *President de Gaulle*, Cyril Cusack, *Gunsmith*, Maurice Denham, *Gen. Colbert*, Vernon Dobtcheff, *Interrogator*, Jacques Francois, *Pascal*, Olga Georges-Picot, *Denise*, Raymond Gerome, *Flavigny*, Barrie Ingham, *St. Clair*, Derek Jacobi, *Caron*, Michel Lonsdale, *Lebel*, Jean Martin, *Wolenski*, Ronald Pickup, *Forger*, Eric Porter, *Col Rodin*, Anton Rodgers, *Bernard*, Delphine Seyrig, *Colette*, Donald Sinden, *Mallinson*, Jean Sorel, *Bastien-Thiry*, David Swift, *Montclair*, Timothy West, *Berthier*. PG. $8,925,000.

Excellent thriller about a professional killer who is hired by revolutionaries to assassinate French President de Gaulle. *The Day of the Jackal* meticulously parallels the plans made by the killer with the search by the police to find him before he succeeds. Despite the obviousness of the outcome and the extremely long running time, *The Day of the Jackal* manages to maintain suspense up to the last minute. This is, by far, Fred Zinneman's finest film and Edward Fox is excellent as the killer, playing him with proper cold-bloodedness.

212 **The Day of the Locust** (1975) ***** Paramount, 144 min. *Dir* John Schlesinger, *Scr* Waldo Salt, based on novel by Nathaniel West, *Cin* Conrad Hall (AN), *Ed* Jim Clark, *Des* Richard MacDonald, *Art* John Lloyd, *Cos* Ann Roth (BFA), *Mus* John Barry, *Prod* Jerome Hellman, *Assoc Prod* Sheldon Schrager.

Cast: Karen Black, *Faye*, Donald Sutherland, *Homer*, Burgess Meredith (AN), *Harry*, William Atherton, *Tod* Geraldine Page, *Big Sister*, Richard Dysart, *Claude Estee*, Bo Hopkins, *Earle Shoop*, Pepe Serna, *Miguel*, Lelia Goldoni, *Mary Dove*, Billy Barty, *Abe*, Jackie Haley, *Adore*, Gloria LeRoy, *Mrs. Loomis*, Jane Hoffman, *Mrs. Odlesh*, Norm Leavitt, *Mr. Odlesh*, Madge Kennedy, *Mrs. Johnson*, Ina Gould, Florence Lake, *Lee Sisters*, Margaret Willey, John War Eagle, *The Gingos*, Natalie Schafer, *Audrey Jennings*, Gloria Stroock, *Alice Estee*, Nita Talbot, *Joan*, Nicholas Cortland, *Projectionist*, Alvin Childress, *Butler*, Paul Stewart, *Halverston*, John Hillerman, *Ned Grote*, William Castle, *Director*, Paul Jabara, *Nightclub Entertainer*, Dick Powell, Jr., *Dick Powell*, Bill Baldwin, *Announcer at Premiere*. R.

Powerful drama set in Hollywood during the 1930's. While most such films are about people who go to Hollywood and achieve success, i.e. *A Star Is Born*, this film takes the other route and concentrates on the many losers. The title refers to these people who converge on that city like locusts. This film was heavily critized for its uncompromising and, sometimes, shocking portrait of society's misfits. *The Day of the Locust* is filled with many extraordinary performances, particularly Burgess Meredith, who gives the performance of his career, as a washed-up vaudevillian. This is John Schlesinger's finest film.

213 **Days of Heaven** (1978) (NB) ***** Paramount, 95 min. *Dir* Terrence Malick (NS, NY, CF), *Scr* Terrence Malick, *Cin* Nestor Almendros (A, NS, LA),

Ed Billy Weber, *Art* Jack Fisk, *Cos* Patricia Norris (AN), *Mus* Ennio Morricone (AN, BFA), *Prod* Bert and Harold Schneider, *Exec Prod* Jacob Brackman.

Cast: Richard Gere, *Bill*, Brooke Adams, *Abby*, Sam Shepard, *The Farmer*, Linda Manz, *Linda*, Robert Wilke, *Farm Foreman*, Jackie Shultis, *Linda's Friend*, Stuart Margolin, *Mill Foreman*, Tim Scott, *Harvest Hand*, Gene Bell, *Dancer*, Doug Kershaw, *Fiddler*, Richard Libertini, *Vaudeville Leader*, Frenchie Lemond, *Vaudeville Wrestler*, Sahbra Markus, *Vaudeville Dancer*, Bob Wilson, *Accountant*, Murial Jolliffe, *Headmistress*, John Wilkinson, *Preacher*, King Cole, *Farm Worker*. PG.

An absolutely beautiful and ravishing masterpiece. *Days of Heaven* is a deceptively simple story of three people, a young man, his girlfriend and his little sister, who go to work in the wheat fields of Texas in 1916. They become involved with their dying boss in an effort to inherit his fortune, which brings about tragic results. Terrence Malick, one of the most original artists in the American cinema, has created a wonderful metaphor for the loss of America's innocence and its maturing in the early part of the century.

214 **Death on the Nile** (1978) ∗∗∗ Paramount, 140 min. *Dir* John Guillermin, *Scr* Anthony Shaffer, based on novel by Agatha Christie, *Cin* Jack Cardiff, *Ed* Malcolm Cooke, *Des* Peter Murton, *Art* Brian and Terry Ackland, *Cos* Anthony Powell (A), *Mus* Nino Rota, *Prod* John Brabourne, Richard Goodwin, *Assoc Prod* Norton Knatchbull.

Cast: Peter Ustinov, *Hercule Poirot*, Jane Birkin, *Louise Bourget*, Lois Chiles, *Linnet Ridgeway*, Bette Davis, *Mrs. Van Schuyler*, Mia Farrow, *Jacqueline de Bellefort*, Jon Finch, *Mr. Ferguson*, Olivia Hussey, *Rosalie Otterbourne*, I.S. Johar, *Manager of the Karnak*, George Kennedy, *Andrew Pennington*, Angela Lansbury, *Mrs. Salome Otterbourne*, Simon MacCorkindale, *Simon Doyle*, David Niven, *Col. Rice*, Maggie Smith, *Miss Bowers*, Jack Warden, *Dr. Bessner*, Harry Andrews, *Barnstaple*, Sam Wanamaker, *Rockford*. PG. $8,800,000. See *Murder on the Orient Express*.

215 **Death Race 2000** (1975) ∗∗∗∗ New World, 78 min. *Dir* Paul Bartel, *Scr* Charles B. Griffith, Robert Thom, *Cin* Tak Fujimoto, *Ed* Tina Hirsch, *Mus* Paul Chihara, *Prod* Roger Corman.

Cast: David Carradine, *Frankenstein*, Simone Griffith, *Annie*, Sylvestor Stallone, *Joe*, Louisa Moritz, *Myra*, Mary Woronov, *Jane*. R. $5,000,000.

Excellent and offbeat science-fiction comic book adventure set in the near future. The title refers to a deadly cross-country road race in which the drivers score points by running over innocent pedestrians. Each driver represents a specific violent film genre, i.e. westerns, horror or gangster films. The entire mood is tongue-in-cheek and Sylvestor Stallone is excellent in an early supporting role as a psychotic gangster type driver. *Deathsport* is a sequel of sorts. Although it is better than many low-budget science fiction features, it lacks the brilliant campy humor of its predecessor.

216 **Death Wish** (1974) ∗∗ Paramount, 93 min. *Dir* Michael Winner, *Scr* Wendell Mayes, based on novel by Brian Garfield, *Cin* Arthur J. Ornitz, *Ed* Bernard Gribble, *Des* Robert Gundlach, *Cos* Joseph G. Aulisi, *Mus* Herbie Hancock, *Prod* Hal Landers, Bobby Roberts, *Co-Prod* Michael Winner.

Cast: Charles Bronson, *Paul Kersey*, Hope Lange, *Joanna Kersey*, Vincent Gardenia, *Frank Ochoa*, Steven Keats, *Jack Toby*, William Redfield, *Sam*

Kreutzer, Stuart Margolin, *Aimes Jainchill*, Stephen Elliott, *Police Commissioner*, Kathleen Tolan, *Carol Toby*, Jack Wallace, *Hank*, Fred Scollay, *District Attorney*, Chris Gampel, *Ives*, Robert Kya-Hill, *Joe Charles* Ed Grover, *Lt. Briggs*, Jeff Goldblum, *Freak 1*, Christopher Logan, *Freak 2*, Gregory Rozakis, *Spraycan*, Floyd Levine, *Desk Sergeant*, Helen Martin, *Alma Lee Brown*, Hank Garrett, *Andrew McCabe*, Christopher Guest, *Patrolman Reilly*. R. $8,800,000.

Average vendetta drama in which Charles Bronson goes on a murdering rampage to avenge the rape of his wife and daughter and the subsequent death of his wife. He prowls the streets of New York murdering any mugger who gets in his way. *Death Wish* is directed with a bit more style than most of Bronson's other films but it really is not much better.

217 **Deathsport** (1978) *** New World, 90 min. *Dir* Allan Arkush, Henry Suso, *Scr* Donald Stewart, Henry Suso, *Story* Frances Doel, *Cin* Gary Graver, *Ed* Larry Bock, *Art* Sharon Compton, *Mus* Andrew Stein, *Chor* George Fullwood, *Prod* Roger Corman.

Cast: David Carradine, *Kaz Oshay*, Claudia Jennings, *Deneer*, Richard Lynch, *Ankar*, William Smithers, *Dr. Karl*, Will Walker, *Marcus*, David McLean, *Lord Zirpola*, Jesse Vint, *Polna*, H.B. Haggarty, *Jailer*, John Himes, *Tritan Pres.*, Jim Galante, *Tritan Guard*, Peter Hooper, *Bakkar*, Brenda Venus, *Adriann*, Gene Hartline, *Sergeant*, Chris Howell, *Officer*, Valerie Rae Clark, *Dancer*. R. See *Death Race 2000*.

218 **The Deep** (1977) ** Columbia, 123 min. *Dir* Peter Yates, *Scr* Peter Benchley, Tracy Keenan Wynn, based on novel by Peter Benchley, *Cin* Christopher Challis, *Ed* Robert Wolfe, *Des* Tony Masters, *Art* John Maxsted, *Cos* Ron Talsky, *Mus* John Barry, *Prod* Peter Guber, *Assoc Prod* George Justin.

Cast: Robert Shaw, *Romer Treece*, Jacqueline Bisset, *Gail Berke*, Nick Nolte, *David Sanders*, Lou Gossett, *Cloche*, Eli Wallach, *Adam Coffin*, Robert Tessier, *Kevin*, Dick Anthony Williams, *Slake*, Earl Maynard, *Ronald*, Bob Minor, *Wiley*, Peter Benchley, *Mate*, Peter Wallach, *Young Adam Coffin*, Colin Shaw, *Young Romer Treece*. PG. $31,300,000.

Disappointing underwater adventure from a novel by Peter Benchley, the author of *Jaws*. A young couple discovers a sunken treasure and drugs and are, hence, pursued by criminals. Many unnecessary details and plot developments were thrown in, such as a long scene involving a deadly eel, apparently to capitalize on *Jaws*. The result is, *The Deep* is far too long to retain any suspense. The underwater photography is well-done, but even that becomes boring after awhile.

219 **The Deer Hunter** (1978) (A, NY) ***** Universal, 183 min. *Dir* Michael Cimino (A, G, LA, D), *Scr* Deric Washburn, *Story* Michael Cimino, Louis Garfinkle, Quinn K. Redeker, Deric Washburn (AN), *Cin* Vilmos Zsigmond (AN, BFA), *Ed* Peter Zinner (A, BFA), *Art* Ron Hobbs, Kim Swados, *Mus* Stanley Myers, *Prod* Michael Cimino, Michael Deeley, John Peverall, Barry Spikings, *Assoc Prod* Joan Carelli, Marion Rosenberg.

Cast: Robert DeNiro (AN), *Michael*, John Cazale, *Stan*, John Savage, *Steven*, Christopher Walken (A, NY), *Nick*, Meryl Streep (AN, NS), *Linda*, George Dzundza, *John*, Chuck Aspergren, *Axel*, Shirley Stoler, *Steven's*

Mother, Rutanya Alda, *Angela*, Pierre Segui, *Julien*, Mady Kaplan, *Axel's Girl*, Amy Wright, *Bridesmaid*, Mary Ann Haenel, *Stan's Girl*, Richard Kuss, *Linda's Father*, Joe Grifasi, *Bandleader*, Christopher Colombi, Jr., *Wedding Man*, Victoria Karnafel, *Sad Looking Girl*, Jack Scardino, *Cold Old Man*, Joe Strand, *Bingo Caller*, Henen Tomko, *Helen*, Paul D'Amato, *Sergeant*. R. $30,425,000.

Magnificent epic drama focusing on three young men (Robert DeNiro, Christopher Walken, John Savage) from a Pennsylvania steel town, who go off to Vietnam. *The Deer Hunter* brilliantly details their lives at home, and how they are later affected by the war. The film is surprisingly complex for a commercial American film, being rich in theme and symbolism, without sacrificing its portrait of a town and its people. Michael Cimino, in only his second film, has created a masterpiece of enormous depth and power.

220 **A Delicate Balance** (1973) ** American Film Theatre, 132 min. *Dir* Tony Richardson, *Scr* Edward Albee, based on his play, *Cin* David Watkin, *Ed* John Victor Smith, *Art* David Brockhurst, *Cos* Margaret Furse, *Prod* Ely A. Landau, *Exec Prod* Neil Hartley.

Cast: Katharine Hepburn, *Agnes*, Paul Scofield, *Tobias*, Lee Remick, *Julia*, Kate Reid, *Claire*, Joseph Cotten, *Harry*, Betsy Blair, *Edna*. PG. See *American Film Theatre*.

221 **Deliverance** (1972) (AN) *** Warner Bros., 109 min. *Dir* John Boorman (AN), *Scr* James Dickey, based on his novel, *Cin* Vilmos Zsigmond, *Ed* Tom Priestley (AN), *Art* Fred Harpman, *Song* "Dueling Banjos" arranged and played by Eric Weissberg with Steve Mandel, *Prod* John Boorman.

Cast: Jon Voight, *Ed*, Burt Reynolds, *Lewis*, Ned Beatty, *Bobby*, Ronny Cox, *Drow*, Bill McKinney, *Mountain Man*, Herbert "Cowboy" Coward, *Toothless Man*, James Dickey, *Sheriff Bullard*, Ed Ramey, *Old Man*, Billy Redden, *Lonny*, Seamon Glass, *First Griner*, Randall Deal, *Second Griner*, Lewis Crone, *First Deputy*, Ken Keener, *Second Deputy*, Johnny Popwell, *Ambulence Driver*, John Fowler, *Doctor*, Kathy Rickman, *Nurse*, Louise Coldren, *Mrs. Biddiford*, Pete Ware, *Taxi Driver*, Hoyt. J. Pollard, *Boy at Gas Station*, Belinda Beatty, *Martha Gentry*, Charlie Boorman, *Ed's Boy*. R.

Interesting, but somewhat overrated film about four Atlanta businessmen who take a weekend canoe trip that ends in disaster. *Deliverance* is well directed and well acted by the four principals (Reynolds, Voight, Beatty and Cox) and is visually impressive, but this is not really one of the most exciting adventure films ever made. There are a few exceptional sequences, but much of the film is repetitious.

222 **Demon Seed** (1977) **** United Artists, 94 min. *Dir* Donald Cammell, *Scr* Roger O. Hirson, Robert Jaffe, based on novel by Dean R. Koontz, *Cin* Bill Butler, *Ed* Francisco Mazzola, *Des* Edward C. Carfagno, *Mus* Jerry Fielding, *Prod* Herb Jaffe.

Cast: Julie Christie, *Susan Harris*, Fritz Weaver, *Alex Harris*, Gerrit Graham, *Walter Gabler*, Berry Kroeger, *Petrosian*, Lisa Lu, *Soon Yen*, Larry J. Blake, *Cameron*, Dana Laurita, *Amy*, Robert Vaughan, *Voice of Proteus IV*, John O'Leary, *Royce*, Alfred Dennis, *Mokri*, David Roberts, *Warner*, Tiffany Potter, Felix Silla, *Babies*. R.

Strange science-fiction drama set in a computerized future. In a bizarre variation of the idea of self-thinking computers, a powerful computer,

Proteus IV, takes over his creator scientist's mechanized home, holding the scientist's wife prisoner and eventually it rapes her. This premise may seem distasteful, but it is surprisingly well handled here, and Julie Christie gives a brilliant performance as the victim of this unspeakable horror. Donald Cammell, who co-directed *Performance* with Nicolas Roeg, is very adept at offbeat subjects.

223 **Desperate Characters** (1971) ** Paramount, 88 min. *Dir* Frank D. Gilroy, *Scr* Frank D. Gilroy, based on novel by Paula Fox, *Cin* Urs Furrer, *Ed* Robert Q. Lovett, *Art* Edgar Lansbury, *Cos* Sally Gifft, *Prod* Frank D. Gilroy, *Co-Prod* Paul Leaf.

  Cast: Shirley MacLaine (BF), *Sophie Bentwood*, Kenneth Mars, *Otto Bentwood*, Gerald O'Loughlin, *Charlie*, Sada Thompson, *Claire*, Jack Somack, *Leon*, Chris Gampel, *Mike*, Mary Ellen Hokanson, *Flo*, Robert Bauer, *Young Man*, Carol Kane, *Young Girl*, Michael Higgens, *Francis Early*. R.

  Well-acted, but overly stagey drama about a dismal day in the life of a miserable middle-aged couple (Shirley MacLaine, Kenneth Mars) living in New York City. *Desperate Characters* depends entirely too much on dialogue, of which there is an overabundance, and the conversations consist of the characters complaining about everything imaginable. After awhile this can become extremely tedious.

224 **The Devils** (1971) *** Britain, Warner Bros., 111 min. *Dir* Ken Russell (NB), *Scr* Ken Russell, based on play by John Whiting and novel *The Devils of Loudun* by Aldous Huxley, *Cin* David Watkin, *Ed* Michael Bradsell, *Art* Robert Cartwright, *Cos* Shirley Russell, *Mus* Peter Maxwell Davies, *Chor* Terry Gilbert, *Prod* Ken Russell, Robert H. Solo, *Assoc Prod* Roy Baird.

  Cast: Vanessa Redgrave, *Sister Jeanne*, Oliver Reed, *Father Grandier*, Dudley Sutton, *Baron de Laubardemont*, Max Adrian, *Ibert*, Gemma Jones, *Madeleine*, Murray Melvin, *Father Mignon*, Michael Gothard, *Father Barre*, Georgina Hale, *Philippe*, Brian Murphy, *Adam*, Christopher Logue, *Cardinal Richelieu*, Graham Armitage, *Louis XIII*, John Woodvine, *Trincant*, Andrew Faulds, *Rangier*, Kenneth Colley, *Legrand*. X.

  Incredibly weird period shocker set in Loudun, France in the 1630's, focusing on a priest (Oliver Reed), who has fathered numerous illegitimate children, and a hunchbacked nun (Vanessa Redgrave), who loves him. *The Devils* contains numerous bizarre sequences including an exorcism of possessed nuns and a graphic burning at the stake. This film manages to make Ken Russell's other films seem tame.

225 **The Devil's Rain** (1975) ** Bryanston, 85 min. *Dir* Robert Fuest, *Scr* James Ashton, Gabe Essoe, Gerald Hopman, *Cin* Alex Phillips, Jr., *Ed* Michael Kahn, *Des* Nikita Knatz, *Prod* James V. Cullen, Michael S. Glick, *Exec Prod* Sandy Howard.

  Cast: Ernest Borgnine, *Corbis*, Eddie Albert, *Dr. Richards*, Ida Lupino, *Mrs. Preston*, William Shatner, *Mark Preston*, Keenan Wynn, *Sheriff Owens*, Tom Skerritt, *Tom Preston*, Joan Prather, *Julie Preston*, Woodrow Chambliss, *John*, John Travolta, *Danny*, Claudio Brooks, *Preacher*, Lisa Todd, *Lilith*, George Sawaya, *Steve Preston*, Erika Carlson, *Aaronessa Fyffe*. PG.

  Disappointing horror film about a hospital researcher (Tom Skerritt) who searches for his missing family in the Southwest and stumbles onto a cult of devil worshippers. The film climaxes with "the devil's rain," which causes the devil worshippers to literally melt. This is the film's highlight, but it is not enough to lift an otherwise dull film.

226 **Diamonds Are Forever** (1971) *** Britain, United Artists, 119 min. *Dir* Guy Hamilton, *Scr* Richard Maibaum, Tom Mankiewicz, based on novel by Ian Fleming. *Cin* Ted Moore, *Ed* Bert Bates, John W. Holmes, *Des* Ken Adam, *Art* Bill Kenney, Jack Maxsted, *Cos* Donfeld, Elsa Fennell, Ted Tetrick, *Sp* Leslie Hillman, Whitney McAustin, Wally Veevers, Albert Whitlock, *Mus* John Barry, *Song* "Diamonds Are Forever," *Mus* John Barry, *Lyrics* Don Black, *Prod* Albert R. Broccoli, Harry Saltzman, *Assoc Prod* Stanley Sopel.

Cast: Sean Connery, *James Bond,* Jill St. John, *Tiffany Case,* Charles Gray, *Ernst Stavros Blofeld,* Lana Wood, *Plenty O'Toole,* Jimmy Dean, *Willard Whyte,* Bruce Cabot, *Saxby,* Bruce Glover, *Wint,* Putter Smith, *Kidd,* Norman Burton, *Felix Leiter,* Joseph Furst, *Dr. Metz,* Bernard Lee, *"M",* Desmond Llewelyn, *"Q",* Laurence Naismith, *Sir Donald Monger,* Burt Metcalf, *Maxwell,* Leonard Barr, *Shady Tree,* Margaret Lacey, *Mrs. Whistler,* Lois Maxwell, *Miss Moneypenny,* Joe Robinson, *Peter Franks,* Donna Garrett, *Bambi,* Trina Parks, *Thumper.* R. $19,620,000.

Sean Connery returns, after a one-film hiatus, as James Bond, the world's most popular secret agent, in *Diamonds Are Forever* and proves that he is still the best actor for the role. *Diamonds Are Forever* is more overtly science fiction than the earlier films and the special effects do not quite measure up, but it is nevertheless one of the most exciting films of the series. Connery again quit and was replaced by Roger Moore, who is good in the role but still lacked the charisma and likable cruelty of Connery. After a shaky start with *Live and Let Die* and *The Man with the Golden Gun*, Moore proved himself in his later films, with *The Spy Who Loved Me* and *Moonraker* being worthy additions to the series.

227 **Diary of a Mad Housewife** (1970) **** Universal, 95 min. *Dir* Frank Perry, *Scr* Eleanor Perry, based on novel by Sue Kaufman, *Cin* Gerald Hirschfeld, *Ed* Sidney Katz, *Des* Peter Dohanos, *Cos* Ruth Morley, *Prod* Frank Perry.

Cast: Carrie Snodgress (AN, GMC), *Tina Balser,* Richard Benjamin, *Jonathan Balser,* Frank Langella (NB), *George Prager,* Lorraine Cullen, *Sylvie Balser,* Frannie Michel, *Liz Balser,* Katherine Meskill, *Charlotte Rady.* R. $6,100,000.

Well-acted story of an average housewife (Carrie Snodgress), who is driven crazy by her overbearing husband (Richard Benjamin) and her daughters, and seeks relief by having an affair with an egocentric writer (Frank Langella). *Diary of a Mad Housewife* attempts to focus on the real problems facing housewives, but this is undermined slightly by a soap opera plot.

228 **A Different Story** (1978) *** Avco Embassy, 107 min. *Dir* Paul Aaron, *Scr* Henry Olek, *Cin* Philip Lathrop, *Ed* Lynn McCallon, *Cos* Robert Demora, *Mus* David Frank, *Songs* Bob Wahler, *Prod* Alan Belkin, *Exec Prod* Michael F. Leone, *Assoc Prod* Joy Shelton Davis, James Freiburger.

Cast: Perry King, *Albert,* Meg Foster, *Stella,* Valerie Curtin, *Phyllis,* Peter Donat, *Sills,* Richard Bull, *Mr. Cooke,* Barbara Collentine, *Mrs. Cooke,* Guerin Barry, *Ned,* Doug Higgens, *Roger,* Lisa James, *Chris,* Eugene Butler,

Sam, Linda Carpenter, *Chastity*, Alan Hunt, *Richard I*, Burk Byrnes, *Richard II*, Eddie C. Dyer, *Bernie,* Richard Altman, *Phyllis' Neighbor,* Richard Seff, *Justice of the Peace,* George Skaff, *Mr. Hashmoni,* Sid Conrad, *Salesman.* PG.

Interesting story of problems facing homosexuals in our society. A gay man (Perry King) and a gay woman (Meg Foster) get married out of necessity. The title *A Different Story* is apt for only the first half of the film, because after that the filmmakers seem to lose their nerve. They predictably fall in love and the film sinks to a mundane story of a typical marriage.

229 **Dillinger** (1973) *** American International, 106 min. *Dir* John Milius, *Scr* John Milius, *Cin* Jules Breener, *Ed* Fred R. Feitshans, Jr., *Art* Trevor Williams, *Mus* Barry DeVorzon, *Prod* Buzz Feitshans, *Exec Prod* Samuel Z. Arkoff, Lawrence A. Gordon, *Assoc Prod* Robert Papazian.

Cast: Warren Oates, *John Dillinger,* Ben Johnson, *Melvin Purvis,* Michelle Phillips, *Billy Frechette,* Cloris Leachman, *Anna Sage,* Harry Dean Stanton, *Homer Van Meter,* Steve Kanaly, *Lester "Pretty Boy" Floyd,* Richard Dreyfuss, *George "Baby Face" Nelson,* Geoffrey Lewis, *Harry Pierpont,* John Ryan, *Charles Mackley,* Roy Jenson, *Samuel Cowley,* Read Morgan, *Big Jim Wollard,* Frank McRae, *Reed Youngblood,* Jerry Summers, *Tommy Carroll,* Terry Leonard, *Theodore "Handsome Jack" Klutas,* Bob Harris, *Ed Fulton.* R.

One of the better gangster films of the 1970's. Warren Oates is excellent as America's most wanted criminal, John Dillinger, and Oates is almost a dead ringer for him. There are some exciting action sequences, but *Dillinger* still lacks the depth of character and the flawless action of Arthur Penn's *Bonnie and Clyde,* the classic of this genre. Screenwriter John Milius made a fine directorial debut with this film.

230 **Dirty Harry** (1971) *** Warner Bros., 101 min. *Dir* Don Siegel, *Scr* Harry Julien Fink, R.M. Fink, Dean Riesner, *Story* Harry Julian Fink, R.M. Fink, *Cin* Bruce Surtees, *Ed* Carl Pingitore, *Art* Dale Hennesy, *Cos* Glenn Wright, *Mus* Lalo Schifrin, *Prod* Don Siegel, *Exec Prod* Robert Daley, *Assoc Prod* Carl Pingitore.

Cast: Clint Eastwood, *Det. Harry Callahan,* Harry Guardino, *Lt. Bressler,* Reni Santoni, *Chico,* Andy Robinson, *Scorpio,* John Larch, *Police Chief,* John Vernon, *Mayor,* John Mitchum, *DeGeorgio,* Mae Mercer, *Mrs. Russell,* Lyn Edgington, *Norma,* Ruth Kobart, *Bus Driver,* Woodrow Parfrey, *Mr. Jaffe,* Josef Sommer, *Rothko* William Patterson, *Bannerman.* R. $17,900,000.

Above average police thriller starring Clint Eastwood as a cop, who wins at all costs breaking any rule necessary. In the first film Harry ruthlessly pursues a mass murderer. The success of *Dirty Harry* led to two inferior sequels. In *Magnum Force* Harry is pitted against a group of vigilantes and in *The Enforcer* it is a group of terrorists. Eastwood is fine in all three films, but the first rises above the others, due to Don Siegel's expert direction.

231 **Dirty Mary Crazy Larry** (1974) * 20th Century–Fox, 93 min. *Dir* John Hough, *Scr* Leigh Chapman, Antonio Santean, based on novel *The Chase* by Richard Unekis, *Cin* Mike Marguleis, *Ed* Chris Holmes, *Mus* Jimmy Haskell, *Prod* Norman T. Herman, *Assoc Prod* Mickey Zide.

Cast: Peter Fonda, *Larry,* Susan George, *Mary,* Adam Rourke, *Deke,* Vic Morrow, *Franklin,* Fred Daniels, *Hank,* Roddy McDowell, *Stanton,* Lynn Borden, *Evelyn,* Adrian Herman, *Cindy,* Janear Hines, *Millie,* Elizabeth

James, *Dispatcher*, William Campbell, *Sur*, John Castranova, *Steve*. PG.
$15,200,000.

Stupid car chase thriller that somehow found a bigger audience than it
deserved. A trio of crooks (Peter Fonda, Susan George, Adam Rourke) hold
up a supermarket and spend most of the film being chased by the authorities.
Dirty Mary Crazy Larry is nothing more than an excuse for a series of car
wrecks, and is not any more interesting than the many other films of this
particular type.

232 **Doc** (1971) *** United Artists, 96 min. *Dir* Frank Perry, *Scr* Pete
Hamill, *Cin* Gerald Hirschfeld, *Ed* Alan Heim, *Des* Gene Callahan, *Cos* Sandy
Cole, *Mus* Jimmy Webb, *Prod* Frank Perry.

Cast: Stacy Keach, *Doc Holliday*, Faye Dunaway, *Kate Elder*, Harris
Yulin, *Wyatt Earp*, Mike Witney, *Ike Clanton*, Denver John Collins, *The Kid*,
Dan Greenberg, *Mr. Clum*, Penelope Allen, *Mattie Earp*, Hedy Sontag, *Alley
Earp*, Bruce M. Fischer, *Billy Clanton*, James Greene, *Frank McLowrey*,
Richard McKenzie, *Sheriff Beham*, John Scanlon, *Barlett*, Antonia Ray, *Con-
cha*, John Bottoms, *Virgil Earp*, Philip Shafer, *Morgan Earp*, Ferdinand
Zogbaum, *James Earp*. R.

Dull European style western that purports to be the true story of the
Gunfight at the O.K. Corral. Historical accuracy is not necessarily an
automatic asset, as *My Darling Clementine*, possibly the least accurate film
on that historic incident, is far superior to *Doc* in every way, having more
depth and character and a true feeling for the West.

233 **Dr. Phibes Rises Again** (1972) *** Britain, American International, 89
min. *Dir* Robert Fuest, *Scr* Robert Blees, Robert Fuest, based on characters
created by William Goldstein, James Whiton, *Cin* Alex Thomson, *Mus* John
Gale *Prod* Louis M. Heyward, *Exec Prod* Samual Z. Arkoff, James H.
Nicholson.

Cast: Vincent Price, *Dr. Phibes*, Robert Quarry, *Biederbeck*, Valli Kemp,
Vulnavia, Fiona Lewis, *Diana*, Peter Cushing, *Captain*, Beryl Reid, *Mrs. Am-
brose*, Terry-Thomas, *Lombardo*, Hugh Griffith, *Ambrose*, Peter Jeffrey, *Insp.
Trout*, John Cater, *Waverly*, Gerald Sim, *Hackett*. PG. See *The Abominable
Dr. Phibes*.

234 **Doctor's Wives** (1971) * Columbia, 100 min. *Dir* George Schaefer, *Scr*
Daniel Taradash, based on novel by Frank G. Slaughter, *Cin* Charles B. Lang,
Ed Carl Kress, *Des* Lyle R. Wheeler, *Cos* Moss Mabry, *Mus* Elmer Bernstein,
Song "The Costume Ball," *Mus* Elmer Bernstein, *Lyrics* Alan and Marilyn
Bergman, *Prod* M.J. Frankovich.

Cast: Dyan Cannon, *Lorrie Dellman*, Richard Crenna, *Pete Brennan*,
Gene Hackman, *Dave Randolph*, Carroll O'Connor, *Joe Gray*, Rachel Roberts,
Della Randolph, Janice Rule, *Amy Brennan*, Diana Sands, *Helen Straughn*,
Cara Williams, *Maggie Gray*, Richard Anderson, *D.A. Douglas*, Ralph
Bellamy, *Jake Porter*, John Colicos, *Mort Dellman*, George Gaynes, *Paul
McGill*, Marian MeCargo, *Elaine McGill*, Scott Brady, *Sgt. Malloy*, Anthony
Costello, *Traynor*, Kristina Holland, *Sybill Carter*, Mark Jenkins, *Lew Saun-
ders*, Vincent Van Lynn, *Barney Harris*, Ernie Barnes, *Dr. Penfield*, Paul
Marin, *Dr. Deemster*, William Bramley, *Dr. Hagstrom*, John Lormer, *Elderly
M.D.* R.

Dreary soap opera that purports to be an honest and revealing indictment of the medical profession. An adulterous doctor's wife, who has affairs with all the other doctors, is found murdered. This story is not even worthy of a second-rate daytime television drama. The true highlights of this awful trash are the repulsive operation scenes; perhaps they are symbolic.

235 **Dog Day Afternoon** (1975) (AN) ***** Warner Bros., 130 min. *Dir* Sidney Lumet (AN), *Scr* Frank Pierson (A, W), based on magazine article by P.F. Kluge, Thomas Moore, *Cin* Victor J. Kemper, *Ed* Dede Allen (AN), *Des* Charles Bailey, *Art* Doug Higgins, *Cos* Anna Hill Johnstone, *Prod* Martin Bregman, Martin Elfand, *Assoc Prod* Robert Greenhut.

Cast: All Pacino (AN, BFA), *Sonny*, John Cazale, *Sal*, Charles Durning (NB), *Moretti*, Chris Sarandon (AN), *Leon*, Sully Boyar, *Mulvaney*, Penny Allen, *Sylvia*, James Broderick, *Sheldon*, Carol Kane, *Jenny*, Beulah Garrick, *Margaret*, Sandra Kazan, *Deborah*, Marcia Jean Kurtz, *Miriam*, Amy Levitt, *Maria*, John Marriott, *Howard*, Estelle Omens, *Edna*, Gary Springer, *Bobby*, Lance Henriksen, *Murphy*, Judith Malina, *Vi*, Dominic Chianese, *Vi's Husband*, Marcia Haufrecht, *Vi's Friend*, Susan Peretz, *Angie*, Floyd Levine, *Phone Cop*, Carmine Foresta, *Carmine*, Thomas Murphy, *Policeman with Angie*, William Bogert, *TV Studio Anchorman*, Ron Cummins, *TV Reporter*, Jay Gerber, *Sam*, Philip Charles Mackenzie, *Doctor* Chu Chu Malave, *Maria's Boyfriend*, Lionel Pina, *Pizza Boy*, Dick Williams, *Limo Driver*. R. $22,500,000.

The best of Sidney Lumet's documents of urban hysteria. Based on a real incident, *Dog Day Afternoon* is the story of a bisexual man (Al Pacino), who attempts to rob a bank, with the help of a slightly moronic friend (John Cazale), to pay for a sex-change operation for his boyfriend. The robbery becomes a three ring circus and is exploited by the medium. Lumet has done a magnificent job in realistically visualizing this outrageous situation, without exaggeration.

236 **$ (Dollars)** (1971) *** Columbia, 119 min. *Dir* Richard Brooks, *Scr* Richard Brooks, *Cin* Petrus Schloemp, *Ed* George Grenville, *Art* Olaf Ivens, Guy Shepperd, *Cos* Johannes Kohner, *Mus* Quincy Jones, *Prod* M.J. Frankovich.

Cast: Warren Beatty, *Joe Collins*, Goldie Hawn, *Dawn Divine*, Gert Frobe, *Mr. Kessell*, Robert Webber, *Attorney*, Scott Brady, *Sarge*, Arthur Brauss, *Candy Man*, Robert Stiles, *Major*, Wolfgang Kieling, *Granich*, Robert Herron, *Bodyguard*, Christiane Maybach, *Helga*, Hans Hunter, *Karl*, Monica Stender, *Berta*, Francoise Blanc, *Stripper*. R.

Interesting caper comedy starring Warren Beatty as a security expert, who robs three safe deposit boxes in a Hamburg bank, assuming he would be safe because the money is illegal. The crooks discover they have been robbed, and subsequently pursue Beatty in a well-done but unfortunately overlong chase. This could have been a much better film, but far too much emphasis is placed on this chase.

237 **The Domino Principle** (1977) ** Avco Embassy, 100 min. *Dir* Stanley Kramer, *Scr* Adam Kennedy, based on his novel, *Cin* Fred Koenekamp, Ernest Laszlo, *Ed* John Burnett, *Des* Bill Creber, *Art* Ron Hobbs, *Cos* Rita Riggs, *Mus* Billy Goldenberg, *Prod* Stanley Kramer, *Exec Prod* Martin Starger, *Assoc Prod* Terry Morse, Jr.

Cast: Gene Hackman, *Roy Tucker*, Candice Bergen, *Ellie Tucker*, Richard Widmark, *Tagge*, Mickey Rooney, *Spiventa*, Edward Albert, *Ross Pine*, Eli Wallach, *Gen. Tom Reser*, Ken Swofford, *Ditcher*, Neva Patterson, *Gaddis*, Jay Novello, *Capt. Ruiz*, Claire Brennan, *Ruby*, Ted Gehring, *Schnaible*, Joseph Perry, *Bowcamp*, Majel Barrett, *Mrs. Schnaible*, Jim Gavin, *Lenny*, George Fisher, *Henemeyer*, Denver Mattson, *Murdock*, Bob Herron, *Brookshire*, Wayne King, *Nebraska*, Charles Horvath, *Harley*, Bear Hudkins, *Truck Driver*, Farnesio De Bernal, *Bank Official*, Patricia Luke, *Travel Agency Girl*, George Sawaya, *Assassination Victim*. R.

Dull assassination thriller starring Gene Hackman as a convict who is broken out of prison by a secret organization to kill an unknown target. Absolutely nothing is explained in *The Domino Principle* and there does not seem to be a logical reason for this secrecy. If Stanley Kramer is attempting to deliver a message with this one, it apparently was lost between inception and completion.

238 **The Don Is Dead** (1973) ** Universal, 115 min. *Dir* Richard Fleischer, *Scr* Marvin H. Albert, based on his novel, *Cin* Richard H. Kline, *Ed* Edward A. Biery, *Mus* Jerry Goldsmith, *Prod* Hal B. Wallis, *Assoc Prod* Paul Nathan.

Cast: Anthony Quinn, *Don Angelo*, Frederic Forrest, *Tony*, Robert Forster, *Frank*, Al Lettieri, *Vince*, Angel Tompkins, *Ruby*, Charles Cioffi, *Orlando*, Jo Anne Meredith, *Marie*, J. Duke Russo, *Don Bruno*, Louis Zorich, *Mitch*, Ina Balin, *Nella*, George Skaff, *Vitto*, Robert Carricart, *Mike Spada*, Anthony Charnota, *Johnny Tresca*, Abe Vigoda, Frank de Kove, Joseph Santos. R.

Standard gangster drama with the Mafia fighting over control of the organization in Las Vagas. *The Don Is Dead* was obviously inspired by the success of *The Godfather*, but it is lacking in everything that made the earlier film so brilliant; subtlety, depth, characterization and style; and Anthony Quinn is a typically exaggerated Mafia boss. Other title, *Beautiful But Deadly*.

239 **Don't Look Now** (1973) ***** Britain/Italy, Paramount, 110 min. *Dir* Nicolas Roeg, *Scr* Chris Bryant, Allan Scott, based on story by Daphne Du Maurier, *Cin* Anthony Richard (BFA), *Ed* Graeme Clifford, *Art* Giovanni Soccol, *Mus* Pino Donaggio, *Prod* Peter Katz, *Exec Prod* Anthony B. Unger, *Assoc Prod* Federico Mueller.

Cast: Julie Christie, *Laura Baxter*, Donald Sutherland, *John Baxter*, Hilary Mason, *Heather*, Clelia Matania, *Wendy*, Massimo Serato, *Bishop*, Renato Scarpa, *Insp. Longhi*, Giorgio Trestini, *Workman*, Leopoldo Trieste, *Hotel Manager*, David Tree, *Anthony Babbage*, Ann Rye, *Mandy Babbage*, Nicholas Salter, *Johnny Baxter*, Sharon Williams, *Christine Baxter*, Bruno Cattaneo, *Det. Sabbione*, Adelina Poerio, *Dwarf*. R.

Superb occult thriller with psychological overtones. A little girl drowns and her father (Donald Sutherland) senses it beforehand. To forget the tragedy, he and his wife (Julie Christie) go to Venice, where he is to restore a church. There they meet two sisters, one of whom is a blind clairvoyant, who claims their daughter is trying to contact them. *Don't Look Now* is an oblique and demanding work, and Nicolas Roeg beautifully constructs the film like a visual puzzle.

240 **Dracula** (1979) *** Universal, 115 min. *Dir* John Badham, *Scr* W.D. Richter, based on play by Hamilton Deane and John L. Balderston from the

novel by Bram Stoker, *Cin* Gilbert Taylor, *Ed* John Bloom, *Des* Peter Murton, *Art* Brian Ackland Snow, *Cos* Julie Harris, *Mus* John Williams, *Prod* Walter Mirisch, *Exec Prod* Marvin E. Mirisch, *Assoc Prod* Tom Pevsner.

Cast: Frank Langella, *Dracula*, Laurence Olivier, *Van Helsing*, Donald Pleasence, *Seward*, Kate Nelligan, *Lucy*, Trevor Eve, *Harker*, Jan Francis, *Mina*, Janine Duvitski, *Annie*, Tony Haygarth, *Renfield*, Teddy Turner, *Swales*, Kristine Howarth, *Mrs. Galloway*, Joe Belcher, *Tom Hindley*, Ted Carroll, *Scarborough Sailer*, Frank Birch, *Harbourmaster*, Gabor Vernon, *Captain of Demeter*, Frank Henson, *Demeter Sailor*, Peter Wallis, *Priest*. R. $12,400,000.

Well-made, but disappointing film version of Broadway play based on Bram Stoker's novel. *Dracula* is not a bad film, by any means; it is at least as good as any other film version of the same story. With all the talent involved this should have been superior to the others, particularly with the ideal casting of Langella in the title role. This story has been told so many times it needed a fresh approach to really succeed, but this is just more of the same.

241 **Drive, He Said** (1971) ** Columbia, 90 min. *Dir* Jack Nicholson, *Scr* Jeremy Larner, Jack Nicholson, based on novel by Jeremy Larner, *Cin* Bill Butler, *Ed* Donn Cambern, Christopher Holmes, Pat Somerset, Robert L. Wolfe, *Des* Harry Gittes, *Mus* David Shire, *Prod* Steve Blauner, Jack Nicholson, *Co-Prod* Harry Gittes, *Exec Prod* Bert Schneider, *Assoc Prod* Fred Roos.

Cast: William Tepper, *Hector Bloom*, Karen Black, *Olive Calvin*, Michael Margotta, *Gabriel*, Bruce Dern, *Coach Bullion*, Robert Towne, *Richard Calvin*, Henry Jaglom, *Conrad*, Mike Warren, *Easly Jefferson*, June Fairchild, *Sylvie*, Don Hammer, *Director of Athletics*, Lynn Bernay, *Dance Instructor*. R.

Confused drama about a college basketball star (William Tepper), who is even more confused than the film. He tries to avoid the draft, he is unable to decide whether to turn pro and he is having an affair with a professor's wife (Karen Black). *Drive, He Said* overreaches itself by covering too many subjects, and says nothing about any of them.

242 **The Driver** (1978) ***** 20th Century–Fox, 91 min. *Dir* Walter Hill, *Scr* Walter Hill, *Cin* Philip Lathrop, *Ed* Tina Hirsh, Robert K. Lambert, *Des* Harry Horner, *Art* David Haber, *Mus* Michael Small, *Prod* Lawrence Gordon, *Assoc Prod* Frank Marshall.

Cast: Ryan O'Neal, *The Driver*, Bruce Dern, *The Detective*, Isabelle Adjani, *The Player*, Ronee Blakely, *The Connection*, Matt Clark, *Red Plainclothesman*, Felice Orlandi, *Gold Plainclothesman*, Joseph Walsh, *Glasses*, Rudy Ramos, *Teeth*, Denny Macko, *Exchange Man*, Frank Bruno, *The Kid*, Will Walker, *Fingers*, Sandy Brown Wyeth, *Split*, Tara King, *Frizzy*, Richard Carey, *Floorman*, Fidel Corona, *Card Player*, Victor Gilmour, *Boardman*, Nick Dimitri, *Blue Mask*, Bob Minor, *Green Mask*. R.

Unusual crime thriller about the greatest of getaway drivers (Ryan O'Neal) and his battle of wits with an obsessive cop (Bruce Dern). *The Driver* is not an ordinary crime film by any means. Walter Hill has taken European style thrillers, which were inspired by American film noir of the 1940's, and has injected it with his own brand of existentialism. He has stripped the genre of all emotion and excesses, creating a masterful crime epic; a film of unprecedented purity.

243 Drum (1976) * United Artists, 102 min. *Dir* Steve Carver, begun by Burt Kennedy, *Scr* Norman Wexler, based on novel by Kyle Onstott, *Cin* Lucien Ballard, *Ed* Carl Kress, *Des* Stan Jolley, *Art* Bill Kenney, *Cos* Ann Roth, *Mus* Charlie Smalls, *Prod* Ralph Serpe.

Cast: Warren Oates, *Hammond*, Isela Vega, *Marianna*, Ken Norton, *Drum*, Pam Grier, *Regine*, Yaphet Kotto, *Blaise*, John Colicos, *Bernard*, Fiona Lewis, *Augusta*, Paula Kelly, *Rachel*, Royal Dano, *Zeke*, Lillian Hayman, *Lucretia*, Rainbeaux Smith, *Sophie*, Alain Patrick, Brenda Sykes, Clay Tanner, Lila Finn, Henry Wills, Donna Garrett, Harvey Parry, May Boss. R. See *Mandingo*.

244 The Duchess and the Dirtwater Fox (1976) ** 20th Century–Fox, 105 min. *Dir* Melvin Frank, *Scr* Melvin Frank, Jack Rose, Barry Sandler, *Story* Barry Sandler, *Cin* Joseph Biroc, *Ed* Frank Bracht, William Butler, *Art* Robert Emmet Smith, Trevor Williams, *Mus* Charles Fox, *Lyrics* Sammy Cahn, Melvin Frank, *Prod* Melvin Frank.

Cast: George Segal, *Charlie Malloy*, Goldie Hawn, *Amanda Quaid*, Conrad Janis, *Gladstone*, Thayer David, *Widdicombe*, Jennifer Lee, *Trollop*, Roy Jenson, *Bloodworth*, Pat Ast, *Dance Hall Girl*, Sid Gould, *Rabbi*, Bob Hoy, Bennie Dobbins, Walter Scott, Jerry Gatlin, *Bloodworth Gang*. PG. $4,975,000.

Fair comedy western about the relationship between a card-sharp (George Segal) and a dance hall girl (Goldie Hawn). Segal and Hawn are good in the title roles, and create a fine romantic team, but the film is very slight and unmemorable. Like many other films of its type, *The Duchess and the Dirtwater Fox* attempts to titillate its audience, but it is far too tame.

245 The Duellists (1977) **** Britain, Paramount, 101 min. *Dir* Ridley Scott (CF-Best first film), *Scr* Gerald Vaughan-Hughes, based on the story *The Duel* by Joseph Conrad, *Cin* Frank Tidy, *Ed* Pamala Powers, *Art* Bryan Graves, *Mus* Howard Blake, *Prod* David Putnam.

Cast: Keith Carradine, *D'Hubert*, Harvey Keitel, *Feraud*, Albert Finney, *Fouche*, Edward Fox, *Col. Reynard*, Cristina Raines, *Adele*, Robert Stephens, *Gen. Treillard*, Tom Conti, *Jacquin*, John McEnery, *Second Major*, Diana Quick, *Laura*, Alun Armstrong, *Lacourbe*, Maurice Colbourne, *Tall Second*, Gay Hamilton, *Maid*, Meg Wynn Owen, *Leonie*, Jenny Runacre, *Mme. de Lionne*, Alan Webb, *Chevalier*. PG.

Beautiful period film about two pompous officers in the Napoleonic Army who take pride to extremes by fighting a continuous duel over a period of many years. Harvey Keitel and Keith Carradine are certainly odd choices to portray French officers, but they are surprisingly effective. *The Duellists* is a visually beautiful film in which Ridley Scott, in his feature film debut, creates some of the most compelling images ever put on film.

246 The Eagle Has Landed (1977) *** Britain, Columbia, 134 min. *Dir* John Sturges, *Scr* Tom Mankiewicz, based on novel by Jack Higgins, *Cin* Peter Allwork, Tony Richmond, *Ed* Irene Lamb, *Des* Peter Murton, *Art* Charles Bishop, *Prod* David Niven, Jr., Jack Winer.

Cast: Michael Caine, *Col. Kurt Steiner*, Donald Sutherland, *Liam Devlin*, Robert Duvall, *Col. Max Radl*, Jenny Agutter, *Molly Prior*, Donald Pleasence, *Heinrich Himmler*, Anthony Quayle, *Adm. Wilhelm Canaris*, Jean Marsh,

Joanna Grey, Sven-Bertil Taube, *Capt. Ritter Newmann*, John Standing, *Father Philip Verecker*, Judy Geeson, *Pamela Verecker*, Treat Williams, *Capt. Harry Clark*, Larry Hagman, *Col. Clarence E. Pitts*, Siegfried Rauch, *Sgt. Brandt*. PG. $4,500,000.

Above average World War II drama about a Nazi plot to kidnap Winston Churchill. Generally espionage war stories of this type have such complicated and convoluted plots, they are nearly impossible to follow, but *The Eagle Has Landed* is different. Although it contains numerous twists, the plot is never hopelessly confusing, and the action is well-paced, moving briskly to its exciting climax.

247 **Earthquake** (1974) * Universal, 129 min. *Dir* Mark Robson, *Scr* George Fox, Mario Puzo, *Cin* Philip Lathrop (AN), *Ed* Dorothy Spencer (AN), *Des* Alexander Golitzen (AN), *Art* E. Preston Ames (AN), *Sp* Frank Brendel, Glen Robinson, Albert Whitlock (A), *Cos* Burton Miller, *Mus* John Williams, *Prod* Mark Robson, *Exec Prod* Jennings Lang.

Cast: Charlton Heston, *Graff*, Ava Gardner, *Remy*, George Kennedy, *Slade*, Lorne Greene, *Royce*, Genevieve Bujold, *Denise*, Richard Roundtree, *Miles*, Marjoe Gortner, *Jody*, Barry Sullivan, *Stockle*, Lloyd Nolan, *Dr. Vance*, Victoria Principal, *Rosa*, Walter Matuschanskayasky (Matthau), *Drunk*, Monica Lewis, *Barbara*, Gabriel Dell, *Sal*, Pedro Armendariz, Jr., *Chevez*, Lloyd Gough, *Cameron*, John Randolph, *Mayor*, Kip Niven, *Walter Russell*, Scott Hylands, *Assistant Caretaker*, Tiger Williams, *Corry*, Donald Moffat, *Dr. Harvey Johnson*, Jesse Vint, *Buck*, Alan Vint, *Ralph*, Lionel Johnston, *Hank*, John Elerick, *Carl Leeds*, John S. Ragin, *Chief Inspector*, George Murdock, *Colonel*. PG. $36,250,000.

Awful disaster film about an earthquake that destroys Los Angeles. *Earthquake* spends so much time attempting to develop a group of inane characters, that seem to be rejects from soap operas, that the audience becomes restless hoping for the earthquake to arrive and kill off these people. Disaster movies depend greatly on their special effects and *Earthquake* also fails on this point, because it is far too easy to pick out the miniatures and the matte shots. This was the first to use the gimmick Sensurround, a sound process that causes vibrations when the sound level is raised.

248 **Echoes of a Summer** (1976) ** Cine Artists, 99 min. *Dir* Don Taylor, *Scr* Robert L. Joseph, *Cin* John Coquillon, *Ed* Michael F. Anderson, *Art* Jack McAdams, *Mus* Terry James, *Prod* Robert L. Joseph, *Exec Prod*. Richard Harris, Sandy Howard.

Cast: Richard Harris, *Eugene*, Lois Nettleton, *Ruth*, Geraldine Fitzgerald, *Sara*, William Windom, *Dr. Hallett*, Brad Savage, *Philip*, Jodie Foster, *Deirdre*. PG.

Standard film about a dying 12 year old girl and how the impending tragedy affects her family. Jodie Foster stars as the girl, coping gallantly with her serious heart ailment. There is far too much emphasis on talk, which fails to bring much substance to a tired and overused premise. Foster's performance is the best thing about the film.

249 **The Effect of Gamma Rays on Man-in-the-Moon Marigolds** (1972) **** 20th Century–Fox, 100 min. *Dir* Paul Newman, *Scr* Alvin Sargent,

based on play by Paul Zindel, *Cin* Adam Holender, *Ed* Evan Lottman, *Des* Gene Callahan, *Cos* Anna Hill Johnstone, *Mus* Maurice Jarre, *Prod* Paul Newman, *Assoc Prod* Frank Caffey.

Cast: Joanne Woodward, *Beatrice*, Nell Potts, *Matilda*, Roberta Wallach, *Ruth*, Judith Lowry, *Nanny*, Richard Venture, *Floyd*, Carolyn Coates, *Mrs. McKay*, Will Hare, *Junk Man*, Estelle Omens, *Caroline*, Jess Osuna, *Sonny*, David Spielberg, *Mr. Goodman*, Ellen Dane, Janice Vickery, Lynn Rogers, *Miss Hanley*, Roger Serbagi, *Charlie*, John Lehne, *Apartment Manager*, Michael Kearney, *Chris Burns*, Dee Victor, *Miss Wyant*. PG.

Strange and superbly acted comedy-drama about a woman coping with failure in her life and her relationship with her two daughters. One of her daughters has won a prize at school for her science project, which is described by the film's odd title, and the film centers on its effect on the family. This plays much better than it sounds, mainly due to the excellent performances of Joanne Woodward, as the mother, and Nell Potts; her real-life daughter; and Roberta Wallach as the two daughters.

250 **The Eiger Sanction** (1975) * Universal, 128 min. *Dir* Clint Eastwood, *Scr* Hal Dresner, Warren B. Murphy, Rod Whitaker, based on novel by Trevanian, *Cin* Frank Stanley, *Ed* Ferris Webster, *Art* Aurelio Crugnola, George Webb, *Cos* Charles Waldo, *Mus* John Williams, *Prod* Robert Daley, *Exec Prod* Richard D. Zanuck, David Brown, A Jennings Lang Presentation.

Cast: Clint Eastwood, *Jonathon Hemlock*, George Kennedy, *Ben Bowman*, Vonetta McGee, *Jemima Brown*, Jack Cassidy, *Miles Mellough*, Heidi Bruhl, *Mrs. Montaigne*, Thayer David, *Dragon*, Reiner Schoene, *Freytag*, Michael Grimm, *Meyer*, Jean-Pierre Bernard, *Montaigne*, Brenda Venus, *George*, Gregory Walcott, *Pope*, Candice Rialson, *Art Student*. R. $7,155,000.

Poor thriller of intrigue, in which a hired killer must eliminate a man on a mountain climbing expedition. This was intended to be a mystery, since no one knows the identity of the intended victim, but *The Eiger Santion* is too predictable to succeed on that level. The film is far too long to hold the viewer's interest, and it lacks the excitement that one expects from Clint Eastwood films.

251 **Electra Glide in Blue** (1973) ** United Artists, 106 min. *Dir* James William Guercio, *Scr* Robert Boris, Michael Butler, *Story* Robert Boris, Rupert Hitzig, *Cin* Conrad Hall, *Ed* Jim Benson, Jerry Greenberg, John F. Link III, *Cos* Rita Riggs, *Mus* James William Guercio, *Prod* James William Guercio.

Cast: Robert Blake, *Wintergreen*, Billy "Green" Bush, *Zipper*, Mitchell Ryan, *Poole*, Jeannine Riley, *Jolene*, Elisha Cook, *Willie*, Royal Dano, *Coroner*, David Wolinski, *Bus Driver*, Peter Cetera, *Zemko*, Terry Kath, *Killer*, Lee Loughnane, *Pig Man*, Walter Parazaider, *Loose Lips*, Joe Samsil, *Ryker*, Jason Clark, *L.A. Detective*, Michael Butler, *Truck Driver*, Susan Forristal, Lucy Angle Guercio, *Ice Cream Girls*, Melissa Green, *Zemko's Girlfriend*, Jim Gilmore, *Detective*, Bob Zemko, *The Beard*. PG.

Disappointing drama about an Arizona motorcycle cop (Robert Blake), who is dissatisfied with his low position, but is unable to advance to detective because of the system. *Electra Glide in Blue* is a police version of the anti-establishment films of the era, and it contains the same flaws that plagued most of those films. It attempts to be realistic and gritty, but instead it comes off as sloppy and aimless.

252 The Electric Horseman (1979) ∗∗∗ Columbia/Universal, 121 min. *Dir* Sydney Pollack, *Scr* Robert Garland, *Story* Shelly Burton, Robert Garland, Paul Gaer, *Cin* Owen Roizman, *Ed* Sheldon Kahn, *Des* Stephen Grimes, *Art* J. Dennis Washington, *Cos* Bernie Pollack, *Mus* Dave Grusin, Songs sung by Willie Nelson, *Prod* Ray Stark, *Assoc Prod* Ronald L. Schwary.

Cast: Robert Redford, *Sonny*, Jane Fonda, *Hallie*, Valerie Perrine, *Charlotta*, Willie Nelson, *Wendell*, John Saxon, *Hunt Sears*, Nicolas Coster, *Fitzgerald*, Allan Arbus, *Danny*, Wilford Brimley, *Farmer*, Will Hare, *Gus*, Basil Hoffman, *Toland*, Timothy Scott, *Leroy*, James B. Sikking, *Dietrich*, James Kline, *Tommy*, Frank Speiser, *Bernie*, Quinn Redeker, *Bud Broderick*, Lois Areno, *Joanna Camden*, Sarah Harris, *Lucinda*, Tasha Zemrus, *Louise*, James Novak, *Dennis*. PG. $31,115,000.

Disappointing comedy-drama of worn-out rodeo cowboy (Robert Redford), who kidnaps a valuable horse to protect it from abuse by its owners. The plot is a little thin, with two many drawn out chase sequences, but the chemistry between Redford and Jane Fonda, as a television reporter who pursues him, is wonderful and saves *The Electric Horseman* from completely sinking, despite the slight predictability of their relationship.

253 11 Harrowhouse (1974) ∗∗ Britain, 20th Century–Fox, 95 min. *Dir* Aram Avakian, *Scr* Jeffrey Bloom, *Adaptation* Charles Grodin, based on novel by Gerald A. Browne, *Cin* Arthur Ibbetson, *Ed* Anne V. Coates, *Art* Peter Mullins, *Cos* Anthony Mendleson, *Mus* Michael J. Lewis, *Prod* Elliott Kastner, *Assoc Prod* Denis Holt.

Cast: Charles Grodin, *Chesser*, Candice Bergen, *Maren*, John Gielgud, *Meecham*, Trevor Howard, *Massey*, James Mason, *Watts*, Helen Cherry, *Lady Bolding*, Jack Watson, *Miller*, Jack Watling, *Fitzmaurice*, Cyril Shaps, *Wildenstein*, Leon Greene, *Toland*, Joe Powell, *Hickey*, Peter Forbes Robertson, *Hotel Manager*, David Rowlands, *Club Manager*. PG.

Dull diamond caper comedy. The overly complex plot involves a diamond salesman (Charles Grodin), who is hired by a wealthy man (Trevor Howard) to rob the vaults of the diamond exchange and is subsequently marked for elimination. Unfortunately, *11 Harrowhouse* falters because of its bland and confusing script, and the story culminates with an obligatory chase sequence.

254 Emperor of the North (1974) ∗∗∗ 20th Century–Fox, 120 min. *Dir* Robert Aldrich, *Scr* Christopher Knopf, *Cin* Joseph Biroc, *Ed* Michael Luciano, *Art* Jack Martin Smith, *Mus* Frank DeVol, *Prod* Stan Hough, *Exec Prod* Kenneth Hyman.

Cast: Lee Marvin, *A Number 1*, Ernest Borgnine, *Shack*, Keith Carradine, *Cigaret*, Charles Tyner, *Cracker*, Malcolm Atterbury, *Hogger*, Simon Oakland, *Policeman*, Harry Caesar, *Coaly*, Hal Baylor, *Yardsman's Helper*, Matt Clark, *Yardlet*, Elisha Cook, *Gray Cat*, Joe di Reda, *Dinger*, Liam Dunn, *Smile*, Diane Dye, *Prudence*, Robert Faulk, *Conductor*, James Goodwin, *Fakir*, Ray Guth, *Preacher*, Sid Haig, *Grease Tail*, Karl Lukas, *Pokey Stiff*, Edward McNally, *Yard Clerk*, John Steadman, *Stew Bum*, Vic Tayback, *Yardman*, Dave Willock, *Groundhog*. PG.

Good but violent tale of honor and survival. The "king of the hobos" (Lee Marvin) vows to prove himself by riding on a freight train guarded by a sadistic railroad cop (Ernest Borgnine). *Emperor of the North* culminates with a well-staged violent confrontation between the two. This is one of Robert Aldrich's better films. Original title *Emperor of the North Pole*.

255 **Empire of the Ants** (1977) * American International, 89 min. *Dir* Bert I. Gordon, *Scr* Jack Turley, based on story by H.G. Wells, *Cin* Reginald Morris, *Ed* Michael Luciano, *Des* Charles Rosen, *Cos* Joanne Haas, *Mus* Dana Kaproff, *Prod* Bert I. Gordon, *Exec Prod* Samuel Z. Arkoff.

Cast: Joan Collins, *Marilyn Fryser*, Robert Lansing, *Dan Stokely*, John David Carson, *Joe Morrison*, Albert Salmi, *Sheriff Kincade*, Jacqueline Scott, *Margaret Ellis*, Pamela Shoop, *Coreen Bradford*, Robert Pine, *Larry Graham*, Edward Power, *Charlie Pearson*, Brooke Palance, *Christine Graham*, Tom Fadden, *Sam Russell*, Irene Tedrow, *Velma Thompson*, Harry Holcombe, *Harry Thompson*, Jack Kosslyn, *Thomas Lawson*, Ilse Earl, *Mary Lawson*, Janie Gavin, *Ginny*, Norman Franklin, *Anson Parker*, Florence McGee, *Phoebe Russell*. PG.

Poor science-fiction thriller about rampaging giant ants that were contaminated by radioactive waste. Insect movies have been out of vogue since the 1950's and for good reason. *Empire of the Ants* is worse than most of its predecessors, due to its poor special effects and its completely unconvincing ants. By comparison, the very similar film *Them!* is a masterpiece.

256 **The End** (1978) ** United Artists, 100 min. *Dir* Burt Reynolds, *Scr* Jerry Belson, *Cin* Bobby Byrne, *Ed* Donn Cambern, *Des* Jan Scott, *Cos* Norman Salling, *Mus* Paul Williams, *Prod* Lawrence Gordon, *Exec Prod* Hank Moonjean.

Cast: Burt Reynolds, *Sonny Lawson*, Dom DeLuise, *Marlon Borunki*, Sally Field, *Mary Ellen*, Strother Martin, *Dr. Kling*, David Steinberg, *Marty Lieberman*, Joanne Woodward, *Jessica*, Norman Fell, *Dr. Krugman*, Myrna Loy, *Maureen Lawson*, Kristy McNichol, *Julie Lawson*, Pat O'Brien, *Ben Lawson*, Robby Benson, *Priest*, Carl Reiner, *Dr. Maneet*, James Best, *Pacemaker Patient*, Jock Mahoney, *Old Man*. R. $20,645,000.

Strange comedy about a dying man who decides to commit suicide, rather than suffering from the pain of the illness. *The End* is a disjointed and confused comedy. The first half is a subtle black comedy about a man facing death, while the second half is an outrageous slapstick comedy with Dom DeLuise as a lunatic friend who agrees to help him out by trying to kill him. Some of this is funny, but the inconsistency destroys the comic pacing.

257 **End of the Road** (1970) *** Allied Artists, 111 min. *Dir* Aram Avakian, *Scr* Aram Avakian, Dennis McGuire, Terry Southern, based on novel by John Barth, *Cin* Gordon Willis, *Ed* Robert Q. Lovett, *Des* John K. Wright III, *Art* Robert Hamlin, *Mus* Teo Macero, *Prod* Stephen F. Kesten, Terry Southern, *Exec Prod* Max L. Raab.

Cast: Stacy Keach, *Jake*, Harris Yulin, *Joe*, Dorothy Tristan, *Rennie*, James Earl Jones, *Doctor*, Grayson Hall, *Peggy*, Ray Brock, *Sniper/Mrs. Dockey*, James Coco, *School Man*, Oliver Clark, *Dog Man*, June Hutchinson, *Miss Banning*, Graham P. Jarvis, *Dr. Carter*, Maeve McGuire, *Shirley*, Joel Oppenheimer, *Chicken Man*, John Pleshette, *Finkle*, Norman Simpson, *Dr. Schott*, Joel Wolfe, *Ticket Seller*. X.

Bizarre black-comedy about an English teacher (Stacy Keach), who after his release from a sanitarium, run by a mad doctor (James Earl Jones), gets a teaching job at a local university. There Keach develops a strange relationship with a professor (Harris Yulin) and his wife (Dorothy Tristan). *End of the Road* is an attempt to make a statement about the times, but it is a bit too weird to clearly make its point.

258 **The Enforcer** (1976) ** Warner Bros., 96 min. *Dir* James Fargo, *Scr* Dean Riesner, Sterling Silliphant, *Story* Gail Morgan Hickman, S.W. Schurr, based on characters created by Harry Julian Fink, R.M. Fink, *Cin* Charles W. Short, *Ed* Joel Cox, Ferris Webster, *Art* Allen E. Smith, *Mus* Jerry Fielding, *Prod* Robert Daley.

Cast: Clint Eastwood, *Harry Callahan*, Harry Guardino, *Lt. Bressler*, Bradford Dillman, *Capt. McKay*, Tyne Daley, *Kate Moore*, John Mitchum, *DiGeorgio*, DeVeren Bookwalter, *Bobby Maxwell*, John Crawford, *The Mayor*. R. $24,000,000. See *Dirty Harry*.

259 **England Made Me** (1973) *** Britain, Cine Globe, 100 min. *Dir* Peter Duffell, *Scr* Desmond Cory, Peter Duffell, based on novel by Graham Greene, *Cin* Ray Parslow, *Ed* Malcolm Cooke, *Des* Tony Woollard, *Art* Peter Young, *Cos* John Furniss, *Mus* John Scott, *Prod* Jack Levin, *Exec Prod* C. Robert Allen, *Assoc Prod* David C. Anderson, Jerome Z. Cline.

Cast: Peter Finch, *Eric Krogh*, Michael York, *Anthony Farrant*, Hildegard Neil, *Kate Farrant*, Michael Hordern, *F. Minty*, Joss Ackland, *Haller*, Tessa Wyatt, *Liz Davidge*, Michael Sheard, *Fromm*, Bill Baskiville, *Stein*, Demeter Bitenic, *Reichminster*, Mira Nikolik, *Nikki*, Vladimir Bacic, *Hartmann*, Maja Papandopulo, *Night Club Singer*, Vladan Zivkovic, *Heinrich*, Crettra Cupar, *Maria*. PG.

Fine drama set in pre-war Nazi Germany. Michael York stars as a young idealistic Englishman, not unlike his character in *Cabaret*, who passes through Germany on his way home from the Far East. He runs into direct conflict with Germany's decadent society, represented by an English financial tycoon (Peter Finch). *England Made Me* is a well acted and finely detailed period film.

260 **Enter the Dragon** (1973) * Warner Bros., 98 min. *Dir* Robert Clouse, *Scr* Michael Allin, *Cin* Gilbert Hubbs, *Ed* Kurt Hirshler, George Watters, *Art* James Wong Sun, *Prod* Paul Heller, Fred Weintraub, *Assoc Prod* Raymond Chow.

Cast: Bruce Lee, *Lee*, John Saxon, *Roper*, Jim Kelly, *Williams*, Shih Kien, *Han*, Bob Wall, *Oharra*, Ahna Capri, *Tania*, Angela Mao Ying, *Su-Lin*, Betty Chung, *Mei Ling*, Geoffrey Weeks, *Braithwaite*, Yang Sze, *Bolo*, Peter Archer, *Parsons*. R. $11,000,000.

Poor martial arts drama that again pits Bruce Lee against every black belt in the Orient. *Enter the Dragon* is considered to be the best of its genre, but if that is the case, then the rest must really be something. Lee's legendary status as a star must rank as one of the great mysteries of the cinema. His abilities in martial arts cannot be denied, but he was a poor screen actor. Surely, many others could have done the same as Lee, and just as well. The action sequences are also unimpressive, as is the case with other films of this genre. They are so ridiculously overdone, that they become dull and predictable.

261 **Equus** (1977) ******* United Artists, 137 min. *Dir* Sidney Lumet, *Scr* Peter Shaffer (AN), based on his play, *Cin* Oswald Morris, *Ed* John Victor Smith, *Des* Tony Walton, *Art* Simon Holland, *Cos* Brenda Dabbs, Patti Unger, Tony Walton, *Mus* Richard Rodney Bennett, *Prod* Elliot Kastner, Lester Persky, *Assoc Prod* Denis Holt.

Cast: Richard Burton (AN, G), *Dr. Dysart*, Peter Firth (AN, G), *Alan Strang*, Colin Blakely, *Frank Strang*, Joan Plowright, *Dora Strang*, Harry Andrews, *Harry Dalton*, Eileen Atkins, *Heather Saloman*, Jenny Agutter (BFA), *Jill Mason*, John Wyman, *The Horseman*, Kate Reid, *Margaret Dysart*, Ken James, *Mr. Pearce*, Elva Mai Hoover, *Miss Raintree*, James Hurdle, *Mr. Davies*, Karen Pearson, *Mary*, David Gardner, *Dr. Bennett*. R.

Interesting psychological suspense story. Richard Burton stars as a psychiatrist who is to examine a young stable boy (Peter Firth) to discover why the boy blinded six horses. The film version of *Equus* is unfortunately more like a filmed play than a true film. Sidney Lumet does demonstrate his uncanny ability with actors by eliciting from Burton his finest performance in a decade, and an equally good performance from Firth.

262 **Escape from Alcatraz** (1979) ******** Paramount, 112 min. *Dir* Don Siegel, *Scr* Richard Tuggle, based on book by J. Campbell Bruce, *Cin* Bruce Surtees, *Ed* Ferris Webster, *Des* Allen Smith, *Prod* Don Siegel, *Exec Prod* Robert Daley, *Assoc Prod* Fritz Manes.

Cast: Clint Eastwood, *Frank Morris*, Patrick McGoohan, *Warden*, Roberts Blossom, *Doc*, Jack Thibeau, *Clarence Anglin*, Fred Ward, *John Anglin*, Paul Benjamin, *English*, Larry Hankin, *Charley Butts*, Bruce M. Fischer, *Wolf*, Frank Ronzio, *Litmus*, Fred Stuthman, *Johnson*, David Cryer, *Wagner*, Madison Arnold, *Zimmerman*. PG. $21,500,000.

An unusually restrained and intelligent Clint Eastwood drama. *Escape from Alcatraz* is based on a true story about the first man to escape from that infamous prison. Don Siegel directs sparingly and economically, dispensing with the excesses one might expect from the genre, especially considering the film's star. The pace is somewhat slow, but the film never becomes boring. This is a pleasant surprise coming from Clint Eastwood.

263 **Escape from the Planet of the Apes** (1971) ****** 20th Century–Fox, 98 min. *Dir* Don Taylor, *Scr* Paul Dehn, based on characters created by Pierre Boulle, *Cin* Joseph Biroc, *Ed* Marion Rothman, *Art* William Creber, Jack Martin Smith, *Mus* Jerry Goldsmith, *Prod* Arthur P. Jacobs, *Assoc Prod* Frank Capra, Jr.

Cast: Roddy McDowell, *Cornelius*, Kim Hunter, *Zira*, Bradford Dillman, *Dr. Lewis Dixon*, Natalie Trundy, *Dr. Stephanie Branton*, Eric Braeden, *Dr. Otto Hasslein*, William Windom, *The President*, Sal Mineo, *Milo*, Albert Salmi, *E-1*, Jason Evers, *E-2*, John Randolph, *Chairman*, Ricardo Montalban, *Armando*, Steve Roberts, *Gen. Brody*, M. Emmet Walsh, *Aide-Capt.*, Roy E. Glenn, Sr., *Lawyer*, Peter Forster, *Cardinal*, Norman Burton, *Army Officer*, William Woodson, *Naval Officer*, Tom Lowell, *Orderly*, Gene Wittington, *Marine Captain*, Donald Elson, *Curator*, Bill Bonds, *TV Newscaster*, Army Archerd, *Referee*, James Bacon, *Gen. Faulkner*, John Alderman, *Corporal*. G. $5,560,000.

See *Beneath the Planet of the Apes*.

264 **Escape to Witch Mountain** (1975) *** Buena Vista, 97 min. *Dir* John Hough, *Scr* Robert Malcolm Young, based on novel by Alexander Key, *Cin* Frank Philips, *Ed* Robert Stafford, *Art* John B. Mansbridge, Al Roelofs, *Cos* Chuck Keehne, Emily Sundby, *Mus* Johnny Mandel, *Prod* Jerome Courtland, *Exec Prod* Ron Miller, A Walt Disney Production.

Cast: Eddie Albert, *Jason*, Ray Milland, *Aristotle Bolt*, Donald Pleasence, *Deranian*, Kim Richards, *Tia*, Ike Eisenmann, *Tony*, Walter Barnes, *Sheriff Purdy*, Reta Shaw, *Mrs. Grindley*, Denver Pyle, *Uncle Bene*, Alfred Ryder, *Astrologer*, Lawrence Montaigne, *Ubermann*, Terry Wilson, *Biff Jenkins*, George Chandler, *Grocer*, Dermott Downs, *Truck*, Shepherd Sanders, *Guru*. G. $9,500,000.

Above average Walt Disney fantasy about a pair of orphans (Kim Richards, Ike Eisenmann), who possess psychic powers, In their search for their true identity they encounter the standard Disney villain (Ray Milland), who wants to exploit their powers. In the sequel, *Return from Witch Mountain*, Bette Davis and Christopher Lee kidnap the two to use their powers for evil purposes. Disney Studios were not exactly known for their originality during the 1970's.

265 **The Europeans** (1979) ** Britain, Levitt-Pickman, 90 min. *Dir* James Ivory, *Scr* Ruth Prawer Jhabvala, based on novel by Henry James, *Cin* Larry Pizer, *Ed* Humphrey Dixon, *Art* Jeremiah Rusconi, *Cos* Judy Moorcraft, *Mus* Richard Robbins, *Prod* Ismail Merchant, *Assoc Prod* Connie Kaiserman.

Cast: Lee Remick, *Eugenia*, Robin Ellis, *Robert Acton*, Wesley Addy, *Mr. Wentworth*, Tim Choate, *Clifford Wentworth*, Lisa Eichhorn, *Gertrude Wentworth*, Nancy New, *Charlotte Wentworth*, Kristin Griffith, *Lizzie Acton*, Helen Stenborg, *Mrs. Anton*, Norman Snow, *Mr. Brandt*, Tim Woodward, *Felix*, Gedda Petry, *Augustine*. G.

Dull period study of manners and morals, in which two "Europeans," actually Americans who grew up in Europe, come to stay with their rich and proper American cousins. The conflict stems from a clash of cultures, but everything is completely played down to the point to total boredom. This is the type of film that pretends to be serious, but has no more substance than an exploitation film.

266 **Evel Knievel** (1971) ** Fanfare, 90 min. *Dir* Marvin Chomsky, *Scr* Alan Caillou, John Milius, *Story* Alan Caillou, *Cin* David Walsh, *Ed* Jack McSweeney, *Art* Norman Houle, *Cos* Arnold Lipin, *Mus* Pat Williams, *Song*, "I Do What I Please," *Mus* Pat Williams, *Lyrics* Bradford Craig, *Prod* George Hamilton, *Exec Prod* Joe Solomon.

Cast: George Hamilton, *Evel Knievel*, Sue Lyon, *Linda*, Bert Freed, *Doc Kincaid*, Rod Cameron, *Charlie Kresson*, Dub Taylor, *Turquoise Smith*, Ron Masak, *Pete*, Hal Baylor, *The Sheriff*, Betty Bronson, *House Mother*, Sylvia Hayes, *Grandma*, Mary Peters, *Marge*. PG. $4,000,000.

Standard biography of famed motorcycle daredevil. Knievel's story in this film never for once seems real, and the film is more of an excuse for some action sequences. The stunts are well-handled and George Hamilton evokes the proper egomania, but the story has the substance of a fan magazine article. *Evel Knievel* nevertheless towers over the later film about Knievel, *Viva Knievel*.

267 **Every Which Way But Loose** (1978) ** Warner Bros., 119 min. *Dir* James Fargo, *Scr* Jeremy Joe Kronsberg, *Cin* Rexford Metz, *Ed* Joel Cox, Ferris Webster, *Art* Elayne Ceder, *Prod* Robert Daley, *Assoc Prod* Jeremy Joe Kronsberg, Fritz Manes.

Cast: Clint Eastwood, *Philo Beddoe*, Sondra Locke, *Lynn Halsey-Taylor*, Geoffrey Lewis, *Orville*, Beverly D'Angelo, *Echo*, Ruth Gordon, *Ma*. PG. $51,800,000.

Dumb, but occasionally funny, Clint Eastwood comedy. In a surprise change, Eastwood dispenses with the usual gritty violence of his other films and turned to slapstick comedy, in a tale about a likable bare-fisted fighter who falls in love with an unlikable country singer. There is very little in the way of plot as *Every Which Way But Loose* just completely wanders aimlessly. Eastwood was mistakenly warned by associates against doing this film, which became his biggest hit.

268 **Everything You Always Wanted to Know About Sex* (*But Were Afraid to Ask)** (1972) ** United Artists, 87 min. *Dir* Woody Allen, *Scr* Woody Allen, based on book by Dr. David Reuben, *Cin* David M. Walsh, *Ed* James T. Heckert, *Des* Dale Hennesy, *Mus* Mundell Lowe, *Prod* Charles H. Joffe, *Exec Prod* Jack Brodsky, *Assoc Prod* Jack Grossberg.

Cast: Woody Allen, *Victor/Fabrizio/Fool/Sperm*, John Carradine, *Dr. Bernardo*, Lou Jacobi, *Sam*, Louise Lasser, *Gina*, Anthony Quayle, *The King*, Tony Randall, *Operator*, Lynn Redgrave, *The Queen*, Burt Reynolds, *Switchboard*, Gene Wilder, *Dr. Ross*, Jack Barry, *Himself*, Erin Fleming, *The Girl*, Elaine Giftos, *Mrs. Ross*, Toni Holt, *Herself*, Robert Q. Lewis, *Himself*, Heather MacRae, *Helen*, Sidney Miller, *George*, Pamela Mason, *Herself*, Regis Philbin, *Himself*, Titos Vandis, *Milos*, Stanley Adams, *Stomach Operator*, Robert Walden, *Sperm*. R. $8,110,000.

The weakest of all of Woody Allen's films. It certainly took nerve to create a film based on an unfilmable book, such as this, but it did not really pay off. Allen's film is divided into seven separate vignettes, each titled from chapters from Dr. David Reuben's book. Some of them are funny, but most surprisingly fall flat. It was a valiant effort, though.

269 **Executive Action** (1973) * National General, 91 min. *Dir* David Miller, *Scr* Dalton Trumbo, *Story* Donald Freed, Mark Lane, *Cin* Robert Steadman, *Ed* George Grenville, Irving Lerner, *Art* Kirk Axtell, *Mus* Randy Edelman, *Prod* Edward Lewis, *Co-Prod* Dan Bessie, Gary Horowitz.

Cast: Burt Lancaster, *Farrington*, Robert Ryan, *Foster*, Will Geer, *Ferguson*, Gilbert Green, *Paulitz*, John Anderson, *Halliday*, Paul Carr, *Gunman Chris*, Colby Chester, *Tim*, Ed Lauter, *Operation Chief Team A*, Walter Brooke, *Smythe*, Sidney Clute, *Depository Clerk*, Deanna Darrin, *Stripper*, Lloyd Gough, *McCadden*, Richard Hurst, *Used Car Salesman*, Robert Karnes, *Man at Rifle Range*, James MacColl, *Oswald Imposter*, Joaquin Martinez, *Art Mendoza*, Dick Miller, Hunter Von Leer, John Brascia, *Riflemen Team B*, Oscar Oncidi, *Jack Ruby*, Tom Peters, *Sergeant*, Paul Sorenson, *Officer Brown*, Sandy Ward, *Policeman*, William Watson, *Technician Team B*, Richard Bull, Lee Delano, *Gunmen Team A*. PG.

Dull assassination thriller based on the theory that John F. Kennedy's assassination was a conspiracy in order to prevent a virtual Kennedy political dynasty. *Executive Action* is more a history lecture than a true drama, and its most dramatic moments are contained in the documentary footage of Kennedy, Stevenson and others that is inserted throughout. The dramatizations themselves are bland, most of which consist of the conspirators sitting in a room plotting the assassination.

270 **The Exorcist** (1973) (AN, G) **** Warner Bros., 121 min. *Dir* William Friedkin (AN, G), *Scr* William Peter Blatty (A, G), based on his novel, *Cin* Owen Roizman (AN), *Ed* Norman Gay, Jordan Leondopoulos, Evan Lottman, Bud Smith (AN), *Des* Bill Malley (AN), *Mus* Jack Nitzsche, *Prod* William Peter Blatty, *Exec Prod* Noel Marshall.

Cast: Ellen Burstyn (AN), *Mrs. MacNeil*, Jason Miller (AN), *Father Karras*, Max Von Sydow, *Father Merrin*, Lee J. Cobb, *Lt. Kinderman*, Kitty Winn, *Sharon*, Linda Blair (AN, G), *Regan MacNeil*, Jack MacGowran, *Burke*, Rev. William O'Malley, *Father Dyer*, Vasiliki Maliaros, *Karras' Mother*, Titos Vandis, *Karras' Uncle*, Wallace Rooney, *Bishop*, Ron Faber, *Assistant Director*, Rev. T. Bermingham, *President of University*. R. $88,500,000.

Excellent horror thriller about a young girl (Linda Blair), who is possessed by a demon. After the failure of doctors to cure her, her mother (Ellen Burstyn) goes to a priest (Jason Miller) to exorcize the demon from the girl. William Friedkin pulled out all the stops in transferring William Peter Blatty's bizarre novel to the screen. *The Exorcist* features some of the most shocking special effects, which contribute to the film's extraordinary power, and made it one of the most controversial films in history.

271 **Exorcist II: The Heretic** (1977) ** Warner Bros., 117 min. *Dir* John Boorman, *Scr* William Goodhart, based on characters created by William Peter Blatty, *Cin* William A. Fraker, *Ed* Tom Priestley, *Des* Richard MacDonald, *Art* Jack Collis, *Cos* Robert de Mora, *Mus* Ennio Morricone, *Prod* John Boorman, Richard Lederer, *Assoc Prod* Charles Orme.

Cast: Linda Blair, *Regan*, Richard Burton, *Father Lamont*, Louise Fletcher, *Dr. Gene Tuskin*, Max von Sydow, *Father Merrin*, Kitty Winn, *Sharon*, Paul Henreid, *The Cardinal*, James Earl Jones, *Older Kokumo*, Ned Beatty, *Edwards*, Belinda Beatty, *Liz*, Rose Portillo, *Spanish Girl*, Barbara Cason, *Mr. Phalor*, Tiffany Kinney, *Deaf Girl*, Joey Green, *Young Kokumo*, Fiseha Dimetros, *Young Monk*, Ken Renard, *Abbot*, Hank Garrett, *Conductor*, Larry Goldman, *Accident Victim*, Bill Grant, *Taxi Driver*, Shane Butterworth, Joely Adams, *Tuskin Children*. R. $13,900,000. See *The Exorcist*.

272 **Eyes of Laura Mars** (1978) **** Columbia, 104 min. *Dir* Irvin Kershner, *Scr* John Carpenter, David Zelag Goodman, *Story* John Carpenter, *Cin* Victor J. Kemper, *Ed* Michael Kahn, *Des* Gene Callahan, *Art* Robert Gundlach, *Cos* Theoni V. Aldredge, *Mus* Artie Kane, *Song* "Prisoner," Karen Lawrence, John DeSautels, Sung by Barbra Streisand, *Prod* Jon Peters, *Exec Prod* Jack H. Harris, *Assoc Prod* Laura Ziskin.

Cast: Faye Dunaway, *Laura Mars*, Tommy Lee Jones, *John Neville*, Brad Dourif, *Tommy Ludlow*, Rene Auberjonois, *Donald Phelps*, Raul Julia, *Michael Reisler*, Frank Adonis, *Sal Volpe*, Lisa Taylor, *Michele*, Darlanne Fluegel, *Lulu*, Rose Gregorio, *Elaine Cassell*, Bill Boggs, *Himself*, Steve Marachuk, *Robert*, Meg Mundy, *Doris Spenser*, Marilyn Meyers, *Shelia Weissman*, Gary Bayer, Mitchell Edmonds, *Reporters*, Michael Tucker, *Bert*. R. $8,600,000.

Excellent occult thriller with Faye Dunaway as a controversial photographer of sex and violence, who has the ability to witness the brutal murders of her models and associates through the eyes of the killer. *Eyes of Laura Mars* is one of the most effective whodunits ever made and many of Irvin Kersher's scenes are absolutely stunning, particularly the climax in which the identity of the killer is revealed.

273 **F.I.S.T.** (1978) *** United Artists, 145 min. *Dir* Norman Jewison, *Scr* Joe Eszterhas, Sylvester Stallone, *Story* Joe Eszterhas, *Cin* Laszlo Kovacs, *Ed* Graeme Clifford, Tony Gibbs, *Des* Richard MacDonald, *Art* Angelo Graham, *Cos* Thalia Phillips, Tony Scarano, Anthea Sylbert, *Mus* Bill Conti, *Prod* Norman Jewison, *Exec Prod* Gene Corman.

Cast: Sylvester Stallone, *Johnny Kovak*, Rod Steiger, *Sen. Madison*, Peter Boyle, *Max Graham*, Melinda Dillon, *Anna Zerinkas*, David Huffman, *Abe Belkin*, Tony LoBianco, *Babe Milano*, Kevin Conway, *Vince Doyle*, Cassie Yates, *Molly*, Peter Donat, *Arthur St. Clarie*, Henry Wilcoxen, *Win Talbot*, John Lehne, *Gant*, Richard Herd, *Mike Monahan*, Elena Karam, *Mrs. Zerinkas*, Ken Kercheval, *Bernie Marr*, Tony Mockus, *Tom Higgens*, Brian Dennehy, *Frank Vasko*, James Karen, *Andrews*. PG. $9,500,000.

Interesting drama about an outspoken laborer who becomes a union organizer and eventually the head of the powerful union, F.I.S.T. (Federation of Inter-State Truckers). Sylvester Stallone is excellent as the Jimmy Hoffa-like union leader and *F.I.S.T.* is a good film up to a point. It tries too hard to be an epic, but its storyline is too weak and it contains too few ideas to achieve that status.

274 **FM** (1978) *** Universal, 110 min. *Dir* John A. Alonzo, *Scr* Ezra Sacks, *Cin* David Myers, *Ed* Jeff Gourson, *Des* Lawrence G. Paull, *Cos* Kent Warner, *Title Song* composed and performed by Steely Dan, *Prod* Rand Holston, *Co-Prod* Robert Larson.

Cast: Michael Brandon, *Jeff Dugan*, Eileen Brennan, *Mother*, Alex Karras, *Doc Holiday*, Cleavon Little, *Prince*, Martin Mull, *Eric Swan*, Cassie Yates, *Laura Coe*, Norman Lloyd, *Carl Billings*, Jay Fenichal, *Bobby Douglas*, James Keach, *Lt. Reach*, Joe Smith, *Albert Driscoll*, Tom Tarpey, *Regis Lamar*, Janet Brandt, *Alice*, Mary Torrey, *Cathy*, Roberta Wallach, *Shari Smith*, Terry Jastrow, *Michael J. Carlyle*, Cissy Wellman, *Maggie*, Robert Patten, *Jack Rapp*, Linda Ronstadt, Jimmy Buffet, Tom Petty, R.E.O Speedwagon. PG.

Well-done comedy-drama that centers on the trials and tribulations of a big city FM rock radio station and climaxes with the disc jockeys blockading themselves inside the station in protest of its pending commercialization. *FM* is similar to *Between the Lines*, but not in the same class, but it does have its moments, and the ensemble cast is excellent. This is the only film directed by cinematographer, John A. Alonzo.

275 **Family Plot** (1976) *** Universal, 120 min. *Dir* Alfred Hitchcock, *Scr* Ernest Lehman, based on novel *Rainbird Pattern* by Victor Canning, *Cin* Leonard J. South, *Ed* J. Terry Williams, *Des* Henry Bumstead, *Cos* Edith Head, *Mus* John Williams, *Prod* Alfred Hitchcock.

Cast: Barbara Harris, *Blanche*, Bruce Dern, *Lumley*, Karen Black, *Fran*, William Devane, *Adamson*, Ed Lauter, *Maloney*, Cathleen Nesbitt, *Julia Rainbird*, Katherine Helmond, *Mrs. Maloney*, Warren J. Kemmerling,

Grandson, Edith Atwater, *Mrs. Clay*, William Price, *Bishop*, Nicholas Colasanto, *Constantine*, Marge Redmond, *Vera Hannigan*, John Lehne, *Andy Bush*, Charles Tyner, *Wheeler*, Alexander Lockwood, *Parson*, Martin West, *Sanger*. PG. $7,540,000.

Disappointing final film from Alfred Hitchcock. *Family Plot* is more comedic than usual as a phoney fortune teller (Harris) and her taxi driver boyfriend (Dern) search for the heir to a family fortune, who happens to be a kidnapper (Devane). This is better than many films of its genre and Harris' performance is a standout, but one would have hoped for more from the master of suspense.

   276 **Farewell, My Lovely** (1975) ******** Avco Embassy, 97 min. *Dir* Dick Richards, *Scr* David Zelag Goodman, based on novel by Raymond Chandler, *Cin* John Alonzo, *Ed* Joel Cox, Walter Thompson, *Des* Dean Tavoularis, *Art* Angelo Graham, *Mus* David Shire, *Prod* Jerry Bruckheimer, George Pappas, *Exec Prod* Jerry Bick, Elliot Kastner.

   Cast: Robert Mitchum, *Philip Marlowe*, Charlotte Rampling, *Mrs. Velma Grayle*, John Ireland, *Nulty*, Sylvia Miles, *Mrs. Florian*, Jack O'Halloran, *Moose Malloy*, Anthony Zerbe, *Brunette*, Harry Dean Stanton, *Billy Rolfe*, Jim Thompson, *Mr. Grayle*, John O'Leary, *Marriott*, Kate Murtagh, *Amthor*, Walter McGinn, *Tommy Ray*, Jimmy Archer, *Georgie*, Joe Spinell, *Nick*, Sylvestor Stallone, *Kelly/Jonnie*, Burton Gilliam, *Cowboy*. R.

   Surprisingly good film version of Raymond Chandler novel, with Robert Mitchum perfect as the hard-boiled detective Philip Marlowe. *Farewell, My Lovely* sticks to the period of the 1940's, but enhances it with the permissiveness of the 1970's without destroying its gloomy atmospheric mood. The minor success of this film prompted a follow-up, a disastrous remake of *The Big Sleep*. All the elements that made the first such a success were completely ignored in the sequel. Mitchum nicely repeats his role as Marlowe, but nothing else seems to work, from its contemporary London setting to its poor script.

   277 **Fast Break** (1979) ****** Columbia, 97 min. *Dir* Jack Smight, *Scr* Sandor Stern, *Story* Marc Kaplan, *Cin* Charles Correll, *Ed* Frank J. Urioste, *Art* Norman Baron, *Mus* James di Pasquale, David Shire, *Prod* Stephen Friedman, *Exec Prod* Jerry Frankel, *Assoc Prod* Jerry Frankel, *Assoc Prod* Jack Grossberg.

   Cast: Gabriel Kaplan, *David Greene*, Harold Sylvester, *D.C.*, Michael Warren, *Preacher*, Bernard King, *Hustler*, Mavis Washington, *Swish*, Reb Brown, *Bull*, Bert Remsen, *Bo Winnegar*, Randee Heller, *Jan*, John Chappell, *Alton Gutkas*, Rhonda Bates, *Enid Cadwallader-Gutkas*, K. Callan, *Ms. Tidwell*, Marty Zagon, *Henry*, Richard Brestoff, *Howard*, Connie Sawyer, *Lottie*. PG.

   Fair comedy vehicle for Gabe Kaplan starring as a basketball coach who is hired to coach the misfit team of a small Nevada college, and Kaplan recruits his best players from the streets of New York City, his home town. *Fast Break* has its humorous moments and it makes the most of Kaplan's personality, but its plot is too predictable, with its obligatory big game, and it plays like a television film.

   278 **Fat City** (1972) ******** Columbia, 100 min. *Dir* John Huston, *Scr* Leonard Gardner, based on his novel, *Cin* Conrad Hall, *Ed* Marguerite

Booth, *Des* Richard Sylbert, *Cos* Dorothy Jeakins, *Mus* Marvin Hamlisch, *Prod* Ray Stark, *Assoc Prod* David Dworski.

Cast: Stacy Keach, *Tully,* Jeff Bridges, *Ernie,* Susan Tyrell (AN), *Oma,* Candy Clark, *Faye,* Nicholas Colasanto, *Ruben,* Art Aragon, *Babe,* Curtis Cokes, *Earl,* Sixto Rodriguez, *Lucero,* Billy Walker, *Wes,* Wayne Mahan, *Buford,* Ruben Navarro, *Fuentes.* PG.

Excellent drama about society's losers. Stacy Keach is superb as an over-the-hill boxer who attempts to make a comeback. *Fat City* centers on a boxer, but it is not a boxing film. Instead it is a sad, but not sentimental, character study focusing on his encounters with others who are down on their luck. There are also excellent supporting performances from Jeff Bridges and Susan Tyrell. This is one of John Huston's best films.

279 **Fiddler on the Roof** (1971) (AN, GMC) *** United Artists, 180 min. *Dir* Norman Jewison (AN), *Scr* Joseph Stein, based on his musical play, adapted from play *Tevye and His Daughters* by Sholom Aleichem, *Cin* Oswald Morris (A), *Ed* Antony Gibbs, Robert Lawrence, *Des* Robert Boyle (AN), *Art* Michael Stringer, *Cos* Joan Bridge, Elizabeth Haffenden, *Mus* Jerry Brock, *Lyrics* Sheldon Harnick, *Mus Adaptation.* John Williams (A), *Chor* Tom Abbott, based on Broadway choreoraphy by Jerome Robbins, *Prod* Norman Jewison, *Assoc Prod* Patrick Palmer.

Cast: Topol (AN, GMC), *Tevye,* Leonard Frey (AN) *Motel,* Paul Mann, *Lazar Wolf,* Michele Marsh, *Hodel,* Paul Michael Glaser, *Perchick,* Norma Crane, *Golde,* Molly Picon, *Yente,* Rosalind Harris, *Tzeitel,* Neva Small, *Chava,* Raymond Lovelock, *Fyedka,* Elaine Edwards, *Shprintze,* Candy Bonstein, *Bielke,* Tutte Lemkow, *The Fiddler,* Zvee Scooler, *Rabbi,* Shimen Ruskin, *Mordcha,* Louis Zorich, *Constable,* Alfie Scopp, *Avram,* Barry Dennen, *Medel,* Howard Goorney, *Nachum,* Vernon Dobtcheff, *Russian Official,* Stella Courtney, *Shandel,* Patience Collier, *Grandma Tzeitel,* Ruth Madoc, *Fruma Sarah.* G. $40,500,000.

Surprisingly good film adaptation of the successful Broadway musical. In one of his better directorial efforts Norman Jewison tightly controls this large scale musical and keeps it from sinking like other film versions of Broadway musicals. What is best though about *Fiddler on the Roof* is the wonderfully charismatic performance of Topal as Tevye, the Jewish milkman living in Russia.

280 **Fighting Mad** (1976) *** 20th Century–Fox, 90 min. *Dir* Jonathan Demme, *Scr* Jonathan Demme, *Cin* Michael Watkins, *Ed* Anthony Magro, *Mus* Bruce Langhorne, *Prod* Roger Corman, *Co-Prod* Evelyn Purcell.

Cast: Peter Fonda, *Tom,* Lynn Lowry, *Lorene,* John Doucette, *Jeff,* Philip Carey, *Pierce,* Scott Glenn, *Charlie,* Kathleen Miller, *Carolee,* Harry Northup, *Sheriff,* Ted Markland, *Hal,* Gino Franco, *Dylan,* Noble Willingham, *Senator.* R.

Above-average vengeance drama starring Peter Fonda as a man who returns to his Arkansas family farm and discovers it is to be taken over by a real estate development company for strip-mining purposes. Fonda refuses to let this happen and declares war on the company. This is a familiar story, but *Fighting Mad* rises above most due to Jonathan Demme's excellent direction.

281 Figures in a Landscape (1971) ** Britain, National General, 118 min.
Dir Joseph Losey, *Scr* Robert Shaw, based on novel by Barry England, *Cin* Henri Alekan, *Ed* Reginald Beck, *Art* Fernando Gonzalez, Ted Tester, *Cos* Susan Yelland, *Mus* Richard Rodney Bennett, *Prod* John Kohn, *Exec Prod* Sir William Piggott-Brown.

Cast: Robert Shaw, *MacConnachie*, Malcolm McDowell, *Ansell*, Henry Woolf, *Helicopter Pilot*, Christopher Malcolm, *Helicopter 1st Observer*, Pamela Brown, *The Widow*, Andrew Bradford, Warrick Sims, Roger Lloyd Pack, Robert East, Tariq Younus, *Soldiers*. PG.

Pretentious existential drama that follows two unknown fugitives (Robert Shaw, Malcolm McDowell), who are running from unknown pursuers through an unknown wasteland. This was intended to be some sort of allegory with several possible meanings, but with a complete lack of details *Figures in a Landscape* proves to be empty and meaningless. Joseph Losey only did this film as an assignment, and not even he could save it.

282 Final Chapter – Walking Tall (1977) * American International, 112 min.
Dir Jack Starrett, *Scr* Howard B. Kreitsek, Samuel A. Peeples, *Cin* Robert B. Hauser, *Ed* Housely Stevenson, *Art* Joe Altadonna, *Cos* Michael W. Hoffman, Chris Zamiara, *Mus* Walter Scharf, *Prod* Charles A. Pratt.

Cast: Bo Svenson, *Buford Pusser*, Margaret Blye, *Luan*, Forrest Tucker, *Grandpa Pusser*, Lurene Tuttle, *Grandma Pusser*, Morgan Woodward, *The Boss*, Libby Boone, *Secretary*, Leif Garrett, *Mike Pusser*, Dawn Lyn, *Dwana Pusser*, Bruce Glover, *Grady Coker*, Taylor Lacher, *Martin*, Sandy McPeak, *Lloyd*, Logan Ramsey, *John*, Robert Phillips, *Johnny*, Clay Tanner, *O.Q.*, David Adams, *Robbie*, Vance Davis, *Aaron*, H.B. Haggerty, *Bulo*, John Malloy, *Producer*. R. $6,350,000. See *Walking Tall*.

283 Fingers (1978) *** Brut, 90 min. *Dir* James Toback, *Scr* James Toback, *Cin* Mike Chapman, *Ed* Robert Lawrence, *Des* Gene Rudolf, *Cos* Albert Wolsky, *Prod* George Barrie.

Cast: Harvey Keitel, *Jimmy*, Tisa Farrow, *Carol*, Jim Brown, *Deems*, Michael V. Gazzo, *Ben*, Marian Seldes, *Mother*, Carole Francis, *Christa*, Georgette Muir, *Anita*, Danny Aiello, *Butch*, Dominick Chianese, *Arthur*, Anthony Siroco, *Riccamonza*, Tanya Roberts, *Julie*, Ed Marinaro, *Gino*, Zack Norman, *Cop*, Murray Mosten, *Dr. Fry*, Jane Elder, *Esther*, Lenny Montana, *Luchino*, Frank Pesche, *Raymond*. R.

Strange thriller about a schizophrenic young man (Harvey Keitel), who is torn between his Mafia family background and his desires to be a classical pianist. Keitel's character is an extremely confused individual, as is the film itself at times. *Fingers* is an interesting directorial debut for James Toback, who does not seem to know the meaning of subtlety, as he takes everything to extremes.

284 Fire Sale (1977) ** 20th Century–Fox, 88 min. *Dir* Alan Arkin, *Scr* Robert Klane, based on his novel, *Cin* Ralph Woolsey, *Ed* Richard Halsey, *Des* James H. Spencer, *Mus* Dave Grusin, *Prod* Marvin Worth.

Cast: Alan Arkin, *Ezra*, Rob Reiner, *Russel*, Vincent Gardenia, *Benny*, Anjanette Comer, *Marion*, Kay Medford, *Ruth*, Barbara Dana, *Virginia*, Sid Caesar, *Zabbar*, Alex Rocco, *Al*, Byron Stewart, *Captain*, Oliver Clark, *Blossom*, Richard Libertini, MacIntyre Dixon, *Painters*, Augusta Dabney, *Mrs.*

Cooper, Don Keefer, *Banker*, Bill Henderson, *Psychiatrist*, John Horn, *Louis*, Sally K. Marr, *Jackie*, Speedy Zapata, *Janitor*, Kimelle Anderson, *Nurse*, Selma Archerd, *Ellie*, Bob Leslie, *Van Driver*, John Hudkins, *Wheelchair Patient*, Viola Harris, *Helen*, Marvin Worth, *Milton*. PG.

Ridiculous, but sometimes funny, black comedy about a crazy department store owner, who plans to burn down his failing store. This is a total hit and miss comedy with a cast of veteran comedy actors, sometimes straining too hard for laughs. *Fire Sale* was apparently an attempt by Alan Arkin to top his earlier directorial effort *Little Murders*. *Fire Sale* is nearly as strange as *Little Murders*, but it lacks the satirically perceptive script that makes *Little Murders* a minor classic.

285 **First Love** (1977) ** Paramount, 91 min. *Dir* Joan Darling, *Scr* David Freeman, Jane Stanton Hitchcock, based on story *Sentimental Education* by Harold Brodkey, *Cin* Bobby Byrne, *Ed* Frank Morriss, *Des* Robert Luthardt, *Prod* David Foster, Lawrence Turman.

Cast: William Katt, *Elgin Smith*, Susan Dey, *Caroline*, John Heard, *David*, Beverly D'Angelo, *Shelley*, Robert Loggia, *John March*, Tom Lacy, *Prod. Oxtan*, Swoosie Kurtz, *Marsha*, June Barrett, *Felicia*, Patrick O'Hara, *Zookeeper*, Judy Kerr, *Secretary*, Jenny Hill, *Girl in Bar*, Virginia Leith, *Mrs. March*, Billy Beck, *Cafeteria Boss*. R.

Dull love story involving two students (William Katt, Susan Dey) at an unnamed college campus. *First Love* purports to be an honest portrayel of young love, with explicit love scenes and frank dialogue, but this is all on the surface. Underneath this is just another sentimental soap opera, which introduces an older man to complicate matters. This was actress Joan Darling's directorial debut.

286 **The Fish That Saved Pittsburgh** (1979) * United Artists, 104 min. *Dir* Gilbert Moses, *Scr* Jaison Starkes, Edmond Stevens, *Story* David Dashev, Gary Stromberg, *Cin* Frank Stanley, *Ed* Peter Zinner, *Art* Herbert Spencer Deverill, *Cos* Patricia Norris, *Mus* Thom Bell, *Chor* Debra Allen, *Prod* David Dashev, Gary Stromberg.

Cast: Julius Erving, *Moses Guthrie*, Jonathan Winters, *H.S. and Harvey Tilson*, Meadowlark Lemon, *Rev. Grady Jackson*, Jack Kehoe, *Setshot*, Margaret Avery, *Toby Millman*, James Bond III, *Tyrone Millman*, Michael V. Gazzo, *Harry the Trainer*, Peter Isackson, *Driftwood*, Nicholas Pryor, *George Bronkington*, M. Emmet Walsh, *Wally Cantrell*, Stockard Channing, *Mona Mondieu*, Flip Wilson, *Coach "Jock" Delaney*, Marvin Albert, *Himself*, George Von Benko, *P.A. Announcer*, Debra Allen, *Ola*, Damien Austin, *Man Ordering*, Alfred Beard, Jr., *Himself*, Dee Dee Bridgewater, *Brandy*, Alix Elias, *Michelle*. PG.

Silly basketball comedy. The skimpy plot involves a lousy team from Pittsburgh, that loses so badly the team eventually walks out. The water boy comes up with a brainstorm of recruiting only players born under the sign of Pisces, which predictably leads them to victory. Most of the film consists of filler, including unexciting basketball games and disco music.

287 **Five Days from Home** (1978) ** Universal, 108 min. *Dir* George Peppard, *Scr* William Moore, *Cin* Harvey Genkins, *Ed* Samuel E. Beetley, *Mus* Bill Conti, *Prod* George Peppard.

Cast: George Peppard, *T.M. Pryor*, Neville Brand, *Insp. Markley*, Sherry Boucher, *Wanda Dulac*, Victor Campos, *Jose Stover*, Robert Donner, *Baldwin*, Ronnie Claire Edwards, *Marian*, Jessie Lee Fulton, *Mrs. Peabody*, William Larsen, *J.J. Bester*, Robert Magruder, *The Colonel*, Savannah Smith, *Georie Haskin*, Don Wyse, *Howie*, Ralph Story, *T.V. Newsman*. PG.

Average thriller starring George Peppard as a convict; he is an ex-cop who killed his wife's lover; with only six days left on his prison term who excapes to see his sick son. Most of the film covers his journey, in which he is pursued by villainous Neville Brand, and introduces an assortment of characters in attempt to add some interest to a somewhat dull script.

288 Five Easy Pieces (1970) (AN, NY) ***** Columbia, 96 min. *Dir* Bob Rafelson (NY), *Scr* Adrien Joyce, *Story* Adrien Joyce, Bob Rafelson (AN), *Cin* Laszlo Kovacs, *Ed* Christopher Holmes, Gerald Shepard, *Prod* Bob Rafelson, Richard Wechsler, *Exec Prod* Bert Schneider.

Cast: Jack Nicholson (AN), *Robert Eroica Dupea*, Karen Black (AN, NY, NB, G), *Rayette Dipesto*, Billy "Green" Bush, *Elton*, Fannie Flagg, *Stoney*, Salley Struthers, *Betty*, Marlena MacGuire, *Twinty*, Richard Stahl, *Recording Engineer*, Lois Smith (NS), *Partita Dupea*, Helena Kallianiotes, *Palm Apodaca*, Toni Basil, *Terry Grouse*, Lorna Thayer, *Waitress*, Susan Anspach, *Catherine Van Ost*, Ralph Waite, *Carl Fidelio Dupea*, William Challee, *Nicholas Dupea*, John Ryan, *Spicer*, Irene Dailey, *Samia Glavia*. R. $8,900,000.

Excellent character study starring Jack Nicholson as an outcast from his bourgeois family, who has given up a promising career in music to work in an oil field. His father becomes ill and Nicholson goes home to visit his family, bringing along his brainless girlfriend (Karen Black). *Five Easy Pieces* is one of the finest films ever made to explore the theme of rebellion against the system, and it does this with subtlety, rather than resorting to obligatory campus protests.

289 The Food of the Gods (1976) * American International, 88 min. *Dir* Bert I. Gordon, *Scr* Bert I. Gordon, based on novel by H.G. Wells, *Cin* Reginald Morris, *Ed* Corky Ehlers, *Art* Graeme Murray, *Mus* Elliot Kaplan, *Prod* Bert I. Gordon, *Exec Prod* Samuel Z. Arkoff.

Cast: Marjoe Gortner, *Morgan*, Pamela Franklin, *Lorna*, Ralph Meeker, *Bensington*, Ida Lupino, *Mrs. Skinner*, John Cypher, *Brian*, Belinda Balaski, *Rita*, Tom Stovall, *Tom*, John McLiam, *Mr. Skinner*. PG. $4,000,000.

Dull science-fiction thriller about giant insects and animals. Marjoe Gortner and John Cypher venture to a remote island, and stumble onto a home owned by John McLiam, who has discovered the "food of the gods," a gooey substance that causes amazing growth. The poor script is matched by the unrealistic special effects. *The Food of the Gods* is reminiscent of the equally poor *Empire of the Ants*.

290 For Pete's Sake (1974) ** Columbia, 90 min. *Dir* Peter Yates, *Scr* Maurice Richlin, Stanley Shapiro, *Cin* Laszlo Kovacs, *Ed* Frank Keller, *Art* Gene Callahan, *Cos* Frank Thompson, *Co-Prod* Martin Erlichman, Stanley Shapiro, *Exec Prod* Phil Feldman.

Cast: Barbra Streisand, *Henry*, Michael Sarrazin, *Peter*, Estelle Parsons, *Helen*, William Redfield, *Fred*, Molly Picon, *Mrs. Cherry*, Louis Zorich, *Nick*, Vivian Bonnell, *Loretta*, Richard Ward, *Bernie*, Heywood Hale Brown, *Judge*

Hiller, Joe Maher, *Mr. Coates*, Vincent Schiavelli, *Check-out Man*, Fred Stuthman, *Loan Officer*, Ed Bakey, *Angelo*, Peter Mamakos, *Dominic*, Norman Marshall, *First Worker*, Joseph Hardy, *Second Cop*, Wil Albert, *Cop as Woman*, Jack Hollander, *Loanshark*, Bill McKinney, *Rocky*. PG. $11,000,000.

Stupid screwball comedy about an extravagant wife of a poor cab driver who gets into debt with the Mafia. *For Pete's Sake* is an obvious attempt to capitalize on the success of *What's Up Doc*, but despite some funny moments, it lacks the wit of its inspiration. Streisand dominates as the fast talking, scatterbrained woman, a character she has perfected, but Sarrizan is not a strong enough foil to make this an interesting romantic team.

291 **For the Love of Benji** (1977) ******* Mulberry Square Productions, 85 min. *Dir* Joe Camp, *Scr* Joe Camp, *Story* Joe Camp, Ben Vaughn, *Cin* Don Reddy, *Ed* Leon Smith, *Des* Harland Wright, *Art* Jack Bennett, *Mus* Euel Box, *Prod* Ben Vaughn, *Exec Prod* Joe Camp.

Cast: Patsy Garrett, *Mary*, Cynthia Smith, *Cindy*, Allen Fiuzat, *Paul*, Ed Nelson, *Chandler*, Art Vasil, *Stellos*, Peter Bowles, *Ronald*, Bridget Armstrong, *Elizabeth*, Mihalis Lambrinos, *Baggage Room Man*. G. $5,000,000. See *Benji*.

292 **The Forbin Project** (1970) ****** Universal, 100 min. *Dir* Joseph Sargent, *Scr* James Bridges, based on novel *Colossus* by D.F. Jones, *Cin* Gene Polito, *Ed* Folmar Blangsted, *Art* Alexander Golitzen, *Mus* Michel Colombier, *Sp* Albert Whitlock, *Prod* Stanley Chase.

Cast: Eric Braeden, *Forbin*, Susan Clark, *Cleo*, Gordon Pinsent, *President*, William Schallert, *Grauber*, Leonid Rostoff, *First Chairman*, George Stanford Brown, *Fisher*, Willard Sage, *Blake*, Alex Rodine, *Kuprin*, Martin Brooks, *Johnson*, Marion Ross, *Angela*, Dolph Sweet, *Missile Commander*, Byron Morrow, *Secretary of State*, Lew Brown, *Peterson*, Sid McCoy, *Secretary of Defense*, Rom Basham, *Harrison*, Robert Cornthwaite, *First Scientist*, James Hong, *Second Scientist*, Sergei Tschernisch, *Translator*. PG.

Another sceince-fiction drama inspired by *2001: A Space Odyssey*. A scientist (Eric Braeden) builds a powerful computer, Colossus, designed to protect the Western world. Colossus discovers a Soviet counterpart, Guardian, and together they take over the world. This is nothing exceptional, with few ideas beyond the interesting premise, and it plays like a television film. Other title, *Colossus the Forbin Project*.

293 **A Force of One** (1979) ***** American Cinema, 90 min. *Dir* Paul Aaron, *Scr* Ernest Tidyman, *Story* Pat Johnson, Ernest Tidyman, *Cin* Roger Shearman, *Ed* Bert Lovitt, *Art* Norman Baron, *Mus* Dick Halligan, *Prod* Alan Belkin, *Exec Prod* Michael F. Leone, *Assoc Prod* Jonathon Sanger.

Cast: Chuck Norris, *Matt*, Jennifer O'Neill, *Mandy Rust*, Clu Gulager, *Dunne*, Ron O'Neal, *Rollins*, James Whitmore, Jr., *Moskowitz*, Clint Ritchie, *Melrose*, Pepe Serna, *Orlando*, Ray Vitte, *Newton*, Taylor Lacher, *Bishop*, Chu Chu Malave, *Pimp*, Kevin Geer, *Johnson*, Eugene Butler, *Murphy*, James Hall, *Moss*, Charles Cyphers, *Dr. Eppis*, Bill Wallace, *Jerry*, Eric Laneuville, *Charlie*. PG. $9,980,000. See *Good Guys Wear Black*.

294 **Force 10 from Naverone** (1978) ******* Britain, American International, 118 min. *Dir* Guy Hamilton, *Scr* Robin Chapman, *Story* Carl Foreman, based on novel by Alistair MacLean, *Cin* Chris Challis, *Ed* Roy Poulton, *Des* Geoffrey Drake, *Cos* Emma Porteous, *Mus* Ron Goodwin, *Prod* Oliver A. Unger, *Co-Prod* Joan R. Sloan, Anthony B. Unger, *Assoc Prod* David Orton.

Cast: Robert Shaw, *Mallory*, Harrison Ford, *Barnsby*, Edward Fox, *Miller*, Barbara Bach, *Maritza*, Franco Nero, *Lescovar*, Carl Weathers, *Weaver*, Richard Kiel, *Drazac*, Angus MacInnes, *Reynolds*, Michael Byrne, *Schroeder*, Alan Badel, *Petrovich*, Christopher Malcolm, *Rogers*, Nick Ellsworth, *Salvone*, Jonathan Blake, *Oberstein*, Michael Sheard, *Bauer*. PG.

Not bad sequel to *The Guns of Naverone*. A group of WWII allied commandos is sent to Yugoslavia to blow up a bridge that is important to the Germans. *Force 10 from Naverone* has an abundance of action, intrigue and plot twists to keep it moving along briskly, and the acting is above average for this type of film, particularly Edward Fox as a demolitions expert.

295 The Fortune (1975) ***** Columbia, 88 min. *Dir* Mike Nichols, *Scr* Adrien Joyce (pseudonym for Carol Eastman), *Cin* John A. Alonzo, *Ed* Stu Linder, *Des* Richard Sylbert, *Art* W. Stewart Campbell, *Mus* David Shire, *Prod* Don Devlin, Mike Nichols, *Exec Prod* Hank Moonjean.

Cast: Jack Nicholson, *Oscar*, Warren Beatty, *Nicky*, Stockard Channing, *Freddie*, Florence Stanley, *Landlady*, Richard B. Shull, *Chief Detective*, Tom Newman, *John the Barber*, John Fiedler, *Photographer*. PG.

Superb period slapstick comedy about two bumbling con men who attempt to cheat a rich heiress. Jack Nicholson and Warren Beatty are perfect as the Laurel & Hardy type pair; generally a difficult transition for dramatic actors to make. Their performances, in conjunction with director Mike Nichols' faultless comic timing, make *The Fortune* one of the funniest and most flawless comedies ever made, but few filmgoers and critics were impressed.

296 40 Carats (1973) ** Columbia, 108 min. *Dir* Milton Katselas, *Scr* Leonard Gershe, based on Jay Allen's adaptation of play by Barillet and Gredy, *Cin* Charles B. Lang, *Ed* David Blewitt, *Des* Robert Clatworthy, *Cos* Jean Louis, *Mus* Michael Legrand, *Prod* M.J. Frankovich.

Cast: Liv Ullman, *Ann Stanley*, Edward Albert, *Peter Latham*, Gene Kelly, *Billy Boylan*, Binnie Barnes, *Maud Ericson*, Deborah Raffin, *Trina Stanley*, Billy "Green" Bush, *J.D. Rogers*, Nancy Walker, *Mrs. Margolin*, Don Porter, *Mr. Latham*, Rosemary Murphy, *Mrs. Latham*, Natalie Schafer, *Mrs. Adams*, Sam Chew, Jr., *Arthur Forbes*, Claudia Jennings, *Gabriella*, Brooke Palance, *Polly*. PG.

Fair film version of Broadway play about a 40 year old woman who falls in love with a 20 year old man while vacationing in Greece. *40 Carats* is a light and pleasant comedy, if one can accept Liv Ullman and Edward Albert in the leads; neither look the age they are supposed to be. It is also worth watching for the supporting performances by Binnie Barnes, Gene Kelly and Billy "Green" Bush.

297 Foul Play (1978) *** Paramount, 116 min. *Dir* Colin Higgins, *Scr* Colin Higgins, *Cin* David M. Walsh, *Ed* Pembroke Herring, *Des* Alfred Sweeney, *Mus* Charles Fox, *Song*, "Ready to Take Chance Again," *Mus* Charles Fox (AN), *Lyrics* Norman Gimbel (AN), *Prod* Edward K. Milkis, Thomas J. Miller, *Assoc Prod* Peter V. Herald.

Cast: Goldie Hawn, *Gloria*, Chevy Chase, *Tony*, Burgess Meredith, *Hennessey*, Rachel Roberts, *Gerda*, Eugene Roche, *Archbishop Thorncrest*, Dudley Moore, *Stanley Tibbets*, Marilyn Sokol, *Stella*, Brian Dennehey,

Fergie, Marc Lawrence, *Stilskin*, Chuck McCann, *Theatre Manager*, Billy Barty, *MacKuen*, Don Calfa, *Scarface*, Bruce Solomon, *Scott*, Cooper Huckabee, *Sandy*, Pat Ast, *Mrs. Venus*, Frances Bay, *Mrs. Russel*. PG. $27,500,000.

Odd, but enjoyable comedy that is the first screen teaming of Chevy Chase and Goldie Hawn. Hawn witnesses a murder and is subsequently followed by the killers, but no one will believe her, until Chevy Chase, as a klutzy detective, comes to her rescue. *Foul Play* becomes complicated, involving a plot to assassinate the Pope, but what really matters is the wonderful chemistry between Chase and Hawn.

298 The Four Musketeers (1975) ***** 20th Century–Fox, 108 min. *Dir* Richard Lester, *Scr* George MacDonald Fraser, based on novel *The Three Musketeers* by Alexander Dumas, *Cin* David Watkin, *Ed* John Victor Smith, *Des* Brian Eatwell, *Cos* Yvonne Blake, Ron Talsky (AN), *Mus* Lalo Schifrin, *Prod* Alexander Salkind, *Exec Prod* Ilya Salkind.

Cast: Michael York, *D'Artagnan*, Oliver Reed, *Athos*, Richard Chamberlain, *Aramis*, Frank Finlay, *Porthos*, Raquel Welch, *Constance*, Christopher Lee, *Rochefort*, Faye Dunaway, *Milady*, Jean-Pierre Cassel, *Louis XIII*, Geraldine Chaplin, *Queen Anne*, Simon Ward, *Lord Buckingham*, Charlton Heston, *Cardinal Richelieu*, Roy Kinnear, *Planchet*, Nicole Calfan, *Kitty*. PG. $8,765,000. See *The Three Musketeers*.

299 Framed (1975) *** Paramount, 106 min. *Dir* Phil Karlson, *Scr* Mort Briskin, based on novel by Mike Misenheimer, Art Powers, *Cin* Jack A. Marta, *Ed* Harry Gerstad, *Des* Stan Jolley, *Cos* Eric Seelig, *Mus* Pat Williams, *Prod* Mort and Joel Briskin.

Cast: Joe Don Baker, *Ron*, Conny Van Dyke, *Susan*, Gabriel Dell, *Vince*, John Marley, *Sal*, Brock Peters, *Sam*, John Larch, *Bundy*, Warren Kemmerling, *Morello*, Paul Mantee, *Frank*, Walter Brooke, *Senator*, Joshua Bryant, *Andrew*, Hunter Von Leer, *Dewey*, Les Lannom, *Gary*, H.B. Haggerty, *Bickford*, Hoke Howell, *Decker*, Lawrence Montaigne, *Deputy Allison*, Red West, *Mallory*, Brenton Banks, *Jeremiah*, Al Hager, *Emmett*, Ken Lester, *Big Jim*, Henry O. Arnold, *Lenny*, Gary Gober, *Kenny* Lloyd Tatum, *Deputy Wilson*, Roy Jenson, *Haskins*. R.

Standard vengeance crime thriller starring Joe Don Baker as a professional gambler, who is framed by some corrupt policeman and sent to prison. Upon his release he sets out after those responsible. The plotline bears a slight resemblance to *Walking Tall* and it is no coincidence that *Framed* has the same star and director. The film is nothing out of the ordinary, but it is well-handled.

300 Fraternity Row (1977) *** Paramount, 101 min. *Dir* Thomas J. Tobin, *Scr* Charles Gary Allison, *Cin* Peter Gibbons, *Ed* Eugene A. Fournier, *Art* James Sbardellati, *Cos* Richard A. Davis, Beverly Ihnen, *Mus* Michael Corner, John Phillips Hutton, Don McLean, Mathew Roe, *Prod* Charles Gary Allison, *Assoc Prod* Thomas W. Joechim, Thomas W. Pope.

Cast: Peter Fox, *Rodger Carter*, Gregory Harrison, *Zac Sterling*, Scott Newman, *Chunk Cherry*, Nancy Morgan, *Jennifer Harris*, Wendy Phillips, *Betty Ann Martin*, Robert Emhardt, *Brother Bob Abernathy*, Robert Matthews, *Lloyd Pope*, Bernard R. Kantor, *Professor*, Cliff Robertson, *Narrator*. PG.

Serious study of college life at an Eastern university in the early 1950's. *Fraternity Row* has its light moments, but it does not compromise in its indictment of fraternities and their prejudices. Its main target is the cruel and sometimes tragic fraternity initiations, known as hazing. This is no *Animal House*. The performances of the young lesser known cast are excellent, particularly Scott Newman, Paul Newman's son, who died not long after the film's release.

301 **Freaky Friday** (1976) *** Buena Vista, 95 min. *Dir* Gary Nelson, *Scr* Mary Rodgers, based on her novel, *Cin* Charles F. Wheeler, *Ed* Cotton Warburton, *Art* John B. Mansbridge, Jack Senter, *Cos* Chuck Keehne, Emily Sundby, *Mus* Johnny Mandel, *Song* "I'd Like to Be You for a Day," Al Kasha, Joel Hirschhorn, *Prod* Ron Miller, A Walt Disney Production.

Cast: Barbara Harris, *Ellen Andrews,* Jodie Foster, *Annabel Andrews,* John Astin, *Bill Andrews,* Patsy Kelly, *Mrs. Schmauss,* Ricki Schreck, *Virginia,* Dick Van Patten, *Harold Jennings,* Sorrell Booke, *Mr. Dilk,* Alan Oppenheimer, *Mr. Joffert,* Kaye Ballard, *Coach Betsy,* Ruth Buzzi, *Opposing Coach,* Marc McClure, *Boris Harris,* Marie Windsor, *Mrs. Murphy,* Sparky Marcus, *Ben Andrews,* Ceil Cabot, *Miss McGuirk,* Brooke Mills, *Mrs. Gibbons,* Karen Smith, *Mary Kay Gilbert,* Marvin Kaplan, *Carpet Cleaner,* Al Molinaro, *Drapery Man,* Iris Adrian, *Bus Passenger,* Barbara Walden, *Mrs. Benson.* G. 11,500,000.

Above average Disney fantasy comedy about personality transference between a mother and daughter. A mother (Barbara Harris) and her daughter (Jodie Foster) become envious of each other and secretly wish they could trade places, and magically they do. What makes *Freaky Friday* most enjoyable is its unintentional suggestiveness, which has Barbara Harris chasing after her daughter's teenage boyfriend. Even so *Freaky Friday* is humorous on the level with which it was intended.

302 **Freebie and the Bean** (1974) **** Warner Bros., 112 min. *Dir* Richard Rush, *Scr* Robert Kaufman, *Story* Floyd Mutrux, *Cin* Laszlo Kovacs, *Ed* Michael McLean, Frederic Steinkamp, *Art* Hilyard Brown, *Mus* Dominic Frontiere, *Prod* Richard Rush, *Exec Prod* Floyd Mutrux.

Cast: James Caan, *Freebie,* Alan Arkin, *Bean,* Loretta Swit, *Meyers' Wife,* Jack Kruschen, *Red Meyers,* Mike Kellin, *Lt. Rosen,* Linda Marsh, *Freebie's Girl,* Paul Koslo, *Whitey,* John Garwood, *Chauffeur,* Alex Rocco, *D.A.,* Valerie Harper, *Bean's Wife.* R. $13,500,000.

Outlandish black slapstick comedy about two unorthodox policemen who will stop at absolutely nothing, including the near destruction of San Francisco, to prove the guilt of a local gangster. The humor is cruel, tasteless and shocking, but somehow it all works. Richard Rush keeps *Freebie and the Bean* moving at a breakneck pace and there is never a dull moment. This may not be for all tastes, but it is among the best of its type.

303 **The French Connection** (1971) (A, G) ***** 20th Century–Fox, 104 min. *Dir* William Friedkin (A, G, D), *Scr* Ernest Tidyman (A, W), based on novel by Robin Moore, *Cin* Owen Roizman (AN), *Ed* Jerry Greenberg (A), *Mus* Don Ellis, *Prod* Philip D'Antoni, *Exec Prod* G. David Shine.

Cast: Gene Hackman (A, NY, NB, G, BFA), *Jimmy "Popeye" Doyle,* Fernando Rey, *Alain Charnier,* Roy Scheider (AN), *Buddy "Cloudy" Russo,* Tony

LoBianco, *Sal Boca*, Marcel Bozzuffi, *Pierre Nicoli*, Frederic De Pasquale, *Devereaux*, Bill Hickman, *Mulderig*, Ann Rebbot, *Marie Charnier*, Harold Gary, *Weinstock*, Arlene Farber, *Angie Boca*, Eddie Egan, *Simonson*, Andre Ernotte, *La Valle*, Sonny Grosso, *Klein*, Pat McDermott, *Chemist*, Alan Weeks, *Drug Pusher*, The Three Degrees, *Themselves*. R. $26,315,000.

Exciting fictionalized account of the largest drug arrest up to that time in the United States. *The French Connection* literally explodes with action, due to the technical wizardry of its director, William Friedkin. The pace is so incredibly fast that one almost misses a few unexplained plot details, which do not seem to matter, anyway. The film's highlight is the dizzying chase sequence that served as model for such scenes in dozens of later films. Gene Hackman gives a brilliant performance as the slightly brutal and obsessive police detective Popeye Doyle, based on real life policeman Eddie Egan. The sequel continues Doyle's pursuit of Charnier the drug dealer, to France. John Frankenheimer emphasizes character over action in *The French Connection II*. This was a noble attempt not to copy the original, but it just does not quite pay off, although, Hackman actually surpasses his earlier portrayel of Doyle.

304 **French Connection II** (1975) *** 20th Century–Fox, 119 min. *Dir* John Frankenheimer, *Scr* Lauri Dillon, Robert Dillon, Alexander Jacobs, *Story* Lauri Dillon, Robert Dillon, inspired by *The French Connection*, *Cin* Claude Renoir, *Ed* Tom Rolf, *Des* Jacques Saulnier, *Art* Georges Glon, Gerard Viard, *Cos* Jacques Fonteray, *Mus* Don Ellis, *Prod* Robert L. Rosen.

Cast: Gene Hackman, *Popeye Doyle*, Fernando Rey, *Charnier*, Bernard Fresson, *Barthelemy*, Jean-Pierre Castaldi, *Raoul Diron*, Charles Millot, *Miletto*, Cathleen Nesbitt, *Old Lady*, Pierre Collet, *Old Pro*, Alexandre Fabre, *Young Tail*, Philippe Leotard, *Jacques*, Jacques Dynam, *Inspector Genevoix*, Raoul Delfosse, *Dutch Captain*, Patrick Florsheim, *Manfredi*. R. $5,620,000. See *The French Connection*.

305 **Frenzy** (1972) ***** Britain, Universal, 116 min. *Dir* Alfred Hitchcock, *Scr* Anthony Shaffer, based on novel *Goodbye Piccadilly, Farewell Leicester Square* by Arthur LaBern, *Cin* Gil Taylor, *Ed* John Jympson, *Des* Sydney Cain, *Art* Robert Laing, *Mus* Ron Goodwin, *Prod* Alfred Hitchcock, *Assoc Prod* William Hill.

Cast: Jon Finch, *Richard Blaney*, Barry Foster, *Robert Rusk*, Barbara Leigh-Hunt, *Brenda Blaney*, Anna Massey, *Babs Milligan*, Alec McCowen, *Chief Inspector Oxford*, Vivian Merchant, *Mrs. Oxford*, Billie Whitelaw, *Hetty Porter*, Clive Swift, *Johnny Porter*, Bernard Cribbins, *Felix Forsythe*, Michael Bates, *Sgt. Spearman*. R. $6,500,000.

Superb murder thriller about an innocent man accused of murder. After some dismal films Alfred Hitchcock made an extraordinary comeback with this, one of this finest films. *Frenzy* contains all the familiar elements of Hitchcock's style that he has perfected over the years; well-paced suspense, black humor, and breathtaking tracking shots. The performances stand out more than in most of his films, particularly Barry Foster, who is the most interesting Hitchcock villain since Robert Walker in *Strangers on a Train*.

306 **The Friends of Eddie Coyle** (1973) *** Paramount, 102 min. *Dir* Peter Yates, *Scr* Paul Manash, based on novel by George V. Higgens, *Cin* Victor J. Kemper, *Ed* Patricia Lewis Jaffe, *Des* Gene Callahan, *Mus* Dave Grusin, *Prod* Paul Manash.

Cast: Robert Mitchum, *Eddie Coyle*, Peter Boyle, *Dillon*, Richard Jordan, *Foley*, Steven Keats, *Jackie Brown*, Alex Rocco, *Scalise*, Joe Santos, *Artie Van*, Mitchell Ryan, *Waters*, Helena Carroll, *Coyle's Wife*, Peter MacLean, Kevin O'Morrison, *Bank Managers*, Carolyn Pickman, *Nancy*, Marvin Lichterman, *Vernon*, James Tolkan, *Contact Man*, Matthew Cowles, *Pete*, Margaret Ladd, *Andrea*, Jane House, *Wanda*, Michael McCleery, *The Kid*. R.

Grimly realistic crime film about cops and mobsters in contemporary Boston. Unlike most films of its genre *The Friends of Eddie Coyle* is more of a character study, that focuses on the people who populate this underworld, than an action film. This is a noble effort, but it does not completely pay off, as a little action might have given the film more balance; even *The Godfather* had a considerable amount of action; because it does grow a bit tedious.

307 **The Frisco Kid** (1979) *** Warner Bros., 122 min. *Dir* Robert Aldrich, *Scr* Michael Elias, Frank Shaw, *Cin* Robert B. Hauser, *Ed* Jack Horger, Irving Rosenblum, Maury Winetrobe, *Des* Terence Marsh, *Mus* Frank DeVol, *Prod* Mace Newfeld, *Exec Prod* Howard W. Koch, Jr.

Cast: Gene Wilder, *Avram*, Harrison Ford, *Tommy*, Ramon Bieri, *Mr. Jones*, Val Bisoglio, *Chief Gray Cloud*, George Ralph DiCenzo, *Darryl Diggs*, Leo Fuchs, *Chief Rabbi*, Penny Peyser, *Rosalie*, William Smith, *Matt Diggs*, Jack Somack, *Samuel Bender*, Beege Barkett, *Sarah Mindl*, Shay Duffin, *O'Leary*. PG. $5,200,000.

Unusual comedy-drama set in the old West. A Polish rabbi (Gene Wilder) on his way to San Francisco to take over a congregation travels on his own through the west. Along the way he befriends an outlaw (Harrison Ford). This offbeat idea could have been the subject for a good film, but unfortunately *The Frisco Kid* runs out of steam too quickly.

308 **From Noon till Three** (1976) *** United Artists, 98 min. *Dir* Frank D. Gilroy, *Scr* Frank D. Gilroy, based on his novel, *Cin* Lucien Ballard, *Ed* Maury Winetrobe, *Des* Robert Clatworthy, *Art* Dick Lawrence, *Cos* Moss Mabry, *Mus* Elmer Bernstein, *Prod* M.J. Frankovich, William Self.

Cast: Charles Bronson, *Graham Dorsey*, Jill Ireland, *Amanda Starbuck*, Douglas V. Fowley, *Buck Bowers*, Stan Haze, *Ape*, Damon Douglas, *Roy*, Hector Morales, *Mexican*, Bert Williams, *Sheriff*, William Lanteau, *Rev. Cabot*, Betty Cole, *Edna*, Davis Roberts, *Sam*, Fred Franklyn, *Postmaster Hall*, Sonny Jones, *Dr. Finger*, Hoke Howell, *Deke*, Howard Brunner, *Mr. Foster*. PG.

Offbeat western comedy about the growth of American myths and legends. Charles Bronson stars as a misfit outlaw, who hides out in the mansion of a rich widow (Jill Ireland). They have a short affair, as the title indicates, and this becomes the basis of an exaggerated best seller which she has written after his supposed death. Bronson is more likable than usual and Ireland almost seems to have acting ability.

309 **The Front** (1976) *** Columbia, 94 min. *Dir* Martin Ritt, *Scr* Walter Bernstein (AN), *Cin* Michael Chapman, *Ed* Sidney Levin, *Art* Charles Bailey, *Cos* Ruth Morley, *Mus* Dave Grusin, *Prod* Martin Ritt, *Exec Prod* Charles Jaffe, *Assoc Prod* Robert Greenhut.

Cast: Woody Allen, *Howard Prince*, Zero Mostel, *Hecky Brown*, Herschel Bernardi, *Phil Sussman*, Michael Murphy, *Alfred Miller*, Andrea

Marcovicci, *Florence Barrett*, Remak Ramsey, *Hennessey*, Marvin Lichterman, *Myer Prince*, Lloyd Gough, *Delaney*, David Margulies, *Phelps*, Joshua Shelley, *Sam*, Norman Rose, *Howard's Attorney*, Danny Aiello, *Danny La Gattuta*, Scott McKay, *Hampton*, Julie Garfield, *Margo*, Charles Kimbrough, *Committee Counselor*, M. Josef Sommer, *Committee Chairman*. PG.

Interesting comedy drama about the Hollywood blacklisting in the McCarthy Era in the 1950's. Woody Allen is excellent, in his first dramatic role, as a cashier who serves as a front for a writer friend who has been blacklisted, because of Communist affiliations. Many of the people involved in the making of *The Front* were themselves blacklisted in the 1950's; i.e. Martin Ritt, Walter Bernstein, Zero Mostel; and this is a subject they obviously cared about. Unfortunately the storyline is a bit weak and the film is unable to sustain itself to the end.

310 **The Front Page** (1974) ******** Universal, 105 min. *Dir* Billy Wilder, *Scr* I.A.L. Diamond, Billy Wilder, based on play by Ben Hecht and Charles MacArthur, *Cin* Jordan S. Cronenweth, *Ed* Ralph E. Winters, *Art* Henry Bumstead, *Cos* Burton Miller, *Mus* Billy May, *Prod* Paul Monash, *Exec Prod* Jennings Lang.

Cast: Jack Lemmon, *Hildy Johnson*, Walter Matthau, *Walter Burns*, Susan Sarandon, *Peggy Grant*, Carol Burnett, *Mollie Malloy*, Vincent Gardenia, *Sheriff*, David Wayne, *Bensinger*, Allen Garfield, *Kruger*, Austin Pendleton, *Earl Williams*, Charles Durning, *Murphy*, Herbert Edelman, *Schwartz*, Martin Gabel, *Dr. Eggelhofer*, Harold Gould, *The Mayor*, Cliff Osmond, *Jacobi*, Dick O'Neill, *McHugh*, Jon Korkes, *Rudy Keppler*, Lou Frizzell, *Endicott*, Paul Benedict, *Plunkett*, Doro Merande, *Jennie*, Noam Pitlick, *Wilson*, Joshua Shelley, *Cab Driver*, Allen Jenkins, *Telegrapher*, John Furlong, *Duffy*, Biff Elliot, *Police Dispatcher*, Barbara Davis, *Myrtle*, Leonard Breman, *Butch*. PG. $7,865,000.

Excellent remake of legendary newspaper comedy. Jack Lemmon and Walter Matthau are excellent as the ace reporter Hildy Brooks and the crusty editor Walter Burns, respectively. Billy Wilder's updating has been heavily criticized for its vulgarities, but this lends a touch of realism to the story and is not out of character. This third version of *The Front Page* is in every way as good as its two predecessors, and may be the definitive version yet.

311 **Fun with Dick and Jane** (1977) ******* Columbia, 95 min. *Dir* Ted Kotcheff, *Scr* Jerry Belson, David Gilber, Mordecai Richler, based on story by Gerald Gaiser, *Cin* Fred Koenekamp, *Ed* Danford B. Greene, *Des* James G. Hulsey, *Cos* Margo Baxley, Donfeld, Lambert E. Marks, *Mus* Lamont Dozier, Ernest Gold, Gene Page, *Prod* Peter Bart, Max Palevsky.

Cast: George Segal, *Dick Harper*, Jane Fonda, *Jane Harper*, Ed McMahon, *Charlie Blanchard*, Dick Gautier, *Doctor Will*, Allan Miller, *Loan Company Manager*, Sean Frye, *Billy Harper*, Hank Garcia, *Raoul Esteban*, John Dehner, *Jane's Father*, Mary Jackson, *Jane's Mother*, Walter Brooke, *Mr. Weeks*, James Jeter, *Immigration Officer*, Maxine Stuart, *Blanchard's Secretary*, Fred Willard, *Bob*, Thalmus Rasulala, *Mr. Johnson*, Ji-Tu Cumbuka, *Guard*. PG. $14,000,000.

Pleasant comedy that updates the children's book characters as a struggling middle-class couple in contemporary society. Dick loses his job, and he and Jane turn to crime when they can't make ends meet. *Fun with Dick and Jane* could have been a more relevant film had the filmmakers attempted to confront their problem seriously, rather than turning this into a crime comedy, but the undeniable chemistry between the two stars make this enjoyable, nevertheless. This was Jane Fonda's comeback film after her "blacklisting" by Hollywood due to her political views.

312 **Funny Lady** (1975) *** Columbia, 136 min. *Dir* Herbert Ross, *Scr* Jay Presson Allen, Arnold Schulman, *Story* Arnold Schulman, *Cin* James Wong Howe (AN), *Ed* Marion Rothman, *Des* George Jenkins, *Cos* Ray Aghayan, Bob Mackie (AN), *Mus Adaptation*. Peter Matz (AN), *Songs* Fred Ebb, John Kander, *Song* "How Lucky Can You Get" by Fred Ebb, John Kander (AN), *Prod* Ray Stark.

Cast: Barbra Streisand, *Fanny Brice*, James Caan, *Billy Rose*, Omar Sharif, *Nick Arnstein*, Roddy McDowell, *Bobby*, Ben Vereen, *Bert Robbins*, Carole Wells, *Norma Butler*, Larry Gates, *Bernard Baruch*, Heidi O'Rourke, *Eleanor Holm*, Samantha Huffaker, *Fran*, Matt Emery, *Buck Bolten*, Joshua Shelley, *Painter*, Corey Fischer, *Conductor*, Garrett Lewis, *Production Singer*, Don Torres, *Man at Wedding*, Raymond Guth, *Buffalo Handler*, Gene Troobnick, *Ned*, Royce Wallace, *Adele*. PG. $19,000,000.

Surprisingly good sequel to the musical biography *Funny Girl*. *Funny Lady* centers on Fanny Brice's relationship with producer Billy Rose and their subsequent marriage. The first half is almost tongue-in-cheek in style, and is far more interesting than the second half, which slows the pace down and becomes a bit too sentimental. Streisand is again excellent as Brice and surprisingly, Caan nearly steals the film from under her nose.

313 **The Fury** (1978) *** 20th Century–Fox, 117 min. *Dir* Brian De Palma, *Scr* John Farris, based on his novel, *Cin* Richard H. Kline, *Ed* Paul Hirsch, *Mus* John Williams, *Prod* Frank Yablans, *Exec Prod* Ron Preissman.

Cast: Kirk Douglas, *Peter*, Amy Irving, *Gillian*, John Cassavetes, *Childress*, Carrie Snodgress, *Hester*, Andrew Stevens, *Robin*, Fiona Lewis, *Susan Charles*, Carol Rossen, *Dr. Ellen Lindstrom*, Charles Durning, *Dr. Jim McKeever*, Joyce Easton, *Katherine Bellaver*, William Finley, *Raymond*, J. Patrick McNamara, *Robertson*, Jane Lambert, *Vivian Nuckles*, Bernie Kuby, *Nuckles*, Rutanya Alda, *Kristen*, Melody Thomas, *Larue*, Hilary Thomas, *Cheryl*, Alice Nunn, *Mrs. Callahan*, Sam Laws, *Blackfish*. R. $12,175,000.

Exciting, but bloody, thriller that mixes telekinesis with espionage. An unknown group attempts to exploit the power of two youths, one of whom is the daughter of a government agent. *The Fury*, unfortunately, works better in parts than as a whole; De Palma's earlier film of telekinesis, *Carrie*, is a far more solid film; but it does contain many extraordinary sequences.

314 **Futureworld** (1976) ** American International, 107 min. *Dir* Richard T. Heffron, *Scr* George Schenck, Mayo Simon, *Cin* Howard Schwartz, *Ed* James Mitchell, *Art* Trevor Williams, *Cos* Ann McCarthy, *Mus* Fred Karlin, *Prod* James T. Aubrey, Richard T. Heffron, Paul N. Lazarus III, *Exec Prod* Samuel Z. Arkoff.

Cast: Peter Fonda, *Chuck Browning*, Blythe Danner, *Tracy Ballard*, Arthur Hill, *Duffy*, Yul Brynner, *Gunslinger*, John Ryan, *Schneider*, Stuart Margolin, *Harry*, Jim Antonio, *Ron*, Allen Ludden, *Game Show MC*, Angela

Greene, *Mrs. Reed*, Robert Cornthwaite, *Mr. Reed*, Darrell Larson, *Eric*, Nancy Bell, *Erica*, John Fujioka, *Mr. Takaguchi*, Dana Lee, *His Aide*, Burt Conroy, *Gen. Karnovski*, Dorothy Konrad, *Mrs. Karnovski*, Alex Rodine, *KGB Man*, Joanna Hall, *Maiden Fair*. PG. $4,000,000. See *Westworld*.

315 **Fuzz** (1972) ** United Artists, 92 min. *Dir* Richard A. Colla, *Scr* Evan Hunter, based on novel by Ed McBain, *Cin* Jacques Marquette, *Ed* Robert Kimble, *Art* Hilyard Brown, *Cos* Dorothy Jeakins, *Mus* Dave Grusin, *Prod* Jack Farren, *Exec Prod* Edward S. Feldman, *Assoc Prod* Charles H. Maguire.

Cast: Burt Reynolds, *Det. Steve Carella*, Jack Weston, *Det. Meyer Meyer*, Tom Skerritt, *Det. Bert King*, Raquel Welch, *Det. Eileen McHenry*, Yul Brynner, *Deaf Man*, James McEachin, *Det. Arthur Brown*, Steve Ihnat, *Det. Andy Parker*, Stewart Moss, *Det. Hal Wallis*, Dan Frazer, *Lt. Byrnes*, Bert Remsen, *Sgt. Murchison*, H. Benny Markowitz, *Patrolman Levine*, James Victor, *Patrolman Gomez*, Roy Applegate, *Patrolman Cramer*, Tom Lawrence, *Patrolman Crosby*, Norman Burton, *Police Commissioner Nelson*, Vince Howard, *Patrolman Marshall*, Jack Lexa, *Patrolman Miscolo*, Britt Leach, Brian Doyle Murray, Harold Oblong, *Detectives*. PG.

Awful police comedy that attempts to recreate the atmosphere of M*A*S*H in a big city precinct. The humor is ridiculous and the jokes are tasteless and fall flat. The filmmakers were not content with an episodic police comedy and forced in a poor subplot involving a super criminal (Yul Brynner), which seems completely out of place with the rest of the film.

316 **Gable and Lombard** (1976) * Universal, 131 min. *Dir* Sidney J. Furie, *Scr* Barry Sandler, *Cin* Jordan S. Cronenweth, *Ed* Argyle Nelson, *Des* Edward C. Carfagno, *Cos* Edith Head, *Mus* Michel Legrand, *Prod* Harry Korshak.

Cast: James Brolin, *Clark Gable*, Jill Clayburgh, *Carole Lombard*, Allen Garfield (Goorwitz), *Louis B. Mayer*, Red Buttons, *Cooper*, Joanne Linville, *Ria*, Melanie Mayron, *Dixie*, Carol McGinnis, *Noreen*, Noah Keen, *Broderick*, Alan D. Dexter, *Sheriff*, S. John Launer, *Judge*, William Bryant, *Colonel*, Alice Backes, *Hedda*, John Lehne, *Kramer*, Karnes, *Gable's Director*, Ross Elliot, *Lombard's Director*, Morgan Brittany, *Vivian Leigh*, Aron Kincaid, *Guest*. R. $6,045,000.

Poor depiction of the romance and marriage of Hollywood stars Clark Gable (James Brolin) and Carole Lombard (Jill Clayburgh). The script seems to be based on a gossip column; it is filled with glaring inaccuracies. Brolin tries too hard to mimic Gable, and Clayburgh is overbearing.

317 **Galileo** (1975) *** Britain, American Film Theatre, 145 min. *Dir* Joseph Losey, *Scr* Barbara Bray, Joseph Losey, based on Charles Laughton's English adaptation of Bertolt Brecht's German play, *Cin* Michael Reed, *Ed* Reginald Beck, *Des* Richard MacDonald, *Mus* Hans Eisler, Richard Hartley, *Prod* Ely Landau, *Exec Prod* Otto Plaschkes.

Cast: Topol, *Galileo*, Edward Fox, *Cardinal Inquisitor*, Colin Blakely, *Priuli*, Georgia Brown, *Ballad Singer's Wife*, Clive Revill, *Ballad Singer*, Margaret Leighton, *Court Lady*, John Gielgud, *Old Cardinal*, Michael Gough, *Sagredo*, Michel Lonsdale, *Cardinal Barberini/Pope*, Richard O'Callaghan, *Fulganzio*, Tim Woodward, *Ludovico*, Judy Parfit, *Angelica Sarti*, John McEnery, *Federzoni*, Patrick Magee, *Cardinal Bellarmin*, Mary Larkin, *Virginia*, Ian Travers, *Andrea (Boy)*, Tom Conti, *Andrea (Man)*. PG. See *American Film Theatre*.

318 The Gambler (1974) *** Paramount, 111 min. *Dir* Karel Reisz, *Scr* James Toback, *Cin* Victor J. Kemper, *Ed* Roger Spottiswoode, *Des* Philip Rosenberg, *Cos* Albert Wolsky, *Mus* Jerry Fielding, based on Gustav Mahler's Symphony No. 1, *Prod* Robert Chartoff, Irwin Winkler.

Cast: James Caan, *Axel*, Paul Sorvino, *Hips*, Lauren Hutton, *Billie*, Morris Carnovsky, *A.R. Lowenthal*, Jacqueline Brookes, *Naomi*, Burt Young, *Carmine*, Carmine Caridi, *Jimmy*, Vic Tayback, *One*, Steven Keats, *Howie*, London Lee, *Monkey*, M. Emmet Walsh, *Las Vegas Gambler*, James Woods, *Bank Officer*, Carl W. Crudup, *Spencer*, Allen Rich, *Bernie*, Stuart Margolin, *Cowboy*, Ric Mancini, *Sal*, Joel Wolfe, *Moe*, Raymond Serra, *Benny*. R.

Powerful, but somewhat pretentious drama about a compulsive gambler. James Caan is excellent as a college professor who is addicted to gambling and seems to also have a death wish. *The Gambler* is flawed by the fact that it attempts to say all gamblers are like this character and have a secret desire to lose. This is a gross oversimplification and *California Split* handles the same subject much better by portraying the complexities in the personalities of such people.

319 The Gang That Couldn't Shoot Straight (1971) ** MGM, 96 min. *Dir* James Goldstone, *Scr* Waldo Salt, based on novel by Jimmy Breslin, *Cin* Owen Roizman, *Ed* Edward A. Biery, *Art* Robert Gundlach, *Cos* Joseph Garibaldi Aulisi, *Mus* Dave Grusin, *Prod* Robert Chartoff, Irwin Winkler.

Cast: Jerry Orbach, *Kid Sally Palumbo*, Leigh Taylor-Young, *Angela Palumbo*, Jo Van Fleet, *Big Momma*, Lionel Stander, *Baccala*, Robert DeNiro, *Mario*, Irving Selbst, *Big Jelly*, Herve Villechaize, *Beppo*, Joe Santos, *Ezmo*, Carmine Caridi, *Tony, the Indian*, Frank Campanella, *Water Buffalo*, Harry Basch, *DeLauria*, Sander Vanocur, *TV Commentator*, Phil Bruns, *Gallagher*, Philip Sterling, *District Attorney Goodman*, Roy Shuman, *Mayor*, Alice Hirson, *Mayor's Wife*, Jack Kehoe, *Scuderi*, Despo, *Mourner*, Sam J. Coppola, *Julie*, James J. Sloyan, *Joey*, Paul Benedict, *Shots O'Toole*, Burt Young, *Willie Quarequio*, Jackie Vernon, *Herman*. PG.

Disappointing gangster comedy starring Jerry Orbach as the leader of a small-time gang of incompetent hoods, who tries to kill a top Mafia boss (Lionel Stander), but bungles his numerous attempts. *The Gang That Couldn't Shoot Straight* has a few funny bits and sight gags, but the script tends to be dull and bogs down most of the film's potential humor.

320 Gator (1976) ** United Artists, 116 min. *Dir* Burt Reynolds, *Scr* William Norton, *Cin* William A. Fraker, *Ed* Harold F. Kress, *Art.* Kirk Axtell, *Mus* Charles Bernstein, *Songs* sung by Jerry Reed, Bobby Goldsboro, *Prod* Arthur Gardner, Jules V. Levy.

Cast: Burt Reynolds, *Gator*, Jack Weston, *Irving Greenfield*, Lauren Hutton, *Aggie Maybank*, Jerry Reed, *Bama McCall*, Alice Ghostly, *Emmeline Cavanaugh*, Dub Taylor, *Mayor Caffrey*, Burton Gilliam, *Smiley*, Mike Douglas, *Governor*, William Engesser, *Bones*, John Steadman, *Ned McKlusky*, Lori Futch, *Suzie McKlusky*. See *White Lightning*. PG. $5,500,000.

321 The Gauntlet (1977) *** Warner Bros., 110 min. *Dir* Clint Eastwood, *Scr* Michael Butler, Dennis Shryack, *Cin* Rexford Metz, *Ed* Joel Cox, Ferris Webster, *Art* Allan E. Smith, *Mus* Jerry Fielding, *Prod* Robert Daley, *Assoc Prod* Fritz Manes.

Cast: Clint Eastwood, *Ben Shockley*, Sondra Locke, *Gus Mally*, Pat Hingle, *Josephson*, William Prince, *Blakelock*, Bill McKinney, *Constable*, Michael Cavanaugh, *Feyderspiel*, Carole Cook, *Waitress*, Mara Corday, *Jail Matron*, Douglas McGrath, *Bookie*, Jeff Morris, *Desk Sergeant*, Samantha Doane, Roy Jenson, Dan Vadis, *Bikers*. R. $17,600,000.

Above average Clint Eastwood thriller about a policeman who must transport a prostitute from jail to trial where she is to appear as a witness in a major crime case. This journey is more difficult than it sounds, as every method possible is used to stop them. The action is sometimes excessive, but that is to be expected from a Clint Eastwood film.

322 **Get Carter** (1971) ** Britain, MGM, 111 min. *Dir* Mike Hodges, *Scr* Mike Hodges, based on novel *Jack's Return Home* by Ted Lewis, *Cin* Wolfgang Suschitzky, *Ed* John Trumper, *Des* Assheton Gorton, *Art* Roger King, *Cos* Vangie Harrison, *Mus* Roy Budd, *Song Lyrics* Jack Fishman, *Prod* Michael Klinger.

Cast: Michael Caine, *Jack Carter*, Ian Hendry, *Eric Paice*, Britt Ekland, *Anna Fletcher*, John Osborne, *Cyril Kinnear*, Tony Beckley, *Peter*, George Sewell, *Con McCarty*, Geraldine Moffatt, *Glenda*, Dorothy White, *Margaret*, Rosemarie Dunham, *Edna* (Landlady), Petra Markham, *Doreen Carter*, Alun Armstrong, *Keith Lacey*, Bryan Mosley, *Cliff Brumby*, Glynn Edwards, *Albert Swift*, Bernard Hepton, *Thorpe*, Terence Rigby, *Gerald Fletcher*, John Bindon, *Sid Fletcher*, Godfrey Quigley, *Eddie Appleyard*, Kevin Brennan, *Harry*, Maxwell Dees, *Vicar*, Liz McKenzie, *Mrs. Brumby*. R.

Average gangster melodrama set in the contemporary British underworld, with Michael Caine as a small-time hood, who searches for those responsible for his brother's death. *Get Carter* seems inspired more by Hollywood film noir of the 1940's than traditional gangster films. The few action sequences are unexceptional and the pacing is slow and tedious. This was remade only one year later as *Hit Man*, a slightly inferior version with an all-black cast.

323 **Get to Know Your Rabbit** (1972) *** Warner Bros., 91 min. *Dir* Brian De Palma, *Scr* Jordan Crittenden, *Cin* John A. Alonzo, *Ed* Peter Colbert, Frank Urioste, *Art* William Malley, *Mus* Jack Elliott, Allyn Ferguson, *Prod* Steve Bernhardt, Paul Gaer, *Assoc Prod* Robert Birnbaum.

Cast: Tom Smothers, *Donald Beeman*, John Astin, *Mr. Turnbull*, Suzanne Zenor, *Paula*, Samantha Jones, *Susan*, Allen Garfield (Goorwitz), *Vic*, Katharine Ross, *Terrific–Looking Girl*, Orson Welles, *Mr. Delasandro*, Hope Summers, *Mrs. Beeman*, Jack Collins, *Mr. Reese*, George Ives, *Mr. Morris*, Robert Ball, *Mr. Weber*, M. Emmet Walsh, *Mr. Wendel*, Helen Page Camp, *Mrs. Wendel*, Pearl Shear, *Flo*, Timothy Carey, *Cop*, Charles Lane, *Mr. Beeman*, Larry D. Mann, *Mr. Seager*, Jessica Myerson, *Mrs. Reese*. R.

Unusual satire starring Tom Smothers as an executive who becomes disgusted with the business world. He quits his job and enrolls in a school for magicians, run by Orson Welles, to start a new career. His attempt to drop out from the establishment fails as his act as a tap dancing magician is soon exploited by his business manager. The film was made in 1970, but it was shelved for two years, because of its weird premise.

324 **The Getaway** (1972) *** National General, 122 min. *Dir* Sam Peckinpah, *Scr* Walter Hill, based on novel by Jim Thompson, *Cin* Lucien Ballard, *Ed* Roger Spottiswoode, Robert Wolfe, *Art* Angelo Graham, Ted Haworth, *Mus* Quincy Jones, *Prod* Mitchell Brower, David Foster.

Cast: Steve McQueen, *Doc McCoy*, Ali MacGraw, *Carol McCoy*, Ben Johnson, *Jack Benyon*, Sally Struthers, *Fran Clinton*, Al Lettieri, *Rudy Butler*, Slim Pickens, *Cowboy*, Richard Bright, *Thief*, Jack Dodson, *Harold Clinton*, Dub Taylor, *Laughlin*, Bo Hopkins, *Frank Jackson*. PG. $18,000,000.

Well-made contemporary gangster film about a couple on the run after robbing a bank. Sam Peckinpah took what could have been a routine action thriller, and turned it into an exciting chase film that surprisingly holds interest for its two hours. This is no *Bonnie and Clyde*, though, but what else is? *The Getaway* is not one of Peckinpah's best films, but it is, ironically, his biggest hit.

325 **Getting Straight** (1970) ** Columbia, 124 min. *Dir* Richard Rush, *Scr* Robert Kaufman, based on novel by Ken Kolb, *Cin* Laszlo Kovacs, *Ed* Maury Winetrobe, *Art* Sydney Z. Litwack, *Mus* Ronald Stein, *Prod* Richard Rush, *Assoc Prod* Paul Lewis.

Cast: Elliott Gould, *Harry Bailey*, Candice Bergen, *Jan*, Jeff Corey, *Dr. Willhunt*, Max Julien, *Ellis*, Robert F. Lyons, *Nich*, Cecil Kellaway, *Dr. Kasper*, Jon Lormer, *Vandenburg*, Leonard Stone, *Lysander*, William Bramley, *Wade Linden*, Jeannie Berlin, *Judy Kramer*, John Rubinstein, *Herbert*, Billie Bird, *Landlady*, Richard Anders, *Dr. Greengrass*, Brenda Sykes, *Luan*, Gregory Sierra, *Garcia*, Jenny Sullivan, *Sheila*, Hilarie Thompson, *Cynthia*, Harrison Ford, *Jake*, Irene Tedrow, *Mrs. Stebbins*, Elizabeth Lane, *Alice Linden*, Joanna Serpe, *Roommate*, Harry Holcombe, *Dean Chesney*, Scott Perry, *Airline Representative*. R. $6,000,000.

Standard 1960's college protest film set at a fictional university. Elliott Gould is excellent as a Vietnam veteran, who has gone back to school for his masters degree and is caught in the middle of the rebelling students and the establishment faculty, which culminates in an exaggerated riot. *Getting Straight* was fashionable at the time of its release, but it is now dated.

326 **The Girl from Petrovka** (1974) ** Universal, 104 min. *Dir* Robert Ellis Miller, *Scr* Chris Bryant, Allan Scott, based on novel by George Feifer, *Cin* Vilmos Zsigmond, *Ed* John F. Burnett, *Art* George C. Webb, *Cos* Deidre Clancy, *Mus* Henry Mancini, *Prod* Richard D. Zanuck, David Brown.

Cast: Goldie Hawn, *Oktyabrina*, Hal Holbrook, *Joe*, Anthony Hopkins, *Kostya*, Gregoire Aslan, *Minister*, Anton Dolin, *Ignatievitch*, Bruno Wintzell, *Alexander*, Zoran Andric, *Leonid*, Hanna Hertelendy, *Judge*, Maria Sokolov, *Old Crone*, Zitto Kazann, *Passport Black Marketeer*, Inger Jensen, *Helga Van Dam*, Raymond O'Keefe, *Minister's Driver*, Richard Marner, *Kremlin Press Official*, Michael Janisch, *Police Chief Valinikov*, Harry Towb, *American Reporter*, Ted Grossman, *Jogging Companion*, Elisa Georgiadis, *Minister's Wife*, Heinz Maracek, *Cafe Waiter*, Anatol Winogradoff, *Shipyard Caretaker*. PG.

Dull love story involving an American correspondent (Hal Holbrook) in Moscow and a Russian girl (Goldie Hawn). *The Girl from Petrovka* resembles, on the surface, *Ninotchka*, complete with humorous comparisons and contrasts between American and Russian culture, but this pales next to Lubitsch's classic, lacking its wit and perception. This film is far beneath the talents of Holbrook and Hawn.

327 Girlfriends (1978) *** Warner Bros., 86 min. *Dir* Claudia Weill, *Scr* Vicki Polon, *Story* Vicki Polon, Claudia Weill, *Cin* Fred Murphy, *Ed* Suzanna Pettit, *Art* Patrizia von Brandenstein, *Mus* Michael Small, *Prod* Claudia Weill, *Co-Prod* Jan Saunders, *Assoc Prod* Pat Churchill, Lilly Kilvert.

Cast: Melanie Mayron, *Susan Weinblatt*, Anita Skinner, *Anne Munroe*, Eli Wallach, *Rabbi Gold*, Christopher Guest, *Eric*, Bob Balaban, *Martin*, Gina Rogak, *Julie*, Amy Wright, *Ceil*, Viveca Lindfors, *Beatrice*, Mike Kellin, *Abe* Jean de Baer, *Terry*, Ken McMillan, *Cabbie*, Russell Horton, *Photo Editor*, Tania Berezin, *Rabbi's Wife*, Kathryn Walker, *Carpel's Receptionist*, Roderick Cook, *Carpel*, Kristoffer Tabori, *Charlie*. PG.

Fine character study that examines the meaning of friendship. Melanie Mayron is excellent as a lonely girl who must cope with the problem of suddenly being left alone after her best friend and roommate get married. The structure of *Girlfriends* is episodic and the ideas are not always strong enough to sustain the film, but this is nevertheless a good directorial debut for Claudia Weill.

328 The Go-Between (1971) (CF) ***** Britain, Columbia, 116 min. *Dir* Joseph Losey, *Scr* Harold Pinter (BFA), based on novel by L.P. Hartley, *Cin* Gerry Fisher, *Ed* Reginald Beck, *Art* Carmen Dillon, *Cos* John Furniss, *Mus* Michael Legrand, *Prod* John Heyman, Norman Priggen, *Exec Prod* Robert Velaise.

Cast: Julie Christie, *Marian Maudsley*, Alan Bates, *Ted Burgess*, Dominic Guard, *Leo Colston*, Margaret Leighton (AN, BFA), *Mrs. Maudsley*, Michael Redgrave, *The Older Leo*, Michael Gough, *Mr. Maudsley*, Edward Fox (BFA), *Hugh Trimingham*, Richard Gibson, *Marcus Maudsley*, Simon Hume-Kendall, *Denys*, Amaryllis Garnett, *Kate*, Roger Lloyd Pack, *Charles*. PG.

Beautiful film that is a visit to the past. Set at the turn of the century, a young boy stays with a friend's family at their huge country estate during the summer. He becomes infatuated with his friend's older sister (Julie Christie) and becomes a go-between delivering messages between her and her secret lover (Alan Bates), who is merely a farmer. *The Go-Between* explores the attitudes toward class differences in the past, with perception and beauty.

329 Go Tell the Spartans (1978) *** Avco Embassy, 114 min. *Dir* Ted Post, *Scr* Wendell Mayes, based on novel *Incident at Muc Wa* by Daniel Ford, *Cin* Harry Stradling, Jr., *Ed* Millie Moore, *Art* Jack Senter, *Mus* Dick Halligan, *Prod* Allan F. Bodoh, Mitchell Cannold, *Exec Prod* Michael Leone, *Assoc Prod* Jesse Corallo.

Cast: Burt Lancaster, *Maj. Asa Barker*, Craig Wasson, *Corp. Stephen Courcey*, Jonathan Goldsmith, *Sgt. Oleonowski*, Marc Singer, *Capt. Al Olivetti*, Joe Unger, *Lt. Raymond Hamilton*, Dennis Howard, *Corp. Abraham Lincoln*, David Clennon, *Lt. Finley Wattsberg*, Evan Kim, *Cowboy*, John Megna, *Corp Ackley*, Hilly Hicks, *Signalman Toffer*, Dolph Sweet, *Gen. Harnitz*, Clyde Kusatsu, *Col. Minh*, James Hong, *Corp Oldman*, Denice Kumagai, *Butterfly*, Tad Horino, *One-Eyed Charlie*, Phong Diep, *Minh's Interpreter*, Ralph Brannen, *Minh's Aid-de-Camp*, Mark Carlton, *Capt. Schlitz*. R.

Interesting, but unexciting war film set in the early days of the Vietnam War. Burt Lancaster is excellent as the head of a group of military advisors who get caught up in the conflict. *Go Tell the Spartans* was lost in the wake of the bigger, more ambitious films on the same subject released in the late 1970's. Although nowhere in the same league as those other films, it should not have been ignored, either.

330 **The Godfather** (1972) (A, G) ***** Paramount, 175 min. *Dir* Francis Coppola (AN, G, D), *Scr* Francis Coppola, Mario Puzo (A, G, W), based on novel by Mario Puzo, *Cin* Gordon Willis, *Ed* William Reynolds, Peter Zinner (AN), *Des* Dean Tavoularis, *Art* Warren Clymer, *Cos* Anna Hill Johnstone (AN), *Mus* Nino Rota, *Prod* Albert S. Ruddy, *Assoc Prod* Gray Frederickson.

Cast: Marlon Brando (A, G), *Don Vito Corleone*, Al Pacino (AN, NS, NB), *Michael Corleone*, James Caan (AN), *Sonny Corleone*, Richard Castellano, *Clemenza*, Robert Duvall (AN, NY), *Tom Hagen*, Sterling Hayden, *Mc-Cluskey*, John Marley, *Jack Woltz*, Richard Conte, *Barzini*, Diane Keaton, *Kay Adams*, Al Lettieri, *Sollozzo*, Abe Vigoda, *Tessio*, Talia Shire, *Connie Rizzi*, Gianni Russo, *Carlo Rizzi*, John Cazale, *Fredo Corleone*, Rudy Bond, *Cuneo*, Al Martino, *Johnny Fontane*, Morgana King, *Mama Corleone*, Lenny Montana, *Luca Brasi*, John Martino, *Paulie Gatto*, Salvatore Corsitto, *Bonasera*, Richard Bright, *Neri*, Alex Rocco, *Moe Greene*, Tony Giorgio, *Bruno Tattaglia*, Vito Scotti, *Nazorine*, Tere Livrano, *Theresa Hagen*, Victor Rendina, *Phillip Tattaglia*, Jeannie Linero, *Lucy Mancini*, Julie Gregg, *Sandra Corleone*, Ardell Sheridan, *Mrs. Clemenza*, Simonetta Stefanelli, *Apollonnia*, Angelo Infanti, *Fabrizio*, Corrado Gaipa, *Don Tommasino*, Franco Citti, *Calo*, Salo Urzi, *Vitelli*. R. $86,275,000.

Magnificent gangster epic chronicling several decades in the life of a New York Mafia family. *The Godfather* and its sequel *The Godfather Part II* must be discussed together as one giant saga, that says more about America than possibly any other film, and comparisons to early gangster films, i.e. *Public Enemy* and *Little Caesar*, would be the equivalent of comparing Chaplin or Keaton to The Bowery Boys. No American film has more richness of character and depth than these films. Francis Coppola was originally just a "hired" director, but somehow he managed to take over and leave his imprint, and then followed it with an even more complex and brilliant sequel. This is the American cinema's great epic, two films of such brilliance that Coppola is the only director working in the U.S. who was able to top them, which he did with *Apocalypse Now*.

331 **The Godfather, Part II** (1974) (A) ***** Paramount, 200 min. *Dir* Francis Coppola (A, NS, D), *Scr* Francis Coppola, Mario Puzo (A, W), based on characters created by Mario Puzo, *Cin* Gordon Willis (NS), *Ed* Barry Malkin, Richard Marks, Peter Zinner, *Des* Dean Tavoularis (A), *Art* Angelo Graham (A), *Cos* Theadora Van Runkle (AN), *Mus* Nino Rota (A), *Additional Mus* Carmine Coppola (A), *Prod* Francis Coppola, *Co−Prod* Gray Frederickson, Fred Roos, *Assoc Prod* Mona Skager.

Cast: Al Pacino (AN, BFA), *Michael Corleone*, Robert De Niro (A), *Vito Corleone*, Robert Duvall, *Tom Hagen*, Diane Keaton, *Kay*, John Cazale, *Fredo Corleone*, Talia Shire (AN), *Connie Corleone*, Lee Strasberg (AN),

Hyman Roth, Michael V. Gazzo (AN), *Frankie Pentangeli*, G.D. Spradlin, *Senator Pat Geary*, Richard Bright, *Al Neri*, Gaston Moschin, *Fanucci*, Tom Rosqui, *Rocco Lampone*, B. Kirby, Jr., *Young Clemenza*, Frank Sivero, *Genco*, Francesca De Sapio, *Young Mama Corleone*, Morgana King, *Mama Corleone*, Mariana Hill, *Deanna Corleone*, Leopoldo Trieste, *Signor Roberto*, Dominic Chianese, *Johnny Ola*, Amerigo Tot, *Michael's Bodyguard*, Troy Donahue, *Merle Johnson*, John Aprea, *Young Tessio*, Joe Spinell, *Willi Cicci*, Abe Vigoda, *Tessio*, Tere Livrano, *Theresa Hagen*, Gianni Russo, *Carlo*, Maria Carta, *Vito's Mother*, Oreste Baldini, *Vito Andolini as a Boy*, Giuseppe Sillato, *Don Francesco*, Mario Cotone, *Don Tommasino*, James Gounaris, *Anthony Corleone*, Fay Spain, *Mrs. Marcia Roth*, Harry Dean Stanton, *F.B.I. Man #1*, David Baker, *F.B.I. Man #2*, Carmine Caridi, *Carmine Rosato*, Danny Aiello, *Tony Rosato*, Carmine Foresta, *Policeman*, Nick Discenza, *Bartender*, Father Joseph Medeglia, *Father Carmelo*, William Bowers, *Senate Committee Chairman*, Phil Feldman, Roger Corman, *Senators*, James Caan, *Sonny Corleone*. R. $30,675,000. See *The Godfather*.

332 **Godspell** (1973) * Columbia, 103 min. *Dir* David Greene, *Scr* David Greene, John-Michael Tebelak, based on stage production by John-Michael Tebelak, *Cin* Richard G. Heimann, *Ed* Alan Heim, *Mus* Stephen Schwartz, *Prod* Edgar Lansburg.

Cast: Victor Garber, *Jesus*, David Haskell, *John/Judas*, Jerry Sroka, *Jerry*, Lynne Thigpen, *Lynne*, Katie Hanley, *Katie*, Robin Lamont, *Robin*, Gilmer McCormick, *Gilmer*, Joanne Jonas, *Joanne*, Merrell Jackson, *Merrell*, Jeffrey Mylett, *Jeffrey*. G.

Silly gospel musical with Jesus and his disciples singing and dancing their way through New York City. This attempt to update Jesus' life and set it in contemporary society is nothing more than ridiculous and pointless. Judging *Godspell* strictly on the level of a musical does not help it at all, either. The songs themselves are all drab, including the hit "Day by Day."

333 **Goin' South** (1978) **** Paramount, 105 min. *Dir* Jack Nicholson, *Scr* Alan Mandel, Al Ramrus, John Herman Shaner, Charles Shyer, *Story* Al Ramrus, John Herman Shanner, *Cin* Nestor Almendros, *Ed* John Fitzgerald Beck, Richard Chew, *Des* Toby Carr Rafelson, *Cos* William Ware Theiss, *Mus* Perry Botkin, Jr., Van Dyke Parks, *Prod* Harry Gittes, Harold Schneider.

Cast: Jack Nicholson, *Henry Moon*, Mary Steenburgen, *Julia Tate*, Christopher Lloyd, *Towfield*, John Belushi, *Hector*, Veronica Cartwright, *Hermine*, Richard Bradford, *Sheriff Kyle*, Jeff Morris, *Big Abe*, Danny DeVito, *Hog*, Tracey Walter, *Coogan*, Gerald H. Reynolds, *Polty*, Luana Anders, *Mrs. Anderson*, George W. Smith, *Mr. Anderson*, Lucy Lee Flippen, *Mrs. Haber*, Ed Begley, Jr., *Mr. Haber*, Maureen Byrnes, *Mrs. Warren*, B.J. Merholz, *Mr. Warren*, Britt Leach, *Parson Weems*, Georgia Schmidt, *Florence*, Nancy Coan Kaclik, *Mrs. Standard*, R.L. Armstrong, *Farmer Standard*. PG. $4,765,000.

Wonderful offbeat comic western starring Jack Nicholson in a strange role as a misfit Gabby Hayes type outlaw, who is saved from hanging by a town ordinance that allows criminals to live if a woman is willing to marry them. Mary Steenburgen is excellent as a spinster who marries Nicholson for his help in her gold mine. *Goin' South* is filled with many hysterical situations and characters and is one of the best films directed by an actor.

334 Going Home (1971) *** MGM, 97 min. *Dir* Herbert B. Leonard, *Scr* Lawrence B. Marcus, *Cin* Fred Jackman, *Ed* Sigmund Neufeld, *Art* Peter Wooley, *Cos* Guy Verhille, *Mus* Bill Walker, *Prod* Herbert B. Leonard, *Assoc Prod* Nicky Blair, Stanley Neufeld.

Cast: Robert Mitchum, *Harry K. Graham*, Brenda Vaccaro, *Jenny*, Jan–Michael Vincent, *Jimmy Graham*, Jason Bernard, *Jimmy (Age 6)*, Sally Kirkland, *Ann Graham*, Joe Attles, *Bible Man*, Lou Gilbert, *Mr. Katz*, Josh Mostel, *Bonelli*, Barbara Brownell, *Betsy*, Carol Gustafson, *Ella*. PG.

Fine drama starring Robert Mitchum as a man who murders his wife, which is unfortunately witnessed by their son. After Mitchum's parole thirteen years later, he is visited by his son, and their tense relationship, which is a mixture of fear and resentment, is the focus of the film. Herbert B. Leonard made a fine directorial debut, and he creates the proper tension with his atmospheric style.

335 Going in Style (1979) **** Warner Bros., 97 min. *Dir* Martin Brest, *Scr* Martin Brest, *Story* Edward Cannon, *Cin* Billy Williams, *Ed* C. Timothy O'Meara, Robert Swink, *Des* Stephen Hendrickson, *Art* Gary Weist, *Cos* Anna Hill Johnstone, *Mus* Michael Small, *Prod* Tony Bill, Fred T. Gallo, *Exec Prod* Leonard Gaines.

Cast: George Burns, *Joe*, Art Carney, *Al*, Lee Strasberg, *Willie*, Charles Hallahan, *Pete*, Pamela Payton-Wright, *Kathy*, Siobhan Keegan, *Colleen*, Brian Neville, *Kevin*, Constantine Hartofolis, *Boy in Park*, Mary Testa, *Teller*, Jean Shevlin, *Mrs. Fein*, James Manis, *Hot Dog Vender*, Margot Stevenson, *Store Cashier*, Tito Goya, *Gypsy Cab Driver*, William Pabst, *Bank Guard*, Christopher Wynkoop, *Bank Manager*. PG. $14,100,000.

Excellent comedy-drama about three old men, who become bored with their lives and decide to rob a bank. *Going in Style* is a far more serious film than one would expect, as it uses a comic premise to examine the problems facing senior citizens in an uncaring society. Martin Brest beautifully and realistically treats a subject that could have easily been mishandled. George Burns gives a surprisingly good dramatic performance as the instigator of the plan.

336 The Golden Voyage of Sinbad (1974) *** Britain, 105 min. *Dir* Gordon Hessler, *Scr* Brian Clemens, *Cin* Ted Moore, *Ed* Roy Watts, *Des* John Stoll, *Art* Fernando Gonzalez, *Sp* Ray Harryhausen, *Mus* Miklos Rozsa, *Prod* Ray Harryhausen, Charles H. Schneer.

Cast: John Phillip Law, *Sinbad*, Caroline Munro, *Margiana*, Tom Baker, *Koura*, Douglas Wilmer, *Vizier*, Martin Shaw, *Rachid*, Gregoire Aslan, *Hakim*, Kurt Christian, *Haroun*, Takis Emmanuel, *Achmed*, John D. Garfield, *Abdul*, Aldo Sambrell, *Omar*. G. $5,000,000.

Fine fantasy about the famed mythical sailor (John Phillip Law) and his search for a golden crown. As is usual with this type of film, the story takes a back seat to the special effects. Ray Harryhausen uses stop-motion photography to full advantage in bringing numerous creatures to life. The sequel *Sinbad and the Eye of the Tiger* starring Patrick Wayne as Sinbad, is inferior to its predeccessor and even Harryhausen's special effects are disappointing.

337 **Goldengirl** (1979) * Avco Embassy, 104 min. *Dir* Joseph Sargent, *Scr* John Kohn, based on novel by Peter Lear, *Cin* Steven Larner, *Ed* George Nicholson, *Art* Syd Litwack, *Mus* Bill Conti, *Prod* Danny O'Donovan, *Exec Prod* Elliot Kastner.

Cast: Susan Anton, *Goldengirl*, James Coburn, *Dryden*, Curt Jurgens, *Serafin*, Leslie Caron, *Dr. Lee*, Robert Culp, *Esselton*, James A. Watson, Jr., *Winters*, Harry Guardino, *Valenti*, Ward Costello, *Cobb*, Michael Lerner, *Sternberg*, John Newcombe, *Armitage*, Julianna Field, *Ingrid*, Sheila DeWindt, *Debbie*, Andrea Brown, *Teammate*, Anette Tannander, *Krull*, Nicholas Coster, *Dr. Dalton*. PG.

Dreadful combination of science-fiction and sports. A mad scientist (Curt Jurgens) raises his daughter (Susan Anton) on drugs in hopes of creating an unbeatable Olympic runner; a plot which predictably backfires. The script is so ridiculous, with a plot that plays like a soap opera, the entire cast seems embarrassed, particularly Anton who is simply dreadful in her first starring role.

338 **Good Guys Wear Black** (1978) ** Mar Vista, 96 min. *Dir* Ted Post, *Scr* Bruce Cohn, Mark Medoff, *Story* Joseph Fraley, *Mus* Craig Safan, *Prod* Allan F. Bodoh, *Exec Prod* Michael Leone.

Cast: Chuck Norris, *John T. Booker*, Anne Archer, *Margaret*, Lloyd Haynes, *Murray*, James Franciscus, *Conrad Morgan*, Dana Andrews, *Government Man*, Jim Backus, *Doorman*. PG. $8,300,000.

Chuck Norris is America's answer to Bruce Lee, as if we needed one, and like his predecessor his talent is restricted entirely to his hands and feet. *Good Guys Wear Black* and *A Force of One* are nothing more than vehicles built entirely around Norris's karate abilities. These films are better directed than their Oriental counterparts and are not as silly, but that is all that can be said.

339 **The Goodbye Girl** (1977) (AN, GMC) *** Warner Bros., 110 min. *Dir* Herbert Ross, *Scr* Neil Simon (AN), *Cin* David M. Walsh, *Ed* John F. Burnett, *Des* Albert Brenner, *Cos* Ann Roth, *Mus* Dave Grusin, *Title Song* written and preformed by David Gates, *Prod* Ray Stark, *Assoc Prod* Roger M. Rothstein.

Cast: Richard Dreyfuss (A, BFA, GMC, LA), *Elliot Garfield*, Marsha Mason (AN), *Paula McFadden*, Quinn Cummings (AN), *Lucy McFadden*, Paul Benedict, *Mark*, Barbara Rhoades, *Donna*, Theresa Merritt, *Mrs. Crosby*, Michael Shawn, *Ronnie*, Patricia Pearcy, *Rhonda*, Gene Castle, *Assistant Choreographer*, Daniel Levans, *Dance Instructor*, Marilyn Sokol, *Linda*, Anita Dangler, *Mrs. Morganweiss*, Victora Boothby, *Mrs. Bodine*. PG. $41,700,000.

Above average Neil Simon comedy about a divorced woman and her daughter who are forced to share an apartment with a temperamental actor. *The Goodbye Girl* is sort of a romantic version of *The Odd Couple* as the man and woman are seemingly incompatible. The results are predictable, but Simon's script is better written than most of his others, and Dreyfuss' performance is outstanding.

340 **The Grasshopper** (1970) *** National General, 95 min. *Dir* Jerry Paris, *Scr* Jerry Belson, Gary Marshall, based on novel *The Passing of Evil* by Mark McShane, *Cin* Sam Leavitt, *Ed* Aaron Stell, *Art* Tambi Larsen, *Cos* Donfeld, *Mus* William Goldenberg, *Prod* Jerry Belson, Garry Marshall.

Cast: Jacqueline Bisset, *Christine*, Jim Brown, *Tommy*, Joseph Cotten, *Richard*, Corbett Monica, *Danny*, Ramon Bieri, *Roosevelt*, Christopher Stone, *Jay*, Roger Garrett, *Buck*, Stanley Adams, *Buddy*, Dick Richards, *Lou*, Tim O'Kelly, *Eddie*, Stefanianna Christopherson, *Libby*, Ed Flanders, *Jack*, Wendy Farrington, *Connie*, Sandi Gaviola, *Kyo*, Eris Sandy, *Vicky*, John David Wilder, *Timmy*, Jay Laskay, *Manny*, Jim Smith, *Larry*, Therese Baldwin, *Gigi*, Chris Wong, *Billy*, Kathalynn Turner, *Ann Marie*, William H. Bassett, *Aaron*, Marc Hannibal, *Walters*, David Duclon, *Miller's Son*. R.

Fine character study of a young woman (Jacqueline Bisset) from Canada, who tries to break into show business, but becomes a Las Vegas showgirl. Her life goes downhill as she gets mixed up with some undesirable characters and she ends up a prostitute. *The Grasshopper* is a bit heavy-handed in its approach, piling on too many tragedies, but it features a fine performance by Bisset.

341 Gravy Train (1974) *** Columbia, 95 min. *Dir* Jack Starrett, *Scr* Bill Kerby, David Whitney, *Cin* Jerry Hirschfeld, *Ed* John Horger, *Des* Stan Jolley, *Prod* Jonathan Taplin, *Exec Prod* Roger Gimbel, *Assoc Prod* Joel Glickman.

Cast: Stacy Keach, *Calvin*, Frederic Forrest, *Russell "Rut"*, Margot Kidder, *Margie*, Barry Primus, *Tony*, Richard Romanus, *Carlo*, Denny Miller, *Rex*, Clay Tanner, *Guy*, Robert Phillips, *Gino*, Jack Starrett, *Rancher*, Lorna Thayer, *TV Interviewer*, Francesca Bellini, *Receptionist*. R.

Offbeat crime comedy about two weird brothers (Stacy Keach, Frederick Forrest), who plan a robbery in hopes of opening a restaurant with their loot. Their plans go awry when they discover they cannot trust the gang that helped them and the two brothers pursue the gang, which culminates in an exciting shootout. Keach and Forrest give excellent performances and bring depth to these odd characters. Other title, *The Dion Brothers*.

342 Gray Lady Down (1978) ** Universal, 111 min. *Dir* David Greene, *Scr* Howard Sackler, James Whittaker, *adaptation* Frank P. Rosenberg, based on novel *Event 1000* by David Lavallee, *Cin* Steven Larner, *Ed* Robert Swink, *Des* William Tuntke, *Sp* Curtis Dickson, *Mus* Jerry Fielding, *Prod* Walter Mirisch.

Cast: Charlton Heston, *Capt. Paul Blanchard*, David Carradine, *Capt. Gates*, Stacy Keach, *Capt. Bennett*, Ned Beatty, *Mickey*, Stephen McHattie, *Murphy*, Ronny Cox, *Cmdr. Samuelson*, Dorien Harewood, *Fowler*, Rosemary Forsyth, *Vickie*, Hilly Hicks, *Page*, Charles Cioffi, *Adm. Barnes*, William Jordan, *Waters*, Jack Rader, *Harkness*, Anthony Ponzini, *Caruso*, Michael O'Keefe, *Harris*, Charlie Robinson, *McAllister*, Christopher Reeve, *Phillips*. PG. $4,060,000.

Dull disaster film about the rescue of a sunken nuclear submarine that is stuck in an ocean canyon off the coast of Connecticut. Charlton Heston stars as the captain of the sub whose tedious wait to be rescued must rival that of the audience's wait for the film to end. David Carradine and Ned Beatty, as the rescuers, do what they can to save the film.

343 Grease (1978) * Paramount, 110 min. *Dir* Randal Kleiser, *Scr* Bronte Woodard, *Adaptation* Allan Carr, based on musical play Warren Casey, Jim Jacobs, *Cin* Bill Butler, *Ed* John F. Burnett, *Des* Phillip Jefferies, *Cos* Albert Wolsky, *Mus Supervision* Bill Oakes, *Chor* Patricia Birch, *Prod* Allan Carr, Robert Stigwood, *Assoc Prod* Neil A. Machlis.

Cast: John Travolta, *Danny,* Olivia Newton-John, *Sandy,* Stockard Channing, *Rizzo,* Jeff Conaway, *Kenickie,* Didi Conn, *Frenchy,* Jamie Donnelly, *Jan,* Dinah Manoff, *Marty,* Barry Pearl, *Doody,* Michael Tucci, *Sonny,* Kelly Ward, *Putzie,* Susan Buckner, *Patty Simcox,* Eddie Deezen, *Eugene,* Lorenzo Lamas, *Tom Chisum,* Dennis C. Stewart, *Leo,* Annette Charles, *Cha Cha,* Dick Patterson, *Mr. Rudie,* Fannie Flagg, *Nurse Wilkin,* Darrell Zwerling, *Mr. Lynch,* Ellen Travolta, *Waitress,* Eve Arden, *Principal McGee,* Frankie Avalon, *Teen Angel,* Joan Blondell, *Vi,* Edd Byrnes, *Vince Fontaine,* Sid Caesar, *Coach Calhoun,* Alice Ghostley, *Mrs. Murdock,* Dody Goodman, *Blanche,* Sha-Na-Na, *Johnny Casino and the Gamblers.* PG. $96,300,000.

Dreadful musical comedy set in the 1950's. How on earth such a mess could have become a box-office blockbuster is certainly a great mystery. *Grease* has all the intelligence and wit of *Beach Blanket Bingo* and the other beach movies of the 1960's. Travolta and Newton-John work well together and there are a few memorable songs, but it would take a lot more to make this a worthwhile movie.

344 Greased Lightning (1977) *** Warner Bros., 96 min. *Dir* Michael Schultz, *Scr* Leon Capetanos, Lawrence DuKore, Melvin Van Peebles, Kenneth Vose, *Cin* George Bouillet, *Ed* Christopher Holmes, Randy Roberts, Bob Wyman, *Art* Jack Senter, *Cos* Celia Bryant, *Mus* Fred Karlin, *Prod* Hannah Weinstein, *Exec Prod* Richard Bell, J. Lloyd Grant, *Assoc Prod* James E. Hinton.

Cast: Richard Pryor, *Wendell Scott,* Beau Bridges, *Hutch,* Pam Grier, *Mary,* Cleavon Little, *Peewee,* Vincent Gardenia, *Sheriff Cotton,* Richie Havens, *Woodrow,* Julian Bond, *Russell,* Earl Hindman, *Beau Welles,* Minnie Gentry, *Wendell's Mother,* Lucy Saroyan, *Hutch's Wife,* Noble Willingham, *Billy Joe Byrnes.* PG. $7,500,000.

Interesting biography of Wendell Scott, the first Black stock-car racing driver, spanning 25 years of his life from his discharge from the army, following WWII, up to his championship race in 1971. *Greased Lightning* is more of a light comedy than a serious biography, but it is well-paced and entertaining. Richard Pryor proves that he can portray another character besides himself.

345 The Great Gatsby (1974) ** Paramount, 144 min. *Dir* Jack Clayton, *Scr* Francis Coppola, based on novel by F. Scott Fitzgerald, *Cin* Douglas Slocombe (BFA), *Ed* Tom Priestley, *Des* John Box (BFA), *Art* Robert Laing, Eugene Rudolf, *Cos* Theoni V. Aldredge (A, BFA), *Mus* Nelson Riddle (A), *Prod* David Merrick, *Assoc Prod* Hank Moonjean.

Cast: Robert Redford, *Jay Gatsby,* Mia Farrow, *Daisy Buchanon,* Bruce Dern, *Tom Buchanon,* Karen Black (G), *Myrtle Wilson,* Scott Wilson, *George Wilson,* Sam Waterston, *Nick Carraway,* Lois Chiles, *Jordan Baker,* Howard DaSilva, *Meyer Wolfsheim,* Roberts Blossom, *Mr. Gatz,* Edward Herrmann, *Klipspringer,* Elliot Sullivan, *Wilson's Friend,* John Devlin, *Gatsby's Bodyguard,* Tom Ewell, *Mourner,* Janet and Louise Arters, *Twins.* PG. $14,200,000.

Disappointing adaptation of F. Scott Fitzgerald novel. The fault lies in the fact that the filmmakers stuck too closely to the book, not realizing the difference between literature and film. What works in literature, quite often, will not translate well to cinema. Visually *The Great Gatsby* is very impressive, but it is just too slow and boring. This is the third film version of the novel and the other two also failed.

346 The Great Northfield, Minnesota Raid (1972) ******** Universal, 91 min. *Dir* Philip Kaufman, *Scr* Philip Kaufman, *Cin* Bruce Surtees, *Ed* Douglas Stewart, *Art* Alexander Golitzen, George Webb, *Cos* Helen Colvig, *Mus* Dave Grusin, *Prod* Jennings Lang, *Assoc Prod* Bruce Graham.

Cast: Cliff Robertson, *Cole Younger*, Robert Duvall, *Jesse James*, Luke Askew, *Jim Younger*, R.G. Armstrong, *Clell Miller*, Dana Elcar, *Allen*, Donald Moffat, *Manning*, John Pearce, *Frank James*, Matt Clark, *Bob Younger*, Wayne Sutherlin, *Charley Pitts*, Robert H. Harris, *Wilcox*, Jack Manning, *Heywood*, Elisha Cook, *Bunker*, Royal Dano, *Gustavson*, Mary Robin Redd, *Kate*, Billy Callaway, *Calliopist*, Arthur Peterson, *Jefferson Jones*, Craig Curtis, *Chadwell*, Barry Brown, *Henry Wheeler*, Liam Dunn, *Drummer*. PG.

Unusual western drama about the famous robbery involving the James and Younger brothers. *The Great Northfield, Minnesota Raid* is more realistic than most westerns with its emphasis on mood and character and the fine detailing of the disastrous raid, which brought about the demise of the notorious outlaws. The acting is excellent particularly Robert Duvall as Jesse James.

347 The Great Santini (1979) ******* Orion, 115 min. *Dir* Lewis John Carlino, *Scr* Lewis John Carlino, based on novel by Pat Conroy, *Cin* Ralph Woolsey, *Ed* Housely Stevenson, *Des* Jack Poplin, *Mus* Elmer Bernstein, *Prod* Charles A. Pratt.

Cast: Robert Duvall (AN), *Bull Meechum*, Blythe Danner, *Lillian Meechum*, Michael O'Keefe (AN), *Ben Meechum*, Lisa Jane Persky, *Mary Anne Meechum*, Julie Ann Haddock, *Karen Meechum*, Brian Andrews, *Matthew Meechum*, Stan Shaw, *Toomer Smalls*, Theresa Merritt, *Arrabelle Smalls*, David Keith, *Red Pettus*, Paul Mantee, *Col. Hedgepath*. PG.

Above-average family drama about a Marine Corps fighter pilot, who applies his authorative military methods to his family. While *The Great Santini* focuses on these family tensions it is an excellent drama, but unfortunately it veers off into an unnecessary subplot involving racial problems. The true highlights are the outstanding performances, particularly those of Robert Duvall, Blythe Danner and Michael O'Keefe.

348 The Great Scout & Cathouse Thursday (1976) ****** American International, 102 min. *Dir* Don Taylor, *Scr* Richard Shapiro, *Cin* Alex Phillips, Jr., *Ed* Sheldon Kahn, *Des* Jack Martin Smith, *Cos* Rene Conley, *Mus* John Cameron, *Prod* Jules Buck, David Korda, *Exec Prod* Samuel Z. Arkoff.

Cast: Lee Marvin, *Sam Longwood*, Oliver Reed, *Joe Knox*, Robert Culp, *Jack Colby*, Elizabeth Ashley, *Nancy Sue*, Strother Martin, *Billy*, Sylvia Miles, *Mike*, Kay Lenz, *Thursday*, Howard Platt, *Vishniac*, Joe Zacha, *Trainer*, Phaedra, *Friday*, Leticia Robles, *Saturday*, Luz Maria Pena, *Holidays*, Erika Carlson, *Monday*, C.C. Charity, *Tuesday*, Ann Verdugo, *Wednesday*. PG.

Dull western slapstick comedy about an aging cowboy (Lee Marvin) and his relationship with a young prostitute (Kay Lenz). There is also a subplot involving the conflict between Marvin and his former partner (Robert Culp). *The Great Scout & Cathouse Thursday* is an attempt at a large-scale comedy but it collapses under the broad slapstick and the multitude of bad jokes.

349 The Great Train Robbery (1979) ******** Britain, United Artists, 111 min. *Dir* Michael Crichton, *Scr* Michael Crichton, based on his novel, *Cin* Geoffrey Unsworth, *Ed* David Bretherton, *Des* Maurice Carter, *Art* Bert Davey, *Cos* Anthony Mendleson, *Mus* Jerry Goldsmith, *Prod* John Foreman, Presented by Dino De Laurentiis.

Cast: Sean Connery, *Edward Pierce*, Donald Sutherland, *Agar*, Lesley-Anne Down, *Miriam*, Alan Webb, *Edgar Trent*, Malcolm Terris, *Henry Fowler*, Robert Lang, *Insp. Sharp*, Wayne Sleep, *"Clean Willy" Williams*, Michael Elphick, *Burgess*, Pamela Salem, *Emily Trent*, Gabrielle Lloyd, *Elizabeth Trent*, Clive Swift, *Mr. Chubb*, James Cossins, *Insp. Harranby*, John Bett, *McPherson*, Peter Benson, *Dispatcher*, Janine Duvitski, *Maggie*. PG. $5,250,000.

Wonderful period caper comedy set in 19th century England. A trio of thieves (Sean Connery, Donald Sutherland, Lesley-Anne Down) plot an impossible robbery of a gold shipment aboard a train. Much of the film comprises the obligatory plans leading up to the robbery, but unlike other films of the type *The Great Train Robbery* is never boring and does not become bogged down with endless details. English title: *The First Great Train Robbery*.

350 The Great Waldo Pepper (1974) ******** Universal, 107 min. *Dir* George Roy Hill, *Scr* William Goldman, *Story* George Roy Hill, *Cin* Robert Surtees, *Ed* William Reynolds, *Art* Henry Bumstead, *Cos* Edith Head, *Prod* George Roy Hill, *Assoc Prod* Robert L. Crawford, A Jennings Lang Production.

Cast: Robert Redford, *Waldo Pepper*, Bo Svenson, *Alex Olsson*, Bo Brundin, *Ernst Kessler*, Susan Sarandon, *Mary Beth*, Geoffrey Lewis, *Newt*, Edward Herrmann, *Ezra Stiles*, Philip Bruns, *Dillhoefer*, Roderick Cook, *Werfel*, Kelly Jean Peters, *Patsy*, Margot Kidder, *Maude*, Scott Newman, *Duke*, James S. Appleby, *Ace*, Patrick W. Henderson, Jr., *Scooter*, James Harrell, *Farmer*, Elma Aicklen, *Farmer's Wife*, Deborah Knapp, *Farmer's Daughter*, John A. Zee, *Director Western Set*, Joe Billings, *Policeman*, Robert W. Winn, *Theatre Manager*, Lawrence Casey, *German Star*, Greg Martin, *Assistant Director*. PG. $10,165,000.

Excellent comedy adventure about a barnstorming pilot (Robert Redford) during the 1920's, who discovers that his kind are becoming outmoded as aviation advances. He travels throughout the midwest, giving rides and putting on air shows, and later turns to stunt flying in movies where he meets his idol, WWI German ace pilot, Ernst Kessler. *The Great Waldo Pepper* is a fine film that examines individuals who are unable to change with the times. George Roy Hill nicely balances comedy and drama in one of his most personal films.

351 The Great Waltz (1972) ***** MGM, 135 min. *Dir* Andrew L. Stone *Scr* Andrew L. Stone, *Cin* Dave Boulton, *Ed* Ernest Walker, *Art* William Albert Havemeyer, *Cos* Emmi Minnich, Josef Wanke, David Walker, *Mus* Johann Strauss, Jr. and Sr., Josef Strauss, Jacques Offenbach, *Mus Adaptation* George Forrest, Robert Craig Wright, *Chor* Onna White, *Prod* Andrew L. Stone, *Assoc Prod* Peter V. Herald.

Cast: Horst Bucholz, *Johann Strauss, Jr.*, Mary Costa, *Jetty Treffz*, Rossano Brazzi, *Baron Tedesco*, Nigel Patrick, *Johann Strauss, Sr.*, Yvonne Mitchell, *Anna Strauss*, James Faulkner, *Josef Strauss*, Vicki Woolf, *Lili Weyl*,

Susan Richardson, *Emilie Trampusch*, George Howe, *Karl Frederick Hirsch*, Lauri Lupino Lane, *Donmayer*, Michael Tellering, *Karl Haslinger*, Willard Parker, *Karl Treffz*, Ingrid Wayland, *Theresa Strauss*. G. See *Song of Norway*.

352 The Great White Hope (1970) ******** 20th Century–Fox, 103 min. *Dir* Martin Ritt, *Scr* Howard Sackler, based on his play, *Cin* Burnett Guffey, *Ed* William Reynolds, *Des* John DeCuir, *Art* Jack Martin Smith, *Cos* Irene Sharaff, *Mus* Lionel Newman, *Chor* Donald McKayle, *Prod* Lawrence Turman.

Cast: James Earl Jones (AN), *Jack Jefferson*, Jane Alexander (AN), *Eleanor*, Lou Gilbert, *Goldie*, Joel Fluellen, *Tick*, Chester Morris, *Pop Weaver*, Robert Webber, *Dixon*, Marlene Warfield, *Clara*, R.G. Armstrong, *Cap'n Dan*, Hal Holbrook, *Cameron*, Beah Richards, *Mama Tiny*, Moses Gunn, *Scipio*, Lloyd Gough, *Smitty*, George Ebeling, *Fred*, Larry Pennell, *Frank Brady*, Roy E. Glenn, Sr., *Pastor*, Bill Walker, *Deacon*, Marcel Dalio, *French Promoter*. PG.

Excellent period drama about black boxer Jack Jefferson (James Earl Jones) and his white mistress (Jane Alexander), who were scorned in the early part of the century. Although there are some fine boxing sequences, *The Great White Hope* is more of a character study focusing on two people, who are trying to survive in a climate of racial prejudice. Jones and Alexander are simply superb.

353 The Greatest (1977) ****** Columbia, 114 min. *Dir* Tom Gries, *Scr* Ring Lardner, Jr., based on book *The Greatest: My Own Story* by Muhammad Ali, Richard Durham, Herbert Muhammad, *Cin* Harry Stradling, Jr., *Ed* Byron Brandt, *Des* Bob Smith, *Cos* Eric Seelig, Sandra Stewart, *Mus* Michael Masser, *Lyrics* Linda Creed, Gerry Goffin, *Prod* John Marshall.

Cast: Muhammad Ali, *Himself*, Ernest Borgnine, *Angelo Dundee*, Lloyd Haynes, *Herbert Muhammad*, John Marley, *Dr. Pacheco*, Robert Duvall, *Bill McDonald*, David Huddleston, *Cruikshank*, Ben Johnson, *Hollis*, James Earl Jones, *Malcolm X*, Dina Merrill, *Velvet Green*, Roger E. Mosley, *Sonny Liston*, Paul Winfield, *Lawyer*, Annazette Chase, *Belinda Ali*, Mira Waters, *Ruby Sanderson*, Phillip MacAllister, *Young Cassius Clay, Jr.*, Arthur Adams, *Cassius Clay, Sr.*, Dorothy Meyer, *Odessa Clay*, Lucille Benson, *Mrs. Fairlie*, Theodore R. Wilson, *Gardener*, Skip Homeier, *Major*, Sally Gries, *Sponsor's Wife*. PG.

Dull biography of world heavyweight boxing champion Muhammad Ali. *The Greatest*, Ali's self-imposed nickname, skims over the highlights of his life without giving much insight into Ali the man. Ali claims to have been acting throughout his colorful boxing career, but he fails to prove that point in this film, giving a somewhat dull performance as himself. This is all very unfortunate as Ali's life and career could be the subject of a truly exciting film.

354 The Greek Tycoon (1978) ****** Universal, 105 min. *Dir* J. Lee Thompson, *Scr* Mort Fine, *Story* Mort Fine, Nico Mastorakis, Win Wells, *Cin* Tony Richmond, *Ed* Alan Strachan, *Des* Michael Stringer, *Mus* Stanley Myers, *Prod* Allen Klein, Ely Landau, *Co-Prod* Nico Mastorakis, Lawrence Myers, *Exec. Prod.* Mort Abrahams, Peter Howard, Les Landau, *Assoc Prod* Eric Rattray.

Cast: Anthony Quinn, *Theo Tomasis*, Jacqueline Bisset, *Liz Cassidy*, Raf Vallone, *Spyros Tomasis*, Edward Albert, *Nico Tomasis*, James Franciscus, *James Cassidy*, Camilla Sparv, *Simi Tomasis*, Marilu Tolo, *Sophia Malalas*, Charles Durning, *Michael Russell*, Luciana Paluzzi, *Paolo Scotti*, Robin

Clarke, *John Cassidy*, Kathryn Leigh Scott, *Nancy Cassidy*, Roland Culver, *Robert Keith*, Tony Jay, *Doctor*, John Bennett, *Servant*, Katherine Schofield, *Helena*, Joan Benham, *Lady Allison*, Linda Thorson, *Angela*, Guy Deghy, *Tahlib*, Jill Melford, *Magda*, Lucy Gutteridge, *Mia*. R. $8,260,000.

Dismal soap opera about the wife of an assassinated American president who marries a Greek shipping tycoon. *The Greek Tycoon* does not name names and purports to be fiction, but it is obvious who this film is based on. There does not seem to be much point in this fictionalization. The acting is only fair and Anthony Quinn is overbearing in the title role.

355 The Grissom Gang (1971) *** Cinerama, 127 min. *Dir* Robert Aldrich, *Scr* Leon Griffiths, based on novel *No Orchids for Miss Blandish* by James Hadley Chase, *Cin* Joseph Biroc, *Ed* Michael Luciano, *Art* James Vance, *Cos* Norma Koch, *Mus* Gerald Fried, *Chor* Alex Romero, *Prod* Robert Aldrich, *Assoc Prod* Walter Blake.

Cast: Kim Darby, *Barbara Blandish*, Scott Wilson, *Slim Grissom*, Tony Musante, *Eddie Hagen*, Robert Lansing, *Dave Fenner*, Irene Dailey, *Ma Grissom*, Connie Stevens, *Anna Borg*, Wesley Addy, *John P. Blandish*, Joey Faye, *Woppy*, Don Keefer, *Doc*, Dotts Johnson, *Johnny Hutchins*, Mort Marshall, *Heinie*, Michael Baseleon, *Connor*, Ralph Waite, *Mace*, Hal Baylor, *Chief McLaine*, Matt Clark, *Bailey*. R.

Above-average crime thriller focusing on the kidnapping of a rich society girl (Kim Darby), during the Depression, by a Ma Barker type gang headed by a sadistic matriarch (Irene Dailey). Their plans become complicated when one of her sons (Scott Wilson) falls in love with the girl. *The Grissom Gang* is slightly sadistic, but Aldrich handles the violence well.

356 The Gumball Rally (1976) ** Warner Bros., 106 min. *Dir* Chuck Bail, *Scr* Leon Capetanos, *Story* Chuck Bail, Leon Capetanos, *Cin* Richard C. Glouner, *Ed* Stuart H. Pappe, Gordon Scott, Maury Winetrobe, *Art* Walter Simonds, *Mus* Dominic Frontiere, *Prod* Chuck Bail, *Assoc Prod* Leon Capetanos.

Cast: Michael Sarrazin, *Bannon*, Norman Burton, *Roscoe*, Gary Busey, *Gibson*, John Durren, *Preston*, Susan Flannery, *Alice*, Harvey Jason, *Lapchick*, Steven Keats, *Kandinsky*, Tim McIntire, *Smith*, Joanne Nail, *Jane*, J. Pat O'Malley, *Barney*, Tricia O'Neil, *Angie*, Lazaro Perez, *Jose*, Nicholas Pryor, *Graves*, Vaughn Taylor, *Andy*, Wally Taylor, *Avila*, Raul Julia, *Franco*. PG. $7,900,000.

Standard cross-country road race comedy. A group of oddball characters periodically assemble for this race and are pursued by an obsessed cop. There is no real story to the film and it is stretched out too long, filling in the gaps with the usual chases and crashes. *The Gumball Rally* is one of several films with the same premise and they all seem like the same film.

357 A Gunfight (1971) ** Paramount, 90 min. *Dir* Lamont Johnson, *Scr* Harold Jack Bloom, *Cin* David Walsh, *Des* Tambi Larsen, *Cos* Mickey Sherwood, *Mus* Laurence Rosenthal, *Title Song* composed and sung by Johnny Cash, *Prod* Harold Jack Bloom, A. Ronald Lubin, *Assoc Prod* Saul Holiff.

Cast: Kirk Douglas, *Will Tenneray*, Johnny Cash, *Abe Cross*, Jane Alexander, *Nora Tenneray*, Raf Vallone, *Francisco Alvarez*, Karen Black, *Jenny Simms*, Eric Douglas, *Bud Tenneray*, Phillip L. Mead, *Kyle*, John Wallwork,

Toby, Dana Elcar, *Marv Green*, Robert J. Wilke, *Cater*, George Le Bow, *Dekker*, James D. Cavasos, *Newt Hale*, Keith Carradine, *Cowboy*. PG.

Boring western about two aging gunfighters (Kirk Douglas, Johnny Cash), who organize a gunfight between the two, to be held in a bullring, and sell tickets to the public. *A Gunfight* certainly has an interesting premise, but unfortunately there is far too much talk and little action, which stretches the build-up to the climactic gunfight out endlessly.

358 **Gumshoe** (1972) ** Britain, Columbia, 88 min. *Dir* Stephen Frears, *Scr* Neville Smith, *Cin* Chris Menges, *Ed* Charles Rees, *Des* Michael Seymour, *Cos* Daphne Dare, *Mus* Andrew Lloyd Webber, *Lyrics* Tim Rice, *Prod* Michael Medwin, *Assoc Prod* David Barber.

Cast: Albert Finney, *Eddie Ginley*, Billie Whitelaw, *Ellen*, Frank Finlay, *William*, Janice Rule, *Mrs. Blankerscoon*, Carolyn Seymour, *Alison*, Fulton Mackay, *Straker*, George Innes, *Bookshop Proprietor*, George Silver, *De Fries*, Billy Dean, *Tommy*, Wendy Richard, *Anne Scott*, Maureen Lipman, *Naomi*, Neville Smith, *Arthur*, Oscar James, *Azinge*, Joey Kenyon, *Joey*, Bert King, *Mal*, Chris Cunningham, *Clifford*, Ken Jones, *Labor Exchange Clerk*, Tom Kempinski, *Psychiatrist*, Harry Hutchinson, *Kleptomaniac*, Ernie Mack and The Saturated Seven, Jason Kane, The Jacksons, Vicki Day, Scott Christian, *Club Artists*. PG.

Fair satire of detective films. Albert Finney stars as a second-rate entertainer, who becomes obsessed with these films and tries to emulate Humphrey Bogart by becoming an amateur sleuth. The makers of *Gumshoe* apparently do not understand this genre, as the film completely misses its target, and the English setting is entirely wrong for such an American subject.

359 **Gus** (1976) *** Buena Vista, 96 min. *Dir* Vincent McEveety, *Scr* Arthur Alsberg, Don Nelson, based on story by Ted Key, *Cin* Frank Phillips, *Ed* Robert Stafford, *Art* John B. Mansbridge, Al Roelofs, *Mus* Robert F. Brunner, *Prod* Ron Miller, A Walt Disney Production.

Cast: Edward Asner, *Hank Cooper*, Don Knotts, *Coach Venner*, Gary Grimes, *Andy Petrovic*, Tim Conway, *Crankcase*, Liberty Williams, *Debbie Kovac*, Dick Van Patten, *Cal Wilson*, Ronnie Schell, *Joe Barnsdale*, Bob Crane, *Pepper*, Johnny Unitas, *Himself*, Dick Butkus, *Rob Cargil*, Harold Gould, *Charles Gwynn*, Tom Bosley, *Spinner*, Dick Enberg, *Atoms Announcer*, George Putnam, *TV Interviewer*, Stu Naham, *L.A. Sportscaster*. G. $9,850,000.

Standard Walt Disney fantasy comedy about a mule that plays football. Edward Asner stars as the owner of a pro football team, who imports a soccer playing mule from Yugoslavia to save his team. The premise is a bit far-fetched and the plot is slightly predictable, but the film is pleasant entertainment. *Gus* is much like the Disney fantasies of the 1960's and is every bit their equal.

360 **Hair** (1979) **** United Artists, 118 min. *Dir* Milos Forman, *Scr* Michael Weller, based on musical play by James Rado, Gerome Ragni, Galt MacDermot, *Cin* Miroslav Ondricek, *Ed* Lynzee Klingman, *Des* Stuart Wurtzel, *Cos* Ann Roth, *Mus* Galt MacDermot, *Lyrics* James Rado, Gerome Ragni, *Chor* Twyla Tharp, *Prod* Michael Butler, Lester Persky, *Assoc Prod* Robert Greenhut.

Cast: John Savage, *Claude*, Treat Williams, *Berger*, Beverly D'Angelo, *Sheila*, Annie Golden, *Jeannie*, Dorsey Wright, *Hud*, Don Dacus, *Woof*, Cheryl Barnes, *Hud's Fiancee*, Richard Bright, *Fenton*, Nicholas Ray, *The General*, Charlotte Rae, *Party Guest*, Miles Chapin, *Steve*, Fern Tailer, *Sheila's Mother*, Charles Deney, *Sheila's Father*, Herman Meckler, *Sheila's Uncle*, Agness Breen, *Sheila's Aunt*, Antonia Rey, *Berger's Mother*, George Manos, *Berger's Father*, Linda Surh, *Vietnamese Girl*, Joe Acord, *Claude's Father*. PG. $6,800,000.

Splendid musical adaptation of legendary 1960's stage musical. *Hair* is no longer topical and hence the film stands as a period piece; a document of the 1960's that wonderfully captures its ideals and rebellious spirit, something that most dramas failed to do. The musical sequences are among the best ever put on film, due considerably to Twyla Tharp's imaginative choreography. Milos Forman again proves that he can portray American society as accurately and as insightful as any American.

361 **Halloween** (1978) ******** Compass International, 93 min. *Dir* John Carpenter, *Scr* John Carpenter, Debra Hill, *Cin* Dean Cundy, *Ed* Charles Burnstein, Tommy Lee Wallace, *Des* Tommy Lee Wallace, *Mus* John Carpenter, *Prod* Debra Hill, *Exec Prod* Irwin Yablans.

Cast: Jamie Lee Curtis, *Laurie*, Donald Pleasence, *Loomis*, Nancy Loomis, *Annie*, P.J. Soles, *Lynda*, Charles Cyphers, *Brackett*, Kyle Richards, *Lindsey*, Brian Andrews, *Tommy*, John Michael Graham, *Bob*, Nancy Stephens, *Marion*, Arthur Malet, *Graveyard Keeper*, Mickey Yablans, *Richie*, Brent LePage, *Lonnie*, Adam Hollander, *Keith*, Robert Phalen, *Dr. Wynn*, Tony Moran, *Michael at 23*, Will Sandin, *Michael at 6*, Sandy Johnson, *Judith*, David Kyle, *Boy Friend*, Peter Griffith, *Laurie's Father*, Jim Windburn, *Stunt*, Nick Castle, *The Shape*. R. $18,500,000.

Excellent murder thriller about a mad slasher who excapes from an institution and terrorizes his hometown on Halloween night. *Halloween* is one of the best and most successful independently made films. Unlike other films of its type, most of which were inspired by this one, the emphasis is more on suspense than on gore and due to John Carpenter's stylish direction *Halloween* contains genuine thrills and sustained tension without resorting to repulsing the audience.

362 **Hammersmith Is Out** (1972) ****** Cinerama, 108 min. *Dir* Peter Ustinov, *Scr* Stanford Whitmore, *Cin* Richard H. Kline, *Ed* David Blewitt, *Cos* Edith Head, *Mus* Dominic Frontiere, Sally Stevens, *Prod* Alex Lucas.

Cast: Elizabeth Taylor (BF), *Jimmie Jean Jackson*, Richard Burton, *Hammersmith*, Peter Ustinov, *Doctor*, Beau Bridges, *Billy Breedlove*, Leon Askin, *Dr. Krodt*, Leon Ames, *Gen. Sam Pembroke*, John Schuck, *Henry Joe*, George Raft, *Guido Scartucci*, Marjorie Eaton, *Princess*, Lisa Jak, *Kiddo*, Linda Gaye Scott, *Miss Quim*, Mal Berger, *Fat Man*, Anthony Holland, *Oldham*, Brook Williams, *Pete Rutter*, Carl Donn, *Cleopatra*, Jose Espinoza, *Duke*. R.

Strange variation of the *Faust* legend starring Richard Burton as a crazed mental patient, who promises a male nurse (Beau Bridges) great wealth and power if he will set him free from the asylum. Bridges lets him escape and through ruthless means, Burton keeps his promise. *Hammersmith Is Out* is a bizarre black comedy, but not all of the humor works.

363 **Handle with Care** (1977) **** Paramount, 98 min. *Dir* Jonathon Demme, *Scr* Paul Brickman, *Cin* Jordan Cronenweth, *Ed* John F. Link II, *Des* Bill Malley, *Cos* Jodie Lynn Tillen, *Mus* Bill Conti, *Exec Prod* Shep Fields, *Assoc Prod* Paul Brickman.

Cast: Paul LeMat, *Blaine (Spider)*, Candy Clark, *Pam (Electra)*, Ann Wedgeworth (NS), *Joyce Rissley*, Bruce McGill, *Dean (Blood)*, Marcia Rodd, *Connie (Dallas Angel)*, Charles Napier, *Harold (Chrome Angel)*, Alix Elias, *Debbie (Hot Coffee)*, Roberts Blossom, *Blaine's Father (Papa Thermadyne)*, Richard Bright, *Garage Owner (Smilin' Jack)*, Ed Begley, Jr., *Priest*, Michael Rothman, *Cochise*, Michael Mahler, *Hustler*, Harry Northup, *Red Baron*, Will Seltzer, *Warlock*. PG.

Wonderful comedy about one man's campaign to end abuse of CB (Citizen's Band) radio in his town. *Handle with Care* may have suffered from guilt by association because of its subject matter, but this is by no means a drive-in feature. The CB's are not merely for comic effect, as in other films, but a device to bring out the true personalities of the film's characters; people who are unable to be themselves without this "mask" to hide behind. This was Jonathon Demme's first important film, but despite its excellent reviews, it failed to find an audience. In a gallant effort to save the film, Paramount changed its original title *Citizens Band* to its present title.

364 **Hannie Caulder** (1971) ** Britain, Paramount, 85 min. *Dir* Burt Kennedy, *Scr* Z.X. Jones, (pseudonym for David Haft, Burt Kennedy), *Story* Peter Cooper, based on characters created by Ian Quicke, Bob Richards, *Cin* Edward Scaife, *Ed* Jim Connock, *Art* Jose Alguero, *Cos* Ray Aghayan, *Mus* Ken Thorne, *Prod* Patrick Curtis, *Exec Prod* Tony Tenser.

Cast: Raquel Welch, *Hannie Caulder*, Robert Culp, *Thomas Luther Price*, Ernest Borgnine, *Emmett Clemens*, Strother Martin, *Rufus Clemens*, Jack Elam, *Frank Clemens*, Christopher Lee, *Bailey*, Diana Dors, *Madame*, Stephen Boyd, *The Preacher*. R.

Dismal western comedy starring Raquel Welch as a female gunslinger on the vengeance trail. Three outlaws (Ernest Borgnine, Strother Martin, Jack Elam) rape her and murder her husband. Welch is taught how to shoot a gun by Robert Culp and she sets out after the three creeps. *Hannie Caulder* is for the most part, dull and predictable, and the characters are exaggerated sterotypes, particularly the three overly repulsive outlaws.

365 **Hanover Street** (1979) ** Britain, Columbia, 109 min. *Dir* Peter Hyams, *Scr* Peter Hyams, *Cin* David Watkin, *Ed* James Mitchell, *Des* Philip Harrison, *Art* Robert Cartwright, Malcolm Middleton, *Cos* Joan Bridge, *Mus* John Barry, *Prod* Paul N. Lazarus III, *Assoc Prod* Harry Benn, Michael Rachmil.

Cast: Harrison Ford, *David Halloran*, Lesley-Anne Down, *Margaret Sellinger*, Christopher Plummer, *Paul Sellinger*, Alec McCowen, *Maj. Trumbo*, Richard Masur, *2nd Lt. Jerry Cimino*, Michael Sacks, *2nd Lt. Martin Hyer*, Patsy Kensit, *Sarah Sellinger*, Max Wall, *Harry Pike*, Shane Rimmer, *Col. Ronald Bart*, Keith Buckley, *Lt. Wells*, Sherrie Hewson, *Phyllis*, Cindy O'Callaghan, *Paula*, Di Trevis, *Elizabeth*, Suzanne Bertish, *French Girl*, Keith Alexander, *Soldier in Barn*. PG.

Sappy love story set in wartorn London. An American WWII bomber pilot (Harrison Ford) meets an English woman (Lesley-Anne Down), and the two fall in love, but she happens to be married to a nice guy (Christopher Plummer). Everything in *Hanover Street* is excessively nice and overly cute. The film only really catches hold in the later part when Ford and Plummer become unlikely partners in an espionage mission, leaving the romance behind.

366 **Hard Times** (1975) ******** Columbia, 92 min. *Dir* Walter Hill, *Scr* Bryan Gindorff, Bruce Henstell, Walter Hill, *Story* Bryan Gindorff, Bruce Henstell, *Cin* Philip Lathrop, *Ed* Roger Spottiswoode, *Art* Trevor Williams, *Mus* Barry DeVorzon, *Prod* Lawrence Gordon, *Exec Prod* Paul Maslansky.

   Cast: Charles Bronson, *Chaney*, James Coburn, *Speed*, Jill Ireland, *Lucy*, Strother Martin, *Poe*, Maggie Blye, *Gayleen*, Michael McGuire, *Gandil*, Robert Tessier, *Jim Henry*, Nick Dimitri, *Street*, Felice Orlandi, *Le Beau*, Bruce Glover, *Doty*, Edward Walsh, *Pettibon*. PG. $4,000,000.

   Charles Bronson's finest film to date. Bronson stars as a bare-knuckled streetfighter in New Orleans during the Depression of the 1930's. *Hard Times* surpasses his other vehicles due to the tight direction by Walter Hill who makes full use of Bronson's screen persona, but without the usual excesses that flawed most of the others. This was an excellent directorial debut for screenwriter Hill, who followed this with a string of superior crime thrillers.

367 **Hardcore** (1979) ******** Columbia, 105 min. *Dir* Paul Schrader, *Scr* Paul Schrader, *Cin* Michael Chapman, *Ed* Tom Rolf, *Des* Paul Sylbert, *Art* Ed O'Donovan, *Mus* Jack Nitzche, *Prod* Buzz Feitshans, *Exec Prod* John Milius.

   Cast: George C. Scott, *Jake Van Dorn*, Peter Boyle, *Andy Mast*, Season Hubley, *Niki*, Dick Sargent, *Wes DeJong*, Leonard Gaines, *Ramada*, David Nichols, *Kurt*, Gary Rand Graham, *Tod*, Larry Block, *Detective Burrows*, Marc Alaimo, *Ratan*, Leslie Ackerman, *Felice*, Charlotte McGinnis, *Beatrice*, Ilah Davis, *Kristen Van Dorn*, Paul Marin, *Joe Van Dorn*, Will Walker, *Jism Jim*, Hal Williams, *Big Dick Blacque*, Bibi Besch, *Mary*. R. $7,025,000.

   Excellent story of a religious man's desperate search for his daughter in the world of pornography. *Hardcore* is much more than just a thriller, as Schrader uses this as a vehicle for his ideas about extremes and how one extreme can cause another. The worlds of religion and pornography are compared and contrasted as both being overly extreme in their attitudes. Kristen rebels against her repressive religious upbringing by going too far to the other extreme. With this film Schrader achieved a unique position, by being the first person to actually offend makers of pornography.

368 **Harold and Maude** (1971) ******** Paramount, 91 min. *Dir* Hal Ashby, *Scr* Colin Higgins, *Cin* John A. Alonzo, *Ed* William A. Sawyer, Edward Warschilka, *Mus* Cat Stevens, *Prod* Colin Higgins, Charles Mulvehill.

   Cast: Bud Cort, *Harold*, Ruth Gordon, *Maude*, Vivien Pickles, *Mrs. Chasen*, Cyril Cusack, *Glaucus*, Charles Tyner, *Uncle Victor*, Ellen Geer, *Sunshine Dore*, Eric Christmas, *Priest*, G. Wood, *Psychiatrist*, Judy Engles, *Candy Gulf*, Shari Summers, *Edith Fern*. R.

   Bizarre black comedy about two lonely people, a 20 year old man and a 79 year old woman, who meet through their common interest in funerals and develop a strange relationship. *Harold and Maude* is one of the weirdest films ever made and Hal Ashby's brilliantly subtle direction prevents the film from going over the edge. The film's comic highlights are Harold's wild fake suicides and his mother's reaction to them.

369 **Harper Valley P.T.A.** (1978) * April Fools, 93 min. *Dir* Richard Bennett, *Scr* George Edwards, Barry Schneider, based on song by Tom T. Hall, *Cin* Willy Kurant, *Ed* Michael Economu, *Cos* Tom Rasmussen, *Mus* Nelson Riddle, *Prod* George Edwards, *Exec Prod* Phil Borack.

Cast: Barbara Eden, *Stella*, Ronny Cox, *Willis*, Nanette Fabray, *Alice*, Susan Swift, *Dee*, Louis Nye, *Kirby*, Pat Paulsen, *Otis*, John Fiedler, *Bobby*, Audrey Christie, *Flora*, DeVara Marcus, *Holly*, Irene Yah Ling Sun, *Myrna*, Louise Foley, *Mavis*, Clint Howard, *Corley*, Jan Teige, Laura Teige, *Reilly Twins*, Pitt Herbert, *Henry*, Faye Dewitt, *Willie Mae*, Molly Dodd, *Olive*, Ron Masak, *Herbie*, Bob Hastings, *Skeeter*. PG. $8,550,000.

The famous hit song from the 1960's about a denounced woman who gets revenge on the local conservative P.T.A. could have been the basis for an interesting social satire, but this film misses that opportunity by a mile. *Harper Valley P.T.A.* is nothing more than a sophomoric slapstick comedy that strains desperately for laughs, highlighted by the use of an elephant to disgrace one P.T.A. member.

370 **The Harrad Experiment** (1973) ** Cinerama, 96 min. *Dir* Ted Post, *Scr* Ted Cassedy, Michael Werner, based on novel by Robert H. Rimmer, *Cin* Richard H. Kline, *Ed* Bill Brame, *Mus* Artie Butler, *Prod* Dennis F. Stevens, *Exec Prod* Noel Marshall, *Assoc Prod* Mel Sokolow.

Cast: James Whitmore, *Philip*, Tippi Hedren, *Margaret*, Don Johnson, *Stanley*, B. Kirby, Jr., *Harry*, Laurie Walters, *Sheila*, Victoria Thompson, *Beth*, Elliot Street, *Wilson*, Sharon Taggart, *Barbara*, Robert Middleton, *Sidney*, Billy Sands, *Jack*, Melody Patterson, *Jeannie*, Maggie Wellman, *Cynthia*, Michael Greene, *Yoga Instructor*, Ron Kolman, *Evan*, Eric Server, Robert C. Ross, *Workmen*, the Ace Trucking Company. R.

Boring drama about sexual relationships in contemporary society, based on a study from an experiment at a coed college. *The Harrad Experiment* alternates between a boring science lecture and a dull soap opera, centering on the relationships of two of the couples involved in the experiment. *Harrad Summer* is an equally dull sequel, in which the participants can apply their knowledge to their life at home.

371 **Harrad Summer** (1974) * Cinerama, 105 min. *Dir* Steven Hillard Stern, *Scr* Morth Thaw, Steven Zacharias, *Cin* Richard Kline, *Ed* Bill Brame, *Mus* Pat Williams, *Prod* Dennis F. Stevens, *Exec Prod* Duke Goldstone.

Cast: Robert Reiser, *Stanley*, Laurie Walters, *Sheila*, Richard Doran, *Harry*, Victoria Thompson, *Beth*, Emaline Henry, *Margaret*, Bill Dana, *Jake*, Jode an Russo, *Paula*, Angela Clarke, *Mrs. Kolasukas*, Tito Vandis, *Kolasukas*, Walter Brooke, *Sam*, Mimi Saffian, *Diane*, Lisa Moore, *Arnae*, James Beach, *Brad*, Pearl Shear, *Fritzi*, Jane Lambert, *Florence*, Marty Allen, *Bert*, Lili Valenty, *Great Grandma*, Sherry Miles, *Dee*, Patrice Rohmer, *Marcia*, Sylvia Waldon, Chuckie Bradley, *Woman's Consciousness Group*. R. See *the Harrad Experiment*.

372 **Harry and Tonto** (1974) *** 20th Century–Fox, 115 min. *Dir* Paul Mazursky, *Scr* Josh Greenfield, Paul Mazursky (AN), *Cin* Michael Butler, *Ed* Richard Halsey, *Des* Ted Haworth, *Cos* Albert Wolsky, *Prod* Paul Mazursky, *Assoc Prod* Tony Ray.

Cast: Art Carney (A, GMC), *Harry*, Ellen Burstyn, *Shirley*, Chief Dan

George, *Old Indian*, Geraldine Fitzgerald, *Jessie*, Larry Hagman, *Eddie*, Arthur Hunnicutt, *Wade*, Phil Bruns, *Burt*, Joshua Mostel, *Norman*, Melanie Mayron, *Ginger*, Dolly Jonah, *Elaine*, Herbert Berghof, *Rivetowski*, Avon Lang, *Leroy*, Barbara Rhodes, *Happy Hooker*, Cliff DeYoung, *Junior*. R. $4,600,000.

Sentimental and bittersweet story of an old man and his cat. After being evicted from his New York apartment Harry goes on a cross-country trip with his cat Tonto to visit each of his children, all of whom prove to be disappointments. *Harry and Tonto* is somewhat reminiscent of Vittorio DeSica's *Umberto D*, but it lacks the older film's brilliant simplicity. *Harry and Tonto* is dominated by the truly superb performance of Art Carney, in his first major screen role.

373 Harry and Walter Go to New York (1976) ** Columbia, 120 min. *Dir* Mark Rydell, *Scr* John Byrum, Robert Kaufman, *Story* John Byrum, Don Devlin, *Cin* Laszlo Kovacs, *Ed* David Bretherton, Don Guidice, *Des* Harry Horner, *Art* Richard Berger, *Cos* Theoni V. Aldridge, *Mus* David Shire, *Lyrics* Alan and Marilyn Bergman, *Prod* Don Devlin, Harry Gittes, *Exec Prod* Tony Bill, *Assoc Prod* Sheldon Shrager.

Cast: James Caan, *Harry Dighby*, Elliott Gould, *Walter Hill*, Michael Caine, *Adam Worth*, Diane Keaton, *Lissa Chestnut*, Charles Durning, *Rufus T. Crisp*, Lesley Ann Warren, *Gloria Fontaine*, Val Avery, *Chatsworth*, Jack Gilford, *Mischa*, Dennis Dugan, *Lewis*, Carol Kane, *Florence*, Kathryn Grody, *Barbara*, David Proval, *Ben*, Michael Conrad, *Billy Gallagher*, Burt Young, *Warden Durgom*, Bert Remsen, *Guard O'Meara*, Ted Cassidy, *Leary*, Michael Greene, *Dan*, James DeCloss, *Barney*, Nicky Blair, *Charley Bullard*, George Greif, *Dutch Herman*, John Hackett, *Ike Marsh*, Phil Kenneally, *Officer O'Reilly*. PG. $4,600,000.

Poor period slapstick comedy about two talentless vaudevillians (Elliot Gould, James Caan) who become involved with a master criminal (Michael Caine). *Harry and Walter Go to New York* had everything going for it; an excellent story, a fine cast and a magnificent recreation of the period; but somehow it just fell apart. The flaw is in the execution, because Mark Rydell tried too hard to wring laughs out of the material. This should have been played more seriously.

374 Harry in Your Pocket (1973) ** United Artists, 103 min. *Dir* Bruce Geller, *Scr* Ron Austin, James David Buchanon, *Cin* Fred Koenekamp, *Ed* Arthur L. Hilton, *Art* William Bates, *Mus* Lalo Schifrin, *Prod* Bruce Geller, *Exec Prod* Alden Schwimmer.

Cast: James Coburn, *Harry*, Michael Sarrazin, *Ray*, Trish Van Devere, *Sandy*, Walter Pidgeon, *Casey*, Michael C. Gwynne, *Fence*, Tony Giorgio, *First Detective*, Michael Sterns, *Second Detective*, Sue Mullen, *Francine*, Duane Bennett, *Salesman*, Stanley Bolt, *Mr. Bates*, Barry Grimshaw, *Bellboy*. PG.

Dull crime thriller focusing on a group of pickpockets. Michael Sarrazin and Trish Van Devere are a young couple, who wish to learn the trade, and they join up with old pros James Coburn and Walter Pidgeon. An obligatory love triangle develops between Sarrazin, Van Devere and Coburn, which complicates their working relationship. There are some interesting moments, highlighting the art, but the film otherwise is pretty standard.

375 The Hawaiians (1970) ** United Artists, 134 min. *Dir* Tom Gries, *Scr* James R. Webb, Based on novel *Hawaii* by James Michener, *Cin* Lucien Ballard, Philip Lathrop, *Ed* Byron Brandt, Ralph Winters, *Des* Cary Odell, *Art* George Chan, *Cos* Bill Thomas (AN), *Mus* Henry Mancini, *Prod* Walter Mirisch, *Assoc Prod* Walter Mirisch, *Assoc Prod* Robert Stambler.

Cast: Charlton Heston, *Whip Hoxworth*, Geraldine Chaplin, *Purity Hoxworth*, John Phillip Law, *Noel Hoxworth*, Tina Chen, *Nyuk Tsin*, Alec McCowen, *Micah Hale*, Mako, *Mun Ki*, Don Knight, *Milton Overpeck*, Miko Mayama, *Fumiko*, Virginia Ann Lee, *Me Li*, Naomi Stevens, *Queen Liliuokalani*, Harry Townes, *American Minister*, Khigh Dhiegh, *Kai Chung*, Keye Luke, *Foo Sen*, James Gregory, *Dr. Whipple, Sr.*, Lyle Bettger, *Jankers*. PG.

Fair sequel to *Hawaii* that continues the story with the return of a sailor (Charlton Heston) to Hawaii to discover his grandfather's fortune has been left to this cousin (Alec McCowen). Heston establishes his own plantation to rival McCowen. *The Hawaiians* is a typically dull historical epic that spans a period of several decades and is more of a soap opera than real history.

376 Hawmps (1976) * Mulberry Square Productions, 126 min. *Dir* Joe Camp, *Scr* William Bickley, Michael Warren, *Story* William Bickley, Joe Camp, Michael Warren, *Cin* Don Reddy, *Ed* Leon Seith, *Des* Harland Wright, *Art* Ned Parsons, *Mus* Euel Box, *Prod* Joe Camp, *Co-Prod* Ben Vaughn, *Exec Prod* A.Z. Smith, *Assoc Prod* H.T. Ardinger, Jr.

Cast: James Hampton, *Howard Clemmons*, Christopher Connelly, *Uriah Tibbs*, Slim Pickens, *Naman Tucker*, Denver Pyle, *Col. Seymour Hawkins*, Gene Conforti, *Hi Jolly*, Mimi Maynard, *Jennifer Hawkins*, Lee de Broux, *Fitzgerald*, Herb Vigran, *Smitty*, Jessie Davis, *Mariachi Singer*, Frank Inn, *Cook*, Larry Swartz, *Cpl. LeRoy*, Mike Travis, *Logan*, Tiny Wells, *Higgens*, Dick Drake, *Drake*, Henry Kendrick, *Col. Zachary*. G. $5,350,000.

Silly Disney-style comedy, based on an historical incident about a U.S. Cavalry experiment, in which they replace horses with camels. This is an interesting premise, but it just simply goes awry with its broad slapstick and sophomoric humor. The biggest flaw though is its length, which is wildly overlong at two hours. *Hawmps* is a bad joke that seems to never end.

377 Head over Heels (1979) ** United Artists, 109 min. *Dir* Joan Micklin Silver, *Scr* Joan Micklin Silver, based on novel *Chilly Scenes of Winter* by Ann Beattie, *Cin* Bobby Byrne, *Ed* Cynthia Scheider, *Des* Peter Jamison, *Cos* Rosanna Norton, *Mus* Len Lauber, *Prod* Griffin Dunne, Mark Metcalf, Amy Robinson.

Cast: John Heard, *Charles*, Mary Beth Hurt, *Laura*, Peter Riegert, *Sam*, Kenneth McMillan, *Pete*, Gloria Grahame, *Clara*, Nora Heflin, *Betty*, Jerry Hardin, *Mr. Patterson*, Tarah Nutter, *Susan*, Mark Metcalf, *Ox*, Allen Joseph, *Blindman*, Frances Bay, *Mrs. Dilillo*, Griffin Dunne, *Dr. Mark*, Alex Johnson, *Elise*, Beverly Booth Rowland, *Woman in Park*, Ann Beattie, *Waitress*, Angela Phillips, *Rebecca*, Margaressa Peach Taylor, *Dancing Nurse*. PG.

Disappointing comedy love story about a government worker (John Heard), who tries desperately to win back his former girlfriend (Mary Beth Hurt). Heard's obsessiveness becomes more annoying to the audience than to Hurt. *Head over Heels* uneasily alternates its tone between comedy and drama and is too reminiscent of Woody Allen's films. Other title *Chilly Scenes of Winter*.

378 The Heartbreak Kid (1972) ***** 20th Century–Fox, 104 min. *Dir* Elaine May, *Scr* Neil Simon, based on story *"A Change of Pace"* by Bruce Jay Friedman, *Cin* Owen Roizman, *Ed* John Carter, *Art* Richard Sylbert, *Cos* Anthea Sylbert, *Mus* Garry Sherman, *Title Song* Cy Coleman, Sheldon Harnick, *Prod* Edgar J. Scherick, *Assoc Prod* Michael Hausman, Erik Lee Preminger.

Cast: Charles Grodin, *Lenny*, Cybill Shepherd, *Kelly*, Jeannie Berlin (AN, NS, NY), *Lila*, Eddie Albert (AN, NS), *Mr. Corcoran*, Audra Lindley, *Mrs. Corcoran*, William Prince, *Colorado Man*, Augusta Dabney, *Colorado Woman*, Mitchell Jason, *Cousin Ralph*, Art Metrano, *Entertainer*, Marilyn Putnam, *Mrs. Kolodny*, Jack Hausman, *Mr. Kolodny*, Erik Lee Preminger, *Pecan Pie Waiter*, Tim Browne, *Kelly's Boyfriend*, Jean Scoppa, *Flower Girl*, Greg Pecque, *Young Boy*, Doris Roberts, *Mrs. Cantrow*. PG. $5,530,000.

Brilliant comedy about a man who falls in love with another woman while on his honeymoon. *The Heartbreak Kid* is Neil Simon's one claim to cinema greatness, which ironically was not an original of Simon's, but an adaptation of a Bruce Jay Friedman short story. Simon tried to write the screenplay in Friedman's style rather than his own, and this is one of the reasons for its success. The script has all the subtle brilliance that Simon's originals lack; he tends to fill his other scripts with stand-up comedians rather than real characters. The cast is superb, particularly Charles Grodin who is so perfect as the title character, that he has the audience believing his lies.

379 Heartland (1979) *** Filmhaus, 93 min. *Dir* Richard Pearce, *Scr* Beth Ferris, *Cin* Fred Murphy, *Ed* Bill Yahraus, *Dir* Patrizia Von Brandenstein, *Art* Carl Copeland, *Cos* Hilary Rosenfeld, *Mus* Charles Gross, *Prod* Beth Ferris, Michael Hausman, *Exec Prod* Annick Smith.

Cast: Rip Torn, *Clyde*, Conchata Ferrell, *Elinore*, Barry Primus, *Jack*, Lilia Skala, *Grandma*, Megan Folson, *Jerrine*, Amy Wright, *Clara*, Jerry Hardin, *Cattlebuyer*, Mary Boyland, *Ma Gillis*, Jeff Boschee, Robert Overholzer, *Land Office Agents*, Bob Sirucek, *Dan*, Marvin Berg, *Justice of Peace*, Gary Voldseth, Mike Robertson, Doug Johnson, *Cowboys*. Not Rated.

Fine frontier drama set in Wyoming in 1910. A young widow (Conchata Farrell) is hired to be a housekeeper for a rancher (Rip Torn) living in the Rockies, and the two eventually marry. *Heartland* is a realistic and unpretentious view of frontier life. This is a low-budget independent feature, but it is a well-made film and a fine debut by director Richard Pearce.

380 Hearts of the West (1975) *** United Artists, 102 min. *Dir* Howard Zieff, *Scr* Bob Thompson, *Cin* Mario Tosi, *Ed* Edward Warschilka, *Art* Robert Luthardt, *Mus* Ken Lauber, *Prod* Tony Bill.

Cast: Jeff Bridges, *Lewis Tater*, Andy Griffith, *Howard Pike*, Donald Pleasence, *A.J. Nietz*, Blythe Danner, *Miss Trout*, Alan Arkin (NY), *Kessler*, Richard B. Shull, *Fat Man*, Herbert Edelman, *Polo*, Alex Rocco, *Earl*, Frank Cady, *Pa Tater*, Anthony James, *Lean Man*, Burton Gilliam, *Lester*, Matt Clark, *Jackson*, Candy Azzara, *Waitress*, Thayer David, *Bank Manager*, Wayne Storm, *Lyle*, Marie Windsor, *Woman in Nevada*. PG.

Fine comedy about a young man who goes to Hollywood, during the 1930's, to become big western writer, but instead becomes a cowboy actor in low-budget westerns. There are many fine performances, particularly Alan Arkin as an eccentric movie director, and there are also many wonderful moments, but *Hearts of the West* has a somewhat thin storyline. Other title *Hollywood Cowboy*.

381 Heaven Can Wait (1978) (AN, GMC) **** Paramount, 101 min. *Dir* Warren Beatty, Buck Henry (AN), *Scr* Warren Beatty, Elaine May (AN), based on play by Harry Segall, *Cin* William A. Fraker (AN), *Ed* Robert C. Jones, Don Zimmerman, *Des* Paul Sylbert (A), *Art* Edwin O'Donovan (A), *Cos* Richard Bruno, Theadora Van Runkle, *Sp* Robert MacDonald, *Mus* Dave Grusin (AN), *Prod* Warren Beatty, *Exec Prod* Howard W. Koch, Jr., Charles H. Maguire.

Cast: Warren Beatty (AN, GMC), *Joe Pendleton*, Julie Christie, *Betty Logan*, James Mason, *Mr. Jordan*, Jack Warden (AN), *Max Corkle*, Charles Grodin, *Tony Abbott*, Dyan Cannon (AN, G), *Julia Farnsworth*, Buck Henry, *The Escort*, Vincent Gardenia, *Krim*, Joseph Maher, *Sisk*, Hamilton Camp, *Bentley*, Arthur Malet, *Everett*, Stephanie Faracy, *Corinne*, Jeannie Linero, *Lavinia*, Harry D.K. Wong, *Gardener*, George J. Manos, *Security Guard*, Larry Block, *Peters*, Frank Campanella, *Conway*, Bill Sorrells, *Tomarken*, Dick Enberg, *T.V. Interviewer*, Dolph Sweet, *Head Coach*, R.G. Armstrong, *General Manager*, Ed Peck, *Trainer*, John Randolph, *Former Owner*, Keene Curtis, *Oppenheim*, William Larson, *Renfield*, William Sylvestor, *Nuclear Reporter*. PG. $49,400,000.

Superior remake of *Here Comes Mr. Jordan*. A football player mistakenly dies before his time and is given another chance in the body of a millionaire. Warren Beatty has put together, as co-director, co-writer, producer and star, one of the finest and most delightful adult fantasies ever made. *Heaven Can Wait* is also one of the few remakes that actually improves on the original; everything from the wonderfully funny script to the faultless cast is better.

382 Hell Up in Harlem (1973) * American International, 96 min. *Dir* Larry Cohen, *Scr* Larry Cohen, *Cin* Fenton Hamilton, *Ed* Franco Guerri, Peter Holmes, *Des* Larry Lurin, *Mus* Fonce Mizell, Freddie Perren, *Prod* Larry Cohen, *Co-Prod* Janelle Cohen, *Exec Prod* Peter Sabiston.

Cast: Fred Williamson, *Tommy*, Julius W. Harris, *Papa Gibbs*, Gloria Hendry, *Helen*, Margaret Avery, *Sister Jennifer*, D'Urville Martin, *Rev. Rufus*, Tony King, *Zach*, Gerald Gordon, *DiAngelo*. R. See *Black Caesar*.

383 Hennessey (1975) ** Britain, American International, 104 min. *Dir* Don Sharp, *Scr* John Gay, *Story* Richard Johnson, *Cin* Ernest Steward, *Ed* Eric Boyd-Perkins, *Des* Ray Simm, *Art* Bert Davey, *Mus* John Scott, *Prod* Peter Snell, *Exec Prod* Samuel Z. Arkoff.

Cast: Rod Steiger, *Hennessy*, Lee Remick, *Kate Brook*, Richard Johnson, *Insp. Hollis*, Trevor Howard, *Cmdr. Rice*, Eric Porter, *IRA Leader Tobin*, Peter Egan, *Hollis' Asst.*, Ian Hogg, *Gerry*, Stanley Lebor, *Hawk*, John Hallam, *Boyle*, Patrick Stewart, *Tilney*, David Collings, *Covey*, John Shrapnel, *Tipaldi*, Hugh Moxey, *Burgess, The M.P.*, Margery Mason, *Housekeeper*, Paul Brennan, *Maguire*, Oliver Maguire, *Mick*. PG

Standard suspense thriller that exploits the problems in Northern Ireland. Rod Steiger stars as an Irish man who plots to blow up the Parliament, with the Royal Family in attendance, because his wife and child were killed in Belfast. Both Scotland Yard and the Irish Republican Army try to stop him, for different reasons. *Hennessey* does manage to build some tension, through the intercutting of both investigations.

384 Herbie Goes to Monte Carlo (1977) ** Buena Vista, 105 min. *Dir* Vincent McEveety, *Scr* Arthur Alsberg, Don Nelson, based on characters created by Gordon Buford, *Cin* Leonard J. South, *Ed* Cotton Warburton, *Art* Perry Ferguson, John B. Mansbridge, *Cos* Chuck Keehne, Emily Sundby, *Mus* Frank De Vol, *Prod* Ron Miller, *Assoc Prod* Jan Williams, A Walt Disney Production.

Cast: Dean Jones, *Jim Douglas*, Don Knotts, *Wheely Applegate*, Julie Sommars, *Diane Darcy*, Jacques Marvin, *Inspector Bouchet*, Roy Kinnear, *Quincey*, Bernard Fox, *Max*, Eric Braeden, *Bruno Von Sickle*, Xavier Saint Macary, *Detective Fontenoy*, Francois Lalande, *Monsieur Ribeaux*, Allan Caillou, *Emile*, Laurie Main, *Duval*, Mike Kulcsar, *Claude*, Johnny Haymer, *Race Official*, Stanley Brock, *Taxi Driver*, Gerard Jugnot, *Waiter*, Jean-Marie Proslier, *Doorman*, Tom McCorry, *Showroom M.C.*, Jean-Jacques Moreau, *Truck Driver*, Yveline Briere, *Girl Friend*, Raoul Delfosse, *Police Captain*, Ed Marcus, *Exhibit M.C.* G. $14,000,000. See *Herbie Rides Again*.

385 Herbie Rides Again (1974) ** Buena Vista, 88 min. *Dir* Robert Stevenson, *Scr* Bill Walsh, based on story by Gordon Buford, *Cin* Frank Phillips, *Ed* Cotton Warburton, *Art* John B. Mansbridge, Walter Tyler, *Cos* Chuck Keehne, Emily Sundby, *Prod* Bill Walsh, A Walt Disney Production.

Cast: Helen Hayes, *Mrs. Steinmetz*, Ken Berry, *Willoughby Whitfield*, Stefanie Powers, *Nicole*, John McIntire, *Mr. Judson*, Keenan Wynn, *Alonzo Hawk*, Huntz Hall, *Judge*, Ivor Barry, *Chauffeur*, Dan Tobin, *Lawyer*, Vito Scotti, *Taxi Driver*, Raymond Bailey, *Lawyer*, Liam Dunn, *Doctor*, Elaine Devry, *Secretary*, Chuck McCann, *Loostgarten*, Richard X. Slattery, *Traffic Commissioner*, Hank Jones, *Sir Lancelot*, Rod McCary, *Red Knight*. G. $17,000,000.

Okay sequel to *The Love Bug*, one of Walt Disney's biggest hits. Herbie, the Volkswagen with a mind of its own, comes to the rescue of a little old lady (Helen Hayes), who tries to save her house from being torn down to be replaced by a new skyscraper. *Herbie Rides Again* lacks the newness possessed by its predecessor as does the third installment *Herbie Goes to Monte Carlo*, in which he races in the famous race.

386 Heroes (1977) *** Universal, 113 min. *Dir* Jeremy Paul Kagan, *Scr* James Carabatsos, *Cin* Frank Stanley, *Ed* Patrick Kennedy, *Des* Charles Rosen, *Mus* Richard Hazard, Jack Nitzsche, *Prod* David Foster, Lawrence Turman.

Cast: Henry Winkler, *Jack Dunne*, Sally Field, *Carol Bell*, Harrison Ford, *Ken Boyd*, Val Avery, *Bus Driver*, Olivia Cole, *Jan Adeox*, Hector Elias, *Dr. Elias*, Dennis Burkley, *Gus*, Tony Burton, *Chef*, Michael Cavanaugh, *Peanuts*, Helen Craig, *Bus Depot Manager*, John P. Finnegan, *Munro*, Betty McGuire, *Mrs. Munro*, John O'Leary, *Ticket Clerk*. PG. $16,885,000.

Interesting comedy-drama about a crazy Vietnam veteran (Henry Winkler), who escapes from the hospital and goes on a cross-country trip to achieve his dream of starting a farm. Along the way he meets a girl (Sally Field), and convinces her to go with him. *Heroes* is not quite as serious a film as it seems to want to be. His lunacy is sometimes exaggerated, but it is at times quite funny.

387 Hester Street (1975) ******** Midwest, 92 min. *Dir* Joan Micklin Silver, *Scr* Joan Micklin Silver, based on the story *Yekl* by Abraham Cahan, *Cin* Kenneth Van Sickle, *Ed* Katherine Wenning, *Mus* William Bolcom, *Prod* Raphael D. Silver.

Cast: Steven Keats, *Jake*, Carol Kane (AN), *Gitl*, Mel Howard, *Bernstein*, Dorrie Kavanaugh, *Mamie*, Stephen Strimpell, *Joe Peltner*, Lauren Frost, *Fanny*, Paul Freedman, *Joey*, Svee Scooler, *Rabbi*, Eda Reiss Merin, *Rabbi's Wife*. PG.

Wonderful period comedy about Jewish immigrants living in New York City. A young woman (Carol Kane) arrives in America to be with her husband (Steven Keats) who has lived in America for 5 years. They are no longer compatible as he has become Americanized and she cannot forsake her old ways. Despite the small budget Joan Micklin Silver, in her feature film debut, beautifully and accurately recreates the period.

388 Hi, Mom! (1970) ******* Sigma III, 87 min. *Dir* Brian De Palma, *Scr* Brian De Palma, Charles Hirsch, *Cin* Robert Elfstrom, *Ed* Paul Hirsch, *Art* Peter Bocour, *Mus* Eric Kaz, *Lyrics* John Andreolli, *Prod* Charles Hirsch.

Cast: Robert DeNiro, *John Rubin*, Charles Durnham, *Superintendent*, Allen Garfield (Goorwitz), *Joe Banner*, Abraham Goren, *Pervert in Theatre*, Lara Parker, *Jeannie Mitchell*, Jennifer Salt, *Judy Bishop*, Gerrit Graham, *Gerrit Wood*, Nelson Peltz, *Playboy*, Peter Maloney, *Pharmacist*, William Daley, *Co-Op Neighbor*, Floyd L. Peterson, *Newscaster*. R.

Unusual black comic satire starring Robert DeNiro as a Vietnam veteran, who works for a pornographic filmmaker, but uses his camara to spy on his neighbors, one of whom (Jennifer Salt) later becomes his wife. *Hi, Mom!* is an early film by Brian De Palma, that satirizes many problems of the times, with such targets as Vietnam, racism and violence. This is a hit and miss comedy, but much of it is quite perceptive.

389 Hickey and Boggs (1972) ****** United Artists, 111 min. *Dir* Robert Culp, *Scr* Walter Hill, *Cin* Wilmer Butler, *Ed* David Berlatsky, *Cos* Bill Thiese, *Mus* Ted Ashford, *Prod* Fouad Said.

Cast: Bill Cosby, *Al Hickey*, Robert Culp, *Frank Boggs*, Rosalind Cash, *Nyona*, Sheila Sullivan, *Edith Boggs*, Isabel Sanford, *Nyona's Mother*, Ta-Ronce Allen, *Nyona's Daughter*, Lou Frizzell, *Lawyer*, Nancy Howard, *Apt. Manager's Wife*, Bernard Nedell, *Used Car Salesman*, Carmen, *Mary Jane*, Louis Moreno, *Quemando (Prisoner)*, Ron Henrique, *Quemando (Florist)*, Cary Sanchez, *Mary Jane's Daughter*, Jason Culp, *Mary Jane's Son*, Robert Mandan, *Mr. Brill*, Michael Moriarty, *Ballard*, Bernie Schwartz, *Bernie*, Denise Renfro, *Brill's Daughter*, Vincent Gardenia, *Papadakis*, Jack Colvin, *Shaw*, James Woods, *Lt. Wyatt*, Ed Lauter, *Ted*, Lester Fletcher, *Rice*, Gil Stuart, *Farrow*, Sil Words, *Mr. Leroy*. PG.

Fair action thriller about two private eyes (Bill Cosby, Robert Culp), who are hired to find a missing woman and inadvertently become involved in the search for money stolen from a Pittsburgh bank. *Hickey and Boggs* takes too long to get started, and the beginning is slightly confusing, with many obtrusive elements. Cosby and Culp, the stars of *I Spy*, are good in their only film teaming, and Culp does a fine job directing the action sequences, but the film does not hold together.

390 High Anxiety (1977) *** 20th Century–Fox, 94 min. *Dir* Mel Brooks, *Scr* Mel Brooks, Ron Clark, Rudy DeLuca, Barry Levinson, *Cin* Paul Lohmann, *Ed* John C. Howard, *Des* Peter Wooley, *Cos* Patricia Norris, *Mus* John Morris, *Prod* Mel Brooks.

Cast: Mel Brooks, *Richard Thorndyke*, Madeline Kahn, *Victoria Brisbane*, Cloris Leachman, *Nurse Diesel*, Harvey Korman, *Dr. Charles Montague*, Ron Carey, *Brophy*, Howard Morris, *Prof. Lilloman*, Dick Van Patten, *Dr. Wentworth*, Jack Riley, *Desk Clerk*, Charlie Callas, *Cocker Spaniel*, Ron Clark, *Zachary Cartwright*, Rudy DeLuca, *Killer*, Barry Levinson, *Bellboy*, Lee Delano, *Norton*, Richard Stahl, *Dr. Baxter*, Darrell Zwerling, *Dr. Eckhardt*, Murphy Dunne, *Piano Player*, Al Hopson, *Man Who Is Shot*, Bob Ridgely, *Flasher*, Albert J. Whitlock, *Arthur Brisbane*. PG. $19,165,000.

Above average Mel Brooks slapstick comedy. After destroying the western and horror genres, Brooks set his sights on a director who is a genre unto himself, Alfred Hitchcock. *High Anxiety* mixes plots, themes and ideas from such Hitchcock thrillers as *Spellbound*, *Vertigo*, *Psycho* and *The Birds* into a surprisingly cohesive satire. Brooks even pokes fun at Hitchcock's technique, such as his extensive camera movement. As is the case in all of Brooks' films the jokes are hit and miss, but this time more hit than usual. Unfortunately, knowledge of Hitchcock's films is necessary for full appreciation.

391 High Plains Drifter (1973) ** Universal, 105 min. *Dir* Clint Eastwood, *Scr* Ernest Tidyman, *Cin* Bruce Surtees, *Ed* Ferris Webster, *Art* Henry Bumstead, *Mus* Dee Barton, *Prod* Robert Daley, *Exec Prod* Jennings Lang.

Cast: Clint Eastwood, *The Stranger*, Verna Bloom, *Sarah Belding*, Mariana Hill, *Callie Travers*, Mitchell Ryan, *Dave Drake*, Jack Ging, *Morgan Allen*, Stefan Gierasch, *Mayor Jason Hobart*, Ted Hartley, *Lewis Belding*, Billy Curtis, *Mordecai*, Geoffrey Lewis, *Stacey Bridges*, Scott Walker, *Bill Borders*, Walter Barnes, *Sheriff Sam Shaw*, Paul Brinegar, *Lutie Naylor*, Richard Bull, *Asa Goodwin*, Robert Donner, *Preacher*, John Hillerman, *Bootmaker*, Anthony James, *Cole Carlin*, William O'Connell, *Barber*, John Quade, *Jake Ross*. R. $7,695,000.

Dull American version of Italian spaghetti westerns. Clint Eastwood, as in some of those earlier films, stars as a mysterious stranger with no name, who is hired to protect a town from a gang of outlaws, sort of a one man version of *The Magnificent Seven*. *High Plains Drifter* is far too cold and sterile and Eastwood as director was inspired by his mentor, the greatly overrated Sergio Leone.

392 The Hindenburg (1975) ** Universal, 125 min. *Dir* Robert Wise, *Scr* Nelson Gidding, *Story* William Levinson, William Link, based on book by Michael M. Mooney, *Cin* Robert Surtees (AN), *Ed* Donn Cambern, *Des* Edward Carfagno (AN), *Cos* Dorothy Jeakins, *Sp* Peter Berkos, Glen Robinson, Albert Whitlock (A), *Mus* David Shire.

Cast: George C. Scott, *Ritter*, Anne Bancroft, *The Countess*, William Atherton, *Boarth*, Roy Thinnes, *Martin Vogel*, Gig Young, *Edward Douglas*, Burgess Meredith, *Emilio Pajetta*, Charles Durning, *Capt. Pruss*, Richard A. Dysart, *Lehmann*, Robert Clary, *Joe Spah*, Rene Auberjonois, *Maj. Napier*,

Peter Donat, *Reed Channing*, Alan Oppenheimer, *Albert Breslau*, Katherine Helmond, *Mrs. Mildred Breslau*, Joanna Moore, *Mrs. Channing*, Stephen Elliott, *Capt. Fellows*, Joyce Davis, *Eleanore Ritter*, Jean Rasey, *Valerie Breslau*, Ted Gehring, *Knorr*, Lisa Pera, *Freda Halle*. PG. $15,105,000.

Boring fictionalized account of the Hindenburg disaster. *The Hindenburg* is based on the theory that the destruction of the dirigible was a result of sabotage and not an accident. This idea is a good start for a movie, but the filmmakers did not know where to go from there, and hence, *The Hindenburg* sunk to the level of the other disaster films, focusing on innocuous characters that are as uninteresting as they are irrelevant.

393 **The Hired Hand** (1971) *** Universal, 93 min. *Dir* Peter Fonda, *Scr* Alan Sharp, *Cin* Vilmos Zsigmond, *Ed* Frank Wazzola, *Art* Lawrence G. Paull, *Cos* Richard Bruno, *Mus* Bruce Langhorne, *Prod* William Hayward, *Exec Prod* Stanley A. Weiss.

Cast: Peter Fonda, *Harry Collings*, Warren Oates, *Arch Harris*, Verna Bloom, *Hannah Collings*, Robert Pratt, *Dan Griffin*, Severn Darden, *McVey*, Ted Markland, *Luke*, Owen Orr, *Mace*, Gray Johnson, *Will*, Rita Rogers, *Mexican Woman*, Al Hopson, *Bartender*, Ann Doran, *Mrs. Sorensen*, Megan Denver, *Janey Collings*, Michael McClure, *Plummer*. PG.

Fine western drama starring Peter Fonda as a cowboy, who is hired by his wife (Verna Bloom), whom he had deserted seven years earlier, to work on her farm. After years of drifting he had become tired of his lifestyle. Their relationship eventually, and predictably, returns to what it had been. *The Hired Hand* is a well-made and easy going western, and it is a good directorial debut for Fonda.

394 **The Hireling** (1973) (CF) **** Britain, Columbia, 95 min. *Dir* Alan Bridges, *Scr* Wolf Mankowitz, based on novel by L.P. Hartley, *Cin* Michael Reed, *Ed* Peter Weatherley, *Des* Natasha Kroll (BFA) *Cos* Phyllis Dalton (BFA), *Mus* Marc Wilkinson, *Prod* Ben Arbeid, *Exec Prod* Terence Baker.

Cast: Robert Shaw, *Leadbetter*, Sarah Miles, *Lady Franklin*, Peter Egan, *Cantrip*, Elizabeth Sellars, *Mother*, Caroline Mortimer, *Connie*, Patricia Lawrence, *Mrs. Hansen*, Petra Markham, *Edith*, Ian Hogg, *Davis*, Christine Hargreaves, *Doreen*, Lyndon Brook, Alison Leggatt. PG.

Fine drama about the relationship between a widow (Sarah Miles) and her chauffeur (Robert Shaw). They become very close during her recovery from a breakdown, and he subsequently falls in love with her. Unfortunately after she is cured she no longer considers him as an equal. *The Hireling*, with its intelligent script and excellent acting, is a clever examination of class barriers in England.

395 **Hit** (1973) *** Paramount, 134 min. *Dir* Sidney J. Furie, *Scr* Alan R. Trustman, David M. Wolf, *Cin* John A. Alonzo, *Ed* Argyle Nelson, *Mus* Lalo Schifrin, *Prod* Harry Korshak, *Exec Prod* Gray Frederickson.

Cast: Billy Dee Williams, *Nick Allen*, Richard Pryor, *Mike Willmer*, Paul Hampton, *Barry Strong*, Gwen Welles, *Sherry Nielson*, Warren Kemmerling, *Dutch Schiller*, Janet Brandt, *Ida*, Sid Melton, *Herman*, David Hall, *Carlin*, Todd Martin, *Crosby*, Norman Burton, *Director*, Jenny Astruc, *Madame Frelou*, Yves Barsacq, *Romain*, Jean-Claude Bercq, *Jean-Baptiste*, Henri Cogan, *Bornou*, Pierre Collet, *Zero*, Robert Lombard, *Mr. Frelou*, Paul Mercy, *Jyras*. R.

Above-average action thriller starring Billy Dee Williams as a Federal agent, who puts together a team of amateur vigilantes for his own personal vendetta against French drug dealers, due to his daughter's death from an overdose. Despite the cast, *Hit* is not a blaxploitation film. Instead it is a straight crime film that mixes elements of *The French Connection* and *The Dirty Dozen*.

396 **Hit Man** (1972) ** MGM, 90 min. *Dir* George Armitage, *Scr* George Armitage, based on novel *Jack's Return Home*, *Cin* Andrew Davis, *Ed* Morton Tubor, *Art* Lynn Griffin, *Mus* H.B. Barnum, *Prod* Gene Corman.

Cast: Bernie Casey, *Tyrone*, Pamela Grier, *Gozelda*, Lisa Moore, *Laural*, Bhetty Waldron, *Ivelle*, Sam Laws, *Sherwood*, Candy All, *Rochelle*, Don Diamond, *Zito*, Edmund Cambridge, *Theotis*, Bob Harris, *Shag*, Rudy Challenger, *Julius*, Tracy Ann King, *Nita*, Christopher Joy, *Leon*, Roger E. Mosley, *Baby Huey*. R. See *Get Carter*.

397 **Hitler: The Last Ten Days** (1973) ** Britain/Italy, Paramount, 106 min. *Dir* Ennio de Concini, *Scr* Ennio de Concini, Marie Pia Fusco, Wolfgang Reinhardt, *English Adaptation* Ivan Moffat, based on book *Last Days of the Chancellery* by Gerhard Boldt, *Cin* Ennio Guarnieri, *Ed* Kevin Connor, *Art* Roy Walker, *Mus* Mischa Spoliansky, *Prod* Wolfgang Reinhardt, *Exec Prod* John Heyman.

Cast: Alec Guinness, *Hitler*, Simon Ward, *Hoffman*, Adolfo Celi, *Krebs*, Diane Cilento, *Hanna*, Gabriele Ferzetti, *Keitel*, Eric Porter, *Von Greim*, Doris Kuntsmann, *Eva Braun*, Joss Ackland, *Burgdorf*, John Barron, *Dr. Stumpfegger*, John Bennett, *Goebbels*, Sheila Gish, *Frau Christian*, Julian Glover, *Fegelein*, Michael Goodliffe, *Weidling*, John Hallam, *Guensche*, Barbara Jefford, *Magda Goebbels*, Mark Kingston, *Bormann*. PG.

Strange drama focusing on the last days of Adolf Hitler's life. Set almost entirely in his bunker, *Hitler: The Last Ten Days* is extremely claustrophobic and tends to become tedious very quickly. Alec Guinness is normally an extremely fine actor, but he is not very convincing as Hitler, who is portrayed as a mild mannered politician rather than a charismatic monster.

398 **Hollywood Boulevard** (1977) *** New World, 83 min. *Dir* Allan Arkush, Joe Dante, *Scr* Patrick Hobby, *Cin* Jamie Anderson, *Ed* Allan Arkush, Joe Dante, Amy Jones, *Art* Jack DeWolfe, *Cos* Jane Rum, *Mus* Andrew Stein, *Prod* Jon Davison, *Assoc Prod* Terri Schwartz.

Cast: Candice Rialson, *Candy Wednesday*, Mary Woronov, *Mary McQueen*, Rita George, *Bobbi Quackenbush*, Jeffrey Kramer, *Patrick Hobby*, Dick Miller, *Walter Paisley*, Richard Doran, *Producer*, Tara Strohmeier, *Jill McBain*, Paul Bartel, *Director*, Jonathan Kaplan, *Scotty*, George Wagner, *Cameraman*, John Kramer, *Duke Mantee*, W.L. Luckey, *Rico Bandello*, Charles B. Griffith, *Mark Dentine*, Joe McBride, *Drive-In Rapist*, Milt Kahn, *Reporter*, Todd McCarthy, *Todd*, Commander Cody and His Lost Planet Airmen, *Themselves*. R.

Bizarre satire of "poverty row" Hollywood and the making of B-movies, particularly those from Roger Corman's own company. The plot defies credibility, as a young actress (Candice Rialson) breaks into B-movies and works on a dim-witted actioner that becomes the setting for mass murder. *Hollywood Boulevard* is in no way meant to be a serious film, as it is filled with the same surrealism and black humor as the films it is satirizing.

399 **The Homecoming** (1973) **** American Film Theatre, 116 min. *Dir* Peter Hall, *Scr* Harold Pinter, based on his play, *Cin* David Watkin, *Ed* Rex Pike, *Des* John Bury, *Art* Jack Stevens, *Cos* Joan Bridge, Elisabeth Haffenden, *Prod* Ely A. Landau, *Exec Prod* Otto Plaschkes.

Cast: Cyril Cusack, *Sam*, Ian Holm, *Lenny*, Michael Jayston, *Teddy*, Vivien Merchant, *Ruth*, Terence Rigby, *Joey*, Paul Rogers, *Max*. PG. See *American Film Theatre*.

400 **The Honeymoon Killers** (1970) ** Cinerama, 107 min. *Dir* Leonard Kastle, *Scr* Leonard Kastle, *Cin* Oliver Wood, *Ed* Richard Brophy, Stan Warnow, *Mus* Gustav Mahler, *Prod* Warren Steibel, *Assoc Prod* Paul Asselin.

Cast: Shirley Stoler, *Martha Beck*, Tony LoBianco, *Ray Fernandez*, Mary Jane Higby, *Janet Fay*, Doris Roberts, *Bunny*, Kip McArdle, *Delphine Downing*, Marilyn Chris, *Myrtle Young*, Dortha Duckworth, *Mrs. Beck*, Barbara Cason, *Evelyn Long*, Ann Harris, *Doris*, Mary Breen, *Rainelle Downing*, Elsa Raven, *Matron*, Mary Engel, *Lucy*, Guy Sorel, *Mr. Dranoff*, Mike Haley, *Jackson*, Diane Asselin, *Severns*, Col. William Adams, *Justice of the Peace*. R.

Grimly realistic murder drama, loosely based on the exploits of real-life killers Martha Beck and Raymond Fernandez, about a couple, who cheat old women out of their life-savings and murder them. *The Honeymoon Killers* is filmed in an almost documentary style and is thus stripped of most dramatic effects. This does not completely pay off, as the film does become somewhat boring.

401 **Hooper** (1978) ** Warner Bros., 99 min. *Dir* Hal Needham, *Scr* Bill Kerby, Thomas Rickman, *Story* Walt Green, Walter S. Herndon, *Cin* Bobby Byrne, *Ed* Donn Cambern, *Art* Hilyard Brown, *Mus* Bill Justis, *Prod* Hank Moonjean.

Cast: Burt Reynolds, *Sonny Hooper*, Jan-Michael Vincent, *Ski*, Sally Field, *Gwen*, Brian Keith, *Jocko*, John Marley, *Max Berns*, James Best, *Cully*, Adam West, *Adam*, Alfie Wise, *Tony*, Robert Klein, *Roger Deal*. PG. $34,900,000.

Silly action film about the world's greatest stuntman. It is certainly understandable why famed stuntman turned director, Hal Needham would want to make a movie tribute to stuntmen, and a good film should have come from his personal devotion to the subject, but this one is not it. *Hooper* is nothing more than another Needham exercise in car chases and wrecks, without one attempt to seriously analyze these people's feelings and motivations.

402 **The Hospital** (1971) *** United Artists, 103 min. *Dir* Arthur Hiller, *Scr* Paddy Chayefsky (A, G, BFA, W), *Cin* Victor J. Kemper, *Ed* Eric Albertson, *Des* Gene Rudolf, *Cos* Frank Thompson, *Mus* Morris Surdin, *Prod* Howard Gottfried, *Assoc Prod* Jack Grossberg.

Cast: George C. Scott (AN), *Dr. Herbert Bock*, Diana Rigg, *Barbara Drummond*, Barnard Hughes, *Drummond*, Richard Dysart, *Dr. Welbeck*, Andrew Duncan, *William Mead*, Nancy Marchand, *Mrs. Christie*, Stephen Elliott, *Sundstrom*, Donald Harron, *Milton Mead*, Roberts Blossom, *Guernsey*, Tresa Hughes, *Mrs. Donavan*, Lenny Baker, *Dr. Schaefer*, Robert Walden, *Dr. Brubaker*, Frances Sternhagen, *Mrs. Cushing*, Lorrie Davis, *Nurse Divine*, Nancy McKay, *Sheilah*, Norman Berns, *Dr. Biegelman*. PG. $9,025,000.

Often brilliant black satire about hospitals, that unfortunately occasionally lapses into silly slapstick. The thin plot revolves around a series of inexplicable deaths that throw the hospital into chaos. George C. Scott gives one of his finest performances as a doctor trying to cope with the confusion, while also being torn between his duty to the hospital and his involvement with the daughter of a crazy patient.

403 **Hot Lead and Cold Feet** (1978) ** Buena Vista, 90 min. *Dir* Robert Butler, *Scr* Arthur Alsberg, Joe McEveety, Don Nelson, based on story by Rod Piffath, *Cin* Frank Phillips, *Ed* Ray de Leuw, *Art* John Mansbridge, Frank T. Smith, *Cos* Ron Talsky, *Mus* Buddy Baker, *Prod* Ron Miller, *Co-Prod* Christopher Hibler, *Assoc Prod* Kevin Corcoran.

Cast: Jim Dale, *Eli/Wild Billy/Jasper Bloodshy*, Karen Valentine, *Jenny*, Don Knotts, *Denver Kid*, Jack Elam, *Rattlesnake*, Darren McGaven, *Mayor Ragsdale*, John Williams, *Mansfield*, Warren Vanders, *Boss Snead*, Debbie Lytton, *Roxanne*, Michael Sharrett, *Marcus*, Dave Cass, *Jack*, Richard Wright, *Pete*, Don "Red" Barry, *Bartender*, Jimmy Van Patten, *Jake*, Gregg Palmer, *Jeff*, Ed Bakey, *Joshua*, John Steadman, *Old Codger*. G. $10,450,000.

Fair Disney western comedy starring Jim Dale in three roles; a wealthy land dealer, who is supposedly dead, and both his sons, who compete with each other over the inheritance. Dale does a fine job handling the three very different characters, but the film does not match his talent. It strains too hard for laughs, and the pacing is slow and dull.

404 **The Hot Rock** (1972) *** 20th Century–Fox, 105 min. *Dir* Peter Yates, *Scr* William Goldman, based on novel by Donald E. Westlake, *Cin* Ed Brown, *Ed* Fred W. Berger, Frank P. Keller (AN), *Des* John Robert Lloyd, *Cos* Ruth Morley, *Mus* Quincy Jones, *Prod* Hal Landers, Bobby Roberts.

Cast: Robert Redford, *Dortmunder*, George Segal, *Kelp*, Ron Leibman, *Murch*, Paul Sand, *Greenberg*, Zero Mostel, *Abe Greenberg*, Moses Gunn, *Dr. Amusa*, William Redfield, *Lt. Hoover*, Topo Swope, *Sis*, Charlotte Rae, *Ma Munch*, Graham Jarvis, *Warden*, Harry Bellaver, *Bartender Rollo*, Seth Allen, *Happy Hippie*, Robert Levine, *Cop at Police Station*, Lee Wallace, *Dr. Strauss*, Robert Weil, *Albert*, Lynne Gordon, *Miasmo*, Grania O'Malley, *Bird Lady*, Fred Cook, *Otto*, Mark Dawson, *Big Museum Guard*, George Bartenieff, Gilbert Lewis, *Museum Guards*, Ed Bernard, Christopher Guest, Charles White, *Policemen*. PG.

Well-made slapstick caper comedy about four clumsy diamond thieves (Redford, Segal, Leibman, Sand), who repeatedly attempt to steal the same diamond. Each robbery attempt is an hilarious set-piece unto itself, highlighted by an assault by the thieves on a police station. Peter Yates has always excelled with action, but in *The Hot Rock* he also proves his ability with comedy.

405 **Hot Stuff** (1979) ** Columbia, 91 min. *Dir* Dom Deluise, *Scr* Michael Kane, Donald E. Westlake, *Cin* James Pergola, *Ed* Neil Travis, *Mus* Patrick Williams, *Title Song* written and performed by Jerry Reed, *Prod* Mort Engelberg, *Exec Prod* Paul Maslansky.

Cast: Dom DeLuise, *Ernie*, Suzanne Pleshette, *Louise*, Jerry Reed, *Doug*, Ossie Davis, *Captain*, Luis Avalos, *Ramon*, Marc Lawrence, *Carmine*, Dick Davalos, *Charles*, Alfie Wise, *Nick*, Bill McCutcheon, *Paully*, Sydney Lassick,

Hymie, Barney Martin, *Kiley,* Pat McCormick, *Cigars,* Sid Gould, *Sid* Carol DeLuise, *Gloria.* PG. $9,020,000.

Silly slapstick comedy about four undercover cops who take over a fencing operation that will hopefully lead them to some major criminals. *Hot Stuff* is purported to be based on fact, but this film probably bears little resemblance to the real operation. This is nothing more than an excuse to introduce a series of weird characters, the thieves who sell the police their stolen goods, and the ending defies credibility.

406 **House Calls** (1978) ** Universal, 98 min. *Dir* Howard Zieff, *Scr* Julius J. Epstein, Alan Mandel, Max Shulman, Charles Shyer, *Story* Julius J. Epstein, Max Shulman, *Cin* David M. Walsh, *Ed* Edward Warschilka, *Des* Henry Bumstead, *Cos* Burton Miller, *Mus* Henry Mancini, *Prod* Arlene Sellers, Alex Winitsky, *Exec Prod* Jennings Lang.

Cast: Walter Matthau, *Dr. Nichols,* Glenda Jackson, *Ann Atkinson,* Art Carney, *Dr. Willoughby,* Richard Benjamin, *Dr. Soloman,* Candice Azzara, *Ellen Grady,* Dick O'Neill, *Irwin Owett,* Thayer David, *Pogostin,* Anthony Holland, *TV Moderator,* Reva Rose, *Mrs. DeVoto,* Sandra Kerns, *Lani Mason,* Brad Dexter, *Quinn,* Jane Connell, *Mrs. Conway,* Lloyd Gough, *Harry Grady,* Gordon Jump, *Dr. O'Brien,* William J. Fiore, *Dr. Sloan,* Taureen Blacque, *Levi,* Charlie Matthau, *Michael Atkinson.* PG. $16,620,000.

Fair hospital comedy about a doctor (Walter Matthau) who has a relationship with one of his patients (Glenda Jackson). *House Calls* is not really an indictment of the medical profession, although there are indications in that direction, but rather a very light romantic comedy, much like those from the 1960's. The script is a letdown, but the cast is excellent, particularly Art Carney as the incompetent chief of staff.

407 **Huckleberry Finn** (1974) * United Artists, 118 min. *Dir* J. Lee Thompson, *Scr* Richard M. Sherman, Robert B. Sherman, based on novel by Mark Twain, *Cin* Laszlo Kovacs, *Ed* Michael F. Anderson, *Des* Philip Jeffries, *Cos* Donfeld, *Mus* Richard M. Sherman, Robert B. Sherman, *Chor* Marc Breaux, *Prod* Arthur P. Jacobs, *Assoc Prod* Robert Greenhut.

Cast: Jeff East, *Huckleberry Finn,* Paul Winfield, *Jim,* Harvey Korman, *King,* David Wayne, *Duke,* Arthur O'Connell, *Col. Grangerford,* Gary Merrill, *Pap,* Natalie Trundy, *Mrs. Loftus,* Lucille Benson, *Wider Douglas,* Kim O'Brien, *Maryjane,* Jean Fay, *Susan,* Ruby Leftwick, *Miss Watson,* Odessa Cleveland, *Jim's Wife,* Joe Boris, *Jason,* Danny Lantrip, *Kyle,* Van Bennett, *Wayne,* Linda Watkins, *Mrs. Grangerford,* Jean Combs, *Miss Emmeline,* Frances Fawcett, *Miss Charlotte,* Suzanne Prystup, *Miss Maryanne.* G. See *Tom Sawyer.*

408 **The Human Factor** (1979) *** Britain, United Artists, 115 min. *Dir* Otto Preminger, *Scr* Tom Stoppard, based on novel by Graham Greene, *Cin* Mike Molloy, *Ed* Richard Trevor, *Art* Ken Ryan, *Cos* Hope Bryce, *Mus* Richard and Gary Logan, *Prod* Otto Preminger, *Exec Prod* Paul Crosfield.

Cast: Nicol Williamson, *Castle,* Richard Attenborough, *Col. Daintry,* Joop Doderer, *Cornelius Muller,* John Gielgud, *Brigadier Tomlinson,* Derek Jacobi, *Davis,* Robert Morley, *Percival,* Ann Todd, *Castle's Mother,* Richard Vernon, *Sir John Hargreaves,* Iman, *Sarah.* R.

Slow espionage thriller about a Secret Service agent (Nicol Williamson), who betrays his native England to help an old friend in Africa. He becomes a double agent by sending secret information to the Soviets, and he is later deported to the U.S.S.R. Most of the film's conflict is inward rather than outward as Williamson anguishes over his deed. This is hardly a great film but, it nearly towers over most of Preminger's films of the past two decades.

409 Hurricane (1979) ** Paramount, 119 min. *Dir* Jan Troell, *Scr* Lorenzo Semple, Jr., based on novel by James Norman Hall, Charles Nordhoff, *Cin* Sven Nykvist, *Ed* Sam O'Steen, *Des* Danilo Donati, *Art* Giorgio Postiglione, *Sp* Joe Day, Aldo Puccini, Glen Robinson, *Mus* Nino Rota, *Chor* Coco, *Prod* Dino De Laurentiis, *Exec Prod* Lorenzo Semple, Jr.

Cast: Jason Robards, *Capt. Bruckner*, Mia Farrow, *Charlotte Bruckner*, Max Von Sydow, *Dr. Bascomb*, Trevor Howard, *Father Malone*, Dayton Ka'Ne, *Matangi*, Timothy Bottoms, *Jack Sanford*, James Keach, *Sgt. Strang*, Richard Sarcione, *Lt. Howard*, Arirau Tekurarere, *Moana*, Willie Myers, *Corp. Morrah*, Nick Rutgers, *Commander Blair*, Nancy Hall Rutgers, *Mrs. Blair*, Manu Tupau, *Samolo*, Simplet Tefane, *Velaga*. PG.

Dull love story, set on the island of East Samoa under the rule of the U.S. Navy, that climaxes with a massive storm. The daughter (Mia Farrow) of the island commander (Jason Robards) falls in love with a native chieftain (Dayton Ka'Ne), but this is nothing more than filler, before the hurricane arrives. The special effects are excellent, but they are not sufficient to make a movie. This is a remake of the John Ford films, which unfortunately was not much good either.

410 Hurry Up, or I'll Be 30 (1973) *** Avco Embassy, 88 min. *Dir* Joseph Jacoby, *Scr* Joseph Jacoby, David Wiltse, *Cin* Burleigh Wartes, *Ed* Stan Warnow, *Mus* Stephen Lawrence, *Lyrics* Bruce Hart, *Songs* sung by Dennis Cooley, *Prod* Joseph Jacoby.

Cast: John Lefkowitz, *George Trapani*, Linda De Coff, *Jackie Tice*, Ronald Anton, *Vince Trapani*, Maureen Byrnes, *Flo*, Danny DeVito, *Petey*, David Kirk, *Mr. Trapani*, Frank Quinn, *Mark Lossier*, Selma Rogoff, *Mrs. Trapani*, George Welbes, *Ken Harris*, Steve Inwood, *Tony*, Faith Langford, *Gypsy Girl/Bar Girl*, Samantha Lynche, *Audition Girl #1*, Susan Peretz, *Miss Walsh*, Bob O'Connell, *Bartender*, Bill Nunnery, *Gas Station Attendant*. R.

Funny and touching comedy about a young man who is a failure in both his job, working for his father, and his social life. As the title suggests he makes one last attempt to achieve success in both before he turns thirty. The humor is very low-key and never overdone as the film surprisingly stays very close to reality. Unknown actor Jeff Lefkowitz is excellent in the lead role, as is the direction by Joseph Jacoby. Neither should have been ignored by the movie industry.

411 Husbands (1970) **** Columbia, 138 min. *Dir* John Cassavetes, *Scr* John Cassavetes, *Cin* Victor Kemper, *Ed* Peter Tanner, *Art* René D'Auriac, *Prod* Al Ruban, *Assoc Prod* Sam Shaw.

Cast: Ben Gazzara, *Harry*, Peter Falk, *Archie*, John Cassavetes, *Gus*, Jenny Runacre, *Mary Tynan*, Jenny Lee Wright, *Pearl Billingham*, Noelle Kao, *Julie*, Leola Harlow, *Leola*, Meta Shaw, *Annie*, John Kullers, *Red*, Delores Delmar, *The Countess*, Paggy Lashbrook, *Diana Mallabee*, Eleanor Zee, *Mrs. Hines*, Claire Malis, *Stuart's Wife*, Lorraine McMartin, *Annie's Mother*, Edgar

Franken, *Ed Weintraub*, Sarah Felcher, *Sarah*, David Rowlands, *Stuart Jackson*. PG.

Excellent drama about three buddies (John Cassavetes, Ben Gazzara, Peter Falk), who are unable to deal with the death of a close friend, so they go on a drunken binge. The entire film documents this binge, detailing their feelings and insights, and how death and growing older affects each of them. As is usual with Cassavetes' own films, *Husbands* is overlong and overly talky, but it is never dull. This is one of his best.

412 Hustle (1975) ** Paramount, 120 min. *Dir* Robert Aldrich, *Scr* Steve Shagan, *Cin* Joseph Biroc, *Ed* Michael Luciano, *Art* Hilyard Brown, *Mus* Frank DeVol, *Prod* Robert Aldrich, *Assoc Prod* William Aldrich.

Cast: Burt Reynolds, *Lt. Phil Gaines*, Catherine Deneuve, *Nicole Britton*, Ben Johnson, *Marty Hollinger*, Paul Winfield, *Sgt. Louis Belgrave*, Eileen Brennan, *Paula Hollinger*, Eddie Albert, *Leo Sellers*, Ernest Borgnine, *Santoro*, Catherine Bach, *Peggy Summer*, Jack Carter, *Herbie Dalitz*, James Hampton, *Bus Driver*, Sharon Kelly, *Gloria Hollinger*, Chuck Hayward, *Morgue Attendant*, David Estridge, *Albino*, Peter Brandon, *Minister*, David Spielberg, *Jerry Bellamy*, Naomi Stevens, *Woman Hostage*, Med Flory, *Albino Beating Cop*. R. $10,390,000.

Dull character study of a policeman who lives with a high class prostitute. *Hustle* appears to be a serious attempt to analyze these people and compare and contrast their life styles, but this film never really rises above a soap opera. To keep things moving a few crime subplots have been thrown in, but they are not any more interesting than the rest of the film.

413 I Love My Wife (1970) * Universal, 95 min. *Dir* Mel Stuart, *Scr* Robert Kaufman, *Cin* Vilis Lapenieks, *Ed* David Saxon, *Art* Alexander Golitzen, George C. Webb, *Cos* Helen Colvig, *Mus* Lalo Schifrin, *Prod* Stan Margulies, *Exec Prod* David L. Wolper, *Assoc Prod* Robert Kaufman.

Cast: Elliott Gould, *Dr. Richard Burrows*, Brenda Vaccaro, *Jody Burrows*, Angel Tompkins, *Helene Donnelly*, Dabney Coleman, *Frank Donnelly*, Joan Tompkins, *Grandma Dennison*, Leonard Stone, *Dr. Neilson*, Helen Westcott, *Mrs. Burrows*, Ivor Francis, *Dr. Korngold*, Al Checco, *Dr. Meyerberg*, Joanna Cameron, *Nurse Sharon*. R.

Dull comedy of adultery starring Elliott Gould as a medical student, who cheats on his wife (Brenda Vaccaro) after she becomes pregnant. Their marriage becomes more strained with time and the birth of their child fails to mend the damage. *I Love My Wife* has a thin and shallow storyline, and its only reason for existence seems to be to capitalize on Gould's popularity.

414 I Never Promised You a Rose Garden (1977) *** New World, 96 min. *Dir* Anthony Page, *Scr* Lewis John Carlino, Gavin Lambert (AN), based on novel by Joanne Greenberg, *Cin* Bruce Logan, *Ed* Garth Craven, *Des* Toby Rafelson, *Cos* Jane Ruhm, *Mus* Paul Chihara, *Prod* Daniel H. Blatt, Terence F. Deane, Michael Hausman, *Exec Prod* Roger Corman, Edger J. Scherick.

Cast: Bibi Anderson, *Dr. Fried*, Kathleen Quinlan, *Deborah Blake*, Ben Piazza, *Mr. Blake*, Lorraine Gary, *Mrs. Blake*, Darlene Craviotto, *Carla*, Reni Santoni, *Hobbs*, Susan Tyrell, *Lee*, Signe Hasso, *Helene*, Norman Alden, *McPherson*, Sylvia Sidney, *Miss Coral*, Martin Bartlett, *Secret Wife of Henry VIII*, Robert Viharo, *Anterrabae*, Jeff Conaway, *Lactamaeon*, Dick Herd, *Dr. Halle*,

Sarah Cunningham, *Mrs. Forbes*, June C. Ellis, *The Spy*, Diane Varsi, *Sylvia*, Patricia Singer, *Kathryn*, Mary Carver, *Eugenia*, Barbara Steele, *Idat*. R. $4,000,000.

Fine drama set in a mental institution, that focuses on a young girl suffering from schizoprenia (Kathleen Quinlan) and the attempts by her psychiatrist (Bibi Anderson) to cure her. This film has been labeled as a female version of *One Flew over the Cuckoo's Nest*, but that comparison is a gross over simplification. *I Never Promised You a Rose Garden* is about mental illness, whereas *Cuckoo's Nest* only uses an institution as its setting; its concerns are elsewhere. Quinlan gives a shattering performance that was surprisingly ignored at award time.

415 I Never Sang for My Father (1970) ******* Columbia, 90 min. *Dir* Gilbert Cates, *Scr* Robert W. Anderson (AN, W), based on his play, *Cin* Morris Hartzband, George Sroetzel, *Ed* Angelo Ross, *Art* Hank Aldrich, *Cos* Theoni V. Aldredge, *Mus* Al Gorgoni, Barry Mann, *Song* "Strangers," *Mus* Barry Mann, Cynthia Weil, *Prod* Gilbert Cates.

Cast: Melvyn Douglas (AN), *Tom*, Gene Hackman (AN), *Gene*, Dorothy Stickney, *Margaret*, Estelle Parsons, *Alice*, Elizabeth Hubbard, *Peggy*, Lovelady Powell, *Norma*, Daniel Keyes, *Dr. Mayberry*, Jon Richards, *Marvin Scott*, Conrad Bain, *Rev. Pell*, Nikki Counselman, *Mary*, Jean Dexter, *Hostess*, Sloane Shelton, *Nurse 1*, Beverly Penberthy, *Special Nurse*, Valerie Ogden, *Nurse 3*, Jim Karen, *Mr. Tucker*, Gene Williams, *Dr. Jensen*. PG.

Fine drama starring Gene Hackman as a middle-aged man, who is still unable to live up the unreasonable expectations of his domineering father (Melvyn Douglas). Their conflict comes to the fore as Hackman must now care for Douglas, who is in his 80's. *I Never Sang for My Father* offers fine insight into these two characters, but the film is a bit stagey. Hackman and Douglas are superb together, however.

416 I Walk the Line (1970) ****** Columbia, 95 min. *Dir* John Frankenheimer, *Scr* Alvin Sargent, based on novel *An Exile* by Madison Jones, *Cin* David M. Walsh, *Ed* Henry Berman, *Art* Albert Brenner, *Cos* Louis Brown, *Mus* Johnny Cash, *Prod* Harold D. Cohen, *Exec Prod* Edward Lewis.

Cast: Gregory Peck, *Sheriff Henry Tawes*, Tuesday Weld, *Alma McCain*, Estelle Parsons, *Ellen-Haney Tawes*, Ralph Meeker, *Carl McCain*, Lonny Chapman, *Bascomb*, Charles Durning, *Hunnicutt*, Jeff Dalton, *Clay McCain*, Freddie McCloud, *Buddy McCain*, Jane Rose, *Elsie*, J.C. Evans, *Grandpa Tawes*, Margaret Ann Morris, *Sybil*, Bill Littleton, *Pollard*, Leo Yates, *Vogel*, Dodo Denney, *Darlene Hunnicutt*. PG.

Dull drama starring Gregory Peck as a Tennessee sheriff, whose life and job become complicated when he has an adulterous affair with a young woman (Tuesday Weld), who happens to be the daughter of a moonshiner. Their relationship is the only interesting aspect, as *I Walk the Line* falls flat when it focuses on the conflict between the law and the moonshiners.

417 I Wanna Hold Your Hand (1978) ******** Universal, 104 min. *Dir* Robert Zemeckis, *Scr* Bob Gale, Robert Zemeckis, *Cin* Donald M. Morgan, *Ed* Frank Morriss, *Art* Peter Jamison, *Cos* Roseanna Norton, *Mus* The Beatles, *Prod* Tamara Asseyev, Alex Rose, *Exec Prod* Steven Spielberg, *Assoc Prod* Bob Gale.

Cast: Nancy Allen, *Pam Mitchell*, Bobby DiCicco, *Tony Smerko*, Marc McClure, *Larry Dubois*, Susan Kendall Newman, *Janis Goldman*, Theresa Saldana, *Grace Corrigan*, Wendie Jo Sperber, *Rosie Petrofsky*, Eddie Deezen, Richard "*Ringo*" Klaus, Christian Juttner, *Peter Plimpton*, Will Jordan, *Ed Sullivan*, Read Morgan, *Peter's Father*, Claude Earl Jones, *Al*, James Houghton, *Eddie*, Michael Hewitson, *Neil*, Dick Miller, *Sgt. Bresner*, Vito Carenzo, *CBS Security Guard*, Luke Andreas, *Police Officer in Alley*, Roberta Lee Carroll, Sherry Lynn, *Cafeteria Girls*, Irene Arranga, *Sheet Girl*, Carole H. Field, *Club Leader*, Nancy Osborne, *Amazon*. PG.

Unusual slapstick comedy about Beatlemania and focusing on a group of teenagers attempting to see The Beatles during their appearance on *The Ed Sullivan Show*. This is perhaps not the most earth shattering of subject matters, but *I Wanna Hold Your Hand* is so well directed, written and acted, by the young cast of unknowns, that it must rank as one of the most intelligent of comedies. Rather than using doubles for The Beatles, the real group appears in videos from the actual show.

418 **I Will...I Will...for Now** (1976) ** 20th Century–Fox, 107 min. *Dir* Norman Panama, *Scr* Albert E. Lewin, Norman Panama, *Cin* John A. Alonzo, *Ed* Robert Lawrence, *Des* Fernando Carrere, *Mus* John Cameron, *Prod* George Barrie.

Cast: Elliott Gould, *Les*, Diane Keaton, *Katie*, Paul Sorvino, *Lou*, Victoria Principal, *Jackie*, Robert Alda, *Dr. Magnus*, Warren Berlinger, *Steve*, Madge Sinclair, *Dr. Williams*, Candy Clark, *Sally*, Carmen Zapata, *Maria*, George Tyne, *Marriage Counsellor*. R.

Stale light marital sex comedy. Elliott Gould and his ex-wife Diane Keaton try to get back together, bound by a contract. That form does not work, either, and they check into a sex clinic, bringing to fore many interrelationships and complications. *I Will...I Will...for Now* is nothing more than a dim-witted 1960's style comedy that is unsuccessfully updated to the 1970's.

419 **Ice Castles** (1978) ** Columbia, 113 min, *Dir* Donald Wrye, *Scr* Gary L. Baim, Donald Wrye, *Cin* Bill Butler, *Ed* Michael Kahn, Melvin Shapiro, Maury Winetrobe, *Des* Joel Schiller, *Cos* Richard Bruno, *Mus* Marvin Hamlisch, *Lyrics* Carole Bayer Sager, *Prod* John Kemeny, *Co-Prod* S. Rodger Olenicoff, *Exec Prod* Rosilyn Heller.

Cast: Lynn-Holly Johnson, *Alexis Winston*, Robby Benson, *Nick Peterson*, Colleen Dewhurst, *Beulah Smith*, Tom Skerritt, *Marcus Winston*, Jennifer Warren, *Deborah Mackland*, David Huffman, *Brian Dockett*, Diane Reilly, *Sandy*, Craig T. McMullen, *Doctor*, Kelsey Ufford, *Ceciel Monchet*, Leonard Lilyholm, *Hockey Coach*, Brian Foley, *Choreographer*, Jean-Claude Bleuze, *French Coach*, Teresa Willmus, *Annette Brashlout*, Diana Holden, *X-Ray Technician*, Michelle McLean, *Skater*, Carol Williams, *TV Producer*. PG. $9,500,000.

Standard sentimental drama about an Olympic hopeful ice skater (Lynn-Holly Johnson), who suffers a terrible accident while training and is subsequently blinded. Robby Benson also stars as her sympathetic boyfriend, who tries to help her through her dilemma. *Ice Castles* is very much like other films of its type, that attempt to wrench tears by hitting squeaky clean characters with a physical tragedy.

420 **The Iceman Cometh** (1973) *** American Film Theatre, 239 min. *Dir* John Frankenheimer, based on play by Eugene O'Neill, Text edited by Thomas Quinn Curtis, *Cin* Ralph Woolsey, *Ed* Harold Kress, *Des* Jack Martin Smith, *Cos* Dorothy Jeakins, *Prod* Ely A. Landau, *Exec Prod* Edward Lewis.

Cast: Lee Marvin, *Hickey*, Fredric March, *Harry Hope*, Robert Ryan, *Larry Slade*, Jeff Bridges, *Don Parritt*, Bradford Dillman, *Willie Oban*, Sorrell Booke, *Hugo Kalmar*, Hildy Brooks, *Margie*, Nancy Juno Dawson, *Pearl*, Evans Evans, *Cora*, Martyn Green, *Captain (Cecil Lewis)*, Moses Gunn, *Joe Mott*, Clifton James, *Pat McGloin*, John McLiam, *Jimmy Tomorrow*, Stephen Pearlman, *Chuck Morello*, Tom Pedi, *Rocky Pioggi*, George Voskovec, *General (Piet Wetjoen)*, Bart Burns, *Moran*, Don McGovern, *Lieb*. PG. See *American Film Theatre*.

421 **If Ever I See You Again** (1978) * Columbia, 105 min. *Dir* Joe Brooks, *Scr* Joe Brooks, Martin Davidson, *Cin* Adam Holender, *Ed* Rich Shaine, *Mus* Joe Brooks, *Prod* Joe Brooks.

Cast: Joe Brooks, *Bob*, Shelley Hack, *Jennifer*, Jimmy Breslin, *Mario*, Jerry Keller, *Steve*, George Plimpton, *Lawrence*, Michael Decker, *Young Bob*, Julie Ann Gordon, *Young Jennifer*, Danielle Brisebois, *Amy*, Branch Emerson, *Jonathan*, Shannon Bolin, *Elsa*, Bob Kaliban, *Supervisor*, Len Gockman, *Executive*, Susan Rubenstein, *Copywriter*, Steve Hiott, *Art Director*, Gordon Ramsey, *Larry*, Vinnie Bell, Eric Weisberg, *Guitarists*, Dan Resin, *Supervisor*, John Nalpern, *Executive*, Malcolm Addey, *Engineer*. PG.

Poor love story about a composer/musician who attempts to win back an old girlfriend he has not seen for years. *If Ever I See You Again* may be the ultimate movie ego trip as Joe Brooks has his hand in nearly everything; director, writer, producer, composer and star. This would have been fine had Brooks had abilities in each of these areas, but unfortunately he fails at all of them. If that were not enough never have two romantic leads been so lacking in charisma.

422 **Images** (1972) *** Britain, Columbia 100 min. *Dir* Robert Altman, *Scr* Robert Altman, *Cin* Vilmos Zsigmond, *Ed* Graeme Clifford, *Des* Leon Ericksen, *Mus* John Williams, *Prod* Tommy Thompson.

Cast: Susannah York (CF), *Cathryn*, René Auberjonois, *Hugh*, Marcel Bozzuffi, *René*, Hugh Millais, *Marcel*, Cathryn Harrison, *Susannah*. R.

Unusual psychological drama about a woman (Susannah York), who may be schizophrenic. She has bizarre hallucinations that may or may not be real. Robert Altman's approach is different as he leaves things open to interpretation by refusing to actually explain her condition. This leaves *Images* slightly muddled, but it is a worthwhile visual experience, nevertheless.

423 **In Praise of Older Women** (1978) ** Canada, Avco Embassy, 108 min. *Dir* George Kaczender, *Scr* Paul Gottlieb, based on novel by Stephen Vizinczey, *Cin* Miklos Lente, *Ed* George Kaczender, Peter Wintonick, *Art* Wolf Kroeger, *Cos* Olga Dimitrov, *Mus* Tibor Polgar, *Prod* Claude Heroux, Robert Lantos, *Exec Prod* Harold Greenberg, Stephen Roth.

Cast: Tom Berenger, *Andras Vayda*, Karen Black, *Maya*, Susan Strasberg, *Bobbie*, Helen Shaver, *Ann MacDonald*, Marilyn Lightstone, *Klari*, Alexandra Stewart, *Paula*, Marianne McIsaac, *Julika*, Alberta Watson, *Mitzi*, Ian Tracey, *Andras Vayda, Jr*. Monique LePage, *Countess*, Mignon Elkins, *Mother Vayda*,

Joan Stuart, *Aunt Alice*, John Bayless, *Glen MacDonald*, Jon Granik, *Tom Horvath*. R.

Dull and repetitive story about a young man who has relationships only with older women. Tom Berenger stars as the man who has found, due to his experience as a child pimp during WWII, that only older women will satisfy him. The film is divided into different episodes, each spotlighting a different woman. Separately these episodes are dull; together they are redundant.

424 **The Incredible Sarah** (1976) ** Britain, Readers Digest, 105 min. *Dir* Richard Fleischer, *Scr* Ruth Wolff, *Cin* Christopher Challis, *Ed* John Jympson, *Des* Elliot Scott (AN), *Art* Norman Reynolds (AN), *Cos* Anthony Mendleson (AN), *Mus* Elmer Bernstein, *Prod* Helen M. Strauss.

Cast: Glenda Jackson, *Sarah Bernhardt*, Daniel Massey, *Sardou*, Yvonne Mitchell, *Mam'selle*, Douglas Wilmer, *Montiguy*, David Langton, *Duc de Morny*, Simon Williams, *Henri de Ligne*, John Castle, *Damala*, Edward Judd, *Jarrett*, Rosemarie Dunham, *Mrs. Bernhardt*, Peter Sallis, *Thierry*, Bridget Armstrong, *Marie*, Margaret Courtenay, *Madame Nathalie*. PG.

Disappointing biography of legendary French stage actress Sarah Bernhardt. *The Incredible Sarah* is more of a series of shrill and bombastic episodes that documents various tantrums, rather than a well-rounded character study that examines Bernhardt the person and the actress. Unfortunately everything is overdone and played too broadly, even by the usually excellent Glenda Jackson.

425 **The In-Laws** (1979) *** Warner Bros., 103 min. *Dir* Arthur Hiller, *Scr* Andrew Bergman, *Cin* David M. Walsh, *Ed* Robert E. Swink, *Des* Pato Guzman, *Mus* John Morris, *Prod* Arthur Hiller, William Sackheim, *Exec Prod* Alan Arkin, *Assoc Prod* Dorothy Wilde.

Cast: Peter Falk, *Vince Ricardo*, Alan Arkin, *Sheldon Kornpett*, Richard Libertini, *General Garcia*, Nancy Dussault, *Carol Kornpett*, Penny Peyser, *Barbara Kornpett*, Arlene Golonka, *Jean Ricardo*, Michael Lembeck, *Tommy Ricardo*, Paul Lawrence Smith, *Mo*, Carmine Caridi, *Angie*, Ed Begley, Jr., *Barry Lutz*, Sammy Smith, *Mr. Hirschorn*, James Hong, *Bing Wong*, Barbara Dana, *Bank Teller*, Rozsika Halmos, *Mrs. Edelman*, Alvaro Carcano, *Edgardo*, Jorge Zepeda, *Carlos*, Sergio Calderon, *Alfonso*. PG. $18,900,000.

Outrageous slapstick farce about a dentist (Alan Arkin), who becomes involved with a crazy CIA agent (Peter Falk). They are drawn together due to the prospective marriage of Arkin's daughter and Falk's son. Falk drags Arkin into a bizarre investigation, which takes them to a South American republic ruled by a looney dictator (Richard Libertini). Arkin and Falk seem like odd choices for a comedy team, but it works splendidly, and their natural rapport adds life to a standard slapstick story.

426 **Inserts** (1976) *** Britain, United Artists, 117 min. *Dir* John Byrum, *Scr* John Byrum, *Cin* Denys Coop, John Harris, *Ed* Mike Bradsell, *Art* John Clark, *Cos* Shirley Russell, *Prod* Davina Belling, Clive Parsons, *Assoc Prod* Harry Benn.

Cast: Richard Dreyfuss, *Boy Wonder*, Jessica Harper, *Cathy*, Stephen Davies, *Rex*, Veronica Cartwright, *Harlene*, Bob Hoskins, *Big Mac*. X.

Unusual drama set in Hollywood in the 1930's. Richard Dreyfuss is superb as a has-been film director who now earns his living making porno films. *Inserts* resembles a filmed stage play as the entire film is set in his decaying mansion. Although pornography is its subject matter, and it did receive an X rating, this is not a pornographic film itself. *Inserts* is a fine underrated film and screenwriter John Byrum made an excellent directorial debut.

427 Interiors (1978) ******** United Artists, 93 min. *Dir* Woody Allen (AN), *Scr* Woody Allen (AN), *Cin* Gordon Willis, *Ed* Ralph Rosenblum, *Des* Mel Brown (AN), *Cos* Joel Schumacher, *Prod* Charles H. Jaffe.

Cast: Kristin Griffith, *Flyn*, Marybeth Hurt, *Joey*, Richard Jordan, *Frederick*, Diane Keaton, *Renata*, E.G. Marshall, *Arthur*, Geraldine Page (AN, BFA), *Eve*, Maureen Stapleton (AN, NY, LA), *Pearl*, Sam Waterston, *Mike*, PG. $4,565,000.

Excellent Bergmanesque drama about a family in turmoil. Woody Allen surprised everyone by making this straight drama. He mistakenly felt that comedies are inferior and cannot be taken seriously. This is simply untrue as some of Allen's comedies rank among the finest films ever made. Allen's motives are no reason to criticize *Interiors*, as he does obtain the desired results. Ingmar Bergman has always been a strong influence on Allen, but it has never been more apparent than in *Interiors*. The great irony, perhaps, is that *Interiors* is actually better than many Bergman films, particularly his later ones.

428 International Velvet (1978) ****** Britain, United Artists, 125 min. *Dir* Bryan Forbes, *Scr* Bryan Forbes, based on novel *National Velvet* by Enid Bagnold, *Cin* Tony Imi, *Ed* Timothy Gee, *Des* Keith Wilson, *Cos* Dorothy Edwards, John Furness, John Hilling, *Mus* Francis Lai, *Prod* Bryan Forbes.

Cast: Tatum O'Neal, *Sarah Brown*, Nanette Newman, *Velvet Brown*, Christopher Plummer, *John Seaton*, Anthony Hopkins, *Capt. Johnson*, Peter Barkworth, *Pilot*, Dinsdale Landon, *Mr. Curtis*, Sarah Bullen, *Beth*, Jeffrey Byron, *Scott Saunders*, Richard Warwick, *Tim*, Daniel Abineri, *Wilson*, Jason White, *Roger*, Martin Neil, *Mike*, Douglas Reith, *Howard*. PG.

Fair sequel to the 1944 film, *National Velvet*. *International Velvet* is set years later with Velvet Brown, Elizabeth Taylor in the first film, as an adult who is preparing her niece (Tatum O'Neal) to follow in her footsteps and become an Olympic rider. The film is overlong and the pace is very slow and somewhat dull. Nanette Newman however gives an excellent performance as Velvet.

429 The Internecine Project (1974) ****** Britain, Allied Artists, 89 min. *Dir* Ken Hughes, *Scr* Barry Levinson, Jonathan Lynn, based on novel by Mort W. Elkind, *Cin* Geoffrey Unsworth, *Ed* John Shirley, *Des* Geoffrey Drake, *Art* David Minty, *Mus* Roy Budd, *Prod* Barry Levinson, *Co-Prod* Andrew Donally, Presented by Emanuel Wolf.

Cast: James Coburn, *Robert Elliot*, Lee Grant, *Jean Robertson*, Harry Andrews, *Albert Parsons*, Ian Hendry, *Alex Hellman*, Michael Jayston, *David Baker*, Keenan Wynn, *E.J. Farnsworth*, Christianne Kruger, *Christina*, Terence Alexander, *Tycoon*, Philip Anthony, *Elliot's Secretary*, David Swift, *Chester Drake*, Julian Glover, *Arnold Pryce Jones*, Ray Callaghan, *Producer*, Geoffrey Burridge, *Floor Manager*, Robert Tayman, *Mixer*, Judy Robinson, *Production Assistant*. PG.

Typical British espionage drama with the usual assortment of agents and intrigue. James Coburn stars as a tycoon who tries to cover up his dark past by eliminating four individuals, who know too much. *The Internecine Project* depends entirely too much on the scenes involving these murders, which cover the film's final third. The method of the murders may be a little too clever, but it is nevertheless, interesting.

430 **Invasion of the Body Snatchers** (1978) ***** United Artists, 115 min. *Dir* Philip Kaufman, *Scr* W.D. Richter, based on novel *The Body Snatchers* by Jack Finney, *Cin* Michael Chapman, *Ed* Douglas Stewart, *Des* Charles Rosen, *Sp* Russ Hessey, Dell Rheaume, *Mus* Denny Zeitlin, *Prod* Robert H. Solo.

Cast: Donald Sutherland, *Matthew Bennell*, Brooke Adams, *Elizabeth Driscoll*, Leonard Nimoy, *Dr. David Kibner*, Veronica Cartwright, *Nancy Bellicec*, Jeff Goldblum, *Jack Bellicec*, Art Hindle, *Geoffrey*, Lelia Goldoni, *Katherine*, Kevin McCarthy, *Running Man*, Don Siegel, *Cab Driver*. $11,135,000.

Magnificent remake of the science-fiction classic of the 1950's. Philip Kaufman took the basic story of humans being transformed into emotionless "pods" and simply pulled out all the stops. This version is a perfect blend of opulence and paranoia, as the viewer is literally plunged into the tense and exciting struggle to retain individuality. The film works on many levels and is such an astounding film that it almost obliterates the original.

431 **The Island at the Top of the World** (1974) *** Buena Vista, 95 min. *Dir* Robert Stevenson, *Scr* John Whedon, based on novel *The Lost Ones* by Ian Cameron, *Cin* Frank Phillips, *Ed* Robert Stafford, *Des* Peter Ellenshaw (AN), *Art* John B. Mansbridge, Al Roelofs, Walter Tyler (AN), *Cos* Bill Thomas, *Sp* Art Cruikshank, Danny Lee, Alan Maley, *Mus* Maurice Jarre, *Prod* Winston Hibler, A Walt Disney Production.

Cast: David Hartman, *Prof. Ivarsson*, Donald Sinden, *Sir Anthony Ross*, Jacques Marin, *Capt. Brieux*, Mako, *Oomiak*, David Gwillim, *Donald Ross*, Agneta Eckemyr, *Freyja*, Gunnar Ohlund, *The Godi*, Lasse Kolstad, *Erik*, Erik Silju, *Torvald*, Rolf Soder, *Lawspeaker*, Torsten Wahlund, *Sven*, Sverre Ousdal, *Gunner*, Niels Hinrichsen, *Sigurd*, Denny Miller, *Town Guard*, Brendan Dillon, *The Factor*, James Almanzar, *French Engineer*, Ivor Barry, *The Butler*, Lee Paul, *Chief of Boat Archers*. G. $10,200,000.

Above-average Disney adventure about an Arctic expedition in 1907, that discovers a colony of Vikings inhabiting an uncharted region. The plot is reminiscent of a Jules Verne type story and Disney pulls it off surprisingly well, due in part to the believable characters and the excellent special effects, particularly a 220 foot dirigible.

432 **The Island of Dr. Moreau** (1977) ** American International, 98 min. *Dir* Don Taylor, *Scr* Al Ramrus, John Herman Shaner, based on novel by H.G. Wells, *Cin* Gerry Fisher, *Ed* Marion Rothman, *Des* Philip Jefferies, *Cos* Richard LaMotte, Emma Porteus, Rita Woods, *Mus* Lawrence Rosenthal, *Prod* Skip Steloff, John Temple-Smith, *Exec Prod* Samuel Z. Arkoff, Sandy Howard.

Cast: Burt Lancaster, *Dr. Moreau*, Michael York, *Braddock*, Nigel Davenport, *Montgomery*, Barbara Carrera, *Maria*, Richard Basehart, *Sayer of* the Law, Nick Cravat, *M'Ling*, The Great John L., *Boarman*, Bob Ozman, *Bullman*, Fumio Demura, *Hyenaman*, Gary Baxley, *Lionman*, John Gillespie, *Tigerman*, David Cass, *Bearman*. PG. $4,000,000.

Fair horror thriller starring Burt Lancaster as a mad scientist conducting bizarre experiments, in which he crosses humans with beasts on a remote island in the Pacific. His half-human beasts eventually rebel against their master. The whole thing is a bit silly and not very well done, but it does feature strong performances by Lancaster and Michael York. This is a remake of *Island of the Lost Souls*.

433 **Islands in the Stream** (1977) *** Paramount, 105 min. *Dir* Franklin J. Schaffner, *Scr* Denne Bart Petitclerc, based on novel by Ernest Hemingway, *Cin* Fred Koenekamp (AN), *Ed* Robert Swink, *Des* William J. Creber, *Mus* Jerry Goldsmith, *Prod* Peter Bart, Max Palevsky.

Cast: George C. Scott, *Thomas Hudson*, David Hemmings, *Eddy*, Gilbert Roland, *Capt. Ralph*, Susan Tyrell, *Lil*, Richard Evans, *Willy*, Claire Bloom, *Audrey*, Julius Harris, *Joseph*, Hart Bochner, *Tom*, Brad Savage, *Andrew*, Michael-James Wixted, *David*, Charles Lampkin, *Constable*, Hildy Brooks, *Helga Ziegner*, Jessica Rains, *Andrea*, Walter Friedel, *Herr Ziegner*. PG. $4,035,000.

Fine drama about a self-exiled artist (George C. Scott) living on an island. He is visited by his three sons, whom he has not seen for four years, and they spend the summer with him. While *Islands in the Stream* is focusing on their relationship it is insightful and perceptive, but it suddenly becomes melodramatic in the final third, in which Scott becomes involved in WWII, with a plot lifted from *To Have and Have Not*.

434 **It Lives Again** (1978) *** Warner Bros., 91 min. *Dir* Larry Cohen, *Scr* Larry Cohen, based on characters created by Larry Cohen, *Cin* Fenton Hamilton, *Ed* Curt Burch, Louis Friedman, Carol O'Blath, *Mus* Bernard Herrmann, *Prod* Larry Cohen, *Assoc Prod* William Wellman, Jr.

Cast: Frederic Forrest, *Eugene Scott*, Kathleen Lloyd, *Judy Scott*, John Ryan, *Frank Davis*, John Marley, *Mallory*, Andrew Duggan, *Dr. Perry*, Eddie Constantine, *Dr. Forest*, James Dixon, *Det. Perkins*. R.

See *It's Alive*.

435 **It's Alive** (1974) *** Warner Bros., 90 min. *Dir* Larry Cohen, *Scr* Larry Cohen, *Cin* Fenton Hamilton, *Ed* Peter Honess, *Mus* Bernard Herrmann, *Prod* Larry Cohen, *Co-Prod* Janelle Cohen, *Exec Prod* Peter Sabiston.

Cast: John Ryan, *Frank*, Sharon Farrell, *Lenore*, Andrew Duggan, *Professor*, Guy Stockwell, *Clayton*, James Dixon, *Perkins*, Michael Ansara, *Captain*, Robert Emhardt, *Executive*, William Wellman, Jr., *Charlie*, Shamus Locke, *Doctor*, Mary Nancy Burnett, *Nurse*, Diana Hale, *Secretary*, Daniel Holzman, *Boy*, Patrick Macallister, Gerald York, Jerry Taft, Gwil Richards, W. Allen York, *Expectant Fathers*. R. $7,100,000.

Bizarre horror shocker about a grotesque newborn baby that kills everyone in the delivery room and goes on a murder spree. *It's Alive* is an above average horror film and better than most films inspired by *The Exorcist*. Naturally the premise is unbelievable, but Larry Cohen has a vivid enough imagination to pull this off. The sequel *It Lives Again* has three killer babies to top the first, but it is more of the same.

436 J.W. Coop (1972) *** Columbia, 112 min. *Dir* Cliff Robertson, *Scr* Cliff Robertson, *Cin* Frank Stanley, *Ed* Alex Beaton, *Mus* Don Randi, Louie Shelton, *Prod* Cliff Robertson, *Assoc Prod* Bruce Graham.

Cast: Cliff Robertson, *J.W. Coop*, Geraldine Page, *Mama*, Christina Ferrare, *Bean*, R.G. Armstrong, *Jim Sawyer*, R.L. Armstrong, *Tooter Watson*, John Crawford, *Rancher*, Wade Crosby, *Billy Sol*, Marjorie Durant Dye, *Big Marge*, Paul Harper, *Warden Morgen*, Son Hooker, *Motorcycle Cop*, Richard Kennedy, *Sheriff*, Bruce Kirby, *Diesel Driver*, Mary Robin Redd, *Bonnie May*, Claude Stroud, *Rodeo Manager*. PG.

Fine drama about an ex-con (Cliff Robertson), who after his release from prison becomes a rodeo cowboy, and through his determination becomes a minor star. *J.W. Coop* features some excellent rodeo action footage and Cliff Robertson not only gives a good performance, but he also succeeds as director, writer and producer.

437 Jabberwocky (1977) ** Britain, Cinema 5, 100 min. *Dir* Terry Gilliam, *Scr* Charles Alverson, Terry Gilliam, *Cin* Terry Bedford, *Ed* Michael Bradsell, *Des* Roy Smith, *Art* Millie Burns, *Cos* Charles Knode, Hazel Pethig, *Mus* De Wolfe, *Prod* Sandy Lieberson, *Exec Prod* John Goldstone, *Assoc Prod* Julian Doyle.

Cast: Michael Palin, *Dennis Cooper*, Max Wall, *King Bruno the Questionable*, Deborah Fallender, *Princess*, John Le Mesurier, *Chamberlain*, Annette Badland, *Griselda Fishfinger*, Warren Mitchell, *Mr. Fishfinger*, Brenda Cowling, *Mrs. Fishfinger*, Harry H. Corbett, Rodney Bewes, *Squires*, Bernard Bresslaw, *Landlord*, Alexandra Dane, *Betsy*, Derek Francis, *Bishop*, Peter Cellier, Frank Williams, Anthony Carrick, *Merchants*, John Bird, *Herald*, Neil Innes, *Herald and Drummer*, Paul Curran, *Mr. Cooper, Sr.*, Graham Crowden, *Fanatics' Leader*, Gordon Rollings, *King's Taster*. PG.

Strange period fantasy comedy about a country bumpkin (Michael Palin), who stupidly decides to hunt down the Jaberwock, a grotesque mythological beast that is terrorizing the countryside. *Jabberwocky* is something of a disappointment coming from Palin and director-writer Terry Gilliam, two members of Monty Python's Flying Circus. The humor is below their normal standards, lacking in wit and intelligence.

438 Jackson County Jail (1976) *** New World, 85 min. *Dir* Michael Miller, *Scr* Donald Stewart, *Cin* Bruce Logan, *Ed* Caroline Ferriol, *Art* Michael McCloskey, *Cos* Cornelia McNamara, *Mus* Loren Newkirk, *Prod* Jeff Begun, *Exec Prod* Roger Corman, *Assoc Prod* Paul Gonsky.

Cast: Yvette Mimieux, *Dinah*, Tommy Lee Jones, *Coley*, Robert Carradine, *Bobby*, Frederic Cook, *Hobie*, Severn Darden, *Sheriff*, Nan Martin, *Allison*, Mary Woronov, *Pearl*, Howard Hessemann, *David*. R.

Interesting drama about an average middle aged woman (Yvette Mimieux) who suddenly finds herself as an escaped prisoner. She is falsely arrested after her car is stolen and is raped while in jail by a psychotic deputy and subsequently escapes with another prisoner (Tommy Lee Jones). *Jackson County Jail* received more praise than most low-budget features, which is ironic because it tends to be more ordinary than most films from New World.

439 Jacques Brel Is Alive and Well and Living in Paris (1975) *** American Film Theatre, 98 min. *Dir* Denis Heroux, *Scr* Eric Blau, based on stage production by Eric Blau and Mort Shuman, *Cin* Rene Verzier, *Ed* Yves Langlois, *Art* Jean Andre, *Cos* Jeannine Virgne, *Mus* Jacques Brel, *Mus. Orchestration* Francois Rauber, *Movement* Moni Yakim, *Prod* Paul Marshall, Cinevideo, *Exec Prod* Claude Heroux, Presented by Ely Landau.

Cast: Elly Stone, Mort Shuman, Joe Masiell, Jacques Brel. PG. See *American Film Theatre*.

440 **Jaws** (1975) (AN) **** Universal, 124 min. *Dir* Steven Spielberg, *Scr* Peter Benchley, Carl Gottlieb, based on novel by Peter Benchley, *Cin* Bill Butler, *Ed* Verna Fields (A), *Des* Joseph Alves, Jr., *Mus* John Williams (A, G), *Underwater Cin* Rexford Metz, *Prod* Richard D. Zanuck, David Brown.

Cast: Roy Scheider, *Brody*, Robert Shaw, *Quint*, Richard Dreyfuss, *Hooper*, Lorraine Gary, *Ellen Brody*, Murray Hamilton, *Vaughn*, Carl Gottlieb, *Meadows*, Jeffrey C. Kramer, *Hendricks*, Susan Backlinie, *Chrissie*, Jonathan Filley, *Cassidy*, Ted Grossman, *Estuary Victim*, Chris Rebello, *Michael Brody*, Jay Mello, *Sean Brody*, Lee Fierro, *Mrs. Kintner*, Jeffrey Voorhees, *Alex Kintner*, Craig Kingsbury, *Ben Gardner*, Dr. Robert Nevin, *Medical Examiner*, Peter Benchley, *Interviewer*. PG. $133,435,000.

Excellent thriller set at an East Coast resort, that is being terrorized by a great white shark. The tension builds gradually and strongly throughout the first half as the shark attacks residents one by one. The second half comprises the shark hunt, in which the three main characters, the police chief (Roy Scheider), a fisherman (Robert Shaw) and a scientist (Richard Dreyfuss), set out in a small boat to find the shark. Due to Steven Spielberg's superb direction, *Jaws* managed to scare millions with its real horrors, without resorting to gratuitous violence.

441 **Jaws 2** (1978) *** Universal, 123 min. *Dir* Jeannot Szwarc, *Scr* Carl Gottlieb, Howard Sackler, based on characters created by Peter Benchley, *Cin* Michael Butler, *Ed* Neil Travis, *Des* Joe Alves, *Art* Stu Campbell, Gene Johnson, *Cos* Laurann Cordero, Gil Loe, *Mus* John Williams, *Prod* Richard D. Zanuck, David Brown, *Assoc Prod* Joe Alves.

Cast: Roy Scheider, *Brody*, Lorraine Gary, *Ellen Brody*, Murray Hamilton, *Mayor Vaughan*, Joseph Mascola, *Peterson*, Jeffrey Kramer, *Hendricks*, Collin Wilcox, *Dr. Elkins*, Ann Dusenberry, *Tina*, Mark Gruner, *Mike*, Barry Coe, *Andrews*, Susan French, *Old Lady*, Gary Springer, *Andy*, Donna Wilkes, *Jackie*, Gary Dubin, *Ed*, John Dukakis, *Polo*, G. Thomas Dunlop, *Timmy*, David Elliot, *Larry*, Marc Gilpin, *Sean*, Keith Gordon, *Doug*, Cynthia Grover, *Lucy*, Ben Marley, *Patrick*, Jerry M. Baxter, *Helicopter Pilot*. PG. $55,610,000. See *Jaws*.

442 **Jenny** (1970) ** Cinerama, 86 min. *Dir* George Bloomfield, *Scr* George Bloomfield, Marvin Luvat, *Story* Diana Gould, *Cin* David Quaid, *Ed* Kent McKinney, *Art* Trevor Williams, *Cos* Ann Roth, *Mus* Michael Small, *Prod* Edgar J. Scherick.

Cast: Marlo Thomas, *Jenny*, Alan Alda, *Delano*, Marian Hailey, *Kay*, Elizabeth Wilson, *Mrs. Marsh*, Vincent Gardenia, *Mr. Marsh*, Stephen Strimpell, *Peter*, Fay Bernardi, *Woman*, Charlotte Rae, *Bella Star*. PG.

Dull comedy-drama about a marriage of convenience. A young filmmaker (Alan Alda), who is trying to avoid the draft, and a pregnant woman (Marlo Thomas) marry in order to solve their mutual problems. *Jenny* tries to be topical by taking on issues of its time, but its treatment is shallow and it has nothing new or relevant to add to those subjects. The plot itself is rather bland, too.

443 Jeremiah Johnson (1972) *** Warner Bros., 107 min. *Dir* Sydney Pollack, *Scr* Edward Anhalt, John Milius, based on novel *Mountain Men* by Vardis Fisher, and story *Crow Killer* by Robert Bunker, Raymond W. Thorp, *Cin* Duke Callaghan, *Ed* Thomas Stanford, *Art* Ted Haworth, *Mus* Tim McIntire, John Rubenstein, *Prod* Joe Wizan, *Assoc Prod* John R. Coonan, Mike Moder.

Cast: Robert Redford, *Jeremiah Johnson*, Will Geer, *Bear Claw*, Stefan Gierasch, *Del Gue*, Allyn Ann McLerie, *Crazy Woman*, Charles Tyner, *Robidoux*, Josh Albee, *Caleb*, Joaquin Martinez, *Paints His Shirt Red*, Paul Benedict, *Reverend*, Matt Clark, *Qualen*, Richard Angarola, *Lebeaux*, Jack Colvin, *Lt. Mulvey*, Delle Bolton, *Swan*. PG. $21,900,000.

Fine western drama starring Robert Redford as a man who becomes disillusioned with civilization and goes off to live out his life as a mountain man. *Jeremiah Johnson* is little more than an episodic adventure that follows his travels, as he braves bitter winters, Indians, and other dangers. The film may wander a little, but it is always interesting.

444 The Jerk (1979) *** Universal, 104 min. *Dir* Carl Reiner, *Scr* Michael Elias, Carl Gottlieb, Steve Martin, *Story*, Carl Gottlieb, Steve Martin, *Cin* Victor J. Kemper, *Ed* Bud Molin, *Des* Jack T. Collis, *Cos* Theadora Van Runkle, *Mus* Jack Elliot, *Prod* William E. McEuen, David V. Picker, *Assoc Prod* Peter MacGregor-Scott.

Cast: Steve Martin, *Navin*, Bernadette Peters, *Marie*, Catlin Adams, *Patty Bernstein*, Mabel King, *Mother*, Richard Ward, *Father*, Dick Anthony Williams, *Taj*, Carl Reiner, *Himself*, Bill Macy, *Stan Fox*, M. Emmet Walsh, *Madman*, Dick O'Neill, *Frosty*, Maurice Evans, *Hobart*, Helena Carroll, *Hester*, Ren Wood, *Elvira*, Pepe Serna, *Punk #1*, Sonny Terry, Brownie McGee, *Blues Singers*, Jackie Mason, *Harry Hartounian*, David Landsberg, *Bank Manager*, Domingo Ambriz, *Father De Cordoba*, Richard Foronjy, Lenny Montana, *Con Men*, Carl Gottlieb, *Iron Balls McGinty*, Clete Roberts, *Announcer*. R. $43,000,000.

Idiotic, but funny vehicle, tailor made for comic Steve Martin's clownish image and talents. *The Jerk* is a rags to riches story with Martin as a moron who inadvertently becomes wealthy due to a strange invention. There are some similarities to the Jerry Lewis comedies of the 1960's, but Martin is essentially an original talent, and Carl Reiner's direction surprisingly holds the silliness together.

445 Jesus Christ Superstar (1973) * Universal, 108 min. *Dir* Norman Jewison, *Scr* Melvyn Bragg, Norman Jewison, based on rock opera with book and lyrics by Tim Rice and music by Andrew Lloyd Webber, *Cin* Douglas Slocombe, *Ed* Anthony Gibbs, *Des* Richard MacDonald, *Art* John Clark, *Cos* Yvonne Blake, *Chor* Rob Iscove, *Prod* Norman Jewison, Robert Stigwood, *Assoc Prod* Patrick Palmer.

Cast: Ted Neeley, *Jesus Christ*, Carl Anderson, *Judas Iscariot*, Yvonne Elliman, *Mary Magdalene*, Barry Dennen, *Pontius Pilate*, Bob Bingham,

Caiaphas, Larry T. Marshall, *Simon Zealotes*, Joshua Mostel, *King Herod*, Kurt Yahgjian, *Annas*, Philip Toubus, *Peter*. G. $13,290,000.

Poor musical rock opera based on popular album and stage show. *Jesus Christ Superstar* is far too ridiculous to be taken seriously, let alone offend anyone, although it did anyway. The entire story is told through musical numbers rather than with dialogue. This is not a flaw in itself except for the fact that its success rests entirely on these musical numbers, none of which are well-done.

446 Joe (1970) *** Cannon, 107 min. *Dir* John G. Avildsen, *Scr* Norman Wexler, (AN), *Cin* John G. Avildsen, *Ed* George T. Norris, *Mus* Bobby Scott, *Prod* David Gil, *Exec Prod* Christopher G. Dewey, Dennis Friedland.

Cast: Peter Boyle, *Joe Curran*, Dennis Patrick, *Bill Compton*, Susan Sarandon, *Melissa Compton*, Audrey Caire, *Joan Compton*, K. Callan, *Mary Lou Curran*, Patrick McDermott, *Frank Russo*, Tim Lewis, *Kid in Soda Shop*, Estelle Omens, *Woman in Bargain Store*, Bob O'Connell, *Man in Bargain Store*, Marlene Warfield, *Bellevue Nurse*, Mary Case, Jenny Paine, *Teeny Boppers*, Reid Cruickshanks, *American Bartender*, Rudy Churney, *Man in Bar*, Robert Emerick, *TV Newscaster*, Gloria Haye, *Janice*, Bo Enivel, *Sam*, Patrick O'Neil, *Bartender at Ginger Man*, Frank Moon, *Gil Richards*, Jeanne M. Lange, *Phyllis*. R. $9,500,000.

Unusual drama about an overbearing bigot (Peter Boyle), who befriends a man (Dennis Patrick), who has accidently killed his daughter's hippie boyfriend. The two men are from entirely different backgrounds, and *Joe* successfully examines the awkwardness of their relationship, while comparing and contrasting their lifestyles and attitudes. Unfortunately *Joe* is flawed by a violent climax that stretches credibility.

447 Joe Kidd (1972) ** Universal, 88 min. *Dir* John Sturges, *Scr* Elmore Leonard, *Cin* Bruce Surtees, *Ed* Ferris Webster, *Art* Henry Bumstead, Alexander Golitzen, *Mus* Lalo Schifrin, *Prod* Sidney Beckerman, *Exec Prod* Robert Daley.

Cast: Clint Eastwood, *Joe Kidd*, Robert Duvall, *Frank Harlan*, John Saxon, *Luis Chama*, Don Stroud, *Lamarr*, Stella Garcia, *Helen Sanchez*, James Wainwright, *Mingo*, Paul Koslo, *Roy*, Gregory Walcott, *Mitchell*, Dick Van Patten, *Hotel Manager*, Lynne Marta, *Elma*, John Carter, *Judge*, Pepe Hern, *Priest*, Joaquin Martinez, *Manolo*, Ron Soble, *Ramon*, Pepe Callahan, *Naco*, Clint Ritchie, *Calvin*, Gil Barreto, *Emilio*, Ed Deemer, *Bartender*, Maria Val, *Vita*, Chuck Hayward, *Eljay*, Michael R. Horst, *Deputy*. PG. $6,330,000.

Dull western starring Clint Eastwood as another mysterious stranger, who is hired by an unscrupulous land baron (Robert Duvall) to lead a group of gunman to assassinate a Spanish-American rebel (John Saxon). *Joe Kidd* has surprisingly little action for an Eastwood western—except for an exciting climax involving a train—and there is very little substance to compensate.

448 Johnny Got His Gun (1971) * Cinemation, 111 min. *Dir* Dalton Trumbo, *Scr* Dalton Trumbo, based on his novel, *Cin* Jules Brenner, *Ed* William P. Dornisch, *Des* Harold Michelson, *Cos* Theadora Van Runkle, *Mus* Jerry Fielding, *Prod* Bruce Campbell, *Assoc Prod* Tony Monaco, Christopher Trumbo.

Cast: Timothy Bottoms, *Joe Bonham*, Kathy Fields, *Kareen*, Marsha Hunt, *Joe's Mother*, Jason Robards, *Joe's Father*, Donald Sutherland, *"Christ"*, Diane Varsi, *The Nurse*, Charles McGraw, *Mike Burkeman*, Eduard Franz, *Col.-Gen. Tillery*, Donald Barry, *Jody Simmons*, Bruce Morrow, *Brigadier General*. PG.

Pretentious anti-war drama that literally wallops an audience with its viewpoint. Good intentions do not necessarily make a good movie. Timothy Bottoms stars as a WWI soldier whose arms and legs are amputated due to a bomb blast injury. Most of *Johnny Got His Gun* takes place inside this character's head; either his voice-over thoughts in his hospital room or his dreams and fantasies, many of which appear to be poor imitations of Fellini. Dalton Trumbo may have been a good writer, but the same cannot be said for his abilities as a director.

449 Joseph Andrews (1977) ** Britain, Paramount, 103 min. *Dir* Tony Richardson, *Scr* Chris Bryant, Allan Scott, *Story* Tony Richardson, based on novel by Henry Fielding, *Cin* David Watkin, *Ed* Thom Noble, *Des* Michael Annals, *Art* Bill Brosie, *Cos* Michael Annals, Arthur Davey, Jean Hunnisett, Patrick Wheatley, *Mus* John Addison, *Songs* Jim Dale, Bob Stewart, *Prod* Neil Hartly.

Cast: Peter Firth, *Joseph Andrews*, Ann-Margret, *Lady Booby*, Michael Hordern, *Parson Adamis*, Beryl Reid, *Mrs. Slipslop*, Jim Dale, *Peddlar*, Natalie Ogle, *Fanny Goodwill*, Peter Bull, *Sir Thomas Booby*, Kenneth Cranham, *Wicked Squire*, Karen Dotrice, *Pamela*, James Villiers, *Mr. Booby*. R.

Dull period farce of mistaken identities. Peter Firth stars in the title role as a young servant in England in the 19th century. The film follows his many escapades,which includes an affair with Lady Booby (Ann-Margret), a woman with a dark past. *Joseph Andrews* is an attempt by Tony Richardson to recapture the magic of his classic *Tom Jones*, another adaptation from Fielding, but this film falls short of that, with its limp and totally witless humor.

450 Juggernaut (1974) *** Britain, United Artists, 109 min. *Dir* Richard Lester, *Scr* Richard DeKoker, *Additional Dialogue* Alan Plater, *Cin* Gerry Fisher, *Ed* Tony Gibbs, *Des* Terence Marsh, *Art* Alan Tomkins, *Prod* Richard DeKoker, *Exec Prod* David V. Picker, *Assoc Prod* Denis O'Dell.

Cast: Richard Harris, *Fallon*, Omar Sharif, *Capt. Brunel*, David Hemmings, *Charlie Braddock*, Anthony Hopkins, *Supt. John McCleod*, Shirley Knight, *Barbara Banister*, Ian Holm, *Nicholas Porter*, Clifton James, *Mr. Corrigan*, Roy Kinnear, *Social Director Curain*, Caroline Mortimer, *Susan McCleod*, Mark Burns, *First Officer Hollingsworth*, John Stride, *Huges*, Freddie Jones, *Mr. Buckland*, Julian Glover, *Commander Marder*, Jack Watson, *Chief Engineer Mallicent*, Roshan Seth, *Azad*, Kenneth Colley, *Detective Brown*, Andrew Bradford, *Third Officer Hardy*. PG.

Above average thriller set aboard a luxury liner that has been sabotaged by a terrorist who has hidden several bombs on the ship. Due to its setting, *Juggernaut* has been mistakenly labeled as a disaster film, but it has nothing in common with those nonsensical films. As a straight thriller this film is nothing out of the ordinary, but Richard Lester's satirical viewpoint makes it more interesting to watch.

451 **Julia** (1977) (AN, BFA) ** 20th Century–Fox, 116 min. *Dir* Fred Zinnemann (AN), *Scr* Alvin Sargent (A, BFA, W), based on story *Pentimento* by Lillian Hellman, *Cin* Douglas Slocombe (AN, BFA, LA), *Ed* Marcel Durham, Walter Murch (AN), *Des* Carmen Dillon, Gene Gallahan, Willy Holt, *Mus* Georges Delerue (AN), *Prod* Richard Roth, *Exec Prod* Julian Derode.

Cast: Jane Fonda (AN, G, BFA, LA), *Lillian Hellman*, Vanessa Redgrave (A, G, LA), *Julia*, Jason Robards (A, LA), *Dashiell Hamett*, Maximilian Schell (AN, NY), *Johann*, Hal Holbrook, *Alan Campbell*, Rosemary Murphy, *Dorothy Parker*, Meryl Streep, *Anne Marie*, Dora Doll, Elizabeth Mortensen, *Train Passengers*, John Glover, *Sammy*, Lisa Pelikan, *Young Julia*, Susan Jones, *Young Lillian*, Cathleen Nesbitt, *Grandmother*, Maurice Denham, *Undertaker*, Gerard Buhr, *Passport Officer*, Stefan Gryft, *"Hamlet"*, Phillip Siegel, *Little Boy*, Molly Urquhart, *Woman*, Antony Carrick, *Butler*. PG. $13,055,000.

Dull film about author Lillian Hellman's relationship with a woman named Julia, a political activist in Europe during the 1930's. *Julia* is just the sort of drivel that excites Hollywood and many critics; it has socially relevant characters constantly chattering about issues, with an overabundance of dialogue; and they swallowed it hook line and sinker. The performances are fine, but none are Oscar worthy. All the praise in the world cannot disguise the fact that *Julia* is a bore.

452 **Junior Bonner** (1972) **** Cinerama, 103 min. *Dir* Sam Peckinpah, *Scr* Jeb Rosebrook, *Cin* Lucien Ballard, *Ed* Robert Wolfe, *Art* Edward S. Haworth, *Mus* Jerry Fielding, *Prod* Joe Wizan, *Assoc Prod* Mickey Borofsky.

Cast: Steve McQueen, *Junior Bonner*, Robert Preston, *Ace Bonner*, Ida Lupino, *Elvira Bonner*, Ben Johnson, *Buck Roan*, Joe Don Baker, *Curly Bonner*, Barbara Leigh, *Charmagne*, Mary Murphy, *Ruth Bonner*, Bill McKinney, *Red Terwiliger*, Sandra Deel, *Nurse Arlis*, Don "Red" Barry, *Homer Rutledge*, Dub Taylor, *Del*, Charles Gray, *Burt*, Matthew Peckinpah, *Tim Bonner*, Sundown Spencer, *Nick Bonner*, Rita Garrison, *Flashie*. PG.

Excellent comedy-drama about an aging rodeo star (Steve McQueen), who returns to his hometown to participate in a local rodeo, but discovers things have changed and he no longer belongs. *Junior Bonner* is almost unique as a film from Sam Peckinpah. It contains no violence, and it proves he can easily survive without it. McQueen gives one of the finest performances of his career and Robert Preston nearly steals the film as his father.

453 **Just You and Me, Kid** (1979) * Columbia, 93 min. *Dir* Leonard Stern, *Scr* Oliver Hailey, Leonard Stern, *Story* Tom Lazarus, *Cin* David Walsh, *Ed* John W. Holmes, *Des* Ron Hobbs, *Art* Sig Tinglof, *Mus* Jack Elliot, *Prod* Irving Fein, Jerome M. Zeitman.

Cast: George Burns, *Bill*, Brooke Shields, *Kate*, Burl Ives, *Max*, Lorraine Gary, *Shirl*, Nicolas Coster, *Harris*, Keye Luke, *Dr. Device*, Carl Ballantine, *Reinhoff the Remarkable*, Leon Ames, *Manduke the Magnificent*, Ray Bolger, *Tom*, John Schuck, *Stan*, Andrea Howard, *Sue*, Christopher Knight, *Roy*, William Russ, *Demesta*, Robert Doran, *Box Boy*. PG.

Unfunny Disney-style comedy about an ex-vaudevillian who hides a runaway teenager in his house. George Burns makes an earnest effort in trying to wring some laughs out of the tired script, and his co-star Brooke Shields is a poor foil; quite a comedown from Gracie Allen. *Just You and Me, Kid* looks more like a television movie, and is a terrible waste of Burns' talent.

454 **Kansas City Bomber** (1972) * MGM, 99 min. *Dir* Jerrold Freedman, *Scr* Calvin Clements, Thomas Rickman, *Story* Barry Sandler, *Cin* Fred Koenekamp, *Ed* David Berlatsky, *Art* Joseph R. Jennings, *Cos* Ronald Talsky, *Mus* Don Ellis, *Prod* Marty Elfand, *Exec Prod* Arthur Gardner, Jules Levy.

Cast: Raquel Welch, *K.C. Carr*, Kevin McCarthy, *Burt Henry*, Helen Kallianotes, *Jackie Burdette*, Norman Alden, *Horrible Hank Hopkins*, Jeanne Cooper, *Vivien*, Mary Kay Pass, *Lovey*, Martine Bartlett, *Mrs. Carr*, Cornelia Sharpe, *Tammy O'Brien*, William Gray Espy, *Randy*, Dick Lane, *Len*, Russ Marin, *Dick Weeks*, Stephen Manley, *Walt*, Jodie Foster, *Rita*, Georgia Schmidt, *Old Woman*, Shelly Novack, Jim Nickerson, *Fans*. PG.

Silly roller derby action film starring Raquel Welch as an up-and-coming star who tries to replace the roller derby queen (Helen Kallianotes). *Kansas City Bomber* promises little and it delivers less. There isn't much of a plot and the characters are mere cardboard stereotypes. This film may be of interest only to fans of this ridiculous sport.

455 **Kelly's Hereos** (1970) *** MGM, 144 min. *Dir* Brian G. Hutton, *Scr* Troy Kennedy Martin, *Cin* Gabriel Figueroa, *Ed* John Jympson, *Des* Jonathan Barry, *Cos* Annia Maria Fea, *Mus* Lalo Schifrin, *Prod* Sidney Beckerman, Gabriel Katzka, *Assoc Prod* Irving L. Leonard.

Cast: Clint Eastwood, *Kelly*, Telly Savalas, *Big Joe*, Don Rickles, *Crapgame*, Donald Sutherland, *Oddball*, Carroll O'Connor, *Gen. Cult*, Gavin McLeod, *Moriarty*, Hal Buckley, *Maitland*, Stuart Margolin, *Little Joe*, Jeff Morris, *Cowboy*, Richard Davalos, *Gutowski*, Perry Lopez, *Petuko*, Tom Troupe, *Job*, Harry Dean Stanton, *Willard*, Dick Balduzzi, *Fisher*, Gene Collins, *Babra*, Len Lesser, *Bellamy*, David Hurst, *Col. Dankhopf*, Fred Pearlman, *Mitchell*, Michael Clark, *Grace*, George Fargo, *Penn*, Dee Pollack, *Jonesy*, George Savalas, *Mulligan*, John Heller, *German Lieutenant*. PG. $5,350,000.

Offbeat WWII caper comedy about a group of American soldiers, who plan a huge gold robbery from a German bank behind enemy lines. *Kelly's Heroes* is filled with many interesting and sometimes weird, characters, particularly Donald Sutherland as an anachronistic hippie tank commander, who surprisingly does not seem too out of place. These characters set *Kelly's Heroes* apart from other films of its type.

456 **Kid Blue** (1973) *** 20th Century– Fox, 100 min. *Dir* James Frawley, *Scr* Edwin Shrake, *Cin* Billy Williams, *Ed* Stefan Arnsten, *Des* Joel Schiller, *Cos* Theodora Van Runkle, *Mus* Tim McIntire, John Rubinstein, *Prod* Marvin Schwartz.

Cast: Dennis Hopper, *Bickford Waner*, Warren Oates, *Reese Ford*, Peter Boyle, *Preacher Bob*, Ben Johnson, *Sheriff Simpson*, Lee Purcell, *Molly Ford*, Janice Rule, *Janet Conforto*, Ralph Waite, *Drummer*, Clifton James, *Mr. Hendricks*, Jose Torvay, *Old Coyote*, Mary Jackson, *Mrs. Evans*, Jay Varela, *Mendoza*, Claude Ennis Starrett, Jr., *Tough Guy*, Warren Finnerty, *Wills*, Howard Hesseman, *Confectionery Man*, Henry Smith, *Joe Cloudmaker*, Bobby Hall, *Bartender*, Melvin Stewart, *Blackman*, Eddy Donno, *Huey*, Owen Orr, Richard Rust, *Train Robbers*. PG.

Unusual comedy western set in the early part of the 20th century. Dennis Hopper stars as an outlaw, who settles in the small town of Dime Box,

Texas, in an attempt to go straight, and runs into an assortment of weirdos. *Kid Blue* is a mild, but pleasant, comedy about a rebel trying to fit into society, but is unable to adjust to it.

457 The Killer Elite (1975) ** United Artists, 122 min. *Dir* Sam Peckinpah, *Scr* Stirling Silliphant, *Cin* Philip Lathrop, *Ed* Garth Craven, Tony De Zarraga, Monte Hellman, *Des* Ted Haworth, *Mus* Jerry Fielding, *Prod* Martin Baum, Arthur Lewis, *Exec Prod* Helmut Dantine.

Cast: James Caan, *Mike Locken*, Robert Duvall, *George Hansen*, Arthur Hill, *Cap Collis*, Bo Hopkins, *Jerome Miller*, Mako, *Chung*, Burt Young, *Mac*, Gig Young, *Weyburn*, Tom Clancy, *O'Leary*, Tiana, *Tommie*, Kate Heflin, *Amy*, Sondra Blake, *Josephine*, Helmut Dantine, *Vorodny*, James Wing Woo, *Tao Yi*, George Kee Cheung, *Bruce*, Simon Tam, *Jimmy Fung*, Rick Alemany, *Ben Otake*, Hank Hamilton, *Hank*, Walter Kelley, *Walter*, Billy J. Scott, *Eddie*, Johnnie Burrell, *Donnie*, Matthew Peckinpah, *Kid*. PG. $4,100,000.

Disappointing thriller about a crippled CIA agent (James Caan), who vows revenge on his former partner (Robert Duvall), who is responsible for his condition. This is one of Sam Peckinpah's lesser efforts and his attitude appears to be flippant, as the actors seem to just throw away the dialogue. The first half is far too slow, charting Caan's recovery and physical rehabilitation, and the action scenes in the second half are below Peckinpah's standards.

458 The Killing of a Chinese Bookie (1976) *** Faces, 135 min. *Dir* John Cassavetes, *Scr* John Cassavetes, *Cin* Fred Elmes, Mike Ferris, *Ed* Tom Cornwell, *Des* Sam Shaw, *Art* Phedon Papamichael, *Prod* Al Ruban, *Assoc Prod* Phil Burton.

Cast: Ben Gazzara, *Cosmo Vitelli*, Timothy Agoglia Carey, *Flo*, Seymour Cassel, *Mort*, Robert Phillips, *Phil*, Morgan Woodward, *John*, John Red Kullers, *Eddie-Red*, Al Ruban, *Marty*, Azizi Johari, *Rachel*, Virginia Carrington, *Betty*, Meade Roberts, *Mr. Sophistication*, Alice Friedland, *Sherry*, Donna Gordon, *Margo*, Haji, *Haji*, Carol Warren, *Carol*, Derna Wong Davis, *Derna*, Kathalina Verniero, *Annie*, Yvette Morris, *Yvette*, Jack Ackerman, *Musical Director*. R.

Unusual crime thriller starring Ben Gazzara as the operator of a sleazy Los Angeles strip-show, who is forced to murder an old Chinese bookie in order to pay off a debt to the syndicate. *The Killing of a Chinese Bookie* is no ordinary thriller. John Cassavetes, as usual, downplays the plot, opting for character and endless improvisation, but it does not entirely work in this setting.

459 King Kong (1976) *** Paramount, 134 min. *Dir* John Guillermin, *Scr* Lorenzo Semple, Jr., based on script by James Creelman, Ruth Rose, from concept of Merian C. Cooper, Edgar Wallace, *Cin* Richard H. Kline (AN), *Ed* Ralph E. Winters, *Des* Mario Chiari, *Art* Archie J. Bacon, David A. Constable, Robert Gundlach, *Cos* Arny Lipin, Moss Mabry, Anthea Sylbert, Fern Weber, *Sp* Carlo Rambaldi, Glen Robinson, Frank Van Der Veer (A), *Mus* John Barry, *Prod* Dino De Laurentiis, *Exec Prod* Federico De Laurentiis.

Cast: Jeff Bridges, *Jack Prescott*, Charles Grodin, *Fred Wilson*, Jessica Lange, *Dwan*, John Randolph, *Capt. Ross*, Rene Auberjonois, *Bagley*, Julius Harris, *Boan*, Jack O'Halloran, *Perko*, Dennis Fimple, *Sunfish*, Ed Lauter,

Carnahan, Jorge Moreno, *Garcia*, Mario Gallo, *Timmons*, John Agar, *City Official*, Kenny Long, *Ape Masked Man*, Rick Baker, *Kong Closeups*. PG. $36,915,000.

Well-made remake of famous horror fantasy film about a giant ape. The basic story remains intact and the main updating is in the dialogue, which is the film's main flaw. In a misguided attempt to be modern the script is filled with silly dialogue, particularly that forced upon Jessica Lange. Technically the film is excellent and the giant ape never looks phoney, opposed to original in which the ape seemed to be inflicted with terminal jitters. Both versions are silly; the only difference is the remake overcomes this with technique.

460 The King of Marvin Gardens (1972) ***** Columbia, 103 min. *Dir* Bob Rafelson, *Scr* Jacob Brackman, *Story* Jacob Brackman, Bob Rafelson, *Cin* Laszlo Kovacs, *Ed* John F. Link II, *Art* Toby Carr Rafelson, *Prod* Bob Rafelson, *Exec Prod* Steve Blauner.

Cast: Jack Nicholson, *David Staebler*, Bruce Dern, *Jason Staebler*, Ellen Burstyn, *Sally*, Julia Anne Robinson, *Jessica*, Benjamin "Scatman" Crothers, *Lewis*, Charles Lavine, *Grandfather*, Arnold Williams, *Rosko*, John Ryan, *Surtees*, Sully Boyer, *Lebowitz*, Josh Mostel, *Frank*, William Pabst, *Bidlack*, Gary Woodrow, *Nervous Man*, Imogene Bliss, *Magda*, Ann Thomas, *Bambi*, Tom Overton, *Spot Operator*. R.

Superb, but odd drama about the pursuit of the American dream. An uncharismatic disc jockey (Jack Nicholson) ventures to Atlantic City to keep hs brother (Bruce Dern), a boisterous gambler with numerous crazy moneymaking schemes, out of trouble. With an unusual touch of subtle surrealism *The King of Marvin Gardens* is Bob Rafelson's most eccentric examination of family relationships and also his best and most neglected film.

461 King of the Gypsies (1978) *** Paramount, 112 min. *Dir* Frank Pierson, *Scr* Frank Pierson, based on book by Peter Maas, *Cin* Sven Nykvist, *Ed* Paul Hirsch, *Des* Gene Callahan, *Art* Jay Moore, *Cos* Anna Hill Johnstone, *Mus* David Grisman, *Chor* Julie Arenal, *Prod* Federico De Laurentiis, A Dino De Laurentiis Presentation.

Cast: Eric Roberts, *Dave Stepanowicz*, Susan Sarandon, *Rose*, Sterling Hayden, *King Zharko Stepanowicz*, Shelley Winters, *Queen Rachel*, Annette O'Toole, *Sharon*, Judd Hirsch, *Groffo*, Annie Potts, *Persa*, Michael V. Gazzo, *Spiro Georgio*, Antonia Rey, *Danitza Georgio*, Daniel Spira, *Zio Miller*, Stephen Mendillo, *Adolf/Mikel*, Joe Zaloom, *Rui Ilanovitch*, Lou Cevetillo, *Pete Stepanowicz*, Zvee Scooler, *Phuro*, David Rounds, *Mr. Kessler*, Michael Higgens, *Judge*, Mary Louise Wilson, *Willie*. R. $4,010,000.

Disappointing saga of life among contemporary Gypsies living in the United States. *King of the Gypsies* promised to be an epic centering on one ethnic group on par with *The Godfather*, but it falls short of that. It wanders too far from its subject, by focusing too much on the problem of one individual who leaves his people to avoid inheriting the title "king" from his grandfather. As it is, *King of the Gypsies* is an above average drama, but it could have been so much more.

462 Klute (1971) *** Warner Bros., 114 min. *Dir* Alan J. Pakula, *Scr* Andy and David Lewis (AN), *Cin* Gordon Willis, *Ed* Carl Lerner, *Art* George

Jenkins, *Cos* Ann Roth, *Mus* Michael Small, *Prod* Alan J. Pakula, *Co-Prod* David Lange, *Exec Prod* C. Kenneth Deland.

Cast: Jane Fonda (A, NS, NY, G), *Bree Daniels*, Donald Sutherland, *John Klute*, Charles Cioffi, *Peter Cable*, Roy Scheider, *Frank Ligourin*, Dorothy Tristan, *Arlyn Page*, Rita Gam, *Trina*, Vivian Nathan, *Psychiatrist*, Nathan George, *Lt. Trask*, Morris Strassberg, *Mr. Goldfarb*, Jean Stapleton, *Goldfarb's Secretary*, Barry Snider, *Berger*, Anthony Holland, *Actor's Agent*, Richard Shull, *Sugarman*, Betty Murray, *Holly Gruneman*. R. $8,000,000.

Overrated and slightly confused thriller about a small town cop (Donald Sutherland), who goes to New York City to find a missing friend. His search leads him to a prostitute (Jane Fonda), with whom he has an affair. Fonda's performance is the film's true highlight, but the plot is weak and the climax is a disappointment. Alan J. Pakula has made better films than this.

463 **Kotch** (1971) *** Cinerama, 114 min. *Dir* Jack Lemmon, *Scr* John Paxton (W), based on novel by Katharine Topkins, *Cin* Richard Kline, *Ed* Ralph E. Winters (AN), *Art* Jack Poplin, *Cos* John Anderson, *Mus* Marvin Hamlisch, *Song* "Life Is What You Make It," *Mus* Marvin Hamlisch (AN, G), *Lyrics* Johnny Mercer (AN, G), *Prod* Richard Carter.

Cast: Walter Matthau (AN), *Joseph P. Kotcher*, Deborah Winters, *Erica Herzenstiel*, Felicia Farr, *Wilma Kotcher*, Charles Aidman, *Gerald Kotcher*, Ellen Geer, *Vera Kotcher*, Darrell Larson, *Vincent Perrin*, Paul Picerni, *Dr. Gaudillo*, Lucy Saroyan, *Sissy*, Jane Connell, *Miss Roberts*, Jessica Rains, *Dr. McKernan*, James E. Brodhead, *Weaver*, Lawrence Linville, *Peter Herzenstiel*, Donald and Dean Kowalski, *Duncan Kotcher*. PG.

Fine comedy-drama starring Walter Matthau as a septuagenarian who is driven crazy by his son and daughter-in-law and moves out on his own. He befriends a pregnant teenager and decides to take care of her. This relationship unfortunately is far less interesting than his conflicts with his own family, but Matthau's superb performance keeps the film on course. *Kotch* is the only film directed by Jack Lemmon.

464 **Kramer Vs. Kramer** (1979) (A, NY, G, LA) ***** Columbia, 105 min. *Dir* Robert Benton (A, NS, LA, D), *Scr* Robert Benton (A, G, W), based on novel by Avery Corman, *Cin* Nestor Almendros (AN), *Ed* Jerry Greenberg (AN), *Des* Paul Sylbert, *Cos* Ruth Morley, *Prod* Stanley R. Jaffe, *Assoc Prod* Richard C. Fischoff.

Cast: Dustin Hoffman (A, NS, NY, G, LA), *Ted Kramer*, Meryl Streep (A, NS, NY, NB, G), *Joanna Kramer*, Jane Alexander (AN), *Margaret Phelps*, Justin Henry (AN), *Billy Kramer*, Howard Duff, *John Shaunessy*, George Coe, *Jim O'Connor*, Jo Beth Williams, *Phyllis Bernard*, Bill Moor, *Gressen*, Howland Chamberlain, *Judge Atkins*, Jack Ramage, *Spencer*, Jess Osuna, *Ackerman*, Nicholas Hormann, *Interviewer*, Ellen Parker, *Teacher*, Shelby Brammer, *Ted's Secretary*, Carol Nadell, *Mrs. Kline*. PG. $61,735,000.

Excellent drama about a divorced man who is suddenly faced with the responsibility of raising his young son and is later forced into a custody battle with his ex-wife. *Kramer Vs. Kramer* raises many issues about male and female equality and double standards in contemporary society, without glossing over them. The four principals (Hoffman, Streep, Alexander and Henry) all give superb performances.

465 The Kremlin Letter (1970) *** 20th Century–Fox, 113 min. *Dir* John Huston, *Scr* Gladys Hill, John Huston, based on novel by Noel Behn, *Cin* Ted Scaife, *Ed* Russell Lloyd, *Des* Ted Haworth, *Art* Elvin Webb, *Cos* John Furniss, *Mus* Robert Drasnin, *Prod* Carter De Haven, Sam Wiesenthal.

Cast: Bibi Anderson, *Erika*, Richard Boone, *Ward*, Nigel Green, *Whore*, Dean Jagger, *Highwayman*, Lila Kedrova, *Sophie*, Michael MacLiammoir, *Sweet Alice*, Patrick O'Neal, *Rone*, Barbara Parkins, *B.A.*, Ronald Radd, *Potkin*, George Sanders, *Warlock*, Raf Vallone, *Puppetmaker*, Max Von Sydow, *Kosnov*, Orson Welles, *Bresnavitch*, Sandor Eles, *Grodin*, Niall MacGinnes, *Erector Set*, Anthony Chinn, *Kitai*, Guy Degny, *Professor*, John Huston, *Admiral*, Fulvia Ketoff, *Sonia*, Vonetta McGee, *Negress*, Marc Lawrence, *Priest*. PG.

Above-average cold war thriller involving an unauthorized treaty between the U.S. and the Soviet Union, known as the "Kremlin Letter," that would require a joint attack by both countries on China. A team of U.S. government agents is formed to stop the letter before it is too late. *The Kremlin Letter* has a convoluted plot, but it is never dull, and it features a fine performance by Richard Boone.

466 Lady Caroline Lamb (1972) ** Britain, United Artists, 123 min. *Dir* Robert Bolt, *Scr* Robert Bolt, *Cin* Oswald Morris, *Ed* Norman Savage, *Art* Carmen Dillon, *Cos* David Walker, *Mus* Richard Rodney Bennett, *Chor* Eleanor Fazan, *Prod* Fernando Ghia, *Exec Prod* Franco Cristaldi, *Assoc Prod* Bernard Williams.

Cast: Sarah Miles, *Lady Caroline Lamb*, Jon Finch, *William Lamb*, Richard Chamberlain, *Lord Byron*, John Mills, *Canning*, Margaret Leighton, *Lady Melbourne*, Pamela Brown, *Lady Bessborough*, Silvia Monti, *Miss Milbanke*, Ralph Richardson, *The King*, Laurence Olivier, *Duke of Wellington*, Peter Bull, *Government Minister*, Charles Carson, *Mr. Potter*, Sonia Dresdel, *Lady Pont*, Nicholas Field, *St. John*, Felicity Gibson, *Girl in Blue*, Robert Harris, *Apothecary*, Richard Hurndall, *Radical Member*. PG.

Dreary historical soap opera involving a major scandal in English society. Sarah Miles stars as the wife of a politician (Jon Finch), who has an affair with Lord Byron (Richard Chamberlain) and does little to hide it from the public. *Lady Caroline Lamb* is no doubt an attempt at presenting a serious historical drama, but the story is overused and tired, and the script is shallow and slightly silly.

467 Lady Sings the Blues (1972) *** Paramount, 144 min. *Dir* Sidney J. Furie, *Scr* Chris Clark, Suzanne DePasse, Terrence McCloy (AN), based on book by Billie Holiday, William Dufty, *Cin* John A. Alonzo, *Ed* Argyle Nelson, *Des* Carl Anderson, *Mus* Michel Legrand, *Prod* Jay Weston, James S. White, *Exec Prod* Berry Gordy.

Cast: Diana Ross (AN), *Billie Holiday*, Billie Dee Williams, *Louis McKay*, Richard Pryor, *Piano Man*, James Callahan, *Reg Hanley*, Paul Hampton, *Harry*, Sid Melton, *Jerry*, Virginia Capers, *Mrs. Holiday*, Yvonne Fair, *Yvonne*, Scatman Crothers, *Big Ben*, Harry Caesar, *Rapist*, Robert L. Gordy, *Hawk*, Milton Selzer, *Doctor*, Ned Glass, *Agent*, Paulene Myers, *Mrs. Edson*, Isabel Sanford, *Madame*, Tracee Lyles, *Prostitute*, Norman Bartold, *Detective*. R. $9,665,000.

Disappointing screen biography of jazz/blues singer Billie Holiday. Diana Ross gives a superb performance, in her film debut, as Holiday, but *Lady Sings the Blues* is plagued with the same problems that flaw other Hollywood biographies. The story is filled with inaccuracies and clichés and cheapens Holiday's life. This is more of a showcase for Ross' talents rather than a biography.

468 The Land That Time Forgot (1975) ** Britain, American International, 90 min. *Dir* Kevin Connor, *Scr* James Cawthorn, Michael Moorcock, based on novel by Edgar Rice Burroughs, *Cin* Alan Hume, *Ed* John Ireland, *Des* Maurice Carter, *Art* Bert Davey, *Mus* Douglas Gamley, *Prod* John Dark, *Exec Prod* Robert E. Greenberg, *Assoc Prod* John Peverall, Presented by Samuel Z. Arkoff.

Cast: Doug McClure, *Bowen Tyler*, John McEnery, *Capt. Von Schoenvorts*, Susan Penhaligon, *Lisa Clayton*, Keith Barron, *Bradley*, Anthony Ainley, *Dietz*, Godfrey James, *Borg*, Bobby Farr, *Ahm*, Declan Mulholland, *Olson*, Colin Farrell, *Whiteley*, Ben Howard, *Benson*, Roy Holder, *Plesser*, Andrew McCulloch, *Sinclair*, Ron Pember, *Jones*, Graheme Mallard, *Deusett*, Andrew Lodge, *Reuther*, Brian Hall, *Schwartz*, Stanley McGeagh, *Hiller*, Peter Sproule, *Hindle*, Steve James, *First Sto-Lu*. PG.

Silly, but enjoyable, adventure yarn about a WWI German submarine, carrying some American survivors of a ship, loses its course and ends up in a prehistoric world inhabited by dinosaurs. The special effects are inferior, but in this type of film that is not overly important. The success of this film led to two similar followups, *At the Earth's Core* and *The People That Time Forgot*, the latter of which is an official sequel.

469 The Landlord (1970) **** United Artists, 110 min. *Dir* Hal Ashby, *Scr* William Gunn, based on novel by Kristin Hunter, *Cin* Gordon Willis, *Ed* William A. Sawyer, *Cos* Domingo A. Rodriguez, *Mus* Al Kooper, *Prod* Norman Jewison.

Cast: Beau Bridges, *Elgar Enders*, Pearl Bailey, *Marge*, Diana Sands, *Fanny*, Lou Gossett, *Copee*, Douglas Grant, *Walter Gee*, Melvin Stewart, *Prof. Duboise*, Lee Grant (AN), *Mrs. Enders*, Walter Brooke, *Mr. Enders*, Susan Anspach, *Susan*, Robert Klein, *Peter*, Will McKenzie, *William, Jr.*, Gretchen Walther, *Doris*, Stanley Green, *Heywood*, Marki Bey, *Lanie*. R.

Excellent comedy about a rich youth (Beau Bridges), who leaves home and purchases an urban tenement. His intentions are to evict the black tenants and turn it into his own pad, but his plans change when he becomes personally involved with these people. *The Landlord* is a character study that works on several levels, touching on the themes of youthful rebellion and race relations. Former film editor Hal Ashby made an auspicious directorial debut with this film.

470 The Last American Hero (1973) **** 20th Century–Fox, 95 min. *Dir* Lamont Johnson, *Scr* William Roberts, based on articles by Tom Wolfe, *Cin* George Silano, *Ed* Robbe Roberts, *Art* Lawrence Paull, *Mus* Charles Fox, *Song* "I Got A Name" sung by Jim Croce, *Prod* John Cutts, William Roberts, *Exec Prod* Joe Wizan.

Cast: Jeff Bridges, *Elroy Jackson, Jr.*, Valerie Perrine, *Marge*, Geraldine Fitzgerald, *Mrs. Jackson*, Ned Beatty, *Hackel*, Gary Busey, *Wayne Jackson*,

Art Lund, *Elroy Jackson, Sr.*, Ed Lauter, *Burton Colt*, William Smith II, *Kyle Kingman*, Gregory Walcott, *Morley*, Tom Ligon, *Lamar*, Ernie Orsatti, *Davie Baer*, Erica Hagen, *Trina*, James Murphy, *Spud*, Lane Smith, *Rick Penny*. PG.

One of the most intelligent films about the subject of auto racing. Jeff Bridges is excellent as Junior Jackson, a moonshiner who becomes a stock car racer to aid his jailed father. Unlike other films about racing, *The Last American Hero* is neither an insipid soap opera nor an excuse for car wrecks, which may explain its box-office failure. Instead it examines the sport from a realistic and cynical viewpoint.

471 Last Days of Man on Earth (1974) ******* Britain, New World, 78 min. *Dir* Robert Fuest, *Scr* Robert Fuest, based on novel *The Final Programme* by Michael Moorcock, *Cin* Norman Warwick, *Ed* Barbara Pokras, Barrie Vince, *Art* Philip Harrison, *Mus* Paul Beaver, Bernard Krause, *Prod* John Goldstone, Sandy Lieberson, *Exec Prod* Roy Baird, David Puttnam.

Cast: Jon Finch, *Jerry*, Jenny Runacre, *Miss Brunner*, Hugh Griffith, *Prof. Hira*, Patrick Magee, *Dr. Baxter*, Sterling Hayden, *Maj. Lindborgh*, Harry Andrews, *John*, Graham Crowden, *Dr. Smiles*, George Coulouris, *Dr. Powys*, Basil Henson, *Dr. Lucas*, Derrick O'Connor, *Frank*, Gilles Milinaire, *Dimitri*, Ronald Lacey, *Shades*, Julie Ege, *Miss Ege*, Sandy Ratcliff, *Jenny*, Sarah Douglas, *Catherine*, Delores Del Mar, *Fortune Teller*. R.

Bizarre science fiction thriller starring Jon Finch as a Nobel winning scientist, who has in his possession a microfilm that contains the answer to immortality. As the world nears its end, he and a woman (Jenny Runacre) become fused together as an ape-like messiah. *Last Days of Man on Earth* mixes black humor and surrealism into one of the strangest films ever made. Other title, *The Final Programme*.

472 The Last Detail (1973) ********* Columbia, 103 min. *Dir* Hal Ashby, *Scr* Robert Towne (AN, BFA), based on novel by Darryl Ponicsan, *Cin* Michael Chapman, *Ed* Robert C. Jones, *Des* Michael Haller, *Cos* Ted Parvin, *Mus* Johnny Mandel, *Prod* Gerald Ayres, *Assoc Prod* Charles Mulvehill.

Cast: Jack Nicholson (AN, NS, NY, BFA, CF), *Buddusky*, Otis Young, *Mulhall*, Randy Quaid (AN), *Meadows*, Clifton James, *Chief Master-at-Arms*, Carol Kane, *Prostitute*, Michael Moriarty, *Marine Duty Officer*, Luana Anders, *Donna*, Kathleen Miller, *Kathleen*, Nancy Allen, *Nancy*, Gerry Salsberg, *Henry*, Don McGovern, *Bartender*, Pat Hamilton, *Madame*, Michael Chapman, *Taxi Driver*, Jim Henshaw, *Sweek*, Derek McGrath, Gilda Radner, Jim Horn, John Castellano, *Nichiren Shoshu Members*. R. $5,000,000.

Excellent comedy-drama about two career sailors (Jack Nicholson, Otis Young), who are assigned to escort a young sailor (Randy Quaid), who was caught stealing, to a military prison. The two are given several days and gradually they begin to sympathize with the kid and try to make his last few days memorable. *The Last Detail* is essentially a road film that opts for realism over potential clichés, particularly in its course toward a logical conclusion that is unusual in this type of film. The language is appropriately raw and the acting is superb, highlighted by one of Nicholson's finest performances.

473 Last Embrace (1979) ******* United Artists, 102 min. *Dir* Jonathon Demme, *Scr* David Shaber, based on novel *13th Man* by Murray Teigh Bloom, *Cin* Tak Fujimoto, *Ed* Barry Malkin, *Des* Charles Rosen, *Art* James A.

Taylor, *Cos* Jane Greenwood, *Mus* Miklos Rozsa, *Prod* Michael Taylor, Dan Wigutow, *Assoc Prod* John Nicolella.

Cast: Roy Scheider, *Harry Hannan*, Janet Margolin, *Ellie Fabian*, John Glover, *Richard Peabody*, Sam Levene, *Sam Urdell*, Charles Napier, *Dave Quittle*, Christopher Walken, *Eckart*, Jacqueline Brookes, *Dr. Coopersmith*, David Marguilies, *Rabbi Drexel*, Andrew Duncan, *Bernie Meckler*, Marcia Rodd, *Adrian*, Gary Goetzman, *Tour Guide*, Lou Gilbert, *Rabbi Jacobs*. R.

Uneven Hitchcock style thriller about a government undercover agent who suffers a mental breakdown following the death of his wife, and subsequently becomes involved in a strange murder mystery. As in many other such thrillers, *Last Embrace* works in parts, but not as a whole. There are some exciting sequences, but the plot does not hold together, particularly the disappointing climax.

474 Last House on the Left (1972) *** Hallmark, 91 min. *Dir* Wes Craven, *Scr* Wes Craven, *Cin* Victor Hurwitz, *Ed* Wes Craven, *Mus* Steve Chapin, David Hess, *Prod* Sean S. Cunningham.

Cast: David Hess, *Krug*, Lacy Grantham, *Phyllis*, Sandra Cassel, *Mari Collingwood*, Marc Sheffler, *Junior*, Jeramie Rain, *Sadie*, Fred Lincoln, *Weasel*, Gaylord St. James, *Dr. Collingwood*, Cynthia Carr, *Mrs. Collingwood*, Ada Washington, *Lady Truckdriver*. R.

Shocking, but effective thriller of murder and mayhem. In a plot borrowed from Ingmar Bergman's *The Virgin Spring*, a group of escaped convicts murder two teenage girls and inadvertently stay in the home of the parents of one of the girls. *Last House on the Left* is cheaply made and it shows, but it does succeed better than most other films of this type in overpowering its audience.

475 The Last Movie (1971) * Universal, 108 min. *Dir* Dennis Hopper, *Scr* Stewart Stern, *Story* Dennis Hopper, Stewart Stern, *Cin* Laszlo Kovacs, *Ed* David Berlatsky, Antranig Mahakian, *Art* Leon Ericksen, *Cos* Gerald Alpert, *Prod* Paul Lewis, *Exec Prod* Michael Gruskoff.

Cast: Dennis Hopper, *Kansas*, Stella Garcia, *Maria*, Julie Adams, *Mrs. Anderson*, Tomas Milian, *Priest*, Don Gordon, *Neville Robey*, Roy Engel, *Mr. Anderson*, Donna Baccala, *Miss Anderson*, Samuel Fuller, *Director*, Poupee Bocar, *Nightclub Singer*, Sylvia Miles, *Script Clerk*. R.

Pretentious drama about the filming of a western in the Peruvian Andes of South America. The film documents the effects the film crew have on the Peruvian villagers. *The Last Movie* is somewhat of a mess and Dennis Hopper's point is very obscure. Hopper was overrated as a director, due to *Easy Rider*, a film with far too many flaws to achieve greatness, and this film solidifies this point.

476 The Last of Sheila (1973) *** Warner Bros., 120 min. *Dir* Herbert Ross, *Scr* Anthony Perkins, Stephen Sondheim, *Cin* Gerry Turpin, *Ed* Edward Warschilka, *Des* Ken Adam, *Art* Tony Roman, *Mus* Billy Goldenberg, *Prod* Herbert Ross, *Exec Prod* Stanley O'Toole.

Cast: Richard Benjamin, *Tom*, Dyan Cannon, *Christine*, James Coburn, *Clinton*, Joan Hackett, *Lee*, James Mason, *Philip*, Ian McShane, *Antony*, Raquel Welch, *Alice*, Yvonne Romain, *Sheila*, Pierro Rosso, *Vittorio*. PG.

Interesting murder whodunit involving a Hollywood producer (James Coburn) who devises an outrageous plan to discover who, among six friends, murdered his wife one year before. He invites the suspects for a cruise aboard his yacht and puts them through many tortuous games. *The Last of Sheila* rises above most murder mysteries as the script keeps one guessing throughout its two hour length, but it is flawed by slightly overdrawn sterotypical characters.

477 **Last of the Red Hot Lovers** (1972) ** Paramount, 98 min. *Dir* Gene Saks, *Scr* Neil Simon, based on his play, *Cin* Victor J. Kemper, *Ed* Maury Winetrobe, *Art* Ben Edwards, *Cos* Albert Wolsky, *Mus* Neal Hefti, *Prod* Howard W. Koch.

Cast: Alan Arkin, *Barney Cashman*, Sally Kellerman, *Elaine*, Paula Prentiss, *Bobby*, Renee Taylor, *Jeannette*, Bella Bruck, *Cashier*, Sandy Balson, *Charlotte*, Frank Loverde, *Mel*, Burt Conroy, *Bert*, Charles Woolf, *Jesse*, Ben Freedman, *Mickey*. PG.

Shrill Neil Simon comedy about a middle-aged man (Alan Arkin), who desperately tries to have an extramarital affair. He invites three different, but crazy, women (Sally Kellerman, Paula Prentiss, Rene Taylor) to his mother's apartment, but unfortunately the characters spend most of the time screaming at each other. This is a bit much to endure, but Arkin does prove he can make anything funny.

478 **The Last Picture Show** (1971) (AN) **** Columbia, 118 min. *Dir* Peter Bogdanovich (AN), *Scr* Peter Bogdanovich, Larry McMurtry (AN, NS, BFA), based on novel by Larry McMurtry, *Cin* Robert Surtees (AN), *Ed* Donn Cambern, *Des* Polly Platt, *Art* Walter Scott Herndon, *Prod* Stephen J. Friedman, *Exec Prod* Bert Schneider, *Assoc Prod* Harold Schneider.

Cast: Timothy Bottoms, *Sonny Crawford*, Jeff Bridges (AN), *Duane Jackson*, Cybill Shepherd, *Jacy Farrow*, Ben Johnson (A, NY, NB, G, BFA), *Sam the Lion*, Cloris Leachman (A, NB, BFA), *Ruth Popper*, Ellen Burstyn (AN, NS, NY), *Lois Farrow*, Eileen Brennan, *Genevieve*, Clu Gulager, *Abilene*, Sam Bottoms, *Billy*, Sharon Taggart, *Charlene Duggs*, Randy Quaid, *Lester Marlow*, Joe Heathcock, *The Sheriff*, Bill Thurman, *Coach Popper*, John Hillerman, *Teacher*. R. $13,110,000.

Excellent drama focusing on a small Texas town during the 1950's. The film dispenses with plot and is more of a slice-of-life drama, examining the lives of the town's inhabitants and how they interrelate. The situations resemble a soap opera on the surface, but *The Last Picture Show* transcends that stigma, by presenting everything in a realistic and believable fashion.

479 **The Last Remake of Beau Geste** (1977) ** Universal, 85 min. *Dir* Marty Feldman, *Scr* Chris Allen, Marty Feldman, *Story* Sam Bobrick, Marty Feldman, *Cin* Gerry Fisher, *Ed* Jim Clark, Arthur Schmidt, *Des* Brian Eatwell, *Art* Les Dilley, *Cos* May Routh, *Mus* John Morris, *Chor* Irving Davies, *Prod* William S. Gilmore, *Exec Prod* George Shapiro, Howard West, *Assoc Prod* Bernard Williams.

Cast: Marty Feldman, *Digby Geste*, Michael York, *Beau Geste*, Ann-Margret, *Flavia Geste*, Peter Ustinov, *Markov*, James Earl Jones, *Sheikh*, Trevor Howard, *Sir Hector*, Henry Gibson, *Gen. Pecheur*, Terry-Thomas, *Governor*, Roy Kinnear, *Boldini*, Spike Milligan, *Crumble*, Avery Schreiber,

Sheikh's Aide/Camel Salesman, Hugh Griffith, *Judge*, Irene Handl, *Miss Worm-wood*, Sinead Cusack, *Isabel Geste*, Henry Polic II, *Capt. Merdmanger*, Ted Cassidy, *Blindman*, Burt Kwouk, *Father Shapiro*, Val Pringle, *Dostoevsky*, Ed McMahon, *Arab Horseman*. PG. $7,625,000.

Absurd slapstick remake, or spoof, of the noted foreign legion saga *Beau Geste*. Much like his directorial mentor, Mel Brooks, Marty Feldman throws in everything but the kitchen sink. *The Last Remake of Beau Geste* is a hodge podge of jokes, routines, puns and anachronisms, some of which work and many of which do not. Buried underneath this mess somewhere is the plot of this satire's inspiration.

480 **The Last Tycoon** (1976) *** Paramount, 122 min. *Dir* Elia Kazan, *Scr* Harold Pinter, based on novel by F. Scott Fitzgerald, *Cin* Victor Kemper, *Ed* Richard Marks, *Des* Gene Callahan (AN), *Art* John Collis (AN), *Cos* Anna Hill Johnstone, *Mus* Maurice Jarre, *Prod* Sam Spiegel.

Cast: Robert DeNiro, *Monroe Stahr*, Tony Curtis, *Rodriguez*, Robert Mit-chum, *Pat Brady*, Jeanne Moreau, *Didi*, Jack Nicholson, *Brimmer*, Donald Pleasence, *Boxley*, Ingrid Boulting, *Kathleen Moore*, Ray Milland, *Fleischaker*, Dana Andrews, *Red Ridingwood*, Theresa Russell, *Cecilia Brady*, Peter Strauss, *Wylie*, Tige Andrews, *Popolos*, Morgan Farley, *Marcus*, John Carradine, *Guide*, Jeff Corey, *Doctor*, Diane Shalet, *Stahr's Secretary*, Seymour Cassell, *Seal Trainer*, Angelica Huston, *Edna*. PG.

Surprisingly good adaptation of F. Scott Fitzgerald's unfinished novel. Although far from being a masterpiece, *The Last Tycoon* is far better than any other film versions of his books. DeNiro is excellent, in an offbeat role, as Monroe Stahr, a soft spoken, but intelligent studio boss, somewhat similar to Irving Thalberg. This was Elia Kazan's first major film in many years and is much more restrained than his earlier films.

481 **The Late Show** (1977) ***** Warner Bros., 94 min. *Dir* Robert Ben-ton, *Scr* Robert Benton (AN), *Cin* Charles Rosher, *Ed* Peter Appleton, Lou Lombardo, *Mus* Ken Wannberg, *Lyrics* Stephen Lehner, *Prod* Robert Altman, *Assoc Prod* Scott Bushnell, Robert Eggenweiler.

Cast: Art Carney (NS), *Ira Wells*, Lily Tomlin, *Margo*, Bill Macy, *Charlie Hatter*, Eugene Roche, *Ron Birdwell*, Joanna Cassidy, *Laura Birdwell*, John Considine, *Lamar*, Ruth Nelson, *Mrs. Schmidt*, John Davey, *Sgt. Dayton*, Howard Duff, *Harry Regan*, PG.

Superb detective thriller about an over-the-hill private eye (Art Carney) who investigates the murder of his partner, which also involves the kidnap-ping of an eccentric woman's (Lily Tomlin) cat. Tomlin forces herself onto Carney as his new partner and the two make a superb screen comedy team. *The Late Show* is far more than just a comedy as Robert Benton has created one of the screen's finest detective films with an exciting, but never overly confusing story, many wonderfully odd characters and a moody film noir atmosphere.

482 **The Laughing Policeman** (1973) ** 20th Century–Fox, 111 min. *Dir* Stuart Rosenberg, *Scr* Thomas Rickman, based on novel by Maj Sjowall and Per Wahloo, *Cin* David Walsh, *Ed* Robert Wyman, *Mus* Charles Fox, *Prod* Stuart Rosenberg.

Cast: Walter Matthau, *Jake Martin*, Bruce Dern, *Leo Larsen*, Lou Gossett, *Larrimore*, Albert Paulsen, *Camerero*, Anthony Zerbe, *Lt. Steiner*, Val Avery, *Pappas*, Cathy Lee Crosby, *Kay Butler*, Mario Gallo, *Bobby Mow*, Joanna Cassidy, *Monica*, Shirley Ballard, *Grace Martin*, William Hansen, *Schwermer*, Jonas Wolfe, *Collins*, Paul Koslo, *Haygood*, Louis Guss, *Gus Niles*, Lee McCain, *Prostitute*, David Moody, *Pimp*, Ivan Bookman, *Rodney*, Cliff James, *Maloney*, Gregory Sierra, *Vickery*, Warren Finnerty, *Ripple*, Matt Clark, *Coroner*. R.

Dreary police thriller about the search for a mass-murderer, who killed a busload of people in San Francisco. Walter Matthau stars as a police detective, who is assigned to unravel the mystery and is aided by Bruce Dern, his loud-mouthed and uncaring partner. The investigation aspect of the plot is somewhat dull and uninteresting, but the performances of Matthau and Dern, as the mismatched partners, breathe some life into it.

483 Law and Disorder (1974) *** Columbia, 103 min. *Dir* Ivan Passer, *Scr* Kenneth Harris Fishman, Ivan Passer, William Richert, *Cin* Arthur J. Ornitz, *Ed* Anthony Protenza, *Art* Gene Rodolf, *Cos* Ann Roth, *Mus* Andy Badale, *Prod* William Richert, *Exec Prod* Michael Medwin, Edgar J. Scherick, *Assoc Prod* Fred C. Caruso, Michael Zivian.

Cast: Carroll O'Connor, *Willie*, Ernest Borgnine, *Cy*, Ann Wedgeworth, *Sally*, Anita Dangler, *Irene*, Leslie Ackerman, *Karen*, Karen Black, *Gloria*, Jack Kehoe, *Elliott*, David Spielberg, *Bobby*, Joe Ragno, *Peter*, Pat Corley, *Ken*, Frank Lucas, *Flasher*, Ed Grover, *Capt. Malloy*, Pepper Wormser, *Yablonsky*, Lionel Pina, *Chico*, Allan Arbus, *Dr. Richter*. R.

Offbeat comedy drama about two harried middle-aged New Yorkers who form an auxillary police force to combat crime in their neighborhood. One would expect such a film to then sink to the level of a vigilante film, such as *Death Wish*, but *Law and Disorder* is too real for that. The film shows genuine insight into the problems of these frustrated people.

484 Lawman (1971) ** United Artists, 99 min. *Dir* Michael Winner, *Scr* Gerald Wilson, *Cin* Bob Paynter, *Ed* Freddie Wilson, *Des* Stan Jolley, *Art* Herbert Westbrook, *Cos* Ron Beck, *Mus* Jerry Fielding, *Prod* Michael Winner.

Cast: Burt Lancaster, *Marshal Jered Maddox*, Robert Ryan, *Marshal Cotton Ryan*, Lee J. Cobb, *Vincent Bronson*, Sheree North, *Laura Shelby*, Joseph Wiseman, *Lucas*, Robert Duvall, *Vernon Adams*, Albert Salmi, *Harvey Stenbough*, J.D. Cannon, *Hurd Price*, John McGiver, *Mayor Sam Bolden*, Richard Jordan, *Crowe Wheelwright*, John Beck, *Jason Bronson*, Ralph Waite, *Jack Dekker*, William Watson, *Choctaw Lee*, Charles Tyner, *Minister*, John Hillerman, *Totts*, Robert Emhardt, *Hersham*, Richard Bull, *Dusaine*, Hugh McDermott, *Moss*, Lou Frizzell, *Cobden*, Walter Brooke, *Luther Harris*, Bill Brimley, *Marc Corman*. PG.

Standard western drama starring Burt Lancaster as a lawman, who arrives in a strange town in order to arrest some men responsible for killing an old man. He runs directly into conflict with the townspeople, who refuse to help him. *Lawman* attempts to be a serious western on the level of *High Noon*, but it is a bit shallow. It does, however, succeed better on a lower level as an action drama.

485 **The Lawyer** (1970) ** Paramount, 120 min. *Dir* Sidney J. Furie, *Scr* Harold Buchman, Sidney J. Furie, *Cin* Ralph Woolsey, *Ed* Argyle Nelson, Jr. *Art* Pato Guzman, *Cos* Ted Parvin, Rita Riggs, *Mus* Malcolm Dodds, *Prod* Brad Dexter.

Cast: Barry Newman, *Tony Petrocelli*, Harold Gould, *Eric P. Scott*, Diana Muldaur, *Ruth Petrocelli*, Robert Colbert, *Jack Harrison*, Kathleen Crowley, *Alice Fiske*, Warren Kemmerling, *Sgt. Moran*, Booth Colman, *Judge Crawford*, Ken Swofford, *Charlie O'Keefe*, E.J. Andre, *F.J. Williamson*, William Sylvester, *Paul Harrison*, Jeff Thompson, *Andy Greer*, Tom Harvey, *Bob Chambers*. R.

Fair courtroom drama loosely based on the Sam Shepperd murder case. Despite the poor odds a determined young lawyer (Barry Newman) defends a doctor, who has been accused of murdering his wife. *The Lawyer* has a gimmick to set it apart from similar films; inserted throughout the film are visualizations of the lawyer's theories of the case. Unfortunately it depends too much on this gimmick.

486 **Le Mans** (1971) ** National General, 106 min. *Dir* Lee H. Katzin, *Scr* Harry Kleiner, *Cin* Rene Guissart, Jr., Robert B. Hauser, *Ed* Ghislaine Des Jonqueres, Don Ernst, John Woodcock, *Des* Phil Abramson, *Cos* Ray Summers, *Mus* Michel Legrand, *Lyrics* Alan and Marilyn Bergman, *Prod* Jack N. Reddish, *Exec Prod* Robert E. Relyea, *Assoc Prod* Alan Levine.

Cast: Steve McQueen, *Michael Delaney*, Siegfried Rauch, *Erich Stahler*, Elga Anderson, *Lisa Belgetti*, Ronald Leigh-Hunt, *David Townsend*, Fred Haltiner, *Johann Ritter*, Luc Merenda, *Claude Aurac*, Christopher Waite, *Larry Wilson*, Louise Edlind, *Anna Ritter*, Angelo Infanti, *Lugo Abratte*, Jean-Claude Bercq, *Paul Jacques Dion*. G. $5,500,000.

Empty racing car saga set at the famed 24 hour French race. Steve McQueen stars as the top Porsche driver, whose main competition is a top Ferrari driver (Siegfried Rauch). That is the extent of this film's drama and conflict, which might as well have been a documentary on the race; much of the film is documentary footage anyway.

487 **Leadbelly** (1976) *** Paramount, 126 min. *Dir* Gordon Parks, Sr., *Scr* Ernest Kinoy, *Cin* Bruce Surtees, *Ed* Harry Howard, *Des* Robert Boyle, *Mus* Fred Karlin, *Prod* Marc Merson, *Exec Prod* David Frost.

Cast: Roger E. Mosley, *Huddie Ledbetter*, Paul Benjamin, *Wes Ledbetter*, Madge Sinclair, *Miss Eula*, Alan Manson, *Prison Chief Guard*, Albert P. Hall, *Dicklikker*, Art Evans, *Blind Lemon Jefferson*, James E. Brodhead, *John Lomax*, John Henry Faulk, *Gov. Neff*, Vivian Bonnell, *Old Lady*, Dana Manno, *Margaret Judd*, Timothy Pickard, *Gray Man*, Lynn Hamilton, *Sally Ledbetter*, Loretta Greene, *Lethe*, Valerie Odell, *Amy*, Rozaa Jean, *Sugar Tit*. PG.

Well-made biography of legendary blues singer Huddie Ledbetter. *Leadbelly* focuses on his early life, told through flashbacks from his last term in prison. Ledbetter is brought to life with a fully rounded characterization due to the excellent performance by Roger E. Mosley. Unfortunely his career as a professional singer is overlooked. At least some part of this aspect of his life would have made the film more complete.

488 **The Legacy** (1979) ** Universal, 100 min. *Dir* Richard Marquand, *Scr* Jimmy Sangster, Patric Tilley, Paul Wheeler, *Story* Jimmy Sangster, *Cin* Dick

Bush, Alan Hume, *Ed* Anne V. Coates, *Des* Disley Jones, *Cos* Shura Cohen, *Mus* Michael J. Lewis, *Prod* David Foster, *Exec Prod* Arnold Kopelson.

Cast: Katharine Ross, *Maggie Walsh*, Sam Elliott, *Pete Danner*, John Standing, *Jason Mountolive*, Ian Hogg, *Harry*, Margaret Tyzack, *Nurse Adams*, Charles Gray, *Karl*, Lee Montague, *Jacques*, Hildagarde Neil, *Barbara*, Marianne Broome, *Maria*, Roger Daltrey, *Clive*, William Abney, *Butler*, Patsy Smart, *Cook*, Mathias Kilroy, *Stable Lad*, Reg Harding, *Gardener*. R. $5,205,000.

Standard horror thriller set in a mansion, where an assortment of obnoxious characters are eliminated one by one. A young couple is forced off the road by a Rolls Royce and are invited to its owner's home. After they arrive, he disappears and they discover they are unable to leave. *The Legacy* mixes elements of *And Then There Were None* with *The Exorcist* and does justice to neither.

489 The Legend of Hell House (1973) ** 20th Century–Fox, 90 min. *Dir* John Hough, *Scr* Richard Matheson, based on his novel *Hell House*, *Cin* Alan Hume, *Ed* Geoffrey Foote, *Des* Ron Fry, *Mus* Delia Derbyshire, Brian Hodgson, *Prod* Albert Fennell, Norman T. Herman, *Exec Prod* James H. Nicholson.

Cast: Pamela Franklin, *Florence Tanner*, Roddy McDowell, *Ben Fischer*, Clive Revill, *Dr. Chris Barrett*, Gayle Hunnicutt, *Ann Barrett*, Roland Culver, *Rudolph Deutsch*, Peter Bowles, *Hanley*. PG.

Average haunted house thriller with the typical story of a group of people who agree to live in a house for one week that is supposedly inhabited by ghosts. *The Legend of Hell House* does work in parts; it has its share of scares and surprises; but the ending disappoints and only succeeds in confusing the situation.

490 Lenny (1974) (AN) ***** United Artists, 112 min. *Dir* Bob Fosse (AN), *Scr* Julian Barry (AN), based on his play, *Cin* Bruce Surtees (AN), *Ed* Alan Heim, *Des* Joel Schiller, *Cos* Albert Wolsky, *Prod* Marvin Worth, *Exec Prod* David V. Picker, *Assoc Prod* Robert Greenhut.

Cast: Dustin Hoffman (AN), *Lenny Bruce*, Valerie Perrine (AN, NY, NB, CF), *Honey Bruce*, Jan Miner, *Sally Marr*, Stanley Beck, *Artie Silver*, Gary Morton, *Sherman Hart*, Rashel Novikoff, *Aunt Mema*, Guy Rennie, *Jack Goldstein*, Frankie Man, *Baltimore Strip Club MC*, Mark Harris, *San Francisco Defense Attorney*, Lee Sandman, *San Francisco Judge*, Susan Malnick, *Kitty Bruce (at 11)*, Martin Begley, *San Francisco Judge*, Phil Philbin, *N.Y. Cop*, Ted Sorrell, Clarence Thomas, *N.Y. Attorneys*, Mike Murphy, *N.Y. District Attorney*, Buddy Boylan, *Marty*, Mickey Gatlin, *San Francisco Cop*, George DeWitt, *Comic*, Judy LaScala, *Chorus Girl*, Glen Wilder, Frank Orsati, *Hunters*, Michelle Young, *Nurse's Aide*. R. $11,600,000.

Powerful and grim biography of controversial nightclub comedian Lenny Bruce, who was denounced in the 1950's and 1960's for his honest and unsubtle comments on society. Dustin Hoffman gives possibly his finest performance as the tortured comic, covering all facets of his personality including his downfall from drugs. Bob Fosse proves that he can handle drama just as well as musicals, although he has yet to depart from entertainment related subjects.

491 Let's Do It Again (1975) ******* Warner Bros., 112 min. *Dir* Sidney Poitier, *Scr* Richard Wesley, *Story* Timothy March, *Cin* Donald M. Morgan, *Ed* Pembroke J. Herring, *Des* Alfred Sweeney, *Mus* Curtis Mayfield, *Prod* Melville Tucker, *Assoc Prod* Pembroke J. Herring.

Cast: Sidney Poitier, *Clyde Williams*, Bill Cosby, *Billy Foster*, Calvin Lockhart, *Biggie Smalls*, John Amos, *Kansas City Mack*, Denise Nicholas, *Beth Foster*, Lee Chamberlain, *Dee Dee Williams*, Mel Stewart, *Ellison*, Julius Harris, *Bubbletop Woodson*, Paul E. Harris, *Jody Tipps*, Val Avery, *Lt. Bottomley*, Jimmie Walker, *Bootney Farnsworth*, Ossie Davis, *Elder Johnson*. PG. $11,800,000. See *Uptown Saturday Night*.

492 The Liberation of L.B. Jones (1970) ****** Columbia, 102 min. *Dir* William Wyler, *Scr* Jesse Hill Ford, Stirling Silliphant, based on novel by Jesse Hill Ford, *Cin* Robert Surtees, *Ed* Carl Kress, *Des* Kenneth A. Reid, *Cos* Vi Alford, Gene Ashman, Seth Banks, *Mus* Elmer Bernstein, *Prod* Ronald Lubin.

Cast: Lee J. Cobb, *Oman Hedgepath*, Anthony Zerbe, *Willie Joe Worth*, Roscoe Lee Browne, *Lord Byron Jones*, Lola Falana, *Emma Jones*, Lee Majors, *Steve Mundine*, Barbara Hershey, *Nella Mundine*, Yaphet Kotto, *Sonny Boy Mosby*, Arch Johnson, *Stanley Bumpas*, Chill Wills, *Mr. Ike*, Zara Cully, *Mama Lavorn*, Favard Nicholas, *Benny*, Joe Attles, *Henry*, Lauren Jones, *Erleen*, Dub Taylor, *Mayor*, Brenda Sykes, *Jelly*, Larry D. Mann, *Grocer*, Ray Teal, *Chief of Police*. R.

Pretentious drama about a racial strife in a small Southern town. *The Liberation of L.B. Jones* attempts to blend together a few different plots, none of which are very interesting, and lead nowhere. William Wyler's usual bland direction does not help, either. This film may have been inspired by *In the Heat of the Night* but in no way compares.

493 The Life and Times of Judge Roy Bean (1972) ******** National General, 120 min. *Dir* John Huston, *Scr* John Milius, *Cin* Richard Moore, *Ed* Hugh S. Fowler, *Art* Tambi Larsen, *Mus* Maurice Jarre, *Song* "Marmalade, Molasses & Honey", *Mus* Maurice Jarre (AN), *Lyrics* Alan & Marilyn Bergman (AN), *Prod* John Foreman.

Cast: Paul Newman, *Judge Roy Bean*, Ava Gardner, *Lily Langtry*, Victoria Principal, *Marie Elena*, Anthony Perkins, *Rev. LaSalle*, Tab Hunter, *Sam Dodd*, John Huston, *Grizzly Adams*, Stacy Keach, *Bad Bob*, Roddy McDowell, *Frank Gass*, Jacqueline Bisset, *Rose Bean*, Ned Beatty, *Tector Crites*, Jim Burk, *Bart Jackson*, Matt Clark, *Nick the Grub*, Steve Kanaly, *Whorehouse Lucky Jim*, Bill McKinney, *Fermel Parlee*. PG. $8,100,000.

Excellent fictionalized biography of the infamous self-proclaimed hanging judge from Texas. *The Life and Times of Judge Roy Bean* is one of the strangest westerns ever made, mixing surrealism and black humor. The film spans many years, highlighting numerous strange and bizarre episodes of his life. Paul Newman gives a wonderful character performance as Bean, and the film is one of John Huston's finest and most underrated films.

494 Lipstick (1976) ****** Paramount, 89 min. *Dir* Lamont Johnson, *Scr* David Rayfiel, *Cin* Bill Butler, William A. Fraker, *Ed* Marion Rothman, *Des* Robert Luthardt, *Mus* Michael Poinareff, *Prod* Freddie Fields.

Cast: Margaux Hemingway, *Chris McCormick*, Chris Sarandon, *Gordon Stuart*, Mariel Hemingway, *Kathy McCormick*, Perry King, *Steve Edison*, Anne

Bancroft, *Carla Bondi*, Robin Gammell, *Nathan Cartwright*, John Bennett Perry, *Martin McCormick*, Franceso, *Photographer*, Bill Burns, *Judge*, Meg Wylie, *Sister Margaret*, Inga Swenson, *Sister Monica*. R. $4,615,000.

Intended as a serious study of rape, *Lipstick* is nothing more than an exploitation revenge thriller on the same level as many drive-in cheapies. The true problems facing rape victims and societies' attitudes are ignored with the film's emphasis centering on cheap thrills, i.e. an extended rape sequence. Famed fashion model Margaux Hemingway makes a poor acting debut allowing her little sister Mariel to easily steal the film from under her.

495 Lisztomania (1975) ******** Britain, Warner Bros., 105 min. *Dir* Ken Russell, *Scr* Ken Russell, *Cin* Peter Suschitzky, *Ed* Stuart Baird, *Art* Philip Harrison, *Cos* Shirley Russell, *Mus. Adaptation* Rick Wakeman, *Prod* Roy Baird, David Puttnam, *Exec Prod* Sanford Lieberson.

Cast: Roger Daltry, *Franz Liszt*, Sara Kestelman, *Princess Carolyn*, Paul Nicholas, *Richard Wagner*, Fiona Lewis, *Countess Marie*, Veronica Quilligan, *Cosima*, Nell Campbell, *Olga*, Andrew Reilly, *Hans*, Ringo Starr, *Pope*, John Justin, *Count d'Agoult*, Anulka Dzuibinska, *Lola Montez*, Imogen Claire, *George Sand*, Peter Brayham, *Bodyguard*, David English, *Captain*. R.

Typical bombastic composer biography from Ken Russell. This time his target is Hungarian Romantic composer Franz Liszt, whom Russell portrays as the world's first music teen idol. As is usual, there is some basis in fact for Russell's ideas and he exaggerates them beyond belief. *Lisztomania* is a hit and miss visual extravaganza that works more in parts than as a whole, but it is worth seeing for its uniquely bizarre images.

496 Little Big Man (1970) ********* National General, 150 min. *Dir* Arthur Penn, *Scr* Calder Willingham, based on novel by Thomas Berger, *Cin* Harry Stradling, Jr., *Ed* Dede Allen, *Des* Dean Tavoularis, *Art* Angelo Graham, *Cos* Dorothy Jeakins, *Mus* John Hammond, *Prod* Stuart Millar, *Assoc Prod* Gene Lasko.

Cast: Dustin Hoffman, *Jack Crabb*, Faye Dunaway, *Mrs. Pendrake*, Martin Balsam, *Allardyce T. Merriweather*, Richard Mulligan, *Gen. George A. Custer*, Chief Dan George (AN, NS, NY), *Old Lodge Skins*, Jeff Corey, *Wild Bill Hickok*, Aimee Eccles, *Sunshine*, Kelly Jean Peters, *Olga*, Carole Androsky, *Caroline*, Robert Little Star, *Little Horse*, Cal Bellini, *Younger Bear*, Tuben Moreno, *Shadow That Comes in Sight*, Steve Shemayne, *Burns Red in the Sun*, William Hickey, *Historian*, James Anderson, *Sergeant*, Jesse Vint, *Lieutenant*, Alan Oppenheimer, *Major*, Thayer David, *Rev. Silas Pendrake*. PG. $15,000,000.

Epic adventure of the old west, as seen through the eyes of Jack Crabb (Dustin Hoffman). His story begins with the slaughter of his family by Indians, who raise him as one of their own and follows his adventures into young adulthood, which culminates with his witnessing of the battle of Little Big Horn. *Little Big Man* is a rarity of its genre; a genuine western epic that never loses sight of its characters. Its episodic structure manages to encompass more different aspects of the old west than possibly any other film.

497 Little Fauss and Big Halsey (1970) ****** Paramount, 99 min. *Dir* Sidney J. Furie, *Scr* Charles Eastman, *Cin* Ralph Woolsey, *Ed* Argyle Nelson, Jr., *Art* Lawrence Paull, *Prod* Albert S. Ruddy.

Cast: Robert Redford, *Big Halsey*, Michael J. Pollard, *Little Fauss*, Lauren Hutton, *Rita Nebraska*, Noah Beery, *Seally Fauss*, Lucille Benson, *Mom Fauss*, Linda Gaye Scott, *Moneth*, Ray Ballard, *Photographer*, Shara St. John, *Marcy*, Erin O'Reilly, *Sylvene McFall*, Ben Archibek, *Rick Nifty*. R.

Fair comedy-drama about an unlikely pair of motorcyclists, a loud-mouthed braggart (Robert Redford) and a shy mechanic (Michael J. Pollard). The two meet at a racetrack and become partners, despite the fact that Redford continually takes advantage of Pollard. The emphasis is more on character than plot, and the film just wanders aimlessly.

498 Little Murders (1971) **** 20th Century–Fox, 110 min. *Dir* Alan Arkin, *Scr* Jules Feiffer, based on his play, *Cin* Gordon Willis, *Ed* Howard Kuperman, *Des* Gene Rudolf, *Cos* Albert Wolsky, *Mus* Fred Kaz, *Prod* Jack Brodsky, *Assoc Prod* Burtt Harris.

Cast: Elliott Gould, *Alfred Chamberlain*, Marcia Rodd, *Patsy Newquist*, Vincent Gardenia, *Mr. Newquist*, Elizabeth Wilson, *Mrs. Newquist*, Jon Korkes, *Kenny*, John Randolph, *Mr. Chamberlain*, Doris Roberts, *Mrs. Chamberlain*, Donald Sutherland, *The Minister*, Lou Jacobi, *The Judge*, Alan Arkin, *The Detective*. R.

Often brilliant black satire of our somewhat violent contemporary society. Jules Feiffer's bizarre surrealistic stage play surprisingly succeeds as a film due to Feiffer's own screen adaptation and the off-the-wall direction by actor Alan Arkin in his directorial debut. Gould is excellent as an apathetic innocent who eventually turns to violence after continually being victimized. Largely ignored at the time of its release, *Little Murders* now stands as a minor classic.

499 A Little Night Music (1977) ** U.S./Austria/Germany, New World, 124 min. *Dir* Harold Prince, *Scr* Hugh Wheeler, Based on stage musical; music and lyrics by Steven Sondheim, based on film *Smiles of a Summer Night* by Ingmar Bergman, *Cin* Arthur Ibbetson, *Ed* John Jympson, *Art* Herta Pischinger, *Cos* Florence Klotz (AN), *Mus Adaptation* Jonathan Tunick (A), *Chor* Patricia Birch, *Prod* Elliot Kastner, *Exec Prod* Heinz Lazek, A Roger Corman Presentation.

Cast: Elizabeth Taylor, *Desiree*, Diana Rigg, *Charlotte*, Len Cariou, *Frederick*, Lesley-Anne Down, *Anne*, Hermione Gingold, *Armfeldt*, Laurence Guittard, *Carl*, Christopher Guard, *Erich*, Chloe Franks, *Fredericka*, Heinz Maracek, *Kurt*, Lesley Dunlop, *Petra*, Jonathan Tunick, *Conductor*, Hubert Tscheppe, *Franz*, Rudolf Schrympf, *Band Conductor*, Franz Schussler, *Mayor*, Johanna Schussler, *Mayoress*. PG.

Dull film version of Stephen Sondheim's stage musical, which was in turn based on Ingmar Bergman's *Smiles of a Summer Night*. The basic premise of a group of characters, whose relationships are interrelated, who meet at a country estate for dinner is intact, but the film is very stuffy and too mannered. The score's most famous song "Send in the Clowns" deserves better than Elizabeth Taylor.

500 The Little Prince (1974) ** Britain, Paramount, 88 min. *Dir* Stanley Donen, *Scr* Alan Jay Lerner, based on story by Antoine de Saint Exupery, *Cin* Christopher Challis, *Ed* Peter Boita, John Guthridge, *Des* John Barry, *Art* Norman Reynolds, *Cos* Tim Goodchild, Shirley Russell, *Mus* Frederick Loewe

(AN, G), *Lyrics* Alan Jay Lerner (AN, G), *Mus Adaptation* Douglas Gamley, Angela Morley (AN), *Song* "Little Prince," *Mus* Frederick Loewe (AN), *Lyrics* Alan Jay Lerner (AN), *Chor* Ronn Forella, Bob Fosse, *Prod* Stanley Donen, *Assoc Prod* A. Joseph Tandet.

Cast: Richard Kiley, *The Pilot*, Steven Warner, *The Little Prince*, Bob Fosse, *The Snake*, Gene Wilder, *The Fox*, Joss Ackland, *The King*, Clive Revill, *The Businessman*, Victor Spinetti, *The Historian*, Graham Crowden, *The General*, Donna McKechnie, *The Rose*. G.

Poor musical adaptation of children's fantasy classic about a little boy from a small distant star, who comes to Earth and befriends a downed pilot. The cast tries their best to breathe life into this stale material, particularly Bob Fosse in his self choreographed "snake in the grass" scene. Unfortunately the songs by Lerner and Loewe are below par and unmemorable and the performance by Stephen Warner is so bland, he seems to be reading his part on sight.

501 **A Little Romance** (1979) *** U.S./France, Orion, 108 min. *Dir* George Roy Hill, *Scr* Allan Burns (AN), based on novel *E Equals MC Squared Mon Amour* by Patrick Cauvin, *Cin* Pierre William Glenn, *Ed* William Reynolds, *Des* Henry Bumstead, *Art* Francois De Lemothe, *Cos* Rosine Delamare, *Mus* Georges Delerue (A), *Prod* Robert L. Crawford, Yves Rousset-Rouard, *Exec Prod* Patrick Kelley.

Cast: Diane Lane, *Lauren*, Thelonious Bernard, *Daniel*, Laurence Olivier, *Julius*, Arthur Hill, *Richard King*, Sally Kellerman, *Kay King*, Broderick Crawford, *Himself*, David Dukes, *George de Marco*, Andrew Duncan, *Bob Duryea*, Claudette Sutherland, *Janet Duryea*, Graham Fletcher-Cook, *Londet*, Ashby Semple, *Natalie*, Claude Brosset, *Michael Michon*, Jacques Maury, *Insp. Leclerc*, Anna Massey, *Ms. Siegel*, Peter Maloney, *Martin*, Dominique Lavanant, *Mme. Corier*. PG. $4,000,000.

Charming adolescent love story about two highly intelligent teenagers, which is simply what its title indicates, *A Little Romance*. The daughter of a jet-set mother meets a French boy in France, who is the only person she can relate to. Many of the characters around them are stereotypes, but the two youths really come alive, due considerably to the wonderful performances of Diane Lane and Thelonious Bernard.

502 **Live and Let Die** (1973) *** Britain, United Artists, 121 min. *Dir* Guy Hamilton, *Scr* Tom Mankiewicz, based on novel by Ian Fleming, *Cin* Ted Moore, *Ed* Bert Bates, Raymond Poulton, John Shirley, *Art* Syd Cain, *Cos* Julie Harris, *Mus* George Martin, *Title Song* Paul and Linda McCartney (AN), performed by Wings, *Chor* Geoffrey Holder, *Prod* Albert R. Broccoli, Harry Saltzman.

Cast: Roger Moore, *James Bond*, Yaphet Kotto, *Kananga/Mr. Big*, Jane Seymour, *Solitaire*, Clifton James, *Sheriff Pepper*, Julius W. Harris, *Tee Hee*, David Hedison, *Leiter*, Gloria Hendry, *Rosie*, Bernard Lee, *"M"*, Lois Maxwell, *Miss Moneypenny*, Tommy Lane, *Adana*, Earl Jolly Brown, *Whisper*, Roy Stewart, *Quarrel*, Lon Satton, *Strutter*. PG. $15,850,000. See *Diamonds Are Forever*.

503 **Logan's Run** (1976) *** United Artists, 118 min. *Dir* Michael Anderson, *Scr* David Zelag Goodman, based on novel by George Clayton Johnson,

William F. Nolan, *Cin* Ernest Laszlo (AN), *Ed* Bob Wyman, *Des* Dale Hennesy (AN), *Cos* Bill Thomas, *Sp* L.B. Abbott, Glen Robinson, Matthew Yuricich, *Mus* Jerry Goldsmith, *Prod* Saul David.

Cast: Michael York, *Logan*, Jenny Agutter, *Jessica*, Richard Jordan, *Francis*, Roscoe Lee Browne, *Box*, Farrah Fawcett-Majors, *Holly*, Peter Ustinov, *Old Man*, Michael Anderson, Jr., *Doc*, Gary Morgan, *Billy*, Denny Arnold, *Runner #1*, Glen Wilder, *Runner #2*, Lara Lindsay, *Woman Runner*, Bob Neil, *First Sanctuary Man*, Randolph Roberts, *Second Sanctuary Man*, Camilla Carr, *Sanctuary Woman*, Greg Michaels, *Ambush Man*, Roger Borden, *Daniel*, Michelle Stacy, *Mary Two*, Ann Ford, *Woman on Lastday*, Laura Hippe, *New You Shop Customer*. PG. $9,500,000.

Entertaining, but mindless science-fiction adventure, set in the year 2274 in a society which eliminates its inhabitants when they reach the age of 30. Michael York stars as a cop whose job is to track down those who try to get away, but suddenly finds himself at that age and must run to survive. The biggest flaws are the special effects which are unconvincing and the sets which are too plastic and phoney.

504 **The Long Goodbye** (1973) ******** United Artists, 112 min. *Dir* Robert Altman, *Scr* Leigh Brackett, based on novel by Raymond Chandler, *Cin* Vilmos Zsigmond (NS), *Ed* Lou Lombardo, *Mus* John Williams, *Prod* Jerry Bick, *Exec Prod* Elliot Kastner, *Assoc Prod* Robert Eggenweiler.

Cast: Elliott Gould, *Philip Marlowe*, Nina Van Pollandt, *Eileen Wade*, Sterling Hayden, *Roger Wade*, Mark Rydell, *Marty Augustine*, Henry Gibson, *Dr. Verringer*, David Arkin, *Harry*, Jim Bouton, *Terry Lennox*, Warren Berlinger, *Morgan*, Jo Ann Brody, *Jo Ann Eggenweiler*, Jack Knight, *Hood*, Pepe Callahan, *Pepe*, Vince Palmieri, Arnold Strong, *Hoods*, Rutanya Alda, Tammy Shaw, *Marlowe's Neighbors*, Jack Riley, *Piano Player*, Ken Sansom, *Colony Guard*, Danny Goldman, *Bartender*, Sybil Scotford, *Real Estate Lady*, Steve Coit, *Detective Farmer*, Tracy Harris, *Detective*, Jerry Jones, *Detective Green*, Rodney Moss, *Clerk*. R.

Excellent satyrical updating of Philip Marlowe that shows the famed detective as being out of place in present day society. Robert Altman literally destroys Raymond Chandler's creation by portraying him as a buffoon who knows less about what's going on than everyone else, a complete reversal of other detective films. Altman's intention was to end what he considered to be a tired old genre, but inadvertently made one of its classics and actually revived it.

505 **The Longest Yard** (1974) ******* Paramount, 120 min. *Dir* Robert Aldrich, *Scr* Tracy Keenan Wynn, *Story* Albert S. Ruddy, *Cin* Joseph Biroc, *Ed* Michael Luciano (AN), *Des* James S. Vance, *Mus* Frank DeVol, *Prod* Albert S. Ruddy, *Assoc Prod* Alan P. Horowitz.

Cast: Burt Reynolds, *Paul Crewe*, Eddie Albert, *Warden Hazen*, Ed Lauter, *Capt. Knauer*, Michael Conrad, *Nate Scarboro*, Jim Hampton, *Caretaker*, Harry Caesar, *Granville*, John Steadman, *Pop*, Charles Tyner, *Unger*, Mike Henry, *Rassmeusen*, Bernadette Peters, *Warden's Secretary*, Pervis Arkins, *Mawabe*, Tony Cacciotti, *Rotka*, Anitra Ford, *Melissa*, Michael Ford, *Announcer*, Joe Kapp, *Walking Boss*, Dick Kiel, *Samson*, Pepper Martin, *Shop Steward*, Mort Marshall, *Assistant Warden*, Ray Nitschke, *Bogdanski*,

Sonny Sixkiller, *Indian*, Bob Tessier, *Shokner*, Sonny Shroyer, *Tannen*, Dino Washington, *Mason*, Ernie Wheelwright, *Spooner*. R. $23,015,000.

Fine comedy drama set in a prison. Burt Reynolds is excellent as a former football player, imprisoned for stealing his girlfriend's car, who is forced by the prison warden (Eddie Albert) to organize a football team consisting of inmates, to play against his guards. Although somewhat predictable *The Longest Yard* is never boring and is one of Robert Aldrich's best macho male dramas.

506 Looking for Mr. Goodbar (1977) *** Paramount, 135 min. *Dir* Richard Brooks, *Scr* Richard Brooks, based on novel by Judith Rossner, *Cin* William A. Fraker (AN), *Ed* George Grenville, *Art* Edward Carfagno, *Cos* Jodie Lynn Tiller, *Mus* Artie Kane, *Prod* Freddie Fields.

Cast: Diane Keaton, *Theresa Dunn*, Tuesday Weld (AN), *Katherine Dunn*, William Atherton, *James Morrissey*, Richard Kiley, *Mr. Dunn*, Richard Gere, *Tony Lopanto*, Alan Feinstein, *Prof. Engle*, Tom Berenger, *Gary Cooper White*, Priscilla Pointer, *Mrs. Dunn*, Laurie Prange, *Brigid Dunne*, Joel Fabiani, *Barney*, Julius Harris, *Black Cat*, Richard Bright, *George*, LeVar Burton, *Cap Jackson*, Marilyn Coleman, *Mrs. Jackson*, Elizabeth Cheshire, *Little Theresa*. R. $16,900,000.

Disappointing thriller about a teacher who spends her evenings picking up strange men in bars, one of whom murders her. Richard Brooks makes the fatal error of turning *Looking for Mr. Goodbar* into a mystery whodunit and loses sight of the story's main purpose, a study of loneliness and desperation. The title refers to her search for "Mr. Right," to escape her from her loneliness. She never finds "Mr. Goodbar," and her search only leads her to disaster. There are many powerful sequences, but overall the film is too long. Brooks succeeds best with the cast, with which he obtains many exceptional performances.

507 The Lords of Flatbush (1974) ** Columbia, 86 min. *Dir* Martin Davidson, Stephen F. Verona, *Scr* Martin Davidson, Gayle Gleckler, Stephen F. Verona, *Additional Dialogue*. Sylvester Stallone, *Cin* Edward Lackman, Joseph Mangine, *Ed* Muffie Meyer, Stan Siegel, *Art* Glenda Miller, *Mus* Joe Brooks, *Additional Mus* Paul Jabara, Paul Nicholas, *Prod* Stephen F. Verona, *Assoc Prod* Richard Millman.

Cast: Perry King, *Chico*, Sylvester Stallone, *Stanley*, Henry Winkler, *Butchey*, Paul Mace, *Wimpy*, Susan Blakely, *Jane*, Maria Smith, *Frannie*, Renee Paris, *Annie*, Paul Jabara, *Crazy Cohen*, Bruce Reed, *Mike*, Frank Stiefel, *Arnie*, Martin Davidson, *Birnbaum*, Joe Stern, *Eddie*, Ruth Klinger, *Mrs. Tyrell*, Joan Neuman, *Miss Molina*, Dolph Sweet, *Rosiello*, Lou Byrne, *Mrs. Bradshaw*, Bill Van Sleet, *Bradshaw*, Margaret Bauer, *Nancy*. PG. $4,000,000.

Interesting comedy-drama about a gang of toughs living in the Flatbush section of Brooklyn, New York in the 1950's. *The Lords of Flatbush* has an episodic structure and just seems to wander with little purpose. Some of these episodes are quite funny but the film does not hold together. The most notable aspect are the early screen appearances of Sylvester Stallone and Henry Winkler.

508 Lost and Found (1979) ** Columbia, 106 min. *Dir* Melvin Frank, *Scr* Melvin Frank, Jack Rose, *Cin* Douglas Slocombe, *Ed* Bill Butler, *Des* Trevor

Williams, *Art* Ted Tester, *Cos* Julie Harris, *Mus* John Cameron, *Prod* Melvin Frank, *Exec Prod* Arnold Kopelson.

Cast: George Segal, *Adam*, Glenda Jackson, *Tricia*, Maureen Stapleton, *Jemmy*, Paul Sorvino, *Reilly*, Hollis McLaren, *Eden*, John Cunningham, *Lenny*, Kenneth Pogue, *Julian*, Janie Sell, *Zelda*, Diana Barrington, *Ellie*, Leslie Carlson, *Jean-Paul*, John Candy, *Carpentier*, James Morris, *Gendarme*, Bruno Engler, *Ski Patrol*, David Bolt, *French Doctor*, Richard Adams, *Attendent*, Roger Periard, *French Lawyer*, Lois Maxwell, *English Woman*, Douglas Campbell, *British Professor*, Mary Pirie, Nicole D'Amour, Denise Baillargeon, *French Nurses*. PG.

Fair reteaming of George Segal and Glenda Jackson with director Melvin Frank. A widowed professor meets a divorced English woman at a ski resort in France, both of whom break their legs. Their relationship begins shakily and predictably they get married. Segal and Jackson, as in their earlier teaming *A Touch of Class*, are excellent together, but the material they are saddled with is rather dull.

509 Lost Horizon (1973) * Columbia, 150 min. *Dir* Charles Jarrott, *Scr* Larry Kramer, based on novel by James Hilton, *Cin* Robert Surtees, *Ed* Maury Winetrobe, *Des* Preston Ames, *Cos* Jean Louis, *Mus* Burt Bacharach, *Lyrics* Hal David, *Chor* Hermes Pan, *Prod* Ross Hunter, *Assoc Prod* Jacques Mapes.

Cast: Peter Finch, *Richard Conway*, Liv Ullman, *Catherine*, Sally Kellerman, *Sally Hughes*, George Kennedy, *Sam Cornelius*, Michael York, *George Conway*, Olivia Hussey, *Maria*, Bobby Van, *Harry Lovett*, James Shigeta, *Brother To-Lenn*, Charles Boyer, *High Lama*, John Gielgud, *Chang*. G.

Poor attempt to transform famed fantasy story into a large musical production. The story of an adventurer who discovers Shangri La, a kingdom in the Himalayan mountains where time stands still, remains intact, but the songs by Bacharach and David are way below their standards and the choreography is ridiculous. The filmmakers have only succeeded in taking a group of fine actors and totally embarrassing them.

510 Lost in the Stars (1974) ** American Film Theatre, 114 min. *Dir* Daniel Mann, *Scr* Alfred Hayes, based on musical play by Maxwell Anderson, Kurt Weill, suggested by novel *Cry the Beloved Country* by Alan Paxton, *Cin* Robert Hauser, *Ed* Walt Hannemann, *Art* Jack Martin Smith, *Mus Supervision*, Alex North, *Prod* Ely Landau, *Exec Prod* Edward Lewis.

Cast: Brock Peters, *Stephen Kumalo*, Melba Moore, *Irina*, Raymond St. Jacques, *John Kumalo*, Clifton Davis, *Absalom*, Paul Rogers, *James Jarvis*, Paulene Myers, *Grace*, Paula Kelly, *Rose*, H.B. Barnum III, *Alex*, Ji-Tu Cumbuka, *Johannes*, Alan Weeks, *Matthew*, John Williams, *Judge*, Ivor Barry, *Carmichael*, Harvey Jason, *Arthur Jarvis*, John Holland, *Van Jarsdale*, John Hawker, *Paulus*, Myrna White, *Linda*, Michael-James Wixted, *Edward Jarvis*, William Glover, *Elana*. G. See *American Film Theatre*.

511 Love and Bullets (1979) ** Britain, Associated Film Distribution, 95 min. *Dir* Stuart Rosenburg, *Scr* Wendell Mayes, John Melson, *Cin* Fred Koenekamp (U.S.), Anthony Richmond (Switzerland), *Ed* Michael F. Anderson, Tom Priestley, Lesley Walker, *Des* John De Cuir, *Art* Colin Grimes, *Cos* Dorothy Jeakins, *Mus* Lalo Schifrin, *Prod* Pancho Kohner.

Cast: Charles Bronson, *Charlie Congers*, Rod Steiger, *Joe Bomposa*, Jill Ireland, *Jackie Pruit*, Strother Martin, *Louis Monk*, Bradford Dillman, *Brickman*, Henry Silva, *Vittorio Farroni*, Paul Koslo, *Huntz*, Sam Chew, *Cook*, Michael V. Gazzo, *Lobo*, Val Avery, *Caruso*, Bill Gray, *Mike Durant*, Andy Romano, *FBI Agent Marty*, Robin Clarke, *FBI Agent George*, Cliff Pellow, *Police Captain*, Lorraine Chase, *Vittorio's Girlfriend*. PG.

Dull action thriller starring Charles Bronson as a cop, who is assigned by the FBI to extradite a gangster's moll, living in Switzerland, and bring her back to the U.S. During their journey he protects her from hitmen sent by the gangster, and he later falls in love with her. *Love and Bullets* is a very tame thriller, that fails to be either serious or exciting.

512 **Love and Death** (1975) **** United Artists, 82 min. *Dir* Woody Allen, *Scr* Woody Allen, *Cin* Ghislain Cloquet, *Ed* Ron Kalish, Ralph Rosenblum, *Art* Willy Holt, *Cos* Gladys De Segonzac, *Mus* Sergei Prokofiev, *Prod* Charles H. Joffe, *Exec Prod* Martin Poll, *Assoc Prod* Fred T. Gallo.

Cast: Woody Allen, *Boris*, Diane Keaton, *Sonja*, George Adet, *Old Nehamkin*, Frank Adu, *Drill Sergeant*, Edmond Ardisson, *Priest*, Feodor Atkine, *Mikhail*, Albert Augier, *Waiter*, Yves Barsacq, *Rimsky*, Lloyd Battista, *Don Francisco*, Jack Bernard, *Gen. Lecoq*, Eva Bertrand, *Woman Hygiene Class*, George Birt, *Doctor*, Yves Brainville, *Andre*, Gerard Buhr, *Servant*, Brian Coburn, *Dimitri*, Henry Coutet, *Minskov*, Patricia Brown, *Cheerleader*, Henry Czarniak, *Ivan*, Despo Diamantidou, *Mother*, Sandor Eles, *Soldier 2*, Luce Fabiole, *Grandmother*, Florian, *Uncle Nikolai*, Jacqueline Fogt, *Ludmilla*, Sol L. Frieder, *Voskovec*, Olga Georges-Picot, *Countess*, Harold Gould, *Anton*, Harry Hankin, *Uncle Sasha*, Jessica Harper, *Natasha*, Tony Jay, *Vladimir Maximovitch*, Tutte Lemkow, *Pierre*, Jack Lenoir, *Krapotkin*, Leib Lensky, *Father Andre*, Ann Lonn Berg, *Olga*, Roger Lumont, *Baker*, Alfred Lutter III, *Young Boris*, Ed Marcus, *Raskov*, Jacques Maury, *Second*, Narcissa McKinley, *Cheerleader*, Aubrey Morris, *Soldier 4*, Denise Peron, *Spanish Countess*, Beth Porter, *Anna*, Alan Rossett, *Guard*, Shimen Ruskin, *Borslov*, Persival Russel, *Berdykov*, Chris Sanders, *Joseph*, Zvee Scooler, *Father*, C.A.R. Smith, *Father Nikolai*, Fred Smith, *Soldier*, Bernard Taylor, *Soldier 3*, Clement-Thierry, *Jacques*, Alan Tilvern, *Sergeant*, James Tolkan, *Napoleon*, Helene Vallier, *Madame Wolfe*, Howard Vernon, *Gen Leveque*, Glenn Williams, *Soldier 1*, Jacob Witkin, *Suskin*. PG. $7,000,000.

Excellent Woody Allen comedy set during the Napoleonic War. Allen plays a schnook who becomes a reluctant soldier in the Russian army and later plots, with his cousin (Diane Keaton), whom he loves, to assassinate Napoleon. The plot, on the surface, resembles a Bob Hope comedy, one of Allen's acknowledged influences, but there is one great difference. *Love and Death* is funny. Allen also succeeds in satirizing both Russian literature, i.e. Tolstoy's *War and Peace*, and Russian film, i.e. Eisenstein's *Potemkin*.

513 **Love and Pain and the Whole Damn Thing** (1973) *** Columbia 110 min. *Dir* Alan J. Pakula, *Scr* Alvin Sargent, *Cin* Geoffrey Unsworth, *Ed* Russell Lloyd, *Art* Enrique Alarcon, *Mus* Michael Small, *Prod* Alan J. Pakula, *Assoc Prod* Thomas Pevsner.

Cast: Maggie Smith, *Lila Fisher*, Timothy Bottoms, *Walter Elbertson*, Don Jaime De Mora y Aragon, *The Duke*, Emiliano Redondo, *Spanish Gentlemen*, Charles Baxter, *Dr. Elbertson*, Margaret Modlin, *Mrs. Elbertson*, May

Heatherley, *Melanie Elbertson*, Lloyd Brimhall, *Carl*, Elmer Modlin, *Dr. Edelheidt*, Andres Monreal, *Tourist Guide*. R.

Offbeat love story about two misfits (Maggie Smith, Timothy Bottoms), who seemingly have little in common other than their mutual shyness. The film starts promisingly, but it later sinks with the introduction of a giant cliché: she is dying of a mysterious disease; from which the film is never able to recover. This could have been a fine comedy, highlighted by the performances of Smith and Bottoms.

514 **Love at First Bite** (1979) ** American International, 96 min. *Dir* Stan Dragoti, *Scr* Robert Kaufman, *Story* Mark Gindes, Robert Kaufman, *Cin* Edward Rosson, *Ed* Mort Fallick, Allan Jacobs, *Des* Serge Krizman, *Mus* Charles Bernstein, *Chor* Alex Romero, *Prod* Joel Freeman, *Exec Prod* George Hamilton, Robert Kaufman, *Assoc Prod* Harold L. Vanarnum, A Melvin Simon Presentation.

Cast: George Hamilton, *Count Dracula*, Susan Saint James, *Cindy Sondheim*, Richard Benjamin, *Dr. Jeff Rosenberg*, Dick Shawn, *Lt. Ferguson*, Arte Johnson, *Renfield*, Sherman Hemsley, *Rev. Mike*, Isabel Sanford, *Judge*, Barry Gordon, *Flashlight Vender*, Ronnie Schell, *Gay in Elevator*, Bob Basso, *TV Repairman*, Bryan O'Byrne, *Priest*, Michael Pataki, *Mobster*, Beverly Sanders, *Lady in Elevator*, Basil Hoffman, *Desk Clerk*, Stanley Brock, *Cab Driver*, Danny Dayton, *Billy*, Robert Ellenstein, *W.V. Man*, David Ketchum, *Customs Inspector*. PG. $20,600,000.

Uneven spoof of Dracula, which places the famed Count in contemporary New York City, where he becomes the victim. George Hamilton proves, as he has always wanted, that he is an excellent comedy actor and does a superb job of mimicking Bela Lugosi. The main problem is the script, which contains some laughs, but not enough for this type of film.

515 **The Love Machine** (1971) * Columbia, 108 min. *Dir* Jack Haley, Jr., *Scr* Samuel Taylor, based on novel by Jacqueline Susann, *Cin* Charles B. Lang, *Ed* David Blewitt, *Des* Lyle R. Wheeler, *Cos* Moss Mabry, *Mus* Artie Butler, *Prod* M.J. Frankovich, *Exec Prod* Irving Mansfield.

Cast: John Phillip Law, *Robin Stone*, Dyan Cannon, *Judith Austin*, Robert Ryan, *Gregory Austin*, Jackie Cooper, *Danton Miller*, David Hemmings, *Jerry Nelson*, Jodi Wexler, *Amanda*, William Roerick, *Cliff Dorne*, Maureen Arthur, *Ethel Evans*, Shecky Greene, *Christie Lane*, Clinton Greyn, *Alfie Knight*, Sharon Farrell, *Maggie Stewart*, Alexandra Hay, *Tina St. Claire*, Eve Bruce, *Amazon Woman*, Greg Mullavey, *Bob Summers*, Edith Atwater, *Mary*, Gene Baylos, *Eddie Flynn*, Ben Lessy, *Kenny Ditto*. R.

Dreary soap opera focusing on the goings on at a television network starring Dyan Cannon as the wife of a network executive, who uses her influence to promote a sleazy newscaster (John Philip Law). Instead of using sex as a contributing factor to network decisions, as in the film *Network*, *The Love Machine* simply revels in it, drowning out any comments it might be attempting.

516 **Love Story** (1970) (AN, G) ** Paramount, 100 min. *Dir* Arthur Hiller (AN, G), *Scr* Erich Segal (AN, G), *Cin* Dick Kratina, *Ed* Robert C. Jones, *Art* Robert Gundlach, *Cos* Pearl Somner, Alice Manougean Martin, *Mus* Francis Lai (A, G), *Prod* Howard G. Minsky, *Exec Prod* David Golden.

Cast: Ali MacGraw (AN, G), *Jenny Cavilleri*, Ryan O'Neal (AN), *Oliver Barrett IV*, Ray Milland, *Oliver Barrett III*, Katherine Balfour, *Mrs. Barrett*, John Marley (AN), *Phil Cavilleri*, Russell Nype, *Dean Thompson*, Sydney Walker, *Dr. Shapely*, Robert Modica, *Dr. Addison*, Walker Daniels, *Ray*, Tommy Lee Jones, *Hank*, John Merensky, *Steve*, Andrew Duncan, *Rev. Blauvelt*, Bob O'Connell, *Doorman*. PG. $50,000,000.

Average love story that inexplicably caused overreaction on both sides. *Love Story* did not deserve to become such a box-office blockbuster, nor did it deserve such adverse criticism from the press, since it is neither better nor worse than most such films. It is a simple story of boy meets girl, and girl dies. Ryan O'Neal and Ali MacGraw are fine in the lead roles.

517 **Lovers and Other Strangers** (1970) *** Cinerama, 106 min. *Dir* Cy Howard, *Scr* Joseph Bologna, David Goodman, Renée Taylor (AN), based on play by Joseph Bologna, Renée Taylor, *Cin* Andrew Laszlo, *Ed* David Bretherton, Sidney Katz, *Des* Ben Edwards, *Cos* Albert Wolsky, *Mus* Fred Karlin, *Song* "For All We Know," *Mus* Fred Karlin (AN), *Lyrics* Robb Royer (Robb Wilson), James Griffin (Arthur James) (A), *Prod* David Susskind, *Assoc Prod* Anthony Loeb.

Cast: Gig Young, *Hal*, Bea Arthur, *Bea*, Bonnie Bedelia, *Susan*, Anne Jackson, *Cathy*, Harry Guardino, *Johnny*, Michael Brandon, *Mike*, Richard Castellano (AN), *Frank*, Bob Dishy, *Jerry*, Marian Hailey, *Brenda*, Joseph Hindy, *Richie*, Anthony Holland, *Donaldson*, Diane Keaton, *Joan*, Cloris Leachman, *Bernice*, Mort Marshall, *Father Gregory*, Anne Meara, *Wilma*. R. $6,750,000.

Fine comedy focusing on the wedding of a young couple (Michael Brandon, Bonnie Bedelia), who decide to marry after living together for 18 months, and the results of bringing their two families together. Many problems in both families are brought out into the open including affairs and divorces. *Lovers and Other Strangers* features many funny characters and subplots, but it is a bit too scattered.

518 **Lovin' Molly** (1974) *** Columbia, 98 min. *Dir* Sidney Lumet, *Scr* Stephen Friedman, based on novel *Leaving Cheyenne* by Larry McMurtry, *Cin* Edward Brown, *Ed* Joanne Burke, *Des* Gene Coffin, *Mus* Fred Hellerman, *Prod* Stephen Friedman, *Assoc Prod* David Golden.

Cast: Blythe Danner, *Molly*, Anthony Perkins, *Gid*, Beau Bridges, *Johnny*, Edward Binns, *Mr. Fry*, Susan Sarandon, *Sarah*, Conrad Fowkes, *Eddie*, Claude Traverse, *Mr. Taylor*, John Henry Faulk, *Mr. Grinsom*. R.

Interesting menage a trois about a liberated woman (Blythe Danner), who is in love with two men (Anthony Perkins, Beau Bridges), who also happen to be close friends. *Lovin' Molly* is divided into three separate sections, spanning several years, beginning in 1925, moving to 1945 and ending in 1964. This is the main problem with the film as it is too weak to cover such a lengthy period and the aging of the three stars is not convincing. Blythe Danner gives an incredible performance and shows what a great range this actress possesses.

519 **Loving** (1970) *** Columbia, 89 min. *Dir* Irvin Kershner, *Scr* Don Devlin, based on novel by J.M. Ryan, *Cin* Gordon Willis, *Ed* Robert Lawrence, *Des* Walter Scott Herndon, *Cos* Albert Wolsky, *Mus* Bernardo Segáll, *Prod* Don Devlin, *Exec Prod* Raymond Wagner.

Cast: George Segal, *Brooks,* Eva Marie Saint, *Selma,* Sterling Hayden, *Lepridon,* Keenan Wynn, *Edward,* Nancie Phillips, *Nelly,* Janis Young, *Grace,* David Doyle, *Will,* Paul Sparer, *Marve,* Andrew Duncan, *Willy,* Sherry Lansing, *Susan,* Roland Winters, *Plommie,* Edgar Stehli, *Mr. Kramm,* Calvin Holt, *Danny,* Mina Kalb, *Diane,* Diana Douglas, *Mrs. Shavelson,* David Ford, *Al,* Roy Scheider, *Skip.* R.

Interesting drama that examines every day middle-class problems. George Segal stars as a free-lance artist, whose life is a shambles. He is dissatisfied with both his work and his dreary family life. *Loving* begins promisingly and is a somewhat realistic examination of contemporary problems, but it occasionally borders on tedium. There is a slightly farcical ending that seems out of place.

520 **Lucky Lady** (1975) ** 20th Century–Fox, 117 min. *Dir* Stanley Donen, *Scr* Willard Huyck, Gloria Katz, *Cin* Geoffrey Unsworth, *Ed* Peter Boita, George Hively, Tom Rolf, *Des* John Barry, *Art* Norman Reynolds, *Mus* Ralph Burns, *Songs* Fred Ebb, John Kander, *Prod* Michael Gruskoff.

Cast: Gene Hackman, *Kibby,* Liza Minnelli, *Claire,* Burt Reynolds, *Walker,* Geoffrey Lewis, *Capt. Aaron Mosley,* John Hillerman, *Christy McTeague,* Robby Benson, *Billy Webber,* Michael Hordern, *Capt. Rockwell,* Anthony Holland, *Mr. Tully,* John McLiam, *Rass Huggins,* Val Avery, *Dolph,* Louis Guss, *Bernie,* William H. Bassett, *Charley,* Emilio Fernandez, *"Ybarra".* PG. $12,695,000.

Disappointing menage a trois period comedy about a trio of rum runners (Gene Hackman, Liza Minnelli, Burt Reynolds). *Lucky Lady* is an episodic film that follows their adventures during the Prohibition, smuggling illegal liquor into the U.S. by boat. The film is an uneasy blend of light slapstick and violence, and the cast tries too hard to be funny.

521 **Luther** (1974) *** Britain, American Film Theatre, 112 min. *Dir* Guy Green, *Scr* Edward Anhalt, based on play by John Osborne, *Cin* Freddie Young, *Ed* Malcolm Cooke, *Des* Peter Mullins, *Cos* Joan Bridge, Elizabeth Haffenden, *Mus* John Addison, *Prod* Ely A. Landau, *Exec Prod* Mort Abrahams.

Cast: Stacy Keach, *Martin Luther,* Partick Magee, *Hans,* Hugh Griffith, *Tetzel,* Robert Stephens, *Von Eck,* Alan Badel, *Cajetan,* Judi Dench, *Katherine,* Leonard Rossiter, *Weinard,* Maurice Denham, *Staupitz,* Julian Glover, *The Knight,* Peter Collier, *Prior,* Thomas Heathcote, *Lucas,* Malcolm Stoddard, *King Charles.* G. See *American Film Theatre.*

522 **M*A*S*H** (1970) (AN, NS, GMC, BFA-United Nations Award, CF) ***** 20th Century–Fox, 116 min. *Dir* Robert Altman (AN), *Scr* Ring Lardner, Jr. (A, W), based on novel by Richard Hooker, *Cin* Harold E. Stine, *Ed* Danford B. Greene (AN), *Art* Arthur Lonergan, Jack Martin Smith, *Mus* Johnny Mandel, *Prod* Ingo Preminger, *Assoc Prod* Leon Ericksen.

Cast: Donald Sutherland, *Hawkeye,* Elliott Gould, *Trapper John,* Tom Skerritt, *Duke,* Sally Kellerman (AN), *Maj. Hot Lips,* Robert Duvall, *Maj. Frank Burns,* Jo Ann Pflug, *Lt. Dish,* René Auberjonois, *Dago Red,* Roger Bowen, *Col. Henry Blake,* Gary Burghoff, *Radar O'Reilly,* David Arkin, *Sgt. Maj. Vollmer,* Fred Williamson, *Spearchucker,* Michael Murphy, *Me Lay,* Kim Atwood, *Ho-Jon,* Tim Brown, *Cpl. Judson,* Indus Arthur, *Lt. Leslie,* John

Schuck, *Painless Pole*, Ken Prymus, *Pfc. Seidman*, Dawne Damon, *Capt. Scorch*, Carl Gottlieb, *Ugly John*, Tamara Horrocks, *Capt. Knocko*, G. Wood, *Gen. Hammond*, Bobby Troup, *Sgt. Gorman*, Bud Cort, *Pvt. Boone*, Danny Goldman, *Capt. Murrhardt*, Corey Fischer, *Capt. Bandini*. R. $36,720,000.

Brilliant anti-war satire focusing on three irreverent army doctors (Donald Sutherland, Elliott Gould, Tom Skerritt) trying to keep their sanity through humor, while stationed at a Mobile Army Surgical Hospital during the Korean War. No film has ever captured the insanity of war so perfectly. Although there are no battle scenes, *M*A*S*H* shows, in sometimes gruesome details, the results of war. Robert Altman's anarchic improvisational style is perfectly suited for the material and *M*A*S*H* is filled with a gallery of some of the most vivid and eccentric characters ever to grace the screen.

523 MacArthur (1977) *** Universal 144 min. *Dir* Joseph Sargent, *Scr* Hal Barwood, Matthew Robbins, *Cin* Mario Tosi, *Ed* George Jay Nicholson, *Des* John J. Lloyd, *Mus* Jerry Goldsmith, *Prod* Frank McCarthy.

Cast: Gregory Peck, *Gen. Douglas MacArthur*, Ed Flanders, *Pres. Truman*, Dan O'Herlihy, *Pres. Roosevelt*, Ivan Boner, *Gen. Sutherland*, Ward Costello, *Gen. Marshall*, Nicolas Coster, *Col. Huff*, Marj Dusay, *Mrs. MacArthur*, Art Fleming, *The Secretary*, Russell D. Johnson, *Adm. King*, Sandy Kenyon, *Gen. Wainwright*, Robert Mandan, *Rep. Martin*, Allan Miller, *Col. Diller*, Dick O'Neill, *Col. Whitney*, Addison Powell, *Adm. Nimitz*, Tom Rosqui, *Gen. Sampson*, G.D. Spadlin, *Gen. Eichelberger*, Kenneth Tobey, *Adm. Halsey*, Garry Walberg, *Gen. Walker*, Lane Allan, *Gen. Marquat*, Barry Coe, *TV Reporter*, Everett Cooper, *Gen. Krueger*, Charles Cyphers, *Gen. Harding*, Manuel De Pina, *Prettyman*, Jesse Dizon, *Castro*, Warde Donovan, *Gen. Shepherd*, John Fujioka, *Emp. Hirohito*, Jerry Holland, *Aide*, Philip Kenneally, *Adm. Doyle*. PG. $9,690,000.

Disappointing biography of the famous and infamous American general. Gregory Peck is fine as Douglas MacArthur, but the character is apparently not interesting enough to sustain such a large production, as in the case of the far superior film, *Patton*. Because of this *MacArthur* drags a bit. The best battle scenes, though, are those between MacArthur and President Truman, brilliantly played by Ed Flanders.

524 Macbeth (1971) (NB) *** Britain, Columbia, 140 min. *Dir* Roman Polanski, *Scr* Roman Polanski, Kenneth Tynan, based on play by William Shakespeare, *Cin* Gilbert Taylor, *Ed* Alistair McIntyre, *Des* Wilfrid Shingleton, *Art* Fred Carter, *Cos* Anthony Mendleson (BFA), *Mus* The Third Ear Band, *Prod* Andrew Braunsberg, Roman Polanski, *Exec Prod* Hugh M. Hefner, *Assoc Prod* Timothy Burrill.

Cast: Jon Finch, *Macbeth*, Francesca Annis, *Lady Macbeth*, Martin Shaw, *Banquo*, Nicholas Selby, *Duncan*, John Stride, *Ross*, Stephan Chase, *Malcolm*, Paul Shelley, *Donalbain*, Terence Baylor, *Macduff*, Andrew Laurence, *Lennox*, Frank Wylie, *Mentieth*, Bernard Archard, *Angus*, Bruce Purchase, *Caithness*, Keith Chegwin, *Fleance*, Noel Davis, *Seyton*, Noelle Rimmington, *Young Witch*, Maisie Farquhar, *Blind Witch*, Elsie Taylor, *First Witch*, Vic Abbott, *Crawdor*. R.

Excellent film version of Shakespeare's play about an ambitious Scots nobleman, driven to murder by his greedy wife. Polanski's version is visually shocking with doses of sex and violence, which is not out of place in this story. This is probably as good as any film based on a Shakespearian play could be, as they do not translate well to film.

525 McCabe and Mrs. Miller (1971) ***** Warner Bros., 121 min. *Dir* Robert Altman, *Scr* Robert Altman, Brian McKay, based on novel *McCabe* by Edmund Naughton, *Cin* Vilmos Zsigmond, *Ed* Lou Lombardo, *Des* Leon Ericksen, *Art* Philip Thomas, *Mus* Leonard Cohen, *Prod* Mitchell Brower, David Foster.

Cast: Warren Beatty, *John McCabe*, Julie Christie (AN), *Constance Miller*, René Auberjonois, *Sheehan*, Hugh Millais, *Dog Butler*, Shelley Duvall, *Ida Coyle*, Michael Murphy, *Sears*, John Schuck, *Smalley*, Corey Fischer, *Mr. Elliott*. R. $4,000,000.

Beautiful atmospheric and poetic western that it treated more like a period film. Warren Beatty stars as a gambler who settles in a Northwest town called Presbyterian Church. There he opens its first bordello and hires a madame (Julie Christie) to run it. The bordello becomes a success and Beatty is forced to prevent takeover from outside business interests that leads to a climax reminiscent of *High Noon*. *McCabe and Mrs. Miller* is not only one of Robert Altman's best films, but is one of the finest westerns ever made.

526 The McKenzie Break (1970) *** United Artists, 108 min. *Dir* Lamont Johnson, *Scr* William Norton, based on novel *The Bowmanville Break* by Sidney Shelley, *Cin* Michael Reed, *Ed* Tom Rolf, *Des* Frank White, *Cos* Tiny Nicholls, *Mus* Riz Ortolani, *Prod* Arthur Gardner, Jules Levy.

Cast: Brian Keith, *Capt. Connor*, Helmut Griem, *Schluetter*, Ian Hendry, *Maj. Perry*, Jack Watson, *Gen. Kerr*, Patrick O'Connell, *Sgt. Cox*, Horst Janson, *Neuchl*, Alexander Allerson, *Von Sperrle*, John Abineri, *Kranz*, Constantin de Goguel, *Lt. Hall*, Tom Kepinski, *Schmidt*, Eric Allan, *Hockbauer*, Caroline Mortimer, *Sgt. Bell*, Mary Larkin, *Cpl. Watt*, Gregg Palmer, *Berger*, Michael Sheard, *Unger*, Ingo Mogendorf, *Fullgrabe*, Franz Van Norde, *Dichter*, Desmond Perry, *Accomplice*, Jim Mooney, *Guard Foss*, Vernon Hayden, *Dispatcher*, Maura Kelly, *Scots Lassie*. PG.

Fine WWII drama set at a British Prisoner-of-War camp in Scotland. Brian Keith stars as an Irish intelligence agent, who is assigned to McKenzie to prevent a potential escape by the German prisoners. The film is a strong and tense battle-of-wits between Keith and the leader of the German prisoners (Helmut Griem). *The McKenzie Break* is one of a few prisoner-of-war dramas set in an Allied camp.

527 The Mackintosh Man (1973) ** Britain, Warner Bros., 100 min. *Dir* John Huston, *Scr* Walter Hill, based on novel *The Freedom Trap* by Desmond Bagley, *Cin* Oswald Morris, *Ed* Russell Lloyd, *Des* Terry Marsh, *Art* Alan Tomkins, *Mus* Maurice Jarre, *Prod* John Foreman, *Assoc Prod* William Hill.

Cast: Paul Newman, *Rearden*, Dominique Sanda, *Mrs. Smith*, James Mason, *Sir George Wheeler*, Harry Andrews, *Mackintosh*, Ian Bannen, *Slade*, Michael Hordern, *Brown*, Nigel Patrick, *Soames-Trevelyan*, Peter Vaughn, *Brunskill*, Roland Culver, *Judge*, Percy Herbert, *Taafe*, Robert Lang, *Jack Summers*, Jenny Runacre, *Gerda*, John Bindon, *Buster*, Hugh Manning, *Prosecutor*, Wolfe Morris, *Malta Police Commissioner*, Noel Purcell,

O'Donovan, Donald Webster, *Jervis*, Keith Bell, *Palmer*, Niall MacGinnis, *Warder*. PG.

Disappointing espionage thriller. Paul Newman is recruited to pose as a jewel thief to work undercover in order to expose a spy in the British government. The plot is extremely convoluted and confusing, and there is an obtrusive twist ending that does not work. There is some action, including a car chase, but it is somewhat dull in comparison to what has been done in other films. This is one of John Huston's least interesting films.

528 **McQ** (1974) ** Warner Bros., 116 min. *Dir* John Sturges, *Scr* Lawrence Roman, *Cin* Harry Stradling, Jr., *Ed* William Ziegler, *Des* Walter Simonds, *Mus* Elmer Bernstein, *Prod* Arthur Gardner, Jules Levy, *Co-Prod* Lawrence Roman, *Exec Prod* Michael Wayne.

Cast: John Wayne, *McQ*, Eddie Albert, *Kosterman*, Colleen Dewhurst, *Myra*, Clu Gulager, *Toms*, David Huddleston, *Pinky*, Jim Watkins, *J.C.*, Al Lettieri, *Santiago*, Julie Adams, *Elaine Forrester*, Roger E. Mosley, *Rosey*, William Bryant, *Stan Boyle*, Joe Tornatore, *LaSalle*, Richard Kelton, *Radical*, Richard Eastham, *Walter Forrester*, Dick Friel, *Bob Mahoney*, Fred Waugh, *Bodyguard*. PG. $4,100,000.

Typical John Wayne vehicle in which the aging star plays a cop who seems to think he is a cowboy. Wayne quits the police force, after a disagreement with his superior, and goes after a drug smuggling ring on his own, armed with an arsenal. Wayne apparently tried to emulate Clint Eastwood, particularly *Dirty Harry*, but *McQ* is nothing but nonsense.

529 **Macon County Line** (1974) ** American International, 89 min. *Dir* Richard Compton, *Scr* Max Baer, Richard Compton, *Story* Max Baer, *Cin* Daniel Lacambre, *Ed* Tina Hirsh, *Art* Roger Pancake, *Cos* Francis Dennis, *Mus* Stu Phillips, *Theme Song* composed and performed by Bobbie Gentry, *Prod* Max Baer, *Exec Prod* Roger Camras, Presented by Samuel Z. Arkoff.

Cast: Alan Vint, *Chris Dixon*, Jesse Vint, *Wayne Dixon*, Cheryl Waters, *Jenny*, Max Baer, *Deputy Reed Morgan*, Geoffrey Lewis, *Hamp*, Joan Blackman, *Carol Morgan*, Sam Gilman, *Deputy Bill*, Timothy Scott, *Lon*, James Gammon, *Elisha*, Leif Garrett, *Luke*, Emile Meyer, *Gurney*, Doodles Weaver, *Augie*. R. $9,100,000.

Dull Southern melodrama based on a true story about three youths who are unwelcome in a small town and are falsely accused of murder. There is a nice twist ending, but it is a long time coming, and *Macon County Line* has little else to offer. A sequel to this film was totally unnecessary, but apparently *Return to Macon County* had to be made anyway.

530 **Made for Each Other** (1971) *** 20th Century–Fox, 107 min. *Dir* Robert B. Bean, *Scr* Joseph Bologna, Renée Taylor, *Cin* William Storz, *Ed* Sonny Mele, *Art* Robert Ramsey, *Cos* Elaine Mangel, *Mus* Trade Martin, *Prod* Roy Townshend, *Exec Prod* Malcolm B. Kahn.

Cast: Renée Taylor, *Pandora (Panda) Gold*, Joseph Bologna, *Gig (Giggy) Pinimba*, Paul Sorvino, *Gig's Father*, Olympia Dukakis, *Gig's Mother*, Helen Verbit, *Pandora's Mother*, Louis Zorich, *Pandora's Father*, Norman Shelly, *"Dr. Furro"*, Ron Carey, Peggy Pope, Susan Brockman, Art Levy, Frieda Wexler, Barbara Levy, Despo, *The Group*. PG.

Offbeat comedy love story about a couple (Renée Taylor, Joseph Bologna), who meet a group therapy session, and who have little in common other than they both are failures. *Made for Each Other* is both funny and real, and it has a fine feeling for these two people, possibly because Taylor and Bologna based the story on their own lives.

531 Magic (1978) *** 20th Century–Fox, 106 min. *Dir* Richard Attenborough, *Scr* William Goldman, based on his novel, *Cin* Victor J. Kemper, *Ed* John Bloom, *Des* Terence Marsh, *Art* Richard Lawrence, *Cos* Ruth Myers, *Mus* Jerry Goldsmith, *Prod* Joseph E. Levine, Richard P. Levine, *Exec Prod* C.O. Erickson.

Cast: Anthony Hopkins, *Corky*, Ann-Margret, *Peggy Ann Snow*, Burgess Meredith, *Ben Greene*, Ed Lauter, *Duke*, Anthony Hopkins (Voice), *Fats*, E.J. Andre, *Merlin*, Jerry Houser, *Cab Driver*, David Ogden Stiers, *Todson*, Lillian Randolph, *Sadie*, Joe Lowry, *Club M.C.*, Beverly Sanders, *Laughing Lady*, I.W. Klein, *Maitre d'*, Stephen Hart, *Captain*, Patrick McCullough, *Doorman*, Bob Hackman, *Father*, Mary Munday, *Mother*, Scott Garrett, *Corky's Brother*, Brad Beesley, *Young Corky*, Michael Harte, *Minister*. R. $13,270,000.

Disappointing murder thriller about a schizophrenic ventriloquist, whose dummy is slowly taking over his personality. Anthony Hopkins is absolutely brilliant in the lead, portraying a man who is gradually losing grasp of reality. Hopkins actually does his own ventriloquism, unlike in the famous film *Dead of Night*, in which the voice of Michael Redgrave's dummy was dubbed. Unfortunately as a thriller *Magic* simply goes nowhere and the ending is anticlimactic.

532 The Magic Christian (1970) *** Britain, Commonwealth United Entertainment, 95 min. *Dir* Joseph McGrath, *Scr* Joseph McGrath, Peter Sellers, Terry Southern, *Additional Material* Graham Chapman, John Cleese, based on novel by Terry Southern, *Cin* Geoffrey Unsworth, *Ed* Kevin Connor, *Des* Assheton Gorton, *Art* George Djurkovic, *Cos* Vangie Harrison, *Mus* Ken Thorne, *Chor* Lionel Blair, *Prod* Denis O'Dell, *Exec Prod* Anthony B. Unger, Henry T. Weinstein.

Cast: Peter Sellers, *Sir Guy Grand*, Ringo Starr, *Youngman Grand*, Isabel Jeans, *Aunt Agnes*, Caroline Balkiston, *Aunt Esther*, Wilfrid Hyde-White, *Klaus*, Richard Attenborough, *Oxford Coach*, Leonard Frey, *Psychiatrist*, Laurence Harvey, *Hamlet*, Christopher Lee, *Vampire*, Spike Milligan, *Warden*, Raquel Welch, *Slave Priestess*. PG.

Irreverent farce about an English millionaire (Peter Sellers), who adopts a bum (Ringo Starr) as his son, and takes him on a bizarre journey through the world of big business and high finance, which culminates in an indescribable cruise aboard a new luxury liner named the "Magic Christian." The surrealistic humor, similar in style to that of Monty Python's Flying Circus, does not always work and its point is not always clear, but the film is so crazy that it is never dull.

533 Magnum Force (1973) ** Warner Bros., 124 min. *Dir* Ted Post, *Scr* Michael Cimino, John Milius, *Story* John Milius, based on characters created by Harry Julian Fink, R.M. Fink, *Cin* Frank Stanley, *Ed* Ferris Webster, *Art* Jack Collis, *Mus* Lalo Schifrin, *Prod* Robert Daley.

Cast: Clint Eastwood, *Harry Callahan*, Hal Holbrook, *Lt. Briggs*, Felton Perry, *Early Smith*, Mitchell Ryan, *Charlie McCoy*, David Soul, *Davis*, Tim Matheson, *Sweet*, Robert Urich, *Grimes*, Kip Niven, *Astrachan*, Christine White, *Carol McCoy*, Adele Yoshioka, *Sunny*. R. $20,100,000. See *Dirty Harry*.

534 **Mahler** (1974) *** Britain, Mayfair, 115 min. *Dir* Ken Russell, *Scr* Ken Russell, *Cin* Dick Bush, *Ed* Michael Bradsell, *Art* Ian Whittaker, *Cos* Shirly Russell, *Mus Adaptation* John Forsythe, *Chor* Gilliam Gregory, *Prod* Roy Baird, *Exec Prod* Sanford Lieberson, David Puttnam.

Cast: Robert Powell, *Gustav Mahler*, Georgina Hale, *Alma Mahler*, Richard Morant, *Max*, Lee Montague, *Bernard Mahler*, Rosalie Crutchley, *Marie Mahler*, Benny Lee, *Uncle Arnold*, Miriam Karlin, *Aunt Rosa*, Angela Down, *Justine*, David Collings, *Hugo Wolf*, Ronald Pickup, *Nick*, Antonia Ellis, *Cosima Wagner*, Dana Gillespie, *Anna Von Mildenburg*, Elaine Delmar, *Princess*, Michael Southgate, *Aloise Mahler*, Gary Rich, *Young Mahler*, Peter Eyre, *Otto*, Sara McLellan, *Putzi*, Claire McLellan, *Glucki*. PG.

Disappointing Ken Russell biography of German Romantic composer Gustav Mahler. His life is told in flashbacks while he is on a train to Vienna, contemplating his past. Robert Powell is excellent casting as the composer, as he bears a striking resemblance to his real-life counterpart. *Mahler* has some of the usual Russell imagery, but it is not as excessive as his other films, and it tends to drag.

535 **Mahogany** (1975) ** Paramount, 109 min. *Dir* Berry Gordy, begun by Tony Richardson, *Scr* John Byrum, based on novel by Toni Amber, *Cin* David Watkin, *Ed* Peter Zinner, *Art* Aurelio Crugnola, Leon Ericksen, *Cos* Diana Ross, *Mus* Michael Masser, *Song* "Theme From Mahogany (Do You Know Where You're Going To)", *Mus* Michael Masser (AN), *Lyrics* Gerry Goffin (AN), *Prod* Jack Ballard, Rob Cohen.

Cast: Diana Ross, *Tracy (Mahogany)*, Billy Dee Williams, *Brian*, Anthony Perkins, *Sean*, Jean-Pierre Aumont, *Christian Rosetti*, Beah Richards, *Florence*, Nina Foch, *Miss Evans*, Marisa Mell, *Carlotta Gavin*, Lenard Norris, *Wil*, Ira Rogers, *Stalker*, Kristine Cameron, *Instructress*, Ted Liss, *Sweatshop Foreman*, Marvin Corman, *Cab Driver*, E. Rodney Jones, *Radio Announcer*, Daniel Daniele, *Guiseppe*, Princess Galitzine, *Herself*, Jacques Stany, *Auctioneer*, Bruce Vilanch, Don Howard, Albert Rosenberg, *Designers*. PG. $6,915,000.

Dull film about an ambitious black woman who rises from the ghetto to become a successful fashion designer, but finds it is lonely at the top. *Mahogany* was intended to be an honest film about the black experience; Tony Richardson was fired for not capturing this; but this film does not even come close to its intentions, as this is nothing more than a soap opera fairy tale, in which color is irrelevant.

536 **Mame** (1974) ** Warner Bros., 132 min. *Dir* Gene Saks, *Scr* Paul Zindel, based on stage musical by Jerry Herman, Jerome Lawrence, Robert E. Lee, and their straight play and novel by Patrick Dennis, *Cin* Philip Lathrop, *Ed* Maury Winetrobe, *Art* Harold Michelson, *Cos* Theadora Van Runkle, *Mus* Jerry Harman, *Mus Adaptation* Billy Byers, Ralph Burns, *Chor* Martin Allen, Onna White, *Prod* James Cresson, Robert Fryer.

Cast: Lucille Ball, *Mame*, Robert Preston, *Beauregard*, Beatrice Arthur, *Vera*, Bruce Davison, *Older Patrick*, Joyce Van Patten, *Sally Cato*, Don Porter, *Mr. Upson*, Audrey Christie, *Mrs. Upson*, Jane Connell, *Agnes Gooch*, Kirby Furlong, *Young Patrick*, John McGiver, *Mr. Babcock*, Doria Cook, *Gloria Upson*, Bobbi Jordan, *Pegeen*, George Chiang, *Ito*. PG. $6,500,000.

Dull musical version of comedy *Auntie Mame*. The original story is intact, with Mame's nephew coming to live with her, but the original film was not as good as its reputation indicates, although it had its moments. Under the gigantic musical production of the remake, the story just sinks. Lucille Ball is normally a fine comedy actress, but she is not eccentric enough to be convincing in the title role.

537 The Maids (1975) ******* Britain, American Film Theatre, 95 min. *Dir* Christopher Miles, *Scr* Robert Enders, Christopher Miles, based on Minos Volanakis' translation of play by Jean Genet, *Cin* Douglas Slocombe, *Ed* Peter Tanner, *Art* Robert Jones, *Mus* Laurie Johnson, *Prod* Robert Enders, *Exec Prod* Bernard Weitzman, *Assoc Prod* Gordon L.T. Scott.

Cast: Glenda Jackson, *Solange*, Susannah York, *Claire*, Vivien Merchant, *Madame*. PG. See *American Film Theatre*.

538 The Main Event (1979) ****** Warner Bros., 112 min. *Dir* Howard Zieff, *Scr* Gail Parent, Andrew Smith, *Cin* Mario Tosi, *Ed* Edward Warschilka, *Des* Charles Rosen, *Cos* Ruth Myers, *Prod* Jon Peters, Barbra Streisand, *Exec Prod* Renee Missel, Howard Rosenman, *Assoc Prod* Jeff Werner.

Cast: Barbra Streisand, *Hillary Kramer*, Ryan O'Neal, *Eddie "Kid Natural" Scanlon*, Paul Sand, *David*, Whitman Mayo, *Percy*, Patti D'Arbanville, *Donna*, Chu Chu Malave, *Luis*, Richard Lawson, *Hector Mantilla*, James Gregory, *Gough*, Richard Altman, *Tour Guide*, Joe Amsler, *Stunt Double Kid*, Seth Banks, *Newsman*, Lindsay Bloom, *Girl in Bed*, Earl Boen, *Nose-Kline*, Roger Bowen, *Owner Sinthia Cosmetics*, Badja Medu Djola, *Heavyweight in Gym*, Rory Calhoun, *Fighter in Kid's Camp*, Sue Casey, *Brenda*, Kristine DeBell, *Lucy*. PG. $26,300,000.

Average battle-of-the-sexes comedy about a down-and-out boxer, whose manager happens to be a woman. *The Main Event* attempts to satirize the use of people as sex objects by reversing the usual situation, with a woman exploitating a man instead of vice versa, but this idea is, unfortunately, almost totally lost in the constant bickering between the two leads. The previous teaming of Streisand and O'Neal, *What's Up Doc*, is much better.

539 A Man Called Horse (1970) ******* National General, 114 min. *Dir* Elliot Silverstein, *Scr* Jack DeWitt, based on story *Man Called Horse* by Dorothy M. Johnson, *Cin* Robert Hauser, *Ed* Philip W. Anderson, Gene Fowler, Jr., *Des* Dennis Lynton Clark, *Art* Phil Barber, *Cos* Edward Marks, Jack Martell, Ted Parvin, *Mus* Leonard Rosenman, *Prod* Sandy Howard, *Assoc Prod* Frank Brill.

Cast: Richard Harris, *Lord John Morgan*, Judith Anderson, *Buffalo Cow Head*, Jean Gascon, *Batise*, Mann Tupou, *Yellow Hand*, Corinna Tsopei, *Running Deer*, Dub Taylor, *Joe*, William Jordan, *Bent*, James Gammon, *Ed*, Edward Little Sky, *Black Eagle*, Lina Marin, *Thorn Rose*, Tamara Garina, *Elk Woman*, Michael Baselson, *He-Wolf*, Manuel Padilla, *Leaping Buck*, Terry Leonard, *Striking Bear*, Iron Eyes Cody, Richard Fools Bull, Ben Eagleman, *Medicine Men*. PG. $6,500,000.

Pretentious western drama about a white man who is captured by Sioux Indians. He is tortured by the Indians, in long grueling scenes, and eventually accepts their lifestyle. This attempt at an honest portrait of American Indians is unfortunately very dull. The sequel *The Return of a Man Called Horse* is a far better film. In this film he teaches the tribe how to defend themselves against invaders. At least this film balances the realism with some genuine excitement.

540 **Man Friday** (1975) *** Britain, Avco Embassy, 115 min. *Dir* Jack Gold, *Scr* Adrian Mitchell, based on novel *Robinson Crusoe*, by Daniel Defoe, *Cin* Alex Phillips, *Ed* Anne V. Coates, *Des* Peter Murton, *Art* Augustine Ytuarte, *Mus* Carl Davis, *Chor* Tino Rodriguez, *Prod* David Korda, *Exec Prod* Jules Buck, Gerald Green.

Cast: Peter O'Toole, *Crusoe*, Richard Roundtree, *Friday*, Peter Cellier, *Carey*, Christopher Cabot, *McBain*, Joel Fluellen, *Doctor*, Sam Sebrooke, *Young Girl*, Stanley Clay, *Young Boy*. PG.

Interesting variation of *Robinson Crusoe*. The classic story has been used as a springboard for an allegory for racial relations and tensions. Crusoe finds Friday washed up on his island after being shipwrecked and takes him in as a slave. Friday begins to ask questions and because of his disillusionment rebels against this white supremecy. Peter O'Toole and Richard Roundtree are excellent in the lead roles.

541 **The Man in the Glass Booth** (1975) **** American Film Theatre, 117 min. *Dir* Arthur Hiller, *Scr* Edward Anhalt, based on play by Robert Shaw, *Cin* Sam Leavitt, *Ed* David Bretherton, *Des* Joel Schiller, *Cos* John A. Anderson, *Prod* Ely Landau, *Exec Prod* Mort Abrahams.

Cast: Maximilian Schell (AN), *Arthur Goldman*, Lois Nettleton, *Miriam Rosen*, Luther Adler, *Presiding Judge*, Lawrence Pressman, *Charlie Cohn*, Henry Brown, *Jack Arnold*, Richard Rasof, *Moshe*, David Nash, *Rami*, Martin Berman, *Uri*, Sy Kramer, *Rudin*, Robert H. Harris, *Dr. Weisberg*, Leonidas Ossetynski, *Samuel*, Lloyd Bochner, *Churchill*, Norbert Schiller, *Schmidt*. PG. See *American Film Theatre.*

542 **Man in the Wilderness** (1971) *** Warner Bros., 105 min. *Dir* Richard C. Sarafian, *Scr* Jack De Witt, *Cin* Gerry Fisher, *Ed* Geoffrey Foote, *Des* Dennis Lynton Clark, *Art* Gumersindo Andres, *Cos* Dennis Lynton Clark, *Mus* Johnny Harris, *Song* "Zach Bass Theme," *Mus* John Bromley, Johnny Harris, *Prod* Sanford Howard, *Assoc Prod* C.O. Erickson.

Cast: Richard Harris, *Zachary Bass*, John Huston, *Capt. Filmore Henry*, Henry Wilcoxen, *Indian Chief*, Percy Herbert, *Fogarty*, Dennis Waterman, *Laurie*, Prunella Ransome, *Grace*, Norman Rossington, *Ferris*, James Doohan, *Benoit*, Bryan Marshall, *Potts*, Ben Carruthers, *Longbow*, Robert Russell, *Smith*, John Bindon, *Coulter*, Bruce M. Fischer, *Wiser*, Dean Selmier, *Russell*. PG.

Fine western tale of survival starring Richard Harris as a scout for a fur trapping expedition in the North West territory in the 1820's, who is mauled by a bear and left for dead. Harris recovers enough to set after the group, led by John Huston, to get his revenge. The film bears some resemblance to *A Man Called Horse*, but it has fewer pretentions and Harris' presence carries the film.

543 **Man of La Mancha** (1972) ** United Artists, 130 min. *Dir* Arthur
Hiller, *Scr* Dale Wasserman, based on his musical play, suggested by novel
Don Quixote by Miguel de Cervantes, *Cin* Giuseppe Rotunno, *Ed* Robert C.
Jones, *Art* Luciano Daniani, *Mus* Mitch Leigh, *Lyrics* Joe Darion, *Mus. Adap-
tation* Lawrence Rosenthal (AN), *Chor* Gillian Lynne, *Prod* Arthur Hiller, *Exec
Prod* Alberto Grimaldi, *Assoc Prod* Saul Chaplin.

Cast: Peter O'Toole (NB), *Don Quixote de la Mancha/Miguel de Cervan-
tes/Alonso Quijana*, Sophia Loren, *Dulcinea/Aldonza*, James Coco, *Sancho
Panzo*, Harry Andrews, *Innkeeper/Governor*, John Castle, *Sanson
Carrasco/Duke*, Brian Blessed, *Pedro*, Ian Richardson, *Padre*, Julie Gregg, *Antonia*, Rosalie Crutchley, *Housekeeper*, Gino Conforti, *Barber*. PG.

Fair film version of Broadway musical based on Cervantes' demented
hero Don Quixote, who attacks a windmill, thinking it is a monster. Peter
O'Toole stars as both Quixote and Cervantes, in which Cervantes is thrown
into prison and tells the story of Quixote as part of his defense. The musical
numbers are lacking in energy and somewhat flat, which sinks the entire film.

544 **Man on a Swing** (1974) *** Paramount, 110 min. *Dir* Frank Perry, *Scr*
David Zelag Goodman, *Cin* Adam Holender, *Ed* Sidney Katz, *Des* Joel
Schiller, *Cos* Ruth Morley, *Mus* Lalo Schifrin, *Prod* Howard B. Jaffe.

Cast: Cliff Robertson, *Lee Tucker*, Joel Grey, *Franklin Wills*, Dorothy
Tristan, *Janet Tucker*, Elizabeth Wilson, *Dr. Anna Willson*, George Voskovec,
Dr. Nicholas Holmar, Ron Weyand, *Dr. Philip Tusco*, Peter Masterson, *Willie
Younger*, Lane Smith, *Ted Ronan*, Joe Ponazecki, *Dan Lloyd*, Christopher
Allport, *Richie Tom Keating*, Patricia Hawkins, *Diana Spenser*, Richard Ven-
ture, *Man in Motel*, Dianne Hull, *Maggie Dawson*, Gil Gerard, *Donald Forbes*,
Richard Dryden, *Mr. Dawson*, Alice Drummond, *Mrs. Dawson*,
Nicholas Pryor, *Paul Kearney*, Penelope Milford, *Evelyn Moore*. PG.

Unusual murder thriller about a cop (Cliff Robertson) who is unable to
solve the murder of a girl and enlists the aid of a charismatic clairvoyant (Joel
Grey). The cop gradually begins to suspect the clairvoyant may be involved
because of his increasingly strange behavior. *Man on a Swing* begins
promisingly, but it falls apart with a disappointing ending. The film does,
however, feature a great performance by Grey.

545 **The Man Who Fell to Earth** (1976) ***** Britain, Cinema 5, 140 min.
Dir Nicolas Roeg, *Scr* Paul Mayersberg, based on novel by Walter Tevis, *Cin*
Anthony Richmond, *Ed* Graeme Clifford, *Mus Director* John Phillips, *Prod*
Michael Deeley, Barry Spikings, *Exec Prod* Si Litvinoff.

Cast: David Bowie, *Thomas Jerome Newton*, Rip Torn, *Nathan Bryce*,
Candy Clark, *Mary Lou*, Buck Henry, *Oliver Farnsworth*, Bernie Casey,
Peters, Jackson D. Kane, *Prof. Canutti*, Rick Riccardo, *Trevor*, Tony Mascia,
Arthur, Linda Hutton, *Elaine*, Hilary Holland, *Jill*, Adrienne Larussa, *Helen*,
Lilybelle Crawford, *Jewelry Store Owner*, Richard Breeding, *Receptionist*,
Albert Nelson, *Waiter*, Peter Prouse, *Peters' Associate*, Capt. James Lovell,
Himself. R.

Beautiful and mysterious science-fiction tale of an alien (David Bowie)
who comes to Earth to find water for his planet, but becomes the head of a
financial empire through his superior intelligence. *The Man Who Fell to Earth*
is an intellectual film rather than an action adventure and the ideas are not

always clear, but Nicolas Roeg has superbly constructed this visually intricate film. Although not really an actor, rock star, Bowie is perfect in the lead role.

546 The Man Who Loved Cat Dancing (1973) ** MGM, 114 min. *Dir* Richard C. Sarafian, *Scr* Eleanor Perry, based on novel by Marilyn Durham, *Cin* Harry Stradling, Jr., *Ed* Tom Rolf, *Art* Edward C. Cafagno, *Cos* Frank Thompson, *Mus* John Williams, *Prod* Eleanor Perry, Martin Poll, *Assoc Prod* T.W. Sewell.

Cast: Burt Reynolds, *Jay*, Sarah Miles, *Catherine*, Lee J. Cobb, *Lapchance*, Jack Warden, *Dawes*, George Hamilton, *Crocker*, Bo Hopkins, *Billy*, Robert Donner, *Dub*, Sandy Kevin, *Ben*, Larry Littlebird, *Iron Knife*, Nancy Malone, *Sudie*, Jay Silverheels, *The Chief*, Jay Varela, *Charlie*, Owen Bush, *Conductor*, Larry Finley, *Bartender*, Sutero Garcia, Jr., *Dream Speaker*. PG.

Fair western adventure chase film about a woman (Sarah Miles), who abandons her stern husband (George Hamilton) and takes up with a likable outlaw (Burt Reynolds). The plot becomes redundant as most of the film consists of the pair being pursued by the husband and his posse. This basic plot was used again in another Reynolds film, *Smokey and the Bandit*, and it did not work there, either.

547 The Man Who Would Be King (1975) **** Britain, Allied Artists, 129 min. *Dir* John Huston, *Scr* Gladys Hill, John Huston (AN), *Cin* Oswald Morris, *Ed* Russell Lloyd (AN), *Des* Alexander Trauner (AN), *Art* Tony Inglis (AN), *Cos* Edith Head (AN), *Mus* Maurice Jarre, *Prod* John Foreman, *Assoc Prod* James Arneth.

Cast: Sean Connery, *Daniel Dravot*, Michael Caine, *Peachy Carnehan*, Christopher Plummer, *Rudyard Kipling*, Saeed Jaffrey, *Billy Fish*, Karroum Ben Bouih, *Kafu-Selim*, Jack May, *District Commissioner*, Doghmi Larbi, *Ootah*, Shakira Caine, *Roxanne*, Mohammed Shamsi, *Babu*, Paul Antrim, *Mulvaney*, Albert Moses, *Ghulan*. PG. $6,500,000.

Wonderful old-fashioned adventure story about two enterprising British officers in 1880 who decide to become the rulers of Kafiristan, an Asian province. *The Man Who Would Be King* is reminiscent of John Huston's earlier film, *The Treasure of the Sierra Madre*, and does not suffer by comparison. Sean Connery and Michael Caine are wonderful together as the two officers and Christopher Plummer is amazing in his brief appearance as Rudyard Kipling.

548 The Man with the Golden Gun (1974) *** Britain, United Artists, 125 min. *Dir* Guy Hamilton, *Scr* Richard Maibaum, Tom Mankiewicz, based on novel by Ian Fleming, *Cin* Ted Moore, Ossie Morris, *Ed* Roy Poulton, *Des* Peter Murton, *Art* John Graysmark, Peter Lamont, *Mus* John Barry, *Lyrics* Don Black, *Prod* Albert R. Broccoli, Harry Saltzman, *Assoc Prod* Charles Orme.

Cast: Roger Moore, *James Bond*, Christopher Lee, *Scaramanga*, Britt Ekland, *Mary Goodnight*, Maud Adams, *Andrea*, Herve Villechaize, *Nick Nack*, Clifton James, *J.W. Pepper*, Soon Taik Oh, *Hip*, Richard Loo, *Hai Fat*, Marc Lawrence, *Rodney*, Bernard Lee, *"M"*, Lois Maxwell, *Miss Moneypenny*, Marne Maitland, *Lazar*, Desmond Llewellyn, *"Q"*, James Cossins, *Colthorpe*, Chan Yiu Lam, *Chula*, Carmen Sautoy, *Saida*, Gerald James, *Frazier*, Michael Osborne, *Navel Lieutenant*, Michael Fleming, *Communications Officer*. PG. $9,400,000. See *Diamonds Are Forever*.

549 **Mandingo** (1975) * Paramount, 127 min. *Dir* Richard Fleischer, *Scr* Norman Wexler, based on novel by Kyle Onstott and play by Jack Kirkland, *Cin* Richard H. Kline, *Ed* Frank Bracht, *Des* Boris Leven, *Cos* Ann Roth, *Mus* Maurice Jarre, *Prod* Dino De Laurentiis, *Exec Prod* Ralph Serpe.

Cast: James Mason, *Maxwell,* Susan George, *Blanche,* Perry King, *Hammond,* Richard Ward, *Agamemnon,* Brenda Sykes, *Ellen,* Ken Norton, *Mede,* Lillian Hayman, *Lucrezia Borgia,* Roy Poole, *Doc Redfield,* Ji-Tu Cumbuka, *Cicero,* Paul Benedict, *Brownlee,* Ben Masters, *Charles,* Ray Spruell, *Wallace,* Louis Turenne, *De Veve,* Duane Allen, *Topaz,* Earl Maynard, *Babouin,* Beatrice Winde, *Lucy,* Debbie Morgan, *Dite,* Irene Tedrow, *Mrs. Redfield.* R. $8,600,000.

Lurid melodrama set in the pre-Civil War South. *Mandingo* is the antithesis of *Gone with the Wind,* but is equally misguided in its perception of the period. In an attempt to be more honest than that overblown soap opera, this film went too far the other way and is nothing more than a series of sleazy overacted episodes of life on a plantation. *Drum* is a continuation of the standards set by the first film.

550 **Manhattan** (1979) (NB, BFA) ***** United Artists, 96 min. *Dir* Woody Allen (NS, NY), *Scr* Woody Allen, Marshall Brickman (AN, BFA), *Cin* Gordon Willis, *Ed* Susan E. Morse, *Des* Mel Bourne, *Cos* Albert Wolsky, *Mus* George Gershwin, *Prod* Charles H. Joffe, *Exec Prod* Robert Greenhut.

Cast: Woody Allen, *Issac Davis,* Diane Keaton, *Mary Wilke,* Michael Murphy, *Yale,* Mariel Hemingway (AN), *Tracy,* Meryl Streep, *Jill,* Anne Byrne, *Emily,* Karen Ludwig, *Connie,* Michael O'Donoghue, *Dennis,* Victor Truro, Tisa Farrow, Helen Hanft, *Party Guests,* Bella Abzug, *Guest of Honor,* Gary Weis, *TV Director,* Kenny Vance, *TV Producer,* Charles Levin, Karen Allen, David Rasche, *TV Actors,* Damion Sheller, *Isaac's Son, Willie,* Wallace Shawn, *Jeremiah,* Mark Linn Baker, Frances Conroy, *Shakespearean Actors,* Bill Anthony, *Porsche Owner #1,* John Doumanian, *Porsche Owner #2,* Ray Serra, *Pizzeria Waiter.* R. $16,960,000.

Brilliant character study focusing on the lives and relationships of a group of New Yorkers. Woody Allen stars as a disenchanted television writer, who drops his girlfriend (Mariel Hemingway), a high school senior, for a flamboyant and overbearing intellectual (Diane Keaton). Allen mixes drama with comedy, without sacrificing his comedic wit, in this film which contains far more insight into people than most straight dramas. Allen was faced with a difficult task of topping his masterpiece *Annie Hall* and *Manhattan* is not only a worthy followup, but it is superior.

551 **Marathon Man** (1976) **** Paramount, 125 min. *Dir* John Schlesinger, *Scr* William Goldman, based on his novel, *Cin* Conrad Hall, *Ed* Jim Clark, *Des* Richard MacDonald, *Art* Jack DeShields, *Mus* Michael Small, *Prod* Sidney Beckerman, Robert Evans.

Cast: Dustin Hoffman, *Babe Levy,* Laurence Olivier (AN, G), *Szell,* Roy Scheider, *Doc Levy,* William Devane, *Janeway,* Marthe Keller, *Elsa,* Fritz Weaver, *Professor,* Richard Bright, *Karl,* Marc Lawrence, *Erhard,* Allen Joseph, *Mr. Levy,* Tito Goya, *Melendez,* Ben Dova, *Szell's Brother,* Lou Gilbert, *Rosenbaum,* Jacques Marin, *LeClerc,* James Wing Woo, *Chen,* Nicole Deslauriers, *Nicole,* Lotta Andor-Palfi, *Old Lady in Street.* R. $16,575,000.

Strange and highly stylized thriller starring Dustin Hoffman as a marathon runner who is drawn into a plot involving missing diamonds by his CIA agent brother (Roy Scheider), and is subsequently pursued by a Nazi madman (Laurence Olivier). There are many extraordinary and tense scenes, sometimes resembling a James Bond film, but *Marathon Man* is better in parts than as a whole.

552 **March or Die** (1977) ** Britain, Columbia, 106 min. *Dir* Dick Richards, *Scr* David Zelag Goodman, *Story* David Zelag Goodman, Dick Richards, *Cin* John Alcott, *Ed* Stanford C. Allen, O. Nicholas Brown, John C. Howard, *Des* Gil Parrondo, *Art* Jose Maria Tapiador, *Mus* Maurice Jarre, *Prod* Jerry Bruckheimer, Dick Richards, *Assoc Prod* Georges-Patrick Salvy-Guide.

Cast: Gene Hackman, *Maj. Foster*, Terence Hill, *Marco*, Max Von Sydow, *Francois*, Catherine Deneuve, *Simone*, Ian Holm, *El Krim*, Rufus, *Sgt. Triand*, Jack O'Halloran, *Ivan*, Marcel Bozzuffi, *Lt. Fontaine*, Andre Penvern, *Top Hat*, Paul Sherman, *Fred*, Vernon Dobtcheff, *Mean Cpl.*, Marne Maitland, *Leon*, Gigi Bonds, *Andre*, Wolf Kahler, Mathias Hell, *Germans*. PG.

Disappointing Foreign Legion saga. *March or Die* is the first serious film in years to deal with that subject and it is a shame that the film is so dull. The visual details are immaculate, but the storyline falls flat, wandering with little purpose, and the characters are one-dimensional. This is a great letdown, considering all the talent involved.

553 **The Marriage of a Young Stockbroker** (1971) ** 20th Century–Fox, 95 min. *Dir* Lawrence Turman, *Scr* Lorenzo Semple, Jr., based on novel by Charles Webb, *Cin* Laszlo Kovacs, *Ed* Frederic Steinkamp, *Des* Pato Guzman, *Cos* Doris Rambeau, Ed Wynigear, *Mus* Fred Karlin, *Song* "Can It Be True", *Lyrics* Tylwyth Kymry, *Prod* Lawrence Turman, *Assoc Prod* Frederic Steinkamp.

Cast: Richard Benjamin, *William Alren*, Joanna Shimkus, *Lisa Alren*, Elizabeth Ashley, *Nan*, Adam West, *Chester*, Patricia Barry, *Dr. Sadler*, Tiffany Bolling, *Girl in the Rain*, Ed Prentiss, *Mr. Franklin*, William Forrest, *Mr. Wylie*, Johnny Scott Lee, *Mark*, Bill McConnell, *Charlie McGuire*, Alma Betran, *Raquel*, Norman Leavitt, *Mr. Van Meter*, Ron Masak, *1st Baseball Fan*, Bob Hastings, *2nd Baseball Fan*, Ken Snell, *Cab Driver*. R.

Disappointing comedy starring Richard Benjamin as a stockbroker, who becomes bored with his job and his marriage, and turns to voyeurism to compensate. The film was apparently intended to be a progression from *The Graduate*, a similar character after a few years of marriage, but its point is too narrow and it lacks the perceptive humor and depth of that classic from the 1960's.

554 **Mary, Queen of Scots** (1971) *** Britain, Universal, 128 min. *Dir* Charles Jarrott, *Scr* John Hale, *Cin* Christopher Challis, *Ed* Richard Marden, *Des* Terence Marsh (AN), *Art* Robert Cartwright (AN), *Cos* Margaret Furse (AN), *Mus* John Barry (AN), *Prod* Hal B. Wallis.

Cast: Vanessa Redgrave (AN), *Mary, Queen of Scots*, Glenda Jackson, *Queen Elizabeth*, Patrick McGoohan, *James Stuart*, Timothy Dalton, *Henry, Lord Darnley*, Nigel Davenport, *Lord Bothwell*, Trevor Howard, *William Cecil*, Daniel Massey, *Robert Dudley, Earl of Leicester*, Ian Holm, *David Riccio*, Andrew Keir, *Ruthven*, Tom Fleming, *Father Ballard*, Katherine Kath,

Catherine De Medici, Beth Harris, *Mary Seton*, Frances White, *Mary Fleming*, Bruce Purchase, *Morton*, Brian Coburn, *Huntly*, Vernon Dobtcheff, *Duc de Guise*, Raf De La Torre, *Cardinal de Guise*, Richard Warner, *Walsingham*, Maria Aitkin, *Lady Bothwell*, Jeremy Bulloch, *Andrew*, Robert James, *John Knox*, Richard Denning, *Francis, King of France*. PG.

Disappointing historical drama focusing on the conflict between Mary Stuart of Scotland (Vanessa Redgrave) and Queen Elizabeth I (Glenda Jackson), and their rivalry over the throne of England. *Mary, Queen of Scots* is typical of historical films in that there is more emphasis on visual details than on substance or accuracy. Redgrave and Jackson are excellent, though, particularly in their confrontations.

555 The Master Gunfighter (1975) * Taylor-Laughlin, 121 min. *Dir* Frank Laughlin, *Scr* Harold Lapland, *Cin* Jack A. Marta, *Ed* Danford Greene, William Reynolds, *Des* Albert Brenner, *Mus* Lalo Schifrin, *Prod* Philip L. Parslow, *Exec Prod* Delores Taylor.

Cast: Tom Laughlin, *Finley*, Ron O'Neal, *Paulo*, Lincoln Kilpatrick, *Jacques*, GeoAnn Sosa, *Chorika*, Barbara Carrera, *Eula*, Victor Campos, *Maltese*, Hector Elias, *Juan*, Michael Lane, *Frewen*, Richard Angarola, *Don Santiago*. PG.

Silly and pretentious western drama starring Tom Laughlin as a peace-loving gunfighter, who kills many people in a fight over a Spanish land grant. Laughlin may have thought that *The Master Gunfighter* was a change of pace from *Billy Jack*, but the two characters are no different, and he substitutes samurai for karate. The film is wildly overlong and total nonsense.

556 A Matter of Time (1976) ** American International, 97 min. *Dir* Vincente Minnelli, *Scr* John Gay, based on novel *Film of Memory* by Maurice Druon, *Cin* Geoffrey Unsworth, *Ed* Peter Taylor, *Des* Veniero Colasanti, John Moore, *Mus* Nino Oliviero, *Prod* J. Edmund Grainger, Jack H. Skirball, *Exec Prod* Samuel Z. Arkoff, Giulio Sbarigia.

Cast: Liza Minnelli, *Nina*, Ingrid Bergman, *The Contessa*, Charles Boyer, *Count Sanziani*, Spiros Andros, *Mario Morello*, Tina Aumont, *Valentina*, Anna Proclemer, *Jeanne Blasto*, Gabrielle Ferzetti, *Antonia Vicaria*, Arnolda Foa, *Pavelli*, Orso Maria Guerrini, *Gabrielle D'Orazio*, Fernando Rey, *Charles Van Maar*. PG.

Dull musical variation of the Cinderella story. Liza Minnelli stars as a maid working in a hotel in Rome, who befriends an old Contessa (Ingrid Bergman). The contessa tells the maid stories of her glamorous past and Minnelli visualizes herself in the stories. *A Matter of Time* is the first screen collaboration of Liza Minnelli and her father Vincente Minnelli, and it is a shame it turned out poorly. Studio tampering is a major factor, but none of the individual scenes are impressive, either.

557 Mean Streets (1973) ***** Warner Bros., 110 min. *Dir* Martin Scorsese, *Scr* Mardik Martin, Martin Scorsese, *Cin* Kent Wakeford, *Ed* Sid Levin, *Prod* Jonathon T. Taplin, *Exec Prod* E. Lee Perry.

Cast: Harvey Keitel, *Charlie*, Robert DeNiro (NS, NY), *Johnny Boy*, David Proval, *Tony*, Amy Robinson, *Teresa*, Richard Romanus, *Michael*, Cesare Danova, *Giovanni*, Vic Argo, *Mario*, Robert Carradine, *Boy with Gun*, David Carradine, *Drunk*, Jeannie Bell, *Diane*, D'Mitch Davis, *Cop*, George

Memmoli, *Joey*, Murray Mosten, *Oscar*, Ken Sinclair, *Sammy*, Harry Northup, *Soldier*, Lois Waldon, *Jewish Girl*, Lenny Scaletta, *Jimmy*, Robert Wilder, *Benton*, Martin Scorsese, *Killer*. R.

Extraordinary gangster drama that examines the lives of low-level hoods and loan sharks. Martin Scorsese's first major film is an intense and odd combination of *The Godfather* and *American Graffiti* that works unbelievably well. *Mean Streets* dispenses with plot and follows the day to day existence of four hoods, which is at times exciting and violent and other times drab. There is an incredible feeling of reality not found in many gangster films. Brilliant performances are given by the entire cast, but Robert DeNiro still manages to steal the film as the irresponsible and slightly psychotic Johnny Boy.

558 **Meatballs** (1979) ** Canada, Paramount, 92 min. *Dir* Ivan Reitman, *Scr* Janis Allen, Len Blum, Dan Goldberg, Harold Ramis, *Cin* Don Wilder, *Ed* Debra Karen, *Art* David Charles, *Cos* Judy Gellman, *Mus* Elmer Bernstein, *Lyrics* Norman Gimbel, *Prod* Dan Goldberg, *Exec Prod* John Dunning, Andre Link, *Assoc Prod* Lawrence Nesis.

Cast: Bill Murray, *Tripper*, Chris Makepeace, *Rudy*, Harvey Atkin, *Morty*, Russ Banham, *Crockett*, Ron Barry, *Lance*, Jack Blum, *Spaz*, Matt Craven, *Hardware*, Kristine DeBell, *A.L.*, Norma Dell'Agnese, *Brenda*, Cindy Girling, *Wendy*, Todd Hoffman, *Wheels*, Keith Knight, *Fink*, Kate Lynch, *Roxanne*, Margot Pinvidic, *Jackie*, Sarah Torgov, *Candace*. PG. $21,200,000.

Fair summer camp comedy that attempts to be another *Animal House*. *Meatballs* is filled with ridiculous and sophomoric humor, most of which does not work. The film is surprisingly laced with awful sentiment involving a shy and lonely kid (Chris Makepiece). *Meatballs* would be an almost total loss if not for the presence of Bill Murray. His dynamic comic persona literally propels the film through the mire.

559 **The Mechanic** (1972) ** United Artists, 100 min. *Dir* Michael Winner, *Scr* Lewis John Carlino, *Cin* Richard Kline, *Ed* Frederick Wilson, *Art* Rodger Maus, *Cos* Lambert Marks, *Mus* Jerry Fielding, *Prod* Lewis John Carlino, Robert Chartoff, Irwin Winkler, *Assoc Prod* Henry Gellis.

Cast: Charles Bronson, *Arthur Bishop*, Keenan Wynn, *Harry McKenna*, Jan-Michael Vincent, *Steve McKenna*, Jill Ireland, *Prostitute*, Linda Ridgeway, *Louise*, Frank DeKova, *Syndicate Head*, Kevin O'Neal, *Cam*, Linda Grant, *Bathtub Girl*, Louise Fitch, *Librarian*, Takayuki Kubota, *Yamoto*, Hank Hamilton, *Kori*, Hiroyasu Fujishima, *Aikido Master*, Michael Hinn, *Rifle Range Attendant*. PG.

Standard crime thriller starring Charles Bronson as a "mechanic," a slang term for a profesional hit man. Jan-Michael Vincent also stars as a young man, who becomes Bronson's assistant in order to learn the trade. *The Mechanic* begins promisingly with an abundance of action, but the film slows down greatly in the second half with dull scenes showing Bronson's lifestyle.

560 **The Medusa Touch** (1978) ** Britain, 110 min. *Dir* Jack Gold, *Scr* John Briley, based on novel by Peter Van Greenaway, *Cin* Arthur Ibbetson, *Ed* Anne V. Coates, *Art* Peter Mullins, *Mus* Michael J. Lewis, *Prod* Anne V. Coates, Jack Gold, *Exec Prod* Aron Milchan, *Assoc Prod* Denis Holt.

Cast: Richard Burton, *Morlar*, Lino Ventura, *Brunel*, Lee Remick, *Zonfeld*, Harry Andrews, *Assistant Commissioner*, Alan Badel, *Barrister*, Marie-

Christine Barrault, *Patricia*, Jeremy Brett, *Parrish*, Michael Hordern, *Fortune Teller*, Gordon Jackson, *Dr. Johnson*, Derek Jacobi, *Publisher*, Robert Lang, *Pennington*. PG.

Dull occult thriller starring Richard Burton as a man with telekinetic powers. After years of just killing individual people, he sets his goals higher and crashes jet liners into buildings. Lee Remick also stars as his psychiatrist, who tries to help him with his minor problem. *The Medusa Touch* is a poor man's *Carrie*, with a muddled script and little suspense.

561 **The Mephisto Waltz** (1971) ** 20th Century–Fox, 108 min. *Dir* Paul Wendkos, *Scr* Ben Maddow, based on novel by Fred Mustard Stewart, *Cin* William W. Spencer, *Ed* Richard Brockway, *Art* Richard Y. Haman, *Cos* Moss Mabry, *Mus* Jerry Goldsmith, *Prod* Quinn Martin, *Assoc Prod* Arthur Fellows.

Cast: Alan Alda, *Myles Clarkson*, Jacqueline Bisset, *Paula Clarkson*, Barbara Parkins, *Roxanne*, Bradford Dillman, *Bill DeLancey*, William Windom, *Dr. West*, Kathleen Widdoes, *Maggie West*, Pamelyn Ferdin, *Abby Clarkson*, Curt Lowens, *Agency Head*, Gregory Morton, *Conductor*, Janee Michelle, *Agency Head's Girl*, Lilyan Chauvin, *Woman Writer*, Khigh Dhiegh, *Zanc Theun*, Alberto Morin, *Bennet*, Berry Kroeger, *Raymont*, Terence Scammell, *Richard*, Curt Jurgens, *Duncan Ely*. R.

Fair occult thriller about a journalist (Alan Alda), who goes to the home of a dying legendary pianist (Curt Jurgens) for an interview. There is an ulterior motive for granting the interview, which involves a satanic cult, and it brings about a change in Alda's personality. *The Mephisto Waltz* is short on thrills, and it is a bit predictable. The story would have been better suited as an episode of *The Twilight Zone*.

562 **Meteor** (1979) * American International, 103 min. *Dir* Ronald Neame, *Scr* Stanley Mann, Edmund H. North, *Cin* Paul Lohmann, *Ed* Carl Kress, *Des* Edward Carfagno, *Art* David Constable, *Cos* Albert Wolsky, *Prod* Arnold Orgolini, Theodore Parvin.

Cast: Sean Connery, *Bradley*, Natalie Wood, *Titiana*, Brian Keith, *Dubov*, Karl Malden, *Sherwood*, Martin Landau, *Adlon*, Roger Robinson, *Hunter*, Bo Brundin, *Manheim*, James Richardson, *Alan*, Katherine DeHetre, *Jan*, Joe Campanella, *Easton*, Michael Zaslow, *Mason*, John McKinney, *Watson*, Henry Fonda, *President*, Richard Dysart, *Secretary of Defense*, John Findlater, *Tom Easton*, Paul Tulley, *Bill Frager*, Allen Williams, *Michael McKendrick*, Gregory Gay, *Russian Premier*, Zitto Kazann, *Hawk-Faced Party Member*, Bibi Besch, *Mrs. Bradley*, Trevor Howard, *Sir Michael Hughes*, Clyde Kusatsu, *Yamashiro*, Burke Byrnes, *Coast Guard Officer*. PG. $6,000,000.

Dull science-fiction disaster film about a giant meteor hurtling toward Earth. Most of the film's drama involves cold war politics, in which both the U.S. and the Soviet Union refuse to admit that each have satellite based missiles. The rest of the time the actors stand around waiting for the inevitable climax, which is itself a great disappointment due to the poor special effects.

563 **Midnight Express** (1978) (AN, G) **** Columbia, 120 min. *Dir* Alan Parker (AN, BFA), *Scr* Oliver Stone (A, W), based on book by Billy Hayes, William Hoffer, *Cin* Michael Seresin, *Ed* Gerry Hambling (AN, BFA), *Des* Geoffrey Kirkland, *Art* Evan Hercules, *Cos* Milena Canonero, Bobby

Lavender, *Mus* Giorgio Moroder (A), *Prod* Alan Marshall, David Puttnam, *Exec Prod* Peter Guber.

Cast: Brad Davis, *Billy Hayes,* Randy Quaid, *Jimmy,* John Hurt (AN, G, BFA), *Max,* Bo Hopkins, *Tex,* Paul Smith, *Hamidou,* Mike Kellin, *Mr. Hayes,* Norbert Wiesser, *Erich,* Irene Miracle (G), *Susan,* Paolo Bonacelli, *Rifki,* Michael Ensign, *Stanley Daniels,* Franco Diogene, *Yesil,* Kevork Milikyan, *Prosecutor,* Mihalis Yannatos, *Translator,* Gigi Ballista, *Chief Judge,* Tony Boyd, *Aslan,* Peter Jeffrey, *Ahmet,* Ahmed El Shenawi, *Negdir,* Zanninos Zanninou, *Turkish Detective,* Dimos Starenios, *Ticket Seller.* R. $15,305,000.

Harrowing drama based on the true experiences of Billy Hayes, an American youth arrested in Turkey and tortured in prison, for attempting to smuggle drugs out of the country. *Midnight Express* is a fictionalization of the incident and is heavily stylized by Alan Parker's atmospheric direction, but it nevertheless powerfully documents the horrors he experienced. Brad Davis is superb in his first starring role.

564 **Midway** (1976) * Universal, 132 min. *Dir* Jack Smight, *Scr* Donald S. Sanford, *Cin* Harry Stradling, Jr., *Ed* Robert Swink, Frank J. Urioste, *Art* Walter Tyler, *Mus* John Williams, *Prod* Walter Mirisch.

Cast: Charlton Heston, *Capt. Matt Garth,* Henry Fonda, *Adm. Chester W. Nimitz,* James Coburn, *Capt. Vinton Maddox,* Glenn Ford, *Rear Adm. Raymond A. Spruance,* Hal Holbrook, *Cmdr. Joseph Rochefort,* Toshiro Mifune, *Adm. Isoroku Yamamoto,* Robert Mitchum, *Adm. William F. Halsey,* Cliff Robertson, *Cmdr. Carl Jessop,* Robert Wagner, *Lt. Cmdr. Ernest L. Blake,* Robert Webber, *Rear Adm. Frank J. Fletcher,* Ed Nelson, *Adm. Harry Pearson,* James Shigeta, *Vice Adm. Chuichi Nagumo,* Christina Kokubo, *Haruko Sakura,* Monte Markham, *Cmdr. Max Leslie,* Biff McGuire, *Capt. Miles Browning,* Kevin Dobson, *Ens. George Gay,* Christopher George, *Lt. Cmdr. C. Wade McClusky,* Glenn Corbett, *Lt. Cmdr. John Waldron,* Gregory Walcott, *Capt. Elliot Buckmaster,* Edward Albert, *Lt. Tom Garth.* PG. $22,330,000.

Boring WWII drama about the famous Pacific battle. *Midway* spends an endless amount of time detailing the plans and preparation of the battle, none of which is very interesting. When the battle itself finally arrives it is a letdown, being a shoddy mixture of documentary and stock footage with the new footage, none of which match, all enhanced by noisy Sensurround. The large cast is no help and seems to be only for marquee value.

565 **Mikey and Nicky** (1976) ***** Paramount, 119 min. *Dir* Elaine May, *Scr* Elaine May, *Cin* Victor J. Kemper, *Ed* John Carter, Sheldon Kahn, *Des* Paul Sylbert, *Mus* John Strauss, *Prod* Michael Hausman, *Exec Prod* Bud Austin.

Cast: Peter Falk, *Mikey,* John Cassavetes, *Nicky,* Ned Beatty, *Kinney,* Rose Arrick, *Annie,* Carol Grace, *Nell,* William Hickey, *Sid Fine,* Sanford Meisner, *Dave Resnick,* Joyce Van Patten, *Jan,* M. Emmet Walsh, *Bus Driver,* Sy Travers, *Hotel Clerk,* Peter Scoppa, *Counter Man,* Virginia Smith, *Jan's Mother,* Jean Shevlin, *Lady on Bus,* Danny Klein, *Harry,* Martin Wolfson, *Candy Store Man,* Eugene Hobgood, *Mel,* David Pendleton, *Bar Patron,* William Gill, *Bartender,* Marilyn Randall, *Shirley,* Reuben Greene, *Franklyn.* R.

Superb gangster character study about friendship and trust. Nicky (John Cassavetes), an overbearing loudmouth, is marked by the mob and seeks the help of Mikey (Peter Falk), the only person he thinks he can trust. Elaine May, somewhat influenced by Cassavetes' directorial style, has fashioned a brilliant and powerful film noir, full of claustrophobia and paranoia. *Mikey and Nicky* is a showcase for the acting talents of Falk and Cassavetes as they totally dominate the film.

566 Minnie and Moskowitz (1971) ******** Universal, 115 min. *Dir* John Cassavetes, *Scr* John Cassavetes, *Cin* Alric Edens, Michael Margulies, Arthur J. Ornitz, *Ed* Fred Knudtson, *Mus* Bob Harwood, *Prod* Al Ruban.

Cast: Gena Rowlands, *Minnie Moore*, Seymour Cassel, *Seymour Moskowitz*, Val Avery, *Zelmo Swift*, Tim Carey, *Morgan Morgan*, Katherine Cassavetes, *Sheba Moskowitz*, Elizabeth Deering, *Girl*, Elsie Ames, *Florence*, Lady Rowlands, *Georgia Moore*, Holly Near, *Irish*, Judith Roberts, *Wife*, John Cassavetes, *Husband*, Jack Danskin, *Dick Henderson*, Eleanor Zee, *Mrs. Grass*, Sean Joyce, *Ned*, David Rowlands, *Minister*. PG.

Oddball comedy romance about two lonely people who have little in common. They meet when Moskowitz (Seymour Cassel), a parking lot attendant, comes to aid Minnie (Gena Rowlands) when her date tries to go too far. This was intended to be John Cassavetes' attempt at a commercial film, but despite its lighter tone *Minnie and Moskowitz* contains much of Cassavetes' stylistic eccentricities. This film demonstrates what a fine actor Cassel is, and how he has been shamefully ignored by the industry.

567 The Missouri Breaks (1976) ********* United Artists, 126 min. *Dir* Arthur Penn, *Scr* Thomas McGuane, *Cin* Michael Butler, *Ed* Dede Allen, Jerry Greenberg, Stephen Rotter, *Des* Albert Brenner, *Art* Stephen Berger, *Cos* Patricia Norris, *Mus* John Williams, *Prod* Elliot Kastner, Robert M. Sherman, *Assoc Prod* Marion Rosenberg.

Cast: Jack Nicholson, *Tom Logan*, Marlon Brando, *Lee Clayton*, Randy Quaid, *Little Tod*, Kathleen Lloyd, *Jane Braxton*, Frederic Forrest, *Cary*, Harry Dean Stanton, *Calvin*, John McLiam, *David Braxton*, John Ryan, *Si*, Sam Gilman, *Hank Rate*, Steve Franken, *Lonesome Kid*, Richard Bradford, *Pete Marker*, James Greene, *Hellsgate Rancher*, Luana Anders, *Rancher's Wife*, Danny Goldman, *Baggage Clerk*, Hunter Von Leer, *Sandy*, Virgil Frye, *Woody*, R.L. Armstrong, *Bob*, Dan Ades, *John Quinn*, Dorothy Newman, *Madame*, Charles Wagenheim, *Freighter*, Vern Chandler, *Vern*. PG. $7,000,000.

Brilliant, but eccentric western. Jack Nicholson, as the leader of a group of cattle rustlers, and Marlon Brando, as a psychotic bounty hunter hired to kill the rustlers, are superb in their only screen teaming. Arthur Penn, in one of his finest achievements, neatly blends straight western action, black humor and social commentary. *The Missouri Breaks* received almost unanimous condemnation from both the press and the public. This can be attributed to the fact that *The Missouri Breaks* completely defies expectations. The expected confrontations between Brando and Nicholson are almost nonexistent. Another reason is its downright weirdness. Brando changes disguises and accents throughout, and at one point he even appears in drag. Of course the whole thing is bizarre, but it does work. It is unfortunate that films that dare to be different are forced to wait years for acceptance. In the western genre a better film than this has never been made.

568 **Mr. Billion** (1977) ** 20th Century–Fox, 91 min. *Dir* Jonathan Kaplan, *Scr* Ken Friedman, Jonathan Kaplan, *Cin* Matthew F. Leonetti, *Ed* O. Nicholas Brown, *Art* Richard Berger, *Cos* Seth Banks, Stephanie Colin, Bill Jobe, Mal Pape, *Mus* Dave Grusin, *Prod* Stephen Bach, Ken Friedman.

   Cast: Terence Hill, *Guido*, Valerie Perrine, *Rosi*, Jackie Gleason, *John*, Slim Pickens, *Duane*, William Redfield, *Leopold*, Chill Wills, *Col. Winkle*, Dick Miller, *Bernie*, R.G. Armstrong, *Sheriff*, Dave Cass, *Boss Kidnapper*, Sam Laws, *Pops*, John Ray McGhee, *Carnell*, Kate Heflin, *Lucy*, Leo Rossi, *Italian Kidnapper*, Bob Minor, *Black Kidnapper*, Frances Heflin, *Mrs. Apple Pie*, Ralph Chesse, *Anthony*. PG.

   Fair chase comedy about an Italian mechanic (Terence Hill), who inherits a fortune. He must get to San Francisco to claim it, but his cross-country trip is more difficult than he expects. Jackie Gleason and Valerie Perrine, as swindlers, are just two of his problems. *Mr. Billion* could have been a good comedy, with its Capraesque premise, but it is nothing more than a series of chases.

569 **Mr. Majestyk** (1974) * United Artists, 103 min. *Dir* Richard Fleischer, *Scr* Elmore Leonard, *Cin* Richard H. Kline, *Ed* Ralph E. Winters, *Mus* Charles Bernstein, *Prod* Walter Mirisch.

   Cast: Charles Bronson, *Vince Majestyk*, Al Lettieri, *Frank Renda*, Linda Cristal, *Nancy Chavez*, Lee Purcell, *Wiley*, Paul Koslo, *Bobby Kopas*, Taylor Lacher, *Gene Lundy*, Frank Maxwell, *Detective McAllen*, Alejandro Rey, *Larry Mendoza*, Jordan Rhodes, *Sheriff Harold Ritchie*, Bert Santos, *Julio Tomaz*, Vern Porter, *Gas Station Attendant*. PG.

   Dim-witted thriller about a Mafia hit man who goes out of his way to kill a melon grower (Charles Bronson), who was responsible for his getting arrested. *Mr. Majestyk* begins by attempting to deal with the plight of migrant workers, but quickly sinks to a ridiculous chase film. The premise simply defies logic, as a professional killer would not risk everything on such a vendetta. The film's highlight is the shooting of a pile of watermelons.

570 **Mixed Company** (1974) ** United Artists, 109 min. *Dir* Melville Shavelson, *Scr* Mort Lachman, Melville Shavelson, *Cin* Stan Lazan, *Ed* Ralph James Hall, Walter Thompson, *Des* Stan Jolley, *Mus* Fred Karlin, *Prod* Melville Shavelson, *Assoc Prod* Mike Moder.

   Cast: Barbara Harris, *Kathy*, Joseph Bologna, *Peter*, Tom Bosley, *Al*, Lisa Gerritsen, *Liz*, Dorothy Shay, *Marge*, Ruth McDevitt, *Miss Bergguist*, Arianne Heller, *Mary*, Stephen Honanie, *Joe*, Haywood Nelson, *Freddie*, Eric Olson, *Rob*, Jina Tan, *Quan*, Bob G. Anthony, *Krause*, Roger Price, *Doctor*, Keith Hamilton, *Milton*. PG.

   Fair comedy about a couple (Barbara Harris, Joseph Bologna), who adopt three children of three different ethnic backgrounds, a black, a Vietnamese, and an American Indian. Having three children of their own already this menagerie naturally causes many complications, including bigotry in and out of the family. *Mixed Company* has an unusual premise, but its treatment is somewhat dull.

571 **The Molly Maguires** (1970) *** Paramount, 124 min. *Dir* Martin Ritt, *Scr* Walter Bernstein, *Cin* James Wong Howe, *Ed* Frank Bracht, *Art* Tambi Larsen (AN), *Cos* Dorothy Jeakins, *Mus* Henry Mancini, *Prod* Walter Bernstein, Martin Ritt.

Cast: Richard Harris, *James McParlan/McKenna*, Sean Connery, *Jack Kehoe*, Samantha Eggar, *Mary Raines*, Frank Finlay, *Davies*, Art Lund, *Frazier*, Anthony Costello, *Frank McAndrew*, Anthony Zerbe, *Dan Daugherty*, Phillip Bourneuf, *Father O'Connor*, Frances Heflin, *Mrs. Frazier*, Bethel Leslie, *Mrs. Kehoe*, Susan Goodman, *Mrs. McAndrew*, Brendan Dillon, *Old Man*, John Alderson, *Jenkins*, Malachy McCourt, *Bartender*, Peter Rogan, *Gomer James*, William Clune, *Franklin Gowen*, Philip Richards, *Gen. Charles Albright*, Karen Machon, *Girl at Football Game*. PG.

Fine historical drama loosely based on fact. Sean Connery stars as the leader of a group of disgruntled Irish coal miners, living in Pennsylvania during the 1870's, who turn to violence to get their point across. Richard Harris also stars as a Pinkerton detective, who infiltrates their secret organization. Unlike many films based on history, *The Molly Maguires* manages to be both dramatic and exciting.

572 **Moment by Moment** (1978) * Universal, 105 min. *Dir* Jane Wagner, *Scr* Jane Wagner, *Cin* Philip Lathrop, *Ed* John F. Burnett, *Des* Harry Horner, *Cos* Albert Wolsky, *Mus* Lee Holdridge, *Prod* Robert Stigwood, *Exec Prod* Kevin McCormick.

Cast: Lily Tomlin, *Trisha*, John Travolta, *Strip*, Andra Akers, *Naomi*, Bert Kramer, *Stu*, Shelley R. Bonus, *Peg*, Debra Feuer, *Stacie*, James Luisi, *Dan Santini*, John O'Leary, *Pharmacist*, Neil Flanagan, *Storekeeper*, Jarvais Hudson, *Gas Station Attendant*, Tom Slocum, *Band Leader*, Michael Consoldane, *Hotel Desk Clerk*, Jo Jordan, *Bookstore Lady*, Joseph Schwab, *Druggist*. R. $8,175,000.

A dismal and boring love story about a relationship between a lonely middle aged woman and a young beach bum. The fault lies in the poor script, which saddles Travolta with ridiculous dialogue, and a plot that never develops beyond Strip appearing and disappearing, forcing Trisha to lengthily search for him twice. It is sad to watch such talents as Tomlin and Travolta totally wasted. The motif of still photographs is used throughout, apparently to represent the film's pace.

573 **Monte Walsh** (1970) **** National General, 108 min. *Dir* William A. Fraker, *Scr* David Zelag Goodman, Lukas Heller, based on novel by Jack Warner Schaefer, *Cin* David M. Walsh, *Ed* Richard Brockway, Raymond Daniels, Gene Fowler, Jr., Robert L. Wolfe, *Des* Albert Brenner, *Cos* Albert Brenner, *Mus* John Barry, *Prod* Hal Landers, Bobby Roberts.

Cast: Lee Marvin, *Monte Walsh*, Jeanne Moreau, *Martine Bernard*, Jack Palance, *Chet Rollins*, Mitch Ryan, *Shorty Austin*, Jim Davis, *Cal Brennan*, Bear Hudkins, *Sonny Jacobs*, Ray Guth, *Sunfish Perkins*, John McKee, *Petey Williams*, Michael Conrad, *Dally Johnson*, Tom Heaton, *Sugar Wyman*, G.D. Spradlin, *Hat Henderson*, Ted Gehring, *Skimpy Eagans*, Bo Hopkins, *Jumpin' Joe Joslin*, Matt Clark, *Rufus Brady*, Billy "Green" Bush, *Powder Kent*, Allyn Ann McLerie, *Mary Eagle*, John McLiam, *Fightin' Joe Hooker*, Leroy Johnson, *Marshal*, Eric Christmas, *Col. Wilson*, Charles Tyner, *Doctor*. PG.

Excellent poetic western starring Lee Marvin as an aging cowboy in the late 1880's, who senses the death of the old west, but refuses to change with the times. *Monte Walsh* is a beautiful film that emphasizes mood and character over plot. This film is atypical of its genre, including an unusual barroom brawl done entirely in close-ups. Noted cinematographer William A. Fraker made a fine directorial debut.

574 Monty Python and the Holy Grail (1975) ******** Britain, Cinema 5, 90 min. *Dir* Terry Gilliam, Terry Jones, *Scr* Graham Chapman, John Cleese, Terry Gilliam, Eric Idle, Terry Jones, Michael Palin, *Cin* Terry Bedford, *Ed* John Hackney, *Mus* Neil Innes, *Additional Mus* De Wolfe, *Prod* Mark Forstater, *Exec Prod* John Goldstone.

Cast: Graham Chapman, John Cleese, Terry Gilliam, Eric Idle, Terry Jones, Michael Palin, Connie Booth, Carol Cleveland, John Young. PG. $5,170,000.

Hysterically funny first film from the six man English comedy troupe Monty Python's Flying Circus. *Monty Python and the Holy Grail* is a send up of medievel times and chivalry, with the group's usual abundance of anachronisms and puns. As in the case of their BBC television the jokes are hit and miss, but those that hit can be quite incredible and perceptive.

575 Monty Python's Life of Brian (1979) ******* Warner Bros., 93 min. *Dir* Terry Jones, *Scr* Graham Chapman, John Cleese, Terry Gilliam, Eric Idle, Terry Jones, Michael Palin, *Cin* Peter Biziou, *Ed* Julian Doyle, *Des and Animation* Terry Gilliam, *Art* Roger Christian, *Cos* Charles Knode, Hazel Pethig, *Mus* Geoffrey Burgon, *Prod* John Goldstone, *Exec Prod* George Harrison, Denis O'Brien, *Assoc Prod* Tim Hampton.

Cast: Graham Chapman, *Brian*, Terry Jones, *Mandy, Mother of Brian*, Ken Colley, *Jesus*, Graham Chapman, John Cleese, Michael Palin, *Wisemen*, Michael Palin, *Mr. Big Nose*, Gwen Taylor, *Mrs. Big Nose*, Eric Idle, *Mr. Cheeky*, Terrence Bayler, *Gregory*, Carol Cleveland, *Mrs. Gregory*, Terry Gilliam, Charles McKeown, *Men Further Forward*, Michael Palin, *Francis*, John Cleese, *Reg*, Eric Idle, *Stan, called Loretta*, Sue Jones-Davis, *Judith*, Eric Idle, *Harry the Haggler*, Gwen Taylor, *Woman with Sick Donkey*, John Young, *Matthias*, Bernard McKenna, Andrew MacLachlin, *Stoner's Helpers*, Neil Innes, *Weedy Samaritan*, John Case, *Gladiator*, George Harrison, *Mr. Papadopoulis*. R. $10,100,000.

Controversial comedy that pokes fun at religion and the Bible. Monty Python's Flying Circus was predictably condemned by every religious group imaginable for this tale of a man, named Brian, who was born at the time of Christ and is mistaken for the Messiah. There are many bizarre and humorous moments, but *The Life of Brian* is not as witty as their first feature film, *Monty Python and the Holy Grail*.

576 Moonraker (1979) ******* Britain, United Artists, 126 min. *Dir* Lewis Gilbert, *Scr* Christopher Wood, based on novel by Ian Fleming, *Cin* Jean Tournier, *Ed* John Glen, *Des* Ken Adam, *Art* Charles Bishop, Max Douy, *Cos* Jacques Fonteray, *Sp* John Evans, Derek Meddings, Paul Wilson (AN), *Mus* John Barry, *Lyrics* Hal David, *Prod* Albert R. Broccoli, *Exec Prod* Michael G. Wilson, *Assoc Prod* William P. Cartlidge.

Cast: Roger Moore, *James Bond*, Lois Chiles, *Holly Goodhead*, Michel Lonsdale, *Drax*, Richard Kiel, *Jaws*, Corinne Clery, *Corinne Dufour*, Bernard Lee, *"M"*, Geoffrey Keen, *Frederick Gray*, Desmond Llewelyn, *"Q"*, Lois Maxwell, *Miss Moneypenny*, Emily Bolton, *Manuela*, Toshiro Suga, *Chang*, Blanche Ravalec, *Dolly*, Jean-Pierre Castaldi, *Pilot Private Jet*, Leila Shenna,

Hostess Private Jet, Walter Gotell, *Gen. Gogol*, Arthur Howard, *Cavendish*, Irka Bochenko, *Blonde Beauty*, Michael Marshall, *Col. Scott*, Douglas Lambert, *Mission Control Director*, Alfie Bass, *Consumptive Italian*. PG. $33,935,000. See *Diamonds are Forever*.

577 More American Graffiti (1979) *** Universal, 111 min. *Dir* B.W.L. Norton, *Scr* B.W.L. Norton, based on characters created by George Lucas, *Cin* Caleb Deschanel, *Ed* Tina Hirsch, *Art* Ray Storey, *Cos* Agnes Rodgers, *Prod* Howard Kazanjian, *Exec Prod* George Lucas.

Cast: Candy Clark, *Debbie Dunham*, Bo Hopkins, *Little Joe*, Ron Howard, *Steve Bolander*, Paul LeMat, *John Milner*, Mackenzie Phillips, *Carol Rainbow*, Charles Martin Smith, *Terry the Toad*, Cindy Williams, *Laurie Bolander*, Ann Bjorn, *Eva*, Richard Bradford, *Major Creech*, John Brent, *Ralph*, Country Joe McDonald, *Country Joe*, Scott Glenn, *Newt*, James Houghton, *Sinclair*, John Lansing, *Lance*, Manuel Padilla, *Carlos*, Ken Place, *Beckwith*, Mary Kay Place, *Teensa*, Tom Ruben, *Eric*, Doug Sahm, *Bobbie*. PG. $9,775,000. See *American Graffiti*.

578 Mother Jugs & Speed (1976) ** 20th Century–Fox, 95 min. *Dir* Peter Yates, *Scr* Tom Mankiewicz, *Story* Stephen Manes, Tom Mankiewicz, *Cin* Ralph Woolsey, *Ed* Frank P. Keller, *Des* Walter Scott Herndon, *Prod* Tom Mankiewicz, Peter Yates, *Exec Prod* Joseph R. Barbera.

Cast: Bill Cosby, *Mother*, Raquel Welch, *Jugs*, Harvey Keitel, *Speed*, Allen Garfield (Goorwitz), *Harry Fishbine*, Larry Hagman, *Murdoch*, L.Q. Jones, *Davey*, Bruce Davison, *LeRoy*, Dick Butkus, *Rodeo*, Milt Kamen, *Barney*, Barra Grant, *Miss Crocker*, Allen Warnick, *Bliss*, Valerie Curtin, *Naomi Fishbine*, Ric Carrott, *Harvey*, Severn Darden, *Moran*, Bill Henderson, *Charles Taylor*, Mike McManus, *Walker*, Toni Basil, *Addict*, Edwin Mills, *Addict's Doctor*, Erica Hagen, *Massage Girl*, Arnold Williams, *Albert*, Charles Knapp, *Man with Zipper*, Linda Geray, *Pregnant Woman*. PG. $7,630,000.

Tasteless black comedy about ambulance drivers, who work for a second-rate ambulance company run by Allen Garfield. *Mother Jugs & Speed* is yet another poor attempt at a M*A*S*H style episodic comedy that uncomfortably alternates between humor and tragedy, and doing neither very well. The film is badly structured, and it almost completely falls apart if not for some good comic performances.

579 Move (1970) ** 20th Century–Fox, 90 min. *Dir* Stuart Rosenberg, *Scr* Stanley Hart, Joel Lieber, based on novel by Joel Lieber, *Cin* William H. Daniels, *Ed* Rita Roland, *Art* Philip Jefferies, Jack Martin Smith, *Cos* Anthea Sylbert, *Mus* Marvin Hamlisch, *Prod* Pandro S. Berman, *Assoc Prod* Kathryn Hereford.

Cast: Elliott Gould, *Hiram Jaffe*, Paula Prentiss, *Dolly*, Genevieve Waite, *Girl*, John Larch, *Mounted Patrolman*, Joe Silver, *Oscar*, Graham Jarvis, *Dr. Picker*, Ron O'Neal, *Peter*, Garrie Beau, *Andrea*, David Burns, *Doorman*, Richard Bull, *Keith*, Mae Questal, *Mrs. Katz*, Aly Wassil, *Gupta*, John Wheeler, *Brown Package*, Rudy Bond, *Detective Sawyer*, Yvonne D'Angiers, *Jeanine*, Amy Thompson, *Miss Landry*, Roger Bowen, *Rabbi*, Stanley Adams, *New Tenant*. R.

Unusual surrealistic comedy about urban paranoia, focusing on a couple (Elliott Gould, Paula Prentiss) and all the problems they encounter by moving from one apartment to another. The premise is far too thin for a feature film, and *Move* might have succeeded as a short. Instead it is stretched out of proportion with completely worthless scenes.

580 **Movie Movie** (1978) **** Warner Bros., 105 min. *Dir* Stanley Donen, *Scr* Larry Gelbart, Sheldon Keller, *Cin* Charles Rosher, Jr. (Dynamite Hands), Bruce Surtees (Baxter's Beauties of 1933), *Ed* George Hively, *Art* Jack Fisk, *Cos* Patricia Norris, *Mus* Ralph Burns, *Lyrics* Larry Gelbart, Sheldon Keller, *Chor* Michael Kidd (Baxter's Beauties of 1933), *Prod* Stanley Donen, *Exec Prod* Martin Starger.

Cast: (Dynamite Hands): George C. Scott, *Gloves Malloy*, Trish Van Devere, *Betsy McGuire*, Harry Hamlin, *Joey Popchik*, Red Buttons, *Peanuts*, Eli Wallach, *Vince Marlowe*, Ann Reinking, *Troubles Moran*, Jocelyn Brando, *Mama Popchik*, Michael Kidd, *Pop Popchik*, Kathleen Beller, *Angie Popchik*, Barry Bostwick, *Johnny Danko*, Art Carney, *Dr. Blaine*, Clay Hodges, *Sailor Lawson*, George P. Wilbur, *Tony Norton*, Peter T. Stader, *Barney Keegle*, (Baxter's Beauties of 1933): George C. Scott, *Spats Baxter*, Barbara Harris, *Trixie Lane*, Barry Bostwick, *Dick Cummings*, Trish Van Devere, *Isobel Stuart*, Red Buttons, *Jinks Murphy*, Eli Wallach, *Pop*, Rebecca York, *Kitty*, Art Carney, *Dr. Bowers*, Maidie Norman, *Gussie*, Jocelyn Brando, *Mrs. Updike*, Charles Lane, *Pennington*, Barney Martin, *Motorcycle Cop*, Dick Winslow, *Tinkle Johnson*, Sebastian Brook, *Fritz*, Jerry Von Hoeltke, *Theatre Workman*, Paula Jones, *Chorus Girl*, John Henry, *Chorus Boy*, John Hudkins, Robert Herron, *Movers*. PG.

Wonderful campy parody of old movies of the 1930's. More than just a movie, this is designed to be a night out at the movies, complete with a double feature and even previews of coming attractions. The two features are a musical spoof of the extravagant Busby Berkely musicals, particularly the Golddiggers films, and a boxing film with all the clichés and stereotypes anyone would want.

581 **The Muppet Movie** (1979) *** Associated Film Distribution, 98 min. *Dir* James Frawley, *Scr* Jack Burns, Jerry Juhl, *Cin* Isidore Mankofsky, *Ed* Chris Greenbury, *Des* Joel Schiller, *Art* Les Gobruegge, *Cos* Gwen Carpetanos, *Cos (Muppets)* Calista Hendrickson, *Mus* Kenny Ascher, Paul Williams (AN), *Song* "The Rainbow Connection," *Mus* Kenny Ascher, Paul Williams (AN), *Prod* Jim Henson, *Co-Prod* David Lazer, *Exec Prod* Martin Starger, Presented by Sir Lew Grade.

Cast: Jim Henson, *Kermit the Frog/Rowlf/Dr. Teeth/Waldorf*, Frank Oz, *Miss Piggy/Fozzie Bear/Animal/Sam the Eagle*, Jerry Nelson, *Floyd Pepper/Crazy Harry/Robin the Frog/Lew Zealand*, Richard Hunt, *Scooter/Statler/Janice/Sweetums/Beaker*, David Goelz, *The Great Gonzo/Zoot/Dr. Bunsen Honeydew*, Charles Durning, *Doc Hooper*, Austin Pendleton, *Max*, Scott Walker, *Frog Killer*. Also featuring: Edgar Bergen, Milton Berle, Mel Brooks, James Coburn, Dom DeLuise, Elliott Gould, Bob Hope, Madeline Kahn, Cloris Leachman, Steve Martin, Richard Pryor, Telly Savalas, Orson Welles, Paul Williams. G. $32,000,000.

Surprisingly witty film featuring the Muppets, the famous television puppet group. The bare storyline features Kermit the Frog, who ventures to Hollywood to become a star. *The Muppet Movie* details his journey, in which he meets all sorts of odd characters, both muppets and humans. This film has equal appeal to adults, due to its intelligent script, and it has much of the charm of *The Wizard of Oz*.

582 Murder by Death (1976) *** Columbia, 94 min. *Dir* Robert Moore, *Scr* Neil Simon, *Cin* David M. Walsh, *Ed* Margaret Booth, *Des* Stephen Grimes, *Cos* Ann Roth, *Mus* Dave Grusin, *Prod* Ray Stark, *Assoc Prod* Roger M. Rothstein.

Cast: Eileen Brennan, *Tess Skeffington*, Truman Capote, *Lional Twain*, James Coco, *Milo Perier*, Peter Falk, *Sam Diamond*, Alec Guinness, *Bensonmum*, Elsa Lanchester, *Jessica Marbles*, David Niven, *Dick Charleston*, Peter Sellers, *Sidney Wang*, Maggie Smith, *Dora Charleston*, Nancy Walker, *Yetta*, Estelle Winwood, *Miss Withers*, James Cromwell, *Marcel*, Richard Narita, *Willie Wang*. PG. $22,000,000.

Above average Neil Simon spoof of detective films. Rather than using only one detective, Simon has created humorous counterparts for Sam Spade, Hercule Poirot, Charlie Chan, Miss Marple and Nick and Nora Charles and throws them together to solve the same murder mystery. *Murder By Death* contains one of Simon's funniest and wittiest scripts with an intentionally confusing plotline that is impossible to decipher.

583 Murder by Decree (1979) *** Canada/Britain, Avco Embassy, 121 min. *Dir* Bob Clark, *Scr* John Hopkins, *Story* Bob Clark, *Cin* Reg Morris, *Ed* Stan Cole, *Des* Harry Pottle, *Cos* Judy Moorcroft, *Prod* Bob Clark, Renee Dupont, *Exec Prod* Len Herberman.

Cast: Christopher Plummer, *Sherlock Holmes*, James Mason, *Dr. Watson*, Donald Sutherland, *Robert Lees*, Genevieve Bujold, *Annie Crook*, David Hemmings, *Inspector Foxborough*, Susan Clark, *Mary Kelly*, Anthony Quayle, *Sir Charles Warren*, John Gielgud, *Lord Salisbury*, Frank Finlay, *Inspector Lestrade*. PG.

Interesting Sherlock Holmes film, in which the famous sleuth investigates Jack the Ripper. *Murder by Decree* has its problems. It is too long, and it tends to wander a bit, plus there is far too much talk, although that is typical of the genre. Where the film does succeed is in the wonderful casting of Christopher Plummer and James Mason as Holmes and Watson, both of whom compare favorably to Basil Rathbone and Nigel Bruce.

584 Murder on the Orient Express (1974) *** Britain, Paramount, 128 min. *Dir* Sidney Lumet, *Scr* Paul Dehn (AN), based on novel by Agatha Christie, *Cin* Geoffrey Unsworth (AN), *Ed* Anne V. Coates, *Des* Tony Walton, *Art* Jack Stephens, *Cos* Tony Walton (AN), *Mus* Richard Rodney Bennett (AN, BFA), *Prod* John Brabourne, Richard Goodwin.

Cast: Albert Finney (AN), *Hercule Poirot*, Lauren Bacall, *Mrs. Hubbard*, Martin Balsam, *Bianchi*, Ingrid Bergman (A, BFA), *Greta Ohlsson*, Jacqueline Bisset, *Countess Andrenyi*, Jean-Pierre Cassel, *Pierre Paul Michel*, Sean Connery, *Col. Arbuthnot*, John Gielgud (BFA), *Beddoes*, Wendy Hiller, *Princess Dragomiroff*, Anthony Perkins, *Hector McQueen*, Vanessa Redgrave, *Mary Debenham*, Rachel Roberts, *Hildegarde Schmidt*, Richard Widmark, *Ratchett*, Michael York, *Count Andrenyi*, Colin Blakely, *Hardman*, George Coulouris, *Dr. Constantine*, Denis Quilley, *Foscarelli*, Vernon Dobtcheff, *Concierge*, Jeremy Lloyd, *A.D.C.*, John Moffatt, *Chief Attendant*. PG. $19,125,000.

Interesting mystery whodunit about a man with a dark past (Richard Widmark), who is found murdered aboard the famous train, which has an overabundance of suspects. *Murder on the Orient Express* is a typical Agatha Christie story with a trick ending. The acting is good, but below the standards of Lumet's films, with one exception. Albert Finney gives an outstanding performance as the eccentric Belgian detective, Hercule Poirot. The follow up *Death on the Nile* is generally as good as the first, but Peter Ustinov cannot compare with Finney as Poirot.

585 **Murphy's War** (1971) *** Britain, Paramount, 106 min. *Dir* Peter Yates, *Scr* Stirling Silliphant, based on novel by Max Catto, *Cin* Douglas Slocombe, *Ed* John Glen, Frank P. Keller, *Des* Disley Jones, *Mus* John Barry, Ken Thorne, *Prod* Micheal Deeley.

Cast: Peter O'Toole, *Murphy*, Sian Phillips, *Dr. Hayden*, Philippe Noiret, *Louis Brezan*, Horst Janson, *Kapitan Lauchs*, John Hallam, *Lt. Ellis*, Ingo Mogendorf, *Lt. Voght*. PG.

Unusual WWII drama starring Peter O'Toole as an Irish aviation mechanic, who is the sole surviving crew member of a British merchant ship that was ruthlessly attacked by a German U-boat. After his recovery, he declares war on the submarine and fights it single-handedly. O'Toole gives a superb performance as the obsessed man, but the film tends to be slow and unexciting.

586 **The Music Lovers** (1971) *** Britain, United Artists, 122 min. *Dir* Ken Russell, *Scr* Melvyn Bragg, based on book *Beloved Friend* by Catherine Drinker Bowen, Barbara Von Meck, *Cin* Douglas Slocombe, *Ed* Michael Bradshell, *Des* Natasha Kroll, *Art* Michael Knight, *Cos* Shirley Russell, *Chor* Terry Gilbert, *Prod* Ken Russell, *Exec Prod* Roy Baird.

Cast: Richard Chamberlain, *Peter Tchaikovsky*, Glenda Jackson, *Nina Milyukova*, Max Adrian, *Nicholas Rubenstein*, Christopher Gable, *Count Anton Chiluvsky*, Kenneth Colley, *Modeste*, Izabella Telezynska, *Madame von Meck*, Maureen Pryor, *Nina's Mother*, Sabina Maydelle, *Sasha Tchaikovsky*, Andrew Faulds, *Davidov*, Bruce Robinson, *Alexei*, Ben Aris, *Young Lieutenant*, Xavier Russell, *Koyola*, Dennis Myers, *Vladimir von Meck*, John Myers, *Anatole von Meck*. R.

Unusual biography of Russian composer Peter Tchaikovsky (Richard Chamberlain), focusing on his marriage to a domineering woman (Glenda Jackson) in an unsuccessful attempt to hide his homosexuality. *The Music Lovers* is the first of Ken Russell's notorious feature film biographies of composers, in which the director defies convention by visually exaggerating details and episodes of their lives.

587 **Mustang Country** (1976) * Universal, 79 min. *Dir* John Champion, *Scr* John Champion, *Cin* J. Barry Herron, *Ed* Douglas Robertson, *Mus* Lee Holdridge, *Prod* John Champion.

Cast: Joel McCrea, *Dan*, Robert Fuller, *Griff*, Patrick Wayne, *Tee Jay*, Nika Mina, *Nika*. G.

Boring family western starring Joel McCrea as an ex-rancher and rodeo cowboy who, with the help of an Indian boy, hunts for a wild stallion. It is hard to believe that McCrea would have come out of retirement for this dismal film. The director and writer, John Champion, obviously had great difficulty stretching this idea to a feature length film and he filled *Mustang Country* with endless dialogue and beautiful scenery.

588 **Myra Breckinridge** (1970) * 20th Century–Fox, 94 min. *Dir* Michael Sarne, *Scr* David Giler, Michael Sarne, based on novel by Gore Vidal, *Cin* Richard Moore, *Ed* Danford B. Greene, *Art* Fred Harpin, *Cos* Edith Head, Theadora Van Runkle, *Mus* Lionel Newman, *Chor* Ralph Beaumont, *Prod* Robert Fryer.

Cast: Raquel Welch, *Myra,* John Huston, *Buck Loner,* Mae West, *Leticia,* Rex Reed, *Young Man,* Farrah Fawcett, *Mary Ann,* Roger C. Carmel, *Dr. Montag,* Roger Herren, *Rusty,* George Furth, *Charlie Flager, Jr.,* Calvin Lockhart, *Irving Amadeus,* Jim Backus, *Doctor,* John Carradine, *Surgeon,* Andy Devine, *Coyote Bill,* Grady Sutton, *Kid Barlow,* Robert Lieb, *Charlie Flager, Sr.,* Skip Ward, *Chance,* Kathleen Freeman, *Bobby Dean Loner,* B.S. Pully, *Tex,* Buck Kartalian, *Jeff,* Monty Landis, *Vince,* Tom Selleck, *Stud,* Peter Ireland, *Student,* Nelson Sardelli, *Mario.* X.

Disgraceful film about a man who goes to Copenhagen for a sex change, and then poses as his widow to gain his/her inheritance. *Myra Breckinridge* is a total travesty and nearly defies description. It is difficult to imagine what was on the minds of the makers of this mess, which must certainly rank as one of the worst films ever made.

589 **Nashville** (1975) (AN, NS, NY, NB) ***** Paramount, 159 min. *Dir* Robert Altman (AN, NS, NY, NB), *Scr* Joan Tewkesbury, *Cin* Paul Lohmann, *Ed* Dennis Hill, Sidney Levin, *Cos* Jules Melillo, *Mus* Richard Baskin, *Song* "I'm Easy", *Mus* Keith Carradine (A, G), *Prod* Robert Altman, *Exec Prod* Martin Starger, Jerry Weintraub, *Assoc Prod* Scott Bushnell, Robert Eggenweiler.

Cast: David Arkin, *Norman,* Barbara Baxley, *Lady Pearl,* Ned Beatty, *Delbert Reese,* Karen Black, *Connie White,* Ronee Blakely (AN, NB), *Barbara Jean,* Timothy Brown, *Tommy Brown,* Keith Carradine, *Tom Frank,* Geraldine Chaplin, *Opal,* Robert Doqui, *Wade,* Shelley Duvall, *L.A. Joan,* Allen Garfield (Goorwitz), *Barnett,* Henry Gibson (NS), *Haven Hamilton,* Scott Glenn, *Pfc. Glenn Kelly,* Jeff Goldblum, *Tricycle Man,* Barbara Harris, *Albuquerque,* David Hayward, *Kenny Fraiser,* Michael Murphy, *John Triplette,* Alan Nicholls, *Bill,* Dave Peel, *Bud Hamilton,* Christina Raines, *Mary,* Bert Remsen, *Star,* Lily Tomlin (AN, NS, NY), *Linnea Reese,* Gwen Welles, *Sueleen Gay,* Keenan Wynn, *Mr. Green,* James Dan Calvert, *Jimmy Reese,* Donna Denton, *Donna Reese,* Merle Kilgore, *Trout,* Carol McGinnis, *Jewel,* Richard Baskin, *Frog,* Sheila Bailey, Patti Bryant, *Smokey Mountain Laurel,* Elliott Gould, Julie Christie, Jonnie Barnett, Vassar Clements, Misty Mountain Boys, Sue Barton, *Themselves.* R. $8,745,000.

Splendid dramatic-musical focusing on the preparations for a rally for a Presidential candidate to be held in Nashville, and the two dozen characters involved, many of whom are country singers. Robert Altman brilliantly interweaves these characters into one masterful kaleidescope and manages to breathe life into all of them. There are many extraordinary performances, particularly those of Ronee Blakely, Henry Gibson, Gwen Welles and Lily Tomlin. Although the film has wall-to-wall country music, one can hate the music and still appreciate the film.

590 Nasty Habits (1977) ** Britain, Brut, 91 min. *Dir* Michael Lindsay-Hogg, *Scr* Robert J. Enders, based on novel *The Abbess of Crewe* by Muriel Spark, *Cin* Douglas Slocombe, *Ed* Peter Tanner, *Art* Robert Jones, *Mus* John Cameron, *Prod* Robert J. Enders, *Exec Prod* George Barrie.

Cast: Glenda Jackson, *Alexandra*, Melina Mercouri, *Gertrude*, Geraldine Page, *Walburga*, Sandy Dennis, *Winifred*, Ann Jackson, *Mildred*, Anne Meara, *Geraldine*, Susan Penhaligon, *Felicity*, Edith Evans, *Hildegarde*, Jerry Stiller, *Priest*, Rip Torn, *Maximilian*, Eli Wallach, *Monsignor*, Suzanna Stone, *Bathildis*, Peter Bromilow, *Baudouin*, Shane Rimmer, *Officer*, Harry Ditson, *Ambrose*, Chris Muncke, *Gregory*. PG.

Disappointing comedy set in a corrupt Philadelphia convent. *Nasty Habits* is a thinly disguised allegory for the Watergate scandal, starring Glenda Jackson as Sister Alexandra an obvious counterpart for President Nixon and with other nuns representing Ford, Kissinger, Dean, etc. This is basically a one-joke movie that wears out very early, because its course and plot are predictable for obvious reasons.

591 National Lampoon's Animal House (1978) **** Universal, 109 min. *Dir* John Landis, *Scr* Douglas Kenney, Chris Miller, Harold Ramis, *Cin* Charles Correll, *Ed* George Folsey, Jr., *Art* John J. Lloyd, *Cos* Deborah Nadoolman, *Prod* Ivan Reitman, Matty Simmons.

Cast: Tim Matheson, *Eric Stratton*, John Belushi, *John Blutarsky*, Peter Riegert, *Donald Schoenstein*, Thomas Hulce, *Larry Kroger*, Stephen Furst, *Kent Dorfman*, Karen Allen, *Katy*, Bruce McGill, *Daniel Simpson Day*, James Widdoes, *Robert Hoover*, John Vernon, *Dean Vernon Wormer*, Cesare Danova, *Mayor Carmine DePasto*, Verna Bloom, *Marion Wormer*, Sarah Holcomb, *Clorette DePasto*, Donald Sutherland, *Dave Jennings*, Mark Metcalf, *Doug Neidermeyer*, James Daughton, *Greg Marmalard*, Mary Louise Weller, *Mandy Pepperidge*, Martha Smith, *Babs Jansen*. R. $74,000,000.

Hysterically funny, but sometimes tasteless comedy, about the adventures of the members of Faber College's worst fraternity and the college's attempt to rid itself of their presence. *National Lampoon's Animal House* is filled with many wonderful comic set pieces and sight gags, but it is flawed by its construction, which could have been tightened up a bit. Although this film is almost cartoonish in concept it does succeed in bringing its many irreverent characters to life.

592 The Nelson Affair (1973) ** Britain, Universal, 118 min. *Dir* James Cellan Jones, *Scr* Terence Rattigan, based on his play *A Bequest to the Nation* *Cin* Gerry Fisher, *Ed* Anne V. Coates, *Des* Carmen Dillon, *Art* Jack Stephens, *Mus* Michel Legrand, *Prod* Hal B. Wallis.

Cast: Glenda Jackson, *Lady Hamilton*, Peter Finch, *Lord Nelson*, Michael Jayston, *Capt. Hardy*, Anthony Quayle, *Lord Minto*, Margaret Leighton, *Lady Nelson*, Dominic Guard, *George Matcham, Jr.*, Nigel Stock, *George Matcham, Sr.*, Barbara Leigh-Hunt, *Catherine Matcham*, Roland Culver, *Lord Barham*, Andre Maranne, *Adm. Villeneuve*, Richard Mathews, *Rev. William Nelson*, Liz Ashley, *Sarah Nelson*, John Nolan, *Capt. Blackwood*. PG.

Fair historical drama about the romance of Lord Nelson (Peter Finch) and Lady Hamilton (Glenda Jackson), and the problems that ensue from this relationship. *The Nelson Affair* is based on a play and it does not transfer well to film. There is far too much reliance on talk, although well handled by Finch and Jackson, it does not serve the story well.

593 The Neptune Factor (1973) * Canada, 98 min. *Dir* Daniel Petrie, *Scr* Jack DeWitt, *Cin* Harry Makin, *Underwater Cin* Lamar Boren, Paul Herberman, *Ed* Stan Cole, *Des* Jack McAdam, Dennis Lynton Clark, *Mus* William McCauley, Lalo Schifrin, *Prod* Sanford Howard, *Exec Prod* Harold Greenberg, David M. Perlmutter.

Cast: Ben Gazzara, *Blake*, Yvette Mimieux, *Leah*, Walter Pidgeon, *Andrews*, Ernest Borgnine, *Mack*, Chris Wiggens, *Captain*, Donnelly Rhodes, *Bob*, Ed McGibbon, *Norton*, Michael J. Reynolds, *Hal*, David Yorkston, *Stephens*, Stuart Gillard, *Bradley*, Mark Walker, *Moulton*, Kenneth Pogue, *Thomas*, Frank Perry, *Sub Captain*, Dan MacDonald, *Hobbs*, Leslie Carlson, *Briggs*, David Renton, *Warrent Officer*, Joan Gregson, *Dobson*, Dave Mann, Hawks, Kay Fujiwara, *Anita*, Richard Whelan, *Radio Officer*. G.

Dim-witted undersea science-fiction adventure. An underwater laboratory at the bottom of the ocean, becomes trapped in a crevasse following an earthquake. A team of rescuers sent to save them stumbles onto an undersea world of giant fish. The film has almost nothing to recommend; the plot is juvenile, the characters are shallow stereotypes and the cast overacts. Other titles, *An Underwater Odyssey* and *The Neptune Disaster*.

594 Network (1976) (AN, LA) **** United Artists, 121 min. *Dir* Sidney Lumet (AN, G, LA), *Scr* Paddy Chayefsky (A, NY, G, LA, W), *Cin* Owen Roizman (AN), *Ed* Alan Heim (AN), *Des* Philip Rosenberg, *Cos* Theoni V. Aldredge, *Mus* Elliot Lawrence, *Prod* Howard Gottfried, *Assoc Prod* Fred Caruso.

Cast: Faye Dunaway (A, G), *Diana Christensen*, William Holden (AN), *Max Schumacher*, Peter Finch (A, G, BFA), *Howard Beale*, Robert Duvall, *Frank Hackett*, Ned Beatty (AN), *Arthur Jensen*, Beatrice Straight (A), *Louise Schumacher*, William Prince, *Edward George Ruddy*, Wesley Addy, *Nelson Chaney*, Arthur Burghardt, *Great Ahmed Kahn*, Bill Burrows, *TV Director*, Kathy Cronkite, *Mary Ann Gilford*, Darryl Hickman, *Bill Herron*, Roy Poole, *Sam Haywood*, Marlene Warfield, *Laureen Hobbs*, Lee Richardson, *Narrator*. R. $13,685,000.

Wildly savage attack on the television medium. A TV news anchorman threatens suicide on the air when his show is canceled, and the network exploits his madness and turns him into a national celebrity. *Network* is more than just a film about television, as it is an allegory for big business and their cutthroat tactics. The film is bombastic and at times too preachy, but Sidney Lumet surprisingly keeps Paddy Chayefsky's incredible and outlandish script from going over the edge and brings out superb performances from the entire cast.

595 The New Centurions (1972) ** Columbia, 103 min. *Dir* Richard Fleischer, *Scr* Stirling Silliphant, based on novel by Joseph Wambaugh, *Cin* Ralph Woolsey, *Ed* Robert C. Jones, *Des* Boris Levin, *Cos* Guy Verhille, *Mus* Quincy Jones, *Prod* Robert Chartoff, Irwin Winkler, *Assoc Prod* Henry Gellis.

Cast: George C. Scott, *Kilvinsky*, Stacy Keach, *Roy*, Jane Alexander, *Dorothy*, Scott Wilson, *Gus*, Rosalind Cash, *Lorrie*, Erik Estrada, *Sergio*, Clifton James, *Whitey*, Richard Kalk, *Milton*, James Sikking, *Sgt. Anders*, Beverly

Hope Atkinson, *Alice*, Burke Byrnes, *Phillips*, Mittie Lawrence, *Gloria*, Isabel Sanford, *Wilma*, William Atherton, *Johnson*, Peter DeAnda, *Gladstone*, Ed Lauter, *Galloway*, Dolph Sweet, *Sgt. Runyon*, Stefan Gierasch, *Landlord*, Carol Speed, *Martha*, Tracee Lyles, *Helen*, Debbie Fresh, *Rebecca*, Michael Lane, *Lumberjack*, Roger E. Mosley, *Truck Driver*, Charles H. Gray, *Bethel*, Read Morgan, *Woodrow Gandy*, Michael DeLano, *Ranatti*, Pepe Serna, *Young Mexican*, Bea Thompkins, *Silverpants*, Hilly Hicks, *Young Black*. R. $7,450,000.

Disappointing drama about contemporary policemen and their every day existence, focusing on two cops; a disillusioned veteran (George C. Scott) and an idealistic rookie (Stacy Keach). The film tries to realistically examine the hardships and pressures of the job, but it throws in a few action sequences when things become dull. *The New Centurions* plays more like a television film.

596 **A New Leaf** (1971) *** Paramount, 102 min. *Dir* Elaine May, *Scr* Elaine May, based on short story *The Green Heart* by Jack Ritchie, *Cin* Gayne Pescher, *Ed* Donald Guidice, Frederick Steinkamp, *Des* Richard Fried, *Art* Warren Clymer, *Cos* Anthea Sylbert, *Prod* Joe Manduke, *Assoc Prod* Florence Nerlinger.

Cast: Walter Matthau, *Henry Graham*, Elaine May, *Henrietta Lowell*, Jack Weston, *Andrew McPherson*, George Rose, *Harold*, William Redfield, *Beckett*, James Coco, *Uncle Harry*, Graham Jarvis, *Bo*, Doris Roberts, *Mrs. Taggart*, Rose Arrick, *Gloria Cunliffe*, Renee Taylor, *Sally Hart*, Mildred Clinton, *Mrs. Heinrich*, Marc Gordon, *John*, Fred Stewart, *Mr. Van Rensaeller*, David Doyle, *Mel*, Jess Osuna, *Frank*, Ida Berlin, *Maid*, Carol Morley, *Girl at Charity Ball*. G.

Disappointing black comedy about a broke playboy (Walter Matthau) who marries a rich klutzy woman (Elaine May) for her money and then plots to murder her. *A New Leaf* is the first American film to have a woman as its director, writer and star, but May disowned the film after it was taken from her by Paramount and re-edited. This may account for the uninspired plot, but the wonderful comic performances of the two leads make this worthwhile, anyway.

597 **New York, New York** (1977) ***** United Artists, 155 min. *Dir* Martin Scorsese, *Scr* Earl MacRauch, Mardik Martin, *Story* Earl MacRauch, *Cin* Laszlo Kovacs, *Ed* Irving Lerner, B. Lovitt, Marcia Lucas, Tom Rolf, *Des* Boris Leven, *Art* Harry R. Kremm, *Cos* Theodora Van Runkle, *Songs* Fred Ebb, John Kander, *Mus Supervision* Ralph Burns, *Chor* Ron Field, *Prod* Robert Chartoff, Irwin Winkler, *Assoc Prod* Gene Kirkwood.

Cast: Robert De Niro, *Jimmy Doyle*, Liza Minnelli, *Francine Evans*, Lionel Stander, *Tony Harwell*, Barry Primus, *Paul Wilson*, Mary Kay Place, *Bernice*, Georgie Auld, *Frankie Harte*, George Memmoli, *Nicky*, Dick Miller, *Palm Club Owner*, Murray Moston, *Horace Morris*, Lenny Gaines, *Artie Kirks*, Clarence Clemons, *Cecil Powell*, Kathi McGinnis, *Ellen Flannery*, Norman Palmer, *Desk Clerk*, Adam Winkler, *Jimmy Doyle, Jr.*, Dimitri Logothetis, *Desk Clerk*, Frank Sivera, *Eddie Di Muzio*, Diahnne Abbott, *Harlem Club Singer*, Joey Forman, *Argumentative Man*, Marge Winkler, *Argumentative Woman*, Steven Prince, *Record Producer*, Don Calfa, *Gilbert*, Bernie Kuby,

Justice of the Peace, Selma Archerd, *Wife of Justice of the Peace*, Bill Baldwin, *Announcer in Moonlit Terrace*, Mary Lindsay, *Hat Check Girl in
Meadows*, William Tole, *Tommy Dorsey*. PG. $6,450,000.

   Splendid musical of the big band era. Martin Scorsese's intended
homage to the Hollywood musicals of the 1940's changed, somewhat, in
production and came out resembling his dark, moody thrillers. *New York,
New York* is essentially a musical film noir. This is also an absorbing
backstage drama as it traces the destruction of a marriage by show business.
This bad marriage also serves as a metaphor for the demise of the big band
era itself. As Francine becomes a successful singer Jimmy's band diminishes
in importance, as did many successful bands, which were forced into the
background by the popularity of their vocalists. The performances of De Niro
and Minnelli, her finest yet, are extraordinary, which is imperative due to the
fact almost no other cast member has much screen time. This is not the light,
cheery, inane musical that everyone had hoped for, and subsequently it
failed with both the critics and the public.
   598 **The Next Man** (1976) *** Allied Artists, 108 min. *Dir* Richard C.
Sarafian, *Scr* Mort Fine, Richard C. Sarafian, Alan Trustman, David M. Wolf,
Story Martin Bregman, Alan Trustman, *Cin* Michael Chapman, *Ed* Aram
Avakian, Robert Lovett, *Des* Gene Callahan, *Cos* Anna Hill Johnstone, *Mus*
Michael Kamen, *Prod* Martin Bregman, *Co-Prod* Burtt Harris.
   Cast: Sean Connery, *Khalil Abdul-Muhsen*, Cornelia Sharpe, *Nicole
Scott*, Albert Paulsen, *Hamid*, Adolfo Celi, *Al Charif*, Marco St. John, *Justin*,
Ted Beniades, *Dedario*, Charles Cioffi, *Fouad*, Salem Ludwig, *Ghassan Kad-
dara*, Tom Klunis, *Hatim Othman*, Jaime Sanchez, *Rodriguez*, Stephen D.
Newman, *Andy Hampses*, Holland Taylor, *TV Interviewer*, Peggy Feury, *Mrs.
Scott*, Patrick Bedford, *Mr. Scott*, Roger Omar Serbagi, *Yassin*, Armand
Dahan, *Abdel-Latif Khaldown*, Charles Randall, *Atif Abbas*, Ian Collier,
Devereaux, Michael Storm, *Salazar*. R.
   Above-average international political thriller. Sean Connery stars as a
Saudi Arabian diplomat who upsets the entire Middle East with his plans to
work peacefully with Israel. A hitlady (Cornelia Sharpe) is sent by Arab
terrorists to eliminate Connery and the two fall in love. The script has its con-
trivances, but the filmmakers managed to make the story exciting and
believable.
   599 **Next Stop, Greenwich Village** (1976) **** 20th Century–Fox, 111
min. *Dir* Paul Mazursky, *Scr* Paul Mazursky, *Cin* Arthur Ornitz, *Ed* Richard
Halsey, *Des* Phil Rosenberg, *Mus* Bill Conti, *Prod* Paul Mazursky, *Co-Prod*
Tony Ray.
   Cast: Lenny Baker, *Larry Lapinsky*, Ellen Greene, *Sarah*, Shelley Winters,
Mrs. Lapinsky, Lois Smith, *Anita*, Christopher Walken, *Robert*, Dori Brenner,
Connie, Antonio Fargas, *Bernstein*, Lou Jacobi, *Herb*, Mike Kellin, *Mr. Lapin-
sky*, Michael Egan, *Herbert*, Denise Galik, *Ellen*, John C. Becher, *Producer
Weinberg*, Jeff Goldblum, *Actor Clyde*, John Ford Noonan, *Barney*, Helen
Hanft, *Herb's Wife*, Rashel Novikoff, *Neighbor Tupperman*, Joe Madden,
Poet Jake, Joe Spinell, *Cop*, Rochelle Oliver, *Abortionist*, Gui Adrisano,
Marco, Carole Manferdini, *Southern Girl*, Rutanya Alda, *Party Guest*. R.
   Wonderful comedy-drama about a group of young intellectuals living in

New York's Greenwich Village during the early 1950's. The central character is Larry Lapinsky, a struggling actor who eventually gets his big break by appearing as a teenage hood in a film. This is one of Mazursky's most autobiographical films, as he was once a struggling actor who appeared in *The Blackboard Jungle*. Mazursky may be the only other American filmmaker, besides Woody Allen, who depicts intellectuals as individuals rather than stereotypes.

600 **Nicholas and Alexandra** (1971) (AN) *** Britain, Columbia, 183 min. *Dir* Franklin J. Schaffner, *Scr* James Goldman, *Additional Dialogue* Edward Bond, based on book by Robert K. Massie, *Cin* Freddie Young (AN), *Ed* Ernest Walter, *Des* John Box (A), *Art* Ernest Archer, Jack Maxsted, Gil Parrondo (A), *Cos* Yvonne Blake, Antonio Castillo (A), *Mus* Richard Rodney Bennett (AN), *Prod* Sam Spiegel.

Cast: Michael Jayston, *Czar Nicholas II*, Janet Suzman (AN), *Alexandra*, Harry Andrews, *Grand Duke Nicholas*, Tom Baker, *Rasputin*, Michael Bryant, *Lenin*, Maurice Denham, *Kokovstov*, Jack Hawkins, *Count Fredericks*, Ian Holm, *Yakovlev*, Curt Jurgens, *German Consul*, John McEnery, *Kerensky*, Roderick Noble, *Alexis*, Laurence Olivier, *Count Witte*, Eric Porter, *Stolypin*, Michael Redgrave, *Sazonov*, Alan Webb, *Yurovsky*, Irene Worth, *Queen Mother*. PG. $6,990,000.

Above-average historical drama focusing on the final fourteen years of the reign of Czar Nicholas II, Russia's last czar, who was overthrown by the Russian Revolution in 1917. *Nicholas and Alexandra* is overlong, and sometimes slow and dull, but it never succumbs to the silliness that destroys most historical epics. The performances, particularly Janet Sizman's, are excellent.

601 **The Nickel Ride** (1974) **** 20th Century–Fox, 106 min. *Dir* Robert Mulligan, *Scr* Eric Roth, *Cin* Jordan Cronenweth, *Ed* O. Nicholas Brown, *Art* Lawrence Paull, *Mus* Dave Grusin, *Prod* Robert Mulligan, *Exec Prod* David Foster.

Cast: Jason Miller, *Cooper*, Linda Haynes, *Sarah*, Victor French, *Paddie*, John Hillerman, *Carl*, Bo Hopkins, *Turner*, Richard Evans, *Bobby*, Bart Burns, *Elias*, Lou Frizzell, *Paulie*, Brendan Burns, *Larry*, Mark Gordon, *Tonozzi*, Harvey Gold, *Chester*, Lee Debroux, *Harry*, Jeanne Lange, *Jeannie*. PG.

Excellent mobster drama starring Jason Miller as a low-level crime boss, who is losing control of his territory, because he is no longer able to deal with his superiors and the problems surrounding him. *The Nickel Ride* is an unusual crime thriller, as it focuses more on mood and atmosphere than action. This is one of Robert Mulligan's finest films.

602 **Nickelodeon** (1976) **** Columbia, 121 min. *Dir* Peter Bogdanovich, *Scr* Peter Bogdanovich, W.D. Richter, *Cin* Laszlo Kovacs, *Ed* William Carruth, *Art* Richard Berger, *Cos* Theadora Van Runkle, *Prod* Robert Chartoff, Irwin Winkler, *Assoc Prod* Frank Marshall.

Cast: Ryan O'Neal, *Leo Harrigan*, Burt Reynolds, *Buck Greenway*, Tatum O'Neal, *Alice Forsythe*, Brian Keith, *H.H. Cobb*, Stella Stevens, *Marty Reeves*, John Ritter, *Franklin Frank*, Jane Hitchcock, *Kathleen Cook*, Harry Carey, Jr., *Dobie*, James Best, *Jim*, George Gaynes, *Reginald Kingsley*, M. Emmet Walsh, *Logan*. PG. $6,000,000.

Excellent celebration of the spirit of moviemaking, set during the pioneer days of the cinema. Bogdanovich intentionally filmed *Nickelodeon* in a broad, slapstick manner to resemble the comedies of that era. Many of the incidents were based on stories told to Bogdanovich in interviews with such directors as John Ford and Howard Hawks. The film was poorly received upon release, but is one of Bogdonovich's best films.

603 **Night Moves** (1975) ******** Warner Bros., 100 min. *Dir* Arthur Penn, *Scr* Alan Sharp, *Cin* Bruce Surtees, *Ed* Dede Allen, *Des* George Jenkins, *Mus* Michael Small, *Prod* Robert M. Sherman.

Cast: Gene Hackman, *Harry Moseby*, Jennifer Warren, *Paula*, Edward Binns, *Ziegler*, Harris Yulin, *Marty Heller*, Kenneth Mars, *Nick*, Janet Ward, *Arlene Iverson*, James Woods, *Quentin*, Anthony Costello, *Marv Ellman*, John Crawford, *Tom Iverson*, Melanie Griffith, *Delly Grastner*, Ben Archibeck, *Charles*, Dennis Dugan, *Boy*, C.J. Hincks, *Girl*, Maxwell Gail, Jr., *Stud*, Susan Barrister, Larry Mitchell, *Ticket Clerks*, Susan Clark, *Ellen*. R.

Excellent detective mystery thriller about a Los Angeles private eye with marital problems, who goes to Florida to find a missing girl. Although he does find her, this is only the beginning of the mystery, for which he never finds the complete answer. *Night Moves* is confusing, but that is the point; the more he finds, the less he knows. Movies reflect their times and this is one of the best Watergate Era films.

604 **Night Watch** (1973) ****** Britain, Avco Embassy, 105 min. *Dir* Brian G. Hutton, *Scr* Tony Williamson, *Additional Dialogue* Evan Jones, based on play by Lucille Fletcher, *Cin* Billy Williams, *Ed* John Jympson, *Art* Peter Murton, *Cos* Valentino, *Mus* John Cameron, *Song* "The Night Has Many Eyes", *Mus* George Barrie, *Lyrics* Sammy Cahn, *Prod* George W. George, Martin Poll, Bernard Straus, *Assoc Prod* David White.

Cast: Elizabeth Taylor, *Ellen Wheeler*, Laurence Harvey, *John Wheeler*, Billie Whitelaw, *Sarah Cooke*, Robert Lang, *Appleby*, Tony Britton, *Tony*, Bill Dean, *Insp. Walker*, Michael Danvers-Walker, *Sgt. Norris*, Rosario Serrano, *Delores*, Pauline Jameson, *Secretary*, Linda Hayden, *Girl in Car*, Kevin Colson, *Carl*, Laon Maybanke, *Florist*. PG.

Standard suspense thriller starring Elizabeth Taylor as a neurotic woman, who claims to have witnessed a murder, but no one will believe her. This premise is stretched out with the usual trick plotting and obligatory red herrings, and culminates with an overly clever twist ending. Taylor gives one of her better performances, but that isn't saying much.

605 **The Nightcomers** (1972) ****** Britain, Avco Embassy, 95 min. *Dir* Michael Winner, *Scr* Michael Hastings, based on novel *Turn of the Screw* by Henry James, *Cin* Robert Paynter, *Ed* Frederick Wilson, *Mus* Jerry Fielding, *Prod* Michael Winner.

Cast: Marlon Brando, *Peter*, Stephanie Beacham, *Miss Jessel*, Thora Hird, *Mrs. Grose*, Harry Andrews, *Master of the House*, Verna Harvey, *Flora*, Christopher Ellis, *Miles*, Anna Palk, *New Governess*. R.

Unusual thriller that serves as a prelude to the incidents in Henry James' *Turn of the Screw*, which was filmed as *The Innocents*, and attempts to explain the reason for the strange behavior of the two children. Marlon Brando stars as a gardener, who corrupts the minds of the children and eventually becomes their victim. The film is somewhat flat and is almost saved by Brando's excellent performance.

606 **Nightwing** (1979) ** Columbia, 105 min. *Dir* Arthur Hiller, *Scr* Steve Shagan, Bud Shrake, Martin Cruz Smith, based on novel by Martin Cruz Smith, *Cin* Charles Rosher, *Ed* John C. Howard, *Des* James Vance, *Mus* Henry Mancini, *Prod* Martin Ransohoff, *Exec Prod* Richard St. Johns, *Assoc Prod* Maggie Abbott, Peter V. Herald.

Cast: Nick Mancuso, *Duran*, David Warner, *Philip*, Kathryn Harrold, *Anne*, Stephen Macht, *Chee*, Strother Martin, *Selwyn*, George Clutesi, *Abner*, Ben Piazza, *Roger*, Donald Hotton, *John*, Charles Hallahan, *Henry*, Judith Novgrod, *Judy*, Alice Hirson, *Claire*, Pat Corley, *Vet*, Charlie Bird, *Beejay*, Danny Zapien, *Joe*, Peter Prouse, *Doctor*, Jose Toledo, *Harold*, Richard Romancito, *Ben*, Flavio Martinez III, *Isla*. PG.

Dull horror thriller about vampire bats that haunt an Indian reservation, with David Warner as an eccentric scientist who tracks them down. This was supposed to induce the same fear as *Jaws* with scares generated by real horrors. The problem is that not only are bats less of a threat to the average person than sharks, but the film itself is not even scarey.

607 **9/30/55** (1977) **** Universal, 101 min. *Dir* James Bridges, *Scr* James Bridges, *Cin* Gordon Willis, *Ed* Jeff Gourson, *Art* Robert Luthardt, *Cos* Kent Warner, *Mus* Leonard Rosenman, *Prod* Jerry Weintraub.

Cast: Richard Thomas, *Jimmy J.*, Susan Tyrrell, *Melba Lou*, Deborah Benson, *Charlotte*, Lisa Blount, *Billie Jean*, Thomas Hulce, *Hanley*, Dennis Quaid, *Frank*, Mary Kai Clark, *Pat*, Dennis Christopher, *Eugene*, Collin Wilcox, *Jimmy J's Mother*, Ben Fuhrman, *Coach*, Ouida White, *Aunt Ethel*, Bryan Scott, *Dickie*, Glen Irby, *Band Director*, Mike Farris, *Edgar*, Tom Bonner, *Radio Announcer*. PG.

Unusual drama examining the effects of James Dean's death (on 9/30/55) on an Arkansas youth (Richard Thomas): it is one of the few films to deal with hero worship and it handles the subject intelligently and sensitively. This film also focuses on the frustrations of youth at the time, paralleling James Dean's own *Rebel without a Cause*.

608 **1941** (1979) **** Universal/Columbia, 120 min. *Dir* Steven Spielberg, *Scr* Bob Gale, Robert Zemeckis, *Story* Bob Gale, John Milius, Robert Zemeckis, *Cin* William A. Fraker (AN), *Ed* Michael Kahn, *Des* Dean Edward Mitzner, *Art* William F. O'Brien, *Cos* Deborah Nadoolman, *Sp* A.D. Flower, William A. Fraker, Gregory Jein (AN), *Mus* John Williams, *Chor* Paul DeRolf, Judy Van Wormer, *Prod* Buzz Feitshans, *Exec Prod* John Milius, *Assoc Prod* Janet Healy, Michael Kahn.

Cast: Dan Aykroyd, *Sgt. Tree*, Ned Beatty, *Ward Douglas*, John Belushi, *Wild Bill Kelso*, Lorraine Gary, *Joan Douglas*, Murray Hamilton, *Claude*, Christopher Lee, *Von Kleinschmidt*, Tim Matheson, *Birkhead*, Toshiro Mifune, *Cmdr. Mitamura*, Warren Oates, *Maddox*, Robert Stack, *Gen. Stilwell*, Treat Williams, *Sitarski*, Nancy Allen, *Donna*, Lucille Benson, *Gas Mama*, Jordan Brien, *Macey*, John Candy, *Foley*, Elisha Cook, *Patron*, Patti LuPone, *Lydia Hedberg*, Penny Marshall, *Miss Fitzroy*, Slim Pickens, *Hollis Wood*, Lionel Stander, *Scioli*, Dub Taylor, *Malcomb*, Joe Flaherty, *M.C.* PG. $23,400,000.

Spectacular slapstick comedy about paranoia striking Los Angeles due to the sighting of a Japanese submarine off the coast, following the attack on Pearl Harbor. *1941* contains some of the most stunning and extravagant sight gags ever filmed, which has been the basis for most of the film's criticism. It was just too overwhelming to inspire the necessary laughs, but this is superficial criticism. Steven Spielberg's immaculate direction beautifully realizes this outlandishly complex film.

609 **99 & 44/100% Dead** (1974) *** 20th Century–Fox, 97 min. *Dir* John Frankenheimer, *Scr* Robert Dillon, *Cin* Ralph Woolsey, *Ed* Harold F. Kress, *Art* Herman Blumenthal, *Cos* Ron Talsky, *Mus* Henry Mancini, *Song* "Easy Baby", *Mus* Henry Mancini, *Lyrics* Alan & Marilyn Bergman, sung by Jim Gilstrap, *Prod* Joe Wizan, *Assoc Prod* Mickey Borofsky.

Cast: Richard Harris, *Harry*, Edmond O'Brien, *Uncle Frank*, Bradford Dillman, *Big Eddie*, Ann Turkel, *Buffy*, Constance Ford, *Dolly*, David Hall, *Tony*, Kathrine Baumann, *Baby*, Janice Heiden, *Clara*, Max Kleven, *North*, Karl Lukas, *Guard*, Anthony Brubaker, *Burt*, Jerry Summers, *Shoes*, Roy Jenson, *Jake*, Bennie Dobbins, *Driver*, Chuck Roberson, *Gunman*, Chuck Connors, *Claw*. PG.

Offbeat and original gangster saga that resembles a live-action comic book. A professional killer (Richard Harris) is hired by a gangster (Edmond O'Brian) as protection in his gang war against rival (Bradford Dillman), who has on his side a vicious killer (Chuck Conners) with a claw for a hand. *99 & 44/100% Dead* is a strange spoof of the genre, and it works quite well.

610 **92 in the Shade** (1975) **** United Artists, 88 min. *Dir* Thomas McGuane, *Scr* Thomas McGuane, *Cin* Michael C. Butler, *Ed* Ed Rothkowitz, *Mus* Michael J. Lewis, *Prod* George Pappas, *Exec Prod* Elliott Kastner.

Cast: Peter Fonda, *Tom Skelton*, Warren Oates, *Nicol*, Margot Kidder, *Miranda*, Elizabeth Ashley, *Jeannie Carter*, Burgess Meredith, *Goldsboro*, Harry Dean Stanton, *Carter*, Sylvia Miles, *Bella*, William Hickey, *Mr. Skelton*, Louise Latham, *Mrs. Skelton*, Joe Spinell, *Ollie*, William Roerick, *Mr. Rudleigh*, Evelyn Russell, *Mrs. Rudleigh*, John Quade, *Roy*, John Heffernan, *Myron*, Warren Kemmerling, *Powell*, Robert Kruse, *Waiter*, Scott Palmer, *Michael*. R.

Unusual comedy thriller starring Peter Fonda as a Florida Keys tourist fishing guide, who runs into conflict with a crazy competitor (Warren Oates). *92 in the Shade* almost entirely avoids plot as it examines the weird characters inhabiting the region. The mood of the film is very strange and is almost totally lacking in emotion. Novelist Thomas McGuane made a fine directorial debut, showing a style so individualistic he has yet to direct again.

611 **No Deposit, No Return** (1976) ** Buena Vista, 112 min. *Dir* Norman Tokar, *Scr* Arthur Alsberg, Don Nelson, *Story* Joe McEveety, *Cin* Frank Phillips, *Ed* Cotton Warburton, *Art* John B. Mansbridge, Jack Senter, *Cos* Chuck Keehne, *Mus* Buddy Baker, *Prod* Ron Miller, *Co-Prod* Joe McEveety, A Walt Disney Production.

Cast: David Niven, *J.W. Osborne*, Darren McGavin, *Duke*, Don Knotts, *Bert*, Herschel Bernardi, *Sgt. Turner*, Barbara Feldon, *Carolyn*, Kim Richards, *Tracy*, Brad Savage, *Jay*, John Williams, *Jameson*, Charlie Martin Smith, *Longnecker*, Vic Tayback, *Big Joe*, Bob Hastings, *Peter*. G. $10,500,000.

Fair Disney comedy about a pair of rich kids (Kim Richards, Brad Savage), who convince two second-rate crooks (Darren McGavin, Don Knotts) to hold them for ransom from their grandfather (David Niven) in order to avoid spending Easter vacation with him. This offbeat premise is unfortunately flawed by a slow and tedious treatment. The only relief comes from some fine comic performances.

612 **Norma Rae** (1979) (AN) *** 20th Century–Fox, 110 min. *Dir* Martin Ritt, *Scr* Harriet Frank, Jr., Irving Ravetch (AN), *Cin* John A. Alonzo, *Ed* Sidney Levin, *Art* Tracy Bousman, *Mus* David Shire, *Song* "It Goes Like It Goes", *Mus* David Shire (A), *Lyrics* Norman Gimbel (A), sung by Jennifer Warnes, *Prod* Tamara Asseyev, Alex Rose.

Cast: Sally Field (A, NS, NY, NB, G, LA, CF), *Norma Rae*, Beau Bridges, *Sonny*, Ron Leibman, *Reuben*, Pat Hingle, *Vernon*, Barbara Baxley, *Leona*, Gail Strickland, *Bonnie Mae*, Morgan Paull, *Wayne Billings*, Robert Broyles, *Sam Bolen*, John Calvin, *Ellis Harper*, Booth Colman, *Dr. Watson*, Lee DeBroux, *Lujan*, James Luisi, *George Benson*, Vernon Weddle, *Rev. Hubbard*, Gilbert Green, *Al London*, Bob Minor, *Lucius White*, Mary Munday, *Mrs. Johnson*, Jack Stryker, *J.J. Davis*, Gregory Walcott, *Lamar Miller*, Noble Willingham, *Leroy Mason*, Lonny Chapman, *Gardner*, Bert Freed, *Sam Dakin*, Bob E. Hannah, *Jed Buffum*, Edith Ivey, *Louise Pickens*, Scott Lawton, *Craig*, Frank McRae, *James Brown*. PG. $11,415,000.

Interesting drama about a woman who helps organize a union in a Southern textile mill. *Norma Rae* does not completely succeed as a socially conscious film about labor vs. management as it is too biased in its attitude. Where it does succeed is in documenting the life of this woman, based on a real person, and how the union affects her, changing from a sheltered individual to one, whose eyes are opened up to the outside world. Sally Field is simply superb in the title role.

613 **The North Avenue Irregulars** (1979) *** Buena Vista, 99 min. *Dir* Bruce Bilson, *Scr* Don Tait, based on book by Reverend Albert Fay Hill, *Cin* Leonard J. South, *Ed* Gordon D. Brenner, *Art* Jack T. Collis, John B. Mansbridge, *Cos* Chuck Keehne, Emily Sundby, *Mus* Robert F. Brunner, *Songs* Al Kasha, Joel Hirschhorn, *Prod* Ron Miller, *Co-Prod* Tom Leetch, *Assoc Prod* Kevin Corcoran. A Walt Disney Production.

Cast: Edward Herrmann, *Michael Hill*, Barbara Harris, *Vicki*, Susan Clark, *Anne*, Karen Valentine, *Jane*, Michael Constantine, *Marv*, Cloris Leachman, *Claire*, Patsy Kelly, *Rose*, Douglas V. Fowley, *Delaney*, Virginia Capers, *Cleo*, Steve Franken, *Tom*, Dena Dietrich, *Mrs. Carlisle*, Dick Fuchs, *Howard*, Herb Voland, *Dr. Fulton*, Alan Hale, *Harry the Hat*, Melora Hardin, *Carmel*, Bobby Rolofson, *Dean*, Frank Campanella, *Max*, Ivor Francis, *Rev. Wainwright*, Louisa Moritz, *Mrs. Gossin*, Majorie Bennett, *Mother Thurber*, Ruth Buzzi, *Dr. Rheems*. G. $9,925,000.

Above-average Walt Disney comedy that has some appeal for adults. A minister (Edward Herrmann) organizes the woman of his small parish to battle local gangsters. The premise is silly, but *The North Avenue Irregulars* has a wittier script than usual from Disney. It does seem to run out of steam toward the end, resorting to standard chase scenes, but most of the film is quite funny.

614 North Dallas Forty (1979) ***** Paramount, 119 min. *Dir* Ted Kot-cheff, *Scr* Peter Gent, Ted Kotcheff, Frank Yablans, based on novel by Peter Gent, *Cin* Paul Lohmann, *Ed* Jay Kamen, *Des* Alfred Sweeney, *Cos* Dorothy Jeakins, *Mus* John Scott, *Prod* Frank Yablans, *Exec Prod* Jack B. Bernstein.

Cast: Nick Nolte, *Phillip Elliott,* Mac Davis, *Maxwell,* Charles Durning, *Coach Johnson,* Dayle Haddon, *Charlotte,* Bo Svenson, *Jo Bob Priddy,* Steve Forrest, *Conrad Hunter,* G.D. Spradlin, *B.A. Strothers,* Dabney Coleman, *Emmett,* Savannah Smith, *Joanne,* Marshall Colt, *Art Hartman,* Guich Koock, *Eddie Rand,* Deborah Benson, *Mrs. Hartman,* James F. Boeke, *Stallings,* John Bottoms, *VIP,* Walter Brooke, *Doctor,* Carlos Brown, *Balford,* Danny J. Bunz, *Tony Douglas,* Jane Daly, *Conrad, Jr.,* Cliff Frazier, *Monroe,* Stanley Grover, *March.* R. $16,100,000.

Superb and brutal satire of professional football, focusing on a team similar to the Dallas Cowboys. Nick Nolte is excellent as the rebellious team member, who runs into conflicts with the coach and the owners who feel he has an attitude problem. *North Dallas Forty* is a savage attack on the sport and realistically, and humorously, documents the abuses and misuses of the players by the owners, who look upon the game as a pure business. The en-tire cast is extraordinary, and this must rank as one of the few truly great sports films.

615 Now You See Him, Now You Don't (1972) *** Buena Vista, 88 min. *Dir* Robert Butler, *Scr* Joseph McEveety, based on story by Robert L. King, *Cin* Frank Phillips, *Ed* Cotton Warburton, *Art* John B. Mansbridge, Walter Tyler, *Cos* Chuck Keehne, Emily Sundby, *Mus* Robert F.Brunner, *Prod* Ron Miller, *Assoc Prod* Joseph L. McEveety, A Walt Disney Production.

Cast: Kurt Russell, *Dexter Riley,* Cesar Romero, *A.J. Arno,* Joe Flynn, *Dean Higgens,* Jim Backus, *Timothy Forsythe,* William Windom, *Lufkin,* Michael McGreevey, *Richard Schuyler,* Joyce Menges, *Debbie Dawson,* Richard Bakalyan, *Cookie,* Alan Hewitt, *Dean Collingsgood,* Kelly Thordsen, *Sgt. Cassidy,* Neil Russell, *Alfred,* George O'Hanlon, *Ted,* John Myhers, *Golfer,* Pat Delany, *Secretary,* Robert Rothwell, *Driver,* Frank Aletter, *TV An-nouncer,* Dave Willock, *Mr. Burns,* Edward Andrews, *Mr. Sampson,* Jack Bender, *Slither Roth,* Frank Welker, *Myles,* Ed Begley, Jr., *Druffle,* Paul Smith, *Road Block Officer,* Billy Casper, Dave Hill, *Professional Golfers.* G. $4,610,000. See *The Computer Wore Tennis Shoes.*

616 Nunzio (1978) *** Universal, 85 min. *Dir* Paul Williams, *Scr* James Andronica, *Cin* Edward R.Brown, *Ed* Johanna Demetrakes, *Des* Mel Bourne, *Art* Richard Fuhrman, *Cos* Ann Roth, *Mus* Lalo Schifrin, *Prod* Jennings Lang.

Cast: David Proval, *Nunzio,* James Andronica, *Jamesie,* Morgana King, *Mrs. Sabatino,* Joe Spinell, *Angelo,* Tovah Feldshuh, *Michelle,* Maria Smith-Caffey, *Carol Sabatino,* Vincent Russo, *JoJo,* Jamie Alba, *Bobby,* Theresa Saldana, *MaryAnn,* Glenn Scarpelli, *Georgie,* Tony Panetta, *Georgie's Friend,* Steve Gucciardo, *Carmine,* Charlet Oberley, *Customer,* Sal Maneri, Anthony Esemplare, *JoJo's Friends,* Sonia Zomina, *Mrs. Shuman,* Crystal Hayden, *Crystal Sabatino,* Vincent Igneri, *Vincent Sabatino,* Tom Quinn, *Pete.* PG.

Sentimental character study about a retarded young man (David Proval), who lives out his dreary existence as a grocery delivery boy, to help support his widowed mother (Morgana King). To forget his problems, he retreats into a world of fantasy. *Nunzio* begins promisingly as a study of loneliness, but it betrays this with a forced uplifting ending.

617 O Lucky Man! (1973) ***** Britain, Warner Bros., 186 min. *Dir* Lindsay Anderson, *Scr* David Sherwin, based on idea by Malcolm McDowell, *Cin* Miroslav Ondricek, *Ed* David Gladwell, Tom Priestley, *Des* Jocelyn Herbert, *Art* Alan Withy, *Mus* Alan Price (BFA), *Prod* Lindsay Anderson, Michael Medwin, *Assoc Prod* Basil Keys.

Cast: Malcolm McDowell, *Mick,* Ralph Richardson, *Sir James/Monty,* Arthur Lowe (BFA), *Duff/Johnson/Munda,* Rachel Roberts, *Gloria/Mme. Paillard/Mrs. Richards,* Helen Mirren, *Patricia,* Dandy Nichols, *Tea Lady/Neighbor,* Mona Washbourne, *Neighbor/Usher/Sister Hallet,* Peter Jeffrey, *Factory Chairman/Prison Governor,* Graham Crowden, *Stewart/ Miller/Meths Drinker,* Philip Stone, *Jeakins/Interrogator/Salvation Army Major,* Alan Price, *Himself,* Wallas Eaton, *Stone/Steiger/Executive/Warder,* Warren Clarke, *M.C./Warner/Male Nurse,* Bill Owen, *Barlow/Superintendent,* Edward Judd, *Oswald,* Pearl Nunez, *Mrs. Naidu,* Mary MacLeod, *Mary Ball/Vicar's Wife,* Michael Bangerter, *William/Interrogator/Released Prisoner,* Michael Medwin, *Duke of Belminster/Captain/Power Studio Technician.* R.

Magnificent picaresque contemporary adventure story about the ups and downs of a coffee salesman (Malcolm McDowell). *O Lucky Man* is an ambitious film of epic proportions that charts his rise, through many extraordinary and bizarre episodes, with continuing musical commentary by Alan Price. This is one of the most brilliant satires of society ever filmed, and is Lindsay Anderson's finest achievement.

618 Obsession (1976) *** Columbia, 98 min. *Dir* Brian DePalma, *Scr* Paul Schrader, *Story* Brian DePalma, *Cin* Vilmos Zsigmond, *Ed* Paul Hirsch, *Art* Jack Senter, *Mus* Bernard Herrmann (AN), *Prod* Harry N. Blum, George Litto, *Exec Prod* Robert S. Bremson.

Cast: Cliff Robertson, *Michael Courtland,* Genevieve Bujold, *Elizabeth Courtland/Sandra Portinari,* John Lithgow, *Robert LaSalle,* Sylvia Kuumba Williams, *Maid,* Wanda Blackman, *Amy Courtland,* Patrick McNamara, *Third Kidnapper,* Stanley J. Reyes, *Inspector Brie,* Nick Kreiger, *Farber,* Stocker Fontelieu, *Dr. Ellman,* Don Hood, *Ferguson,* Andrea Esterhazy, *D'Annunzio.* PG. $4,000,000.

Well-made suspense thriller about a man who falls in love with a young woman (Genevieve Bujold), who is a dead ringer for his murdered wife, who, along with his daughter, had been kidnapped years earlier. *Obsession* is a graceful blend of mystery and romance, with a subtle suggestion of incest, but it misses greatness by backing away from its subject.

619 Ode to Billy Joe (1976) *** Warner Bros., 105 min. *Dir* Max Baer, *Scr* Herman Raucher, based on song by Bobbie Gentry, *Cin* Michael Hugo, *Ed* Frank E. Morriss, *Art* Philip Jeffries, *Mus* Michel Legrand, *Prod* Max Baer, Roger Camras, *Assoc Prod* Mark Sussman.

Cast: Robby Benson, *Billy Joe McAllister,* Glynnis O'Connor, *Bobbie Lee Hartley,* Joan Hotchkis, *Mrs. Hartley,* Sandy McPeak, *Mr. Hartley,* James Best, *Dewey Barksdale,* Terence Goodman, *James Hartley,* Becky Brown, *Becky Thompson,* Sempson Hemphill, *Brother Taylor,* Ed Shelnut, *Coleman*

Stroud, Eddie Tair, *Tom Hargitay*, William Hallberg, *Dan McAllister*, Frannye Capelle, *Belinda Wiggs*, Rebecca Jernigan, *Mrs. Thompson*, Ann Martin, *Mrs. Hunicutt*, Will Long, *Trooper Bash*, John Roper, *Trooper Ned*. PG. $11,600,000.

Surprisingly good film version of Bobbie Gentry's hit song from the 1960's. The film attempts to finish the story by explaining why Billy Joe McAllister did jump off the bridge. This is the film's major flaw, as this explanation tends to be silly and melodramatic. This aside, *Ode to Billy Joe* is a fine and realistic portrait of life in a small Southern town during the 1950's with good performances from Robby Benson and Glynnis O'Connor as the star-crossed lovers.

620 **The Odessa File** (1974) *** Britain/Germany, Columbia, 128 min. *Dir* Ronald Neame, *Scr* George Markstein, Kenneth Ross, based on novel by Frederick Forsyth, *Cin* Oswald Morris, *Ed* Ralph Kemplen, *Des* Rolf Zehetbauer, *Cos* Monika Bauert, *Mus* Andrew Lloyd Webber, *Prod* John Woolf, *Co-Prod* John R. Sloan.

Cast: Jon Voight, *Peter Miller*, Maximilian Schell, *Edward Roschmann*, Maria Schell, *Fran Miller*, Mary Tamm, *Sigi*, Derek Jacobi, *Klaus Wenzer*, Peter Jeffrey, *David Porath*, Klaus Lowitsch, *Gustav MacKensen*,Kurt Meisel, *Alfred Oster*, Hans Messemer, *Gen. Glucks*, Garfield Morgan, *Israeli General*, Shmuel Rodensky, *Simon Wiesenthal*, Ernst Schroder, *Werner Deilman*, Gunter Strack, *Kunik*, Noel Willman, *Franz Bayer*, Martin Brandt, *Marx*, Hans Caninenberg, *Dr. Ferdinand Schultz*, Heinz Ehrenfreund, *Shapira*, Alexander Golling, *Colonel*. PG. $6,000,000.

Above average international thriller about a German reporter (Jon Voight), who pursues a business tycoon, who is a former Nazi (Maximilian Schell). This long complex film moves very briskly to its climax, which contains a genuine surprise ending. Voight is excellent and his German accent never seems phoney. *The Odessa File* is a good film, but it is nevertheless inferior to the earlier Forsyth adaptation, *The Day of the Jackal*.

621 **The Offense** (1973) *** Britain, United Artists, 112 min. *Dir* Sidney Lumet, *Scr* John Hopkins, *Cin* Gerry Fisher, *Ed* John Victor Smith, *Art* John Clark, *Prod* Denis O'Dell.

Cast: Sean Connery, *Johnson*, Trevor Howard, *Cartwright*, Vivien Merchant, *Maureen*, Ian Bannen, *Baxter*, Derek Newark, *Jessard*, John Hallam, *Panton*, Peter Bowles, *Cameron*, Ronald Radd, *Lawson*, Anthony Sagar, *Hill*, Howard Goorney, *Lambeth*, Richard Moore, *Garrett*, Maxine Gordon, *Janie*. R.

Powerful psychological drama starring Sean Connery as a police officer, who goes too far in his interrogation of a child molester (Ian Bannen) and beats him to death. Connery cracks due to a traumatic experience in his childhood. *The Offense* does not back off from its touchy subject and the acting is superb, but it suffers a bit from staginess.

622 **Oh, God!** (1977) ** Warner Bros., 97 min. *Dir* Carl Reiner, *Scr* Larry Gelbart, based on novel by Avery Corman, *Cin* Victor Kemper, *Ed* Bud Molin, *Art* Jack Senter, *Mus* Jack Elliot, *Prod* Jerry Weintraub.

Cast: George Burns, *God*, John Denver, *Jerry Landers*, Teri Garr, *Bobbie Landers*, Donald Pleasence, *Dr. Harmon*, Ralph Bellamy, *Sam Raven*, William Daniels, *George Summers*, Barnard Hughes, *Judge Baker*, Paul Sorvino, *Rev. Willie Williams*, Barry Sullivan, *Priest*, Dinah Shore, *Herself*, Jeff Corey, *Rabbi*, George Furth, *Briggs*, David Ogden Stiers, *Mr. McCarthy*, Titos Vandis, *Greek Bishop*. PG. $31,440,000.

Dull comedy about God, in the person of George Burns, coming to Earth and picking a grocery clerk to deliver his message. This comedy is so light that it resembles an ordinary television movie. Burns is very funny in the role, which has him deliver what is essentially a Burns-style comedy routine, but Paul Sorvino as an overpowering evangelist steals the film.

623 **Oklahoma Crude** (1973) ******* Columbia, 108 min. *Dir* Stanley Kramer, *Scr* Marc Norman, *Cin* Robert Surtees, *Ed* Folmar Blangsted, *Des* Alfred Sweeney, *Cos* Bill Thomas, *Mus* Henry Mancini, *Song* Henry Mancini, Hal David, Sung by Anne Murray, *Prod* Stanley Kramer, *Assoc Prod* Ivan Volkman.

Cast: George C. Scott, *Mase*, Faye Dunaway, *Lena*, Jack Palance, *Hellman*, John Mills, *Cleon*, William Lucking, *Marion*, Harvey Jason, *Wilcox*, Ted Gehring, *Wobbly*, Cliff Osmond, *Massive Man*, Rafael Campos, *Jimmy*, Woodrow Parfrey, *Lawyer*, John Hudkins, *Bloom*, Harvey Parry, *Bliss*, Bob Herron, *Dulling*, Jerry Brown, *Rucker*, Jim Burk, *Moody*, Henry Wills, *Walker*, Hal Smith, *C.R. Miller*, Cody Bearpaw, *Indian*, James Jeter, *Strapp*, Larry D. Mann, *Deke Watson*, John Dierkes, *Farmer*, Karl Lukas, *Hobo 1*, Wayne Storm, *Hobo 2*, Billy Varga, *Cook*. PG.

Entertaining comedy-drama with Faye Dunaway as the owner of an oil well, who hires George C. Scott to help prevent it from being swallowed up by an oil conglomerate, represented by villainous Jack Palance. This is one of the few Stanley Kramer films that does not hit an audience over the head with a preachy message, and for that reason *Oklahoma Crude* rises above his others.

624 **Old Boyfriends** (1979) ******* Avco Embassy, 103 min. *Dir* Joan Tewkesbury, *Scr* Leonard Schrader, Paul Schrader, *Cin* William A. Fraker, *Ed* Bill Reynolds, *Art* Peter Jamison, *Cos* Suzanne Grace, Tony Faso, *Mus* David Shire, *Prod* Edward R. Pressman, Michele Rappaport, *Exec Prod* Paul Schrader.

Cast: Talia Shire, *Diane Cruise*, Richard Jordan, *Jeff Turrin*, Keith Carradine, *Wayne Van Til*, John Belushi, *Eric Katz*, John Houseman, *Dr. Hoffman*, Buck Henry, *Art Kopple*, Nina Jordan, *Kylan Turrin*, Gerritt Graham, *Sam the Fisherman*, P.J. Soles, *Sandy*, Bethel Leslie, *Mrs. Van Til*, Joan Hotchkis, *Pamela Shaw*, William Bassett, *David Brinks*. R.

Interesting psychological drama about a confused woman who tries to relive her past by visiting her old boyfriends. Each meeting leads to a different result, one of which is quite tragic. There appears to be a point to all this, but it is never quite clear. The performances are, however, all excellent, particularly that of Talia Shire, who proves she can succeed nicely without her brother, Francis Coppola, or *Rocky*.

625 **Oliver's Story** (1978) ****** Paramount, 92 min. *Dir* John Korty, *Scr* John Korty, Erich Segal, based on novel by Erich Segal, *Cin* Arthur Ornitz, *Ed* Stuart H. Pappe, *Art* Robert Gundlach, *Cos* Peggy Farrell, *Mus* Lee Holdridge, "Oliver's Theme" composed by Francis Lai, *Prod* David V. Picker.

Cast: Ryan O'Neal, *Oliver Barrett*, Candice Bergen, *Marcie Bonwit*, Nicola Pagett, *Joanna Stone*, Edward Binns, *Phil Cavilleri*, Benson Fong, *John Hsiang*, Charles Haid, *Stephen Simpson*, Kenneth McMillan, *James Francis*, Ray Milland, *Mr. Barrett*, Josef Sommar, *Dr. Dienhart*, Sully Boyar, *Mr. Gentilano*, Swoosie Kurtz, *Gwen Simpson*, Meg Mundy, *Mrs. Barrett*, Beatrice Winde, *Waltereen*, Sol Schwade, *Arlie*, Father Frank Toste, *Father Giametti*, Cynthia McPherson, *Anita*, Gloria Irizarry, *Cleaning Woman*, Louise Turenne, *Waiter*, Victor Gil de la Madrid, *Newscaster*. PG. $8,460,000. See *Love Story*.

626 **The Omega Man** (1971) *** Warner Bros., 98 min. *Dir* Boris Sagal, *Scr* John William Corrington, Joyce H. Corrington, based on novel *I Am Legend* by Richard Matheson, *Cin* Russell Metty, *Ed* William Ziegler, *Art* Arthur Loel, Walter M. Simonds, *Cos* Margo Baxley, Bucky Rous, *Mus* Ron Granier, *Prod* Walter Seltzer.

Cast: Charlton Heston, *Robert Neville*, Anthony Zerbe, *Matthias*, Rosalind Cash, *Lisa*, Paul Koslo, *Dutch*, Lincoln Kilpatrick, *Zachary*, Eric Laneuville, *Richie*, Jill Giraldi, *Little Girl*, Anna Aries, *Woman in Cemetery Crypt*, DeVeren Bookwalter, John Dierkes, Monika Henreid, Linda Redfearn, Forrest Wood, *Family Members*, Brian Tochi, *Tommy*. PG. $4,000,000.

Above-average science fiction drama set after the destruction of civilization, due to germ warfare between Russia and China. Charlton Heston stars as an uncontaminated survivor, who lives in a barricaded apartment to protect himself from marauding mutants. *The Omega Man* takes a familiar theme of survival in a post-apocalyptic world and packs it with more excitement than unusual.

627 **The Omen** (1976) *** 20th Century–Fox, 111 min. *Dir* Richard Donner, *Scr* David Seltzer, *Cin* Gilbert Taylor, *Ed* Stuart Baird, *Art* Carmen Dillon, *Mus* Jerry Goldsmith (AN), *Song*, "Ave Satani", *Mus* Jerry Goldsmith (AN), *Prod* Harvey Bernhard, *Exec Prod* Mace Newfeld.

Cast: Gregory Peck, *Robert*, Lee Remick, *Katherine Thorn*, David Warner, *Jennings*, Billie Whitelaw, *Mrs. Baylock*, Leo McKern, *Archaeologist*, Harvey Stevens, *Damien*, Patrick Troughton, *Father Brennan*, Martin Benson, *Father Spiletto*, Anthony Nicholls, *Dr. Becker*, Holly Palance, *Young Nanny*, John Stride, *Psychiatrist*, Robert MacLeod, Sheila Raynor, *House Staff*. R. $28,545,000.

Exciting horror thriller about a child who happens to be the anti-Christ. Gregory Peck stars as an American ambassador, who under advice from a priest switches his newborn baby. Five years later strange things begin to occur, all centered around his son, Damien. *The Omen* has many scenes of violence, none of which are gratuitous, but they are brilliantly conceived and quite memorable. This film mixes the theme of Satanism, made popular by *The Exorcist*, with the visual style of a gothic horror thriller. The sequel *Damien, The Omen II*, continues the boy's life in his teens, but has none of the style of its predecessor.

628 **On a Clear Day You Can See Forever** (1970) *** Paramount, 129 min. *Dir* Vincente Minnelli, *Scr* Alan Jay Lerner, based on musical play by Alan Jay Lerner, Burton Lane, *Cin* Harry Stradling, *Ed* David Bretherton, *Des* John De Cuir, *Cos* Cecil Beaton, Arnold Scaasi, *Mus* Burton Lane, *Lyrics* Alan

Jay Lerner, *Mus Adaptation* Nelson Riddle, *Chor* Howard Jeffrey, *Prod* Howard W. Koch.

Cast: Barbra Streisand, *Daisy Gamble*, Yves Montand, *Dr. Marc Chabot*, Bob Newhart, *Dr. Mason Hume*, Larry Blyden, *Warren Pratt*, Simon Oakland, *Dr. Conrad Fuller*, Jack Nicholson, *Tad Pringle*, John Richardson, *Robert Tentrees*, Pamela Brown, *Mrs. Fitzherbert*, Irene Handl, *Winnie Wainwhistle*, Roy Kinnear, *Prince Regent*, Peter Crowcroft, *Divorce Attorney*, Byron Webster, *Prosecuting Attorney*, Mabel Albertson, *Mrs. Hatch*, Laurie Main, *Lord Percy*. G.

Unusual musical starring Barbra Streisand as a woman, who goes to a psychiatrist (Yves Montand) to curb her smoking habit. While she is under hypnosis, he discovers that she may be a reincarnation of a 19th century English noblewoman. The premise is odd for a musical, but it surprisingly works, particularly in the fine period scenes. Streisand is excellent in the dual role.

629 Once in Paris (1978) *** Leigh-McLaughlin, 100 min. *Dir* Frank D. Gilroy, *Scr* Frank D. Gilroy, *Cin* Claude Saunier, *Ed* Robert Q. Lovett, *Mus* Mitch Leigh, *Prod* Frank D. Gilroy, *Co-Prod* Gerard Croce, Manny Fuchs.

Cast: Wayne Rogers, *Michael Moore*, Gayle Hunnicutt, *Susan Townsend*, Jack Lenoir, *Jean-Paul Barbet*, Philippe March, *Marcel Thery*, Clement Harari, *Abe*, Tanya Lopert, *Eve Cartling*, Marthe Mercadier, *Mme. Barbet*, Yves Massard, *First Man at Party*, Sady Rebbot, *Second Man at Party*, Matt Carney, *Lars Brady*, Doris Roberts, *Brady's Ex-Wife*, Gerard Croce, *Monsieur Farny*, Victoria Ville, *Mme. Farny*. Not Rated.

Interesting drama about an American screenwriter (Wayne Rogers), who goes to Paris to work on a script for a film set to go into production. The main focus of *Once in Paris* is on his relationships with an Englishwoman (Gayle Hunnicutt), with whom he falls in love even though he is married, and his chauffeur (Jack Lenoir), whom he befriends. This is a nice pleasant film, but it is very slight in ambition.

630 Once Is Not Enough (1975) * Paramount, 121 min. *Dir* Guy Green, *Scr* Julius J. Epstein, based on novel by Jacqueline Susann, *Cin* John A. Alonzo, *Ed* Rita Roland, *Des* John DeCuir, *Cos* Moss Mabry, *Mus* Henry Mancini, *Prod* Howard W. Koch, *Exec Prod* Irving Mansfield.

Cast: Kirk Douglas, *Mike Wayne*, Alexis Smith, *Deidre Granger*, David Janssen, *Tom Colt*, George Hamilton, *David Milford*, Melina Mercouri, *Karla*, Gary Conway, *Hugh*, Brenda Vaccaro (AN, G), *Linda*, Deborah Raffin, *January*, Lillian Randolph, *Mabel*, Renata Vanni, *Maria*, Mark Roberts, *Rheingold*, John Roper, *Franco*, Leonard Sachs, *Dr. Peterson*, Jim Boles, *Scotty*. R. $8,870,000.

Dreadful soap opera focusing on a group of ridiculous stereotypical jet-setters. Kirk Douglas stars as a has-been movie producer who does anything for his daughter (Deborah Raffin), including marrying a rich woman (Alexis Smith) just to support her. This woman is also having a love affair with another woman (Melina Mercouri). *Once Is Not Enough* is in reality a very tame film, not the shocker it was purported to be, and it is also very dull.

631 The One and Only (1978) *** Paramount, 98 min. *Dir* Carl Reiner, *Scr* Steve Gordon, *Cin* Victor J. Kemper, *Ed* Bud Molin, *Des* Edward Carfagno,

Mus Patrick Williams, *Prod* Steve Gordon, David V. Picker, *Exec Prod* Robert Halmi.

Cast: Henry Winkler, *Andy Schmidt*, Kim Darby, *Mary Crawford*, Gene Saks, *Sidney Seltzer*, William Daniels, *Mr. Crawford*, Harold Gould, *Hector Moses*, Polly Holliday, *Mrs. Crawford*, Herve Villechaize, *Milton Miller*, Bill Baldwin, *Announcer in Des Moines*, Anthony Battaglia, *Little Andy*, Ed Begley, Jr., *Arnold the King*, Brandon Cruz, *Sherman*, Charles Frank, *Paul Harris*, Will Seltzer, *Eddie*. PG. $12,190,000.

Surprisingly effective comedy about an obnoxious and conceited, but unsuccessful, actor (Henry Winkler), who turns to wrestling when he can't find work. *The One and Only* follows his life from college, where he meets the girl he later marries (Kim Darby), to his stardom as a Gorgeous George-type wrestler. This character in reality is so loathesome that Winkler, director Carl Reiner, and scriptor Steve Gordon have performed a minor miracle in bringing him to life.

632 One Flew Over the Cuckoo's Nest (1975) (A, G, BFA) ***** 129 min. *Dir* Milos Forman (A, G, BFA, D), *Scr* Bo Goldman, Lawrence Hauben (A, G, W), based on novel by Ken Kesey, *Cin* Bill Butler (AN), William A. Fraker, Haskell Wexler (AN), *Ed* Richard Chew, Sheldon Kahn, Lynzee Klingman (AN), *Des* Paul Sylbert, *Art* Edwin O'Donovan, *Mus* Jack Nitzsche (AN), *Prod* Michael Douglas, Saul Zaentz, *Assoc Prod* Martin Fink.

Cast: Jack Nicholson, (A, NS, NY, NB, G, BFA), *R.P. McMurphy*, Louise Fletcher (A, G, BFA), *Nurse Ratched*, William Redfield, *Harding*, Michael Berryman, *Ellis*, Brad Dourif (AN), *Billy Bibbit*, Peter Brocco, *Col. Matterson*, Dean R. Brooks, *Dr. Spivey*, Alonzo Brown, *Miller*, Sherman "Scatman" Crothers, *Turkle*, Mwako Cumbuku, *Warren*, Danny De Vito, *Martini*, William Duell, *Sefelt*, Josip Elic, *Bancini*, Lan Fendors, *Nurse Itsu*, Nathan George, *Washington*, Ken Kenny, *Beans Garfield*, Mel Lambert, *Harbor Master*, Sydney Lassick, *Cheswick*, Kay Lee, *Night Supervisor*, Christopher Lloyd, *Taber*, Dwight Marfield, *Ellsworth*, Ted Markland, *Hap Arlish*, Louisa Moritz, *Rose*, Phil Roth, *Woolsey*, Will Sampson, *Chief Bromden*, Mimi Sarkisian, *Nurse Pilbow*, Vincent Schiavelli, *Fredrickson*, Marya Small, *Candy*, Delos V. Smith, Jr., *Scanlon*, Tin Welch, *Ruckley*. R. $59,165,000.

Superb study of rebellion in a mental institution. Jack Nicholson gives one of his best performances as a prisoner who pretends to be insane so he can be transferred to an institution where he thinks life will be easier. There he encounters the evil and misguided Nurse Ratched (Louise Fletcher) and his disrupting of the hospital's normal routine leads to a tragic conclusion. Milos Forman not only has brought out superb performances from the entire cast, many of whom are nonprofessionals, but he has fashioned a brilliant allegory of authoritative society.

633 One of Our Dinosaurs Is Missing (1975) * Britain, Buena Vista, 93 min. *Dir* Robert Stevenson, *Scr* Bill Walsh, based on novel *The Great Dinosaur Robbery*, By David Forrest, *Cin* Paul Beeson, *Ed* Hugh Scaife, *Art* Michael Stringer, *Mus* Ron Goodwin, *Prod* Bill Walsh, A Walt Disney Production.

Cast: Peter Ustinov, *Hnup Wan*, Helen Hayes, *Hettie*, Clive Revill, *Quon*, Derek Nimmo, *Lord Southmere*, Joan Sims, *Emily*, Bernard Bresslaw,

Fan Choy, Natasha Pyne, *Susan*, Roy Kinnear, *Superintendent Grubbs*, Joss Ackland, *B.J. Spence*, Deryck Guyler, *Harris*, Andrew Dove, *Lord Castleberry*, Max Harris, *Truscott*. G. $4,775,000.

Dull Disney comedy about the search for a vital microfilm hidden somewhere in the bones of a dinosaur skeleton at the British Natural History Museum. Chinese secret agents steal the entire skeleton and they are subsequently pursued by English nannies led by Helen Hayes. The whole thing is silly and not well handled; the slapstick is too broad and the actors overplay their parts.

634 **One on One** (1977) ** Warner Bros., 98 min. *Dir* Lamont Johnson, *Scr* Robby Benson, Jerry Segal, *Cin* Donald M. Morgan, *Ed* Robbe Roberts, *Art* Sherman Laudermilk, *Cos* Donfeld, *Mus* Charles Fox, *Lyrics* Paul Williams, *Songs* performed by Seals and Crofts, *Prod* Martin Hornstein, *Assoc Prod* Ron Windred.

Cast: Robby Benson, *Henry Steele*, Annette O'Toole, *Janet Hays*, G.D. Spradlin, *Coach Moreland Smith*, Gail Strickland, *B.J. Rudolph*, Melanie Griffith, *Hitchhiker*, James G. Richardson, *Malcolm*, Hector Morales, *Gonzales*, Cory Faucher, *Tom*. PG. $13,100,000.

Dismal drama about a misfit college basketball player who is harassed by his coach. This was intended to be an uplifting sports film that would arouse an audience to root for an underdog, much like *Rocky*. Unfortunately, as played by Robby Benson, this mistreated player comes off as a moron who deserves to be thrown off the team. G.D. Spradlin as the coach gives the film's best performance and should gain audience sympathy.

635 **The Onion Field** (1979) *** Avco Embassy, 126 min. *Dir* Harold Becker, *Scr* Joseph Wambaugh, based on his book, *Cin* Charles Rosher, *Ed* John W. Wheeler, *Des* Brian Eatwell, Joe Hubbard, *Mus* Eumir Deodato, *Prod* Walter Coblenz.

Cast: John Savage, *Karl Hettinger*, James Woods, *Greg Powell*, Franklyn Seales, *Jimmy Smith*, Ted Danson, *Ian Campbell*, Ronny Cox, *Pierce Brooks*, David Huffman, *D.A. Phil Halpin*, Christopher Lloyd, *Jailhouse Lawyer*, Diane Hull, *Helen Hettinger*, Priscilla Pointer, *Chrissie Campbell*, Beege Barkett, *Greg's Woman*, Richard Herd, *Beat Cop*, Le Tari, *Emmanuel McFadden*, Richard Venture, *Glenn Bates*, Lee Weaver, *Billy*, Phillip R. Allen, *D.A. Marshall Schulman*, Pat Corley, *Jimmy's Lawyer #2*, K. Callan, *Mrs. Powell*, Sandy McPeak, *Mr. Powell*, Lillian Randolph, *Nana*, Ned Wilson, *LAPD Captain*, Jack Rader, *IAD Captain*, Raleigh Bond, *Judge #2*, Stanley Grover, *Greg's Lawyer #2*, Michael Pataki, *D.A. Dino Fulgoni*, Steve Conte, *Prison Guard #1*. R. $5,000,000.

Disappointing story, based on a true incident of the murder of a California policeman and the subsequent trial in which the killer defends himself and makes a mockery of the judicial system. *The Onion Field* unfortunately skips over the several courtroom scenes, leaving the details of the trial confused and muddled. Where this film does succeed is in the documentation of the gradual breakdown of the murdered cop's partner, due to his feeling of guilt.

636 **The Only Game in Town** (1970) * 20th Century–Fox, 113 min. *Dir* George Stevens, *Scr* Frank D.Gilroy, based on his play, *Cin* Henri Decae, *Ed*

John W. Holmes, William Sands, Pat Shade, *Art* Herman Blumenthal, Auguste Capelier, *Cos* Mia Fonssagrives, Vicki Tiel, *Mus* Maurice Jarre, *Prod* Fred Kohlmar.

Cast: Elizabeth Taylor, *Fran*, Warren Beatty, *Joe Grady*, Charles Braswell, *Lockwood*, Hank Henry, *Tony*, Olga Valery, *Woman with Purple Wig*. PG.

Dreary love story, set in Las Vegas, about a gambler (Warren Beatty) and a chorus girl (Elizabeth Taylor). *The Only Game in Town* is extremely dull as it is little more than Beatty and Taylor talking in a room. This could be acceptable had they had something interesting to say, but they do not. The main reason for the overabundance of indoor scenes is the fact that the film was shot in Paris rather than Las Vegas.

637 **Opening Night** (1977) *** Faces, 144 min. *Dir* John Cassavetes, *Scr* John Cassavetes, *Cin* Al Ruban, *Ed* Tom Cornwell, *Art* Brian Ryman, *Cos* Alexandra Corwin-Hankin, *Mus* Bo Harwood, *Prod* Al Ruban, *Exec Prod* Sam Shaw, *Assoc Prod* Michael Lally.

Cast: Gena Rowlands (BF), *Myrtle Gordon*, John Cassavetes, *Maurice Aarons*, Ben Gazzara, *Manny Victor*, Joan Blondell, *Sarah Goode*, Paul Stewart, *David Samuels*, Zohra Lampert, *Dorothy Victor*, Laura Johnson, *Nancy Stein*, John Tuell, *Gus Simmons*, Ray Powers, *Jimmy*, John Finnegan, *Prop Man*, Louise Fitch, *Kelly*, Fred Draper, *Leo*, Katherine Cassavetes, *Vivian*, Lady Rowlands, *Melva Drake*. Not Rated.

Interesting drama about a strange actress (Gena Rowlands), who is on the verge of a breakdown, while preparing for a Broadway play. She reflects on her personal life after witnessing a tragedy. Although Cassavetes focuses on show people rather than average middle-class people. *Opening Night* is much like his other films, and Rowlands gives another excellent performance.

638 **Orca** (1977) ** Paramount, 92 min. *Dir* Michael Anderson, *Scr* Sergio Donati, Luciano Vincenzoni, *Cin* Ted Moore, *Underwater Cin* Vittorio Dragonetti, *Ed* John Bloom, Marion Rothman, Ralph E. Winters, *Des* Mario Garbuglia, *Art* Ferdinando Giovannoni, Boris Juraga, *Cos* Jost Jakob, Philippe Pickford, *Mus* Ennio Morricone, *Lyrics* Coro Connors, *Prod* Luciano Vincenzoni, Presented by Dino De Laurentiis.

Cast: Richard Harris, *Nolan*, Charlotte Rampling, *Rachel*, Will Sampson, *Umilak*, Bo Derek, *Annie*, Keenan Wynn, *Novak*, Robert Carradine, *Ken*, Scott Walker, *Swain*, Peter Hooten, *Paul*, Wayne Heffley, *Priest*, Vincent Gentile, *Gas Station Man*, Don "Red" Barry, *Dock Worker*. PG. $9,430,000.

Silly adventure film about a whale that seeks revenge on a shark-hunter (Richard Harris), who has harpooned its mate. Harris decides to fight back and it becomes a battle of wits between man and whale. Except for some truly fine special effects scenes, *Orca* is boring, with much of the dialogue consisting of a science lecture about whales.

639 **The Organization** (1971) ** United Artists, 107 min. *Dir* Don Medford, *Scr* James R. Webb, based on character created by John Ball, *Cin* Joseph Biroc, *Ed* Ferris Webster, *Des* James F. McGuire, *Art* George B. Chan, *Cos* Angela Alexander, Wes Jefferies, John K. Lemons, *Prod* Walter Mirisch.

Cast: Sidney Poitier, *Lt. Virgil Tibbs*, Barbara McNair, *Valerie Tibbs*, Sheree North, *Gloria Morgan*, Gerald S. O'Loughlin, *Lt. Jack Pecora*, Raul

Julia, *Juan Mendoza*, Ron O'Neal, *Joe Paraley*, Lani Miyazaki, *Annie Sekido*, Allen Garfield, (Goorwitz), *Benjy*, Bernie Hamilton, *Lt. Jessup*, Fred Beir, *Bob Alford*, Graham Jarvis, *William Martin*, James A. Watson, Jr., *Stacy Baker*, Charles H. Gray, *Morgan*, Jarion Monroe, *Larry French*, Daniel Travanti, *Sgt. Chassman*, Billy "Green" Bush, *Dave Thomas*, Maxwell Gail, Jr., *Rudy*, George Spell, *Andy Tibbs*, Wanda Spell, *Ginny Tibbs*. PG. See *They Call Me Mr. Tibbs*.

640 **The Other** (1972) *** 20th Century–Fox, 100 min. *Dir* Robert Mulligan, *Scr* Tom Tryon, based on his novel, *Cin* Robert Surtees, *Ed* Folmar Blangsted, O. Nicholas Brown, *Des* Albert Brenner, *Cos* Joanne Haas, Tommy Welsh, *Mus* Jerry Goldsmith, *Prod* Robert Mulligan, *Exec Prod* Tom Tryon, *Assoc Prod* Don Kranze.

Cast: Chris Udvarnoky, *Niles Perry*, Martin Udvarnoky, *Holland Perry*, Uta Hagan, *Ada*, Diana Muldaur, *Alexandra*, Norma Connolly, *Aunt Vee*, Victor French, *Angelini*, Loretta Leversee, *Winnie*, Lou Frizzell, *Uncle George*, Portia Nelson, *Mrs. Rowe*, Jenny Sullivan, *Torrie*, John Ritter, *Rider*, Jack Collins, *Mr. P.C. Pretty*, Ed Bakey, *Chan-Yu*, Clarence Crow, *Russell*. PG.

Interesting mystery thriller focusing on two strange twin brothers, who are direct opposites. One is mischievous and a trouble-maker, while the other brother is more level-headed, but there is a reason for their differences. *The Other* is deliberately paced and slowly builds to its surprise conclusion. The thrills are more cerebral, without resorting to physical violence.

641 **The Other Side of Midnight** (1977) ** 20th Century–Fox, 165 min. *Dir* Charles Jarrott, *Scr* Herman Raucher, Daniel Taradash, based on novel by Sidney Sheldon, *Cir* Fred Koenekamp, *Ed* Donn Cambern, Harold F. Kress, *Des* John DeCuir, *Cos* Irene Sharaff (AN), *Mus* Michel Legrand, *Prod* Frank Yablans, *Exec Prod* Howard W. Koch, Jr.

Cast: Marie-France Pisier, *Noelle Page*, John Beck, *Larry Douglas*, Susan Sarandon, *Catherine Douglas*, Raf Vallone, *Constantin Demeris*, Clu Gulager, *Bill Fraser*, Christian Marquand, *Armand Gautier*, Michael Lerner, *Barbet*, Sorrell Booke, *Lanchon*, Anthony Ponzini, *Co-Pilot Metaxes*, Louis Zorich, *Demonides*, Charles Cioffi, *Chotas*, Dimitra Arliss, *Sister Teresa*, Jan Arvan, *Warden*, Josette Banzet, *Madame Rosa*, John Chappell, *Doc Peterson*, Eunice Christopher, *Female Guard*, Roger Etienne, *Jacques Page*. R. $18,410,000.

Above average, but overlong, trashy soap opera about a French woman who spends years plotting revenge on an American soldier, who had jilted her in World War II. This rises slightly above other potboilers, mainly due to the performance of Marie-France Pisier, who dominates the film, as the French woman. Pisier, a great actress, deserved better than this for her first American starring role, but she does her best to make this a worthy film.

642 **The Other Side of the Mountain** (1975) * Universal, 103 min. *Dir* Larry Peerce, *Scr* David Seltzer, based on *A Long Way Up* by E.G. Valens, *Cin* David M. Walsh, *Ed* Eve Newman, *Cos* Grady Hunt, *Mus* Charles Fox, *Song*, "Richard's Window" Charles Fox, Norman Gimbel (AN), Sung by Olivia Newton-John, *Prod* Edward S. Feldman.

Cast: Marilyn Hassett, *Jill Kinmont*, Beau Bridges, *Dick Buek*, Belinda J. Montgomery, *Audra-Jo*, Nan Martin, *June Kinmont*, William Bryant, *Bill Kinmont*, Dabney Coleman, *Dave McCoy*, Bill Vint, *Buddy Warner*, Hampton

Fancher, *Lee Zadroga*, William Roerick, *Dr. Pittman*, Don Brenner, *Cookie,* Walter Brooke, *Dean*, Jocelyn Jones, *Linda Meyers*, Greg Mabrey, *Bob Kinmont*, Tony Becker, *Jerry Kinmont*, Griffin Dunne, *Herbie Johnson*, Warren Miller, *Dr. Enders*, Robin Pepper, *Skeeter Werner*, Brad Savage, *Boy in Wheelchair*. PG. $18,475,000.

Poor biography of Olympic hopeful skier Jill Kinmont, who was paralyzed in a tragic skiing accident. Her heroic story is given the ususal Hollywood treatment and emerges as an insipid and overly sentimental soap opera. The first half is merely bad, but the second half, which has her fall in love with a daredevil, is simply dreadful. The result is predictable and was only intended to wrench more tears from the audience. In the sequel Jill gets married and finally finds true happiness. An end title explaining her fate would have sufficed.

643 **The Other Side of the Mountain Part 2** (1978) * Universal, 105 min. *Dir* Larry Peerce, *Scr* Douglas Day Stewart, *Cin* Ric Waite, *Ed* Walter Hannemann, Eve Newman, *Art* William Campbell, *Mus* Lee Holdridge, *Lyrics* Molly-Ann Leikin, songs sung by Merrily Webber, *Prod* Edward S. Feldman, *Assoc Prod* Donna R. Dubrow.

Cast: Marilyn Hassett, *Jill Kinmont*, Timothy Bottoms, *John Boothe*, Nan Martin, *June Kinmont*, Belinda J. Montgomery, *Audra-Jo*, Gretchen Corbett, *Linda*, William Bryant, *Bill Kinmont*, James A. Bottoms, *Mr. Boothe*, June Dayton, *Mrs. Boothe*, Curtis Credel, *Roy Boothe*, Carole Tru Foster, *Beverly Boothe,* Charles Frank, *Mel*, George Petrie, *Doctor in Los Angeles*. PG. $7,345,000. See *The Other Side of the Mountian*.

644 **Our Time** (1974) ** Warner Bros., 90 min. *Dir* Peter Hyams, *Scr* Jane C. Stanton, *Cin* Jules Brenner, *Ed* James Mitchell, *Art* Peter Wooley, *Mus* Michel Legrand, *Prod* Richard A. Roth.

Cast: Pamela Sue Martin, *Abby*, Betsy Slade, *Muffy*, Parker Stevenson, *Michael*, George O'Hanlon, Jr., *Malcolm*, Karen Balkin, *Laura*, Debralee Scott, *Ann*, Nora Heflin, *Emmy*, Kathryn Holcomb, *Helen*, Roderick Cook, *Headmaster*, Edith Atwater, *Mrs. Pendleton*, Marijane Maricle, *Miss Picard*, Meg Wyllie, *Nurse*, Mary Jackson, *Miss Moran*, Carol Arthur, *Gym Teacher*, Hope Summers, *Biology Teacher*, Jerry Hardin, *Keats*, Robert Walden, *Frank*, Michael Gray, *Buzzy*. PG.

Dull drama set at a Massachussets girls' boarding school in 1955. The film focuses on two particular girls (Pamela Sue Martin, Betsy Slade) and their experiences with boys. *Our Time* was intended to be a realistic portrait of the girls' sexual awakening, but it is nothing more than a teeny bopper soap opera. Other title, *Death of Her Innocence*.

645 **The Out-of-Towners** (1970) *** Paramount, 98 min. *Dir* Arthur Hiller, *Scr* Neil Simon, *Cin* Andrew Laszlo, *Ed* Fred Chulack, *Art* Charles Bailey, *Cos* Forrest T. Butler, Grace Harris, *Mus* Quincy Jones, *Prod* Paul Nathan.

Cast: Jack Lemmon, *George Kellerman*, Sandy Dennis, *Gwen Kellerman*, Sandy Baron, *TV Man*, Anne Meara, *Woman in Police Station*, Robert Nichols, *Man in Plane*, Ann Prentiss, *Airline Stewardess*, Graham Jarvis, *Murray*, Ron Carey, *Boston Cab Driver*, Phil Bruns, *Officer Meyers*, Carlos Montalban, *Cuban Diplomat*, Billy Dee Williams, *Boston Lost and Found,*

Anthony Holland, *Hotel Night Clerk*, Paul Dooley, *Hotel Day Clerk*, Robert King, *Boston Agent*, Johnny Brown, *Waiter on Train*, Dolph Sweet, *Police Sergeant*, Jack Crowder, *Police Officer*, Jon Korkes, Robert Walden, *Looters*, Richard Libertini, *Boston Baggage Man*. G. $7,250,000.

Above average Neil Simon comedy about the horrors that befall a businessman (Jack Lemmon) and his wife (Sandy Dennis), while in New York City for a job interview. Simon piles on one tragedy after another, almost to the point of excess, but Lemmon's reactions to each new situation are comic gems, and his dynamic performance holds *The Out-of-Towners* together.

646 **The Outfit** (1973) ** MGM, 102 min. *Dir* John Flynn, *Scr* John Flynn, based on novel by Richard Stark, *Cin* Bruce Surtees, *Ed* Ralph E. Winters, *Art* Tambi Larsen, *Mus* Jerry Fielding, *Prod* Carter De Haven.

Cast: Robert Duvall, *Macklin*, Karen Black, *Bett Harrow*, Joe Don Baker, *Cody*, Robert Ryan, *Mailer*, Timothy Carey, *Menner*, Richard Jaeckel, *Chemey*, Sheree North, *Buck's Wife*, Felice Orlandi, *Frank Orlandi*, Marie Windsor, *Madge Coyle*, Jane Greer, *Alma*, Henry Jones, *Doctor*, Joanna Cassidy, *Rita*, Tom Reese, *1st Man*, Elisha Cook, *Carl*, Bill McKinney, *Buck*, Anita O'Day, *Herself*, Archie Moore, *Packard*, Tony Young, *Accountant*, Roland LaStarza, *Hit Man*, Edward Ness, *Ed Macklin*, Roy Roberts, *Bob Caswell*. PG.

Standard contemporary gangster thriller. Robert Duvall stars as an ex-con, who seeks revenge on a syndicate boss (Robert Ryan) for killing his brother, who had robbed Ryan's bank. With the help of an old friend (Joe Don Baker), and girlfriend (Karen Black), Duvall begins robbing all of Ryan's operations. *The Outfit* is nothing new, and it ends with predictable mayhem.

647 **Outlaw Blues** (1977) ** Warner Bros., 100 min. *Dir* Richard T. Heffron, *Scr* B.W.L. Norton, *Cin* Jules Brenner, *Ed* Scott Conrad, Danford B. Green, *Art* Jack Marty, *Cos* Rosanna Norton, *Mus* Charles Bernstein, *Prod* Steve Tisch, *Exec Prod* Paul Heller, Fred Weintraub, *Assoc Prod* Eve Monley.

Cast: Peter Fonda, *Bobby Ogden*, Susan Saint James, *Tina Waters*, John Crawford, *Chief Cavenaugh*, James Callahan, *Garland Dupree*, Michael Lerner, *Hatch*, Steve Fromholz, *Elroy*, Richard Lockmiller, *Associate Warden*, Matt Clark, *Billy Bob*, Jan Rita Cobler, *Cathy Moss*, Gene Rader, *Leon Warback*, Curtis Harris, *Big Guy*, Jerry Greene, *Disc Jockey*, Dave Helfert, *Anchorman*, Jeffrey Friedman, *Newsman*, James N. Harrel, *Cop Chauffeur*. PG. $4,200,000.

Fair comedy chase thriller about a country singer on the run. Peter Fonda, after being released from prison, tracks down another singer (James Callahan), who has stolen one of his songs. When Callahan is accidently shot in a scuffle, Fonda becomes a target for a manhunt, but he is aided by Susan St. James, a member of Callahan's Group. *Outlaw Blues* is pleasant entertainment, but the direction and pacing are dull.

648 **The Outlaw Josey Wales** (1976) *** Warner Bros., 135 min. *Dir* Clint Eastwood, *Scr* Sonia Chernus, Philip Kaufman, based on novel *Gone to Texas* by Forrest Carter, *Cin* Bruce Surtees, *Ed* Ferris Webster, *Des* Tambi Larsen, *Mus* Jerry Fielding (AN), *Prod* Robert Daley.

Cast: Clint Eastwood, *Josey Wales*, Chief Dan George, *Lone Watie*, Sondra Locke, *Laura Lee*, Bill McKinney, *Terrill*, John Vernon, *Fletcher*, Paula

Trueman, *Grandma Sarah*, Sam Bottoms, *Jamie*, Geraldine Keams, *Little Moonlight*, Woodrow Parfrey, *Carpetbagger*, Joyce Jameson, *Rose*, Sheb Wooley, *Cobb*, Royal Dano, *Ten Spot*, Matt Clark, *Kelly*, John Verros, *Chato*, Will Sampson, *Ten Bears*, William O'Connell, *Carstairs*, John Quade, *Comanchero Leader*. PG. $13,500,000.

Above average vengeance western. Clint Eastwood stars as a farmer, living after the Civil War, who seeks revenge for the murder of his family by Union soldiers, and subsequently becomes an outlaw. This moody, episodic film is well directed by Eastwood and has more depth than most films of its genre. *The Outlaw Josey Wales* may be slightly overlong, but it is still Eastwood's best western.

649 **Over the Edge** (1979) ** Orion, 95 min. *Dir* Jonathan Kaplan, *Scr* Charlie Hass, Tim Hunter, *Cin* Andrew Davis, *Ed* Robert Bargere, *Des* Jim Newport, *Mus* Sol Kaplan, *Prod* George Litto.

Cast: Michael Kramer, *Carl*, Pamela Ludwig, *Cory*, Matt Dillon, *Richie*, Vincent Spano, *Mark*, Tom Fergus, *Claude*, Harry Northup, *Doberman*, Andy Romano, *Fred*, Ellen Geer, *Sandra*, Richard Jamison, *Cole*, Julia Pomeroy, *Julia*, Tiger Thompson, *Johnny*. PG.

Standard rebellious youth film set in a suburban development. This change of setting from the urban streets does not add any relevance to the subject, as *Over the Edge* is nothing more than a mindless and manipulative action film. The film also has the audacity to castigate a cop for defending himself against a youth who pulls a gun on him. Many of the cast members overact terribly and the whole film is misguided.

650 **The Owl and the Pussycat** (1970) *** Columbia, 96 min. *Dir* Herbert Ross, *Scr* Buck Henry, based on play by Bill Manhoff, *Cin* Harry Stradling, Andrew Laszlo, *Ed* Margaret Booth, John F. Burnett, *Des* John Robert Lloyd, *Art* Philip Rosenberg, Robert Wightman, *Cos* Ann Roth, *Mus* Richard Halligan, *Prod* Ray Stark, *Assoc Prod* George Justin.

Cast: Barbra Streisand, *Doris*, George Segal, *Felix*, Robert Klein, *Barney*, Allen Garfield (Goorwitz), *Dress Shop Proprietor*, Roz Kelly, *Eleanor*, Jacques Sandulescu, *Rapzinsky*, Jack Manning, *Weyderhaus*, Grace Carney, *Mrs. Weyderhaus*, Barbara Anson, *Miss Weyderhaus*, Kim Chan, *Theatre Cashier*, Stan Gottlieb, *Coatcheck Man*, Joe Madden, *Old Man Neighbor*, Fay Sappington, *Old Woman Neighbor*, Evelyn Land, *Barney's Girl*, Dominic T. Barto, *Man in Bar*, Marshall Ward, Tom Atkins, Stan Bryant, *Gang in Car*. R. $11,645,000.

Fine comedy character study about the relationship of an introverted book clerk (George Segal) and a bombastic prostitute (Barbra Streisand). *The Owl and the Pussycat* is almost entirely a two character film, that nearly dispenses with plot and focuses more on their mismatched relationship. The script tends to be more shrill and vulgar than witty, but Segal and Streisand somehow make it work.

651 **The Panic in Needle Park** (1971) *** 20th Century–Fox, 110 min. *Dir* Jerry Schatzberg, *Scr* Joan Didion, John Gregory Dunne, based on novel by James Mills, *Cin* Adam Holender, *Ed* Evan Lottman, *Art* Murray P. Stern, *Cos* Jo Ynocencio, *Prod* Dominick Dunne, *Assoc Prod* Roger M. Rothstein.

Cast: Al Pacino, *Bobby*, Kitty Winn (CF), *Helen*, Alan Vint, *Hotch*,

Richard Bright, *Hank*, Keil Martin, *Chico*, Michael McClanathan, *Sonny*, Warren Finnerty, *Sammy*, Marcia Jean Kurtz, *Marcie*, Raul Julia, *Marco*, Angie Ortega, *Irene*, Larry Marshall, *Mickey*, Paul Mace, *Whitey*, Nancy MacKay, *Penny*, Gil Rogers, *Robins*, Joe Santos, *Di Bono*, Paul Sorvino, *Samuels*. R.

Powerful drama about drug addiction. Al Pacino is superb, in his first starring role, as a junkie, who introduces his girlfriend (Kitty Winn) to his decadent world filled with other junkies, thieves, etc. and nearly destroys her in the process. *The Panic in Needle Park* is one of the best films on the subject and is sort of a drug version of *The Days of Wine and Roses*.

652 **The Paper Chase** (1973) * * * 20th Century–Fox, 112 min. *Dir* James Bridges, *Scr* James Bridges (AN), based on novel by John Jay Osborn, Jr., *Cin* Gordon Willis, *Ed* Walter Thompson, *Art* George Jenkins, *Prod* Rodrick Paul, Robert C. Thompson.

Cast: Timothy Bottoms, *Hart*, Lindsay Wagner, *Susan*, John Houseman (A, NB, G), *Kingsfield*, Graham Beckel, *Ford*, Edward Hermann, *Anderson*, Bob Lydiard, *O'Connor*, Craig Richard Nelson, *Bell*, James Naughton, *Kevin*, Regina Buff, *Asheley*, David Clennon, *Toombs*, Lenny Baker, *Moss*. PG. $4,000,000.

Well-made comedy-drama set at Harvard Law School. *The Paper Chase* does an excellent job of documenting the pressures and the hardships of college, possibly better than any other film, but then it throws in an extraneous love story involving the lead character and young woman, who just happens to be his tough professor's daughter. This unfortunately damages what could have been a great film. The classroom scenes, dominated by the banter between the student (Timothy Bottoms) and his professor (John Houseman), are absolute gems; it is unfortunate the rest of the film could not have been on the same level.

653 **Paper Moon** (1973) * * * * Paramount, 102 min. *Dir* Peter Bogdanovich, *Scr* Alvin Sargent (AN, W), based on novel *Addie Pray* by Joe David Brown, *Cin* Laszlo Kovacs, *Ed* Verna Fields, *Des* Polly Platt, *Prod* Peter Bogdanovich.

Cast: Ryan O'Neal, *Moses Pray*, Tatum O'Neal (A), *Addie Loggins*, Madeline Kahn (AN), *Trixie Delight*, John Hillerman, *Deputy Hardin/Bootlegger*, P.J. Johnson, *Imogene*, Burton Gilliam, *Floyd*, Randy Quaid, *Leroy*, Dorothy Forster, *Widow Huff*, Jesse Lee Fulton, *Miss Ollie*, Jim Harrell, *Minister*, Lila Waters, *Minister's Wife*, Noble Willingham, *Robertson*, Bob Young, *Gas Station Attendant*, Jack Saunders, *Station Master*, Liz Ross, *Widow Pearl Morgan*, Yvonne Harrison, *Widow Marie Bates*, Ed Reed, *Lawman*. PG. $16,560,000.

Charming Depression-era comedy about a pair of con-artists and their travels through the midwest. Ryan O'Neal and his real-life daughter Tatum O'Neal, in a splendid movie debut, are excellent together as a phoney Bible salesman and a little girl, who may or may not be his daughter. He becomes stuck with her because he owes her money, but soon discovers she is a better con-artist than he is. Bogdanovich filmed *Paper Moon*, in black-and white to evoke the style of the films of the thirties and to give it a somewhat realistic tone.

654 **Papillon** (1973) * * * Allied Artists, 150 min. *Dir* Franklin J. Schaffner, *Scr* Lorenzo Semple, Jr., Dalton Trumbo, based on book by Henri Charriere, *Cin* Fred Koenekamp, *Ed* Robert Swink, *Des* Anthony Masters, *Art* Jack Maxsted, *Mus* Jerry Goldsmith (AN), *Prod* Robert Dorfman, Franklin J. Schaffner, *Exec Prod* Ted Richmond.

Cast: Steve McQueen, *Papillon*, Dustin Hoffman, *Dega*, Victor Jory, *Indian Chief*, Don Gordon, *Julot*, Anthony Zerbe, *Leper Colony Chief*, Robert Deman, *Maturette*, Woodrow Parfrey, *Clusiot*, Bill Mumy, *Lariot*, George Coulouris, *Dr. Chatal*, Ratna Assan, *Zoraima*, William Smithers, *Warden Barrot*, Gregory Sierra, *Antonio*, Barbara Morrison, *Mother Superior*, Ellen Moss, *Nun*, Don Hanmer, *Butterfly Trader*, Dalton Trumbo, *Commandant*. PG. $22,500,000.

Disappointing epic of real-life exploits of Henri Charriere (Papillon), the man who escaped from Devils Island. Life on Devil's Island is seemingly well documented as the audience is assaulted with one horror after another. *Papillon's* main fault lies in its characterizations. Charriere's character, an essential ingredient, is almost totally lost under the huge production, and the part of Dega was unnecessarily increased merely to fill the role with a major star. This film, however, does succeed as a prison drama, although it does tend to go too far at times.

655 **Paradise Alley** (1978) * * * * * Universal, 107 min. *Dir* Sylvester Stallone, *Scr* Sylvester Stallone, *Cin* Laszlo Kovacs, *Ed* Eve Newman, *Des* John W. Corso, *Art* Deborah Beaudet, *Cos* Sandra Berke, Lambert Marks, *Mus* Bill Conti, *Prod* John F. Roach, *Exec Prod* Edward Pressman, *Assoc Prod* Arthur Chobanian.

Cast: Sylvester Stallone, *Cosmo Carboni*, Armand Assante, *Lenny*, Lee Canalito, *Victor*, Kevin Conway, *Stich*, Anne Archer, *Annie*, Joe Spinell, *Burp*, Aimee Eccles, *Susan Chow*, Terry Funk, *Frankie the Thumper*, Joyce Ingalls, *Bunchie*, Frank McRae, *Big Glory*, Tom Waits, *Mumbles*. PG.

Superb period comedy about three brothers (Sylvester Stallone, Armand Assante, Lee Canalito) struggling to get out of the slums of New York's Hell Kitchen during the 1940's. Stallone cooks up a wild scheme turning Canalito into a wrestler and he drags in Assante to assist. *Paradise Alley* is an odd film that mixes in stylistic touches of Damon Runyan and Federico Fellini. Stallone made a surprisingly effective directorial debut.

656 **The Parallax View** (1974) * * * * Paramount, 100 min. *Dir* Alan J. Pakula, *Scr* David Giler, Lorenzo Semple, Jr. based on novel by Loren Singer, *Cin* Gordon Willis, *Ed* Jack Wheeler, *Art* George Jenkins, *Cos* Frank Thompson, *Mus* Michael Small, *Prod* Alan J. Pakula, *Exec Prod* Gabriel Katzka, *Assoc Prod* Charles Maguire.

Cast: Warren Beatty, *Frady*, Paula Prentiss, *Lee Carter*, William Daniels, *Austin*, Walter McGinn, *Jack*, Hume Cronyn, *Rintels*, Kelly Thordsen, *L.D.*, Chuck Waters, *Assassin (Busboy)*, Earl Hindman, *Red*, Bill Joyce, *Sen. Carroll*, Bettie Johnson, *Mrs. Carroll*, Bill McKinney, *Art* Joanna Harris, *Chrissy*, Ted Gehring, *Schecter*, Lee Pulford, *Shirley*, Doria Cook, *Gale*, Jim Davis, *Hammond*, Joan Lemmo, *Organist*, Anthony Zerbe, *Schwartzkopf*, Kenneth Mars, *Turner*. R.

Exciting thriller based on theories of the Kennedy assassinations. Warren

Beatty is excellent as a newspaper reporter who investigates the mysterious deaths of all the witnesses to the assassination of a U.S. Senator and uncovers a conspiracy involving a secret company, the Parallax Corp., that trains assassins. This is one of Alan J. Pakula's finest achievements, but it was unfairly neglected at the time of its release.

657 **Part 2, Sounder** (1976) ** Gamma III, 98 min. *Dir* William Graham, *Scr* Lonne Elder III, based on novel by William H. Armstrong, *Cin* Urs. B. Furrer, *Ed* Sid Levin, *Des* Walter Scott Herndon, *Mus* Taj Mahal, *Prod* Terry Nelson, *Exec Prod* Robert B. Radnitz.

Cast: Harold Sylvester, *Nathan*, Ebony Wright, *Rebecca*, Taj Mahal, *Ike*, Annazette Chase, *Camille*, Darryl Young, *David*, Erica Young, *Josie*, Ronald Bolden, *Earl*, Barbara Chaney, *Mrs. Boatwright*, Kuumba, *Harriet*, Ted Airhart, *Perkins*, Walter Breaux, *Stranger*, Harry Franklin, Sr., *Rev. Josephs*. G. See *Sounder*.

658 **Part 2, Walking Tall** (1975) ** American International, 109 min. *Dir* Earl Bellamy, *Scr* Howard B. Kreitsek, *Cin* Keith Smith, *Ed* Art Seid, *Art* Phil Jeffries, *Mus* Walter Scharf, *Prod* Charles A. Pratt.

Cast: Bo Svenson, *Buford*, Luke Askew, *Pinky*, Noah Beery, *Carl*, John Chandler, *Ray*, Robert DoQui, *Obra*, Bruce Glover, *Grady*, Richard Jaeckel, *Stud*, Brooke Mills, *Ruby*, Logan Ramsey, *John*, Angel Tompkins, *Marganne*, Lurene Tuttle, *Grandma*, William Bryant, *FBI Agent*, Leif Garrett, Dawn Lyn, *Pusser Children*. PG. $9,400,000. See *Walking Tall*.

659 **Pat Garrett and Billy the Kid** (1973) *** MGM, 106 min. *Dir* Sam Peckinpah, *Scr* Rudolph Wurlitzer, *Cin* John Coquillon, *Ed* David Berlatsky, Garth Craven, Tony de Zarraga, Richard Halsey, Roger Spottiswoode, Robert L. Wolfe, *Art* Ted Haworth, *Mus* Bob Dylan, *Prod* Gordon Carroll.

Cast: James Coburn, *Pat Garrett*, Kris Kristofferson, *Billy the Kid*, Richard Jaeckel, *Sheriff Kip McKinney*, Katy Jurado, *Mrs. Baker*, Chill Wills, *Lemeul*, Jason Robards, *Gov. Wallace*, Bob Dylan, *Alias*, Slim Pickens, *Sheriff Baker*, R.G. Armstrong, *Ollinger*, Luke Askew, *Eno*, John Beck, *Poe*, Richard Bright, *Holly*, Matt Clark, *J.W. Bell*, Rita Coolidge, *Maria*, Jack Dodson, *Howland*, Jack Elam, *Alamosa Bill*, Emilio Fernandez, *Paco*, Paul Fix, *Maxwell*, L.Q. Jones, *Black Harris*, Jorge Russek, *Silva*, Charlie Martin Smith, *Bowdre*, Harry Dean Stanton, *Luke*, Claudia Bryar, *Mrs. Horrell*, John Chandler, *Norris*, Mike Mikler, *Denver*, Aurora Clavel, *Ida*, Rutanya Alda, *Ruthie*, Walter Kelley, *Rupert*, Rudy Wurlitzer, *O'Folliard*, Elisha Cook, Jr., *Cody*, Gene Evans, *Horrell*, Donnie Fritts, *Beaver*, Dub Taylor, *Josh*, Don Levy, *Sackett*. R.

Underrated Sam Peckinpah western about lawman Parrett's pursuit of outlaw Billy the Kid, his former friend. *Pat Garrett and Billy the Kid* is far from perfect; it is not as tightly structured as Sam Peckinpah's best films. This is possibly due to the well publicized tampering by MGM, who supposedly re-edited the film on their own. In its present form, though, it is an above average western, with fine performances by Coburn and Kristofferson in the title roles.

660 **Patton** (1970) (A, NB) **** 20th Century–Fox, 170 min. *Dir* Franklin J. Schaffner (A, D), *Scr* Francis Coppola, Edmund H. North (A, W), based on factual material by Ladislas Farago, Omar N. Bradley, *Cin* Fred Koenekamp

(AN), *Ed* Hugh S. Fowler (A), *Art* Urie McCleary, Gil Parrando (A), *Mus* Jerry Goldsmith (AN), *Prod* Frank McCarthy, *Assoc Prod* Frank Coffey.

Cast: George C. Scott (A, NS, NY, NB, G), *Gen. George S. Patton, Jr.,* Karl Malden, *Gen. Omar N. Bradley,* Stephen Young, *Capt. Chester B. Hansen,* Michael Strong, *Brig. Gen. Hobert Carver,* Michael Bates, *Field Marshal Sir Bernard L. Montgomery,* Karl Michael Vogler, *Field Marshal Erwin Rommel,* Cary Loftin, *Gen. Bradley's Driver,* Albert Dumortier, *Moroccan Minister,* Frank Latimore, *Lt. Col. Henry Davenport,* Morgan Paull, *Capt. Richard N. Jensen,* Bill Hickman, *Gen. Patton's Driver,* Patrick J. Zurica, *1st Lt. Alexander Stiller,* James Edwards, *Sgt. William G. Meeks,* Lawrence Dobkin, *Col. Gaston Bell,* David Bauer, *Lt. Gen. Harry Buford,* John Barrie, *Air Vice-Marshal Sir Arthur Coningham,* Richard Muench, *Col. Gen. Alfred Jodl,* Siegfried Rauch, *Capt. Oskar Steiger,* Edward Binns, *Maj. Gen. Walter Beddell Smith,* Tim Considine, *Soldier who gets slapped.* PG. $28,100,000.

Spectacular film biography of the famous and infamous American WWII combat general. George C. Scott gives a classic performance in the title role and manages the miracle of bringing the character to life despite the film's magnitude. Not even the magnificent battle sequences and the huge arsenal of hardware can compete with Scott's commanding presence. *Patton* examines both sides of his personality, without making moral judgments about him.

661 **Payday** (1973) ******* Cinerama, 103 min. *Dir* Daryl Duke, *Scr* Don Carpenter, *Cin* Richard Glouner, *Ed* Richard Halsey, *Songs* Shel Silverstein, Ian and Sylvia Tyson, Bob Smith and Tommy McKinney, *Prod* Martin Fink, *Co-Prod* Don Carpenter, *Exec Prod* Ralph J. Gleason.

Cast: Rip Torn, *Maury Dann,* Ahna Capri, *Mayleen,* Elayne Heilveil, *Rosamond,* Michael C. Gwynne, *Clarence,* Jeff Morris, *Tally,* Cliff Emmich, *Chauffer,* Henry O. Arnold, *Ted,* Walter Bamberg, *Bridgeway,* Linda Spatz, *Sandy,* Eleanor Fell, *Galen Dann,* Clara Dunn, *Mama Dann,* Earle Trigg, *Disc Jockey,* Mike Edwards, *Restaurant Manager,* Winton McNair, *Highway Policeman.* R.

Interesting drama about an egotistical country music singer. The difficulties and hazards of show business and being on the road are well documented in *Payday,* showing how it can take its toll on human beings, particularly those who do not achieve their goals of success. The real highlight, though, is Rip Torn's brilliant performance as a thoroughly unlikable singer, who is unable to deal with this failure.

662 **Peeper** (1975) ****** 20th Century–Fox, 87 min. *Dir* Peter Hyams, *Scr* W.D. Richter, based on novel *Deadfall* by Keith Laumer, *Cin* Earl Rath, *Ed* James Mitchell, *Des* Albert Brenner, *Mus* Richard Clements, *Prod* Robert Chartoff, Irwin Winkler.

Cast: Michael Caine, *Tucker,* Natalie Wood, *Ellen Prendergast,* Thayer David, *Frank Prendergast,* Liam Dunn, *Billy Pate,* Dorothy Adams, *Mrs. Prendergast,* Timothy Agoglia Carey, *Sid,* Don Calfa, *Rosie,* Michael Constantine, *Anglich,* Snag Werris, *Burlesque Comic,* Liz Renay, *Burlesque Dancer,* Guy Marks, *Man in Alley,* Margo Winkler, *Lady with Luggage.* PG.

Okay period spoof of detective films. Michael Caine stars as a private eye who is hired by Michael Constantine to find his long-lost daughter, so she can get his inheritance. He encounters a strange family where Constantine's daughter may or may not be living. *Peeper* succeeds more in evoking the late 1940's, than as a spoof, as the humor is too light and inconsequential.

663 The People That Time Forgot (1977) ** Britain, American International, 90 min. *Dir* Kevin Connor, *Scr* Patrick Tilley, based on novel by Edgar Rice Burroughs, *Cin* Alan Hume, *Ed* John Ireland, Barry Peters, *Des* Maurice Carter, *Art* Bery Davey, Fernando Gonzalez, *Cos* Brenda Dabbs, *Mus* John Scott, *Prod* John Dark.

Cast: Patrick Wayne, *Ben*, Doug McClure, *Bowen*, Sarah Douglas, *Charley*, Dana Gillespie, *Ajor*, Thorley Walters, *Norfolk*, Shane Rimmer, *Hogan*, Tony Britton, John Hallam, Dave Prowse, Gaylord Reid, Kiram Shah, Richard Parmentier, Jimmy Ray, Tony McHale. PG. See *The Land That Time Forgot*.

664 A Perfect Couple (1979) *** 20th Century–Fox, 111 min. *Dir* Robert Altman, *Scr* Robert Altman, Allan Nicholls, *Cin* Edmond L. Koons, *Ed* Tony Lombardo, *Mus* Allan Nicholls, *Prod* Robert Altman, *Exec Prod* Tommy Thompson, *Assoc Prod* Scott Bushnell, Robert Eggenweiler.

Cast: Paul Dooley, *Alex*, Marta Heflin, *Sheila*, Titos Vandis, *Panos*, Belita Moreno, *Eleousa*, Henry Gibson, *Fred*, Dimitra Arliss, *Athena*, Allan Nicholls, *Dana 115*, Ann Ryerson, *Skye 147*, Pappy Lagos, *Melpomeni*, Dennis Franz, *Costa*, Margery Bond, *Wilma*, Mona Golabek, *Mona*, Terry Wills, *Ben*, Susan Blakeman, *Penelope*, Melanie Bishop, *Star*. PG.

Odd comedy love story about two people who meet through a dating service. The two come from entirely different backgrounds, she is a member of a large musical group and he is from a conservative Greek family. *A Perfect Couple* benefits most from Robert Altman's wonderful direction, although this is one of his weakest films, which makes the most of the film's deadpan humor. The major flaw is the overabundance of musical sequences, stemming from the woman's group.

665 Performance (1970) **** Britain, Warner Bros., 106 min. *Dir* Donald Cammell, Nicolas Roeg, *Scr* Donald Cammell, *Cin* Nicolas Roeg, *Ed* Antony Gibbs, *Art* John Clark, *Mus* Jack Nitzsche, *Song* "Memo from Turner", *Mus* Mick Jagger, *Prod* Sanford Lieberson, *Assoc Prod* David Cammell.

Cast: James Fox, *Charles*, Mick Jagger, *Turner*, Anita Pallenberg, *Pherber*, Michele Breton, *Lucy*, Ann Sidney, *Dana*, John Bindon, *Moody*, Stanley Meadows, *Rosebloom*, Allen Cuthbertson, *Lawyer*, Anthony Morton, *Dennis*, Johnny Shannon, *Harry*, Anthony Valentine, *Joey*, Ken Colley, *Tony*, John Sterland, *Chauffeur*, Laraine Wickens, *Lorraine*. X.

Bizarre and controversial film about a gangster marked for death by the mob, who hides in a communal apartment building run by Mick Jagger. *Performance* is a very strange film and can best be described as a gangster rock musical. It is filled with surrealistic fantasy musical sequences much in the style of Ken Russell. Made in 1968, it sat on the shelf for two years.

666 Pete 'n' Tillie (1972) *** Universal, 100 min. *Dir* Martin Ritt, *Scr* Julius J. Epstein (AN), based on novella *Witch's Milk* by Peter De Vries, *Cin* John A. Alonzo, *Ed* Frank Bracht, *Art* George Webb, *Cos* Edith Head, *Mus* John Williams, *Prod* Julius J. Epstein, *Exec Prod* Jennings Lang.

Cast: Walter Matthau, *Pete*, Carol Burnett, *Tillie*, Geraldine Page (AN), *Gertrude*, Barry Nelson, *Burt*, René Auberjonois, *Jimmy Twitchell*, Lee H.

Montgomery, *Robbie*, Henry Jones, *Mr. Tucker*, Kent Smith, *Father Keating*, Philip Bourneuf, *Dr. Willett*, Whit Bissell, *Minister*, Timothy Blake, *Lucy Lund*. PG. $7,970,000.

Unusual love story about two lonely middle-aged people (Walter Matthau, Carol Burnett), who marry and experience extreme marital difficulties, which are exacerbated by the death of their nine year old son. *Pete 'n' Tillie* is primarily a serious and sometimes sad film, but it does have its moments of humor, mostly provided by Matthau's wisecracking character, and the mixture is well balanced. Burnett is an excellent foil to Matthau.

667 **Pete's Dragon** (1977) ** Buena Vista, 134 min. *Dir* Don Chaffey, *Scr* Malcolm Marmorstein, based on story by S.S. Field, Seton I. Miller, *Cin* Frank Philips, *Ed* Gordon D. Brenner, *Art* John B. Mansbridge, Jack Martin Smith, *Cos* Bill Thomas, *Mus* Al Kasha, Joel Hirschhorn (AN), *Mus Adaptation* Irwin Kostal (AN), *Song* "Candle on the Water", *Mus* Al Kasha, Joel Hirschhorn (AN), *Chor* Onna White, *Prod* Jerome Courtland, Ron Miller; Walt Disney Prod.

Cast: Sean Marshall, *Pete*, Helen Reddy, *Nora*, Jim Dale, *Dr. Terminus*, Mickey Rooney, *Lampie*, Red Buttons, *Hoagy*, Shelly Winters, *Lena Gogan*, Jane Kean, *Miss Taylor*, Jim Backus, *The Mayor*, Charles Tyner, *Merle*, Jeff Conaway, *Willie*, Gary Morgan, *Grover*, Cal Bartlett, *Paul*, Charlie Callas, *Voice of Elliott*. G. $16,100,000.

Standard Disney fantasy comedy about an orphan boy, who runs away from his foster family and is befriended by a 12 foot tall clumsy dragon named Elliot. *Pete's Dragon* nicely mixes an animated dragon into the live-action, but it depends too much on this gimmick. Without it the story is nothing more than a tired musical, with the cast trying too hard for laughs.

668 **Phantasm** (1979) *** Avco Embassy, 90 min. *Dir* Don Coscarelli, *Scr* Don Coscarelli, *Cin* Don Coscarelli, *Ed* Don Coscarelli, *Des* S. Tyler, *Art* David Gavin Brown, *Mus* Fred Myrow, Malcolm Seagrave, *Prod* Don Coscarelli, *Co-Prod* Paul Pepperman.

Cast: Michael Baldwin, *Mike*, Bill Thornbury, *Jody*, Regie Bannister, *Reggie*, Lathy Lester, *Lavender*, Terrie Kalbus, *Granddaughter*, Ken Jones, *Caretaker*, Susan Harper, *Girlfriend*, Lynn Eastman, *Sally*, David Arntzen, *Toby*, Ralph Richmond, *Bartender*, Bill Cone, *Tommy*, Laura Mann, *Double Lavender*, Mary Ellen Shaw, *Fortune Teller*, Myrtle Scotton, *Maid*, Angus Scrimm, *Tall Man*. R. $6,000,000.

Outlandish horror film focusing on the bizarre goings on at a cemetery. A boy goes to the funeral of a friend, who was murdered, and discovers something strange about a nearby mausoleum. He drags his older brother into his investigation, where they encounter gnomes, a zombie-like tall man and a deadly flying metal ball. Filmed like a nightmare and as logical.

669 **Phantom of the Paradise** (1974) **** 20th Century–Fox, 91 min. *Dir* Brian DePalma, *Scr* Brian DePalma, *Cin* Larry Pizer, *Cin. (TV Wedding Sequence)* Robert Elfstrom, James Signorelli, *Ed* Paul Hirsh, *Des* Jack Fisk, *Mus* Paul Williams (AN), *Mus Adaptation* George Aliceson Tipton, Paul Williams (AN), *Chor* William Shephard, *Prod* Edward R. Pressman, *Exec Prod* Gustave Berne.

Cast: Paul Williams, *Swan*, William Finley, *Winslow the Phantom*, Jessica Harper, *Phoenix*, George Memmoli, *Philbin*, Gerrit Graham, *Beef*, Jeffrey

Comanor, Archie Hahn, Harold Oblong, *The Juicy Fruits/The Beach Bums/The Undeads*, Gene Gross, *Warden*, Henry Calvert, *Nightwatchman*, Ken Carpenter, Sam Forney, *Stagehands*. PG.

Excellent rock horror musical that mixes elements of *The Phantom of the Opera* and *Faust*. A songwriter's rock composition is stolen by a music mogul (Paul Williams), who also has sold his soul to the devil. After being disfigured in prison, the songwriter comes back to haunt the Paradise, a magnificent rock place. *The Phantom of the Paradise* is bizarre and outlandish, and Brian DePalma injects the film with incredible energy. This should have become a major cult film, as it is far superior to *The Rocky Horror Picture Show*.

670 **A Piece of the Action** (1977) *** Warner Bros., 134 min. *Dir* Sidney Poitier, *Scr* Charles Blackwell, *Story* Timothy March, *Cin* Donald M. Morgan, *Ed* Pembroke J. Herring, *Des* Alfred Sweeney, *Cos* Marie V. Brown, David Rawley, *Mus* Curtis Mayfield, *Prod* Melville Tucker, *Assoc Prod* Pembroke J. Herring, Kris Keiser.

Cast: Sidney Poitier, *Manny Durrell*, Bill Cosby, *Dave Anderson*, James Earl Jones, *Joshua Burke*, Denise Nicholas, *Lila French*, Hope Clarke, *Sarah Thomas*, Tracy Reed, *Nikki McLean*, Titos Vandis, *Bruno*, Frances Foster, *Bea Quitman*, Jason Evers, *Ty Shorter*, Marc Lawrence, *Louis*, Ja'net Dubois, *Nellie Bond*. PG. $6,700,000. See *Uptown Saturday Night*.

671 **The Pink Panther Strikes Again** (1976) *** United Artists, 103 min. *Dir* Blake Edwards, *Scr* Blake Edwards, Frank Waldman, *Cin* Harry Waxman, *Ed* Alan Jones, *Mus* Henry Mancini, Song "Come to Me", *Mus* Henry Mancini, *Lyrics* Don Black (AN), sung by Tom Jones, *Prod* Blake Edwards.

Cast: Peter Sellers, *Inspector Clouseau*, Herbert Lom, *Dreyfus*, Colin Blakely, *Alec Drummond*, Leonard Rossiter, *Quinlin*, Lesley-Anne Down, *Olga*, Burt Kwouk, *Kato*, Andre Maranne, *Francois*, Marne Maitland, *Deputy Commissioner*, Richard Vernon, *Dr. Fassbender*, Michael Robbins, *Jarvis*, Briony McRoberts, *Margo Fassbender*, Dick Crocket, *President*, Byron Kane, *Secretary of State*. PG. $20,005,000. See *The Return of the Pink Panther*.

672 **Piranha** (1978) *** New World, 92 min. *Dir* Joe Dante, *Scr* John Sayles, *Story* Richard Robinson, John Sayles, *Cin* Jamie Anderson, *Ed* Joe Dante, Mark Goldblatt, *Art* Bill Mellin, Kerry Mellin, *Mus* Pino Donaggio, *Prod* Jon Davison, *Co-Prod* Chako Van Leeuwen, *Exec Prod* Roger Corman, Jeff Schechtman.

Cast: Heather Menzies, *Maggie*, Bradford Dillman, *Paul*, Kevin McCarthy, *Dr. Joak*, Keenan Wynn, *Jack*, Dick Miller, *Buck*, Barbara Steele, *Dr. Mengers*, Belinda Balaski, *Betsy*, Melody Thomas, *Laura*, Bruce Gordon, *Col. Waxman*, Barry Brown, *Trooper*, Paul Bartel, *Dumont*, Shannon Collins, *Suzie*, Shawn Nelson, *Whitney*, Richard Deacon, *Earl*. R. $4,000,000.

Above average spoof of *Jaws*. Heather Menzies and Bradford Dillman, while searching for several missing persons discover a modern day mad scientist (Kevin McCarthy), who has accidently unleashed a super breed of piranhas that were to be used in the Vietnam War. *Piranha* is better than most films of this type due to its excellent script and its eccentric sense of humor.

673 **Pipe Dreams** (1976) ** Avco Embassy, 87 min. *Dir* Stephen Verona, *Scr* Stephen Verona, *Cin* Steve Larner, *Ed* Robert L. Estrin, *Cos* Glenda Ganis, *Mus* Dominic Frontiere, *Prod* Stephen Verona, *Exec Prod* Barry Hankerson.

Cast: Gladys Knight, *Maria Wilson*, Barry Hankerson, *Rob Wilson*, Bruce French, *The Duke*, Sherry Bain, *Loretta*, Mike Tippit, *Mike Thompson*, Altovise Davis, *Lydia*, Sylvia Hayes, *Sally*, Frank McRae, *Moose*, Carol Ita White, *Rosey Rottencrotch*, Bobbi Shaw, *Slimey Sue*, Arnold Johnson, *Johnny Monday*, Robert Corso, *Mini-Guinea*, Sally Kirkland, *Two-Street Betty*, Redmond Gleeson, *Hollow Legs*. PG.

Dull love story about a woman (Gladys Knight), who attempts to win back her husband (Barry Hankerson), who is working on the Alaska pipeline. The Alaska locales are a nice change of pace, but they are used too much to fill in the holes in a weak story. Knight makes a fine film debut, and her husband ironically is played by her real-life husband.

674 **Play It Again Sam** (1972) ******* Paramount, 87 min. *Dir* Herbert Ross, *Scr* Woody Allen, based on his play, *Cin* Owen Roizman, *Ed* Marion Rothman, *Des* Ed Wittstein, *Cos* Anna Hill Johnstone, *Mus* Billy Goldenberg, *Additional Mus* Oscar Peterson, *Prod* Arthur P. Jacobs, *Exec Prod* Charles Joffe, *Assoc Prod* Frank Capra, Jr.

Cast: Woody Allen, *Allan*, Diane Keaton, *Linda*, Tony Roberts, *Dick*, Jerry Lacy, *Bogart*, Susan Anspach, *Nancy*, Jennifer Salt, *Sharon*, Joy Bang, *Julie*, Viva, *Jennifer*, Mari Fletcher, *Dream Sharon*, Diana Davila, *Girl in Museum*, Suzanne Zenor, *Discotheque Girl*, Michael Greene, Ted Markland, *Hoods*. PG. $5,755,000.

Fine comedy starring Woody Allen as a recently divorced man, who is unable to cope with being single. Throughout the film the ghost of Humphrey Bogart gives Allen advice on meeting women. *Play It Again Sam* is more gimmicky than Allen's other films and lacks their crazy brilliance, but there are, however, many hilarious sequences and some clever movie references, such as an ending lifted from *Casablanca*.

675 **Play It As It Lays** (1972) ***** Universal, 99 min. *Dir* Frank Perry, *Scr* Joan Didion, John Gregory Dunne, based on novel by Joan Didion *Cin* Jordan Cronenweth, *Ed* Sidney Katz, *Des* Pato Guzman, *Cos* Joel Schumacher, *Prod* Frank Perry, *Co-Prod* Dominick Dunne.

Cast: Tuesday Weld, *Maria*, Anthony Perkins, *B.Z.*, Tammy Grimes, *Helene*, Adam Roarke, *Carter*, Ruth Ford, *Carlotta*, Eddie Firestone, *Benny Austin*, Diana Ewing, *Susannah*, Paul Lambert, *Larry Kulick*, Chuck McCann, *Abortionist's Assistant*, Severn Darden, *Hypnotist*, Tony Young, *Johnny Waters*, Richard Anderson, *Les Goodwin*, Elizabeth Claman, *The Chickie*, Mitzi Hoag, *Patsy*, Tyne Daley, *Journalist*, Roger Ewing, *Nelson*, Richard Ryal, *Apartment Manager*, John Finnegan, *Frank*, Darlene Conley, *Kate's Nurse*, Arthur Knight, Albert Johnson, *Themselves*, Allan Warnick, *TV Panelist*. R.

Dismal study of emptiness in Hollywood. Tuesday Weld stars as an actress whose life is meaningless; she has a retarded child, her director-husband ignores her and she has numerous love affairs. *Play It As It Lays* is meant to be a serious attack on the pretentiousness of these people, but the film completely fails because it is itself, pretentious.

676 **Play Misty for Me** (1971) ******* Universal, 102 min. *Dir* Clint Eastwood, *Scr* Jo Heims, Dean Reisner, *Story* Jo Heims, *Cin* Bruce Surtees, *Ed* Carl Pingitore, *Art* Alexander Golitzen, *Cos* Helen Colvig, *Mus* Dee Barton, *Prod* Robert Daley, *Assoc Prod* Bob Larson, A Jennings Lang Presentation.

Cast: Clint Eastwood, *Dave Garland*, Jessica Walter, *Evelyn Draper*, Donna Mills, *Tobie Williams*, John Larch, *Sgt. McCallum*, Jack Ging, *Dr. Frank Dewan*, Irene Hervey, *Madge Brenner*, James McEachin, *Al Monte*, Clarice Taylor, *Birdie*, Don Siegel, *Murphy the Bartender*, Duke Everts, *Jay Jay*. R. $5,415,000.

Unusual murder thriller starring Clint Eastwood as a harried radio disc jockey. One of his listeners (Jessica Walter) continually requests the song "Misty". After they meet, she moves in with him, and literally takes over his life. He is unable to get rid of her and later discovers she is psychotic. *Play Misty for Me* is an intelligent and well-paced thriller, that builds to an exciting climax. This was Eastwood's directorial debut.

677 **Players** (1979) * Paramount, 120 min. *Dir* Anthony Harvey, *Scr* Arnold Schulman, *Cin* James Crabe, *Ed* Randy Roberts, *Des* Richard Sylbert, *Cos* Richard Bruno, *Mus* Jerry Goldsmith, *Prod* Robert Evans, *Exec Prod* Arnold Schulman, *Assoc Prod* Tommy Cook.

Cast: Ali MacGraw, *Nicole*, Dean-Paul Martin, *Chris*, Maximilian Schell, *Marco*, Pancho Gonzalez, *Pancho*, Steven Guttenberg, *Rusty*, Melissa Prophet, *Ann*, Drew Denny, *Chris at 10*, Ian Altman, *Rusty at 10*, David Gilruth, *Chauffer*, Ilie Nastase, John McEnroe, Guillermo Vilas, Ion Tiriac, Don Maskell, Tom Gullikson, John Lloyd, Denis Ralston, Vijay Amritraj, Jim McManus, John Alexander, David Pate, Jorge Mendoza. *Themselves*. PG.

Poor drama about a professional tennis player's relationship with an irresponsible older woman, which is complicated by her relationship with a wealthy man. *Players* is nothing more than a dismal soap opera, interspersed with numerous overlong and boring tennis scenes. Dean-Paul Martin gives an acceptable performance, but he is a better tennis player than an actor; he did his own playing. The performances of the rest of the cast, however, range from mediocre to poor.

678 **Plaza Suite** (1971) *** Paramount, 114 min. *Dir* Arthur Hiller, *Scr* Neil Simon, based on his play, *Cin* Jack Marta, *Ed* Frank Bracht, *Art* Arthur Lonergan, *Cos* Jack Bear, *Mus* Maurice Jarre, *Prod* Howard W. Koch.

Cast One: Walter Matthau, *Sam Nash*, Maureen Stapleton, *Karen Nash*, Jose Ocasio, *Waiter*, Dan Ferrone, *Bellhop*, Louise Sorel, *Miss McCormack*. *Two*: Walter Matthau, *Jesse Kiplinger*, Barbara Harris, *Muriel Tate*. *Three*: Walter Matthau, *Roy Hubley*, Lee Grant, *Norma Hubley*, Jeannie Sullivan, *Mimsey Hubley*, Tom Carey, *Borden Eisler*. PG. $4,000,000.

Above-average Neil Simon comedy. *Plaza Suite* has three separate vignettes, each set in the same New York hotel and each starring Walter Matthau. With these short stories Simon is able to go full force without burning out. All three stories are intelligent and witty, particularly the third in which Matthau is the harried father of a bride-to-be, who refuses to come out of the bathroom. *Plaza Suite* is superior to Simon's west coast version *California Suite*.

679 **Pocket Money** (1972) **** National General, 102 min. *Dir* Stuart Rosenberg, *Scr* Terrence Malick, based on novel *Jim Kane* by J.P.S. Brown, *Cin* Laszlo Kovacs, *Ed* Robert Wyman, *Prod* John Foreman.

Cast: Paul Newman, *Jim Kane*, Lee Marvin, *Leonard*, Strother Martin, *Garrett*, Christine Belford, *Adelita*, Kelly Jean Peters, *Wife*, Fred Graham, *Herb*, Wayne Rogers, *Stretch*. PG.

Unusual contemporary western-comedy about two men who become involved with crooked cattle men. *Pocket Money* is such a relaxed comedy that the entire thing seems to be a complete throwaway. This is the type of film that has to grow on you, but audiences generally overlook such films. Newman is superb in an offbeat role as a somewhat slow cowboy, as is Marvin as his friend who aids him. Much of the tone of the film can be attributed to Malick's witty, but low-key script.

680 **Portnoy's Complaint** (1972) * Warner Bros., 101 min. *Dir* Ernest Lehman, *Scr* Ernest Lehman, based on novel by Philip Roth, *Cin* Philip Lathrop, *Ed* Sam O'Steen, Gordon Scott, *Des* Robert F. Boyle, *Cos* Moss Mabry, *Mus* Michel Legrand, *Prod* Ernest Lehman.

Cast: Richard Benjamin, *Alexander Portnoy*, Karen Black, *The Monkey*, Lee Grant, *Mrs. Portnoy*, Jack Somack, *Mr. Portnoy*, Jeannie Berlin, *Bubbles*, Jill Clayburgh, *Naomi*, D.P. Barnes, *Dr. Spielvogel*, Francesca DeSapio, *Lina*, Kevin Conway, *Smolka*, Lewis J. Stadlen, *Mandel*, Renee Lippin, *Hannah*, Jessica Rains, *Opening Girl*, Eleanor Zee, *Woman in Hospital*. R.

Dismal comedy about a young man (Richard Benjamin), who is unable to cope with his Jewish upbringing and his domineering mother (Lee Grant), which is responsible for his sexual hang-ups. *Portnoy's Complaint* nearly fails completely, with its poor treatment and awful script, but Karen Black manages a good performance, nevertheless. Noted screenwriter Ernest Lehman made an inauspicious debut as director.

681 **The Poseidon Adventure** (1972) ** 20th Century–Fox, 117 min. *Dir* Ronald Neame, *Scr* Wendell Mayes, Stirling Silliphant, based on novel by Paul Gallico, *Cin* Harold E. Stine (AN), *Ed* Harold F. Kress (AN), *Des* William Creber (AN), *Cos* Paul Zastupnevich (AN), *Mus* John Williams (AN), *Song* "The Morning After", Al Kasha, Joel Hirschhorn (A), *Prod* Irwin Allen, *Assoc Prod* Sidney Marshall.

Cast: Gene Hackman (BFA), *Rev. Frank Scott*, Ernest Borgnine, *Rogo*, Red Buttons, *Martin*, Carol Lynley, *Nonnie*, Roddy McDowell, *Acres*, Stella Stevens, *Linda Rogo*, Shelley Winters, (AN, G), *Belle Rosen*, Jack Albertson, *Manny Rosen*, Leslie Nielson, *Captain*, Pamela Sue Martin, *Susan*, Arthur O'Connell, *Chaplain*, Eric Shea, *Robin*, Fred Sadoff, *Linarcos*, Sheila Mathews, *Nurse*, Jan Arvan, *Doctor*, Byron Webster, *Purser*, John Crawford, *Chief Engineer*, Bob Hastings, *M.C.*, Erik Nelson, *Tinkham*. PG. $42,000,000.

Stupid and implausible disaster film. *The Poseidon Adventure* may be enjoyable if one can ignore the fact that tidal waves technically cannot capsize ocean liners and if it is not bothersome to witness characters in peril who spend too much time bickering among themselves. Both the dialogue and the acting are overwrought and exaggerated, but this soap opera nevertheless found an audience. The sequel, which has two groups fighting over the ship's valuable cargo, is so stupid it must rank as one of the all time camp classics.

682 **Posse** (1975) *** Paramount, 92 min. *Dir* Kirk Douglas, *Scr* Christopher Knopf, William Roberts, *Story* Christopher Knopf, *Cin* Fred Koenekamp, *Ed* John W. Wheeler, *Des* Lyle Wheeler, *Mus* Maurice Jarre, *Prod* Kirk Douglas, *Exec Prod* Phil Feldman.

Cast: Kirk Douglas, *Marshall Nightingale*, Bruce Dern, *Jack Strawhorn*, Bo Hopkins, *Wesley*, James Stacy, *Hellman*, Luke Askew, *Krag*, David

Canary, *Pensteman*, Alfonso Arau, *Peppe*, Katherine Woodville, *Mrs. Cooper*, Mark Roberts, *Mr. Cooper*, Beth Brickell, *Mrs. Ross*, Dick O'Neill, *Wiley*, Bill Burton, *McCanless*, Louise Elias, *Rains*, Gus Greymountain, *Reyno*, Allan Warnick, *Telegrapher*, Roger Behrstock, *Sheriff*. PG.

Unusual western drama about a U.S. Marshall (Kirk Douglas), who tracks down an outlaw (Bruce Dern) in order to help fulfill his political ambitions. Douglas and his deputies move in on a small town and practically take over, which causes much indifference and leads to a surprise conclusion. Douglas did a fine job as both director and star.

683 The Possession of Joel Delaney (1972) ** Paramount, 105 min. *Dir* Waris Hussein, *Scr* Grimes Grice, Matt Robinson, *Cin* Arthur Ornitz, *Ed* John Victor Smith, *Des* Peter Murton, *Art* Philip Rosenberg, *Cos* Frank Thompson.

Cast: Shirley MacLaine, *Norah*, Perry King, *Joel*, Michael Hordern, *Dr. Reichman*, Earle Hyman, *Charles*, Robert Burr, *Ted*, Miriam Colon, *Vernonica*, Lovelady Powell, *Erika*, Edmundo Rivera Alvarez, *Don Pedro*, Teodorino Bello, *Mrs. Perez*, David Elliott, *Peter Benson*, Jose Fernandez, *Tonio Perez*, Ernesto Gonzales, *Handsome Seance Subject*, Aukie Herger, *Mr. Perez*, Paulita Iglesias, *Female Bruja*, Lisa Kohane, *Carrie Benson*, Marita Lindholm, *Marta*, Barbara Trentham, *Sherry*, Peter Turgeon, *Brady*. R.

Silly thriller starring Shirley MacLaine as a woman who tries to deal with her younger brother (Perry King), who is possessed by the soul of a dead Puerto Rican murderer. *The Possession of Joel Delaney* certainly lives up to its ridiculous premise, and it could have succeeded as a comedy, but unfortunately it is a drama. As a thriller it is a very flat, lacking the necessary thrills and tension.

684 Pretty Baby (1978) ***** Paramount, 109 min. *Dir* Louis Malle, *Scr* Polly Platt, *Story* Louis Malle, Polly Platt, based on material in *Storyville* by Al Rose, *Cin* Sven Nykvist, *Ed* Suzanne Baron, Suzanne Fenn, *Des* Trevor Williams, *Cos* Mina Mittelman, *Mus Adaptation* Jerry Wexler (AN), *Special Photography* Maureen Lambray, *Prod* Louis Malle.

Cast: Susan Sarandon, *Hattie*, Brooke Shields, *Violet*, Keith Carradine, *Bellocq*, Frances Faye, *Nell*, Antonio Fargas, *Piano Player*, Gerrit Graham, *Highpockets*, Mae Mercer, *Mama Moseberry*, Diana Scarwid, *Frieda*, Barbara Steele, *Josephine*, Matthew Anton, *Red Top*, Secret Scott, *Flora*, Cheryl Markowitz, *Gussie*, Susan Manskey, *Fanny*, Laura Zimmerman, *Agnes*, Miz Mary, *Odette*, Don Hood, *Alfred Fuller*, Pat Perkins, *Ola Mae*, Von Eric Perkins, *Nonny*, Sasha Holliday, *Justine*, Lisa Shames, *Antonia*, Harry Braden, *Harry*, Philip H. Sizeler, *Senator*, Don K. Lutenbacher, *Violet's First Customer*. R. $4,195,000.

Outstanding period film about life in a brothel, set in the Storyville section of New Orleans in 1917. The entire film is told from the viewpoint of a 12 year old girl, the daughter of a prostitute, who becomes a prostitute herself and later moves in with a photographer. *Pretty Baby* is a strong example of Louis Malle's ability to take a shocking subject matter, and deal with it tastefully without compromising on the details.

685 Prime Cut (1972) *** National General, 91 min. *Dir* Michael Ritchie, *Scr* Robert Dillon, *Cin* Gene Polito, *Ed* Carl Pingatore, *Art* Bill Malley, *Cos* Patricia Norris, *Mus* Lalo Schifrin, *Prod* Joe Wizan, *Exec Prod* Kenneth Evans, *Assoc Prod* Mickey Birofsky.

Cast: Lee Marvin, *Nick Devlin*, Gene Hackman, *"Mary Ann"*, Angel Tompkins, *Clarabelle*, Gregory Walcott, *Weenie*, Sissy Spacek, *Poppy*, Janit Baldwin, *Violet*, William Morey, *Shay*, Clint Ellison, *Delaney*, Howard Platt, *Shaughnessy*, Les Lannom, *O'Brien*, Eddie Egan, *Jake*, Therse Reinch, *Jake's Girl*, Bob Wilson, *Reaper Driver*, Gordon Signor, *Brockman*, Gladys Watson, *Milk Lady*, Hugh Gillin, Jr. *Desk Clerk*, E. Lund, *Mrs. O'Brien*, David Savage, *Ox-Eye*, Craig Chapman, *Farmer Bob*, Jim Taksas, *Big Jim*, Wayne Savagne, *Freckle Face*. PG.

Interesting gangster thriller starring Lee Marvin as a Chicago hit man, who is sent to Kansas City to eliminate a repulsive and trouble-making gangster (Gene Hackman). *Prime Cut* is unusual for a gangster film in that it has a rural, rather than an urban backdrop. The film is extremely violent and relies too heavily on shocks, but it is well-made, nevertheless.

686 The Prisoner of Second Avenue (1975) *** Warner Bros., 105 min. *Dir* Melvin Frank, *Scr* Neil Simon, based on his play, *Cin* Philip Lathrop, *Ed* Bob Wyman, *Art* Preston Ames, *Cos* Joel Schumacher, *Mus* Marvin Hamlisch, *Prod* Melvin Frank.

Cast: Jack Lemmon, *Mel*, Anne Bancroft, *Edna*, Gene Saks, *Harry*, Elizabeth Wilson, *Pauline*, Florence Stanley, *Pearl*, Maxine Stuart, *Belle*, Ed Peck, *Man Upstairs*, Gene Blakely, *Charlie*, Ivor Francis, *Psychiatrist*, Stack Pierce, *Detective*. PG.

Above average Neil Simon comedy about the numerous problems that befall a middle-aged New York couple. It starts with the loss of the husband's job, and later as things become worse, he seemingly suffers a breakdown. *The Prisoner of Second Avenue* could be *The Out-of-Towners* years later, as the premises are quite similar. Lemmon and Bancroft are excellent and are able to bring believability to Simon's sometimes overwrought script.

687 The Prisoner of Zenda (1979) ** Britain, Universal, 108 min. *Dir* Richard Quine, *Scr* Dick Clement, Ian La Frenais, based on novel by Anthony Hope, as dramatized by Edward Rose, *Cin* Arthur Ibbetson, *Ed* Byron "Buzz" Brandt, *Des* John J. Lloyd, *Cos* Susan Yelland, *Mus* Henry Mancini, *Prod* Walter Mirisch, *Assoc Prod* Peter MacGregor-Scott.

Cast: Peter Sellers, *Rudolf IV/Rudolf V/Syd*, Lynne Frederick, *Princess Flavia*, Lionel Jeffries, *Gen. Sapt*, Elke Sommer, *The Countess*, Gregory Sierra, *The Count*, Jeremy Kemp, *Duke Michael*, Catherine Schell, *Antionette*, Simon Williams, *Fritz*, Stuart Wilson, *Rupert of Hentzau*, Norman Rossington, *Bruno*, John Laurie, *Archbiship*, Graham Stark, *Erik*, Michael Balfour, *Luger*, Arthur Howard, *Deacon*, Ian Abercrombie, *Johann*, Michael Segal, *Conductor*. PG. $4,890,000.

Fair comedy version of classic story starring Peter Sellers as both a king and his exact double, who poses as the king as a part of a plot by the king's brother (Jeremy Kemp) to obtain the throne. *The Prisoner of Zenda* fails as a period adventure and as a comedy, as there is little excitement and most of the humor falls flat, despite the gallant efforts of Sellers.

688 The Private Life of Sherlock Holmes (1970) **** U.S./Britain, United Artists, 125 min. *Dir* Billy Wilder, *Scr* I.A.L. Diamond, Billy Wilder, *Cin* Christopher Challis, *Ed* Ernest Walter, *Des* Alexander Trauner, *Art* Tony Inglis, *Cos* Julie Harris, *Mus* Miklos Rozsa, *Chor* David Blair, *Prod* Billy Wilder, *Assoc Prod* I.A.L. Diamond.

Cast: Robert Stephens, *Sherlock Holmes*, Colin Blakely, *Dr. John Watson*, Irene Handl, *Mrs. Hudson*, Stanley Holloway, *First Gravedigger*, Christopher Lee, *Mycroft Holmes*, Genevieve Page, *Gabrielle Valladon*, Clive Revill, *Rogozhin*, Tamara Toumanova, *Petrova*, George Benson, *Insp. Lestrade*, Catherine Lacey, *Old Lady*, Mollie Maureen, *Queen Victoria*, Peter Madden, *Von Tirpitz*, Robert Cawdron, *Hotel Manager*, Michael Elwyn, *Cassidy*, Michael Balfour, *Cabby*, Frank Thornton, *Porter*, James Copeland, *Guide*, Alex McCrindle, *Baggageman*, Kenneth Benda, *Minister*, Graham Armitage, *Wiggins*, Eric Francis, *Second Gravedigger*. PG.

Unusual Sherlock Holmes film that is more of a character study than a mystery thriller. The film focuses on Holmes as a person and examines different traits only suggested in earlier films, such as drug addiction and the possibility of homosexuality. The film also shows Holmes' fallibility as a detective, by giving him a case he is unable to solve. This is the only Sherlock Holmes film to aspire to greatness.

689 **The Promise** (1979) ** Universal, 98 min. *Dir* Gilbert Cates, *Scr* Garry Michael White, *Story* Paul Heller, Fred Weintraub, *Cin* Ralph Woolsey, *Ed* Peter E. Berger, *Art* William Sandell, *Mus* David Shire, *Song* Theme from *The Promise* ("I'll Never Say Goodbye"), *Mus* David Shire (AN), *Lyrics* Alan and Marilyn Bergman (AN), *Prod* Paul Heller, Fred Weintraub, *Exec Prod* Tully Friedman, *Assoc Prod* Eva Monley.

Cast: Kathleen Quinlan, *Nancy/Marie*, Stephen Collins, *Michael*, Beatrice Straight, *Marion*, Laurence Luckinbill, *Dr. Gregson*, William Prince, *Calloway*, Michael O'Hare, *Ben*, Bibi Besch, *Dr. Allison*, Robin Gammell, *Dr. Wickfield*, Katherine DeHetre, *Wendy*, Paul Ryan, *Dr. Fenton*, Tom O'Neill, *Painter*, Kirchy Prescott, *Nurse*, John Allen Vick, Dan Leegant, *Cab Drivers*, Jerry Walter, *Cal*, Bob Hirschfeld, *Dr. Meisner*, Alan Newman, *Barker*, Carey Loftin, Max Balchowsky, Mickey Gilbert, *Truck Drivers*. PG. $6,470,000.

Dreary soap opera about lost love. A young couple (Kathleen Quinlan, Stephen Collins) is involved in a car accident. Because she believes Quinlan is not good enough for her son, Collins' mother (Beatrice Straight) tells him Quinlan has died. They meet later, after she has had plastic surgery, but he does not recognize her, even though the audience can. *The Promise* is silly and sentimental, and the story defies credibility.

690 **Prophecy** (1979) * Paramount, 102 min. *Dir* John Frankenheimer, *Scr* David Seltzer, *Cin* Harry Stradling, Jr., *Ed* Tom Rolf, *Des* William Craig Smith, *Cos* Ray Summers, *Mus* Leonard Rosenman, *Prod* Robert L. Rosen, *Assoc Prod* Alan Levine.

Cast: Robert Foxworth, *Bob*, Talia Shire, *Maggie*, Armand Assante, *Hawks*, Richard Dysart, *Isely*, Victoria Racino, *Ramona*, George Clutesi, *M'Rai*, Tom McFadden, *Pilot*, Evans Evans, *Cellist*, Burke Byrnes, *Father*, Mia Bendixsen, *Girl*, Johnny Timko, *Boy*, Everett L. Creach, *Kelso*, Charles H. Gray, *Sheriff*. PG. $10,500,000.

Poor attempt at a serious ecological horror film in which mercury poisoning from a paper plant transforms animals into horrible creatures. *Prophecy* was intended to be a warning of the probable results of continued pollution of our natural resources. This is certainly a noble idea, but this film does not even come close to its apparent intentions and is no better than those similarly themed monster movies of the 1950's. One expects better from a director of the calibre of John Frankenheimer.

691 Promises in the Dark (1979) ** Orion, 115 min. *Dir* Jerome Hellman, *Scr* Loring Mandel, *Cin* Adam Holender, *Ed* Bob Wyman, *Des* Walter Scott Herndon, *Cos* Ann Roth, *Mus* Leonard Rosenman, *Prod* Jerome Hellman, *Exec Prod* Sheldon Shrager.

Cast: Marsha Mason, *Dr. Alexandra Kendall*, Ned Beatty, *Bud Koenig*, Susan Clark, *Fran Koenig*, Michael Brandon, *Dr. Jim Sandman*, Kathleen Beller, *Buffy Koenig*, Paul Clemens, *Gerry Hulin*, Donald Moffat, *Dr. Walter McInerny*, Philip Sterling, *Dr. Frucht*, Bonnie Bartlett, *Nurse Farber*, James Noble, *Dr. Blankenship*, Arthur Rosenberg, *Emergency Room Doctor*, Peggy McCay, *Mrs. Pritkin*, Robert Doran, *Alan*, Lenora May, *Sue*, Alexandra Johnson, *Ellie*, Fran Bennett, *Emergency Room Nurse*. PG.

Downbeat film about a girl (Kathleen Beller) dying of cancer and how, with the help of a compassionate doctor (Marsha Mason), she deals with the inevitable. *Promises in the Dark* is a well-made and sometimes realistic film about death, but that is the core of its fault. Spending nearly two hours watching a girl slowly die is hardly a subject that will generate much interest.

692 Psychic Killer (1975) ** Avco Embassy, 90 min. *Dir* Raymond Danton, *Scr* Mike Angel, Greydon Clark, Raymond Danton, *Cin* Herb Pearl, *Ed* Mike Brown, *Art* Joel Leonard, *Mus* William Kraft, *Prod* Mardi Rustam, *Exec Prod* Mohammed Rustam.

Cast: Jim Hutton, *Arnold*, Paul Burke, *Det. Morgan*, Julie Adams, *Laura*, Nehemiah Persoff, *Dr. Gubner*, Neville Brand, *Lemonowski*, Aldo Ray, *Anderson*, Della Reese, *Mrs. Gibson*, Rod Cameron, *Dr. Commanger*, Joe Della Sorte, *Sanders*, Harry Holcomb, *Judge*, Robyn Raymond, *Jury Foreman*, Judith Brown, *Anne*, Mary Wilcox, *Martha*, Bill Quinn, *Coroner*, Whit Bissell, *Dr. Taylor*, Stack Pierce, *Emilio*, Greydon Clark, *Sowash*. PG.

Dull occult thriller about a psycho who kills with his mind. *Psychic Killer* is sort of an occult version of Alfred Hitchocock's *Psycho*, lifting many of its plot details, even including a shower sequence. Jim Hutton is good, in one of his rare dramatic roles, as the killer with a mother fixation. This film lacks both the depth and the witty intelligence of Hitchcock's classic, concentrating more on gratuitous violence.

693 The Public Eye (1972) *** Britain, 95 min. *Dir* Carol Reed, *Scr* Peter Schaffer, based on his play, *Cin* Christopher Challis, *Ed* Anne V. Coates, *Des* Terence Marsh, *Art* Robert Cartwright, *Cos* Julie Harris, *Mus* John Barry, *Prod* Hal. B. Wallis, *Assoc Prod* Paul Nathan.

Cast: Mia Farrow, *Belinda*, Topol, *Christoforou*, Michael Jayston, *Charles*, Margaret Rawlings, *Mrs. Sidley*, Annette Crosbie, *Miss Framer*, Dudley Foster, *Mayhew*, Michael Aldridge, *Sir Philip Crouch*, Michael Barrington, *Scrampton*, Neil McCarthy, *Parkinson*. G.

Fine comedy about a Greek private detective (Topol), who is hired by a stuffy Englishman (Michael Jayston) to follow his wife (Mia Farrow), whom he suspects of having an affair. Farrow is not having an affair, but she and Topol meet and strike a relationship. The outcome is very predictable, but *The Public Eye* is nevertheless a pleasant comedy, due to the intelligent script and the pairing of Topol and Farrow.

694 **Pulp** (1972) *** Britain, United Artists, 95 min. *Dir* Michael Hodges, *Scr* Michael Hodges, *Cin* Ousama Rawi, *Ed* John Glen, *Des* Patrick Downing, *Art* Darrell Lass, *Cos* Gitt Magrini, *Mus* George Martin, *Prod* Michael Klinger.

Cast: Michael Caine, *Mickey King*, Mickey Rooney, *Preston Gilbert*, Lionel Stander, *Ben Dinuccio*, Lizabeth Scott, *Princess Betty Cippola*, Nadia Cassini, *Liz Adams*, Al Lettieri, *Miller*, Dennis Price, *Mysterious Englishman*, Amerigo Tot, *Sotgio*, Leopoldo Trieste, *Marcovic*, Robert Sacchi, *Jim Norman*, Joe Zammit Cordina, *Santana*, Ave Ninchi, *Chambermaid*, Werner Hasselman, Louise Lambert, *American Tourists*. PG.

Well-made thriller starring Michael Caine as a pulp novelist, who is hired by a retired gangster movie actor (Mickey Rooney) to ghostwrite his autobiography. Rooney is murdered to prevent him from exposing a scandal from his past and Caine investigates the mystery. *Pulp* is a fine spoof of detective films, with a clever premise and many movie in-jokes.

695 **The Pursuit of Happiness** (1971) ** Columbia, 93 min. *Dir* Robert Mulligan, *Scr* Jon Boothe, George L. Sherman, based on novel by Thomas Rogers, *Cin* Dick Kratina, *Ed* Folmar Blangsted, *Art* George Jenkins, *Cos* Ann Roth, *Mus* Dave Grusin, *Prod* David Susskind, *Assoc Prod* Alan Shayne.

Cast: Michael Sarrazin, *William Popper*, Barbara Hershey, *Jane Kauffman*, Arthur Hill, *John Popper*, Ruth White, *Mrs. Popper*, E.G. Marshall, *Daniel Lawrence*, Robert Klein, *Melvin Lasher*, Sada Thompson, *Ruth Lawrence*, David Doyle, *James Moran*, Barnard Hughes, *Judge Vogel*, Peter White, *Terence Lawrence*, Tom Rosqui, *Defense Attorney Keller*, William Devane, *Pilot*, Gilbert Lewis, *George Wilson*, Albert Henderson, *McArdle*, Ralph Waite, *Det. Cromie*, Charles Durning, *Guard*. PG.

Fair drama about a rebellious youth (Michael Sarrazin), who accidently runs over a woman. His refusal to cooperate makes his situation worse than it would have been, and he is sent to prison. *The Pursuit of Happiness* stretches credibility and is just too illogical, in relation to the protagonist's unnecessary stubbornness, to be taken seriously.

696 **Puzzle of a Downfall Child** (1971) ** Universal, 104 min. *Dir* Jerry Schatzberg, *Scr* Adrien Joyce, *Story* Adrien Joyce, Jerry Schatzberg, *Cin* Adam Holender, *Ed* Evan Lottman, *Art* Richard Bianchi, *Cos* Terry Leong, *Mus* Michael Small, *Prod* John Foreman, *Assoc Prod* Frank Caffey, A Jennings Lang Presentation.

Cast: Faye Dunaway, *Lou Andreas Sand*, Barry Primus, *Aaron*, Viveca Lindfors, *Pauline Galva*, Barry Morse, *Dr. Galba*, Roy Scheider, *Mark*, Ruth Jackson, *Barbara Casey*, John Heffernan, *Dr. Sherman*, Sydney Walker, *Psychiatrist*, Clark Burckhalter, *Davy Bright*, Shirley Rich, *Peggy McCavage*, Emerick Bronson, *Falco*, Barbara Carrera, *T.J. Brady*. R.

Interesting drama starring Faye Dunaway as a former fashion model, who retires to an isolated beach house to escape the pressures that led to a breakdown. She reflects on her past by relating the events of her life to an old photographer friend (Barry Primus). Unfortunately the film never rises above a soap opera, with its numerous clichés and stereotypes. Fashion photographer Jerry Schatzberg debuted as director, but he has done better work since.

697 Quackser Fortune Has a Cousin in the Bronx (1970) **** UMC, 90 min. *Dir* Waris Hussein, *Scr* Gabriel Walsh, *Cin* Gilbert Taylor, *Ed* Bill Blunden, *Art* Herbert Smith, *Mus* Michael Dress, *Prod* John H. Cushingham, Mel Howard, *Exec Prod* Sidney Glazier.

Cast: Gene Wilder, *Quackser Fortune*, Margot Kidder, *Zazel Pierce*, Eileen Colgan, *Betsy Bourke*, Seamus Ford, *Mr. Fortune*, May Ollis, *Mrs. Fortune*, Liz Davis, *Kathleen Fortune*, Caroline Tully, *Vera Fortune*, Paul Murphy, *Damien*, David Kelly, *Tom Maguire*, Tony Doyle, *Mike*, John Kelly, *Tim*. R.

Unusual comedy about a manure salesman (Gene Wilder) living in Dublin, Ireland. Wilder is sort of a misfit, who spends his time following horses, and collecting their manure to sell as fertilizer. He later falls for an American college girl (Margot Kidder), which later causes him great humiliation. The humor is very low-keyed and subtle, somewhat reminiscent of Truffaut.

698 Quadrophenia (1979) *** Britain, World Northal, 120 min. *Dir* Franc Roddam, *Scr* Dave Humphries, Franc Roddam, Martin Stellman, based on rock opera by The Who, *Cin* Brian Tufano, *Ed* Mike Taylor, *Des* Simon Holland, *Musical Directors* John Entwhistle, Pete Townsend, *Prod* Roy Baird, Bill Curbishley, *Exec Prod* The Who (Roger Daltrey, John Entwhistle, Keith Moon, Pete Townsend), *Assoc Prod* John Peverall.

Cast: Phil Daniels, *Jimmy*, Mark Wingett, *Dave*, Philip Davis, *Chalky*, Leslie Ash, *Steph*, Garry Cooper, *Pete*, Toyah Wilcox, *Monkey*, Sting, *Ace*, Trevor Laird, *Ferdy*, Gary Shail, *Spider*, Kate Williams, *Jimmy's Mother*, Michael Elphick, *Jimmy's Father*, Raymond Winston, *Kevin*. R.

Powerful drama based on The Who's second rock opera. Rather than producing a surrealistic rock musical, as in the film version of their first rock opera *Tommy*, The Who opted for a straight drama, and it works. Phil Daniels is excellent as a confused and rebellious "Mod", a group of youths who rebelled against the "Rockers", greaser types in leather jackets. The film nicely documents the clash between these two groups in England during the early 1960's. A bit of knowledge of rock history is helpful in understanding this film, which is even more difficult to understand, because of the thick English accents.

699 Quintet (1979) **** 20th Century–Fox, 100 min. *Dir* Robert Altman, *Scr* Robert Altman, Frank Barhydt, Patricia Resnick, *Story* Robert Altman, Lionel Chetwynd, Patricia Resnick, *Cin* Jean Boffety, *Ed* Dennis M. Hill, *Des* Leon Ericksen, *Art* Wolf Kroegar, *Cos* Scott Bushnell, *Mus* Tom Pierson, *Prod* Robert Altman, *Exec Prod* Tommy Thompson, *Assoc Prod* Allan Nicholls.

Cast: Paul Newman, *Essex*, Vittorio Gassman, *St. Christopher*, Fernando Rey, *Grigor*, Bibi Andersson, *Ambrosia*, Brigitte Fossey, *Vivia*, Nina Van Pallandt, *Deuca*, David Langton, *Goldstar*, Tom Hill, *Francha*, Monique Mercure, *Redstone's Mate*, Craig Richard Nelson, *Redstone*, Maruska Stankova, *Jaspera*, Anne Gerety, *Aeon*, Michael Maillot, *Obelus*, Max Fleck, *Wood Supplier*, Francoise Berd, *Charity House Woman*. R.

Excellent, but bizarre, science-fiction story that is set in a frozen city in the future. The "Quintet" of the title is a nearly incomprehensible game played by the city's inhabitants. This is a game of survival, in which the last one alive is the winner. Altman never explains the rules, a fact which angered many critics, and it really is not necessary, because the game seems to represent life and death. *Quintet* is one of the bleakest views of the future ever put on film, and one of Altman's best films.

700 **R.P.M.** (1970) * Columbia, 92 min. *Dir* Stanley Kramer, *Scr* Erich Segal, *Cin* Michel Hugo, *Ed* William A. Lyon, *Des* Robert Clatworthy, *Cos* Moss Mabry, *Mus* Perry Botkin, Jr., Barry DeVorzon, *Additional Lyrics* Melanie, songs sung by Melanie, *Prod* Stanley Kramer, *Assoc Prod* George Glass.

Cast: Anthony Quinn, *Perez*, Ann-Margret, *Rhoda*, Gary Lockwood, *Rossiter*, Paul Winfield, *Dempsey*, Graham Jarvis, *Thatcher*, Alan Hewitt, *Hewlitt*, Ramon Bieri, *Brown*, John McLiam, *Rev. Blauvelt*, Don Keefer, *Dean Cooper*, Donald Moffat, *Perry Howard*, Norman Burton, *Coach McCurdy*, John Zaremba, *Tyler*, Inez Pedroza, *Estella*, Teda Bracci, Linda Meiklejohn, Bruce Fleischer, David Ladd, John David Wilder, *Bradjose*, Raymond Cavaleri, Henry Brown, Jr. Frank Alesia, Robert Carricart, Jr., *Students*. R.

Dismal college protest film that lives up to its ridiculously cutesy title, which stands for Revolutions Per Minute. Anthony Quinn stars as the head of a university, who betrays his liberal beliefs by calling in the police to arrest some campus radicals. Perhaps this film is autobiographical as Stanley Kramer has a tendency to take on important subjects and then betrays them.

701 **Rabbit, Run** (1970) ** Warner Bros., 94 min. *Dir* Jack Smight, *Scr* Howard B. Kreitsek, based on novel by John Updike, *Cin* Philip Lathrop, *Ed* Archie Marshek, *Art* Al Sweeney, *Prod* Howard B. Kreitsek, *Assoc Prod* Joanne Dean.

Cast: James Caan, *Rabbit Angstrom*, Carrie Snodgress, *Janice Angstrom*, Anjonette Comer, *Ruth*, Jack Albertson, *Marty Tothero*, Arthur Hill, *Rev. Jack Eccles*, Henry Jones, *Mr. Angstrom*, Carmen Matthews, *Mrs. Springer*, Virginia Vincent, *Margaret*, Nydia Westman, *Mrs. Smith*, Marc Antony Van Der Nagel, *Nelson*, Josephine Hutchinson, *Mrs. Angstrom*, Don Keefer, *Mr. Springer*, Margot Stevenson, *Mrs. Tothero*, Sondra Scott, *Miriam Angstrom*, Ken Kercheval, *Barney*. R.

Dismal drama starring James Caan as a former high school basketball star, who is unable to adjust to adulthood. He cannot get a decent job, because of his lack of skills, and his wife (Carrie Snodgress) is an alcoholic. She accidently drowns their baby, but he is blamed. *Rabbit Run* is very uneven. It tries to be realistic, but it too often sinks to melodrama.

702 **Rabbit Test** (1978) * Avco Embassy, 84 min. *Dir* Joan Rivers, *Scr* Jay Redack, Joan Rivers, *Cin* Lucien Ballard, *Ed* Stanford C. Allen, *Art* Robert Kinoshita, *Mus* Peter Carpenter, Mike Post, *Prod* Edgar Rosenberg, *Assoc Prod* Melissa Rosenberg.

Cast: Billy Crystal, *Lionel*, Joan Prather, *Segoynia*, Alex Rocco, *Danny*, Doris Roberts, *Mrs. Carpenter*, Edward Ansara, *Newscaster*, Imogene Coca, *Madam Marie*, Jane Connell, *Anthropologist*, Keene Curtis, *Dr. Lasse-Braun*, Norman Fell, *Segoynia's Father*, Fannie Flagg, *President's Wife*, Jack Fletcher, *The Pope*, Alice Ghostley, *Nurse Tunn*, George Gobel, *President of U.S.*, Roosevelt Grier, *Taxi Driver*, Paul Lynde, *Dr. Vidal*, Murray Matheson, *Dr. Lowell*, Roddy McDowell, *Gypsy Grandmother/Dr. Fishbind*, Sheree North, *Mystery Lady*, Tom Poston, *Minister*, Charlotte Rae, *Cousin Clare*, Joan

Rivers, *Second Nurse*, Sab Shimono, *Chinese Leader*, Mary Steelsmith, *Melody Carpenter*, Jimmie Walker, *Umbuto*. PG. $4,700,000.

An unintentionally unfunny comedy about a man who becomes pregnant. Joan Rivers is one of many comics to attempt to follow in the footsteps of Woody Allen and Mel Brooks by making the transition to film director. In Rivers' case, this transition is a total failure as not one joke or comedy situation succeeds. *Rabbit Test* is certainly one of the worst films ever made.

703 **Race with the Devil** (1975) ** 20th Century–Fox, *Dir* Jack Starrett, *Scr* Wes Bishop, Lee Frost, *Cin* Robert Jessup, *Ed* Allan Jacobs, *Mus* Leonard Rosenman, *Prod* Paul Maslansky.

Cast: Peter Fonda, *Roger*, Warren Oates, *Frank*, Loretta Swit, *Alice*, Lara Parker, *Kelly*, R.G. Armstrong, *Sheriff*, Clay Tanner, *Delbert*, Carol Blodgett, *Ethel*, Ricci Ware, *Ricci Ware*, James N. Harrell, *Gun Shop Owner*, Paul A. Partain, *Cal Mathers*, Karen Miller, *Kay*, Arky Blue, *Arky Blue*, Jack Starrett, *Gas Station Attendant*, Phil Hoover, *Mechanic*, Wes Bishop, *Deputy Dave*. PG. $5,820,000.

Fair action thriller about two couples, who accidently stumble onto a cult of devil worshippers, while on vacation in Texas. *Race with the Devil* begins with an interesting premise, but it quickly disintegrates into a standard chase film, as the devil worshippers spend the rest of the film pursuing the two couples. The action sequences are just average for this type of film.

704 **Rafferty and the Gold Dust Twins** (1975) ** Warner Bros., 91 min. *Dir* Dick Richards, *Scr* John Kaye, *Cin* Ralph Woolsey, *Ed* Walter Thompson, *Art* Joel Schiller, *Mus* Artie Butler, *Prod* Michael Gruskoff, Art Linson.

Cast: Alan Arkin, *Rafferty*, Sally Kellerman, *Mac Beachwood*, Mackenzie Phillips, *Frisbee*, Alex Rocco, *Blackjack Kibitzer*, Charlie Martin Smith, *Soldier*, Harry Dean Stanton, *Billy Winston*, Earl Smith, *Bandleader*, John McLiam, *Mac's Father*, Richard Hale, *Jesus Freak*, Ed Peck, *Blackjack Player*, Lilian Randolph, *Student Driver*. R.

Fair road comedy about two females (Sally Kellerman, Mackenzie Phillips), who kidnap a nervous driving instructor (Alan Arkin), at gunpoint, and force him to take them from Los Angeles to Arizona. *Rafferty and the Gold Dust Twins* attempts to be realistic by focusing on society's losers, but the film is too weird and silly for that. There is no real plot as it follows the adventures of the three and their growing friendship.

705 **Rage** (1972) ** Warner Bros., 99 min. *Dir* George C. Scott, *Scr* Philip Friedman, Dan Kleinman, *Cin* Fred Koenekamp, *Ed* Michael Kahn, *Art* Frank Sylos, *Prod* Fred Weintraub, *Exec Prod* Leon Fromkees, J. Ronald Getty.

Cast: George C. Scott, *Dan Logan*, Richard Basehart, *Dr. Cardwell*, Martin Sheen, *Maj. Holliford*, Barnard Hughes, *Dr. Spencer*, Nicolas Beauvy, *Chris Logan*, Paul Stevens, *Col. Franklin*, Stephen Young, *Maj. Reintz*, Kenneth Tobey, *Col. Nickerson*, Robert Walden, *Dr. Janeway*, William Jordan, *Maj. Cooper*. PG.

Dull vendetta drama with George C. Scott waging a one-man-war against the military, after his son dies from exposure to chemicals. *Rage* could have been a good action thriller, but most of the time is spent on boring talk, which does little to help put forth its obvious message. Scott made his directorial debut with this film.

706 **The Railway Children** (1971) ******* Britain, Universal, 106 min. *Dir* Lionel Jeffries, *Scr* Lionel Jeffries, based on novel by E. Nesbit, *Cin* Arthur Ibbetson, *Ed* Teddy Darvas, *Art* John Clark, *Cos* Elsa Fennell, *Mus* Johnny Douglas, *Prod* Robert Lynn.

Cast: Dinah Sheridan, *Mother*, Bernard Cribbens, *Perks*, William Mervyn, *Old Gentlemen*, Iain Cuthbertson, *Father*, Jenny Agutter, *Bobbie*, Sally Thomsett, *Phyllis*, Peter Bromilow, *Doctor*, Ann Lancaster, *Ruth*, Gary Warren, *Peter*, Gordon Whiting, *Russian*, Beatrix MacKey, *Aunt Emma*, Debbie Davies, *Mrs. Perks*, David Lodge, *Bandmaster*, Christopher Witty, *Jim*, Brenda Cowling, *Mrs. Viney*, Paddy Ward, *Cart Man*, Erik Chitty, *Photographer*, Sally James, *Maid*, Dominic Allen, *C.I.D. Man*. G.

Above-average family film focusing on three children, whose father has been taken to prison for treason. Their mother takes them to live in a small Yorkshire village, and they spend most of their time playing at a nearby railway line. Unlike most family films *The Railway Children* is intelligent and never juvenile. British character Lionel Jeffries debuted as director.

707 **Rancho Deluxe** (1975) ******* United Artists, 93 min. *Dir* Frank Perry, *Scr* Thomas McGuane, *Cin* William A. Fraker, *Ed* Sid Katz, *Art* Michael Haller, *Mus* Jimmy Buffett, *Prod* Elliott Kastner.

Cast: Jeff Bridges, *Jack McKee*, Sam Waterston, *Cecil Colson*, Elizabeth Ashley, *Cora Brown*, Charlene Dallas, *Laura Beige*, Clifton James, *John Brown*, Slim Pickens, *Henry Beige*, Harry Dean Stanton, *Curt*, Richard Bright, *Burt*, Patti D'Arbanville, *Betty Fargo*, Maggie Wellman, *Mary Fargo*, Bert Conway, *Wilber Fargo*, Anthony Palmer, *Karl*, Joseph Sullivan, *Dizzy*, Helen Craig, *Mrs. Castle*, Ronda Copland, *Dee*. R.

Offbeat contemporary western comedy. A rancher (Clifton James) hires a detective (Slim Pickens) to catch a pair of cattle rustlers (Jeff Bridges, Sam Waterson). *Rancho Deluxe* was intended to be quirky and eccentric, but Frank Perry's direction is just too ordinary. Some of the odd humor of Thomas McGuane's script does manage to seep through, though. McGuane used the story again in *The Missouri Breaks*, which had the benefit of Arthur Penn's truly wild treatment.

708 **Real Life** (1979) ******** Paramount, 99 min. *Dir* Albert Brooks, *Scr* Albert Brooks, Monica Johnson, Harry Shearer, *Cin* Eric Saarinen, *Ed* David Finfer, *Art* Linda Marder, Linda Spheeris, *Mus* Mort Lindsay, *Prod* Penelope Spheeris, *Exec Prod* Norman Epstein, Jonathan Kovlar.

Cast: Albert Brooks, *Himself*, Charles Grodin, *Warren Yeager*, Frances Lee McCain, *Jeanette Yeager*, J.A. Preston, *Dr. Ted Cleary*, Matthew Tobin, *Dr. Howard Hill*, Lisa Urette, *Lisa Yeager*, Robert Stirrat, *Eric Yeager*, David Spielberg, *Dr. Jeremy Nolan*, Jennings Lang, *Martin Brand*, Norman Bartold, *Isaac Steven Hayward*. PG.

Superb comedy about a filmmaker, who moves in with an average family to film their lives, which he subsequently destroys. *Real Life* is a perceptive satire specifically aimed at the PBS series about the Loud family, but is about documentaries in general. The main point is that film cannot record true reality, because it automatically changes with the presence of a camera. Albert Brook's hysterically funny performance dominates, as he portrays himself as a selfish egotistical filmmaker. Brooks also made his directorial debut with this film, and of the contemporary comedian-directors he ranks second only to Woody Allen.

709   The Reincarnation of Peter Proud (1975)   *** American International, 104 min. *Dir* J. Lee Thompson, *Scr* Max Ehrlich, based on his novel, *Cin* Victor J. Kemper, *Ed* Michael Anderson, *Art* Jack Martin Smith, *Mus* Jerry Goldsmith, *Prod* Frank P. Rosenberg, *Exec Prod* Charles A. Pratt.

Cast: Michael Sarrazin, *Peter Proud*, Jennifer O'Neill, *Ann Curtis*, Margot Kidder, *Marcia Curtis*, Cornelia Sharpe, *Nora*, Paul Hecht, *Dr. Goodman*, Tony Stephano, *Jeff Curtis*, Norman Burton, *Dr. Spear*, Anne Ives, *Ellen*, Debralee Scott, *Suzy*. R. $5,000,000.

Above average occult thriller. The complex plot involves a man (Michael Sarrizan), who is the reincarnation of a man murdered by his wife (Margot Kidder), and has a relationship with the woman's daughter (Jennifer O'Neill), who is in a sense his daughter. *The Reincarnation of Peter Proud* concentrates more on character than most films of its type, and still manages some thrills along the way.

710   Remember My Name (1978)   *** Columbia, 94 min. *Dir* Alan Rudolph, *Scr* Alan Rudolph, *Cin* Tak Fujimoto, *Ed* William A. Sawyer, Thomas Walls, *Mus* Alberta Hunter, *Prod* Robert Altman.

Cast: Geraldine Chaplin, *Emily*, Anthony Perkins, *Curry*, Moses Gunn, *Pike*, Berry Berenson, *Barbara*, Jeff Goldblum, *Nudd*, Timothy Thomerson, *Jeff*, Alfre Woodard, *Rita*, Marilyn Coleman, *Teresa*, Jeffrey S. Perry, *Harry*, Carlos Brown, *Rusty*, Dennis Franz, *Franks*. R.

Strange thriller starring Geraldine Chaplin as an ex-convict, who inexplicably terrorizes both a couple (Anthony Perkins, Berry Berenson) and a dime store manager (Jeff Goldblum) and his clerk (Alfre Woodard). She lives in a dilapidated apartment and has an affair with the building manager (Moses Gunn). *Remember My Name* is not an ordinary thriller, as Alan Rudolph's obscure style drains it of any emotion or excitement.

711   Report to the Commissioner (1975)   ** United Artists, 112 min. *Dir* Milton Katselas, *Scr* Abby Mann, Ernest Tidyman, based on novel by James Mills, *Cin*, Mario Tosi, *Ed* David Blewitt, *Des* Robert Clatworthy, *Cos* Anna Hill Johnstone, *Mus* Elmer Bernstein, *Prod* M.J. Frankovich.

Cast: Michael Moriarty, *Beauregard "Bo" Lockley*, Yaphet Kotto, *Richard "Crunch" Blackstone*, Susan Blakely, *Patty Butler*, Hector Elizondo, *Capt. d'Angelo*, Tony King, *Thomas "Stock" Henderson*, Michael McGuire, *Lt. Hanson*, Edward Grover, *Capt. Strichter*, Dana Elcar, *Chief Perna*, Bob Balaban, *Joey Egan*, William Devane, *Asst D.A. Jackson*, Stephen Elliott, *Police Commissioner*, Richard Gere, *Bill*, Vic Tayback, *Lt. Seidensticker*, Albert Seedman, *Det. Schulman*, Noelle North, *Samatha*, Bebe Drake Hooks, *Dorothy*. PG.

Unusual police suspense thriller about a misfit police officer, who mistakenly tracks down an undercover cop (Susan Blakely), and accidently causes her death. *Report to the Commissioner* tries to mix social commentary with realistic action and the mix does not always work. The structure of the film is weak and too many scenes are performed at an extremely hyper level.

712   Return from Witch Mountain (1978)   ** Buena Vista, 93 min. *Dir* John Hough, *Scr* Malcolm Marmorstein, based on characters created by Alexander Key, *Cin* Frank Phillips, *Ed* Bob Bring, *Art* John B. Mansbridge, Jack

Senter, *Mus* Lalo Schifrin, *Prod* Jerome Courtland, Ron Miller, *Assoc Prod* Kevin Corcoran, A Walt Disney Production.

Cast: Bette Davis, *Letha,* Christopher Lee, *Victor,* Kim Richards, *Tia,* Ike Eisenmann, *Tony,* Jack Soo, *Mr. Yokomoto,* Christian Juttner, *Dazzler,* Dick Bakalyan, *Eddie,* Poindexter, *Crusher,* Anthony James, *Sickle,* Ward Costello, *Mr. Clearcole,* Brad Savage, *Muscles,* Jeffrey Jacquet, *Rocky.* G. $7,375,000. See *Escape to Witch Mountain.*

713 **The Return of a Man Called Horse** (1976) *** United Artists, 125 min. *Dir* Irvin Kershner, *Scr* Jack DeWitt, based on characters created by Dorothy M. Johnson, *Cin* Owen Roizman, *Ed* Michael Kahn, *Mus* Laurence Rosenthal, *Prod* Terry Morse, Jr., *Exec Prod* Sandy Howard.

Cast: Richard Harris, *John Morgan,* Gale Sondergaard, *Elk Woman,* Geoffrey Lewis, *Zenas Morro,* Bill Lucking, *Tom Gryce,* Jorge Luke, *Running Bull,* Claudio Brook, *Chemin d'Fer,* Enrique Lucero, *Raven,* Jorge Russek, *Blacksmith,* Ana De Sade, *Moonstar,* Pedro Damien, *Standing Bear,* Humberto Lopez-Pineda, *Thin Dog,* Patricia Reyes, *Grey Thorn,* Regino Herrerra, *Lame Wolf,* Rigobert Rico, *Owl,* Alberto Mariscal, *Red Cloud.* PG. See *A Man Called Horse.*

714 **The Return of the Pink Panther** (1975) *** United Artists, 115 min. *Dir* Blake Edwards, *Scr* Blake Edwards, Frank Waldman, *Cin* Geoffrey Unsworth, *Ed* Tom Priestley, *Art* Peter Mullins, *Mus* Henry Mancini, *Lyrics* Hal David, *Prod* Blake Edwards, *Assoc Prod* Tony Adams.

Cast: Peter Sellers, *Inspector Clouseau,* Christopher Plummer, *Sir Charles Litton,* Catherine Schell, *Claudia Litton,* Herbert Lom, *Chief Inspector Dreyfus,* Burt Kwouk, *Cato,* Peter Arne, *Col. Sharki,* Gregoire Aslan, *Chief of Police,* Peter Jeffrey, *Gen. Wadafi,* David Lodge, *Jean Duval,* Eric Pohlmann, *Fat Man,* Andre Maranne, *Francois (Dreyfus' Aide),* Jean Bluthal, *Begger,* Victor Spinetti, *Concierge,* Mike Grady, *Bell Boy,* Carol Cleveland, *Sari Lady,* Jeremy Hawk, *Jealous Escort.* G. $25,390,000.

After a decade of failures Blake Edwards successfully revived the "Pink Panther" series starring Peter Sellers as the bumbling Inspector Clouseau. The three from the 1970's *The Return of the Pink Panther, The Pink Panther Strikes Again* and *The Revenge of the Pink Panther* are every bit as good as the two originals. The Edwards/Sellers collaboration is responsible for some of the funniest sight gags to ever grace the screen. Unfortunately these films are uneven because less care was taken with the other characters, and the films fall flat when Sellers is not on the screen.

715 **Return to Macon County** (1975) * American International, 90 min. *Dir* Richard Compton, *Scr* Richard Compton, *Cin* Jacques Marquette, *Ed* Corky Ehlers, *Mus* Robert O. Ragland, *Prod* Elliot Schick, *Exec Prod* Samuel Z. Arkoff.

Cast: Nick Nolte, *Bo Hollinger,* Don Johnson, *Harley McKay,* Robin Mattson, *Junell,* Robert Viharo, *Sgt. Whittaker,* Eugene Daniels, *Tom,* Matt Greene, *Peter,* Devon Ericson, *Betty,* Ron Prather, *Steve,* Philip Crews, *Larry,* Laura Sayer, *Libby,* Walt Guthrie, *Big Man in Coffee Shop,* Mary Ann Hearn, *Pat,* Sam Kilman, *Cook,* Bill Moses, *Sheriff Jackson,* Pat O'Connor, *Officer Harris,* Maurice Hunt, *Motel Owner,* Kim Graham, *Girl in Car,* Don Higdon, *Boy in Car.* PG. See *Macon County Line.*

716 Revenge of the Pink Panther (1978) *** United Artists, 98 min. *Dir* Blake Edwards, *Scr* Ron Clark, Blake Edwards, Frank Waldman, based on story by Blake Edwards, *Cin* Ernie Day, *Ed* Alan Jones, *Des* Peter Mullins, *Art* John Siddall, *Cos* Tiny Nichols, *Mus* Henry Mancini, *Prod* Blake Edwards, *Exec Prod* Tony Adams.

Cast: Peter Sellers, *Inspecter Clouseau*, Herbert Lom, *Dreyfus*, Dyan Cannon, *Simone Legree*, Robert Webber, *Douvier*, Burt Kwouk, *Cato*, Paul Stewart, *Scallini*, Robert Loggia, *Marchione*, Graham Stark, *Auguste Balls*, Sue Lloyd, *Claude Russo*, Tony Beckley, *Guy Algo*, Valerie Leon, *Tanya*. PG. $25,000,000. See *Return of the Pink Panther*.

717 Rhinoceros (1974) *** American Film Theatre, 101 min. *Dir* Tom O'Horgan, *Scr* Julian Barry, based on play by Eugene Ionesco, *Cin* Jim Crabe, *Ed* Bud Smith, *Des* Jack Martin Smith, *Cos* Noel Taylor, *Mus* Galt MacDermot, *Prod* Ely A. Landau, *Exec Prod* Edward Lewis.

Cast: Zero Mostel, *John*, Gene Wilder, *Stanley*, Karen Black, *Daisy*, Robert Weil, *Carl*, Joe Silver, *Norman*, Marilyn Chris, *Mrs. Bingham*, Robert Fields, *Logician*, Melody Santangelo, *Young Woman*, Lou Cutell, *Cashier*, Don Calfa, *Waiter*, Kathryn Harkin, *Lady with Cat*, Lorna Thayer, *Restaurant Owner*, Howard Morton, *Doctor*, Percy Rodrigues, *Mr. Nicholson*. PG. See *American Film Theatre*.

718 Rich Kids (1979) *** United Artists, 96 min. *Dir* Robert M. Young, *Scr* Judith Ross, *Cin* Ralf D. Bode, *Ed* Edward Beyer, *Art* David Mitchell, *Cos* Hilary M. Rosenfeld, *Mus* Craig Doerge, *Songs* Craig Doerge, Allan Nichols, *Prod* George W. George, Michael Hauseman, *Exec Prod* Robert Altman.

Cast: Trini Alvarado, *Franny Philips*, Jeremy Levy, *Jamie Harris*, Kathryn Walker, *Madeleine Philips*, John Lithgow, *Paul Philips*, Terry Kiser, *Ralph Harris*, David Selby, *Steve Sloan*, Roberta Maxwell, *Barbara Peterfreund*, Paul Dooley, *Simon Peterfreund*, Diane Stilwell, *Stewardess*, Dianne Kirksey, *Ralph's Secretary*, Irene Worth, *Madeleine's Mother*, Olympia Dukakis, *Lawyer*, Jill Eikenberry, *Juilliard Student*. PG.

Fine comedy about upper-middle class youths, and how they cope with the divorce of their parents. *Rich Kids* focuses on two particular kids (Trini Alvarado, Jeremy Levy) and their friendship based on their common despair. The film is intelligent and witty, particularly in its portrayal of the youths. Unfortunately the film, at times, is clichéd with the kids seemingly wiser than their foolish parents.

719 Rio Lobo (1970) ** National General, 114 min. *Dir* Howard Hawks, *Scr* Leigh Brackett, Burton Wohl, based on story by Burton Wohl, *Cin* William Clothier, *Ed* John Woodcock, *Des* Robert E. Smith, *Cos* Luster Bayless, Ted Parvin, *Mus* Jerry Goldsmith, *Prod* Howard Hawks, *Assoc Prod* Paul Helmick.

Cast: John Wayne, *Cord McNally*, Jorge Rivero, *Pierre Cordona*, Jennifer O'Neill, *Shasta*, Jack Elam, *Phillips*, Victor French, *Ketcham*, Susana Dosamantes, *Maria Carmen*, Chris Mitchum, *Tuscarora*, Mike Henry, *Sheriff Hendricks*, David Huddleston, *Dr. Jones*, Bill Williams, *Sheriff Cronin*, Edward Faulkner, *Lt. Harris*, Sherry Lansing, *Amelita*, Dean Smith, *Bitey*, Robert Donner, *Whitey*, Jim Davis, *Riley*, Peter Jason, *Lt. Forsythe*, Robert Rothwell, Chuck Courtney, George Plimpton, *Whitey's Henchmen*. G. $4,250,000.

Fair western starring John Wayne as an ex-Union Army officer, who tracks down the men who murdered one of his junior officers during the Civil War. *Rio Lobo* is the final installment of an unofficial Howard Hawks trilogy, following *Rio Bravo* (1959) and *El Dorado* (1967), the best of the three, all of which contain similiar plots and characters. This film is inferior to its two predecessors, and is a disappointing final film for Hawks.

720 **The Ritz** (1976) **** Warner Bros., 90 min. *Dir* Richard Lester, *Scr* Terrence McNally, based on his play, *Cin* Paul Wilson, *Ed* John Bloom, *Des* Philip Harrison, *Cos* Vangie Harrison, *Mus* Ken Thorne, *Prod* Denis O'Dell.

Cast: Jack Weston, *Gaetano Proclo*, Rita Moreno, *Googie Gomez*, Jerry Stiller, *Carmine Vespucci*, Kaye Ballard, *Vivian Proclo*, F. Murray Abraham, *Chris*, Paul B. Price, *Claude*, Treat Williams, *Michael Brick*, John Everson, *Tiger*, Christopher J. Brown, *Duff*, Dave King, *Abe*, Bessie Love, *Maurine*, Tony DeSantis, *Sheldon Farenthold*, George Coulouris, *Old Man Vespucci*. R.

Excellent farce set in a New York gay bathhouse. Jack Weston is marked for murder by his gangster brother-in-law, Jerry Stiller, and hides out in the bathhouse, thinking it is a regular hotel. Richard Lester excels at this type of slapstick humor and he keeps things moving at a frenetic pace. Rita Moreno steals the film as a talentless singer, performing at the bathhouse.

721 **Robin and Marian** (1976) **** Britain, Columbia, 106 min. *Dir* Richard Lester, *Scr* James Goldman, *Cin* David Watkin, *Ed* John Victor Smith, *Des* Michael Stringer, *Art* Gil Parrando, *Cos* Yvonne Blake, *Mus* John Barry, *Prod* Denis O'Dell, *Exec Prod* Richard Shepherd.

Cast: Sean Connery, *Robin Hood*, Audrey Hepburn, *Maid Marian*, Robert Shaw, *Sheriff of Nottingham*, Richard Harris, *King Richard*, Nicol Williamson, *Little John*, Denholm Elliott, *Will Scarlet*, Kenneth Haigh, *Sir Ranulf*, Ronnie Barker, *Friar Tuck*, Ian Holm, *King John*, Bill Maynard, *Mercadier*, Esmond Knight, *Old Defender*, Veronica Quilligan, *Sister Mary*. PG. $4,000,000.

Excellent adventure film about the last days of Robin Hood and Maid Marian. *Robin and Marian* begins 20 years later, with Robin and Little John returning from the Crusades only to find that Marian is a nun and the Sheriff of Nottingham is still after him. This film is slightly schizophrenic. James Goldman's screenplay is romantic in tone, but Richard Lester's satyrical direction tends to destroy that mood.

722 **Rock 'n' Roll High School** (1979) **** New World, 93 min. *Dir* Allan Arkush, *Scr* Russ Dvonch, Joseph McBride, Richard Whitley, *Story* Allan Arkush, Joe Dante, *Cin* Dean Cundey, *Ed* Larry Bock, Gail Werbin, *Art* Marie Kordus, *Cos* Jack Buehler, *Chor* Siana Lee Hall, *Prod* Michael Finnell, *Exec Prod* Roger Corman.

Cast: P.J. Soles, *Riff Randell*, Vincent Van Patten, *Tom*, Clint Howard, *Eaglebauer*, Dey Young, *Kate*, Mary Woronov, *Miss Togar*, Paul Bartel, *McGree*, Dick Miller, *Police Chief*, Alix Elias, *Coach Steroid*, Don Steele, *Screamin' Steve*, Loren Lester, *Hansel*, Daniel Davies, *Gretel*, Lynn Farrell, *Angel Dust*, Herbie Braha, *Manager*, Grady Sutton, *School Board President*, Chris Somma, *Shawn*, Marla Rosenfield, *Cheryl*, Barbara Ann Walters, *Cafeteria Lady*, Terry Soda, *Norma*, Joe Van Sickle, *Cop*, The Ramones, *Themselves*. PG.

Wonderfully absurd rock musical that features the New Wave rock group The Ramones. The skimpy plot centers on Riff Randell (P.J. Soles) whose love for The Ramones disrupts Vince Lombardi High School. This slightly warped updating of the teen musicals of the 1960's at least has a happy ending; the nice girl and the nice guy finally get together and Riff Randell blows up the school. Who could ask for more? This is possibly the best film to emerge from Roger Corman's company during the 1970's and not surprisingly gained a large cult following.

723 **Rocky** (1976) (A, G, LA) ******** United Artists, 119 min. *Dir* John G. Avildsen (A, D), *Scr* Sylvester Stallone (AN), *Cin* James Crabe, *Ed* Scott Conrad, Richard Halsey (A), *Des* Bill Cassidy, *Art* James H. Spencer, *Cos* Robert Cambel, Joanne Hutchinson, *Mus* Bill Conti, *Song*, "Gonna Fly Now", *Mus* Bill Conti (AN), *Lyrics* Carol Connors, Ayn Robbins, (AN), *Prod* Robert Chartoff, Irwin Winkler, *Exec Prod* Gene Kirkwood.

Cast: Sylvester Stallone (AN), *Rocky*, Talia Shire (AN, NY, NB), *Adrian*, Burt Young (AN), *Paulie*, Carl Weathers, *Apollo*, Burgess Meredith (AN), *Mickey*, Thayer David, *Jergens*, Joe Spinell, *Gazzo*, Joe Frazier, *Himself*, Judi Letizia, *Marie*, Jimmy Gambina, *Mike*, Bill Baldwin, *Fight Announcer*, Al Silvani, *Cut Man*, George Memmoli, *Ice Rink Attendant*, Diana Lewis, George O'Hanlon, *TV Commentators*, Larry Carroll, *TV Interviewer*, Billy Sands, *Club Fight Announcer*. PG. $55,890,000.

Uplifting drama about a small-time boxer whose life is going nowhere until he is given a shot at the heavyweight championship. *Rocky* is basically a Cinderella story and surprisingly it works, despite its sentiment. Sylvester Stallone's story ironically parallels his own fight for movie stardom. Stallone followed this with *Rocky II* in which he gets another shot at the title. This film is more like a remake than a sequel, but it is a fine film nevertheless.

724 **The Rocky Horror Picture Show** (1975) ****** Britain, 20th Century–Fox, 100 min. *Dir* Jim Sharman, *Scr* Richard O'Brien, Jim Sharman, based on stage musical by Richard O'Brien, *Cin* Peter Suschitzky, *Ed* Graeme Clifford, *Des* Brian Thomson, *Cos* Sue Blane, *Mus* Richard O'Brien, *Prod* Michael White, *Exec Prod* Lou Adler, *Assoc Prod* John Goldstone.

Cast: Tim Curry, *Dr. Frank N. Furter*, Susan Sarandon, *Janet*, Barry Bostwick, *Brad*, Richard O'Brien, *Riff Raff*, Patricia Quinn, *Magenta*, Little Nell, *Columbia*, Jonathan Adams, *Dr. Scott*, Peter Hinwood, *Rocky Horror*, Meatloaf, *Eddie*, Charles Gray, *Criminolgist*. R. $12,215,000.

Fair rock musical spoof of *Frankenstein* and other horror movies. A young average couple (Barry Bostwick, Susan Sarandon) is caught in a heavy rainstorm and stops at a castle to use the phone. There they encounter a group of bizarre characters, led by Frank N. Furter, a bisexual version of Dr. Frankenstein. Some of the musical sequences are fine, but the storyline is weak and not well structured. Surprisingly this silly film became a huge cult success, playing for years at midnight showings.

725 **Rocky II** (1979) ******* United Artists, 119 min. *Dir* Sylvester Stallone, *Scr* Sylvester Stallone, *Cin* Bill Butler, *Ed* Danford B. Greene, *Art* Richard Berger, *Mus* Bill Conti, *Prod* Robert Chartoff, Irwin Winkler, *Assoc Prod* Arthur Chobanian.

Cast: Sylvester Stallone, *Rocky Balboa*, Talia Shire, *Adrian*, Burt Young, *Paulie*, Carl Weathers, *Apollo Creed*, Burgess Meredith, *Mickey*, Tony Burton, *Apollo's Trainer*, Joe Spinell, *Gazzo*, Leonard Gaines, *Agent*, Sylvia Meals, *Mary Anne Creed*, Frank McRae, *Meat Foreman*, Al Silvani, *Cutman*, John Pleshette, *Director*, Stu Nahan, *Announcer*, Bill Baldwin, *Commentator*, Jerry Ziesmer, *Salesman*, Paul J. Micale, *Father Carmine*. PG. $43,050,000. See *Rocky*.

726 **Roller Boogie** (1979) * United Artists, 103 min. *Dir* Mark L. Lester, *Scr* Barry Schneider, *Story* Irwin Yablans, *Cin* Dean Cundey, *Ed* Howard Kunin, *Art* Keith Michl, *Mus* Bob Esty, *Songs* Michele Aller, Michael Brooks, Bob Esty, *Chor* David Winters, *Prod* Bruce Cohn Curtis, *Exec Prod* Irwin Yablans, *Assoc Prod* Joseph Wolf.

Cast: Linda Blair, *Terry*, Jim Bray, *Bobby* Beverly Garland, *Mrs. Barkley*, Roger Perry, *Barkley*, Jimmy Van Patten, *Hoppy*, Kimberly Beck, *Lana*, Rick Sciacca, *Complete Control*, Sean McClory, *Jammer*, Mark Goddard, *Thatcher*, Albert Insinnia, *Gordo*, Stoney Jackson, *Phones*, M.G. Kelly, *J.D.*, Chris Nelson, *Franklin*, Patrick Wright, *Sgt. Danner*, Dorothy Meyer, *Ada*, Shelley Golden, *Mrs. Potter*, Bill Ross, *Nick*, Carey Fox, *Sonny*, Nina Axelrod, *Bobby's Friend*. PG.

Silly youth oriented film that attempts to capitalize on the roller disco craze. A rich girl (Linda Blair) runs away from home to join the wonderful world of roller disco in Venice, California. There are the normal complications with gangsters who want to close down the disco, but the kids rally, a la Busby Berkeley, to save it. *Roller Boogie* is total nonsense!

727 **Rollerball** (1975) ** United Artists, 129 min. *Dir* Norman Jewison, *Scr* William Harrison, based on his short story *Rollerball Murders*, *Cin* Douglas Slocombe, *Ed* Anthony Gibbs, *Des* John Box, *Art* Robert Laing, *Cos* Julie Harris, *Prod* Norman Jewison, *Assoc Prod* Patrick Palmer.

Cast: James Caan, *Jonathan E.*, John Houseman, *Bartholomew*, Maud Adams, *Ella*, John Beck, *Moonpie*, Moses Gunn, *Cletus*, Pamela Hensley, *Mackie*, Barbara Trentham, *Daphne*, Ralph Richardson, *Librarian*, Shane Rimmer, *Team Executive*, Alfred Thomas, *Team Trainer*, Burnell Tucker, *Jonathan's Captain of Guard*, Angus MacInnes, *Jonathan's Guard #1*, Rick Le Parmentier, *Bartholomew's Aide*, Burt Kwouk, *Oriental Doctor*, Rober Ito, *Oriental Instructor*, Nancy Blair, *Girl in Library*, Loftus Burton, Abi Gouhad, *Black Reporters*. R. $9,050,000.

Disappointing science-fiction thriller about a brutal futuristic sport that combines motorcycles with roller derby. *Rollerball* purports to attack violence in both sports and society, but the film comes alive only in the violent action scenes centering on the deadly sport. This could have been a good action film had the filmmakers been content to keep it on that level, but they felt compelled to complicate matters with statements about capitalism and corporate control of society, which slows the pace to a grinding halt.

728 **Rollercoaster** (1977) *** Universal, 119 min. *Dir* James Goldstone, *Scr* Richard Levinson, William Link, *Story* Richard Levinson, William Link, Sanford Sheldon, based on story by Tommy Cook, *Cin* David M. Walsh, *Ed* Edward A. Biery, Richard Sprague, *Des* Henry Bumstead, *Cos* Burton Miller, *Mus*

Lalo Schifrin, *Prod* Jennings Lang, *Exec Prod* Howard G. Kazanjian, *Assoc Prod* Tommy Cook.

Cast: George Segal, *Harry Calder*, Richard Widmark, *Hoyt*, Timothy Bottoms, *Young Man*, Henry Fonda, *Simon Davenport*, Harry Guardino, *Keefer*, Susan Strasberg, *Fran*, Helen Hunt, *Tracy Calder*, Dorothy Tristan, *Helen*, Harry Davis, *Benny*, Stephen Pearlman, *Lyons*, Gerald Rowe, *Wayne Moore*, Wayne Tippit, *Christie*, Michael Bell, *Demerest*, Charlie Tuna, *Rock Concert M.C.* PG. $10,110,000.

Good cat-and-mouse thriller involving a battle of wits between a civic inspector (George Segal) and an extortionist (Timothy Bottoms), who blows up rollercoasters. The outcome is a little predictable, but *Rollercoaster* still manages to maintain suspense as Segal races to stop the man before he strikes again. *Rollercoaster* was released with Sensurround, which adds little to the film, but it does not hinder it, either.

729 **Rolling Thunder** (1977) *** American International, 99 min. *Dir* John Flynn, *Scr* Heywood Gould, Paul Schrader, *Cin* Jordan Cronenweth, *Ed* Frank P. Keller, *Art* Steve Burger, *Mus* Barry DeVorzon, *Prod* Norman T. Herman, *Exec Prod* Lawrence Gordon.

Cast: William Devane, *Maj. Charles Rane*, Tommy Lee Jones, *Johnny Vohden*, Linda Haynes, *Linda Forchet*, Lisa Richards, *Janet*, Dabney Coleman, *Maxwell*, James Best, *Texan*, Cassie Yates, *Candy*, Lawrason Driscoll, *Clif*, Jordan Gerler, *Mark*, Luke Askew, *Slim*, James Victor, *Lopez*, Jane Abbott, *Sister*. R.

Above-average vendetta drama about a returning Vietnam veteran, who vows revenge on a gang of killers responsible for the deaths of his wife and son. *Rolling Thunder's* examination of the stress suffered by prisoners of war is a bit shallow and clichéd, but it does succeed as an action thriller due to the brisk direction of John Flynn and the performance of William Devane.

730 **The Romantic Englishwoman** (1975) **** Britain/France, New World, 115 min. *Dir* Joseph Losey, *Scr* Tom Stoppard, Thomas Wiseman, based on novel by Thomas Wiseman, *Cin* Gerry Fisher, *Ed* Reginald Beck, *Des* Richard MacDonald, *Cos* Ruth Myers, *Mus* Richard Hartley, *Prod* Daniel M. Angel, *Assoc Prod* Richard F. Dalton, Presented by Roger Corman.

Cast: Glenda Jackson, *Elizabeth*, Michael Caine, *Lewis*, Helmut Berger, *Thomas*, Beatrice Romand, *Catherine*, Nathalie Delon, *Miranda*, Michel Lonsdale, *Swan*, Marcus Richardson, *David*, Kate Nelligan, *Isabel*, Rene Kolldehof, *Herman*, Anna Steele, *Annie*, Bill Wallis, *Hendrik*, Julie Peasgood, *New Nanny*, David DeKeyser, *George*, Phil Brown, *Mr. Wilson*, Marcella Markham, *Mrs. Wilson*. R.

Excellent comedy-drama starring Michael Caine and Glenda Jackson as a writer and his wife, who are having marital problems. Jackson goes off to Europe where she meets a gigolo (Helmut Berger), but her affair may be more imagined by Caine than reality. *The Romantic Englishwoman* is one of Joseph Losey's finest psychological examinations of English bourgeoisie. Losey nicely mixes in humor without harming his usual graceful and elegant visual style.

731 **Rooster Cogburn** (1975) * Universal, 107 min. *Dir* Stuart Millar, *Scr* Martin Julien, based on character created by Charles Portis, *Cin* Harry

Stradling, Jr., *Ed* Robert Swink, *Art* Preston Ames, *Cos* Edith Head, *Mus* Lawrence Rosenthal, *Prod* Hal B. Wallis.

Cast: John Wayne, *Rooster Cogburn*, Katharine Hepburn, *Eula*, Anthony Zerbe, *Breed*, Strother Martin, *McCoy*, Richard Jordan, *Hawk*, John McIntire, *Judge Parker*, Paul Koslo, *Luke*, Jack Colvin, *Red*, Jon Lormer, *Rev. Goodnight*, Richard Romancito, *Wolf*, Lane Smith, *Leroy*, Warren Vanders, *Babgy*, Jerry Gatlin, *Nose*. PG. $8,020,000.

Dismal sequel to *True Grit*. John Wayne repeats his offbeat role as Rooster Cogburn and is teamed for the first time with Katharine Hepburn in a film that appears to be a poor western version of *The African Queen*. One would assume that even with the inferior script *Rooster Cogburn* would be worth watching due to its two stars, but Wayne and Hepburn spend so much time arguing they resemble *The Bickersons*.

732 **The Rose** (1979) ******** 20th Century–Fox, 134 min. *Dir* Mark Rydell, *Scr* Bo Goldman, Bill Kerby, *Cin* Vilmos Zsigmond, *Ed* C. Timothy O'Meara, Robert L. Wolfe (AN), *Des* Richard MacDonald, *Art* Jim Schoppe, *Cos* Theoni V. Aldredge, *Mus* Paul A. Rothchild, *Song* "The Rose", *Mus* Amanda Mc-Broom (G), *Chor* Toni Basil, *Prod* Aaron Russo, Marvin Worth, *Exec Prod* Tony Ray.

Cast: Bette Midler (AN, GMC), *Rose*, Alan Bates, *Rudge*, Frederic Forrest (AN), *Dyer*, Harry Dean Stanton, *Billy Ray*, Barry Primus, *Dennis*, David Keith, *Mal*, Sandra McCabe, *Sarah*, Will Hare, *Mr. Leonard*, Rudy Bond, *Monty*, Don Calfa, *Don Frank*, James Keane, *Dealer*, Doris Roberts, *Rose's Mother*, Sandy Ward, *Rose's Father*. R. $22,620,000.

Powerful drama about the downfall of a female rock star, loosely based on the life of Janis Joplin. *The Rose*, better than almost any film, documents the hardships of constantly being on the road, constantly having to perform, and how this can take its toll on people. Bette Milder gives a staggeringly good performance – a particularly astonishing accomplishment for a film debut – as the singer, realistically depicting her drug scenes without exaggeration.

733 **Rosebud** (1975) ****** United Artists, 126 min. *Dir* Otto Preminger, *Scr* Erik Lee Preminger, *Additional Dialogue* Marjorie Kellogg, based on novel by Paul Bonnecarrere, Joan Jemingway, *Cin* Denys Coop, *Ed* Thom Noble, Peter Thornton, *Des* Michael Seymour, *Art* Simon Holland, *Mus* Laurent Petitgirard, *Prod* Otto Preminger.

Cast: Peter O'Toole, *Larry Martin*, Richard Attenborough, *Sloat*, Cliff Gorman, *Hamlekh*, Claude Dauphin, *Fargeau*, John V. Lindsay, *Sen. Donovan*, Peter Lawford, *Lord Carter*, Amidou, *Kirkbane*, Raf Vallone, *George Nikolaos*, Adrienne Corri, *Lady Carter*, Josef Shiloa, *Hacam*, Brigitte Ariel, *Sabine*, Isabelle Huppert, *Helene*, Lalla Ward, *Margaret*, Kim Cattral, *Joyce*, Debra Berger, *Gertrude*, Georges Beller, *Patrice*, Francoise Brion, *Melina Nikolaos*, Julian Pettifer, *Himself*, Edward Behr, *Himself*. PG.

Dull international thriller about Arab terrorists. A group of PLO terrorists kidnap five wealthy girls aboard a yacht, named "Rosebud". The film cuts back and forth between the captors and the efforts of the CIA to find them. *Rosebud* has little excitement and concentrates too heavily on dialogue. John

Lindsay, former mayor of New York, makes an embarrassing film debut.

734 **Royal Flash** (1975) *** Britain, 20th Century–Fox, 99 min. *Dir* Richard Lester, *Scr* George MacDonald Fraser, based on his novel, *Cin* Geoffrey Unsworth, *Ed* John Victor Smith, *Des* Terence Marsh, *Art* Alan Tomkins, *Mus* Ken Thorne, *Prod* David V. Picker, Denis O'Dell.

Cast: Malcolm McDowell, *Flashman*, Alan Bates, *Rudi von Sternberg*, Florinda Bolkan, *Lola Montez*, Oliver Reed, *Otto von Bismarck*, Britt Ekland, *Duchess Irma*, Lionel Jeffries, *Kraftstein*, Tom Bell, *de Gautet*, Joss Ackland, *Sapten*, Christopher Cazenove, *Hansen*, Roy Kinnear, *Old Roue*, Alistair Sim, *Mr. Greig*, Michael Hordern, *Headmaster*. PG.

Above average period satire about the adventures of Flashman, a 19th century English rogue. Malcolm McDowell stars as the Flashman, who is forced by Bismarck (Oliver Reed) and Sternberg (Alan Bates) to impersonate a Prussian nobleman who is to marry Duchess Irma (Britt Eckland). *Royal Flash* has a complicated plot, but it moves briskly, due to Richard Lester's lightning paced direction. This resembles his other period satire *The Three Musketeers*, but it is not quite as brilliant.

735 **The Ruling Class** (1972) ***** Britain, Avco Embassy, 154 min. *Dir* Peter Medak, *Scr* Peter Barnes, based on his play, *Cin* Ken Hodges, *Ed* Ray Lovejoy, *Des* Peter Murton, *Mus* John Cameron, *Chor* Eleanor Fazan, *Prod* Jules Buck, Jack Hawkins, *Assoc Prod* David Korda, Presented by Joseph E. Levine.

Cast: Peter O'Toole (AN, NB), *14th Earl of Gurney*, Alastair Sim, *Bishop Lampton*, Arthur Lowe, *Tucker*, Harry Andrews, *13th Earl of Gurney*, Coral Browne, *Lady Claire*, Michael Bryant, *Dr. Herber*, Nigel Green, *McKyle*, William Mervyn, *Sir Charles*, Carolyn Seymour, *Grace*, James Villiers, *Dinsdale*, Hugh Burden, *Matthew Peake*, Graham Crowden, *Truscott*, Kay Walsh, *Mrs. Piggot-Jones*, Patsy Byrne, *Mrs. Treadwell*, Joan Cooper, *Nurse Brice*, James Grout, *Inspector*. R.

Outlandish and powerful black-comedy about an aristocratic Englishman who thinks he is Jesus Christ. *The Ruling Class* is one of the most savage attacks on British aristocracy ever put on film. The cruelty and coldness of the upper class is brilliantly put across as O'Toole is scorned as a freakish outcast while he preaches love as Christ, but is later welcomed back with open arms when he takes on the personality of Jack the Ripper. The total unpredictability of this film is one of its strong points; one moment it is a comedy and then without warning it becomes a musical or even a horror film. O'Toole gives possibly the finest performance of his career as this slightly confused individual.

736 **Russian Roulette** (1975) ** Avco Embassy, 93 min. *Dir* Lou Lombardo, *Scr* Tom Ardies, Stanley Mann, Arnold Margolin, based on novel *Kosygin is Coming* by Tom Ardies, *Cin* Brian West, *Ed* Richard Marden, *Art* Roy Walker, *Mus* Michael J. Lewis, *Prod* Jerry Bick, *Exec Prod* Elliott Kastner, *Assoc Prod* Dennis Holt, Marion Segal.

Cast: George Segal, *Shaver*, Christina Raines, *Bogna*, Bo Brundin, *Vostik*, Denholm Elliott, *Petapiece*, Gordon Jackson, *Hardison*, Peter Donat, *McDermott*, Richard Romanus, *Ragulia*, Nigel Stock, *Ferguson*, Val Avery,

Henke, Louise Fletcher, *Midge,* Jacques Sandulescu, *Gorki,* Graham Jarvis, *Benson,* Constantin de Goguel, *Samuel,* Wally Marsh, *Taggart,* Hagan Beggs, *Kavinsky,* Douglas McGrath, *Lars.* PG.

Fair cold war thriller about a fictitious plot to assassinate Soviet Premier Alexei Kosygin, during his visit to Vancouver, B.C. in 1970. George Segal stars as a Canadian Mountie who attempts to prevent the assassination plot perpetrated by members of the KGB. *Russian Roulette* is hardly in the same class as *The Day of the Jackal,* lacking both its pacing and suspense.

737 **Ryan's Daughter** (1970) ** Britain, MGM, 192 min. *Dir* David Lean, *Scr* Robert Bolt, *Cin* Freddie Young (A), *Ed* Norman Savage, *Des* Stephen Grimes, *Art* Roy Walker, *Cos* Jocelyn Rickards, *Mus* Maurice Jarre, *Prod* Anthony Havelock-Allan, *Assoc Prod* Roy Stevens.

Cast: Robert Mitchum, *Charles Shaughnessy,* Sarah Miles (AN), *Rosy,* Trevor Howard, *Father Collins,* Christopher Jones, *Randolph Doryan,* John Mills (A), *Michael,* Leo McKern, *Tom Ryan,* Barry Foster, *Tim O'Leary,* Archie O'Sullivan, *McCardle,* Marie Kean, *Mrs. McCardle,* Evin Crowley, *Maureen,* Barry Jackson, *Corporal,* Douglas Sheldon, *Driver,* Ed O'Callaghan, *Bernard,* Philip O'Flynn, *Paddy,* Niall O'Brian, *Joseph,* Owen O'Sullivan, *Peter,* Niall Toibin, *O'Keffe,* Emmet Bergin, *Sean,* May Cluskey, *Storekeeper,* Annie Dalton, *Old Woman.* R. $14,640,000.

Standard period love story that is wildly blown out of proportion. A young woman (Sarah Miles) marries a dull schoolteacher (Robert Mitchum), and her boring life causes her to have an affair with an English soldier (Christopher Jones.) The townspeople discover her infidelity and castigate her. There is little else to this giant epic other than beautiful scenery. It is almost as if David Lean tried to combine two of his films; *Brief Encounter* on the scale of *Lawrence of Arabia.*

738 **A Safe Place** (1971) ** Columbia, 94 min. *Dir* Henry Jaglom, *Scr* Henry Jaglom, *Cin* Dick Kratina, *Ed* Pieter Bergema, *Cos* Barbara Flood, *Exec Prod* Bert Schneider.

Cast: Tuesday Weld, *Susan/Noah,* Orson Welles, *The Magician,* Jack Nicholson, *Mitch,* Philip Proctor, *Fred,* Gwen Welles, *Bari,* Dov Lawrence, *Larry,* Fanny Birkenmaier, *The Maid,* Richard Finnochio, Barbara Flood, Roger Garrett, Jordon Hahn, Francesca Hilton, Julie Robinson, Jennifer Walker, *The Friends,* Rhonda Alfaro, *Little Girl in Rowboat,* Sylvia Zapp, *5 Year Old Susan.* PG.

Strange drama about a young woman (Tuesday Weld), who retreats into her childhood, where she feels safe, to escape from her troubled life. She even turns her New York apartment into a playroom. *A Safe Place* is perhaps too weird and heavy-handed for its own good, as its point is too obscure. Henry Jaglom made his directorial debut with this film.

739 **The Sailor Who Fell from Grace with the Sea** (1976) ** Britain, Avco Embassy, 105 min. *Dir* Lewis John Carlino, *Scr* Lewis John Carlino, based on novel by Yukio Mishima, *Cin* Douglas Slocombe, *Ed* Anthony Gibbs, *Des* Ted Haworth, *Art* Brian Ackland-Snow, *Cos* Lee Poll, *Mus* John Mandel, *Prod* Martin Poll, *Assoc Prod* David White.

Cast: Sarah Miles, *Anne Osborne,* Kris Kristofferson, *Jim Cameron,*

Jonathan Kahn, *Jonathan Osborne*, Margo Cunningham, *Mrs. Palmer*, Earl
Rhodes, *Chief*, Paul Tropea, *Number 2*, Gary Lock, *Number 4*, Stephen
Black, *Number 5*, Peter Clapham, *Richard Pettit*, Jennifer Tolman, *Mary
Ingram*. R. $7,000,000.

Visually stunning and graceful, but ultimately boring and misguided,
love story about a relationship between an American sailor and a British
woman with a jealous son. Where this film really goes wrong is the attempt
to transport a Japanese novel to an English setting, without regard for the vast
difference in culture; the Japanese attitudes in the novel are completely out
of place in England. The pace is very slow and the few shocking scenes do
not liven up the proceedings.

740 **St. Ives** (1976) ** Warner Bros., 93 min. *Dir* J. Lee Thompson, *Scr*
Barry Beckerman, based on novel *The Procane Chronicle* by Oliver Bleeck,
Cin Lucien Ballard, *Ed* Michael F. Anderson, *Des* Philip M. Jefferies, *Mus* Lalo
Schifrin, *Prod* Stanley Canter, Pancho Kohner.

Cast: Charles Bronson, *St. Ives*, John Houseman, *Procane*, Jacqueline
Bisset, *Janet*, Maximilian Schell, *Constable*, Harry Guardino, *Deal*, Harris
Yulin, *Oller*, Dana Elcar, *Blunt*, Michael Lerner, *Myron Green*, Dick O'Neill,
Counterman, Elisha Cook, *Eddie*, Val Bisoglio, *Finley*, Burr DeBenning,
Officer Frann, Daniel J. Travanti, *Parisi*. PG.

Dull murder thriller starring Charles Bronson as a former police reporter
who is hired by John Houseman to help recover some stolen papers, but
along the way several people are killed. *St. Ives* is different from other Bronson films of this type, as it has little violence. This would be fine had the script
been worthwhile, but as it stands a little violence would have been a
welcome relief.

741 **Saint Jack** (1979) *** New World, 112 min. *Dir* Peter Bogdanovich,
Scr Peter Bogdanovich, Howard Sackler, Paul Theroux, based on novel by
Paul Theroux, *Cin* Robby Muller, *Ed* William Carruth, *Art* David Ng, *Prod*
Roger Corman, *Exec Prod* Hugh M. Hefner, Edward L. Rissien.

Cast: Ben Gazzara, *Jack Flowers*, Denholm Elliot, *William Leigh*, James
Villiers, *Frogget*, Joss Ackland, *Yardley*, Rodney Bewes, *Smale*, Mark
Kingston, *Yates*, Lisa Lu, *Mrs. Yates*, Monika Subramanian, *Monika*, Judy Lim,
Judy, George Lazenby, *Senator*, Peter Bogdanovich, *Eddie Schuman*, Joseph
Noel, *Gopi*, Ong Kian Bee, *Hing*, Tan Yan Meng, *Little Hing*, Andrew Chua,
Andrew. R.

Unusual drama set in the seamy underworld of Singapore. Ben Gazzara
is excellent as an independent pimp who runs into conflict with the local
mob. *Saint Jack* had the potential of greatness, because of its colorfully flamboyant main character, perfectly embodied by Gazzara. Unfortunately the
storyline is not worthy of the character, and the film goes nowhere.

742 **Same Time Next Year** (1978) *** Universal, 119 min. *Dir* Robert
Mulligan, *Scr* Bernard Slade (AN), based on his play, *Cin* Robert Surtees (AN),
Ed Sheldon Kahn, *Des* Henry Bumstead, *Mus* Marvin Hamlisch, *Song* "The
Last Time I Felt Like This", *Mus* Marvin Hamlisch (AN), *Lyrics* Alan and Marilyn
Bergman (AN), sung by Johnny Mathis, Jane Oliver, *Prod* Morton Gottlieb,
Walter Mirisch.

Cast: Ellen Burstyn (AN), *Doris*, Alan Alda, *George*, Ivan Bonar, *Chalmers*, Bernie Kurby, *Waiter*, Cosmo Sardo, *Second Waiter*, David Northcut, *Pilot #1*, William Cantrell, *Pilot #2*. PG. $13,460,000.

Fine comedy drama about two married people, but not to each other, who have an affair at a resort in Northern California in 1951, and decide to meet at the same time each year. The film is divided into four separate sections detailing the changes in the couple over the years and the changes in society around them. *Same Time Next Year* is a little too stagebound, but it has a strong script and excellent performances by the two leads to carry it through.

743 Saturday Night Fever (1977) ***** Paramount, 119 min. *Dir* John Badham, *Scr* Norman Wexler, based on story by Nik Cohn, *Cin* Ralph D. Bode, *Ed* David Rawlins, *Des* Charles Bailey, *Cos* Jennifer Nichols, Patricia Von Brandenstein, *Mus* Barry, Robin and Maurice Gibb (The Bee Gees), David Shire, *Chor* Lester Wilson, *Prod* Robert Stigwood, *Exec Prod* Kevin McCormick.

Cast: John Travolta (AN, NB), *Tony Manero*, Karen Lynn Gorney, *Stephanie*, Barry Miller, *Bobby C*, Joseph Cali, *Joey*, Paul Pape, *Double J*, Bruce Ornstein, *Gus*, Donna Pescow, *Annette*, Val Bisoglio, *Frank Manero, Sr.*, Julie Bovasso, *Flo*, Martin Shaker, *Frank, Jr.*, Nina Hansen, *Grandmother*, Lisa Peluso, *Linda*, Sam J. Coppola, *Fusco*, Denny Dillon, *Doreen*, Bert Michaels, *Pete*, Donald Gantry, *Jay Langhart*, Monte Rock III, *Disco DJ*. R. $74,100,000.

Excellent drama about a New York youth (John Travolta), whose only relief from his seemingly wasted existence is dancing in a neighborhood disco. He is trapped in his environment and lifestyle, which includes a dull job at a paint store and socializing with his degenerate friends. *Saturday Night Fever* seems throughout to be heading for a giant cliché, with its climactic dance contest, but even there it pulls a surprise twist. The film beautifully and realistically captures his lifestyle and is a movie of its time. Travolta proved to be a commanding presence in his first starring role.

744 The Savage Is Loose (1974) ** Campbell Devon, 114 min. *Dir* George C. Scott, *Scr* Max Ehrlich, Frank DeFelitta, *Cin* Alex Phillips, Jr., *Ed* Michael Kahn, *Mus* Gil Melle, *Prod* George C. Scott, *Exec Prod* Robert E. Relyea.

Cast: George C. Scott, *John*, Trish Van Devere, *Maida*, John David Carson, *David*, Lee H. Montgomery, *Young David*. R.

Dull adventure about a family, a couple and a young son, shipwrecked on a tropical island, where they are forced to live out their existence. *The Savage Is Loose* tends to be pretentious and attempts to cover such serious themes as incest. The small cast is excellent, but there is little in this overlong tale of survival to retain audience interest.

745 Save the Tiger (1973) *** Paramount, 100 min. *Dir* John G. Avildsen, *Scr* Steve Shagan (AN, W), *Cin* Jim Crabe, *Ed* David Bretherton, *Art* Jack Collis, *Mus* Marvin Hamlisch, *Prod* Steve Shagan, *Exec Prod* Edward S. Feldman.

Cast: Jack Lemmon (A), *Harry Stoner*, Jack Gilford (AN), *Phil Greene*, Laurie Heineman, *Myra*, Norman Burton, *Fred* Patricia Smith, *Janet Stoner*, Thayer David, *Charlie Robbins*, William Hansen, *Meyer*, Harvey Jason, *Rico*,

Liv Von Linden, *Ula*, Lara Parker, *Margo*, Eloise Hardt, *Jackie*, Janina, *Dusty*, Ned Glass, *Sid* Pearl Shear, *Cashier*, Bliff Elliot, *Tiger Petitioner*, Ben Freedman, *Taxi Driver*, Madeline Lee, *Receptionist*. R.

Interesting drama about a middle-aged man who suffers from a mental breakdown. The cause of his problem is never completely clear, but it appears to be from male menopause; he is constantly living in the past and is unable to deal with the present and his loss of youth. Jack Lemmon's powerful performance totally dominates *Save the Tiger* and makes the viewer almost forget any of the problems in the script.

746 **Scarecrow** (1973) (CF) ******** Warner Bros., 112 min. *Dir* Jerry Schatzberg, *Scr* Garry Michael White, *Cin* Vilmos Zsigmond, *Ed* Evan Lottman, *Des* Al Brenner, *Cos* Jo Ynocencio, *Mus* Fred Myrow, *Prod* Robert M. Sherman.

Cast: Gene Hackman, *Max*, Al Pacino, *Lion*, Dorothy Tristan, *Coley*, Ann Wedgeworth, *Frenchy*, Richard Lynch, *Riley*, Eileen Brennan, *Darlene*, Penny Allen, *Annie*, Richard Hackman, *Mickey*, Al Cingolani, *Skipper*, Rutanya Alda, *Woman in Camper*. R. $4,300,000.

Excellent character study of a pair of drifters who meet on the road and become friends out of their mutual loneliness. The structure is episodic as *Scarecrow* follows their exploits and travels from one situation to another. By dispensing with a plot *Scarecrow* more successfully emphasizes character development and concentrates on their friendship as it grows from its shaky beginnings. Gene Hackman and Al Pacino are excellent in their offbeat roles as Max and Lion, and *Scarecrow* ranks as Jerry Schatzberg's finest film to date.

747 **Scavenger Hunt** (1979) ****** 20th Century–Fox, 116 min. *Dir* Michael Schultz, *Scr* Henry Harper, Stephen A. Vail, *Cin* Ken Lamkin, *Ed* Christopher Holmes, *Art* Richard Berger, *Mus* Billy Goldenberg, *Prod* Stephen A. Vail, *Co-Prod* Paul Maslansky, *Exec Prod* Melvin Simon, *Assoc Prod* Hana Cannon, Craig S. Yace.

Cast: Richard Benjamin, *Stuart*, James Coco, *Henri*, Scatman Crothers, *Sam*, Ruth Gordon, *Arvilla*, Cloris Leachman, *Mildred*, Cleavon Little, *Jackson*, Roddy McDowell, *Jenkins*, Robert Morley, *Bernstein*, Richard Mulligan, *Marvin*, Tony Randall, *Henry*, Dirk Benedict, *Jeff*, Willie Aames, *Kenny*, Stephanie Faracy, *Babette*, Stephen Furst, *Merle*, Richard Masur, *Georgie*, Meat Loaf, *Scum*, Pat McCormick, *Barker*, Vincent Price, *Parker*, Avery Schreiber, *Zoo Keeper*, Liz Torres, *Lady Zero*, Carol Wayne, *Nurse*. PG.

Poor all-star slapstick comedy. A dying game manufacturer (Vincent Price) devises an outlandish scavenger hunt, for which the winner will inherit his $200,000,000 estate. The participants are divided into groups and most of the movie is spent on this ridiculous search for junk, which cause numerous complications. *Scavenger Hunt* is nothing more than a series of unfunny sight gags and silly chases.

748 **Scream Blacula Scream** (1973) ****** American International, 96 min. *Dir* Bob Kelljan, *Scr* Maurice Jules, Raymond Koenig, Joan Torres, *Story* Raymond Koenig, Joan Torres, *Cin* Isadore Mankofsky, *Ed* Fabian Tordjmann, *Art* Alfeo Bocchicchio, *Mus* Bill Marx, *Prod* Joseph T. Naar, A Samuel Z. Arkoff Presentation.

Cast: William Marshall, *Manuwalde*, Pam Grier, *Lisa*, Don Mitchell, *Justin*, Michael Conrad, *Sheriff*, Richard Lawson, *Willis*, Lynne Moody, *Denny*, Beverly Gill, *Maggie*, Bernie Hamilton, *Ragman*, Barbara Rhoades, *Elaine*, Janee Michelle, *Gloria*, Don Blackman, *Doll Man*, Van Kirksey, *Prof. Walston*, Arnold Williams, *Louis*. PG. See *Blacula*.

749 Scrooge (1970) ******* National General, 115 min. *Dir* Ronald Neame, *Scr* Leslie Bricusse, based on the novel *A Christmas Carol* by Charles Dickens, *Cin* Oswald Morris, *Ed* Peter Weatherley, *Des* Terence Marsh (AN), *Art* Bob Cartwright (AN), *Cos* Margaret Furse (AN), *Mus* Leslie Bricusse (AN), *Mus Adaptation* Ian Frazer, Herbert W. Spencer (AN), *Song* "Thank You Very Much", *Mus* Leslie Bricusse (AN), *Chor* Paddy Stone, *Prod* Robert H. Solo, *Exec Prod* Leslie Bricusse, *Assoc Prod* David Orton.

Cast: Albert Finney (GMC), *Scrooge*, Alec Guinness, *Marley's Ghost*, Edith Evans, *Ghost of Christmas Past*, Kenneth More, *Ghost of Christmas Present*, Michael Medwin, *Nephew*, Lawrence Naismith, *Fezziwig*, David Collings, *Bob Cratchit*, Anton Rodgers, *Tom Jenkins*, Suzanne Neve, *Isabel*, Frances Cuka, *Mrs. Cratchit*, Derek Francis, Roy Kinnear, *Portly Gentlemen*, Mary Peach, *Nephew's Wife*, Paddy Stone, *Ghost of Christmas Yet to Come*, Kay Walsh, *Mrs. Fezziwig*, Richard Beaumont, *Tiny Tim*. G.

Disappointing musical version of Charles Dickens' *A Christmas Carol*, starring Albert Finney as the title character, who hates Christmas, but changes after he is shown his future and where his miserly ways will lead him. Finney is excellent, and it is unfortunate that the film fails to measure up to his performance; this is attributable in part to the dull and obtrusive songs.

750 The Seduction of Joe Tynan (1979) ******* Universal, 107 min. *Dir* Jerry Schatzberg, *Scr* Alan Alda, *Cin* Adam Holender, *Ed* Evan Lottman, *Art* David Chapman, *Cos* Jo Ynocencio, *Mus* Bill Conti, *Prod* Martin Bregman, *Exec Prod* Louis A. Stroller.

Cast: Alan Alda, *Joe Tynan*, Barbara Harris, *Ellie*, Meryl Streep (NS, NY, NB), *Karen Traynor*, Rip Torn, *Sen. Kittner*, Melvyn Douglas, *Sen. Birney*, Charles Kimbrough, *Francis*, Carrie Nye, *Aldena Kittner*, Blanche Baker, *Janet*, Adam Ross, *Paul Tynan*, Chris Arnold, *Jerry*, Maurice Copeland, *Edward Anderson*, Robert Christian, *Arthur Briggs*, Maureen Anderman, *Joe's Secretary*, Merv Griffin, *Himself*, John Badila, *Reporter on TV*. R. $11,405,000.

Well-made political drama about an ambitious liberal U.S. Senator, who seems to handle his political affairs better than his private life. The "seduction" in the title refers to his need for success and power. The film realistically portrays his relationship with his family and the problems incurred by his public life, without offering easy and pat solutions. Joe Tynan seems to be loosely based on Ted Kennedy, and if there are any doubts watch for the scene where he drives the golf cart into the water.

751 Sergeant Pepper's Lonely Hearts Club Band (1978) ***** Universal, 111 min. *Dir* Michael Schultz, *Scr* Henry Edwards, *Cin* Owen Roizman, *Ed* Christopher Holmes, *Des* Brian Eatwell, *Cos* May Routh, *Mus* John Lennon, Paul McCartney, arranged by George Martin, *Chor* Patricia Birch, *Prod* Robert Stigwood, *Exec Prod* Dee Anthony, *Assoc Prod* Bill Oakes.

Cast: Peter Frampton, *Billy Shears*, Barry Gibb, *Mark Henderson*, Robin Gibb, *Dave Henderson*, Maurice Gibb, *Bob Henderson*, Frankie Howerd, *Mean Mr. Mustard*, Paul Nicholas, *Dougie Shears*, Donald Pleasence, *B.D. Brockhurst*, Sandy Farina, *Strawberry Fields*, Dianne Steinberg, *Lucy*, Steve Martin, *Dr. Maxwell Edison*, Aerosmith, *Future Villain*, Alice Cooper, *Father Sun*, Earth Wind & Fire, *Benefit Performers*, Billy Preston, *Sgt. Pepper*, Stargard, *The Diamonds*, George Burns, *Mr. Kite*, Carel Struycken, *The Brute*, Patti Jerome, *Saralinde Shears*, Max Showalter, *Ernest Shears*, John Wheeler, *Mr. Fields*. PG. $12,960,000.

Poor attempt to turn the legendary Beatles album "Sergeant Pepper's Lonely Hearts Club Band" into a musical comedy fantasy. The storyline is nonsensical, and the acting by the leads is poor; Frampton and Barry, Robin and Maurice Gibb (The Bee Gees) do not even appear comfortable in front of the camera. The updated versions of Beatles songs from "Sergeant Pepper" and other albums are greatly inferior to the originals. It is dangerous to tamper with The Beatles.

752 **Semi-Tough** (1977) ** United Artists, 108 min. *Dir* Michael Ritchie, *Scr* Walter Bernstein, based on novel by Dan Jenkins, *Cin* Charles Rosher, Jr., *Ed* Richard A. Harris, *Des* Walter Scott Herndon, *Cos* Theoni V. Aldredge, *Mus* Jerry Fielding, *Prod* David Merrick.

Cast: Burt Reynolds, *Billy Clyde Puckett*, Kris Kristofferson, *Shake Tiller*, Jill Clayburgh, *Barbara Jane Bookman*, Robert Preston, *Big Ed Bookman*, Bert Convy, *Friedrich Bismark*, Roger E. Mosley, *Puddin*, Lotte Lenya, *Clara Pelf*, Richard Masur, *Phillip Hooper*, Carl Weathers, *Dreamer Tatum*, Brian Dennehy, *T.J. Lambert*, Mary Jo Catlett, *Carlene*, Joe Kapp, *Hose Manning*, Ron Silver, *Vlada*, Jim McKrell, *McNair*, Peter Bromilow, *Interpreter*, Norman Alden, *Coach Parks*, Fred Stuthman, *Minister*, Janet Brandt, *Dressmaker*, William Wolf, *Fitter*, Jenifer Shaw, *Stewardess*, Kevin Furry, *Puddin, Jr.*, Ava Roberts, *Puddin's Wife*. R. $22,810,000.

Disappointing satire of professional football. *Semi-Tough* unfortunately wanders from its intended target and concentrates too heavily on attacking EST type group therapy. With all the talent involved, this could have been an excellent sports film on par with *North Dallas Forty*, particularly considering Michael Ritchie's predilection for subjects involving competition. Bert Convy as the ruthless head of the therapy group steals the film.

753 **The Sentinel** (1977) ** Universal, 92 min. *Dir* Michael Winner, *Scr* Jeffrey Konvitz, based on his novel, *Cin* Dick Kratina, *Ed* Bernard Gribble, Terence Rawlings, *Des* Philip Rosenberg, *Cos* Peggy Farrell, *Mus* Gil Melle, *Prod* Jeffrey Konvitz, Michael Winner.

Cast: Christina Raines, *Alison Parker*, Chris Sarandon, *Michael Lerman*, Martin Balsam, *Professor*, John Carradine, *Halliran*, Jose Ferrer, *Robed Figure*, Ava Gardner, *Miss Logan*, Arthur Kennedy, *Franchino*, Burgess Meredith, *Chazen*, Sylvia Miles, *Gerde*, Deborah Raffin, *Jennifer*, Eli Wallach, *Gatz*, Christopher Walken, *Rizzo*, Jerry Orbach, *Film Director*, Beverly D'Angelo, *Sandra*, Hank Garrett, *Brenner*, Robert Gerringer, *Hart*, Nana Tucker, *Girl at End*, Tom Berenger, *Man at End*, William Hickey, *Perry*, Gary Allen, *Malcolm Stinnett*, Tresa Hughes, *Rebecca Stinnett*. R. $4,630,000.

Overly gruesome and perverse horror film. A television commercial actress moves into an apartment building that is the gateway to hell. This sounds promising, but *The Sentinel* becomes just another haunted house thriller with the usual clichés, i.e. creaking doors, swinging chandeliers and mysterious footsteps. The climax resembles Tod Browning's *Freaks*, with the appearance of a group of grotesquely deformed people. Rather than being scarey *The Sentinel* is merely repulsive.

754 **Serpico** (1973) ******** Paramount, 130 min. *Dir* Sidney Lumet, *Scr* Waldo Salt, Norman Wexler (AN, W), based on book by Peter Maas, *Cin* Arthur J. Ornitz, *Ed* Dede Allen, Richard Marks, *Des* Charles Bailey, *Art* Douglas Higgens, *Mus* Mikis Theodorakis, *Prod* Martin Bregman, A Dino De Laurentiis Presentation.

Cast: Al Pacino (AN, NB, G), *Frank Serpico*, John Randolph, *Chief Green*, Jack Kehoe, *Tom Keough*, Biff McGuire, *Capt. McClain*, Barbara Eda-Young, *Laurie*, Cornelia Sharpe, *Leslie*, Tony Roberts, *Bob Blair*, Allan Rich, *D.A.*, Norman Ornellas, *Rubello*, Ed Grover, *Lombardo*, Gene Gross, *Capt. Tolkin*, James Tolkin, *Steiger*, Lewis J. Stadlen, *Berman*, John Lehne, *Gilbert*, M. Emmet Walsh, *Gallagher*, George Ede, *Daley*, Charles White, *Commissioner Delaney*. R. $14,600,000.

Excellent biography of Frank Serpico, a New York cop whose refusal to take bribes opened up a major scandal of police corruption. *Serpico* is more of a character study than a crime thriller, but it does mix in some fine gritty action scenes to balance the story. The film also serves as a fine metaphor of the opposition of society to non-conformity. Al Pacino gives an outstanding performance as Serpico.

755 **The Seven-Per-Cent Solution** (1976) ******* Universal, 113 min. *Dir* Herbert Ross, *Scr* Nicholas Meyer (AN), based on his novel, *Cin* Oswald Morris, *Ed* Chris Barnes, *Des* Ken Adam, *Art* Peter Lamont, *Cos* Alan Barrett (AN), *Mus* John Addison, *Song*, "The Madam's Song", *Mus* Stephen Sondheim, *Prod* Hebert Ross, *Exec Prod* Arlene Sellers, Alex Winitsky, *Assoc Prod* Stanley O'Toole.

Cast: Nicol Williamson, *Sherlock Holmes*, Alan Arkin, *Sigmund Freud*, Vanessa Redgrave, *Lola Deveraux*, Robert Duvall, *Dr. Watson*, Laurence Olivier, *Prof. Moriarty*, Joel Grey, *Lowenstein*, Samantha Eggar, *Mary Watson*, Jeremy Kemp, *Baron von Leinsdorf*, Charles Gray, *Mycroft Holmes*, Georgia Brown, *Mrs. Freud*, Regine, *Madame*, Anna Quayle, *Freda*, Jill Townsend, *Mrs. Holmes*, John Bird, *Berger*, Alison Leggatt, *Mrs. Hudson*, Frederick Jaeger, *Marker*, Erik Chitty, *Butler*. PG. $5,870,000.

Unusual period comedy that mixes history and fiction. Sherlock Holmes (Nicol Williamson) and Sigmund Freud (Alan Arkin) team up to help each other with their problems, Holmes' cocaine addiction and the disappearances of one of Freud's patients. This is a film of enormous promise, with interesting characterizations by Williamson and Arkin, but the story is thin and runs out of steam.

756 **1776** (1972) ****** Columbia, 141 min. *Dir* Peter H. Hunt, *Scr* Peter Stone, based on his stage play, music by Sherman Edwards, *Cin* Harry Stradling, Jr. (AN), *Ed* Florence Williamson, William Ziegler, *Art* George Jenkins, *Cos* Patricia Zipprodt, *Mus* Sherman Edwards, *Chor* Onna White, *Prod* Jack L. Warner.

Cast: William Daniels, *John Adams*, Howard Da Silva, *Benjamin Franklin*, Ken Howard, *Thomas Jefferson*, John Cullum, *Edward Rutledge*, Roy Poole, *Stephen Hopkins*, David Ford, *John Hancock*, Ronald Holgate, *Richard Henry Lee*, Ray Middleton, *Col. McKean*, William Hansen, *Caesar Rodney*, Ralston Hill, *Thomson*, William Duell, *McNair*, Virginia Vestoff, *Abigail Adams*, Blythe Danner, *Martha Jefferson*, Stephen Nathan, *Courier*. G.

Fair film version of Broadway musical about the Declaration of Independence. Admittedly this story does not lend itself well to musicalization, but the filmmakers could have probably done a better job than this. The film's strongest point is in its casting, particularly William Daniels, Howard Da Silva and Ken Howard, who are ideal in their roles. With all the potential subjects for musicals, why pick on American history?

757 **The Seven-Ups** (1973) *** 20th Century–Fox, 103 min. *Dir* Philip D'Antoni, *Scr* Alexander Jacobs, Albert Ruben, *Story* Sonny Grosso, *Cin* Urs Furrer, *Ed* Gerald Greenberg, *Des* Ed Wittstein, *Cos* Joseph G. Aulisi, *Prod* Philip D'Antoni, *Exec Prod* Barry Weitz, Kenneth Utt, *Assoc Prod* Gerald Greenberg.

Cast: Roy Scheider, *Buddy Manucci*, Tony Lo Bianco, *Vito*, Larry Haines, *Max Kalish*, Victor Arnold, *Barilli*, Jerry Leon, *Mingo*, Ken Kercheval, *Ansel*, Richard Lynch, *Moon*, Bill Hickman, *Bo*, Ed Jordan, *Bruno*, David Wilson, *Bobby*, Robert Burr, *Lt. Hanes*, Rex Everhart, *Gilson*, Matt Russo, *Festa*, Lou Polan, *Coltello*, Joe Spinell, *Toredano*, William Shust, *Henry Parten*, Roger Serbagi, *Mickey Parten*, Frances Chaney, *Sara Kalish*. PG. $4,500,000.

Exciting police-action thriller, Roy Scheider stars as the leader of an unorthodox plain clothes police squad that is as brutal as the criminals they pursue. There is very little in the way of substance and the plot is a bit skimpy, but the action makes up for this, particularly a spectacular car chase sequence that rivals the one from *The French Connection*.

758 **Shaft** (1971) *** MGM, 100 min. *Dir* Gordon Parks, Sr., *Scr* John D. F. Black, Ernest Tidyman, based on novel by Ernest Tidyman, *Cin* Urs Furrer, *Ed* Hugh A. Robertson, *Art* Emanuel Gerard, *Cos* Joe Aulisi, *Mus* Isaac Hayes (AN, G), *Song* "Theme from Shaft", *Mus* Isaac Hayes (A), *Prod* Joel Freeman, *Assoc Prod* David Golden.

Cast: Richard Roundtree, *John Shaft*, Moses Gunn, *Bumpy Jones*, Charles Cioffi, *Lt. Vic Androzzi*, Christopher St. John, *Ben Buford*, Gwenn Mitchell, *Ellie Moore*, Lawrence Pressman, *Tom Hannon*, Victor Arnold, *Charlie*, Sherri Brewer, *Marcy*, Rex Robbins, *Rollie*, Camille Yarbrough, *Dina Greene*, Margaret Warncke, *Linda*, Joseph Leon, *Byron Leibowitz*, Arnold Johnson, *Cul*, Dominic Barto, *Patsy*, George Strus, *Carmen*, Edmund Hashim, *Lee*, Drew Bundini Brown, *Willy*, Tommy Lane, *Leroy*, Al Kirk, *Sims*, Shimen Ruskin, *Dr. Sam*, Antonio Fargas, *Bunky*. R. $7,750,000.

Above-average crime thriller starring Richard Roundtree as a black private eye in Harlem, who is hired by a black gangster to recover his kidnapped daughter. *Shaft* is an action packed thriller with an excellent performance by Roundtree. This is one of the best of the blaxploitations films of the early 1970's and its success led to two sequels; *Shaft's Big Score*, a worthy follow-up with Shaft investigating the murder of a friend, and *Shaft in Africa*, an inferior and slightly unbelievable film, with Shaft fighting slave traders in Africa.

759 **Shaft in Africa** (1973) ** MGM, 112 min. *Dir* John Guillermin, *Scr* Stirling Silliphant, based on characters created by Ernest Tidyman, *Cin* Marcel Grignon, *Ed* Max Benedict, *Des* John Stoll, *Mus* Johnny Pate, *Prod* Roger Lewis, *Assoc Prod* Rene Dupont.

Cast: Richard Roundtree, *John Shaft*, Frank Finlay, *Amafi*, Vonetta McGee, *Aleme*, Neda Arneric, *Jazar*, Debebe Eshetu, *Wassa*, Spiros Focas, *Sassari*, Jacques Herlin, *Perreau*, Jho Jhenkins, *Ziba*, Willie Jonah, *Oyo*, Adolfo Lastretti, *Piro*, Marne Maitland, *Col. Gondar*, Frank McRae, *Osiat*. R. See *Shaft*.

760 **Shaft's Big Score** (1972) *** MGM, 104 min. *Dir* Gordon Parks, Sr., *Scr* Ernest Tidyman, *Cin* Urs Furrer, *Ed* Harry Howard, *Art* Emanuel Gerard, *Cos* Joe Aulisi, *Mus* Gordon Parks, Sr., *Songs* Isaac Hayes, Gordon Parks, Sr., *Sung by* Isaac Hayes, O.C. Smith, *Prod* Roger Lewis, Ernest Tidyman, *Assoc Prod* David Golden, A Stirling Silliphant-Roger Lewis Production.

Cast: Richard Roundtree, *John Shaft*, Moses Gunn, *Bumpy Jonas*, Drew Bundi Brown, *Willy*, Joseph Mascolo, *Mascola*, Kathy Imrie, *Rita*, Wally Taylor, *Kelly*, Julius W. Harris, *Bollin*, Rosalind Miles, *Arna*, Joe Santos, *Pascal*, Angelo Nazzo, *Al*, Don Blakely, *Johnson*, Melvin Green, Jr., *Junior Gillis*, Thomas Anderson, *Preacher*, Evelyn Davis, *Old Lady*, Richard Pittman, *Kelly's Hood #1*, Robert Kya-Hill, *Cal Asby*. R. See *Shaft*.

761 **The Shaggy D.A.** (1976) *** Buena Vista, 91 min. *Dir* Robert Stevenson, *Scr* Don Tait, suggested by the novel *The Hound of Florence* by Felix Salten, *Cin* Frank Philips, *Ed* Bob Bring, Norman Palmer, *Art* Perry Ferguson, John B. Mansbridge, *Cos* Chuck Keehne, Emily Sundby, *Mus* Buddy Baker, *Prod* Bill Anderson, *Exec Prod* Ron Miller, A Walt Disney Production.

Cast: Dean Jones, *Wilby Daniels*, Tim Conway, *Tim*, Suzanne Pleshette, *Betty Daniels*, Keenan Wynn, *John Slade*, Jo Anne Worley, *Katrina Muggelberg*, Dick Van Patten, *Raymond*, Shane Sinutko, *Brian Daniels*, Vic Tayback, *Eddie Roschak*, John Myhers, *Adm. Brenner*, Dick Bakalyan, *Freddie*, Warren Berlinger, *Dip*, Ronnie Schell, *TV Director*, Jonathan Daly, *TV Interviewer*, John Fiedler, *Howie Clemmings*, Hans Conried, *Prof. Whatley*, George Kirby, *Dog Character Voices*. G. $10,550,000.

Good sequel to Walt Disney's *The Shaggy Dog*. The story is very similar to the original, in which a boy, through the powers of a magic ring, turns into a sheep dog. In this film a young D.A. (Dean Jones) finds the ring which puts him into some ridiculous, but funny situations. This is a kind of comic fantasy that only Disney would make, and they do a good job of it.

762 **Shampoo** (1975) ***** Columbia, 109 min. *Dir* Hal Ashby, *Scr* Warren Beatty, Robert Towne (AN, NS, W), *Cin* Laszlo Kovacs, *Ed* Robert C. Jones, *Des* Richard Sylbert (AN), *Art* Stu Campbell (AN), *Mus* Paul Simon, *Prod* Warren Beatty.

Cast: Warren Beatty, *George*, Julie Christie, *Jackie*, Goldie Hawn, *Jill*, Lee Grant (A), *Felicia*, Jack Warden (AN), *Lester*, Tony Bill, *Johnny Pope*, Carrie Fisher, *Lorna*, Jay Robinson, *Norman*, George Furth, *Bank Officer*, Brad Dexter, *Senator*, William Castle, *Producer*. R. $22,000,000.

Superb *Rules of the Game* style comedy of manners and morals, about a Beverly Hills hairdresser who has relationships with his clientele. Set in 1968 at the time of Richard Nixon's election, *Shampoo* is a portrait of the times, as total dishonesty permeates throughout these character's lives. The entire cast is superb, particularly Warren Beatty, who also produced and co-wrote the wonderfully sharp script. Hal Ashby, in one of his finest achievements, directed in a whirlwind style never allowing the proceedings to slow down for even a moment. This is one of the best and most intelligent comedies of the decade.

763 Shamus (1973) *** Columbia, 98 min. *Dir* Buzz Kulik, *Scr* Barry Beckerman, *Cin* Victor J. Kemper, *Ed* Walter Thompson, *Art* Philip Rosenberg, *Cos* Frank Thompson, *Mus* Jerry Goldsmith, *Prod* Robert M. Weitman, *Assoc Prod* Jim Di Gangi.

Cast: Burt Reynolds, *McCoy*, Dyan Cannon, *Alexis*, John Ryan, Col. *Hardcore*, Joe Santos, *Lt. Promuto*, Georgio Tozzi, *Dottore*, Ron Weyand, *Hume*, Larry Block, *Springy*, Beeson Carroll, *Bolton*, Kevin Conway, *The Kid*, Kay Frye, *Bookstore Girl*, John Glover, *Johnnie*, Merwin Goldsmith, *Schnook*, Melody Santangelo, *First Woman*, Irving Selbst, *Heavy*, Alex Wilson, *Felix*, Tony Amato, Jr., *Willie*, Lou Martell, *Rock*, Marshall Anker, *Dealer*, Bert Bertram, *Doorman*, Jimmy Kelly, *Grifter*. PG.

Fine detective thriller starring Burt Reynolds as a private eye, who is hired by a millionaire to find a man involved in a diamond theft. The plot is extremely convoluted and confusing, and there are many extraneous characters and plot developments. *Shamus*, however, remains interesting because of its brisk pace and its exciting action focusing on numerous attempts on Reynold's life.

764 Sheila Levine Is Dead and Living in New York (1975) * Paramount, 113 min. *Dir* Sidney J. Furie, *Scr* Gail Parent, Kenny Solms, based on novel by Gail Parent, *Cin* Donald M. Morgan, *Ed* Argyle Nelson, *Des* Fernando Carrere, *Cos* Ron Talsky, *Mus* Michel Legrand, *Prod* Harry Korshak.

Cast: Jeannie Berlin, *Sheila Levine*, Roy Scheider, *Sam Stoneman*, Rebecca Dianna Smith, *Kate*, Janet Brandt, *Bernice*, Sid Melton, *Manny*, Charles Woolf, *Wally*, Leda Rogers, *Agatha*, Jack Bernardi, *Uncle Herm*, Allen Secher, *Rabbi*, Talley Parker, *Rochchelle*, Jon Miller, *Norman*, Noble Willingham, *Principal*, Richard Rasof, *Attendant*, Evelyn Russell, *Miss Burke*, Don Carrara, *Harold*, Sharon Martin Goldman, *Melissa*, Karen Anders, *Aunt Min*. PG.

Dismal comedy-drama about a shy Jewish American princess (Jeannie Berlin) trying to survive in New York City. Berlin meets Roy Scheider in a singles bar and they spend the night together. She falls in love with him, but the feeling is not mutual. The film is dull and overlong and the characters are stereotypes, particularly that of Berlin's, which is more annoying than sympathetic.

765 The Shootist (1976) **** Paramount, 99 min. *Dir* Don Siegel, *Scr* Scott Hale, Miles Hood Swarthout, based on novel by Glendon Swarthout, *Cin* Bruce Surtees, *Ed* Douglas Stewart, *Des* Robert Boyle (AN), *Cos* Luster Bayless, Moss Mabry, Edna Taylor, *Mus* Elmer Bernstein, *Prod* M.J. Frankovich, William Self, Presented by Dino De Laurentiis.

Cast: John Wayne, *J.B. Books*, Lauren Bacall, *Bond Rogers*, Ron Howard, *Gillom Rogers*, Bill McKinney, *Cobb*, James Stewart, *Dr. Hostetler*, Richard Boone, *Sweeney*, Hugh O'Brian, *Pulford*, Harry Morgan, *Marshall*, John Carradine, *Beckum*, Sheree North, *Serepta*, Richard Lenz, *Dobkins*, Scatman Crothers, *Moses*, Gregg Palmer, *Ambusher*, Alfred Dennis, *Barber*, Dick Winslow, *Streetcar Driver*, Melody Thomas, *Streetcar Passenger*, Kathleen O'Malley, *Schoolteacher*. PG, $5,985,000.

Excellent western drama about a gunfighter dying from cancer, who decided to go out in glory. After nearly a decade of dismal films, John Wayne came charging with this western classic that must rank as one of the finest, easily equalling his efforts with John Ford and Howard Hawks. *The Shootist* almost parallels Wayne himself, beginning with clips of his early films representing the life of this film's character, and ironically proved to be his final film.

766 Short Eyes (1977) *** Paramount, 104 min. *Dir* Robert M. Young, *Scr* Miguel Pinero, based on his play, *Cin* Peter Sova, *Ed* Edward Beyer, *Des* Joe Babas, *Cos* Paul Martino, *Mus* Curtis Mayfield, *Prod* Lewis Harris, *Exec Prod* Marvin Stuart, *Assoc Prod* Martin Hirsh, Walker Stuart.

Cast: Bruce Davison, *Clark Davis*, Jose Perez, *Juan*, Nathan George, *Ice*, Don Blakely, *El Raheem*, Shawn Elliott, *Paco*, Tito Goya, *Cupcakes*, Joe Carberry, *Longshore*, Kenny Steward, *Omar*, Bob Maroff, *Mr. Nett*, Keith Davis, *Mr. Brown*, Miguel Pinero, *Go Go*, Willie Hernandez, *Cha Cha*, Tony De Benedetto, *Tony*, Bob O'Connell, *Mr. Allard*, Mark Margolis, *Mr. Morrison*, Richard Matamoros, *Gomez*, Curtis Mayfield, *Pappy*, Freddie Fender, *Johnny*. R.

Fine drama about life in a prison, The film focuses on a child-molester (Bruce Davison), known by the slang term "short eyes", and how he is castigated by his fellow criminals, who look upon his deed as the lowest of all crimes. *Short Eyes* is generally realistic; it was filmed on location in the Men's House of Detention in New York; and properly claustrophobic, but it is flawed by staginess.

767 The Shout (1979) *** Britain, Films Incorporated, 97 min. *Dir* Jerry Skolimowski, *Scr* Michael Austin, Jerzy Skolimowski, based on story by Robert Graves, *Cin* Mike Malloy, *Ed* Barrie Vince, *Art* Simon Holland, *Prod* Jeremy Thomas, *Assoc Prod* Michael Austin.

Cast: Alan Bates, *Crossley*, Susannah York, *Rachel*, John Hurt, *Anthony*, Robert Stephens, *Chief Medical Officer*, Tim Curry, *Robert*, Julian Hough, *Vicar*, Carol Drinkwater, *Cobbler's Wife*, Nick Stringer, *Cobbler*, John Rees, *Inspector*, Susan Woolridge, *Harriet*. R.

Bizarre psychological thriller starring Alan Bates as a mysterious stranger, who moves in with an experimental composer (John Hurt) and his wife (Susannah York). With unknown motives Bates begins to take over. He also has an unusual power, a loud deafening scream known as "the shout". *The Shout* is not for all tastes, and will certainly disappoint those who require easy answers, but it is a worthwhile and unusual experience.

768 Shout at the Devil (1976) ** Britain, American International, 128 min. *Dir* Peter Hunt, *Scr* Stanley Price, Alistair Reid, Wilber Smith, based on novel by Wilbur Smith, *Cin* Mike Reed, *Ed* Michael Duthie, *Art* Ernie Archer, Bob

Laing, *Mus* Maurice Jarre, *Prod* Michael Klinger, *Assoc Prod* Stanley Sopel, Robert Sterne.

Cast: Lee Marvin, *Flynn*, Roger Moore, *Sebastian*, Barbara Parkins, *Rosa*, Rene Koldehoff, *Fleischer*, Ian Holm, *Mohammed*, Karl Michael Vogler, *Von Kleine*, Horst Janson, *Kyller*, Gernot Endemann, *Braun*, Maurice Denham, *Mr. Smythe*, Jean Kent, *Mrs. Smythe*, Heather Wright, *Cynthia*, Bernard Horsfall, *Capt. Joyce*, Robert Lang, *Capt. Henry*, Peter Copley, *Adm. Howe*, Murray Melvin, *Lt. Phipps*, Geoff Davidson, *Mackintosh*, Gerard Paquis, *French Pilot*, George Coulouris, *El Keb*, Renu Setna, *Mr. Raji*. PG.

Fair WWI adventure about two men (Lee Marvin, Roger Moore), who attempt to destroy a German cruiser in the need of repairs, hidden in a South East African delta. This is essentially an old-fashioned action film, which is the source of its flaws. The film is shallow and overlong while the characters are pretentious and too broad. The few well done action scenes are little compensation.

769 **Showdown** (1973) ** Universal, 99 min. *Dir* George Seaton, *Scr* Theodore Taylor, *Story* Hank Fine, *Cin* Ernest Laszlo, *Ed* John W. Holmes, *Art* Henry Bumstead, Alexander Golitzen, *Cos* Edith Head, *Mus* David Shire, *Prod* George Seaton, *Assoc Prod* Donald Roberts.

Cast: Rock Hudson, *Chuck*, Dean Martin, *Billy*, Susan Clark, *Kate*, Donald Moffat, *Art* John McLiam, *P.J.*, Charles Baca, *Martinez*, Jackson Kane, *Clem*, Ben Zeller, *Perry*, John Richard Gill, *Earl*, Philip L. Mead, *Jack*, Rita Rogers, *Girl*, Vic Mohica, *Big Eye*, Raleigh Gardenhire, *Joe*, Ed Begley, Jr., *Pook*, Dan Boydston, *Rawls*. PG.

Standard western drama about two boyhood friends (Dean Martin, Rock Hudson), who end up on opposite sides of the law. Hudson is a sheriff who must hunt down Martin, a train robber, but in the end decides to help him. This idea has been used many times before, mainly in crime films, and although it may be a slight novelty in westerns, *Showdown* is hardly much different from many other westerns.

770 **Silent Movie** (1976) *** 20th Century–Fox, 86 min. *Dir* Mel Brooks, *Scr* Mel Brooks, Ron Clark, Rudy DeLuca, Barry Levinson, *Story* Ron Clark, *Cin* Paul Lohmann, *Ed* Stanford C. Allen, John C. Howard, *Des* Al Brenner, *Mus* John Morris, *Prod* Michael Hertzberg.

Cast: Mel Brooks, *Mel Funn*, Marty Feldman, *Marty Eggs*, Dom DeLuise, *Dom Bell*, Bernadette Peters, *Vilma Kaplan*, Sid Caesar, *Studio Chief*, Harold Gould, *Engulf*, Ron Carey, *Devour*, Carol Arthur, *Pregnant Lady*, Liam Dunn, *News Vender*, Fritz Feld, *Maitre'd*, Chuck McCann, *Studio Gate Guard*, Yvonne Wilder, *Studio Chief's Secretary*, Valerie Curtin, *Intensive Care Nurse*, Arnold Soboloff, *Acupuncture Man*, Patrick Campbell, *Hotel Bellhop*, Harry Ritz, *Man in Tailor Shop*, Charlie Callas, *Blind Man*, Henny Youngman, *Fly-in-Soup-Man*, Eddie Ryder, *British Officer*, Al Hopson, Rudy Deluca, Barry Levinson, Howard Hesseman, Lee Delano, Jack Riley, *Executives*, Burt Reynolds, James Caan, Liza Minnelli, Anne Bancroft, Paul Newman, Marcel Marceau, *Themselves*. PG. $21,240,000.

Unusual slapstick comedy that is exactly what its title says; a silent movie. It took a director who either has a lot of nerve or is crazy, to pull off such a stunt. Mel Brooks fits both descriptions and his stunt surprisingly works. *Silent Movie* is a satire of Hollywood, focusing on the efforts of a comedy director to make the first silent movie in decades. This film is about itself, much in the same manner as Fellini's *8½*.

771 The Silent Partner (1979) ******* Canada, EMC Film Corp., 103 min. *Dir* Daryl Duke, *Scr* Curtis Hanson, based on novel *Think of a Number* by Anders Bodelson, *Cin* Billy Williams, *Des* Trevor Williams, *Mus* Oscar Peterson, *Prod* Joel B. Michaels, Stephen Young, *Exec Prod* Garth H. Drabinsky, Presented by Mario Kassar, Andrew Vajna.

Cast: Elliott Gould, *Miles Cullen*, Susannah York, *Julie*, Christopher Plummer, *Reikle*, Celine Lomez, *Elaine*, Michael Kirby, *Packard*, Ken Pogue, *Detective*, John Candy, *Simonson*, Gail Dahms, *Louise*, Michael Donaghue, *Berg*, Jack Duffy, *Fogelman*, Nancy Simmonds, *Girl in Sauna*, Nuala Fitzgerald, *Mrs. Skinner*, Guy Sanvido, *Locksmith*, Aino Perkskanen, *Mrs. Evanchuck*, Michele Rosen, *Young Woman in Bank*. R.

Fine thriller about a bank teller (Elliott Gould), who outsmarts a sadistic bank robber (Christopher Plummer). Gould discovers the robbery plan beforehand and pulls a switch, keeping the money himself. Plummer discovers what happened and begins to terrorize Gould, turning the film into a clever battle-of-wits thriller, with occasional bursts of violence. Plummer gives a great performance as one of the most vicious villains to ever grace the screen.

772 Silent Running (1972) ******* Universal, 89 min. *Dir* Douglas Trumbull, *Scr* Steve Bochco, Michael Cimino, Derec Washburn, *Cin* Charles F. Wheeler, *Ed* Aaron Stell, *Sp* John Dykstra, Douglas Trumbull, Steve Yuricich, *Mus* Peter Schikele, *Songs* sung by Joan Baez, *Prod* Michael Gruskoff, *Assoc Prod* Martin Hornstein.

Cast: Bruce Dern, *Lowell*, Cliff Potts, *Wolf*, Ron Rifkin, *Barker*, Jesse Vint, *Keenan*, Steven Brown, Mark Persons, Cheryl Sparks, Larry Whisenhunt, *Drones*. PG.

Unusual ecological science-fiction thriller. Bruce Dern becomes obsessed with the greenhouses aboard his spaceship, the Valley Forge, and protects them at all costs. When he and his fellow crew members receive orders to destroy the greenhouses, he goes berserk and kills the other crew members. This is not enough to fill a feature film and *Silent Running* drags considerably. The spectacular special effects almost compensate for the lack of substance. This was special effects wizard, Douglas Trumbull's first attempt at directing.

773 Silver Bears (1977) ******* Columbia, 113 min. *Dir* Ivan Passer, *Scr* Peter Stone, based on novel by Paul E. Erdman, *Cin* Anthony Richmond, *Ed* Bernard Gribble, *Art* Edward Marshall, *Mus* Claude Bolling, *Prod* Arlene Sellers, Alex Winitsky.

Cast: Michael Caine, *Doc Fletcher*, Cybill Shepherd, *Debbie Luckman*, Louis Jourdan, *Prince di Siracusa*, Stephane Audran, *Shireen Firdausi*, Tom Smothers, *Donald Luckman*, David Warner, *Agha Firdausi*, Martin Balsam, *Joe Fiore*, Jay Leno, *Albert Fiore*, Tony Mascia, *Marvin Skinner*, Charles Gray, *Charles Cook*, Joss Ackland, *Henry Foreman*, Jeremy Clyde, *Nick Topping*. PG.

Overly complex, but well-made comedy thriller. Several swindles are interrelated as Michael Caine opens a phoney bank in Switzerland for American gangster Martin Balsam, which a major banker wants to buy as a front. This is all complicated by a plot involving a silver-mine in Iran. The storyline is next to impossible to sort out, but it is so well paced it does not really matter. *Silver Bears* is a pleasant light comedy.

774 Silver Streak (1976) *** 20th Century–Fox, 113 min. *Dir* Arthur Hiller, *Scr* Colin Higgins, *Cin* David M. Walsh, *Ed* David Bretherton, *Des* Alfred Sweeney, *Sp* Fred Cramer, *Mus* Henry Mancini, *Prod* Edward K. Milkis, Thomas L. Miller, *Exec Prod* Martin Ransohoff, Frank Yablans.

Cast: Gene Wilder, *George Caldwell*, Jill Clayburgh, *Hilly Burns*, Richard Pryor, *Grover Muldoon*, Patrick McGoohan, *Roger Devereau*, Ned Beatty, *Sweet*, Clifton James, *Sheriff Chauncey*, Ray Walston, *Mr. Whiney*, Stefan Gierasch, *Johnson (Prof. Schreiner)*, Len Birman, *Chief*, Valerie Curtin, *Plain Jane*, Richard Kiel, *Reace (Goldtooth)*, Lucille Benson, *Rita Babtree*, Scatman Crothers, *Ralston*, Fred Willard, *Jerry Jarvis*, Delos V. Smith, *Burt*. PG. $30,020,000.

Well-made comedy mystery set almost entirely aboard a train. Gene Wilder stars as a writer who thinks he has seen a dead body, and in his personal investigation uncovers a plot involving art thieves. He is thrown off the train a few times, but he manages to get back on, bringing with him Richard Pryor. *Silver Streak* is an exciting, fast-paced comedy, that is most notable for the first screen teaming of Wilder and Pryor.

775 Sinbad and the Eye of the Tiger (1977) ** Columbia, 112 min. *Dir* Sam Wanamaker, *Scr* Beverly Cross, *Story* Beverly Cross, Ray Harryhausen, *Cin* Ted Moore, *Ed* Roy Watts, *Des* Geoffrey Drake, *Art* Fred Carter, Fernando Gonzales, *Cos* Cynthia Tingey, *Sp* Ray Harryhausen, *Mus* Roy Budd, *Prod* Ray Harryhausen, Charles H. Schneer.

Cast: Patrick Wayne, *Sinbad*, Taryn Power, *Dione*, Margaret Whiting, *Zenobia*, Jane Seymour, *Farah*, Patrick Troughton, *Melanthius*, Kurt Christian, *Rafi*, Nadim Sawaiha, *Hassan*, Damien Thomas, *Kassim*, Bruno Barnabe, *Balsora*, Bernard Kay, *Zabid*, Salami Coker, *Maroof*, David Sterne, *Aboo-Seer*. G. $7,700,000. See *The Golden Voyage of Sinbad*.

776 Sisters (1973) *** American International, 92 min. *Dir* Brian De Palma, *Scr* Brian De Palma, Louisa Rose, *Story* Brian De Palma, *Cin* Gregory Sandor, *Ed* Paul Hirsch, *Des* Gary Weist, *Mus* Bernard Herrmann, *Prod* Edward R. Pressman, *Assoc Prod* Lynn Pressman, Robert Rohdie.

Cast: Margot Kidder, *Danielle Breton*, Jennifer Salt, *Grace Collier*, Charles Durning, *Joseph Larch*, Bill Finley, *Emil Breton*, Lisle Wilson, *Philip Woode*, Barnard Hughes, *Mr. McLennon*, Mary Davenport, *Mrs. Collier*, Dolph Sweet, *Det. Kelley*. R.

Fine murder thriller about a nitwit female reporter (Jennifer Salt), who witnesses a murder from her own apartment. The plot involves a psychotic Siamese twin (Margot Kidder), who takes on the personality of her dead sister. *Sisters* is one of De Palma's more overt homages to Alfred Hitchcock, combining elements from *Psycho* and *Rear Window*.

777 Skatetown, U.S.A. (1979) * Columbia, 98 min. *Dir* William A. Levey, *Scr* Nick Castle, *Story* Nick Castle, Lorin Dreyfuss, William A. Levey, *Cin*

Donald M. Morgan, *Ed* Gene Fowler, Jr., *Art* Larry Wiemer, *Cos* Betsy Heimann, Bob Labansat, *Mus* Miles Goodman, *Chor* Bob Banas, *Prod* Lorin Dreyfuss, William A. Levey, *Exec Prod* Peter E. Strauss.

Cast: Scott Baio, *Richie*, Flip Wilson, *Harvey Ross*, Ron Palillo, *Frankey*, Ruth Buzzi, *Elvira*, Dave Mason, *Himself*, Greg Bradford, *Stan*, Maureen McCormick, *Susan*, Patrick Swayze, *Ace*, Billy Barty, *Jimmy*, Kelly Lang, *Allison*, David Landsberg, *Irwin*, Lenny Bari, *Alphonse*, Murray Langston, *The Drunk*, Bill Kirchenbauer, *Skatetown Doctor*, Denny Johnston, *Wizard*, Vic Dunlop, *Ripple*. PG.

Dim-witted roller disco comedy. The film's entire premise consists of a big contest at the disco and the conflict between the good contestant (Greg Bradford) and the bad contestant (Patrick Swayze). This thin storyline holds together what is essentially a variety show, filled with numerous dance and comedy routines, all with a seemingly endless barrage of bad music. This was the first film to capitalize on the craze, and even it was too late.

778 Skin Game (1971) *** Warner Bros., 102 min. *Dir* Paul Bogart, *Scr* Pierre Marton (pseudonym for Peter Stone), based on story by Richard A. Simmons, *Cin* Fred Koenekamp, *Ed* Walter Thompson, *Art* Herman Blumenthal, *Mus* David Shire, *Prod* Harry Keller, *Exec Prod* Meta Rosenberg.

Cast: James Garner, *Quincy Drew*, Lou Gossett, *Jason O'Rourke*, Susan Clark, *Ginger*, Brenda Sykes, *Naomi*, Edward Asner, *Plunkett*, Andrew Duggan, *Calloway*, Henry Jones, *Sam*, Neva Patterson, *Mrs. Claggart*, Parley Baer, *Mr. Claggart*, George Tyne, *Bonner*, Royal Dano, *John Brown*, J. Pat O'Malley, *William*, Joel Fluellen, *Abram*, Napoleon Whiting, *Ned*, Juanita Moore, *Viney*, Dort Clark, *Pennypacker*, Robert Foulk, *Sheriff*. PG.

Unusual western comedy starring James Garner and Lou Gossett as a pair of con artists. They pose as master and slave and Garner sells Gossett to various slave traders, and Gossett later escapes to rejoin Garner. *Skin Game* takes on a sensitive subject and handles it humorously, without ever becoming insulting. Both Garner and Gossett give superb performances.

779 Sky Riders (1976) ** U.S./Greece, 20th Century–Fox, 91 min. *Dir* Douglas Hickox, *Scr* Jack DeWitt, Stanley Mann, Garry Michael White, *Cin* Ousama Rawi, *Aerial Cin* Jim Freeman, Greg MacGillivray, *Ed* Malcolm Cooke, *Art* Terry Ackland-Snow, *Mus* Lalo Schifrin, *Prod* Terry Morse, Jr., *Exec Prod* Sandy Howard.

Cast: James Coburn, *McCabe*, Susannah York, *Ellen*, Robert Culp, *Bracken*, Charles Aznavour, *Nikolidis*, Werner Pochath, *No. 1*, Zouzou, *No. 6*, Kenneth Griffith, *Wasserman*, Harry Andrews, *Auerbach*, John Beck, Ernie Orsatti, Steven Keats, Henry Brown, Cherie Latimer, Barbara Trentham, Simon Harrison, Stephanie Matthews, Anthony Antypas, Telis Zottos. PG.

Silly thriller involving the kidnap of the wife (Susannah York) of an American businessman (Robert Culp) and their children, by terrorists in Greece. Their rescue is conceived by her ex-husband (James Coburn) with the use of hang gliders. The film is little more than an excuse for the hang gliding footage, which does not generate any more excitement than a documentary on the subject. The plot involving the kidnap is standard.

780 Skyjacked (1972) ** MGM, 100 min. *Dir* John Guillermin, *Scr* Stanley R. Greenberg, based on novel *Hijacked* by David Harper, *Cin* Harry

Stradling, Jr., *Ed* Robert Swink, *Art* Edward C. Carfagno, *Cos* Jack Bear, *Mus* Perry Botkin, Jr., *Prod* Walter Seltzer.

Cast: Charlton Heston, *Henry O'Hara,* Yvette Mimieux, *Angela Thacher,* James Brolin, *Jerome K. Weber,* Claude Akins, *Sgt. Ben Puzo,* Jeanne Crain, *Mrs. Clara Shaw,* Susan Dey, *Elly Brewster,* Roosevelt Grier, *Gary Brown,* Mariette Hartley, *Harriet Stevens,* Walter Pidgeon, *Sen. Arne Lindner,* Ken Swofford, *John Bimonte,* Leslie Uggams, *Lovejoy Wells,* Ross Elliott, *Harold Shaw,* Nicholas Hammond, *Peter Lindner,* Mike Henry, *Sam Allen,* Jayson William Kane, *William Reading,* Toni Clayton, *Jane Burke,* John Hillerman, *Walter Brandt,* Kelley Miles, *Hazel Martin,* John Fiedler, *Robert Grundig,* Maureen Connell, *Mrs. O'Hara.* PG. $6,750,000.

Silly thriller about a commercial airline that is hijacked to Russia. The film begins as a mystery, with a bomb placed aboard the plane by one of the passengers. Unfortunately the identity of this psychotic passenger is obvious nearly from the beginning. *Skyjacked* is yet another drama focusing on a group of innocuous characters in jeopardy, with poor results.

781 **Slap Shot** (1977) ******** Universal, 123 min. *Dir* George Roy Hill, *Scr* Nancy Dowd, *Cin* Victor Kemper, *Ed* Dede Allen, *Art* Henry Bumstead, *Cos* Tom Bronson, *Mus. Supervision* Elmer Bernstein, *Prod* Stephen Friedman, Robert J. Wunsch, *Assoc Prod* Robert L. Crawford.

Cast: Paul Newman, *Reggie Dunlop,* Strother Martin, *Joe McGrath,* Michael Ontkean, *Ned Braden,* Jennifer Warren, *Francine Dunlop,* Lindsay Crouse, *Lily Braden,* Andrew Duncan, *Jim Carr,* Jeff Carlson, *Jeff Hanson,* Steve Carlson, *Steve Hanson,* David Hanson, *Jack Hanson,* Yvon Barrette, *Denis Le Mieux,* Allan Nicholls, *Upton,* Brad Sullivan, *Wanchuck,* Stephen Mendillo, *Jim Ahern,* Yvon Ponton, *Drouin,* Matthew Cowles, *Charlie,* Kathryn Walker, *Anita McCambridge,* Melinda Dillon, *Suzanne,* M. Emmet Walsh, *Dickie Dunn,* Swoosie Kurtz, *Shirley,* Paul D'Amato, *Tim Mc-Cracken,* Ned Dowd, *Ogilthorpe,* Nancy Dowd, *Andrea,* Paul Dooley, *Hyannisport Announcer.* R. $14,305,000.

Excellent black comedy about ice hocky. Paul Newman is excellent as the player-coach of a losing minor league team, who discovers violence is the answer to winning. He recruits three crazy brothers and turns his team into a gang of hooligans, who not only win but attract the fans. *Slap Shot* satirizes violence in sports, which seems to be its main appeal. Unlike most films about team sports, *Slap Shot* is briskly paced and exciting.

782 **Slaughterhouse-Five** (1972) ********* Universal, 104 min. *Dir* George Roy Hill, *Scr* Stephen Geller, Based on novel by Kurt Vonnegut, Jr., *Cin* Miroslav Ondricek, *Ed* Dede Allen, *Des* Henry Bumstead, *Art* Alexander Golitzen, George Webb, *Mus* Glenn Gould, *Prod* Paul Monash, *Exec Prod* Jennings Lang.

Cast: Michael Sacks, *Billy Pilgrim,* Ron Leibman, *Paul Lazzaro,* Eugene Roche, *Derby,* Sharon Gans, *Valencia,* Valerie Perrine, *Montana Wildhack,* Roberts Blossom, *Wild Bob Cody,* Sorrell Booke, *Lionel Merble,*Kevin Conway, *Weary,* Gary Waynesmith, *Stanley,* John Dehner, *Rumford,* Stan Gottlieb, *Hobo,* Perry King, *Robert,* Friedrich Ledebur, *German Leader,* Nick Belle, *Young German Coward,* Henry Bumstead, *Eliot Rosewater,* Lucille Benson, *Billy's Mother,* Gilmer McCormick, *Lily,* Holly Near, *Barbara,* Richard

Schaal, *Campbell*, Karl Otto Alberty, *German Guard Group 2*, Tom Wood, *Englishman*. R.

Excellent fantasy comic satire about an average man (Michael Sacks), who drifts back and forth in time. He exists in three distinctly different places: war-torn Dresden during WWII, his contemporary and bland married life, and in the future on the planet Tralfamadore where he is to mate with a Hollywood starlet (Valerie Perrine) in a large see-through dome. Adapting novels of this type to the screen is a difficult task, but director George Roy Hill and scripter Stephen Geller have done a magnificent job in visualizing Vonnegut's novel.

783 **Sleeper** (1973) ******** United Artists, 88 min. *Dir* Woody Allen, *Scr* Woody Allen, *Cin* David Walsh, *Ed* Ralph Rosenblum, *Des* Dianne Wager, *Art* Dale Hennesy, *Cos* Joel Schumacher, *Prod* Jack Grossberg, *Exec Prod* Charles H. Joffe.

Cast: Woody Allen, *Miles Monroe*, Diane Keaton, *Luna*, John Beck, *Erno*, Marya Small, *Dr. Nero*, Bartlett Robinson, *Dr. Orva*, Mary Gregory, *Dr. Melik*, Chris Forbes, *Rainer*, Peter Hobbs, *Dr. Dean*, Spencer Milligan, *Jeb*, Stanley Ross, *Sears*, Whitney Rydbeck, *Janus*, Don Keefer, *Dr. Tryon*. PG. $8,055,000.

Hilarious science-fiction comedy about a man who awakens 100 years into the future after being accidently frozen during a visit to the hospital. This is not really a spoof of the genre as Allen's main target appears to be present day society, with a strong emphasis on his usual themes of love and sex. *Sleeper* was Allen's first well sustained comedy and is notable for his first pairing with Diane Keaton, creating one of screen history's great romantic comedy teams.

784 **Sleuth** (1972) ******** Britain, 20th Century–Fox, 138 min. *Dir* Joseph L. Mankiewicz, *Scr* Anthony Shaffer, based on his play, *Cin* Oswald Morris, *Ed* Richard Marden, *Des* Ken Adam, *Art* Peter Lamont, *Cos* John Furniss, *Mus* John Addison (AN), *Prod* Morton Gottlieb, *Assoc Prod* David Middlemas.

Cast: Laurence Olivier (AN, NY), *Andrew Wyke*, Michael Caine (AN), *Milo Tindle*. PG. $5,605,000.

Excellent cat-and mouse thriller about a man who invites his wife's lover to his mansion and forces him into participating in some deadly games in order to get revenge. Despite the fact that *Sleuth* never transcends its theatrical origins, it succeeds as cinema mainly due to the brilliant performances of Olivier as the husband and Caine as the wife's lover and Anthony Shaffer's sharp and witty script.

785 **Slither** (1973) ****** MGM, 97 min. *Dir* Howard Zieff, *Scr* W.D. Richter, *Cin* Laszlo Kovacs, *Ed* David Bretherton, *Art* Dale Hennessy, *Mus* Tom McIntosh, *Prod* Jack Sher, *Assoc Prod* W.D. Richter.

Cast: James Caan, *Dick Kanipsia*, Peter Boyle, *Barry Fenaka*, Sally Kellerman, *Kitty Kopetzky*, Louise Lasser, *Mary Fenaka*, Allen Garfield (Goorwitz), *Vncent J. Palmer*, Richard B. Shull, *Harry Moss*, Alex Rocco, *Man with Ice Cream*, Seamon Glass, *Farmer in Truck*, Wayne Storm, *Highway Patrolman*, Diana Darrin, *Band Singer*, Stuart Nisbet, *Buddy*, Edwina Gough, *Bingo Player*, Al Dunlap, *Man in Men's Room*, James Joseph, *Short Order Cook*, Virginia Sale, *Bingo Caller*, Alex Henteloff, *Man at Phone Booth*, Len Lesser, *Jogger*, Garry Woodrow, *Man with Camera*. PG.

Fair caper comedy starring James Caan as an ex-con who, through his friendship with an embezzler (Richard B. Shull), becomes involved in a search for a hidden fortune. The film becomes a long chase involving vans and trailers, and it subsequently bogs the film down. *Slither* features a fine array of odd-ball characters, but the humor is underplayed to the point of listlessness.

786 **Slow Dancing in the Big City** (1978) *** United Artists, 101 min. *Dir* John G. Avildsen, *Scr* Barra Grant, *Cin* Ralf Bode, *Ed* John G. Avildsen, *Art* Henry Shrady, *Cos* Ruth Morley, *Mus* Bill Conti, *Chor* Anne Ditchdurn, Robert North, *Prod* John G. Avildsen, Michael Levee, *Assoc Prod* George Manasse.

Cast: Paul Sorvino, *Lou Friedlander*, Anne Ditchdurn, *Sarah Gantz*, Nicolas Coster, *David*, Anita Dangler, *Franny*, Hector Jaime Mercado, *Roger*, Thaao Penghlis, *Christopher*, Linda Selman, *Barbara*, G. Adam Gifford, *Marty*, Tara Mitton, *Diana*, Dick Carballo, *George*, Jack Ramage, *Dr. Foster*, Daniel Faraldo, *T.C.* PG.

Well-made love story about a newspaper columnist (Paul Sorvino), who falls for a ballet dancer (Anne Ditchdurn), who has moved into his run-down apartment building. There are some obtrusive sub-plots that interfere with the main story, but *Slow Dancing in the Big City* features a superb performance by Sorvino as a Jimmy Breslin-type writer, and Ditchdurn is touching in her film debut.

787 **A Small Town in Texas** (1976) *** American International, 95 min. *Dir* Jack Starrett, *Scr* William Norton, *Cin* Bob Jessup, *Ed* Jodie Copelan, John C. Horger, Larry L. Mills, *Art* Elayne Ceder, *Mus* Charles Bernstein, *Prod* Joe Solomon, *Exec Prod* Louis S. Arkoff.

Cast: Timothy Bottoms, *Poke*, Susan George, *Mary Lee*, Bo Hopkins, *Duke*, Art Hindle, *Boogie*, John Karlen, *Lenny*, Morgan Woodward, *C.J. Crane*, Patrice Rohmer, *Trudy*, Hank Rolike, *Cleotus*, Buck Fowler, *Bull Parker*, Clay Tanner, *Junior*. PG.

Above average Southern action drama. Timothy Bottoms stars as an ex-con, who returns to his hometown to be with his girlfriend (Susan George) and their son. He also seeks vengeance on the sheriff (Bo Hopkins), who put him in jail and who is also involved with George. *A Small Town in Texas* is primarily an action chase film, but it rises above most due to its believable characters and fine acting.

788 **Smile** (1975) **** United Artists, 113 min. *Dir* Michael Ritchie, *Scr* Jerry Belson, *Cin* Conrad Hall, *Ed* Richard Harris, *Cos* Patricia Norris, *Prod* Michael Ritchie, *Exec Prod* Jerry Belson, *Assoc Prod* Tim Zinnemann.

Cast: Bruce Dern, *"Big Bob" Freelander*, Barbara Feldon, *Brenda DiCarlo*, Michael Kidd, *Tommy French*, Geoffrey Lewis, *Wilson Shears*, Nicholas Pryor, *Andy DiCarlo*, Colleen Camp, *Connie Thompson/Miss Imperial County*, Joan Prather, *Robin Gibson/Miss Angelope County*, Denise Nickerson, *Shirley Tolstoy/Miss San Diego*, Annette O'Toole, *Doria Houston/Miss Anaheim*, Maria O'Brien, *Maria Gonzales*, Titos Vandis, *Emile Eidleman*, Eric Shea, *"Little Bob" Freelander*. PG.

Excellent satire of beauty pageants focusing on the final week of preparations for a Young American Miss Pageant held in the town of Santa

Rosa, California. The fine cast is headed by Bruce Dern as an obnoxious mobile home salesman, who is a contest judge, and Barbara Feldon as the girls' hostess. *Smile* has more on its mind than merely these contests, as it offers hysterical insight into small town America and the American dream.

789 Smokey and the Bandit   (1977)   *   Universal, 97 min. *Dir* Hal Needham, *Scr* Lee Barrett, Alan Mandel, Charles Shyer, *Story* Robert L. Levy, Hal Needham, *Cin* Bobby Byrne, *Ed* Walter Hanneman, Angelo Ross, *Art* Mark Mansbridge, *Mus* Dick Feller, Bill Justis, Jerry Reed, *Songs* sung by Jerry Reed, *Prod* Mort Engleberg, *Exec Prod* Robert L. Levy.

Cast: Burt Reynolds, *Bandit*, Sally Field, *Carrie*, Jerry Reed, *Cledus*, Jackie Gleason, *Sheriff Buford T. Justice*, Mike Henry, *Junior*, Paul Williams, *Little Enos*, Pat McCormick, *Big Enos*, Alfie Wise, *Patrolman-Traffic Jam*, George Reynolds, *Brandford*, Macon McCalman, *Mr. B*, Linda McClure, *Waynette*, Susan McIver, *Hot Pants*, Michael Mann, *Branford's Deputy*, Lamar Jackson, *Sugar Bear*, Ronnie Gay, *Georgia Trooper*, Quinnon Sheffield, *Alabama Trooper*. PG. $61,055,000.

Dim-witted comedy that is nothing more than one long car chase. Burt Reynolds in a characteristic role, portrays Bandit, a legendary driver who, along with his partner, transport beer illegally across state lines. Their journey is interrupted by troopers and a runaway bride, who is being pursued by a crazed sheriff. The endless crashes and mugging by the stars are intended to be funny, but there isn't one shred of wit or intelligence to be found anywhere. This was the first film directed by stunt coordinator Hal Needham, and this is nothing more than an excuse for some fancy stunts.

790 Snowball Express   (1972)   **   Buena Vista, 99 min. *Dir* Norman Tokar, *Scr* Arnold Margolin, Jim Parker, Don Tait, based on novel *Chateau Bon Vivant* by Frankie and John O'Rear, *Cin* Frank Phillips, *Ed* Robert Stafford, *Art* John B. Mansbridge, Walter Tyler, *Mus* Robert F. Brunner, *Prod* Ron Miller, *Assoc Prod* Tom Leetch, A Walt Disney Production.

Cast: Dean Jones, *Johnny Baxter*, Nancy Olson, *Sue Baxter*, Harry Morgan, *Jesse McCord*, Keenan Wynn, *Martin Ridgeway*, Johnny Whitaker, *Richard Baxter*, Michael McGreevey, *Wally Perkins*, George Lindsey, *Double L. Dingman*, Kathleen Cody, *Chris Baxter*, Mary Wickes, *Miss Wiggington*, David White, *Mr. Fowler*, Dick Van Patten, *Mr. Carruthers*, Alice Backes, *Miss Obelvie*, Joanna Phillips, *Naomi Voight*, John Myhers, *Mr. Manescue*. G. $7,100,000.

Standard Disney slapstick comedy about a New York accountant (Dean Jones) who leaves the city to take over a broken down Colorado resort hotel he inherited from his uncle, which he tries gallantly to turn into a nice ski lodge. *Snowball Express* climaxes with a slapstick ski chase, which seems to be the real purpose of an otherwise dull film.

791 Soldier Blue   (1970)   *   Avco Embassy, 112 min. *Dir* Ralph Nelson, *Scr* John Gay, based on novel *Arrow in the Sun* by Theodore V. Olsen, *Cin* Robert Hauser, Arthur J. Ornitz (UN), *Ed* Alex Beaton, *Art* Frank Arrigo, *Cos* Ted Parvin, *Mus* Roy Budd, *Prod* Gabriel Katzka, Harold Loeb, *Exec Prod* Joseph E. Levine, *Assoc Prod* William S. Gilmore, Jr.

Cast: Candice Bergen, *Cresta Marybelle Lee*, Peter Strauss, *Pvt. Honus Grant*, Donald Pleasence, *Isaac*, John Anderson, *Col. Iverson*, Jorge Rivero,

Spotted Wolf, Dana Elcar, *Capt. Battles,* James Hampton, *Pvt. Menzies,* Mort Mills, *Sgt. O'Hearn,* Bob Carraway, *Lt. McNair,* Martin West, *Lt. Spingarn,* Jorge Russek, *Running Foy,* Marco Antonio Arzate, *Kiowa Brave,* Ron Fletcher, *Lt. Mitchell,* Barbara Turner, *Mrs. Long,* Aurora Clavell, *Indian Woman.* R.

Dismal pro-Indian western loosely based on the Sand Creek Massacre of Indians by the U.S. Cavalry. The intentions of the film are admirable, but *Soldier Blue* comes off as nothing more than a sadistic exercise in violence, due to its poor treatment. The attitudes are far too black and white, with the white men portrayed as a bunch of rampaging sadists, instead of human beings. *Little Big Man* covered the same subject with far more intelligence.

792 **Somebody Killed Her Husband** (1978) *** Columbia, 97 min. *Dir* Lamont Johnson, *Scr* Reginald Rose, *Cin* Andrew Laszlo, *Ed* Barry Malkin, *Des* Ted Haworth, *Art* David Chapman, *Cos* Joseph G. Aulisi, *Mus* Alex North, *Song,* "Love Keeps Getting Stronger Every Day," *Mus* Neil Sedaka, *Lyrics* Howard Greenfield, sung by Neil Sedaka, *Prod* Martin Poll, *Assoc Prod* William Craven, A Melvin Simon Production.

Cast: Farrah Fawcett-Majors, *Jenny Moore,* Jeff Bridges, *Jerry Green,* John Wood, *Ernest Van Santen,* Tammy Grimes, *Audrey Van Santen,* John Glover, *Hubert Little,* Patricia Elliot, *Helene,* Mary McCarty, *Flora,* Laurence Guittard, *Preston Moore,* Vincent Robert Santa Lucia, *Benjamin,* Beeson Carroll, *Frank Danziger,* Eddie Lawrence, *Other Neighbor,* Arthur Rhytis, *Customer,* Jean-Pierre Stewart, *Man in Beret,* Terri DuHaime, *Lulu's Mother.* PG.

Well-made comedy suspense thriller starring Jeff Bridges and Farrah Fawcett-Majors as an adulterous couple who become prime suspects when her husband is found murdered in the kitchen. In their efforts to clear themselves, with their own investigation, they uncover more than just murder. Bridges and Fawcett-Majors are well paired as the couple in jeopardy, and the film moves briskly to its exciting climax, a chase through a department store.

793 **Something for Everyone** (1970) *** National General, 110 min. *Dir* Harold Prince, *Scr* Hugh Wheeler, based on novel *The Cook* by Harry Kressing, *Cin* Walter Lassally, *Ed* Barry Peters, Ralph Rosenblum, *Art* Otto Pischinger, *Cos* Florence Klotz, *Mus* John Kander, *Prod* John P. Flaxman.

Cast: Angela Lansbury, *Countess Herthe von Ornstein,* Michael York, *Conrad Ludwig,* Anthony Corlan, *Helmuth von Ornstein,* Heidelinde Weis, *Annaliese Plesche,* Eva Maria Meineke, *Mrs. Plesche,* John Gill, *Mr. Plesche,* Jane Carr, *Lotte von Ornstein,* Despo, *Bobby,* Wolfrid Lier, *Klaus,* Walter Janssen, *Father Georg,* Klaus Havenstein, *Rudolph.* R.

Unusual black comedy starring Michael York as an opportunist, who gains access to the castle of a countess (Angela Lansbury) by becoming a footman and gradually takes over her staff and family, using every means, including sexual. *Something for Everyone* has a potentially shocking premise, but it is very tastefully handled. Broadway director Harold Prince made a fine feature film debut.

794 **Something Short of Paradise** (1979) ** American International, 91 min. *Dir* David Helpern, Jr., *Scr* Fred Barron, *Cin* Walter Lassally, *Ed* Frank

Bracht, *Art* William De Seta, *Mus* Mark Snow, *Prod* Lester Berman, James C. Gutman, *Exec Prod* Michael Ingber, Herbert Swartz, Presented by Samuel Z. Arkoff.

Cast: Susan Sarandon, *Madeliene*, David Steinberg, *Harris*, Jean-Pierre Aumont, *Jean-Fidel*, Marilyn Sokol, *Ruthie*, Joe Grifasi, *Barney*, Robert Hilt, *Edgar*, David Rasche, *David*, Bob Kaliban, *George*, Ted Pugh, *Frank*, Ann Robey, *Gail*, William Francis, *Hotel Manager*, Adrienne Jalbert, *Fru-Fru*, Terrence O'Hara, *Donny*, Fred Nassif, *Desk Clerk*, Sonya Jennings, *Beth*, Ellen March, *Lisa*, Loretta Tupper, *Alice*, Martha Sherrill, *Mrs. Peel*. PG.

Dull comedy love story about the relationship of a theatre manager (David Steinberg) and a magazine writer (Susan Sarandon). *Something Short of Paradise* is an obvious attempt to cover the same ground that Woody Allen has perfected, by focusing on intellectuals and their relationships. Intellectuals are difficult to portray on the screen with any depth, and the film's title may be an apt description.

795 Sometimes a Great Notion (1971) *** Universal, 113 min. *Dir* Paul Newman, *Scr* John Gay, based on novel by Ken Kesey, *Cin* Richard Moore, *Ed* Bob Wyman, *Art* Philip Jefferies, *Cos* Edith Head, *Mus* Henry Mancini, *Song* "All His Children", *Mus* Henry Mancini, *Lyrics* Alan and Marilyn Bergman, *Prod* John C. Foreman, *Assoc Prod* Frank Caffey.

Cast: Paul Newman, *Hank Stamper*, Henry Fonda, *Henry Stamper*, Lee Remick, *Viv Stamper*, Michael Sarrazin, *Leeland Stamper*, Richard Jaeckel (AN), *Joe Ben Stamper*, Linda Lawson, *Jan Stamper*, Cliff Potts, *Andy Stamper*, Sam Gilman, *John Stamper*, Lee De Broux, *Willard Eggleston*, Jim Burk, *Biggy Newton*, Roy Jenson, *Elwood*, Joe Maross, *Floyd Evenwrite*, Roy Poole, *Jonathan Draeger*, Charles Tyner, *Les Gibbons*. PG. $4,100,000.

Standard drama about a logging family in Oregon starring Henry Fonda as the father and Paul Newman and Michael Sarrazin as his sons. The family defies a local strike and desperately tries to keep the business going. *Sometimes a Great Notion* is well-made and at times exciting, but the characters tend to be stereotypes. Richard Jaeckel steals the film, giving one of his finest performances. Other title, *Never Give an Inch*.

796 Song of Norway (1970) * Cinerama, 142 min. *Dir* Andrew L. Stone, *Scr* Andrew L. Stone, based on play by George Forrest, Milton Lazarus, Robert Wright, and unpublished play by Homer Curran, *Cin* Davis Boulton, *Ed* Virginia Stone, *Art* William Albert Havemeyer, *Cos* Fiorella Miriani, David Walker, *Mus. Adaptation* George Forrest, Robert Wright, *Chor* Lee Theodore, *Prod* Andrew L. Stone, Virginia Stone.

Cast: Toraly Maurstad, *Edvard Grieg*, Florence Henderson, *Nina Grieg*, Christina Schollin, *Therese Berg*, Frank Porretta, *Rikard Nordraak*, Harry Secombe, *Bjornsterne Bjornson*, Robert Morley, *Berg*, Edward G. Robinson, *Krogstad*, Elizabeth Larner, *Mrs. Bjornson*, Oscar Homolka, *Engstrand*, Frederick Jaeger, *Henrik Ibsen*, Henry Gilbert, *Franz Liszt*, Richard Wordsworth, *Hans Christian Andersen*. G. $4,450,000.

Silly musical biography of Norwegian composer Edvard Grieg. *Song of Norway* is filled with dismal and phoney sweetness, and the film does not even do justice to Grieg's music. Unfortunately Andrew L. Stone, who is no Ken Russell, did not learn from this mistake and consequently followed this travesty with an equally poor film on the life of Johann Strauss, Jr., titled *The Great Waltz*.

797 Sorcerer (1977) ***** Paramount/Universal, 121 min. *Dir* William Friedkin, *Scr* Walon Green, based on novel *The Wages of Fear* by George Arnaud, *Cin* Dick Bush, John M. Stephens, *Ed* Bud Smith, *Des* John Box, *Art* Roy Walker, *Cos* Anthony Powell, *Mus* Tangerine Dream, *Prod* William Friedkin, *Assoc Prod* Bud Smith.

Cast: Roy Scheider, *Scanlon/"Dominguez"*, Bruno Cremer, *Victor Manzon/"Serrano"*, Francisco Rabal, *Nilo*, Amidou, *Kassem/"Martinez"*, Ramon Bieri, *Corlette*, Peter Capell, *Lartigue*, Karl John, *Marquez*, Frederick Ledebur, *Carlos*, Chico Martinez, *Bobby Del Rios*, Joe Spinell, *Spider*, Randy Jurgensen, *Vinnie*, Rosario Almontes, *Agrippa*, Richard Holley, *Billy White*, Anne Marie Descott, *Blanche*, Jean-Luc Bideau, *Pascal*, Jacques Francois, *Lefevre*, Andre Falcon, *Guillot*, Gerard E. Murphy, *Donnelly*, Desmond Crofton, *Boyle*, Henry Diamond, *Murray*, Ray Dittrich, *Ben*, Frank Gio, *Marty*, Gus Allegretti, *Carlo Ricci*. PG.

Brilliant remake of Henri-Georges Clouzot's *The Wages of Fear*, *Sorcerer* is an existential thriller of survival. Four men accused of various crimes are hiding out in a dismal South American village. They attempt to escape from their self-exile by transporting nitroglycerine by trucks through treacherous jungles to an oil well fire. *Sorcerer* may not be a horror film in the conventional sense, but Friedkin documents this desperate struggle for freedom as if it were an escape from hell itself. The prologue showing the original crimes of the four men is a bit slow, but once the action reaches South America, *Sorcerer*, with some absolutely incredible sequences, becomes one of the most powerful visions of hell ever put on film.

798 Sounder (1972) (AN) *** 20th Century–Fox, 105 min. *Dir* Martin Ritt, *Scr* Lonne Elder III (AN), based on novel by William H. Armstrong, *Cin* John A. Alonzo, *Ed* Sid Levin, *Art* Walter Herndon, *Cos* Nedra Watt, *Mus* Taj Mahal, *Prod* Robert B. Radnitz.

Cast: Cicely Tyson (AN, NS, NB), *Rebecca Morgan*, Paul Winfield (AN), *Nathan Lee Morgan*, Kevin Hooks, *David Lee Morgan*, Carmen Mathews, *Mrs. Boatwright*, Taj Mahal, *Ike*, James Best, *Sheriff Young*, Yvonne Jarrell, *Josie Mae Morgan*, Eric Hooks, *Earl Morgan*, Sylvia "Kuumba" Williams, *Harriett*, Janet MacLachlen, *Camille*, Teddy Airhart, *Mr. Perkins*, Rev. Thomas N. Phillips, *Preacher*, Judge William Thomas Bennett, *Judge*, Inez Durham, *Court Clerk*, Spencer Bradford, *Clarence*, Myrl Sharkey, *Mrs. Clay*. G. $8,725,000.

Fine period drama about a black sharecropping family living in Louisiana during the Depression. The story involves the imprisonment of the father (Paul Winfield) for stealing a ham to feed his family, and how the mother (Cicely Tyson) pulls her family through the crisis. *Sounder* is superbly acted and well-written, but it tends to be sentimental. In the inferior sequel *Part II Sounder* the family becomes involved in building a schoolhouse.

799 Soylent Green (1973) ** MGM, 97 min. *Dir* Richard Fleischer, *Scr* Stanley R. Greenberg, based on novel by Harry Harrison, *Cin* Richard H. Kline, *Ed* Samuel E. Beetley, *Art* Edward C. Carfagno, *Cos* Pat Barto, *Mus* Fred Myrow, *Prod* Walter Seltzer, Russell Thacher.

Cast: Charlton Heston, *Thorn*, Leigh Taylor-Young, *Shirl*, Chuck Conners, *Tab*, Joseph Cotten, *Simonson*, Brock Peters, *Hatcher*, Paula Kelly, *Martha*, Edward G. Robinson, *Sol Roth*, Stephen Young, *Gilbert*, Mike Henry, *Kulozik*, Lincoln Kilpatrick, *Priest*, Roy Jenson, *Donovan*, Leonard Stone, *Charles*, Whit Bissell, *Santini*, Celia Lovsky, *Exchange Leader*, Jane Dulo, *Mrs. Santini*, Dick Van Patten, *Usher*, Tim Herbert, *Brady*, John Dennis, *Wagner*, Jan Bradley, *Bandana Woman*, Carlos Romero, *New Tenant*, Pat Houtchens, *Fat Guard*. PG.

Dull science-fiction mystery thriller set in a vastly overcrowded future. Charlton Heston stars as a policeman, who in his investigation of a murder discovers a government secret involving "soylent green," a mysterious food source. The makers of *Soylent Green* try so hard to deliver a serious ecological message that they apparently forgot to devise an interesting plot with which to carry this message.

800 **Sparkle** (1976) ** Warner Bros., 98 min. *Dir* Sam O'Steen, *Scr* Joel Schumacher, *Story* Howard Rosenman, Joel Schumacher, *Cin* Bruce Surtees, *Ed* Gordon Scott, *Art* Peter Wooley, *Mus* Curtis Mayfield, *Chor* Lester Wilson, *Prod* Howard Rosenman, *Exec Prod* Peter Brown, Beryl Vertue.

Cast: Philip M. Thomas, *Stix*, Irene Cara, *Sparkle*, Lonette McKee, *Sister*, Dwan Smith, *Delores*, Mary Alice, *Effie*, Dorian Harewood, *Levi*, Tony King, *Satin*, Beatrice Winde, *Mrs. Waters*, Paul Lambert, *Moe*, Joyce Easton, *Lee*, DeWayne Jessie, *Ham*, Norma Miller, *Doreen*. PG.

Disappointing drama about three sisters (Irene Cara, Lonette McKee, Dwan Smith), who form a singing group during the 1950's. *Sparkle* seems like a serious attempt at a realistic backstage musical drama, but the plot is filled with the usual assortment of clichés and stereotypes. One sister has the promise of success (Cara), while another ends up in the gutter, and along the way there are the usual problems with drugs and gangsters.

801 **Special Delivery** (1976) *** American International, 98 min. *Dir* Paul Wendkos, *Scr* Don Gazzaniga, *Cin* Harry Stradling, Jr., *Ed* Housely Stevenson, *Art* Jack Poplin, *Mus* Lalo Schifrin, *Prod* Richard Berg, *Exec Prod* Charles A. Pratt.

Cast: Bo Svenson, *Jack Murdock*, Cybill Shepherd, *Mary Jane*, Tom Atkins, *Zabelski*, Sorrell Booke, *Bank Manager Zane*, Gerrit Graham, *Swivat*, Michael C. Gwynne, *Carl Graff*, Jeff Goldblum, *Snake*, Robert Ito, *Mr. Chu*, Lynnette Mettey, *Marj*, Richard Drout Miller, *Artie*, John Quade, *Barney*, Vic Tayback, *Wyatt*, Edward Winter, *Pierce*, Kim Richards, *Juliette*. PG.

Offbeat crime comedy about an unsuccessful bank robbery by a group of Vietnam vets. Bo Svenson stars as the one member of the group who gets away, but in the confusion he hides the money in a nearby mailbox. Recovering the money becomes a difficult task, particularly with the interference of two witnesses; an artist (Cybill Shepherd) and pusher (Michael C. Gwynne). *Special Delivery* is a well-made and fast-paced comedy.

802 **S*P*Y*S** (1974) * 20th Century–Fox, 87 min. *Dir* Irvin Kershner, *Scr* Lawrence J. Cohen, Fred Freeman, Mal Marmorstein, *Cin* Gerry Fisher, *Ed* Keith Palmer, *Des* Michael Seymour, *Art* Richard Rambeau, *Cos* Sue Yelland, *Mus* Jerry Goldsmith, *Prod* Robert Chartoff, Irwin Winkler, *Assoc Prod* Bob Lawrence.

Cast: Elliott Gould, *Griff*, Donald Sutherland, *Brulard*, Zouzou, *Sybil*, Joss Ackland, *Martinson*, Kenneth Griffith, *Lippet*, Vladek Sheybal, *Borisenko*, Kenneth J. Warren, *Grubov*, Yuri Borienko, *Yuri*, Michael Petrovitch, *Sevitsky*, Pierre Oudry, *Gaspar*, Jacques Marin, *Lafayette*, Shane Rimmer, *Hessler*, Xavier Gelin, *Paul*, George Pravada, *Russian Coach*. PG. $5,205,000.

Bland comedy about two incompetent CIA agents (Donald Sutherland, Elliott Gould) who are on the run due to mishandling a defection of a Russian ballet dancer. It is obvious from its title that *S*P*Y*S* is a foolish attempt to emulate *M*A*S*H*, including the reteaming of its two stars, but that style is out of place in a thriller. This is a terrible waste of talent, particularly the two stars and director Irvin Kershner, who is capable of much better work.

803 **A Star Is Born** (1976) (GMC) ** Warner Bros., 140 min. *Dir* Frank R. Pierson, *Scr* Joan Didion, John Gregory Dunne, Frank R. Pierson, based on story by Robert Carson, William Wellman, *Cin* Robert Surtees (AN), *Ed* Peter Zinner, *Des* Polly Platt, *Art* William Hiney, *Cos* Seth Banks, Shirley Strahm, *Mus* Kenny Ascher, Paul Williams (G), *Mus Adaptation* Roger Kellaway (AN), *Song*, "Evergreen", *Mus* Paul Williams (A, G), *Lyrics* Barbra Streisand (A, G), *Chor* David Winters, *Prod* Jon Peters, *Exec Prod* Barbra Streisand.

Cast: Barbra Streisand (G), *Esther Hoffman*, Kris Kristofferson (G), *John Norman Howard*, Gary Busey, *Bobby Ritchie*, Paul Mazursky, *Brian*, Oliver Clark, *Gary Danziger*, Vanetta Fields, Clydie King, *The Oreos*, Marta Heflin, *Quentin*, M.G. Kelly, *Bebe Jesus*, Sally Kirkland, *Photography*, Joanne Linville, *Freddie*, Uncle Rudy, *Mo*. R. $37,100,000.

Fair remake of the famed film about Hollywood. In this version the setting has been switched to the world of rock music, but the basic story of the destruction of a show business marriage remains intact. Perhaps the story is tired and overused; this is the fourth version; but nothing in *A Star Is Born* seems fresh. Barbra Streisand's shrill personality, which dominates the film, contributes to bringing the film down.

804 **Star Trek – The Motion Picture** (1979) *** Paramount, 132 min. *Dir* Robert Wise, *Scr* Harold Livingston, *Story* Alan Dean Foster, based on television series created by Gene Roddenberry, *Cin* Richard H. Kline, *Ed* Todd Ramsey, *Des* Harold Michelson (AN), *Art* Leon Harris, Joe Jennings, John Vallone (AN), *Sp* John Dykstra, Grant McCune, Dave Stewart, Robert Swarthe, Douglas Trumbull, Richard Yuricich (AN), *Mus* Jerry Goldsmith (AN), *Prod* Gene Roddenberry, *Assoc Prod* Jon Povill.

Cast: William Shatner, *Capt. Kirk*, Leonard Nimoy, *Mr. Spock*, DeForest Kelley, *Dr. McCoy*, James Doohan, *Scotty*, George Takei, *Sulu*, Majel Barrett, *Dr. Chapel*, Walter Koenig, *Chekov*, Nichelle Nichols, *Uhura*, Persis Khambatta, *Ilia*, Stephen Collins, *Decker*, Mark Lenard, *Klingon Captain*, Billy Van Zandt, *Alien Boy*, Grace Lee Whitney, *Janice Rand*. G. $56,000,000.

Spectacular, but slightly disappointing film version of the popular television series from the late 1960's. The film was not plagued with the budget limitations suffered by the series and the film contains magnificent special effects. There are some genuinely interesting ideas put forth, that are worthy of the best episodes of the series. The main problem is the pace, which is far too slow, particularly when the camera ogles the Enterprise and the interior of the alien spacecraft.

805 **Star Wars** (1977) (AN, LA) ******** 20th Century–Fox, 121 min. *Dir* George Lucas (AN), *Scr* George Lucas (AN), *Cin* Gilbert Taylor, *Ed* Richard Chew, Paul Hirsh, Marcia Lucas (A), *Des* John Barry (A), *Art* Leslie Dilley, Norman Reynolds (A), *Cos* John Mollo (A), *Sp* Robert Blalock, John Dykstra, Richard Edlund, Grant McCune, John Stears (A), *Mus* John Williams (A, G, BFA), *Prod* Gary Kurtz.

Cast: Mark Hamill, *Luke Skywalker*, Harrison Ford, *Han Solo*, Carrie Fisher, *Princess Leia*, Peter Cushing, *Grand Moff Tarkin*, Alec Guinness (AN), *Ben (Obi-Wan) Kenobi*, Anthony Daniels, *See Threepio (C3PO)*, Kenny Baker, *Artoo-Detoo (R2D2)*, Peter Mayhew, *Chewbacca*, David Prowse, *Lord Darth Vader*, Phil Brown, *Uncle Owen Lars*, Shelagh Fraser, *Aunt Beru Lars*, Jack Purvis, *Chief Jawa*, Alex McCrindle, *Gen. Dodonna*, Eddie Byrne, *Gen. Willard*, Drewe Henley, *Red Leader*, Dennis Lawson, *Red Two*, Garrick Hagon, *Red Three*, Jack Klaff, *Red Four*, William Hootkins, *Red Six*, Angus McInnis, *Gold Leader*, Jeremy Sinden, *Gold Two*, Graham Ashley, *Gold Five*, Don Henderson, *Gen. Taggi*, Richard LeParmentier, *Gen. Motti*, Leslie Schofield, *Commander #1*, James Earl Jones, *Voice of Darth Vader*. PG. $185,140,000.

Spectacular space opera adventure. Luke Skywalker, a young farm boy, sets out to rescue Princess Leia, who has been kidnapped by the evil Darth Vader. That is the basic premise of this live-action, cartoon version of the basic theme of good vs. evil. What *Star Wars* lacks in substance, it more than makes up for in exuberance. The real star is the special effects, which set a new standard in film.

806 **Stardust** (1974) ******* Britain, Columbia, 113 min. *Dir* Michael Apted, *Scr* Ray Connolly, *Cin* Tony Richmond, *Ed* Mike Bradsell, *Mus* Dave Edmunds, David Puttnam, Stray Cats, *Prod* Sanford Lieberson, David Puttnam, *Exec Prod* Roy Baird, *Assoc Prod* Gavrik Losey, Presented by Nat Cohen.

Cast: David Essex, *Jim MacLaine*, Adam Faith, *Mike*, Larry Hagman, *Porter Lee Austin*, Ines Des Longchamps, *Danielle*, Rosalind Ayres, *Jeanette*, Marty Wilde, *Colin Day*, Edd Byrnes, *TV Interviewer*, Keith Moon, *J.D.*, Dave Edmunds, *Alex*, Paul Nicholas, *Johnny*, Karl Howman, *Stevie*, Rick Lee Parmentier, *Felix Hoffman*, Peter Duncan, *Kevin*, John Normington, *Harrap*, James Hazeldine, *Brian*, Dave Daker, *Ralph Woods*, Anthony Naylor, *Keith Nolan*, Charlotte Cornwell, *Sally Potter*, Rose Marie Klespitz, *Lucille*. R. See *That'll Be the Day*.

807 **Start the Revolution Without Me** (1970) ******* Warner Bros., 98 min. *Dir* Bud Yorkin, *Scr* Lawrence J. Cohen, Fred Freeman, *Cin* Jean Tournier, *Ed* Ferris Webster, *Art* Francois de Lamothe, *Cos* Alan Barrett, *Mus* John Addison, *Prod* Bud Yorkin, *Exec Prod* Norman Lear, *Assoc Prod* Edward Stephenson.

Cast: Gene Wilder, *Claude/Philippe*, Donald Sutherland, *Charles/Pierre*, Hugh Griffith, *King Louis*, Jack MacGowran, *Jacques*, Billie Whitelaw, *Queen Marie*, Victor Spinetti, *Duke d'Escargot*, Orson Welles, *Himself*, Helen Fraser, *Mimi*, Ewa Aulin, *Christina*, Harry Fowler, *Marcel*, Rosalind Knight, *Helen DeSisi*, Murray Melvin, *Blind Man*, Ken Parry, *Dr. Boileau*, Jacques Maury, *Lt. Sorel*, Maxwell Shaw, *Duke DeSisi*, Graham Stark, *Andre Coupe*, Barry Lowe, *Sergeant*, George A. Cooper, *Dr. Duval*, Michael Rothwell, *Paul Duval*, Denise Coffey, *Anne Duval*. PG.

Well-made period farce about mistaken identity, set during the French Revolution. Donald Sutherland and Gene Wilder star as two separate sets of twins, who are mixed up at birth. This leaves one Sutherland and Wilder as aristocratic brothers and another Sutherland and Wilder as peasant brothers, causing many humorous complications. The stars are good in their dual roles, and Hugh Griffith steals the film as the nitwit king.

808 **Starting Over** (1979) ******* Parmount, 106 min. *Dir* Alan J. Pakula, *Scr* James L. Brooks, based on novel by Dan Wakefield, *Cin* Sven Nykvist, *Ed* Marion Rothman, *Des* George Jenkins, *Cos* John Boxer, *Mus* Marvin Hamlisch, *Prod* James L. Brooks, Alan J. Pakula, *Assoc Prod* Isabel M. Halliburton, Douglas Z. Wick.

Cast: Burt Reynolds, *Phil Potter*, Jill Clayburgh (AN), *Marilyn Holmberg*, Candice Bergen (AN), *Jessica Potter*, Charles Durning, *Mickey Potter*, Frances Sternhagen, *Marva Potter*, Austin Pendleton, *Paul*, Mary Kay Place, *Marie*, MacIntyre Dixon, *Dan Ryan*, Jay Sanders, *Larry*, Richard Whiting, *Everett*, Sturgis Warner, *John Morganson*, Alfie Wise, Wallace Shawn, *Workshop Members*, Mary C. Wright, Daniel Stern, George Hirsch, *Students*, Ian Martin, *Doorman*. PG. $19,100,000.

Fine comedy about a recently divorced man coping with loneliness. Burt Reynolds stars as a writer, who divorces his overbearing and talentless singer-songwriter wife (Candice Bergen). He falls for a shy teacher (Jill Clayburgh), but their relationship becomes complicated by the return of his wife. The storyline is slight, but most of the humor grows naturally out of the characters, without resorting to one-liners. It is unfortunate that Reynolds does not do more of these comedies, instead of mindless car chase films.

809 **Stay Hungry** (1976) ******** United Artists, 102 min. *Dir* Bob Rafelson, *Scr* Charles Gaines, Bob Rafelson, based on novel by Charles Gaines, *Cin* Victor J. Kemper, *Ed* John F. Link II, *Des* Toby Carr Rafelson, *Mus* Byron Berline, Bruce Langhorne, *Prod* Bob Rafelson, Harold Schneider.

Cast: Jeff Bridges, *Craig Blake*, Sally Field, *Mary Tate Farnsworth*, Arnold Schwarzenegger, *Joe Santo*, R. G. Armstrong, *Thor Erickson*, Robert Englund, *Franklin*, Helena Kallianiotes, *Anita*, Robert E. Mosley, *Newton*, Woodrow Parfrey, *Craig's Uncle*, Scatman Crothers, *Butler*, Kathleen Miller, *Dorothy Stephens*, Fannie Flagg, *Amy Walterson*, Joanna Cassidy, *Joe Mason*, Richard Gilliland, *Hal Foss*, Ed Begley, Jr., *Lester*, John David Carson, *Halsey*, Joe Spinell, *Jabo*, Cliff Pellow, *Walter Jr.*, Dennis Fimple, *Bubba*, Mayf Nutter, *Packman*. R.

Unusual comedy-drama about a wealthy Southern youth (Jeff Bridges), who is sent by some associates to a run-down gym to purchase it for a major development. The owner (R.G. Armstrong) refuses to sell and Bridges becomes attracted to the world of bodybuilding. *Stay Hungry* is an excellent character study that perceptively compares and contrasts these opposite worlds, much like Rafelson's earlier film *Five Easy Pieces*, and is enhanced by some truly eccentric characters and humor.

810 **The Steagle** (1971) ****** Avco Embassy, 90 min. *Dir* Paul Sylbert, *Scr* Paul Sylbert, based on novel by Irvin Faust, *Cin* Burnett Guffey, *Ed* Thomas Stanford, *Art* William Campbell, Bill Malley, *Cos* Anthea Sylbert, *Mus* Fred Myrow, *Prod* Jim Di Gangi, *Exec Prod* Frank P. Rosenberg.

Cast: Richard Benjamin, *Dr. Harold Weiss*, Chill Wills, *Tall-Guy McCoy*, Cloris Leachman, *Rita Weiss*, Jean Allison, *Florence Maguire*, Suzanne Charny, *Marcy*, Ivor Francis, *Clergyman*, Susan Tyrrell, *Louise*, Jack Bernardi, *Marty Panesh*, Susan Kussman, *Joan*, Peter Hobbs. *Dr. Worthington Payne*, Joe Bernard, *Max Levine*, Anita Alberts, *Loretta*, Frank Christi, *Mr. Forbes*, Dianne Ladd, *Mrs. Forbes*, Harold Reynolds, *Dr. Plymile*, John Hiestand, *Matt Mayhew*. R.

Unusual comedy starring Richard Benjamin as a college professor, who retreates into a world of fantasy to escape from his dull life. The Cuban Missile Crisis in 1962 causes him to crack, and he begins to live out his fantasies. *The Steagle* has some interesting ideas, but unfortunately not enough for a feature-length film. Benjamin, however, gives a fine comic performance. This was set designer Paul Sylbert's directorial debut.

811 **Steelyard Blues** (1973) ** Warner Bros., 92 min. *Dir* Alan Myerson, *Scr* David S. Ward, *Cin* Laszlo Kovacs, Stevan Larner, *Ed* Donn Cambern, Robert Grovener, *Art* Vincent Cresciman, *Mus* Paul Butterfield, Nick Gravenites, David Shire, *Lyrics* Michael Bloomfield, Nick Gravenites, *Prod* Tony Bill, Michael and Julia Phillips, *Exec Prod* Donald Sutherland.

Cast: Jane Fonda, *Iris*, Donald Sutherland, *Veldini*, Peter Boyle, *Eagle*, Garry Goodrow, *Duval*, Howard Hesseman, *Frank Veldin*, John Savage, *The Kid*, Richard Schaal, *Zoo Director*, Melvin Stewart, *Black Man in Jail*, Morgan Upton, *Police Captain*, Roger Bowen, *Fire Commissioner*, Howard Storm, *Health Inspector*, Jessica Myerson, *Savage Rose*, Dan Barrows, *Rocky*, Nancy Fish, *Pool Hall Waitress*, Lynn Bernay, *Bar Waitress*, Edward Greenberg, *Rookie Cop*. PG.

Fair counter-culture comedy about a group of social outcasts, who attempt to restore an old navy amphibious plane. They are unable to find all the necessary parts, which forces them to stage a raid on a nearby naval base. *Steelyard Blues* has some nice comic touches, but much of the humor falls flat. This type of film belongs to the era of the late 1960's and was already dated upon release.

812 **The Stepford Wives** (1975) ** Columbia, 114 min. *Dir* Bryan Forbes, *Scr* William Goldman, based on novel by Ira Levin, *Cin* Owen Roizman, *Ed* Timothy Gee, *Des* Gene Callahan, *Mus* Michael Small, *Prod* Edgar J. Scherick, *Exec Prod* Gustave M. Berne.

Cast: Katharine Ross, *Joanna*, Paula Prentiss, *Bobby*, Peter Masterson, *Walter*, Nanette Newman, *Carol*, Patrick O'Neal, *Dale Coba*, Tina Louise, *Charmaine*, Carol Rosson, *Dr. Fancher*, William Prince, *Artist*, Paula Trueman, *Welcome Wagon Lady*, Remak Ramsay, *Atkinson*, John Aprea, *Policeman*. PG. $4,000,000.

Slow science-fiction suspense thriller about the strange occurrences in the town of Stepford, Connecticut. Katharine Ross, her husband (Peter Masterson) and their children leave the pressures of New York to live in quiet suburbia. Ross befriends Paula Prentiss, and the two discover the other wives are being turned into robots. *The Stepford Wives* is a sterile version of *Invasion of the Body Snatchers*, but it has some interesting and satirical comments on male and female roles in society. Unfortunately the story takes far too long to get started.

813 **The Sting** (1973) (A, NB) ***** Universal, 129 min. *Dir* George Roy Hill (A, D), *Scr* David S. Ward (A), *Cin* Robert Surtees (AN), *Ed* William Reynolds (A), *Art* Henry Bumstead (A), *Cos* Edith Head (A), *Mus* Adaptation Marvin Hamlisch (A), *Prod* Tony Bill, Michael and Julia Phillips, A Richard D. Zanuck-David Brown Production.

   Cast: Paul Newman, *Henry Gondorff*, Robert Redford (AN), *Johnny Hooker*, Robert Shaw, *Doyle Lonnegan*, Charles Durning, *Lt. Snyder*, Ray Walston, *Singleton*, Eileen Brennan, *Billie*, Harold Gould, *Kid Twist*, John Heffernan, *Niles*, Dana Elcar, *FBI Agent*, Jack Kehoe, *Erie Kid*, Dimitra Arliss, *Loretta*. PG. $78,965,000.

   Magnificent period comedy about a pair of con artists (Paul Newman, Robert Redford), who pull off an elaborate scam in order to bilk a gangster (Robert Shaw). The plot is as elaborate as the con itself, moving along with many twists and turns following Newman and Redford as they set Shaw up for the final pay-off. Many critics have complained that the plot actually makes little sense, but this simply is not true, as every piece fits neatly into the puzzle. (The screenwriter won an Academy Award.) The *Sting* is one of the few truly great entertainment films.

814 **The Stone Killer** (1973) *** Columbia, 96 min. *Dir* Michael Winner, *Scr* Gerald Wilson, based on novel *A Complete State of Death* by John Gardner, *Cin* Richard Moore, *Ed* Frederick Wilson, *Art* Ward Preston, *Mus* Roy Budd, *Prod* Michael Winner, A Dino De Laurentiis Presentation.

   Cast: Charles Bronson, *Torrey*, Martin Balsam, *Vescari*, David Sheiner, *Lorenz*, Norman Fell, *Daniels*, Ralph Waite, *Mathews*, Eddie Firestone, *Armitage*, Walter Burke, *J.D.*, David Moody, *Lipper*, Charles Tyner, *Psychiatrist*, Paul Koslo, *Langley*, Stuart Margolin, *Lawrence*, John Ritter, *Hart*, Byron Morrow, *Police Chief*, Jack Colvin, *Jumper*, Frank Campanella, *Calabriese*, Alfred Ryder, *Champion*, Gene Woodbury, *Paul Long*, Harry Basch, *Mossman*, Jan Arvan, *Vechetti*, Lisabeth Hush, *Helen*, Mary Cross, *Waitress*, Kelly Miles, *Gerry Wexton*, Christina Raines, *Mathew's Daughter*, Robert Emhardt, *Fussy Man*. R.

   Exciting crime thriller starring Charles Bronson as a cop, who uncovers a Mafia murder plot. A gang boss (Martin Balsam) seeks revenge for a 40 year old incident and recruits Viet Nam vets to handle the murders. The story is a little strained and it defies believability, but the action is so fast and exciting, particularly the climactic shootout, it obliterates the flaws.

815 **Straight Time** (1978) **** Warner Bros., 114 min. *Dir* Ulu Grosbard, *Scr* Jeffrey Boam, Edward Bunker, Alvin Sargent, based on novel *No Beast So Fierce* by Edward Bunker, *Cin* Owne Roizman, *Ed* Sam O'Steen, Randy Roberts, *Des* Stephen Grimes, *Art* Dick Lawrence, *Mus* David Shire, *Prod* Stanley Beck, Tim Zinneman, *Exec Prod* Howard B. Pine, *Assoc Prod* Gail Mutrux.

   Cast: Dustin Hoffman, *Max Dembo*, Theresa Russell, *Jenny Mercer*, Harry Dean Stanton, *Jerry Schue*, Gary Busey, *Willy Darin*, M. Emmet Walsh, *Earl Frank*, Sandy Baron, *Manny*, Kathy Bates, *Selma Darin*, Edward Bunker, *Mickey*, Stuart I. Benton, *Salesman #1*, Barry Cahill, *Salesman #2*, Corey Rand, *Carlos*, James Ray, *Manager*, Fran Ryan, *Cafe Owner*, Rita Taggart, *Carol Schue*. R.

A superb and grimly realistic examination of a criminal. *Straight Time* is an unusual and possibly unique crime film. Max Dembo is a criminal, and that is just the way he is. No apologies or excuses are made for his actions and society or a bad childhood is never blamed. Dustin Hoffman, who originally attempted to also direct this film, gives one of his finest performances. *Straight Time* failed with both critics and the public, because it is just too real and logical for a typical crime film, but opinion will likely change.

816 **Straw Dogs** (1971) ***** Britain, Cinerama, 118 min. *Dir* Sam Peckinpah, *Scr* David Zelag Goodman, Sam Peckinpah, based on novel *The Siege of Trencher's Farm* by Gordon M. Williams, *Cin* John Coquillon, *Ed* Paul Davies, Tony Lawson, Robert Spottiswoode, *Des* Ray Simm, *Art* Ken Bridgeman, *Cos* Tiny Nicholls, *Mus* Jerry Fielding, *Prod* Daniel Melnick, *Assoc Prod* James Swann.

Cast: Dustin Hoffman, *David Sumner*, Susan George, *Amy Sumner*, Peter Vaughn, *Tom Hedden*, David Warner, *Henry Niles*, T.P. McKenna, *Maj. Scott*, Del Henney, *Charlie Venner*, Ken Hutchinson, *Scutt*, Colin Welland, *Rev. Hood*, Jim Norton, *Cawsey*, Sally Thomsett, *Janice*, Donald Webster, *Riddaway*, Len Jones, *Bobby Hedden*, Michael Mundell, *Bertie Hedden*, Peter Arne, *John Niles*, Robert Keegan, *Harry Ware*, June Brown, *Mrs. Hedden*, Chloe Franks, *Emma Hedden*, Cherina Mann, *Mrs. Hood*. R. $4,000,000.

Powerful drama starring Dustin Hoffman as a meek mathematician, who must defend his English country home against a group of intruders. Hoffman is a pacifist by nature, but he is suddenly forced to reexamine his ideals in order to protect himself and his home. *Straw Dogs* is an extremely violent film, but its violence is not without purpose. Peckinpah is known for his expertise with cinematic violence, and this film is one of his finest.

817 **The Strawberry Statement** (1970) ** MGM, 103 min. *Dir* Stuart Hagmann, *Scr* Israel Horovitz, based on novel *The Strawberry Statement: Notes of a College Revolutionary* by James Simon Kunen, *Cin* Ralph Woolsey, *Ed* Marjorie Fowler, Roger J. Roth, Fredric Steinkamp, *Art* Preston Ames, George W. Davis, *Cos* Norman Burza, Ricky Roberts, *Mus* Ian Freebairn-Smith, *Prod* Robert Chartoff, Irwin Winkler.

Cast: Bruce Davison, *Simon*, Kim Darby, *Linda*, Bud Cort, *Coxswain*, Murray MacLeod, *George*, Tom Foral, *Coach*, Danny Goldman, *Charlie*, Kristina Holland, *Irma*, Bob Balaban, *Elliot, The Organizer*, Kristin Van Buren, *Filing Room Girl*, Israel Horovitz, *Dr. Benton*, James Simon Kunen, *Chairman*, James Coco, *Grocer*, Eddra Gale, *Dean's Secretary*, Michael Margotta, *Swatch*, Bob Benjamin, *Man*, Jeannie Berlin, *Clipboard Girl*, Carol Bagasarian, *Telephone Girl*, Bert Remsen, *Policeman*, Jon Hill, Jess Walton, Andrew Parks, *Students*. R.

Fair film about college protests in the 1960's. Bruce Davison stars as an apathetic student, who is drawn into the protest by his interest in a girl (Kim Darby), but eventually he himself becomes committed to the ideals. *The Strawberry Statement* is as anarchic as its subject matter, and it falls apart, trying unsuccessfully to mix several styles.

818 **The Strongest Man in the World** (1975) ** Buena Vista, 92 min. *Dir* Vincent McEveety, *Scr* Herman Groves, Joseph L. McEveety, *Cin* Andrew

Jackson, *Ed* Cotton Warburton, *Art* John B. Mansbridge, Jack Senter, *Cos* Chuck Keehne, Emily Sundby, *Mus* Robert F. Brunner, *Prod* Bill Anderson, A Walt Disney Production.

Cast: Kurt Russell, *Dexter*, Joe Flynn, *Dean Higgens*, Eve Arden, *Harriet*, Cesar Romero, *A.J. Arno*, Phil Silvers, *Krinkle*, Dick Van Patten, *Harry*, Harold Gould, *Dietz*, Michael McGreevey, *Schuyler*, Dick Bakalyan, *Cookie*, William Schallert, *Quigley*, Benson Fong, *Ah Fong*, James Gregory, *Chief Blair*. G. $6,875,000. See *The Computer Wore Tennis Shoes*.

819 Stunts (1977) ** New Line Cinema, 90 min. *Dir* Mark L. Lester, *Scr* Barney Chen, Dennis Johnson, *Story*, Michael Harpster, Raymond Lafaro, Robert Shaye, *Cin* Bruce Logan, *Ed* Corky Ehlers, *Mus* Michael Kamen, *Prod* Raymond Lafaro, William Panzer, *Exec Prod* Peter S. Davis, Robert Shaye, *Assoc Prod* Mark Fleischman.

Cast: Robert Forster, *Glen Wilson*, Fiona Lewis, *B.J. Parswell*, Joanna Cassidy, *Patti*, Darrell Fetty, *Dave*, Bruce Glover, *Chuck Johnson*, Jim Luisi, *Blake*, Richard Lynch, *Pete*, Candice Rialson, *Judy*, Malachi Throne, *Earl*, Ray Sharkey, *Paul*. PG.

Standard action film about the mysterious murders of stuntmen. Robert Forster stars as the brother of a murdered stuntman, who takes his place on the set of an action movie in production in order to catch the psycho who is sabotaging the stunts. Stunts is more of an action thriller than a serious drama about Hollywood. Some of the action scenes are well-done, but the storyline seems better suited for television.

820 Such Good Friends (1971) ** Paramount, 101 min. *Dir* Otto Preminger, *Scr* Esther Dale (pseudonym for Elaine May), *Adaptation* David Shaber, based on novel by Lois Gould, *Cin* Gayne Rescher, *Ed* Harry Howard, *Des* Rouben Ter-Arutunian, *Cos* Hope Bryce Preminger, Ron Talsky, *Mus* Thomas Z. Shepard, *Song* "Suddenly, It's All Tomorrow", *Mus* Thomas Z. Shepard, *Lyrics* Robert Brittan, *Prod* Otto Preminger, *Assoc Prod* Erik Preminger, Nat Rudich.

Cast: Dyan Cannon, *Julie Messinger*, James Coco, *Dr. Timmy Spector*, Jennifer O'Neill, *Miranda Graham*, Ken Howard, *Cal Whiting*, Nina Foch, *Mrs. Wallman*, Laurence Luckinbill, *Richard Messinger*, Louise Lasser, *Marcy Berns*, Burgess Meredith, *Bernard Kalman*, Sam Levene, *Uncle Eddie*, William Redfield, *Barney Halstead*, James Beard, *Dr. Mahler*, Rita Gam, *Doria Perkins*, Nancy Guild, *Molly Hastings*, Elaine Joyce, *Marion Spector*, Nancy R. Pollack, *Aunt Harriet*, Doris Roberts, *Mrs. Gold*. R.

Dreary comedy about a troubled contemporary married couple (Dyan Cannon, Laurence Luckinbill). When he goes to a hospital, she discovers he has been unfaithful by having affairs with most of their female friends. She decides to get revenge by also being unfaithful. *Such Good Friends* is yet another poor attempt by Otto Preminger to be fashionable with the times, but the humor is more vulgar than witty.

821 The Sugarland Express (1974) *** Universal, 108 min. *Dir* Steven Spielberg, *Scr* Hal Barwood, Matthew Robbins (CF), *Story* Hal Barwood, Matthew Robbins, Steven Spielberg, *Cin* Vilmos Zsigmond, *Ed* Edward M. Abroms, Verna Fields, *Art* Joseph Alves, Jr., *Mus* John Williams, *Prod* Richard D. Zanuck, David Brown.

Cast: Goldie Hawn, *Lou Jean,* Ben Johnson, *Capt. Tanner,* Michael Sacks, *Slide,* William Atherton, *Clovis,* Gregory Walcott, *Mashburn,* Steve Kanaly, *Jessup,* Louise Latham, *Mrs. Looby,* Harrison Zanuck, *Baby Langston,* A.L. Camp, *Mr. Nocker,* Jessie Lee Fulton, *Mrs. Nocker,* Dean Smith, *Russ Berry,* Ted Grossman, *Dietz,* Bill Thurman, *Hunter,* Kenneth Hudgins, *Standby,* Buster Danials, *Drunk,* Jim Harrell, *Mark Feno,* Frank Steggall, *Logan Waters,* Roger Ernest, *Hot Jock #1,* Guich Koock, *Hot Jock #2,* Merrill L. Connally, *Looby.* PG.

Unusual and unbelievable chase film that surprisingly is based on a real incident. A woman helps her husband break out of prison in a effort to get back their baby, which has been adopted. Along the way they kidnap a state trooper and are subsequently pursued by a long convoy of troopers. Although *The Sugarland Express* is essentially one long chase the script is extremely intelligent and there is far more concentration on character than in other such films. Goldie Hawn is superb as the woman and Steven Spielberg made a fine feature film debut.

822 **Summer of '42** (1971) *** Warner Bros., 102 min. *Dir* Robert Mulligan, *Scr* Herman Raucher (AN), *Cin* Robert Surtees (AN). *Ed* Folmar Blangsted, *Des* Albert Brenner, *Mus* Michel Legrand (A, BFA), *Prod* Richard A. Roth, *Assoc Prod* Don Kranze.

Cast: Gary Grimes, *Hermie,* Jennifer O'Neill, *Dorothy,* Jerry Houser, *Oscy,* Oliver Conant, *Benjie,* Katherine Allentuck, *Aggie,* Christopher Norris, *Miriam,* Lou Frizzell, *The Druggest,* Walter Scott, *Dorothy's Husband,* Maureen Stapleton, *Voice of Hermie's Mother,* Robert Mulligan, *Narrator.* R. $20,500,000.

Fine drama about growing up, set during the 1940's. Gary Grimes stars as a teenager, who becomes infatuated with an older woman (Jennifer O'Neill), whose husband has gone off to war. Her anguish leads her to have a brief affair with Grimes. *Summer of '42* is sensitive and sometimes sentimental, but never overly so, and it has a fine sense of the period. The sequel, *Class of '44,* follows Grimes to college: it is well-made, but is not in the same class with its predecessor.

823 **Summer Wishes, Winter Dreams** (1973) ** Columbia, 93 min. *Dir* Gilbert Cates, *Scr* Stewart Stern, *Cin* Gerald Hirschfeld, *Ed* Sidney Katz, *Des* Peter Dohanos, *Cos* Anna Hill Johnstone, *Mus* Johnny Mandel, *Prod* Jack Brodsky.

Cast: Joanne Woodward (AN, NY, BFA), *Rita Walden,* Martin Balsam, *Harry Walden,* Sylvia Sidney (AN, NB), *Mrs. Pritchett,* Dorie Brenner, *Anna,* Win Forman, *Fred Goody,* Tresa Hughes, *Betty Goody,* Peter Marklin, *Joel,* Ron Richards, *Bobby Walden,* Charlotte Oberley, *Waitress,* Minerva Pious, *Mrs. Bimberg,* Helen Ludlam, *Grandmother,* Grant Code, *Grandfather,* Sol Frieder, *Mr. Goldblatt.* PG.

Dull character study focusing on the dreary existence of a middle-aged couple (Joanne Woodward, Martin Balsam), who go off to Bastogne, where he was during WWII, to rejuvenate their lives after the death of her mother (Sylvia Sidney). *Summer Wishes, Winter Dreams* tries to be poignant, but the film is little more than endless talk. The performances are excellent, however.

824 **Sunburn** (1979) *** Paramount, 101 min. *Dir* Richard C. Sarafian, *Scr* James Booth, John Daley, Stephen Oliver, based on novel *The Bind* by Stanley Ellin, *Cin* Alex Phillips, Jr., *Ed* Geoff Foot, *Des* Ted Tester, *Art* Augustin Ituarte, *Cos* Moss Mabry, *Mus* John Cameron, *Prod* John Daly, Gerald Green, *Exec Prod* Jay Bernstein, John Quested.

Cast: Charles Grodin, *Jake,* Farrah Fawcett, *Ellie,* Art Carney, *Marcus,* Joan Collins, *Nera,* William Daniels, *Crawford,* John Hillerman, *Webb,* Eleanor Parker, *Mrs. Thoran,* Keenan Wynn, *Mark Elmes,* Robin Clarke, *Karl,* Joan Goodfellow, *Joanna,* Jack Kruschen, *Gela,* Alejandro Rey, *Fons,* Jorge Luke, *Vasquez,* Seymour Cassel, *Dobbs,* Joanna Lehmann, *Mamie,* Alex Sharpe, *Kunz,* Bob Orrison, *Milan,* Deloy White, *Dr. Kellogg.* P.

Pleasant comedy thriller involving the mysterious death of an industrialist. An insurance investigator (Charles Grodin) hires a woman (Farrah Fawcett) to pose as his wife for his undercover investigation of the murder in Acapulco. *Sunburn* was intended to be a vehicle built around Fawcett, but it surprisingly works very well due to her good comic performance and her excellent pairing with Grodin, who is the film's real star.

825 **Sunday Bloody Sunday** (1971) (BFA, G-English Language Foreign Film) *** Britain, United Artists, 110 min. *Dir* John Schlesinger (AN, BFA), *Scr* Penelope Gilliatt (AN, NS, NY, W), *Cin* Billy Williams, *Ed* Richard Marden (BFA), *Des* Luciana Arrighi, *Art* Norman Dorme, *Cos* Jocelyn Richards, *Mus* Ron Geesin, *Prod* Joseph Janni, *Assoc Prod* Teddy Joseph.

Cast: Glenda Jackson (AN, BFA), *Alex Greville,* Peter Finch (AN, NS, BFA), *Dr. Daniel Hirsh,* Murray Head, *Bob Elkin,* Peggy Ashcroft, *Mrs. Greville,* Maurice Denham, *Mr. Greville,* Vivian Pickles, *Alva Hodson,* Frank Windsor, *Bill Hodson,* Thomas Baptiste, *Prof. Johns,* Tony Britton, *George Harding,* Harold Goldblatt, *Daniel's Father,* Hannah Norbert, *Daniel's Mother,* Jon Finch, *Scotsman.* R.

Fine drama about an unusual love triangle. A doctor (Peter Finch) and an employment counselor (Glenda Jackson) are in love with the same man (Murray Head). The subject of homosexuality is sensitively handled and never exploited, and the characters never sink to the level of stereotypes. This could have been a great film if the storyline were stronger, but it lacks a needed punch.

826 **The Sunshine Boys** (1975) (GMC) *** United Artists, 111 min. *Dir* Herbert Ross, *Scr* Neil Simon (AN, W), based on his play, *Cin* David M. Walsh, *Ed* Margaret Booth, John F. Burnett, *Des* Albert Brenner (AN), *Prod* Ray Stark, *Assoc Prod* Roger M. Rothstein.

Cast: Walter Matthau (AN, GMC), *Willy Clark,* George Burns (A), *Al Lewis,* Richard Benjamin (G), *Ben Clark,* Lee Meredith, *Stage Nurse,* Carol Arthur, *Doris,* Rosetta LeNoire, *Nurse,* Jennifer Lee, *Helen,* F. Murray Abraham, *Mechanic,* Howard Hesseman, *Commercial Director,* Jim Cranna, *TV Director,* Ron Rifkin, *TV Floor Manager,* Fritz Feld, Jack Bernardi, *Men at Audition,* Garn Stephens, *Stage Manager,* Santos Morales, *Desk Clerk,* Archie Hahn, *Assistant at Audition.* PG. $7,200,000.

Fine bittersweet comedy about two old vaudevillians (Walter Matthau, George Burns), who reunite after many years of hatred. Richard Benjamin also stars as Matthau's nephew, who brings the two together for a television appearance. *The Sunshine Boys* is one of Neil Simon's best films, because his usual abundance of one-liners is not out of place when spoken by two comedians, and the three stars all give excellent performances. Simon based the characters on Smith and Dale.

827 **The Super Cops** (1974) *** MGM, 94 min. *Dir* Gordon Parks, Sr., *Scr* Lorenzo Semple, Jr., based on book by L.H. Whittmore, *Cin* Dick Kratina, *Ed* Harry Howard, *Art* Stephen Hendrickson, *Prod* William Belasco.

Cast: Ron Leibman, *Greenberg*, David Selby, *Hantz*, Sheila E. Frazier, *Sara*, Pat Hingle, *Lt. Novick*, Dan Frazier, *Krasna*, Joseph Sirola, *Lt. O'Shaughnessy*, Arny Freeman, *Judge Kellner*, Bernard Kates, *D.A. Heller*, Alex Colon, *Carlos*, Charles Turner, *Joe Hayes*, Ralph Wilcox, *John Hayes*, Al Fann, *Frank Hayes*, David Greenberg, *Detective Bassoff*, Robert Hantz, *Detective Neel*, Norman Bush, *Billy*, Arthur French, *Victor*, Tamu, *Girl*. R.

Typical police thriller about real-life New York undercover cops, Greenberg and Hantz, who were known on the streets as Batman and Robin due to their daring exploits. Unfortunately *The Super Cops* is not as wild as it should have been in order to faithfully recreate the craziness of the pair. This could have been another *French Connection* with the proper treatment, but as it stands, it is merely a better than average action film.

828 **Super Fly** (1972) *** Warner Bros., 96 min. *Dir* Gordon Parks, Jr., *Scr* Phillip Fenty, *Cin* James Signorelli, *Ed* Bob Brady, *Cos* Nate Adams, *Mus* Curtis Mayfield, *Prod* Sig Shore, *Assoc Prod* Irving Stimler.

Cast: Ron O'Neal, *Priest*, Carl Lee, *Eddie*, Sheila Frazier, *Georgia*, Julius W. Harris, *Scatter*, Charles McGregor, *Fat Freddie*, Nate Adams, *Dealer*, Polly Niles, *Cynthia*, Yvonne Delaine, *Mrs. Freddie*, Henry Shapiro, *Robbery Victim*, K.C., *Pimp*, Jim Richardson, *Junkie*, The Curtis Mayfield Experience. R. $6,300,000.

Well-made crime thriller about a drug pusher (Ron O'Neal), who decides to pull off one big killing before going straight, but he finds quitting is more difficult than he has anticipated. *Super Fly* has been criticized for supposedly glorifying drug pushers, but it really makes no moral judgments. In the inferior sequel *Super Fly T.N.T.*, O'Neal becomes mixed up in foreign politics and sells guns rather than drugs.

829 **Superfly T.N.T.** (1973) * Paramount, 87 min. *Dir* Ron O'Neal, *Scr* Alex Haley, *Story* Ron O'Neal, Sig Shore, *Cin* Robert Gaffney, *Ed* Bob Brady, *Des* Giuseppe Bassan, *Mus* Osibisa, *Prod* Sig Shore.

Cast: Ron O'Neal, *Priest*, Roscoe Lee Browne, *Dr. Lamine Sonko*, Sheila Frazier, *Georgia*, Robert Guillaume, *Jordan Gaines*, Jacques Sernas, *Matty Smith*, William Berger, *Lefevre*, Roy Bosler, *Customs Man*, Silvio Nardo, *George*, Olga Bisera, *Lisa*, Rik Boyd, *Rik*, Dominic Barto, *Rand*, Minister Dem, *General*, Jeannie McNeill, *Riding Instructress*, Dan Davis, *Pilot*, Luigi Orso, *Crew Chief*, Ennio Catalfamo, *Photographer*, Francesco Rachini, *Warehouse Custodian*. R. See *Superfly*.

830 **Superman** (1978) **** Warner Bros., 143 min. *Dir* Richard Donner, *Scr* Robert Benton, David Newman, Leslie Newman, Mario Puzo, based on characters created by Joel Shuster, Jerry Siegal, *Cin* Geoffrey Unsworth, *Ed* Stuart Baird (AN), *Des* John Barry, *Cos* Yvonne Blake, *Sp* Les Bowie, Colin Chilvers, Denys Coop, Roy Field, Derek Meddings, Zoran Perisic (A, BFA),

Mus John Williams (AN), *Prod* Pierre Spengler, *Exec Prod* Ilya Salkind, *Assoc Prod* Charles F. Greenlaw, Presented by Alexander Salkind.

Cast: Christopher Reeve, *Superman/Clark Kent*, Gene Hackman, *Lex Luthor*, Marlon Brando, *Jor-El*, Margot Kidder, *Lois Lane*, Jackie Cooper, *Perry White*, Ned Beatty, *Otis*, Glenn Ford, *Pa Kent*, Phyllis Thaxter, *Ma Kent*, Susannah York, *Lara*, Valerie Perrine, *Eve Teschmacher*, Marc McClure, *Jimmy Olsen*, Maria Schell, *Vond-Ah*, Trevor Howard, *First Elder*, Jeff East, *Young Clark Kent*, Harry Andrews, *Second Elder*, Terence Stamp, *Gen. Zod*, Jack O'Halloran, *Non*, Sarah Douglas, *Ursa*. PG. $82,500,000.

Excellent filmization of the famous comic book hero. *Superman* traces the super hero's history beginning on the doomed planet Krypton. The early sections of the film involving Krypton and Superman's growing up on the Kent farm are a bit slow, but they are probably necessary. The film really gets going when he starts his job as the "mild mannered reporter" for the *Daily Planet*. This section introduces all of the familiar characters and has Superman battling the evil Lex Luthor. The casting of these characters is superb and the actors really bring them to life, particularly Christopher Reeve who is equally convincing as Kent and as Superman.

831 **Support Your Local Gunfighter** (1971) ** United Artists, 92 min. *Dir* Burt Kennedy, *Scr* James Edward Grant, *Cin* Harry Stradling, Jr., *Ed* Bill Gulick, *Art* Phil Barber, *Cos* Lambert Marks, Pat Norris, *Mus* Jack Elliott, Allyn Ferguson, *Prod* William Finnegan, *Exec Prod* Burt Kennedy.

Cast: James Garner, *Latigo Smith*, Suzanne Pleshette, *Patience Barton*, Jack Elam, *Jug May*, Joan Blondell, *Jenny*, Harry Morgan, *Taylor Barton*, Marie Windsor, *Goldie*, Henry Jones, *Ez*, John Dehner, *Col. Ames*, Chuck Conners, *Swifty Morgan*, Dub Taylor, *Doc Schultz*, Kathleen Freeman, *Mrs. Perkins*, Ellen Corby, *Abigail*, Dick Curtis, *Bud Barton*, Herb Vigran, *Fat*, John Wheeler, *Croupier*, Mike Wagner, *Bartender*, Ben Cooper, *Colorado*, Willis Bouchey, *McLaglen*, Grady Sutton, *Storekeeper*, Walter Burke, *Morris*, Gene Evans, *Butcher*, Terry Wilson, *Thug*, Roy Glenn, *Headwaiter*, Virginia Capers, *Maid*, Pedro G. Gonzales, *Ortiz*. G.

Fair follow-up to western comedy *Support Your Local Sheriff*. In this installment James Garner deserts a madame, who wishes to marry him, and settle in the town of Purgatory, where he is mistaken for a gunfighter. The film has the same style of broad humor of its predecessor, which was slightly overrated, and is nearly as good, mainly due to Garner's fine underplaying.

832 **The Swarm** (1978) * Warner Bros., 116 min. *Dir* Irwin Allen, *Scr* Stirling Silliphant, based on novel by Arthur Herzog, *Cin* Fred J. Koenekamp, *Ed* Harold F. Kress, *Des* Stan Jolley, *Cos* Paul Zastupnevich (AN), *Sp* L.B. Abbott, *Mus* Jerry Goldsmith, *Prod* Irwin Allen.

Cast: Michael Caine, *Brad Crane*, Katharine Ross, *Helena*, Richard Widmark, *Gen. Slater*, Richard Chamberlain, *Dr. Hubbard*, Olivia de Havilland, *Maureen*, Ben Johnson, *Felix*, Lee Grant, *Anne MacGregor*, Jose Ferrer, *Dr. Andrews*, Patty Duke Astin, *Rita*, Slim Pickens, *Jud Hawkins*, Bradford Dillman, *Maj. Baker*, Fred MacMurray, *Clarence*, Henry Fonda, *Dr. Krim*, Cameron Mitchell, *Gen. Thompson*, Christian Juttner, *Paul Durant*, Morgan Paull, *Dr. Newman*, Alejandro Rey, *Dr. Martinez*, Don "Red" Barry, Pete Harris. PG. $7,700,000.

Ridiculous thriller about a swarm of South American killer bees heading toward the U.S. *The Swarm* must rank as one of the shoddiest major films to ever come from Hollywood, and everyone involved should have known better. The giant swarm is obviously nothing more than a group of dots painted onto the celluloid, which will hardly cause any audience tension. The subplots are so silly that the only audience relief comes when the bees attack the innocuous characters, miraculously without even leaving a trace on their skin.

833 **Swashbuckler** (1976) *** Universal, 101 min. *Dir* James Goldstone, *Scr* Jeffrey Bloom, *Story* Paul Wheeler, *Cin* Philip Lathrop, *Ed* Edward A. Biery, *Des* John Lloyd, *Cos* Burton Miller, *Mus* John Addison, *Chor* Geoffrey Holder, *Prod* Jennings Lang, *Exec Prod* Elliot Kastner, *Assoc Prod* William S. Gilmore, Jr.

Cast: Robert Shaw, *Ned Lynch*, James Earl Jones, *Nick Debrett*, Peter Boyle, *Lord Durant*, Genevieve Bujold, *Jane Barnet*, Beau Bridges, *Maj. Folly*, Geoffrey Holder, *Cudjo*, Avery Schreiber, *Polonski*, Tom Clancy, *Mr. Moonbeam*, Anjelica Huston, *Woman of Dark Visage*, Bernard Behrens, *Sir James Barnet*, Dorothy Tristan, *Alice*, Mark Baker, *Lute Player*, Kip Niven, *Willard Culverhill*, Tom Fitzsimmons, *Corporal*, Louisa Horton, *Lady Barnet*, Sid Haig, *Bald Pirate*, Robert Ruth, *Bearded Pirate*, Robert Morgan, *Peglegged Pirate*, Jon Cedar, *Pirate Gun Captain*. R.

Enjoyable pirate comedy that recalls the swashbucklers of the past. Robert Shaw and James Earl Jones star as two "good" pirates who attempt to rid Jamaica of the tyranny of its evil governor (Peter Boyle). *Swashbuckler* is all hokum and its not particularly clever, but in all honesty it is at least as good as most of Errol Flynn's not so brilliant swashbucklers.

834 **Sweet Revenge** (1976) *** United Artists, 89 min. *Dir* Jerry Schatzberg, *Scr* Marilyn Goldin, B.J. Perla, *Story* B.J. Perla, *Cin* Vilmos Zsigmond, *Ed* Richard Fetterman, Evan Lottman, *Art* Bill Kenney, *Mus* Paul Chihara, *Prod* Jerry Schatzberg.

Cast: Stockard Channing, *Dandy*, Sam Waterston, *LeClerq*, Norman Matlock, *John T*, Richard Doughty, *Andy*, Franklyn Ajaye, *Edmund*, Ed E. Villa, *Greg*, Evan Lottman, *Bailiff*. PG.

Fine character study of a female car thief (Stockard Channing), who becomes involved with a public defender (Sam Waterston), who is in love with her. The film has a good balance of comedy and drama, and features an excellent performance by Channing. *Sweet Revenge* was considered unsalable by the studio and was originally shelved, which is truly unfortunate. Original title, *Dandy, The All-American Girl*.

835 **T.R. Baskin** (1971) ** Paramount, 90 min. *Dir* Herbert Ross, *Scr* Peter Hyams, *Cin* Gerald Hirschfeld, *Ed* Maury Winetrobe, *Des* Albert Brenner, *Mus* Jack Ellison, *Prod* Peter Hyams.

Cast: Candice Bergen, *T.R. Baskin*, Peter Boyle, *Jack Mitchell*, James Caan, *Larry Moore*, Marcia Rodd, *Dayle Wigoda*, Erin O'Reilly, *Kathy*, Howard Platt, *Arthur*, William Wise, *Gary*, Jane Alderman, *Marsha*, Joy Mandel, *Linda*, Fawne Harriman, *Alice*, Hope Hommersand, *Eilene*, Mariann Walters, *Cab Driver*. PG.

Pretentious drama about a small town girl (Candice Bergen), who settles in Chicago to make a life for herself. The film wanders aimlessly detailing her many relationships with men, most of which are told through flashbacks, in a failed attempt to comment on contemporary society. *T.R. Baskin* is very dull, partially due to its bland cinéma vérité visual style.

836 **The Taking of Pelham One Two Three** (1974) *** United Artists, 104 min. *Dir* Joseph Sargent, *Scr* Peter Stone, based on novel by John Godey, *Cin* Owen Roizman, *Ed* Gerald Greenberg, Robert Q. Lovett, *Art* Gene Rudolf, *Cos* Anna Hill Johnstone, *Mus* David Shire, *Prod* Gabriel Katzka, Edgar J. Scherick, *Assoc Prod* Stephen F. Kesten.

Cast: Walter Matthau, *Lt. Garber*, Robert Shaw, *Blue*, Martin Balsam, *Green*, Hector Elizondo, *Grey*, Earl Hindman, *Brown*, Tony Roberts, *Warren LaSalle*, James Broderick, *Denny Doyle*, Dick O'Neill, *Correll*, Lee Wallace, *The Mayor*, Tom Pedi, *Caz Dolowicz*, Beatrice Winde, *Mrs. Jenkins*, Jerry Stiller, *Lt. Rico Patrone*, Nathan George, *Patrolman James*, Rudy Bond, *Police Commissioner*, Kenneth McMillan, *Borough Commander*, Doris Roberts, *Mayor's Wife*, Julius Harris, *Insp. Daniels*. R.

Exciting action film about the hijacking of a subway train under the streets of New York City. The gang of highjackers, led by Robert Shaw, seizes the train and holds it for ransom for $1,000,000. Most of the film is a battle of wits between Shaw and Walter Matthau, a Transit Authority detective. The two stars give excellent performances and prevent the abundance of talk from slowing down the film.

837 **Taking Off** (1971) **** Universal, 93 min. *Dir* Milos Forman, *Scr* Jean-Claude Carriere, Milos Forman, John Guare, John Klein, *Cin* Miroslav Ondricek, *Ed* John Carter, *Art* Robert Wightman, *Cos* Peggy Farrell, *Prod* Alfred W. Crown, *Assoc Prod* Michael Hausman.

Cast: Lynn Carlin, *Lynn Tyne*, Buck Henry, *Larry Tyne*, Linnea Heacock, *Jeannie Tyne*, Georgia Engel, *Margot*, Tony Harvey, *Tony*, Audra Lindley, *Ann Lockston*, Paul Benedict, *Ben Lockston*, Vincent Schiavelli, *Mr. Schiavelli*, David Gittler, *Jamie*, Ike and Tina Turner, *Themselves*, Rae Allen, *Mrs. Divito*, Corinna Cristobal, *Corinna Divito*, Allen Garfield (Goorwitz), *Norman*, Barry Del Rae, *Schuyler*, Frank Berle, *Committee Man*, Phillip Bruns, *Policeman*, Carly Simon, *Audition Singer*. R.

Fine satire of the generation gap. A teenage girl (Linnea Heacock) runs away from home and goes to an audition for rock singers. In their search for her, her parents (Lynn Carlin, Buck Henry) are opened up to new experiences, including marijuana and strip poker. *Taking Off* is a perceptive comedy that avoids many of the numerous clichés involving the subject. This is the first American film by Czechoslovakian film director Milos Forman.

838 **The Tamarind Seed** (1974) ** Britain, Avco Embassy, 123 min. *Dir* Blake Edwards, *Scr* Blake Edwards, based on novel by Evelyn Anthony, *Cin* Freddie Young, *Ed* Ernest Walter, *Art* Harry Pottle, *Mus* John Barry, *Prod* Ken Wales, *Assoc Prod* Johnny Goodman.

Cast: Julie Andrews, *Judith Farrow*, Omar Sharif, *Feodor Sverdlov*, Anthony Quayle, *Jack Loder*, Daniel O'Herlihy, *Fergus Stephenson*, Sylvia Sims, *Margaret Stephenson*, Oscar Homolka, *Gen. Golitsyn*, Bryan Marshall, *George MacLeod*, David Baron, *Richard Paterson*, Celia Bannerman, *Rachel*

Paterson, Roger Dann, *Col. Moreau*, Sharon Duce, *Sandy Mitchell*, George Mikell, *Maj. Sukalov*, Kate O'Mara, *Anna Skriabina*, Constantin De Goguel, *Dimitri Memenov*. PG.

Dull espionage love story starring Julie Andrews as a British civil servant, who meets and falls in love with a Russian agent (Omar Sharif), while on vacation in the Caribbean. Sharif has more than romance on his mind, as he attempts to turn her into an agent. Blake Edwards has always had difficulty with drama, and it definitely shows in *The Tamarind Seed*. Perhaps it should have been played for laughs.

839 **Taxi Driver** (1976) (AN, CF) ***** Columbia, 113 min. *Dir* Martin Scorsese (NS), *Scr* Paul Schrader, *Cin* Michael Chapman, *Ed* Marcia Lucas, Tom Rolf, Melvin Shapiro, *Art* Charles Rosen, *Mus* Bernard Herrmann (AN, BFA), *Prod* Michael And Julia Phillips.

Cast: Robert DeNiro (AN, NS, NY, LA), *Travis Bickle*, Cybill Shepherd, *Betsy*, Peter Boyle, *Wizard*, Jodie Foster (AN, NS, BFA), *Iris*, Albert Brooks, *Tom*, Leonard Harris, *Palantine*, Harvey Keitel, *Sport*, Norman Matlock, *Charlie T*, Harry Northup, *Doughboy*, Joe Spinell, *Personnel Officer*, Diahnne Abbott, *Concession Girl*, Steven Prince, *Andy, Gun Salesman*, Martin Scorsese, *Passenger Watching Silhouette*. R. $11,600,000.

Magnificent drama about a psychotic anti-social cab driver. *Taxi Driver* powerfully documents this character's descent into madness, which culminates in a bloody climax. Director Scorsese and scriptor Schrader deliberately leave out details of his personality, creating a more ambiguous and complex film. Scorsese's direction adds new meaning to the word intensity; DeNiro is about the only one who could play this chilling character. *Taxi Driver* is one of the most misunderstood and controversial films ever made. It is very shocking and will upset many viewers, but it is the most brilliant descent into hell ever put on film.

840 **Telefon** (1977) *** United Artists, 103 min. *Dir* Don Siegel, *Scr* Peter Hyams, Stirling Silliphant, based on novel by Walter Wager, *Cin* Michael Butler, *Ed* Douglas Stewart, *Des* Ted Haworth, *Art* William F. O'Brien, *Cos* Luster Bayless, Jane Robinson, Edna Taylor, *Mus* Lalo Schifrin, *Prod* James B. Harris.

Cast: Charles Bronson, *Borzov*, Lee Remick, *Barbara*, Donald Pleasence, *Dalchimsky*, Tyne Daly, *Putterman*, Alan Badel, *Col Malchenko*, Patrick Magee, *Gen. Strelsky*, Sheree North, *Marie Wills*, Frank Marth, *Harley Sandburg*, Helen Page Camp, Ray Jenson, *The Starks*, Jacqueline Scott, Ed Bakey, *The Hasslers*, John Mitchum, *Bascom*, Iggie Wolfington, *Rev. Diller*. PG. $4,350,000.

Above average cold war thriller. A group of hardline Stalinists reactivate a 20 year old Soviet plot, in which several undercover agents were planted in the U.S. ready to blow up key sites at any time, through posthypnotic suggestion. Charles Bronson and Lee Remick are two spies, who must stop Donald Pleasence from triggering these agents. *Telefon* nicely blends action with the obvious romance of the two leads.

841 **Tell Me That You Love Me, Junie Moon** (1970) ** Paramount, 113 min. *Dir* Otto Preminger, *Scr* Marjorie Kellogg, based on her novel, *Cin* Boris Kaufman, *Ed* Henry Berman, Dean O. Ball, *Des* Lyle Wheeler, *Cos* Ronald Talsky, *Mus* Philip Springer, *Prod* Otto Preminger, *Assoc Prod* Nat Rudich.

Cast: Liza Minnelli, *Junie Moon*, Ken Howard, *Arthur*, Robert Moore, *Warren*, James Coco, *Mario*, Kay Thompson, *Gregory*, Fred Williamson, *Beach Boy*, Ben Piazza, *Jesse*, Emily Yancy, *Solana*, Leonard Frey, *Guiles*, Clarice Taylor, *Minnie*, James Beard, *Sidney Wyner*, Julie Bovasso, *Ramona*, Gina Collins, *Lila*, Barbara Logan, *Mother Moon*, Nancy Marchand, *Nurse Oxford*, Lynn Milgrin, *Nurse Holt*. PG.

Dreary comedy-drama about three misfits, a physically scarred girl (Liza Minnelli), an epileptic (Ken Howard) and a paraplegic homosexual (Richard Moore), who meet at a hospital and decide to live together. The film fails to be sensitive and realistic, due to Otto Preminger's heavy handed treatment, which is far too broad, and the characters never rise above stereotypes.

842 **10** (1979) **** Orion, 120 min. *Dir* Blake Edwards, *Scr* Blake Edwards, *Cin* Frank Stanley, *Ed* Ralph E. Winters, *Des* Rodger Maus, *Cos* Pat Edwards, *Mus* Henry Mancini (AN), *Lyrics* Carol Bayer Sager, Robert Wells, *Prod* Tony Adams, Blake Edwards.

Cast: Dudley Moore, *George*, Julie Andrews, *Sam*, Bo Derek, *Jenny*, Robert Webber, *Hugh*, Dee Wallace, *Mary Lewis*, Sam Jones, *David*, Brian Dennehy, *Bartender*, Max Showalter, *Reverend*, Rad Daly, *Josh*, Nedra Volz, *Mrs. Kissel*, James Noble, *Fred Miles*, Virginia Kiser, *Ethel Miles*, John Hawker, *Covington*, Deborah Rush, *Dental Assistant*, Don Calfa, *Neighbor*. R. $36,000,000.

Excellent comedy about a man, who is suffering from mid-life crisis and drops everything to pursue an idyllic young woman on her honeymoon in Mexico. Blake Edwards has had a very uneven career and his comedy talent seemed to only take hold in his collaboration with Peter Sellers in the "Pink Panther" series, at lease until *10*. Edwards must have found the same inspiration with Dudley Moore, who is Sellers' equal as an all-around comedy actor. *10* is one of Edwards' most solid and consistently funny films.

843 **The Terminal Man** (1974) ** Warner Bros., 104 min. *Dir* Mike Hodges, *Scr* Mike Hodges, based on novel by Michael Crichton, *Cin* Richard H. Kline, *Ed* Robert Wolfe, *Art* Fred Harpman, *Cos* Nino Novarese, *Prod* Mike Hodges, *Assoc Prod* Michael Dryhurst.

Cast: George Segal, *Harry Benson*, Joan Hackett, *Dr. Janet Ross*, Richard A. Dysart, *Dr. John Ellis*, Jill Clayburgh, *Angela Black*, Donald Moffat, *Dr. Arthur McPherson*, Matt Clark, *Gerhard*, Michael C. Gwynne, *Dr. Robert Morris*, Norman Burton, *Det. Capt. Anders*, William Hansen, *Dr. Ezra Manon*, James Sikking, *Ralph Friedman*, Ian Wolfe, *The Priest*, Gene Borkan, Burke Byrnes, *Benson's Guards*, Jim Antonio, *Richards*, Jordan Rhodes, *Questioner #1*, Dee Carroll, *Night Nurse*, Jason Wingreen, *Instructor*, Steven Kanaly, *Edmonds*, Fred Sadoff, *Police Doctor*, Robert Ito, *Anesthetist*, Victor Argo, *Orderly*, Lee DeBroux, *Reporter*. PG.

Dull science fiction thriller about a scientist (George Segal), who has computers hooked to his brain, with tragic results. He is transformed into a homicidal maniac and goes on a murder spree. *The Terminal Man* is cold and unemotional and is too slowly paced to generate the needed thrills. Segal's excellent performance is the only thing to recommend. Michael Crichton's novels do not seem to translate well to film.

844 The Texas Chainsaw Massacre (1974) *** Bryanston, 83 min. *Dir* Tobe Hooper, *Scr* Kim Henkel, Tobe Hooper, *Cin* Daniel Pearl, *Ed* Larry Carroll, Sallye Richardson, *Art* Robert A. Burns, *Mus* Wayne Bell, Tobe Hooper, *Prod* Tobe Hooper, *Exec Prod* Jay Parsley, *Assoc Prod* Kim Henkel, Richard Saenz.

Cast: Marilyn Burns, *Sally*, Allen Danziger, *Jerry*, Paul A. Partain, *Franklin*, William Vail, *Kirk*, Teri McMinn, *Pam*, Edwin Neal, *Hitchhiker*, Jim Siedow, *Old Man*, Gunnar Hansen, *Leatherface*, John Dugan, *Grandfather*, Jerry Lorenz, *Pickup Driver*. R.

Powerful and shocking drama, based on a true story, about a family of psychopaths that murder a group of youths. *The Texas Chainsaw Massacre* is an extremely deceptive film, because some of its images and situations are so ghastly they make the film seem bloodier than it really is. This film has become a major cult film and has spawned numerous inferior imitations.

845 Thank God It's Friday (1978) * Columbia, 100 min. *Dir* Robert Klane, *Scr* Barry Armyan Bernstein, *Cin* James Crabe, *Ed* Richard Halsey, *Song* "Last Dance", *Mus* Paul Jabara (A), *Prod* Rob Cohen, *Exec Prod* Neil Bogart.

Cast: Valerie Landsburg, *Frannie*, Terri Nunn, *Jeannie*, Chick Vennera, *Marv*, Donna Summer, *Nicole*, Ray Vitte, *Bobby*, Mark Lonow, *Dave*, Andrea Howard, *Sue*, Jeff Goldblum, *Tony*, Robin Menker, *Maddy*, Debra Winger, *Jennifer*, John Friedrich, *Ken*, Paul Jabara, *Carl*, Marya Small, *Jackie*, Chuck Sacci, *Gus*, Hilary Beane, *Shirley*, DeWayne Jessie, *Floyd*, The Commodores. PG. $7,300,000.

Ridiculous musical comedy that consists entirely of one night in a gaudy and noisy disco. *Thank God It's Friday* is in reality a dim-witted variety show, rather than a true movie. Comedy routines and musical numbers serve as substitutes for a script, with little attempt at an intelligent storyline. This could be partially acceptable if the routines rose above stupidity, and the music was more than mere noise.

846 That'll Be the Day (1973) *** Britain, Mayfair, 90 min. *Dir* Claude Whatham, *Scr* Ray Connolly, *Cin* Peter Suschitzky, *Ed* Michael Bradsell, *Art* Brian Morris, *Prod* Sanford Lieberson, David Puttnam, *Exec Prod* Roy Baird, Presented by Nat Cohen.

Cast: David Essex, *Jim MacLaine*, Ringo Starr, *Mike*, Rosemary Leach, *Mrs. MacLaine*, James Booth, *Mr. MacLaine*, Billy Fury, *Stormy*, Keith Moon, *J.D.*, Rosalind Ayres, *Jeanette*, Robert Lindsay, *Terry*, Beth Morris, *Jean*, James Ottaway, *Granddad*, Verna Harvey, *Wendy*, Erin Geraghty, *Joan*, Deborah Watling, *Sandra*, Patti Love, *Sandra's Friend*, Daphne Oxenford, *Mrs. Sutcliffe*, Bernard Severn, *Sutcliffe*, Kim Braden, *Charlotte*. PG.

Well-made nostalgic film set in the late 1950's. Rock star David Essex stars as a working class youth, who has an uncertain future. His story is continued in *Stardust*, in which he becomes the leader of a successful rock group and eventually a legendary rock star. Both films are realistic and well-made, and Essex proves to be a fine actor.

847 There Was a Crooked Man... (1970) *** Warner Bros., 122 min. *Dir* Joseph L. Mankiewicz, *Scr* Robert Benton, David Newman, *Cin* Harry Stradling, Jr., Gene Milford, *Art* Edward Carrere, *Cos* Anna Hill Johnstone, *Mus* Charles Strouse, *Title Song*, *Mus* Lee Adams, Charles Strouse, *Prod* Joseph L. Mankiewicz.

Cast: Kirk Douglas, *Paris Pitman, Jr.*, Henry Fonda, *Woodward Lopeman*, Hume Cronyn, *Dudley Whinner*, Warren Oates, *Floyd Moon*, Burgess Meredith, *Missouri Kid*, Arthur O'Connell, *Mr. Lomax*, Martin Gabel, *Warden LeGoff*, John Randolph, *Cyrus McNutt*, Michael Blodgett, *Coy Cavendish*, Claudia McNeil, *Madame*, Alan Hale, Jr., *Tobaccy*, Victor French, *Whiskey*, Lee Grant, *Mrs. Bullard*, Jeanne Cooper, *Prostitute*, C.K. Yang, *Ah-Ping Woo*, Bert Freed, *Skinner*, Gene Evans, *Col. Wolff*, Pamela Hensley, *Edwina*, Barbara Rhoades, *Miss Brundage*. R.

Unusual western drama starring Kirk Douglas as an outlaw sent to prison for a robbery and Henry Fonda as the arresting sheriff, who later becomes the warden of the same Arizona prison. Douglas and Fonda are excellent as the adversaries, and the film has a fine mix of comedy and drama, with some social commentary about prison reform thrown in.

848 There'a a Girl in My Soup (1970) ****** Britain, Columbia, 96 min. *Dir* Roy Boulting, *Scr* Terence Frisby, *Additional Dialogue*, Peter Kortner, based on play by Terence Frisby, *Cin* Harry Waxman, *Ed* Martin Charles, *Art* John Howell, *Cos* Vangie Harrison, *Mus* Mike D'Abo, *Prod* John Boulting, M.J. Frankovich, *Exec Prod* John Dark.

Cast: Peter Sellers, *Robert Danvers*, Goldie Hawn, *Marion*, Tony Britton, *Andrew*, Nicky Henson, *Jimmy*, John Comer, *John*, Diana Dors, *John's Wife*, Gabrielle Drake, *Julia*, Geraldine Sherman, *Caroline*, Judy Campbell, *Lady Heather*, Nicola Pagett, *Clare*, Christopher Cazenove, *Nigel*, Robin Parkinson, Ray Skelton, *Reporters*, Carolyn Seymour, *Nigel's Girlfriend*, Raf De La Torre, *Leguestier*. R. $4,500,000.

Fair comedy starring Peter Sellers as a middle-aged television gourmet, who becomes disenchanted with growing older and tries to regain his youth by living it up, which includes having an affair with a young kooky woman (Goldie Hawn). *There's a Girl in My Soup* has a few fine comic moments, due to the excellent underplaying of Sellers, but the film is very uneven.

849 They Call Me Mr. Tibbs (1970) ****** United Artists, 108 min. *Dir* Gordon Douglas, *Scr* Alan R. Trustman, James R. Webb, *Story* Alan R. Trustman, based on character created by John Dudley Ball, *Cin* Gerald Finnerman, *Ed* Bud Molin, *Art* Addison Hehr, *Mus* Quincy Jones, *Prod* Herbert Hirschman, *Exec Prod* Walter Mirisch.

Cast: Sidney Poitier, *Virgil Tibbs*, Martin Landau, *Rev. Logan Sharpe*, Barbara McNair, *Valerie Tibbs*, Anthony Zerbe, *Rice Weedon*, Jeff Corey, *Capt. Marden*, David Sheiner, *Herbert Kenner*, Juano Hernandez, *Mealie*, Norma Crane, *Marge Garfield*, Edward Asner, *Woody Garfield*, Ted Gehring, *Sgt. Deutsch*, Beverly Todd, *Puff*, Linda Towne, *Joy Sturges*, George Spell, *Andrew*, Wanda Spell, *Gineer*. PG.

Fair sequel to *In the Heat of the Night* with Sidney Poitier recreating his role of black detective Virgil Tibbs. He investigates the murder of a girl, in which a priest-friend (Martin Landau) may be guilty. This is nothing more than a standard cop film, that's only reason for existing is the character of Tibbs, who returned in an equally dull film, titled *The Organization*, to battle drug dealers in San Francisco.

850 They Might Be Giants (1971) ****** Universal, 88 min. *Dir* Anthony Harvey, *Scr* James Goldman, based on his play, *Cin* Victor J. Kemper, *Ed* Gerald

Greenberg, *Des* John Robert Lloyd, *Cos* Ann Roth, *Mus* John Barry, *Prod* John Foreman, *Assoc Prod* Frank Coffey.

Cast: Joanne Woodward, *Dr. Mildred Watson*, George C. Scott, *Justin Playfair*, Jack Gilford, *Wilbur Peabody*, Lester Rawlins, *Blevins Playfair*, Ron Weyand, *Dr. Strauss*, Kitty Winn, *Grace*, Peter Fredericks, *Grace's Boyfriend*, Sudie Bond, *Maud*, Jenny Egan, *Miss Finch.* G.

Unusual comedy starring George C. Scott as a mentally ill patient, who is suffering from delusions of grandeur; he thinks he is Sherlock Holmes. His brother wants to have him committed and hires a female psychiatrist (Joanne Woodward) to examine him. Her name just happens to be Dr. Watson. This opens the film up to many comic possibilities, but unfortunately it misses them. Scott and Woodward give excellent performances, though.

851 **They Only Kill Their Masters** (1972) ** MGM, 97 min. *Dir* James Goldstone, *Scr* Lane Slate, *Cin* Michel Hugo, *Ed* Edward A. Biery, *Art* Lawrence G. Paull, *Mus* Perry Botkin, Jr., *Prod* William Belasco, *Assoc Prod* Barry Mendelson.

Cast: James Garner, *Abel*, Katharine Ross, *Kate*, Hal Holbrook, *Watkins*, Harry Guardino, *Streeter*, June Allyson, *Mrs. Watkins*, Christopher Connelly, *John*, Tom Ewell, *Walter*, Peter Lawford, *Campbell*, Edmond O'Brien, *George*, Arthur O'Connell, *Ernie*, Ann Rutherford, *Gloria*, Art Metrano, *Malcolm*, Harry Basch, *Mayor*, PG.

Dull mystery thriller starring James Garner as a small town police chief investigating the death of a woman, who was apparently killed by her dog. As is predictable, Garner discovers there is far more to her death, but his investigation leads to a very disappointing and ridiculous conclusion. Garner's persona is the best aspect of *They Only Kill Their Masters*, which seems better suited for television.

852 **The Thief Who Came to Dinner** (1973) ** Warner Bros., 105 min. *Dir* Bud Yorkin, *Scr* Walter Hill, based on novel by Terence Lore Smith, *Cin* Philip Lathrop, *Ed* John C. Harger, *Des* Polly Platt, *Mus* Henry Mancini, *Prod* Bud Yorkin, *Assoc Prod* D. Michael Moore.

Cast: Ryan O'Neal, *Webster*, Jacqueline Bisset, *Laura*, Warren Oates, *Dave*, Jill Clayburgh, *Jackie*, Charles Cioffi, *Henderling*, Ned Beatty, *Deams*, Austin Pendleton, *Zukovsky*, Gregory Sierra, *Dynamite*, Michael Murphy, *Ted* John Hillerman, *Laxker*, Alan Oppenheimer, *Insurance Man*, Margaret Fairchild, *Mrs. Donner*, Jack Manning, *Tom*, Richard O'Brien, *Sgt. Del Conte*, George Morfogen, *Rivera*. PG.

Fair comedy crime thriller starring Ryan O'Neal as a jewel thief, who poses as a member of high society in order to aid in plotting his thefts. Warren Oates co-stars as a cop, who knows O'Neal is guilty, but is unable to prove it. *The Thief Who Came to Dinner* is poorly paced and totally lacking in energy, and the characters and the humor tend to be flat.

853 **Thieves Like Us** (1974) *** United Artists, 123 min. *Dir* Robert Altman, *Scr* Robert Altman, Calder Willingham, Joan Tewkesbury, based on novel by Edward Anderson, *Cin* Jean Boffety, *Ed* Lou Lombardo, *Prod* Jerry Bick, *Assoc Prod* Robert Eggenweiler, Thomas Hal Philips.

Cast: Keith Carradine, *Bowie*, Shelly Duvall, *Keechie*, John Schuck, *Chicamaw*, Bert Remsen, *T-Dub*, Louise Fletcher, *Mattie*, Ann Latham, *Lula*,

Tom Skerritt, *Dee Mobley*, Al Scott, *Capt. Stammers*, John Roper, *Jasbo*, Mary Waits, *Noel*, Rodney Lee, Jr., *James Mattingly*, William Watters, *Alvin*. R.

Unusual period crime thriller about a Bonnie and Clyde-type couple on the run. A young prisoner (Keith Carradine) escapes with a slightly psychotic criminal (John Schuck) to join his partner (Bert Remsen) in a series of bank robberies. He falls for a young woman (Shelly Duvall) and leaves the gang in an attempt to go straight. Robert Altman, as in his other films, has taken a specific genre and ignores all its rules. *Thieves Like Us* contains little action and concentrates more on character.

854 **Three Days of the Condor** (1975) *** Paramount, 117 min. *Dir* Sydney Pollack, *Scr* David Rayfiel, Lorenzo Semple, Jr., based on novel *Six Days of the Condor* by James Grady, *Cin* Owen Roizman, *Ed* Don Guidice, Frederic Steinkamp (AN), *Des* Stephen Grimes, *Art* Gene Rudolf, *Cos* Theoni V. Aldredge, *Mus* Dave Grusin, *Prod* Stanley Schneider.

Cast: Robert Redford, *Turner*, Faye Dunaway, *Kathy*, Cliff Robertson, *Higgens*, Max Von Sydow, *Joubert*, John Houseman, *Mr. Wabash*, Addison Powell, *Atwood*, Walter McGinn, *Barber*, Tina Chen, *Janice*, Michael Kane, *Wicks*, Don McHenry, *Dr. Lappe*, Michael Miller, *Fowler*, Jess Osuna, *Mitchell*, Dino Narizzano, *Thomas*, Helen Stenberg, *Mrs. Russell*, Patrick Gorman, *Martin*, Hansford Rowe, Jr., *Jennings*, Carlin Glynn, *Mae Barber*, Hank Garrett, *Mailman*, Arthur French, *Messenger*, Jay Devlin, *Tall Thin Man*. R. $20,015,000.

Well-made action thriller about a CIA researcher (Robert Redford), who suddenly becomes a fugitive from the CIA, when he discovers corruption within the organization. *Three Days of the Condor* is essentially a chase film from the beginning, in which Redford discovers the mass-murder of his research unit. Unlike most such films, the protagonist's survival depends more on his wits than on violence. Sydney Pollack, not generally known as an action director, handles the action scenes very well.

855 **The Three Musketeers** (1974) ***** 20th Century–Fox, 107 min. *Dir* Richard Lester, *Scr* George MacDonald Fraser, based on novel by Alexander Dumas, *Cin* David Watkin, *Ed* John Victor Smith, *Mus* Michel Legrand, *Prod* Alexander Salkind.

Cast: Michael York, *D'Artagnan*, Oliver Reed, *Athos*, Richard Chamberlain, *Aramis*, Frank Finlay, *Porthos*, Raquel Welch (GMC), *Constance*, Christopher Lee, *Rochefort*, Jean-Pierre Cassel, *Louis XIII*, Geraldine Chaplin, *Anne of Austria*, Simon Ward, *Buckingham*, Faye Dunaway, *Milady*, Charlton Heston, *Cardinal Richelieu*, Spike Milligan, *M. Bonancieux*, Roy Kinnear, Nicole Calfan, Sybil Danning. PG. $11,435,000.

Splendid film adaptation of Alexander Dumas' classic novel. Richard Lester has created a masterpiece of slapstick comedy, without sacrificing the qualities of the story, and he completely stays within the confines of the period without resorting to cheap anachronisms for laughs. Lester manages to make it all seem original with his usual dose of satirical cynicism, mixed with his superb comic timing. Originally filmed as one long epic *The Three Musketeers* was released in two equally brilliant parts, *The Three Musketeers* and *The Four Musketeers*. After numerous screen versions, it's about time someone got it right.

856 **Three Women** (1977) ***** 20th Century–Fox, 122 min. *Dir* Robert Altman, *Scr* Robert Altman, *Cin* Charles Rosher, *Ed* Dennis Hill, *Art* James D. Vance, *Mus* Gerald Busby, *Prod* Robert Altman.

Cast: Shelly Duvall (LA, CF), *Millie*, Sissy Spacek (NY), *Pinky*, Janice Rule, *Willie*, Robert Fortier, *Edgar*, Ruth Nelson, John Cromwell, *Pinky's Parents*, Sierra Pecheur, *Bunweill*, Craig Richard Nelson, *Mr. Maas*, Maysie Hoy, Belita Moreno, *Hospital Attendants*, Leslie Ann Hudson, Patricia Ann Hudson, *Hospital Twins*, Beverly Ross, *Deidre*, John Davey, *Dr. Norton*. PG.

Beautiful surrealistic film about personality transference. Two young lonely women (Shelley Duvall, Sissy Spacek), who work at a senior citizen's health center, become friends and share an apartment. Spacek idolizes Duvall and after a suicide attempt Spacek takes on Duvall's personality. Robert Altman based this film on a dream he had and the film plays like one. *Three Women* is reminiscent of Bergman's *Persona*, but unlike that overrated classic, it is merely confusing rather than confused.

857 **Thunder and Lightning** (1977) *** 20th Century–Fox, 93 min. *Dir* Corey Allen, *Scr* William Hjortsberg, *Cin* James Pergola, *Ed* Anthony Redman, *Cos* Dyke Davis, *Mus* Andy Stein, *Prod* Roger Corman.

Cast: David Carradine, *Harley*, Kate Jackson, *Nancy Sue*, Roger C. Carmel, *Ralph, Jr.*, Sterling Holloway, *Hobe*, Ed Barth, *Rudi*, Ron Feinberg, *Bubba*, George Murdock, *Jake*, Pat Cranshaw, *Taylor*, Charles Napier, *Jim Bob*, Hope Pomerance, *Mrs. Hunnicutt*, Malcolm Jones, *Rainey*. PG.

Above-average moonshine chase film set in the Florida everglades. David Carradine stars as a moonshiner, who is in competition with Roger C. Carmel, who also happens to be the father of Carradine's girlfriend, Kate Jackson. *Thunder and Lightning* has a very skimpy plot, but it is filled with many exciting chases, both in cars and on water, and the pacing keeps things moving briskly.

858 **Thunderbolt and Lightfoot** (1974) *** United Artists, 115 min. *Dir* Michael Cimino, *Scr* Michael Cimino, *Cin* Frank Stanley, *Ed* Ferris Webster, *Art* Tambi Larsen, *Mus* Dee Barton, *Prod* Robert Daley.

Cast: Clint Eastwood, *Thunderbolt*, Jeff Bridges (AN), *Lightfoot*, George Kennedy, *Red Leary*, Geoffrey Lewis, *Goody*, Catherine Bach, *Melody*, Gary Busey, *Curly*, Jack Dodson, *Vault Manager*, Gene Elman, *Tourist*, Burton Gilliam, *Welder*, Roy Jenson, *Dunlop*, Claudia Lennear, *Secretary*, Bill McKinney, *Crazy Driver*, Vic Tayback, *Mario*. R. $9,100,000.

Above-average Clint Eastwood action film. The plot involves the search for hidden loot, in which Eastwood and his new partner Jeff Bridges are forced to team up with Eastwood's sadistic old colleague George Kennedy and his partner Geoffrey Lewis. *Thunderbolt and Lightfoot* has its quota of action, but there is a stronger emphasis on character than in most other Eastwood films. This was Michael Cimino's first film.

859 **THX-1138** (1971) *** Warner Bros., 88 min. *Dir* George Lucas, *Scr* George Lucas, Walter Murch, *Story* George Lucas, *Cin* Albert Kihn, Dave Myers, *Ed* George Lucas, *Des* Michael Haller, *Cos* Donald Longhurst, *Mus* Lalo Schifrin, *Prod* Francis Coppola, Lawrence Sturhahn, *Assoc Prod* Ed Folger.

Cast: Robert Duvall, *THX*, Donald Pleasence, *SEN*, Pedro Colley, *SRT*, Maggie McOmie, *LUH*, Ian Wolfe, *PTO*, Sid Haig, *NCH*, Marshall Efron, *TWA*, John Pearce, *DWY*, Johnny Weismuller, Jr., Robert Feero, *Chrome Robots*, Irene Forrest, *IMM*, Claudette Blessing, *ELC*. PG.

Strange science-fiction drama set in a sterile underground society, where sex is forbidden. Robert Duvall stars as a man who rebels against the system. *THX-1138* is slow and deliberately paced, but it has many compelling images and scenes, including a tense chase scene through the city's tunnels. This was George Lucas' feature film debut, which he based on his award winning student film.

860 **Time After Time** (1979) ******** Britain, Warner Bros., 112 min. *Dir* Nicholas Meyer, *Scr* Nicholas Meyer, *Story* Karl Alexander, Steve Hayes, *Cin* Paul Lohmann, *Ed* Donn Cambern, *Des* Edward C. Carfagno, *Sp* Jim Blount, Larry Fuentes, *Mus* Miklos Rozsa, *Prod* Herb Jaffe, *Assoc Prod* Steven-Charles Jaffe.

Cast: Malcolm McDowell, *H.G. Wells*, David Warner, *Stevenson*, Mary Steenburgen, *Amy*, Charles Cioffi, *Lt. Mitchell*, Andonia Katsaros, *Mrs. Turner*, Patti D'Arbanville, *Shirley*, Geraldine Baron, *Carol*, Kent Williams, *Assistant*, James Garrett, *Edwards*, Keith McConnell, *Harding*, Leo Lewis, *Richardson*, Karin Mary Shea, *Jenny*, Lauri Main, *Insp. Greyson*, Joseph Maher, *Adams*. PG. $6,300,000.

Excellent science-fiction adventure that mixes history and fiction. H.G. Wells (Malcolm McDowell) invents a time machine, but Jack the Ripper (David Warner) takes it into the future, stopping in present day San Francisco. Wells discovers the killer's whereabouts and sets out after him, where he meets and falls in love with a bank teller (Mary Steenburgen). *Time After Time* is a wonderful romantic thriller, that nicely balances humor and tension, while at the same time examining the differences between the past and the present.

861 **Tom Sawyer** (1973) ****** United Artists, 104 min. *Dir* Don Taylor, *Scr* Richard M. and Robert B. Sherman, based on novel *The Adventures of Tom Sawyer* by Mark Twain, *Cin* Frank Stanley, *Ed* Marion Rothman, *Des* Philip Jefferies (AN), *Cos* Donfeld (AN), *Mus* Richard M. and Robert B. Sherman (AN), *Chor* Danny Daniels, *Prod* Arthur P. Jacobs, *Exec Prod* Walter Bien, *Assoc Prod* Frank Capra, Jr.

Cast: Johnny Whitaker, *Tom Sawyer*, Celeste Holm, *Aunt Polly*, Warren Oates, *Muff Potter*, Jeff East, *Huckleberry Finn*, Jodie Foster, *Becky Thatcher*, Lucille Benson, *Widder Douglas*, Henry Jones, *Mr. Dobbins*, Noah Keen, *Judge Thatcher*, Dub Taylor, *Clayton*, Richard Eastham, *Doc Robinson*, Sandy Kenyon, *Constable Clemens*, Joshua Hill Lewis, *Cousin Sidney*, Susan Joyce, *Cousin Mary*, Steve Hogg, *Ben Rogers*, Kunu Hank, *Injun Joe*. G. $5,000,000.

Well-made but juvenile musical version of Mark Twain's classic novel. The original story remains basically intact, but in this film version it is too genteel, despite the generally fine cast and the authentic settings. The relatively minor success of this *Tom Sawyer* led to a natural sequel, *Huckleberry Finn*, which is however a total shambles and far more juvenile than its predecessor.

862 **Tommy** (1975) *** Britain, Columbia, 111 min. *Dir* Ken Russell, *Scr* Ken Russell, based on rock opera by Peter Townsend, *Cin* Dick Bush, Robin Lehman, Ronnie Taylor, *Ed* Stuart Baird, *Des* Paul Dufficey, *Art* John Clark, *Mus* Peter Townsend, John Entwhistle, Keith Moon, *Prod* Ken Russell, Robert Stigwood, *Exec Prod* Christopher Stamp, Beryl Vertue.

Cast: Roger Daltrey, *Tommy*, Ann-Margret (AN, G), *Nora Walker*, Oliver Reed, *Frank Hobbs*, Elton John, *Pinball Wizard*, Eric Clapton, *Preacher*, Keith Moon, *Uncle Ernie*, Jack Nicholson, *Specialist*, Robert Powell, *Capt. Walker*, Paul Nicholas, *Cousin Kevin*, Tina Turner, *Acid Queen*, Barry Winch, *Young Tommy*, Victoria Russell, *Sally Simpson*, The Who (Roger Daltrey, John Entwhistle, Keith Moon, Peter Townsend). PG. $16,000,000.

Bizarre film musical based on the legendary rock opera by The Who. Roger Daltrey, the lead singer of the group, stars in the title role as a young man who is deaf, dumb and blind due to a childhood trauma, and becomes a new messiah. The outlandishness of the story lends itself well to Ken Russell's surrealistic directorial style. The story is told entirely through its musical sequences, as *Tommy* contains no dialogue.

863 **Tora! Tora! Tora!** (1970) ** U.S./Japan, 20th Century—Fox, 143 min. *Dir* Richard Fleischer, Kinji Fukasaku, Toshio Masuda, *Scr* Larry Forrester, Ryuzo Kikushima, Hideo Oguni based on books by Ladislas Farago and Gordon W. Prange, *Cin* Osami Furuya, Sinsaku Himeda, Masamichi Satoh, Charles F. Wheeler (AN), *Ed* Inoue Chikaya, Pembroke J. Herring, James E. Newcom (AN), *Art* Richard Day, Taizoh Kawashima, Toshiro Muraki, Jack Martin Smith (AN), *Mus* Jerry Goldsmith, *Prod* Elmo Williams, *Assoc Prod* Keinosuke Kubo, Otto Lang, Masayuki Takagi.

Cast: Martin Balsam, *Adm. Kimmel*, Soh Yamamura, *Adm. Yamamoto*, Jason Robards, *Gen. Short*, Joseph Cotten, *Henry Stimson*, Tatsuya Mihashi, *Cmdr. Genda*, E.G. Marshall, *Lt. Col. Bratton*, Takahiro Tamura, *Lt. Cmdr. Fuchida*, James Whitmore, *Adm. Halsey*, Eijiro Tono, *Adm. Nagumo*, Wesley Addy, *Lt. Cmdr. Kramer*, Shogo Shimada, *Ambassador Nomura*, Frank Aletter, *Lt. Cmdr. Thomas*, Koreya Senda, *Prince Konoye*, Leon Ames, *Frank Knox*, Junya Usami, *Adm. Yoshida*, Richard Anderson, *Capt. John Earle*, Kazuo Kitamura, *Foreign Minister Matsuoka*, Keith Andres, *Gen. George C. Marshall*, Edward Andrews, *Adm. Stark*, Neville Brand, *Lt. Kaminsky*, Leora Dana, *Mrs. Kramer*, Asao Uchida, *Gen. Tojo*, George Macready, *Cordell Hull*. G. $14,530,000.

Overlong and drawn out historical drama about the truth behind the Japanese attack on Pearl Harbor. *Tora! Tora! Tora!* is extremely detailed and very realistic, but that unfortunately is the source of its flaws. The film tends to be dull and totally lacking in drama, resembling a history lecture, until the climactic battle, which is one of the most spectacular and breathtaking ever filmed.

864 **A Touch of Class** (1973) (AN) *** Britain, Avco Embassy, 106 min. *Dir* Melvin Frank, *Scr* Melvin Frank, Jack Rose (AN), *Cin* Austin Dempster, *Ed* Bill Butler, *Des* Terry Marsh, *Art* Alan Tompkins, *Mus* John Cameron (AN), *Song* "All That Love Went to Waste", *Mus* George Barrie (AN), *Lyrics* Sammy Cahn (AN), *Prod* Melvin Frank.

Cast: George Segal (GMC), *Steve Blackburn*, Glenda Jackson (A, GMC), *Vicki Allessio*, Paul Sorvino, *Walter Menkes*, Hildegard Neil, *Gloria Blackburn*, Cec Linder, *Wendell Thompson*, K. Callan, *Patty Menkes*, Mary Barclay, *Marsha Thompson*, Michael Elwyn, *Cecil*, Nadim Sawalha, *Night Hotel Manager*, Ian Thompson, *Derek*, Eve Karpf, *Miss Ramos*, David De Keyser, *Dr. Alvarez*, Gaye Brown, *Dora French*. PG. $8,400,000.

Fine situation comedy about infidelity. A married American man (George Segal), living in London, meets and falls in love with a divorced Englishwoman (Glenda Jackson). Segal takes Jackson on a disastrous rendezvous in Spain, but they continue their affair back in London, with Segal running back and forth between Jackson and his wife. *A Touch of Class* is a nice pleasant comedy, featuring fine performances by Segal and Jackson, but is hardly the great film it was thought to be.

865 **The Towering Inferno** (1974) (AN) ** 20th Century–Fox/Warner Bros., 165 min. *Dir* John Guillermin, Irwin Allen (action sequences only), *Scr* Stirling Silliphant, based on novels *The Tower* by Richard Martin Stern, and *The Glass Inferno* by Frank M. Robinson and Thomas N. Scortia, *Cin* Joseph Biroc, Fred Koenekamp (A), *Ed* Carl Kress, Harold F. Kress (A), *Des* William Creber (AN), *Art* Ward Preston (AN), *Cos* Paul Zastupnevich, *Mus* John Williams (AN), *Sp* A.D. Flowers, Logan Frazee, *Prod* Irwin Allen, *Assoc Prod* Sidney Marshall.

Cast: Steve McQueen, *Michael O'Hallorhan*, Paul Newman, *Doug Roberts*, William Holden, *James Duncan*, Faye Dunaway, *Susan Franklin*, Fred Astaire (AN, G), *Harlee Claiborne*, Susan Blakely, *Patty Simmons*, Richard Chamberlain, *Roger Simmons*, Jennifer Jones, *Lisolette Mueller*, O.J. Simpson, *Jernigan*, Robert Vaughn, *Senator Gary Parker*, Robert Wagner, *Dan Bigelow*, Susan Flannery, *Lorrie*, Sheila Matthews, *Paula Ramsay*, Norman Burton, *Will Giddings*, Jack Collins, *Mayor Robert Ramsey*, Don Gordon, *Kappy*, Felton Perry, *Scott*, Gregory Sierra, *Carlos*, Ernie Orsatti, *Mark*. PG. $50,000,000.

Spectacular, but idiotic disaster film. A fire breaks out in the world's tallest building, trapping a group of rich stereotypes on the top floor at a party. The special effects are better than average for this kind of film, but that does not compensate for the poor script, which contains inane dialogue, cardboard characters (possibly intentional since cardboard burns quickly), and implausible situations, e.g. tanks atop the building that contain enough water to fill the Pacific Ocean. With this film the disaster genre reached its peak and quickly died afterwards.

866 **Trackdown** (1976) * United Artists, 98 min. *Dir* Richard T. Heffron, *Scr* Paul Edwards, *Story* Ivan Nagy, *Cin* Gene Polito, *Ed* Anthony De Marco, *Art* Vincent M. Cresciman, *Mus* Charles Bernstein, *Prod* Bernard Schwartz.

Cast: Jim Mitchum, *Jim*, Karen Lamm, *Betsy*, Anne Archer, *Barbara*, Erik Estrada, *Chucho*, Cathy Lee Crosby, *Lynn*, Vince Cannon, *Johnny*, John Kerry, *Sgt. Miller*, Robert Rodriguez, *Feo*, Ernie Wheelwright, *Rosey*, Zitto Kazann, *Curtain*, Elizabeth Chauvet, *Billie*. R.

Dull thriller about a cowboy (Jim Mitchum) searching through the sleazy streets of Los Angeles for his runaway teenage sister (Karen Lamm), who has become a prostitute. If not for the nudity and violence *Trackdown* would resemble a television film. The story is shallow and unexciting and Mitchum's dull screen persona is no consolation.

867 The Train Robbers (1973) * Warner Bros., 92 min. *Dir* Burt Kennedy, *Cin* William H. Clothier, *Ed* Frank Santillo, *Art* Alfred Sweeney, *Mus* Dominic Frontiere, *Prod* Michael Wayne.

Cast: John Wayne, *Lane*, Ann-Margret, *Mrs. Lowe*, Rod Taylor, *Grady*, Ben Johnson, *Jessie*, Christopher George, *Calhoun*, Bobby Vinton, *Ben Young*, Jerry Gatlin, *Sam Turner*, Ricardo Montalban, *Pinkerton Man*. PG.

Absolutely dismal western adventure. John Wayne has made some bad films in his career, but this must rank as his worst. The unbelievably simple plot consists of Wayne and his friends riding off to recover some stolen gold and then riding back, which is interspersed with occasional bits of stupid dialogue. The filmmakers did not even attempt to make this film look good; their apathy is obvious.

868 The Traveling Executioner (1970) *** MGM, 95 min. *Dir* Jack Smight, *Scr* Garrie Batesman, *Cin* Philip Lathrop, *Ed* Neil Travis, *Art* Edward Carfagno, George W. Davis, *Cos* Norman Burza, Kitty Mager, Edward Marks, Marilyn Matthews, *Mus* Jerry Goldsmith, *Prod* Jack Smight.

Cast: Stacy Keach, *Jonas Candide*, Marianna Hill, *Gundred Hezallerliebst*, Bud Cort, *Jimmy*, Graham Jarvis, *Doc Prittle*, James J. Sloyan, *Piquant*, M. Emmet Walsh, *Warden Brodski*, John Bottoms, *Lawyer*, Ford Rainey, *Stanley Mae*, James Greene, *Gravey Combs*, Sammy Reese, *Priest*, Stefan Gierasch, *Willy Hezallerliebst*, Logan Ramsey, *La Follette*, Charles Tyner, *Virgil*, William Mims, *Lynn*, Val Avery, *Jake*, Walter Barnes, *Sheriff*, Charles Briggs, *Zak*. R.

Fine period black comedy starring Stacy Keach as the title character, who travels around the country with his own electric chair charging prisons for his services. Unfortunately he falls in love with one of his prospective victims (Marianna Hill). *The Traveling Executioner* is certainly an unusual film and is quite funny, despite its potentially offensive subject. This is one of Jack Smight's best films.

869 Travels with My Aunt (1972) **** Britain, MGM, 109 min. *Dir* George Cukor, *Scr* Jay Presson Allen, Hugh Wheeler, based on novel by Graham Greene, *Cin* Douglas Slocombe (AN), *Ed* John Bloom, *Des* John Box (AN), *Art* Robert W. Laing, Gil Parrando (AN), *Cos* Anthony Powell (A), *Mus* Tony Hatch, *Prod* James Cresson, George Cukor, Robert Fryer.

Cast: Maggie Smith (AN), *Aunt Augusta*, Alec McCowen, *Henry*, Lou Gossett, *Wordsworth*, Robert Stevens, *Visconti*, Cindy Williams, *Tooley*, Robert Flemyng, *Crowder*, Jose Luis Lopez Vazquez, *Dambreuse*, Raymond Gerome, *Mario*, Daniel Emilfork, *Hakim*, Corrine Marchand, *Louise*, John Hamill, *Crowder's Man*, David Swift, *Detective*, Bernard Holley, *Bobby*, Valerie White, *Mme. Dambreuse*, Antonio Pica, *Elegant Man*, Alex Savage, *Minister*, Olive Behrendt, *Madame*, Nora Norman, *Stripper*. PG.

Wonderful comedy following the crazy adventures of an eccentric English woman (Maggie Smith), who takes her bewildered nephew (Alec McCowen) along, after meeting for the first time at his mother's funeral. In her efforts to change her nephew's conservative attitudes, she involves him in some wacky illegal schemes. Smith is ideal as the crazy aunt and McCowen is equally good as the stuffy nephew. This is one of Cukor's best films.

870 **Treasure of Matecumbe** (1976) * Buena Vista, 117 min. *Dir* Vincent McEveety, *Scr* Don Tait, based on novel *A Journey to Matecumbe* by Robert Lewis Taylor, *Cin* Frank Phillips, *Ed* Cotton Warburton, *Des* Robert Clatworthy, *Art* John B. Mansbridge, *Cos* Shelby Anderson, *Mus* Buddy Baker, *Chor* Burch Mann, *Prod* Bill Anderson, *Exec Prod* Ron Miller, A Walt Disney Production.

Cast: Robert Foxworth, *Jim*, Joan Hackett, *Lauriette*, Peter Ustinov, *Dr. Snodgrass*, Vic Morrow, *Spangler*, Johnny Doran, *Davie*, Billy Attmore, *Thad*, Jane Wyatt, *Aunt Effie*, Robert DoQui, *Ben*, Mills Watson, *Catrell*, Val De Vargas, *Charlie*, Virginia Vincent, *Aunt Lou*, Don Knight, *Skaggs*, Dub Taylor, *Sheriff Forbes*, Dick Van Patton, *Gambler*. G. $4,675,000.

Poor Disney adventure film set in the 19th century, in which a group of people search for buried treasure near the Florida Keys, with the aid of a map. *Treasure of Matacumbe* begins slowly, with endless exposition that spans the first half of the film, and when the film finally gets going it almost completely falls apart, due to the very poor special effects.

871 **The Trial of Billy Jack** (1974) * Taylor-Laughlin, 170 min. *Dir* Frank Laughlin, *Scr* Frank and Teresa Christina, *Cin* Jack A. Marta, *Ed* Michael Economou, George Grenville, Michael Karr, Jules Nayfack, Tom Rolf, *Art* George W. Troast, *Cos* Moss Mabry, *Mus* Elmer Bernstein, *Prod* Joe Cramer, *Assoc Prod* Robert Schultz, Beverly Walker.

Cast: Tom Laughlin, *Billy Jack*, Delores Taylor, *Jean Roberts*, Victor Izay, *Doc*, Teresa Laughlin, *Carol*, William Wellman, Jr., *National Guardsman*, Russell Lane, *Russell*, Michelle Wilson, *Michelle*, Geo Anne Sosa, *Joanne*, Lynn Baker, *Lynn*, Riley Hill, *Rosner*, Sparky Watt, *Sheriff Cole*, Gus Greymountain, *Blue Elk*, Sacheen Littlefeather, *Patsy Littlejohn*, Michael Ballard, *Danny*, Jack Stanley, *Grandfather*, Bong Soo Han, *Master Han*, Rolling Thunder, *Thunder Mountain*, Sandra Ego, *Indian Maiden*, Trinidad Hopkins, *Vision Maiden*, Marianne Hall, *Alicia*, Johnny West, *Turning Water*, Buffalo Horse, *Little Bear*, Dennis O'Flaherty, *Defense Attorney*, George Aguilar, *Elk's Shadow*, Pepper Rogers, *Third Trooper*, Teda Bracci, *Teda*, Susan Sosa, *Sunshine*, Michael J. Shigezane, *Karate Expert*. PG. $24,000,000. See *Billy Jack*.

872 **Tropic of Cancer** (1970) *** Paramount, 87 min. *Dir* Joseph Strick, *Scr* Betty Botley, Joseph Strick, based on book by Henry Miller, *Cin* Alain Derobe, *Ed* Sidney Myers, Silvia Sarner, *Mus* Stanley Myers, *Prod* Joseph Strick, *Assoc Prod* Betty Botley, Michael Rittener.

Cast: Rip Torn, *Henry Miller*, James Callahan, *Fillmore*, Ellen Burstyn, *Mona*, David Bauer, *Carl*, Laurence Ligneres, *Ginette*, Phil Brown, *Van Norden*, Dominique Delpierre, *Vite Cheri*, Stuart De Silva, *Ranji*, Raymond Gerome, *M. Le Censeur*, Gisele Grimm, *Germaine*, Ginette LeClerc, *Madame Hamilton*, Francois Lugagne, *Irene*, Magali Noel, *The Princess*, Sheila Steafel, *Tania*, Elliot Sullivan, *Packover*, Sabine Sun, *Elsa*, Henry Miller, *Spectator*. X.

Fine film based on Henry Miller's autobiographical account of his life in Paris during the 1930's. *Tropic of Cancer* is a series of comic vignettes, detailing the sexual escapades and the impoverished existence of the expatriate writer (Rip Torn), in which he is forced to sponge off his friends. Although the film focuses on the seamy side of life, it is not pornographic.

873 **The Turning Point** (1977) (AN, NB, G) ** 20th Century–Fox, 119 min. *Dir* Herbert Ross (AN, G, LA), *Scr* Arthur Laurents (AN, W), *Cin* Robert Surtees (AN), *Ed* William Reynolds (AN), *Des* Albert Brenner (AN), *Cos* Tony Faso, Jennifer Parsons, Albert Wolsky, *Mus Adaptation* John Lanchbery, *Prod* Arthur Laurents, Herbert Ross, *Exec Prod* Nora Kaye.

Cast: Anne Bancroft (AN, NB), *Emma*, Shirley MacLaine (AN), *Deedee*, Tom Skerritt (NB), *Wayne*, Leslie Browne (AN), *Emilia*, Mikhail Baryshnikov (AN), *Yuri*, Martha Scott, *Adelaide*, Antoinette Sibley, *Sevilla*, Alexandra Danilova, *Dahkarova*, Starr Danias, *Carolyn*, Marshall Thompson, *Carter*, James Mitchell, *Michael*, Scott Douglas, *Freddie*, Daniel Levans, *Arnold*, Jurgen Schneider, *Peter*, Anthony Zerbe, *Rosie*, Phillip Saunders, *Ethan*, Lisa Lucas, *Janina*. PG. $17,060,000.

Overrated ballet drama that sinks to the level of a soap opera. Two women, one a ballet star (Anne Bancroft) and the other a housewife (Shirley MacLaine), who had been rival dancers reunite after many years apart. This leads to conflict as their mutual jealousies are brought out into the open. Bancroft and MacLaine give strong performances, but they can't overcome the shallow script which glosses over the problems of the women.

874 **The Twelve Chairs** (1970) *** UMC, 94 min. *Dir* Mel Brooks, *Scr* Mel Brooks, based on novel by Ilya Arnoldovich Ilf, Yevgeniy Petrov, *Cin* Djordje Nikolic, *Ed* Alan Heim, *Art* Mile Nikolic, *Mus* John Morris, *Prod* Michael Hertzberg, *Exec Prod* Sidney Glazier.

Cast: Ron Moody, *Vorobyaninov*, Frank Langella (NB), *Ostap Bender*, Dom DeLuise, *Father Fyodor*, Mel Brooks, *Tikon*, Bridget Brice, *Young Woman*, Robert Bernal, *Curator*, David Lander, *Engineer Bruns*, Andreas Voutsinas, *Nikolai Sestrin*, Vlada Petric, *Sevitsky*, Diana Coupland, *Madame Bruns*. PG.

Fine slapstick comedy set in Russia in 1927. Ron Moody stars as a former nobleman, who searches for a fortune in jewels hidden by his mother in one of twelve matching chairs, which have been separated. *The Twelve Chairs* is a well-made comedy and is surprisingly well-acted. This is one of Mel Brooks' best films and is not flawed by his usual exaggerations.

875 **Twilight's Last Gleaming** (1977) *** Allied Artists, 146 min. *Dir* Robert Aldrich, *Scr* Ronald M. Cohen, Edward Huebsch, based on novel *Viper 3* by Walter Wager, *Cin* Robert Hauser, *Ed* Michael Luciano, *Des* Rolf Zehetbauer, *Mus* Jerry Goldsmith, *Prod* Merv Adelson, *Exec Prod* Helmit Jedele.

Cast: Burt Lancaster, *Lawrence Dell*, Richard Widmark, *Martin MacKenzie*, Charles Durning, *President David T. Stevens*, Melvyn Douglas, *Zachariah Guthrie*, Paul Winfield, *Powell*, Burt Young, *Garvas*, Joseph Cotten, *Arthur Renfrew*, Roscoe Lee Browne, *James Forrest*, Gerald S. O'Loughlin, *Michael O'Rourke*, Richard Jaeckel, *Capt. Stanford Towne*, Vera Miles, *Victoria Stevens*, William Marshall, *William Klinger*, Charles Aidman, *Col. Bernstein*, Leif Erickson, *Ralph Whittaker*, Charles McGraw, *Peter Crane*, Simon Scott, *Phil Spencer*, Morgan Paull, *1st Lt. Louis Cannellis*, William Smith, *Hoxey*, Bill Walker, *Willard*. R. $4,500,000.

Well-done thriller about a group of renegades who take over a missile silo in an attempt to blackmail the United States into admitting the truth about its involvement in the Vietnam War. *Twilight's Last Gleaming* may be a message movie, but it is never overly preachy or boring, despite its longer than average running time. Burt Lancaster is excellent as the leader of the blackmailers, but Gerald S. O'Loughlin, as a Presidential aide, nearly steals the film. This is one of the finest films from noted action director Robert Aldrich.

876 **Two-Lane Blacktop** (1971) *** Universal, 102 min. *Dir* Monte Hellman, *Scr* Will Corry, Rudolph Wurlitzer, *Story* Will Corry, *Cin* Jack Deerson, *Ed* Monte Hellman, *Cos* Charles Knight, *Prod* Michael S. Laughlin.

Cast: James Taylor, *The Driver*, Warren Oates, *G.T.O.*, Laurie Bird, *The Girl*, Dennis Wilson, *The Mechanic*, David Drake, *Needles Station Attendant*, Richard Ruth, *Needles Station Mechanic*, Rudolph Wurlitzer, *Hot Rod Driver*, Jaclyn Hellman, *Driver's Girl*, Bill Keller, *Texas Hitchhiker*, Harry Dean Stanton, *Oklahoma Hitchhiker*, Don Samuels, Charles Moore, *Texas Policeman*, Tom Green, *Boswell Station Attendant*, W.H. Harrison, *Parts Store Owner*, Alan Vint, *Man in Roadhouse*, Illa Ginnaven, *Waitress in Roadhouse*. R.

Unusual drama about two California youths (James Taylor, Dennis Wilson) driving a souped up 1955 Chevy, who are challenged to a race to Washington, D.C. by a loud-mouthed braggart (Warren Oates), but eventually the participants begin to lose interest in the race. *Two-Lane Blacktop* wanders aimlessly, but that is part of the film's point, in its examination of their wasted lives.

877 **Two-Minute Warning** (1976) ** Universal, 115 min. *Dir* Larry Peerce, *Scr* Alan Hume, based on novel by George LaFountaine, *Cin* Gerald Hirschfeld, *Ed* Walter Hannemann, Eve Newman, *Art* Herman A. Blumenthal, *Mus* Charles Fox, *Prod* Edward S. Feldman.

Cast: Charlton Heston, *Holly*, John Cassavetes, *Button*, Martin Balsam, *McKeever*, Beau Bridges, *Mike Ramsay*, Marilyn Hassett, *Lucy*, David Janssen, *Steve*, Jack Klugman, *Sandman*, Gena Rowlands, *Janet*, Walter Pidgeon, *Pickpocket*, Brock Peters, *Paul*, David Groh, *Al*, Mitchell Ryan, *Priest*, Joe Kapp, *Charlie Tyler*, Pamela Bellwood, *Peggy Ramsay*, Jon Korkes, *Jeffrey*, William Bryant, *Lt. Calloway*, Allan Miller, *Mr. Green*, Andy Sidaris, *TV Director*, Ron Sheldon, Stanford Blum, *Assistant TV Directors*, Warren Miller, *Sniper*. R. $9,110,000.

Dim-witted thriller about a psychotic sniper, who kills off a group of people at a crowded football stadium. The build-up is so long and drawn out and the characters are so flat and innocuous, with irrelevant and uninteresting personal details about their problems, that it becomes a relief when the sniper begins shooting. The only plus to this film is the lack of phoney psychology about the killer's motives.

878 **Two Mules for Sister Sara** (1970) *** Universal, 113 min. *Dir* Don Siegel, *Scr* Albert Maltz, *Story* Budd Boetticher, *Cin* Gabriel Figueroa, *Ed* Juan Jose Marino, Robert F. Shugrue, *Art* Rodriguez Granada, *Cos* Carlos Chavez, Helen Colvig, *Mus* Ennio Morricone, *Prod* Carroll Case, Martin Rackin.

Cast: Shirley MacLaine, *Sara*, Clint Eastwood, *Hogan*, Manolo Fabregas, *Col. Betran*, Alberto Morin, *Gen. LeClaire*, Armando Silvestre, *First American*, John Kelly, *Second American*, Enrique Lucero, *Third American*, David

Estuardo, *Juan*, Ada Carrasco, *Juan's Mother*, Poncho Cordoba, *Juan's Father*, Jose Chavez, *Horacio*. PG. $4,900,000.

Fine western drama focusing on a cowboy (Clint Eastwood), who comes to the aid of a nun (Shirley MacLaine) only to later discover she is really a prostitute in disguise. *Two Mules for Sister Sara* is mostly episodic, detailing their travels across the Mexican desert, but there are some fine action sequences and Eastwood and MacLaine are well-paired.

879 **Ulzana's Raid** (1972) *** Universal, 103 min. *Dir* Robert Aldrich, *Scr* Alan Sharp, *Cin* Joseph Biroc, *Ed* Michael Luciano, *Art* James Vance, *Mus* Frank DeVol, *Prod* Carter De Haven, *Assoc Prod* Alan Sharp.

Cast: Burt Lancaster, *McIntosh*, Bruce Davison, *Lt. Garnett DeBuin*, Jorge Luke, *Ke-Ni-Tay*, Richard Jaeckel, *Sergeant*, Joaquin Martinez, *Ulzana*, Lloyd Bochner, *Capt. Gates*, Karl Swenson, *Rukeyser*, Douglass Watson, *Maj. Cartwright*, Dran Hamilton, *Mrs. Riordan*, John Pearce, *Corporal*, Gladys Holland, *Mrs. Rukeyser*, Margaret Fairchild, *Mrs. Ginsford*, Aimee Eccles, *McIntosh's Indian Woman*, Richard Bull, *Ginsford*, Otto Reichow, *Steegmeyer*, Dean Smith, *Horowitz*, Larry Randles, *Mulkearn*. R.

Above-average western drama starring Burt Lancaster as a frontier scout, who must lead a patrol, headed by a young and inexperienced army officer (Bruce Davison), to round up some renegade Apaches. *Ulzana's Raid* is much like many other message westerns of the time, but because of Aldrich's expert direction it lacks the heavy-handedness that flaws most of the others.

880 **Undercovers Hero** (1975) *** Britain, United Artists, 95 min. Roy Boulting, *Scr* Roy Boulting, Leo Marks, *Cin* Gil Taylor, *Ed* Martin Charles, *Art* John Howell, *Mus* Neil Rhoden, *Prod* John Boulting, *Assoc Prod* John Palmer.

Cast: Peter Sellers, *Gen. Latour/Maj. Robinson/Schroeder/Hitler/Prince Kyoto/President of France*, Lila Kedrova, *Mdm. Grenier*, Curt Jurgens, *Gen. Von Grotjahn*, Beatrice Romand, *Marie-Claude*, Jenny Hanley, Francoise Pascal, Gabriella Licudi, Rula Lenska, Daphne Lawson, Carolle Rousseau, Hylette Adolphe, *Grenier's Girls*, Nicholas Loukes, *Schroeder's Aide*, Vernon Dobtcheff, *Priest*, Patricia Burke, *Mother Superior*. R.

Unusual black comedy set in WWII about the prostitutes of a French bordello who battle Nazis in their own way. Peter Sellers does his usual good job of mimickry in six different and bizarre roles. *Undercovers Hero*, although almost unanimously condemned, is an enjoyable comedy for those who are not shocked by the premise. Other title, *Soft Beds and Hard Battles*.

881 **An Unmarried Woman** (1978) (AN) **** 20th Century–Fox, 124 min. *Dir* Paul Mazursky, *Scr* Paul Mazursky (AN, NS, NY, LA), *Cin* Arthur Ornitz, *Ed* Stuart H. Pappe, *Des* Pato Guzman, *Cos* Albert Wolsky, *Mus* Bill Conti, *Prod* Paul Mazursky, Tony Ray.

Cast: Jill Clayburgh (AN), *Erica*, Alan Bates, *Saul*, Michael Murphy, *Martin*, Cliff Gorman, *Charlie*, Pat Quinn, *Sue*, Kelly Bishop, *Elaine*, Lisa Lucas, *Patti*, Linda Miller, *Jeannette*, Andrew Duncan, *Bob*, Daniel Seltzer, *Dr. Jacobs*, Matthew Arkin, *Phil*, Penelope Russianoff, *Tanya*, Novella Nelson, *Jean*, Raymond J. Barry, *Edward*, Ivan Karp, *Herb Rowan*, Jill Eikenberry, *Claire*, Michael Tucker, *Fred*, Paul Mazursky, *Hal*. R. $13,615,000.

Excellent drama examining the problems facing a divorced woman. *An Unmarried Woman* begins with what appears to be an ideal marriage, but the husband later confesses to having an affair with another woman. The film realistically deals with this traumatic experience and the change undergone in her life. This realism fades somewhat in the last part, focusing on her affair with an artist, but it does not detract too much. Jill Clayburgh gives a superb performance, encompassing all of the woman's emotions.

882 **Up in Smoke** (1978) ** Paramount, 86 min. *Dir* Lou Adler, *Scr* Tommy Chong, Cheech Marin, *Cin* Gene Polito, *Ed* Scott Conrad, Lou Lombardo, *Art* Leon Ericksen, *Prod* Lou Adler, Lou Lombardo, *Assoc Prod* John Beug.

Cast: Cheech Marin, *Pedro*, Tommy Chong, *Man*, Strother Martin, *Mr. Stoner*, Edie Adams, *Tempest Stoner*, Stacy Keach, *Sgt. Stedenko*, Tom Skerritt, *Strawberry*, Val Avery, *Factory Boss*, Zane Buzby, *Jade East*, Anne Wharton, *Debbie*, Louisa Moritz, *Gloria*. R. $28,300,000.

A mess of a comedy that occasionally succeeds, despite itself. Cheech and Chong, a famed underground comedy team, made their movie debut with *Up in Smoke*, after enjoying many years of success with records and concerts. There is no real plot, and the film just wanders from one situation to another. Supposedly their scripts are only a few pages, and it certainly appears to be the case here. *Up in Smoke* is strictly for their fans; few others will be impressed.

883 **Up the Sandbox** (1972) *** National General, 97 min. *Dir* Irvin Kershner, *Scr* Paul Zindel, based on novel by Anne Richardson Roiphe, *Cin* Gordon Willis, *Ed* Robert Lawrence, *Des* Harry Horner, *Mus* Billy Goldenberg, *Prod* Robert Chartoff, Irwin Winkler.

Cast: Barbra Streisand, *Margaret Reynolds*, David Selby, *Paul Reynolds*, Jane Hoffman, *Mrs. Yussim*, John C. Becher, *Mr. Yussim*, Jacobo Morales, *Fidel Castro*, Iris Brooks, *Vicki*, Barbara Rhodes, *Dr. Bowden*. R.

Unusual comedy-drama starring Barbra Streisand as a harried housewife and mother, who retreats into a world of fantasy, which includes such bizarre sequences as her seduction by Fidel Castro, to escape from her dreary existence. *Up the Sandbox* is an interesting examination of the problems facing women, but it sometimes strains too hard for laughs. Streisand gives a fine and unusually restrained performance.

884 **Uptown Saturday Night** (1974) *** Warner Bros., 104 min. *Dir* Sidney Poitier, *Scr* Richard Wesley, *Cin* Fred J. Koenekamp, *Ed* Pembroke J. Herring, *Des* Alfred Sweeney, *Mus* Tom Scott, *Title Song* Tom Scott, Morgan Ames, sung by Dobie Gray, *Prod* Melville Tucker.

Cast: Sidney Poitier, *Steve Jackson*, Bill Cosby, *Wardell Franklin*, Harry Belafonte, *Geechie Dan Beauford*, Calvin Lockhart, *Silky Slim*, Flip Wilson, *The Reverend*, Richard Pryor, *Sharp Eye Washington*, Rosalind Cash, *Sarah Jackson*, Roscoe Lee Browne, *Congressman Lincoln*, Paula Kelly, *Leggy Peggy*, Lee Chamberlin, *Madame Zenobia*, Johnny Sekka, *Geechie's Henchman*, Lincoln Kilpatrick, *Slim's Henchman #1*, Ketty Lester, *Irma Franklin*, Don Marshall, *Slim's Henchman #2*, Harold Nicholas, *Little Seymour*. PG. $7,400,000.

Well made comedy crime thriller that is a black version of *The Sting* with a touch of *The Godfather* mixed in. Two friends, a factory worker (Sidney Poitier) and a cab driver (Bill Cosby), track down a stolen lottery ticket that they lost in a hold-up at a gambling club. Not all of the humor works and the pace is too slow, but some of the performers, particularly Cosby and Richard Pryor make up for this. Poitier and Cosby reteamed twice for *Let's Do It Again*, in which Poitier hypnotizes Jimmy Walker into becoming a boxing champ, and *A Piece of the Action*, in which Poitier and Cosby are forced to work at a youth center to stay out of jail.

885 **Valentino** (1977) ******** Britain, United Artists, 132 min. *Dir* Ken Russell, *Scr* Mardik Martin, Ken Russell, *Cin* Peter Suschitsky, *Ed* Stuart Baird, *Art* Philip Harrison, *Cos* Shirley Russell, *Mus* Stanley Black, Ferde Grofe, *Prod* Robert Chartoff, Irwin Winkler, *Assoc Prod* Harry Benn.

Cast: Rudolf Nureyev, *Valentino*, Leslie Caron, *Nazimova*, Michele Phillips, *Natasha Rambova*, Carol Kane, *"Fatty's" Girl*, Felicity Kendal, *June Mathis*, Seymour Cassel, *George Ullman*, Peter Vaughn, *Rory O'Neil*, Huntz Hall, *Jesse Lasky*, David De Keyser, *Joseph Schenck*, Alfred Marks, *Richard Rowland*, Anton Diffring, *Baron Long*, Jennie Linden, *Agnes Ayres*, William Hootkins, *"Fatty"*, Bill McKinney, *Jail Cop*, Don Fellows, *George Melford*, John Justin, *Sidney Olcott*, Linda Thorson, *Billie Streeter*, June Bolton, *Bianca De Saulles*, Penny Milford, *Lorna Sinclair*, Dudley Sutton, *Willie*, Robin Brent Clarke, *Jack De Saulles*, Anthony Dowell, *Vaslav Nijinsky*. R.

Bizarre biography of the famous silent screen star. As in his biographical films about composers, Ken Russell has taken details of Valentino's life and exaggerates them in a surrealistic extravaganza. Famed ballet dancer Rudolf Nureyev is an odd choice for the role of Valentino, and although he has little acting ability, he has a surprisingly strong screen charisma. *Valentino* is certainly not an ordinary Hollywood biography but in its own way it is one of the most truthful.

886 **Vanishing Point** (1971) ****** 20th Century–Fox, 107 min. *Dir* Richard C. Sarafian, *Scr* Guillermo Cain, *Story* Malcolm Hart, *Cin* John A. Alonzo, *Ed* Stefan Arnsten, *Prod* Norman Spencer, *Exec Prod* Michael Pearson.

Cast: Barry Newman, *Kowalski*, Cleavon Little, *Super Soul*, Dean Jagger, *Prospector*, Victoria Medlin, *Vera*, Paul Koslo, *Young Cop*, Bob Donner, *Older Cop*, Timothy Scott, *Angel*, Gilda Texter, *Nude Rider*, Anthony James, *First Male Hitch-hiker*, Arthur Malet, *Second Male Hitch-hiker*, Karl Swenson, *Clerk at Delivery Agency*, Severn Darden, *J. Hovah*, Delaney & Bonnie & Friends, *J. Hovah's Singers*, Lee Weaver, *Jake*, Cherie Foster, *First Girl*, Valerie Kairys, *Second Girl*, Tom Reese, *Sheriff*, Owen Bush, *Communications Officer*. PG. $5,005,000.

Unbelievable car chase film starring Barry Newman as a man who delivers cars from Denver to San Francisco. During one of his deliveries, he bets he can reach his destination in only 15 hours. A blind black disc jockey (Cleavon Little) discovers the chase and broadcasts its details over the radio, turning Newman into a folk hero. This interesting premise unfortunately is merely an excuse for chases and wrecks.

887 **Vigilante Force** (1976) ******* United Artists, 89 min. *Dir* George Armitage, *Scr* George Armitage, *Cin* William Cronjager, *Ed* Morton Tubor, *Art* Jack Fisk, *Mus* Gerald Fried, *Prod* Gene Corman.

Cast: Kris Kristofferson, *Aaron*, Jan-Michael Vincent, *Ben*, Victoria Principal, *Linda*, Bernadette Peters, *Dee*, Brad Dexter, *Mayor*, Judson Pratt, *Harry*,

David Doyle, *Homer*, Anthony Carbone, *Freddie*, Andrew Stevens, *Paul*, Shelly Novack, *D.O.*, Paul X. Gleason, *Michael*, John Steadman, *Shakey*, Lilyan McBride, *Boots*, James Lydon, *Tom*. PG.

Unusual action thriller set in a boom town plagued with anarchy. Jan-Michael Vincent brings in his Vietnam vet brother Kris Kristofferson to supplement the police force. Kristofferson becomes power mad and takes over the town. *Vigilante Force*, unlike most low-budget action films, has ideas to justify its violence. The film is a political allegory with the theme that authoritarianism is not the alternative to anarchy. Unfortunately the execution is not up to its ideas.

888 **The Villain** (1979) * Columbia, 93 min. *Dir* Hal Needham, *Scr* Robert G. Kane, *Cin* Bobby Byrne, *Ed* Walter Hannemann, *Art* Carl Anderson, *Mus* Bill Justis, *Prod* Mort Engleberg, *Exec Prod* Paul Maslansky.

Cast: Kirk Douglas, *Cactus Jack*, Ann-Margret, *Charming Jones*, Arnold Schwarzenegger, *Handsome Stranger*, Paul Lynde, *Nervous Elk*, Foster Brooks, *Bank Clerk*, Ruth Buzzi, *Damsel in Distress*, Jack Elam, *Avery Simpson*, Strother Martin, *Parody Jones*, Robert Tessier, *Mashing Finger*, Mel Tillis, *Telegraph Agent*, Laura Lizer Sommers, *Working Girl*. PG. $9,930,000.

Dull western chase comedy. The entire film consists of a villainous cowboy (Kirk Douglas), who pursues a dim-witted good guy (Arnold Schwartzenegger), but his plans continually go awry. *The Villain* is an attempt at a live-action version of the Road Runner cartoons, but the humor tends to be bland and sophomoric. This also resembles Hal Needham's other mindless chase film, *Smokey and the Bandit*.

889 **Viva Knievel** (1977) * Warner Bros., 106 min. *Dir* Gordon Douglas, *Scr* Norman Katkov, Antonio Santillan, *Story* Antonio Santillan, *Cin* Fred Jackman, *Ed* Harold Kress, *Des* Ward Preston, *Cos* Paul Zastupnevich, *Mus* Charles Bernstein, *Prod* Stan Hough, *Exec Prod* Sherrill C. Corwin.

Cast: Evel Knievel, *Himself*, Gene Kelly, *Will Atkins*, Lauren Hutton, *Kate Morgan*, Red Buttons, *Ben Andrews*, Leslie Nielsen, *Stanley Millard*, Frank Gifford, *Himself*, Sheila Allen, *Sister Charity*, Cameron Mitchell, *Barton*, Eric Olson, *Tommy Atkins*, Albert Salmi, *Cortland*, Dabney Coleman, *Ralph Thompson*, Ernie Orsatti, *Norman Clark*, Sidney Clute, *Andy*, Robert Tafur, *Gov. Garcia*, Marjoe Gortner, *Jessie*. PG.

Poor biographical film loosely based on life of famed daredevil, Evel Knievel, which ironically stars Knievel as himself. This is the second film based on his life and the first, *Evel Knievel*, a merely average film, is far superior to this travesty. The script is silly, containing numerous unintentional laughs, and Knievel proves that portraying oneself can be quite a difficult task.

890 **Voices** (1979) ** United Artists, 106 min. *Dir* Robert Markowitz, *Scr* John Herzfeld, *Cin* Alan Metzger, *Ed* Danford B. Green, *Art* Richard Bianchi, *Cos* John Boxer, *Mus* Jimmy Webb, *Chor* Stuart Hodes, *Prod* Joe Wizan, *Assoc Prod* Betty Gumm.

Cast: Michael Ontkean, *Drew Rothman*, Amy Irving, *Rosemarie Lemon*, Alex Rocco, *Frank Rothman*, Barry Miller, *Raymond Rothman*, Herbert Berghof, *Nathan Rothman*, Viveca Lindfors, *Mrs. Lemon*, Allan Rich, *Montrose Meier*, Joseph Cali, *Pinky*, Rik Colitti, *String*, Jean Ehrlich, *Snowflake*,

Thurman Scott, *Patterson*, Melonie Mazman, *Debbie*, Arva Holt, *Helen*, Richard Kendall, *Scott Gunther*, Mary Serrano, *Cheryl*, Thom Christopher, *Paul Janssen*. PG.

Average love story about a truck driver with ambitions of becoming a professional singer (Michael Ontkean), and a deaf girl (Amy Irving). *Voices* has more humor than other films of its type, mostly in its depiction of Ontkean's obnoxious family, but when it focuses on the relationship of Ontkean and Irving its sinks to a level of nothing but cliché and is filled with drippy sentiment.

891 **Voyage of the Damned** (1976) ** Britain, Avco Embassy, 155 min. *Dir* Stuart Rosenberg, *Scr* David Butler, Steve Shagan (AN), based on book by Max Morgan-Witts, Gordon Thomas, *Cin* Billy Williams, *Ed* Tom Priestley, *Des* Wilfred Shingleton, *Art* Jack Stephens, *Cos* Betty Adamson, John Billing, Phyllis Dalton, *Mus* Lalo Schifrin (AN), *Prod* Robert Fryer, *Assoc Prod* Bill Hill.

Cast: Faye Dunaway, *Denise Kreisler*, Max Von Sydow, *Capt. Schroeder*, Oskar Werner, *Dr. Kreisler*, Malcolm McDowell, *Max Gunter*, Orsen Welles, *Estedes*, James Mason, *Remos*, Lee Grant (AN), *Lillian Rosen*, Ben Gazzara, *Morris Troper*, Katharine Ross (G), *Mira Hauser*, Luther Adler, *Prof. Weiler*, Paul Koslo, *Aaron Pozner*, Michael Constantine, *Clasing*, Nehemiah Persoff, *Mr. Hauser*, Jose Ferrer, *Benitez*, Fernando Rey, *Cuban President*, Lynne Frederick, *Anna Rosen*, Maria Schell, *Mrs. Hauser*, Helmut Griem, *Otto Schiendick*, Victor Spinetti, *Dr. Strauss*, Julie Harris, *Alice Feinchild*, Janet Suzman, *Leni Strauss*, Wendy Hiller, *Rebecca Weiler*, Sam Wanamaker, *Carl Rosen*, Denholm Elliott, *Adm. Canaris*. PG.

Dull factual drama about a shipload of Jews expelled from Nazi Germany en route to Cuba, where they are to be refused entry as a Nazi propaganda stunt. *Voyage of the Damned* may have been a true story, but the film comes off as another *Ship of Fools* type melodrama, skipping over several interrelated vignettes and the numerous stereotypical and uninvolving characters.

892 **W.C. Fields and Me** (1976) ** Universal, 111 min. *Dir* Arthur Hiller, *Scr* Bob Merrill, based on book by Carlotta Monti, Cy Rice, *Cin* David M. Walsh, *Ed* John C. Howard, *Des* Robert Boyle, *Cos* Edith Head, *Mus* Henry Mancini, *Prod* Jay Weston.

Cast: Rod Steiger, *W.C. Fields*, Valerie Perrine, *Carlotta*, John Marley, *Bannerman*, Jack Cassidy, *John Barrymore*, Bernadette Peters, *Melody*, Dana Elcar, *Dockstedter*, Paul Stewart, *Ziegfeld*, Billy Barty, *Ludwig*, Allan Arbus, *La Cava*, Milt Kamen, *Chasen*, Louis Zorich, *Gene Fowler*, Andrew Parks, *Claude*, Hank Rolike, *Leon*, Kenneth Tobey, *Parker*, Paul Mantee, *Edward*, Elizabeth Thompson, *Woman Patient*, Eddie Firestone, *Private Detective*, Linda Purl, *Ingenue*, Clay Tanner, *Assistant Director*, George Loras, *Schmidt*. PG.

Disappointing biography of the famed screen comedian, as seen through the eyes of his long-time secretary Carlotta Monti. Recreating W.C. Fields on screen is a difficult task, without it seeming like an impressionist's comedy routine, but unfortunately that is the result in *W.C. Fields and Me*. Rod Steiger tries hard to mimmick Fields, but he never gets into the character, which also can be blamed on the shallow script.

893 **W.W. and the Dixie Dancekings** (1975) *** 20th Century–Fox, 91 min. *Dir* John G. Avildsen, *Scr* Thomas Rickman, *Cin* James Crabe, *Ed* Richard Halsey, Robbe Roberts, *Art* Lawrence G. Paull, *Mus* Dave Grusin, *Prod* Stanley S. Cantor, *Exec Prod* Steve Shagan.

Cast: Burt Reynolds, *W.W. Bright,* Art Carney, *Deacon Gore,* Conny Van Dyke, *Dixie,* Jerry Reed, *Wayne,* Ned Beatty, *Country Bull,* James Hampton, *Junior,* Don Williams, *Leroy,* Richard D. Hurst, *Butterball,* Sherman G. Lloyd, *Elton Bird,* Bill McCutcheon, Mel Tillis, Fred Stuthman, *Gas Station Attendants,* Furry Lewis, *Uncle Furry,* Mort Marshall, *Hester Tate,* Sherry Mathis, *June Ann,* Hal Needham, *Patrolman,* Nancy Andrews, *Rosie,* Peg Murray, *Della.* PG. $7,790,000.

Fine comedy about a con man (Burt Reynolds), who poses as the manager of a country music group to hide from the law. He becomes attached to the musicians, who do not realize the truth, and tries to go straight by really helping them. This is mainly a vehicle for Reynolds, and his screen persona is used to full advantage, but this time without resorting to endless chases.

894 **Walk Proud** (1979) ** Universal, 102 min. *Dir* Robert Collins, *Scr* Evan Hunter, *Cin* Bobby Byrne, *Ed* Douglas Stewart, *Art* William F. Campbell, *Mus* Robby Benson, Don Peake, *Prod* Lawrence Turman.

Cast: Robby Benson, *Emilio,* Sarah Holcomb, *Sarah Lassiter,* Henry Darrow, *Mike Serrano,* Pepe Serna, *Cesar,* Trinidad Silva, *Dagger,* Ji-Tu Cumbuka, *Sgt. Gannett,* Lawrence Pressman, *Henry Lassiter,* Domingo Ambriz, *Cowboy,* Brad Sullivan, *Jerry Kelsey,* Irene De Bari, *Mrs. Mendez,* Elroy Phil Casados, *Hugo,* Daniel Faraldo, *El Tigre,* Tony Alvarenga, *Paco,* Stephen Morrell, *Hippo,* Benjie Bancroft, *Police Guard,* Lee Fraser, *Johnny,* Gary Cervantes, *Carlos,* Tim Culbertson, *Guard,* Panchito Gomez, *Manuel.* PG.

Fair drama about a Chicano street gang member (Robby Benson) who falls in love with a white upper middle class girl, causing the predictable conflicts. *Walk Proud* is not like other such films released the same year, as its main concern is the *Romeo and Juliet* plot, rather than action. Benson does not have a strong enough screen presence nor the acting range, to carry the film.

895 **Walking Tall** (1973) ** Cinerama, 125 min. *Dir* Phil Karlson, *Scr* Mort Briskin, *Cin* Jack A. Marta, *Ed* Harry Gerstad, *Des* Stan Jolley, *Cos* Phyllis Garr, Oscar Rodriguez, *Mus* Walter Scharf, *Title Song* Don Black, Walter Scharf, sung by Johnny Mathis, *Technical Consultant* Buford Pusser, *Prod* Mort Briskin, *Exec Prod* Charles A. Pratt, *Assoc Prod* Joel Briskin.

Cast: Joe Don Baker, *Buford Pusser,* Elizabeth Hartman, *Pauline Pusser,* Gene Evans, *Sheriff Al Thurman,* Noah Beery, *Grandpa Pusser,* Brenda Benet, *Luan Paxton,* John Brascia, *Prentiss Parley,* Bruce Glover, *Grady Coker,* Arch Johnson, *Buel Jaggers,* Felton Perry, *Obra Eaker,* Richard X. Slattery, *Arno Purdy,* Rosemary Murphy, *Callie Hacker,* Lynn Borden, *Margie Ann,* Ed Call, *Lutie McVeigh,* Sidney Clute, *Sheldon Levine,* Douglas V. Fowley, *Judge Clarke,* Don Keefer, *Dr. Lamar Stivers,* Sam Laws, *Willie Rae Lockman,* Pepper Martin, *Zolan Dicks,* John Myhers, *Lester Dickens,* Logan Ramsey, *John Witter,* Kenneth Tobey, *Augie McCullah,* Lurene Tuttle, *Grandma Pusser.* R. $17,000,000.

Average biography of legendary sheriff, Buford Pusser. This could have made an interesting film, but the filmmakers turned Pusser's life into another violent, Southern, vendetta melodrama, in which a wronged man gets revenge on a group of stereotyped villains. On that level *Walking Tall* is better than most, but it could obviously have been so much more. Joe Don Baker does give an excellent performance as Pusser. The sequels were generally more of the same, but were not as well done, and Bo Svenson is miscast as Pusser.

896 **The Wanderers** (1979) *** Orion, 113 min. *Dir* Philip Kaufman, *Scr* Philip Kaufman, Rose Kaufman, based on novel by Richard Price, *Cin* Michael Chapman, *Ed* Stuart H. Pappe, Ronald Roose, *Art* Jay Moore, *Cos* Robert de Mora, *Prod* Martin Ransohoff, *Exec Prod* Richard R. St. Johns, *Assoc Prod* Fred C. Caruso.

Cast: Ken Wahl, *Richie*, John Friedrich, *Joey*, Karen Allen, *Nina*, Toni Kalem, *Despie Galasso*, Alan Rosenberg, *Turkey*, Jim Youngs, *Buddy*, Tony Ganios, *Perry*, Linda Manz, *Peewee*, William Andrews, *Emilio*, Erland Van Lidth de Jeude, *Terror*, Val Avery, *Mr. Sharp*, Dolph Sweet, *Chubby Galasso*, Michael Wright, *Clinton*, Burtt Harris, *Marine Recruiter*, Samm-Art Williams, *Roger*, Dion Albanese, *Teddy Wong*, Olympia Dukakis, *Joey's Mom*. R.

Unusual street gang comedy focusing on an Italian-American youth gang living in the Bronx in the 1960's. *The Wanderers* has its share of action and violence, but its style is reminiscent of *American Graffiti* in its comedic portrait of growing up in the 1960's. Philip Kaufman's visual style is like his classic *Invasion of the Body Snatchers*, but the script is slightly muddled and overreaches itself.

897 **The War Between Men and Women** (1972) ** National General, 110 min. *Dir* Melville Shavelson, *Scr* Danny Arnold, Melville Shavelson, suggested by writings and drawings of James Thurber, *Cin* Charles F. Wheeler, *Ed* Frank Bracht, *Des* Stan Jolley, *Mus* Marvin Hamlisch, *Animation* Robert Dranko, *Prod* Danny Arnold.

Cast: Jack Lemmon, *Peter Wilson*, Barbara Harris, *Terry Kozlenko*, Jason Robards, *Stephen Kozlenko*, Herb Edelman, *Howard Mann*, Lisa Gerritsen, *Linda Kozlenko*, Moosie Drier, *David Kozlenko*, Severn Darden, *Dr. Harris*, Lisa Eilbacher, *Caroline Kozlenko*, Lucille Meredith, *Mrs. Schenker*, Ruth McDevitt, *Elderly Woman*, Joey Faye, *Florist Delivery Man*, Alan DeWitt, *Man*, John Zaremba, *Minister*, Rick Gates, *Bernie*, Lea Marmer, *Old Hag*, Janya Brannt, *Nurse*, Dr. Joyce Brothers, *Herself*, William Hickman, *Large Gentleman*, Olive Dunbar, Margaret Muse, *Women at Literary Tea*. PG.

Fair battle-of-the-sexes comedy loosely based on the life of writer-cartoonist James Thurber. Jack Lemmon stars as the Thurber character, who marries a woman (Barbara Harris) with three kids and a dog. The structure is too episodic due to its comic strip source and the film's sentiment drowns its humor, but Lemmon and Harris try their best with the material.

898 **The Warriors** (1979) ***** Paramount, 90 min. *Dir* Walter Hill, *Scr* Walter Hill, David Shaber, based on novel by Sol Yurick, *Cin* Andrew Laszlo, *Ed* David Holden, *Art* Don Swanagan, Bob Wightman, *Cos* Bobbie Mannix, Mary Ellen Winston, *Mus* Barry DeVorzon, *Prod* Lawrence Gordon, *Exec Prod* Frank Marshall, *Assoc Prod* Joel Silver.

Cast: Michael Beck, *Swan*, James Remar, *Ajax*, Thomas Waites, *Fox*, Dorsey Wright, *Cleon*, Brian Tyler, *Snow*, David Harris, *Cochise*, Tom McKitterick, *Cowboy*, Marcelino Sanchez, *Rembrandt*, Terry Michos, *Vermin*, Deborah Van Valkenburgh, *Mercy*, David Patrick Kelly, *Luther*, Roger Hill, *Cyrus*, Lynn Thigpen, *D.J.*, Ginny Ortiz, *Candy Store Girl*. R. $14,500,000.

Powerful drama about street gangs in New York. The film begins with a massive conference in Central Park held by a charismatic gang leader named Cyrus, in an attempt to unite all the gangs to take over the entire city. Cyrus is assassinated and The Warriors, a Coney Island gang, are blamed. Most of the film documents their desperate journey home, while being pursued by every gang in the city and the New York police. The violence is plentiful and beautifully stylized, but it is never gratuitous or shocking. *The Warriors* is one of Walter Hill's finest existential dramas and it resembles an odyssey from Greek mythology.

899 **Watermelon Man** (1970) ******* Columbia, 97 min. *Dir* Melvin Van Peebles, *Scr* Herman Raucher, *Cin* W. Wallace Kelley, *Ed* Carl Kress, *Art* Malcolm C. Bert, Sydney Z. Litwack, *Cos* Gene Ashman, Edna Taylor, *Mus* Melvin Van Peebles, *Prod* John B. Bennett, *Exec Prod* Leon Mirell.

Cast: Godfrey Cambridge, *Jeff Gerber*, Estelle Parsons, *Althea Gerber*, Howard Caine, *Townsend*, D'Urville Martin, *Bus Driver*, Mantan Moreland, *Counterman*, Kay Kimberly, *Erica*, Kay E. Kuter, *Dr. Wainwright*, Scott Garrett, *Burton Gerber*, Erin Moran, *Janice Gerber*, Irving Selbst, *Johnson*, Emil Sitka, *Delivery Man*, Lawrence Parke, *First Passenger*, Karl Lucas, *Policeman #2*, Ray Ballard, *Third Passenger*, Robert Dagny, *Second Passenger*. R.

Unusual fantasy comedy about a bigoted white man (Godfrey Cambridge), who wakes up one morning and discovers he has turned black. Suddenly the tables are turned and he is now on the receiving end of racial hatred. The premise is clever, a bizarre variation of *Gentlemen's Agreement*, but the storyline runs out of steam. Unfortunately Cambridge's makeup is imperfect and he is unconvincing as a white man.

900 **The Way We Were** (1973) ******* Columbia, 118 min. *Dir* Sydney Pollack, *Scr* Arthur Laurents, based on his novel, *Cin* Harry Stradling, Jr. (AN), *Ed* Margaret Booth, *Des* Stephen Grimes (AN), *Cos* Dorothy Jeakins, Moss Mabry (AN), *Mus* Marvin Hamlisch (A), *Song* "The Way We Were", *Mus* Marvin Hamlisch (A, G), *Lyrics* Alan & Marilyn Bergman (A, G), *Prod* Ray Stark, *Assoc Prod* Richard Roth.

Cast: Barbra Streisand (AN), *Katie*, Robert Redford, *Hubbell*, Bradford Dillman, *J.J.*, Lois Chiles, *Carol Ann*, Patrick O'Neal, *George Bissinger*, Viveca Lindfors, *Paula Reisner*, Allyn Ann McLerie, *Rhea Edwards*, Murray Hamilton, *Brooks Carpenter*, Herb Edelman, *Bill Verso*, Diana Ewing, *Vicki Bissinger*, Sally Kirkland, *Pony Dunbar*, Marcia Mae Jones, *Peggy Vanderbilt*, Don Keefer, *Actor*, George Gaynes, *El Morocco Captain*. PG. $25,000,000.

Interesting, but slightly overblown love story. The film begins in the 1930's where Robert Redford, an apathetic Wasp, and Barbra Streisand, a left-wing activist, meet at college, and despite their differences, fall in love. They marry and end up in Hollywood, where the film culminates with the blacklistings of the 1950's. *The Way We Were* tries to be a socially relevant film, but it is overextending itself and it simply falls apart. Despite all this, the film does manage to be entertaining on a simpler level.

901 **A Wedding** (1978) ******** 20th Century–Fox, 125 min. *Dir* Robert Altman, *Scr* Robert Altman, John Considine, Allan Nicholls, Patricia Resnick, *Story* Robert Altman, John Considine, *Cin* Charles Rosher, *Ed* Tony Lombardo, *Prod* Robert Altman, *Exec Prod* Tommy Thompson, *Assoc Prod* Scott Bushnell, Robert Eggenweiler.

Cast, The Groom's Family: Lillian Gish, *Nettie Sloan*, Ruth Nelson, *Beatrice Sloan Cory*, Ann Ryerson, *Victoria Cory*, Desi Arnaz Jr., *Dino Corelli, The Groom*, Belita Moreno, *Daphne Corelli*, Vittorio Gassman, *Luigi Corelli*, Nina Van Pollandt, *Regina Corelli*, Virginia Vestoff, *Clarice Sloan*, Dina Merrill, *Antoinette Sloan Goddard*, Pat McCormick, *Mackenzie Goddard*, Luigi Proietti, *Little Dino*.

The Bride's Family: Carol Burnett, *Tulip Brenner*, Paul Dooley, *Snooks Brenner*, Amy Stryker, *Muffin Brenner, The Bride*, Mia Farrow, *Buffy Brenner*, Dennis Christopher, *Hughie Brenner*, Mary Seibel, *Aunt Marge Spar*, Margaret Ladd, *Ruby Spar*, Gerald Busby, *David Ruteledge*, Peggy Ann Garner, *Candice Ruteledge*, Mark R. Deming, *Matthew Ruteledge*, David Brand, Chris Brand, Amy Brand, Jenny Brand, Jeffrey Jones, Jay D. Jones, Courtney MacArthur, Paul D. Keller III, *Ruteledge Children*.

The Corelli House Staff: Cedric Scott, *Randolph*, Robert Fortier, *Jim Habor, Gardener*, Maureen Steindler, *Libby Clinton, Cook. The Wedding Staff:* Geraldine Chaplin, *Rita Billingsley*, Mona Abbound, *Melba Lear*, Viveca Lindfors, *Ingrid Hellstrom*, Lauren Hutton, *Flo Farmer*, Allan Nicholls, *Jake Jacobs*, Maysie Hoy, *Casey*, John Considine, *Jeff Kuykendall*, Patricia Resnick, *Redford*, Margery Bond, *Lombardo*, Dennis Franz, *Koons*, Harold C. Johnson, *Oscar Edwards*, Alexander Sopenar, *Victor*.

The Friends and Guests: Howard Duff, *Dr. Jules Meecham*, John Cromwell, *Bishop Martin*, Bert Remsen, *William Williamson*, Pam Dawber, *Tracy Farrell*, Gavan O'Hirlihy, *Wilson Briggs*, Craig Richard Nelson, *Capt. Reedley Roots*, Jeffrey S. Perry, *Bunky Lemay*, Marta Heflin, *Shelby Munker*, Lesley Rogers, *Rosie Bean*, Timothy Thomerson, *Russell Bean*, Beverly Ross, *Nurse Janet Schulman*, David Fitzgerald, *Kevin Clinton*, Susan Kendall Newman, *Chris Clinton*. PG. $4,785,000.

Well-made comic satire focusing entirely on a lavish wedding and the two bourgeois families involved. Altman merely uses the setting of a wedding as a springboard for numerous ideas on society and family relationships, and he takes his usual plotless structure and examines the dozens of characters and how they interrelate. This is a difficult task and Altman manages to bring them all to life, although *A Wedding* lacks the epic brilliance of *Nashville*.

902 **Welcome to L.A.** (1976) ******** United Artists, 106 min. *Dir* Alan Rudolph, *Scr* Alan Rudolph, *Cin* Dave Myers, *Ed* William A. Sawyer, Tom Walls, *Mus* Richard Baskin, *Prod* Robert Altman.

Cast: Keith Carradine, *Carroll*, Sally Kellerman, *Ann*, Geraldine Chaplin, *Karen*, Harvey Keitel, *Ken*, Lauren Hutton, *Nona*, Viveca Lindfors, *Susan*, Sissy Spacek, *Linda*, Denver Pyle, *Carl*, John Considine, *Jack*, Richard Baskin, *Eric*. R.

Unusual comedy-drama focusing on a group of oddball characters living in Los Angeles. *Welcome to L.A.* is a kaleidescopic portrait of a city and its people, examining their empty lives and relationships. Alan Rudolph, in an excellent directorial debut, was obviously influenced by his mentor Robert Altman, but his style is more original than derivative.

903 **Westworld** (1973) *** MGM, 91 min. *Dir* Michael Crichton, *Scr* Michael Crichton, *Cin* Gene Polito, *Ed* David Bretherton, *Art* Herman Blumenthal, *Mus* Fred Karlin, *Prod* Paul N. Lazarus III, *Assoc Prod* Michael I. Rachmil.

Cast: Richard Benjamin, *Peter Martin,* James Brolin, *John Blane,* Yul Brynner, *Gunslinger,* Norman Bartold, *Medieval Knight,* Alan Oppenheimer, *Chief Supervisor,* Victoria Shaw, *Medieval Queen,* Dick Van Patten, *Banker,* Linda Scott, *Arlette,* Steve Franken, *Technician,* Michael Mikler, *Black Knight,* Terry Wilson, *Sheriff,* Majel Barrett, *Miss Carrie,* Anne Randall, *Servant Girl,* Julie Marcus, *Girl in Dungeon,* Sharyn Wynters, *Apache Girl,* Anne Bellamy, *A Middle-Aged Woman,* Chris Holter, *A Stewardess,* Charles Seel, *A Bellhop,* Wade Crosby, *A Bartender,* Nora Marlowe, *The Hostess.* PG. $7,000,000.

Interesting science-fiction thriller about an adult amusement park where people can safely live out their fantasies. James Brolin and Richard Benjamin are excellent as two businessmen who play cowboys until the system goes haywire and they are pursued by a robot gunslinger (Yul Brynner). The theme of automation gone berserk is a familiar one, but the approach is fresh. Noted SF novelist Michael Crichton made a fine directorial debut with this film. In the sequel, *Futureworld,* the robots clone humans to completely take over. *Futureworld* is somewhat dull and lacks both the suspense and the excitement of its predecessor.

904 **What's Up Doc** (1972) *** Warner Bros., 94 min. *Dir* Peter Bogdanovich, *Scr* Robert Benton, David Newman, Buck Henry (W), *Story* Peter Bogdanovich, *Cin* Laszlo Kovacs, *Ed* Verna Fields, *Des* Polly Platt, *Art* Herman A. Blumenthal, *Mus* Artie Butler, *Prod* Peter Bogdanovich, *Assoc Prod* Paul Lewis.

Cast: Barbra Streisand, *Judy Maxwell,* Ryan O'Neal, *Howard Bannister,* Kenneth Mars, *Hugh Simon,* Austin Pendleton, *Frederick Larrabee,* Sorrell Booke, *Harry,* Stefan Gierasch, *Fritz,* Mabel Albertson, *Mrs. Van Hoskins,* Michael Murphy, *Smith,* Graham Jarvis, *Bailiff,* Madeline Kahn, *Eunice Burns,* Liam Dunn, *Judge,* Phil Roth, *Jones,* John Hillerman, *Kaltenborn,* George Morfogen, *Rudy,* Randy Quaid, *Prof. Hosquith,* M. Emmet Walsh, *Arresting Officer,* Eleanor Zee, *Banquet Receptionist,* Kevin O'Neal, *Delivery Boy.* G. $28,000,000.

Contemporary screwball-comedy about a musicologist (O'Neal) who gets involved with a first class kook (Streisand). They subsequently become embroiled in a plot involving stolen jewels, which leads to a climactic slapstick chase through the streets of San Francisco. Bogdanovich has always acknowledged the influence of such directors as Ford, Hawks and Hitchcock, but *What's Up Doc* is more than just a homage to Hawks' *Bringing Up Baby,* but without Hawks's expert comic timing. Although not a great film, this at least rises above most other slapstick comedies.

905 When a Stranger Calls (1979) ******** Columbia, 97 min. *Dir* Fred Walton, *Scr* Steve Feke, Fred Walton, *Cin* Don Peterson, *Ed* Sam Vitale, *Des* Elayne Barbara Ceder, *Mus* Dana Kaproff, *Prod* Doug Chapin, Steve Feke, *Exec Prod* Barry Krost, Melvin Simon, *Assoc Prod* Larry Kostroff.

Cast: Charles Durning, *John Clifford*, Carol Kane, *Jill Johnson*, Tony Beckley, *Curt Duncan*, Colleen Dewhurst, *Tracy*, Steven Anderson, *Stephen Lockart*, Carmen Argenziano, *Dr. Mandrakis*, Rutanya Alda, *Mrs. Mandrakis*, Ron O'Neal, *Lt. Charlie Garber*, Rachel Roberts, *Dr. Monk*, Sarah Dammann, *Bianca Lockart*, Richard Bail, *Stevie Lockart*, Joe Reale, *Bartender*, John Tobyansen, *Bar Customer*. R. $11,400,000.

Excellent murder thriller about a psychotic killer who terrorizes a baby sitter. *When a Stranger Calls* should not be confused with those other mad slasher movies that flooded the market following the success of *Halloween*. One of the differences with this film is its emphasis on character and suspense rather than inventive methods of killing. The entire cast is excellent particularly Charles Durning as the detective and Tony Beckley who brings much depth and sympathy to his role as the psychotic killer. Fred Walton deserves enormous credit for taking a cliché idea and turning it into a worthy film.

906 When the Legends Die (1972) ******* 20th Century–Fox, 105 min. *Dir* Stuart Miller, *Scr* Robert Dozier, based on novel by Hal Borland, *Cin* Richard H. Kline, *Ed* Louis San Andres, *Art* Angelo Graham, *Mus* Glenn Paxton, *Songs* Bo Goldman, Glenn Paxton, *Prod* Stuart Millar, *Co-Prod* Gene Lasko.

Cast: Richard Widmark, *Red Dillon*, Frederic Forrest, *Tom Black Bull*, Luana Anders, *Mary*, Vito Scotti, *Meo*, Herbert Nelson, *Dr. Wilson*, John War Eagle, *Blue Elk*, John Cruber, *Tex Walker*, Gary Walberg, *Superintendent*, Jack Mullaney, *Gas Station Attendant*, Malcolm Curley, *Benny Grayback*, Roy Engle, *Sam Turner*, Rex Holman, *Neil Swenson*, Mel Gallagher, *Cowboy*, Tillman Box, *Young Tom Black Bull*, Sondra Pratt, *Angie*, Verne Muehlstedt, *Harold*, Evan Stevens, *George*. PG.

Fine drama about an Indian youth (Frederic Forrest), who is taken from his reservation and turned into a rodeo star by a ruthless and drunken manager (Richard Widmark). Forrest becomes disillusioned by his success and society, and returns to his reservation. The story may not be original, but its treatment is fresh, and Widmark and Forrest are excellent.

907 Where Does It Hurt? (1972) ****** Cinerama, 90 min. *Dir* Rod Amateau, *Scr* Rod Amateau, Budd Robinson, based on their novel *The Operator*, *Cin* Brick Marquand, *Ed* Tony Mora, Stan Rabjohn, *Art* Mike Haller, *Mus* Keith Allison, *Prod* Rod Amateau, Bill Schwartz, *Exec Prod* Josef Shafel.

Cast: Peter Sellers, *Albert Hopfnagel*, Jo Ann Pflug, *Alice*, Rick Lenz, *Lester*, Harold Gould, *Dr. Zerny*, Hope Summers, *Nurse Throttle*, Eve Bruce, *LaMarr*, Kathleen Freeman, *Mrs. Mazzini*, Norman Alden, *Katzen*, Keith Allison, *Hinkley*, William Elliot, *Oscar*, Jeanne Byron, *Dr. Kincaid*, Paul Lambert, *Dr. Pinikhes*, Brett Halsey, *Dr. Quagliomo*, Albert Reed, *Dr. Radcliffe*, J. Edward McKinley, *Commissioner*, Marvin Miller, *Catering Manager*, Pat Morita, *Nishimoto*, Jack Mullaney, *Male Secretary*. R.

Interesting black comedy that savagely attacks hospitals. Peter Sellers stars as the corrupt hospital administrator, who would prefer that his surgeons perform unnecessary operations than none at all. *Where Does It Hurt?* may be far fetched, and some of its humor is forced, but it does offer some funny insights into hospital attitudes, and the ending is a gem.

908 **Where's Poppa?** (1970) *** United Artists, 87 min. *Dir* Carl Reiner, *Scr* Robert Klane, *Cin* Jack Priestley, *Ed* Chic Ciccolini, Bud Molin, *Art* Warren Clymer, *Cos* Albert Wolsky, *Mus* Jack Elliott, *Lyrics* Norman Gimbel, *Prod* Jerry Tokofsky, Marvin Worth.

Cast: George Segal, *Gordon Hocheiser*, Ruth Gordon, *Mrs. Hocheiser*, Trish Van Devere, *Louise*, Ron Leibman, *Sidney Hocheiser*, Tom Atkins, *First Policeman*, Florence Tarlow, *Secretary*, Jane Hoffman, *First Woman*, Helen Martin, *Capable Woman*. R.

Bizarre black comedy about a middle-aged lawyer (George Segal), who tries to cope with living with his senile mother (Ruth Gordon). Life with her becomes so unbearable, he is driven to plotting her murder. *Where's Poppa?* promises a bit more than it delivers. Although it does not compromise on its touchy subject matter and there are some hysterically funny scenes, it is unable to keep the lunacy at its high pitch, throughout.

909 **Which Way Is Up?** (1977) ** Universal, 94 min. *Dir* Michael Schultz, *Scr* Cecil Brown, Carl Gottlieb, based on film *The Seduction of Mimi* by Lina Wertmuller, *Cin* John A. Alonzo, *Ed* Danford B. Greene, *Des* Lawrence G. Paull, *Mus* Mark Davis, Paul Riser, *Prod* Steve Krantz, *Assoc Prod* Michael Chinich.

Cast: Richard Pryor, *Leroy Jones/Rufus Jones/Rev. Thomas*, Lonette McKee, *Vanetta*, Margaret Avery, *Annie Mae*, Morgan Woodward, *Mr. Mann*, Marilyn Coleman, *Sister Sarah*, Bebe Drake-Hooks, *Thelma*, Gloria Edwards, *Janelle*, Ernesto Hernandez, *Jose*, DeWayne Jessie, *Sugar*, Morgan Roberts, *Henry*, Diane Rodriguez, *Estrella*, Dolph Sweet, *The Boss*, Danny Valdez, *Chuy*, Luis Valdez, *Ramon*, Pat Ast, *Hooker*, Timothy Thomerson, *Tour Guide*. R. $9,565,000.

Uneven comedy featuring Richard Pryor in three separate roles, all of whom tend to be repulsive. The central character is that of a worker in an orange grove, who becomes a labor organizor. Pryor also appears as this character's shrill father and a hypocritical preacher. *Which Way Is Up?* is poorly structured and the humor is more tasteless than funny.

910 **Whiffs** (1975) * 20th Century–Fox, 90 min. *Dir* Ted Post, *Scr* Malcolm Marmorstein, *Cin* David Walsh, *Ed* Robert Lawrence, *Art* Fernando Carrere, *Mus* John Cameron, *Song* "Now That We're In Love", *Mus* George Barrie (AN), *Lyrics* Sammy Cahn (AN), *Prod* George Barrie, *Assoc Prod* Don Erickson.

Cast: Elliott Gould, *Dudley Frapper*, Eddie Albert, *Col Lockyer*, Harry Guardino, *Chops*, Godfrey Cambridge, *Dusty*, Jennifer O'Neill, *Scottie*, Alan Manson, *Sgt. Poultry*, Donald Barry, *Post*, Richard Masur, *Lockyer's Aide*, Howard Hesseman, *Gopian*, Matt Greene, *Sentry*, James Brown, *Trooper*. PG.

Limp comedy starring Elliott Gould as a military guinea pig for germ warfare tests. The humor is unbearably ridiculous, in which the supposed big laughs stem from mugging by the stars and sophomoric dialogue. This is the type of slapstick comedy that Jerry Lewis was known for in the 1960's, but next to *Whiffs* Lewis' films are great artistic achievements.

911 **The White Dawn** (1974) *** Paramount, 109 min. *Dir* Philip Kaufman, *Scr* James Houston, Tom Rickman, *Adaptation* Martin Ransohoff, based on novel by James Houston, *Cin* Michael Chapman, *Ed* Douglas Stewart, *Mus* Henry Mancini, *Prod* Martin Ransahoff, *Assoc Prod* Don Guest, James Houston.

Cast: Warren Oates, *Billy*, Timothy Bottoms, *Daggett*, Lou Gossett, *Portagee*. R.

Interesting drama about three whalers who are stranded in the Arctic in the 1890's and are taken in by a tribe of Eskimos, with tragic results. *The White Dawn* does make a gallant effort to be a serious examination of the difference in cultures, but as in the similarly themed *A Man Called Horse* the film tends to drag somewhat.

912 **White Lightning** (1973) *** United Artists, 101 min. *Dir* Joseph Sargent, *Scr* William Norton, *Cin* Edward Rosson, *Ed* George Nicholson, *Mus* Charles Bernstein, *Prod* Arthur Gardner, Jules V. Levy.

Cast: Burt Reynolds, *Gator McKlusky*, Jennifer Billingsly, *Lou*, Ned Beatty, *Sheriff Connors*, Bo Hopkins, *Roy Boone*, Matt Clark, *Dude Watson*, Louise Latham, *Martha Culpepper*, Diane Ladd, *Maggie*, R.G. Armstrong, *Big Bear*, Conlan Carter, *Deputy*, Dabbs Greer, *Pa McKluskey*, Lincoln Demyan, *Superintendent Simms*, John Steadman, *Skeeter*, Iris Korn, *Ma McKluskey*, Stephanie Burchfield, *Jenny*, Barbara Muller, *Louella*, Robert Ginnaven, *Harvey*, Faye Martin, *Sister Linda Fay*, Richard Allin, Bill Bond, *Treasury Agents*, Glenn Wilder, *Junior*, Kathy Finley, *Student*, Dick Ziker, Buddy Joe Hooker, *Highway Patrolman*. PG. $6,105,000.

Well-made vendetta drama about a convict who, for personal reasons, aids the Feds in getting a crooked sheriff. This is possibly the best of Burt Reynold's Southern action dramas. *White Lightning* has all the elements of his other films–plenty of action, chases and moonshine—but they are not exaggerated to cartoon-like levels. The sequel *Gator*, pits Reynolds against a gangster who runs an entire town. This film is greatly inferior to its predecessor.

913 **White Line Fever** (1975) *** Columbia, 89 min. *Dir* Jonathan Kaplan, *Scr* Ken Friedman, Jonathan Kaplan, *Cin* Fred Koenekamp, *Ed* O. Nicholas Brown, *Art* Sydney Litwack, *Mus* David Nichtern, *Prod* John Kemeny, *Exec Prod* Mort Litwack, Gerald Schneider.

Cast: Jan-Michael Vincent, *Carrol Jo Hummer*, Kay Lenz, *Jerri Hummer*, Slim Pickens, *Duana Haller*, L.Q. Jones, *Buck Wessle*, Don Porter, *Josh Cutler*, Sam Laws, *Pops*, Johnny Ray McGhee, *Cornell*, Leigh French, *Lucy*, R.G. Armstrong, *Prosecutor*, Martin Kove, *Clem*, Jamie Anderson, *Jamie*, Ron Nix, *Deputy*, Dick Miller, *Birdie*, Arnold Jeffers, *Reporter*, Curgie Pratt, *Defense Lawyer*, John David Garfield, *Witness Miller*. PG. $6,000,000.

Above average action thriller about an Air Force vet (Jan-Michael Vincent), who becomes an independent trucker. He runs into problems with the trucking industry and discovers it is difficult to remain honest. The truckers naturally try to stop him, and it results in the obligatory violence. This is pretty standard, but director Jonathan Kaplan handles it well.

914 **Who Is Harry Kellerman and Why Is He Saying Those Terrible Things About Me?** (1971) *** National General, 108 min. *Dir* Ulu Grosbard, *Scr*

Herb Gardner, *Cin* Victor J. Kemper, *Ed* Barry Malkin, *Des* Harry Horner, *Cos* Anna Hill Johnstone, *Mus* Shel Silverstein, *Prod* Herb Gardner, Ulu Grosbard, *Assoc Prod* Fred C. Caruso.

Cast: Dustin Hoffman, *Georgie Soloway*, Barbara Harris (AN), *Allison Densmore*, Jack Warden, *Dr. Moses*, David Burns, *Georgie's Father*, Dom DeLuise, *Irwin*, Gabriel Dell, *Sid*, Betty Walker, *Georgie's Mother*, Rose Gregorio, *Gloria*, Regina Baff, *Ruthie Tresh*, Ed Zimmerman, *Halloran*, Amy Levitt, *Susan*, Joseph R. Sicari, *Marty*. PG.

Unusual comedy about a successful rock singer-composer (Dustin Hoffman), who has difficulty coping with getting older and the emptiness of fame. To make things worse he believes a man named Harry Kellerman is trying to destroy his reputation. The film is a fine study of the pressures of stardom, but it tends to ramble a bit. Barbara Harris gives a superb performance as Hoffman's girlfriend.

915 Who Is Killing the Great Chefs of Europe? (1978) ******* U.S./West Germany, 112 min. *Dir* Ted Kotcheff, *Scr* Peter Stone, based on novel *Someone Is Killing the Great Chefs of Europe* by Nan and Ivan Lyons, *Cin* John Alcott, *Art* Werner Achmann, *Cos* Judy Moorcroft, *Mus* Henry Mancini, *Prod* William Aldrich.

Cast: George Segal, *Robby*, Jacqueline Bisset, *Natasha*, Robert Morley, *Max*, Jean-Pierre Cassel, *Kohner*, Philippe Noiret, *Moulineau*, Jean Rochefort, *Grandvilliers*, Luigi Proietti, *Ravello*, Stefano Satta Flores, *Fausto Zoppi*, Madge Ryan, *Beecham*, Frank Windsor, *Blodgett*, Peter Sallis, *St. Claire*, Tim Barlow, *Doyle*, John LeMesurier, *Dr. Deere*, Joss Ackland, *Cantrell*, Jean Gaven, *Salpetre*, Daniel Emilfork, *Saint-Juste*, Jacques Marin, *Massenet*, Jacques Balutin, *Chappermain*, Jean Paredes, *Brissac*, Kenneth Fortescue, *Director*. PG. $6,000,000.

Well-made light black-comedy mystery about the murders of some of Europe's finest chefs. George Segal stars as an overbearing fast food businessman, who pursues Jacqueline Bisset, his ex-wife, who is the world's greatest dessert chef and also a potential victim. This is a fast-paced and witty comedy, and it features a superb performance by Robert Morley as a world renowned gourmet.

916 Who'll Stop the Rain? (1978) ******** United Artists, 125 min. *Dir* Karel Reisz, *Scr* Judith Roscoe, Robert Stone, based on novel *Dog Soldiers* by Robert Stone, *Cin* Richard H. Kline, *Ed* John Bloom, *Mus* Laurence Rosenthal, *Prod* Herb Jaffe, Gabriel Katzka.

Cast: Nick Nolte, *Ray*, Tuesday Weld, *Marge*, Michael Moriarty, *John*, Anthony Zerbe, *Antheil*, Richard Masur, *Danskin*, Ray Sharkey, *Smitty*, Gail Strickland, *Chairman*, Charles Haid, *Eddy*, David O. Opatoshu, *Bender*. R.

Excellent adventure thriller starring Nick Nolte as a soldier who smuggles drugs into the U.S. from Vietnam for a correspondent (Michael Moriarty). Nolte contacts Moriarty's wife (Tuesday Weld), and they are then pursued by some corrupt F.B.I. agents, who want the drugs for themselves. *Who'll Stop the Rain?* should have been a more shocking and horrowing film, but it is nevertheless a well made adventure, highlighted by the outstanding performance of Nolte, who is possibly the cinema's finest existential hero since Humphrey Bogart.

917 The Wilby Conspiracy (1975) ** Britain, United Artists, 101 min. *Dir* Ralph Nelson, *Scr* Rod Amateau, Harold Nebenzal, based on novel by Peter Driscoll, *Cin* John Coquillon, *Ed* Ernest Walter, *Des* Harold Pottle, *Art* John Hoesli, *Mus* Stanley Myers, *Prod* Martin Baum, *Exec Prod* Helmut Dantine.

Cast: Sidney Poitier, *Shack Twala*, Michael Caine, *Keogh*, Nicol Williamson, *Horn*, Prunella Gee, *Rina Nierkirk*, Persis Khambatta, *Peris Ray*, Saeed Jaffrey, *Mukerjee*, Ryk De Gooyer, *Van Heerden*, Rutger Hauer, *Blane Nierkirk*, Joseph De Graf, *Wilby*, Helmut Dantine, *Prosecutor*, Brian Epsom, *Judge*, Abdullah Sunado, *Headman in Masai Village*, Freddy Achiang, *Shepherd Boy*, Patrick Allen, *District Commandant*, Archie Duncan, *Gordon*. PG.

Above average political thriller of racial turmoil in South Africa. An activist (Sidney Poitier) and an Englishman (Michael Caine), who accidently become involved, are on the run from the law and are pursued by a bigoted policeman (Nicol Williamson). *The Wilby Conspiracy* is nothing more than a chase thriller masquerading as a socially relevant film. The three stars, particularly Williamson, give better performances than this deserves.

918 The Wild Party (1975) *** American International, 100 min. *Dir* James Ivory, *Scr* Walter Marks, based on narrative poem by Joseph Moncure March, *Cin* Walter Lassally, *Ed* Kent McKinney, *Art* David Nichols, *Cos* Ronald Kolodgie, Ralph Lauren, Ron Talsky, *Mus* Laurence Rosenthal, *Lyrics* Walter Marks, *Dance Mus* Louis St. Louis, *Chor* Patricia Birch, *Prod* Ismail Merchant, *Exec Prod* Joseph Beruh, Edgar Lansbury, *Assoc Prod* George Manasse.

Cast: James Coco, *Jolly Grimm*, Raquel Welch, *Queenie*, Perry King, *Dale Sword*, Tiffany Bolling, *Kate*, Royal Dano, *Tex*, David Dukes, *James Morrison*, Dena Dietrich, *Mrs. Murchison*, Regis Cordic, *Mr. Murchison*, Jennifer Lee, *Madeline True*, Marya Small, *Bertha*, Bobo Lewis, *Wilma*, Annette Ferra, *Nadine*, Eddie Laurence, *Kreutzer*. R.

Unusual drama set at wild Hollywood party in the 1920's. James Coco stars as a once popular movie comic, loosely based on Fatty Arbuckle, who throws this party to help begin his comeback. As in the real party thrown by Arbuckle, this ends in tragedy. Coco gives an outstanding performance in this well made, but somewhat overly talky dramatic musical.

919 The Wild Rovers (1971) ** MGM, 106 min. *Dir* Blake Edwards, *Scr* Blake Edwards, *Cin* Philip Lathrop, *Ed* John F. Burnett, *Art* George W. Davis, Addison Hehr, *Cos* Jack Bear, *Mus* Jerry Goldsmith, *Song* "Wild Rover", *Mus* Jerry Goldsmith, *Lyrics* Ernie Sheldon, *Prod* Blake Edwards, Ken Wales.

Cast: William Holden, *Ross Bodine*, Ryan O'Neal, *Frank Post*, Karl Malden, *Walter Buckman*, Lynn Carlin, *Sada Billings*, Tom Skerritt, *John Buckman*, Joe Don Baker, *Paul Buckman*, James Olson, *Joe Billings*, Leora Dana, *Nell Buckman*, Moses Gunn, *Ben*, Victor French, *Sheriff*, Rachel Roberts, *Maybell*, Sam Gilman, *Hansen*, Charles Gray, *Savage*, William Bryant, *Hereford*, Jack Garner, *Cap Swilling*. PG.

Fair western about a pair of cowboys (William Holden, Ryan O'Neal), who suddenly decide to rob a bank, and become pursued outlaws. Most of the film documents their getaway to Mexico, while focusing on their relationship. *The Wild Rovers* tries to emulate both *Butch Cassidy and the*

Sundance Kid and *The Wild Bunch*, but it has none of the brilliance of either film. Holden and O'Neal give fine performances, but they cannot match the charismatic pairing of Newman and Redford.

920 **Willard** (1971) ****** Cinerama, 95 min. *Dir* Daniel Mann, *Scr* Gilbert A. Ralston, based on novel *Ratman's Notebooks* by Stephen Gilbert, *Cin* Robert B. Hauser, *Ed* Warren Low, *Art* Howard Hollender, *Cos* Dorothy Barkley, Eric Seeling, *Mus* Alex North, *Prod* Mort Briskin, *Exec Prod* Charles A. Pratt.

Cast: Bruce Davison, *Willard Stiles*, Ernest Borgnine, *Al Martin*, Elsa Lanchester, *Henrietta Stiles*, Sondra Locke, *Joan*, Michael Dante, *Brandt*, Jody Gilbert, *Charlotte Stassen*, Joan Shawlee, *Alice*, William Hansen, *Mr. Barskin*, J. Pat O'Malley, *Jonathan Farley*, John Myhers, *Mr. Carlson*, Helen Spring, *Mrs. Becker*, Pauline Drake, *Ida Stassen*, Almira Sessions, *Carrie Smith*, Alan Baxter, *Mr. Spencer*, Sherry Presnell, *Mrs. Spencer*, Lola Kendrick, *Mrs. Martin*. PG. $9,300,000.

Unusual drama about a young lonely man (Bruce Davison), whose only solace is in his friendship with his pet rats. Willard decides to get revenge on those who have mistreated him, and he trains his army of rats to be killers. *Willard* is better than most films of its type, but that is not saying much. The lead rat proved so charismatic he was given his own film, a dull sequel titled *Ben*.

921 **Willy Wonka and the Chocolate Factory** (1971) ******* 98 min. *Dir* Mel Stuart, *Scr* Roald Dahl, based on his novel *Charlie and the Chocolate Factory*, *Cin* Arthur Ibbetson, *Ed* David Saxon, *Art* Harper Goff, *Cos* Ille Sievers, *Mus* Leslie Bricusse, Anthony Newley (AN), *Mus Adaptation* Walter Scharf (AN), *Chor* Howard Jeffrey, *Prod* Stan Margulies, David L. Wolper.

Cast: Gene Wilder, *Willy Wonka*, Jack Albertson, *Grandpa Joe*, Peter Ostrum, *Charlie Bucket*, Michael Bollner, *Augustus Gloop*, Ursula Reit, *Mrs. Gloop*, Denise Nickerson, *Violet Beauregarde*, Leonard Stone, *Mr. Beauregarde*, Julie Dawn Cole, *Veruca Salt*, Roy Kinnear, *Mr. Salt*, Paris Themmen, *Mike Teevee*, Dodo Denny, *Mrs. Teevee*, Diana Sowle, *Mrs. Bucket*, Aubrey Wood, *Mr. Bill*, David Battley, *Mr. Turkentine*, Gunter Meissner, *Mr. Slugworth*, Peter Capell, *Tinker*, Werner J. Heyking, *Jopeck*, Ernest Ziegler, *Grandpa George*, Dora Altmann, *Grandma Georgina*, Franziska Liebing, *Grandma Josephine*. G.

Above-average children's fantasy comedy starring Gene Wilder as the owner of a strange chocolate factory. As part of a contest he takes some obnoxious children and their parents on a tour through his factory, where he teaches them a lesson. This is an odd film for its type, as it tends to be slightly sadistic in its treatment, but that is part of the film's charm.

922 **The Wind and the Lion** (1975) ******** United Artists, 119 min. *Dir* John Milius, *Scr* John Milius, *Cin* Billy Williams, *Ed* Robert L. Wolfe, *Des* Gil Parrando, *Art* R. Antonio Paton, *Cos* Richard E. LaMotte, *Mus* Jerry Goldsmith (AN), *Prod* Herb Jaffe, *Assoc Prod* Phil Rawlins.

Cast: Sean Connery, *Raisuli*, Candice Bergen, *Eden Pedecaris*, Brian Keith, *Theodore Roosevelt*, John Huston, *John Hay*, Geoffrey Lewis, *Cummere*, Steve Kanaly, *Capt. Jerome*, Vladek Sheybal, *The Bashaw*, Nadim Sawalha, *Sherif of Wazan*, Roy Jenson, *Adm. Chadwick*, Deborah Baxter, *Alice Roosevelt*, Jack Cooley, *Quentin Roosevelt*, Chris Aller, *Kermit*

Roosevelt, Simon Harrison, *William Pedecaris*, Polly Gottesman, *Jennifer Pedecaris*. PG. $5,000,000.

Excellent period adventure, loosely based on a real incident, about a Berber Chieftain (Sean Connery), who kidnaps an American woman (Candice Bergen) and her two children in 1904, which causes an international crisis. This leads to a battle of wits between the Chieftain and Pres. Theodore Roosevelt, superbly played by Brian Keith. *The Wind and the Lion* is a wonderful blend of action and romance, and is John Milius' finest film.

923 **Winter Kills** (1979) ******** Avco Embassy, 97 min. *Dir* William Richert, *Scr* William Richert, based on novel by Richard Condon, *Cin* Vilmos Zsigmond, *Ed* David Bretherton, *Des* Robert Boyle, *Art* Norman Newberry, *Cos* Robert De Mora, *Mus* Maurice Jarre, *Prod* Fred Caruso, *Exec Prod* Leonard J. Goldberg, Robert Sterling, *Assoc Prod* John Stark.

Cast: Jeff Bridges, *Nick*, John Huston, *Pa Kegan*, Anthony Perkins, *John Cerruti*, Sterling Hayden, *Z.K.*, Eli Wallach, *Joe*, Dorothy Malone, *Emma*, Tomas Milian, *Frank*, Belinda Bauer, *Yvette*, Ralph Meeker, *Baker*, Toshiro Mifune, *Keith*, Donald Moffat, *Captain*, David Spielberg, *Miles*, Brad Dexter, *Heller*, Peter Brandon, *Doctor*, Michael Thoma, *Ray*. PG.

Outlandish black comedy about political assassination. Jeff Bridges stars as a member of a wealthy political family, loosely based on the Kennedy family, who investigates the assassination of his brother, who had been President of the U.S. *Winter Kills* had the promise of being a terrible film, partially due to its problem-filled production history, but it turned out to be one of the most pleasant surprises of the decade. William Richert, in his directorial debut, proved to be a wildly original talent.

924 **Wise Blood** (1979) ******** U.S./West Germany, New Line Cinema, 108 min. *Dir* John Huston, *Scr* Benedict Fitzgerald, based on novel by Flannery O'Connor, *Cin* Gerald Fisher, *Ed* Roberto Silvi, *Des* Sally Fitzgerald, *Cos* Sally Fitzgerald, *Mus* Alex North, *Prod* Michael and Kathy Fitzgerald.

Cast: Brad Dourif, *Hazel Motes*, Ned Beatty, *Hoover Shoates*, Harry Dean Stanton, *Asa Hawks*, Daniel Shor, *Enoch Emery*, Amy Wright, *Sabbath Lilly*, Mary Nell Santacroce, *Landlady*, John Huston, *Grandfather*. Not Rated.

Strange comedy-drama about a young man (Brad Dourif), home from the war, who through his association with a blind preacher, becomes a preacher for the Church Without Christ. Dourif's obsessiveness leads to a powerful and tragic conclusion. *Wise Blood* is a perceptive portrait of these odd, but real people and is one of John Huston's finest films.

925 **The Wiz** (1978) ****** Universal, 133 min. *Dir* Sidney Lumet, *Scr* Joel Schumacher, based on book *The Wonderful Wizard of Oz* by L. Frank Baum and musical *The Wiz*, book by William F. Brown and music and lyrics by Charlie Smalls, *Cin* Oswald Morris (AN), *Ed* Dede Allen, *Des* Tony Walton (AN), *Art* Philip Rosenberg (AN), *Cos* Tony Walton (AN), *Mus Adaptation*, Quincy Jones (AN), *Chor* Louis Johnson, *Assistant Chor* Carlton Johnson, Mabel Robinson, *Prod* Rob Cohen, *Exec Prod* Ken Harper, *Assoc Prod* Burtt Harris.

Cast: Diana Ross, *Dorothy*, Michael Jackson, *Scarecrow*, Nipsey Russell, *Tinman*, Ted Ross, *Lion*, Mabel King, *Evillene*, Theresa Merritt, *Aunt Em*, Thelma Carpenter, *Miss One*, Lena Horne, *Glinda the Good*, Richard Pryor,

The Wiz, Stanley Greene, *Uncle Henry*, Clyde J. Barrett, *Subway Peddler*, Carlton Johnson, *Head Winkie*, Harry Madsen, *Cheetah*, Glory Van Scott, *Rolls Royce Lady*, Vicki Baltimore, *Green Lady*. G. $13,610,000.

Disappointing film version of the hit Broadway musical. *The Wiz* is an updating of the children's classic *The Wizard of Oz*, but with an all black cast. This appears to have been an attempt at a socially relevant film that sets the problems of blacks in today's society to music, and this is where it fails. Its strengths, though, are its well-done fantasy and musical sequences, and *The Wiz* should not have strained to be more.

926 A Woman Under the Influence (1974) **** Faces International, 155 min. *Dir* John Cassavetes (AN), *Scr* John Cassavetes, *Cin* Mitch Breif, *Ed* David Armstrong, Elizabeth Bergeron, Tom Cornwell, Sheila Viseltear, *Art* Phedon Papamichael, *Mus* Bo Harwood, *Prod* Sam Shaw.

Cast: Peter Falk, *Nick Longhetti*, Gena Rowlands (AN, NB, G), *Mabel Longhetti*, Matthew Cassel, *Tony Longhetti*, Matthew Laborteaux, *Angelo Longhetti*, Christina Grisanti, *Maria Longhetti*, Katherine Cassavetes, *Mama Longhetti*, Lady Rowlands, *Martha Mortensen*, Fred Draper, *George Mortensen*, O.G. Dunn, *Garson Cross*, Mario Gallo, *Harold Jensen*, Eddie Shaw, *Doctor Zepp*, Angelo Grisanti, *Vito Grimaldi*. Not Rated. $6,115,000.

Excellent drama about a housewife who is unable to cope with her everyday problems and suffers a mental breakdown. Gena Rowlands gives a magnificent performance as the suffering wife, who possesses more nervous tics than anyone imaginable. Peter Falk is also excellent as the husband who tries to understand her dilemma but instead contributes to it. *A Woman Under the Influence*, although very long, is a solid film and the best from John Cassavetes.

927 Women in Love (1970) (G-English Language Foreign Film) ***** Britain, United Artists, 129 min. *Dir* Ken Russell (AN), *Scr* Larry Kramer (AN), based on novel by D.H. Lawrence, *Cin* Billy Williams (AN), *Ed* Michael Bradsell, *Cos* Shirley Russell, *Mus* Georges Delerue, *Chor* Terry Gilbert, *Prod* Larry Kramer, Martin Rosen, *Assoc Prod* Roy Baird.

Cast: Alan Bates, *Rupert Birkin*, Oliver Reed, *Gerald Crich*, Glenda Jackson (A, NS, NY, NB), *Gudrun Brangwen*, Jennie Linden, *Ursula Brangwen*, Eleanor Bron, *Hermione Roddice*, Alan Webb, *Mr. Crich*, Vladek Sheybal, *Loerke*, Catherine Wilmer, *Mrs. Crich*, Sarah Nicholls, *Winifred Crich*, Sharon Gurney, *Laura Crich*, Christopher Gable, *Tibby Lupton*, Michael Gough, *Mr. Brangwen*, Norma Shebeare, *Mrs. Brangwen*, Nike Arrighi, *Contessa*, James Laurenson, *Minister*, Michael Graham Cox, *Palmer*, Richard Heffer, *Loerke's Friend*, Michael Garratt, *Maestro*. R.

Outlandish and brilliant period film focusing on the relationships of two Englishmen (Oliver Reed, Alan Bates) with two sisters (Glenda Jackson, Jennie Linden). There is only a slight plot, but Ken Russell's breathtakingly surrealistic style propels *Women in Love* beyond most films. There are many outstanding sequences, including Jackson's dance before a herd of cattle and a nude wrestling match between Reed and Bates. This is Russell's first major film and also his finest.

928 Won Ton Ton, The Dog Who Saved Hollywood (1976) * Paramount, 92 min. *Dir* Michael Winner, *Scr* Cy Howard, Arnold Schulman, *Cin* Richard

H. Kline, *Ed* Bernard Gribble, *Art* Ward Preston, *Mus* Neal Hefty, *Prod* David V. Picker, Arnold Schulman, Michael Winner.

Cast: Bruce Dern, *Grayson Potchuck*, Madeline Kahn, *Estie Del Ruth*, Art Carney, *J.J. Fromberg*, Phil Silvers, *Murray Fromberg*, Teri Garr, *Fluffy Peters*, Ron Leibman, *Rudy Montague*, Augustus von Schumacher, *Won Ton Ton*. PG.

Silly period Hollywood comedy about a dog movie star, loosely patterned after Rin Tin Tin, that saves a studio from financial ruin during the 1920's. The film is little more than a series of witless and dull sight gags, with a parade of dozens of cameo appearances that serve little purpose beyond marquee value. What can one expect from a film in which the dog gives the best performance?

929 **The World's Greatest Athlete** (1973) *** Buena Vista, 92 min. *Dir* Robert Scheerer, *Scr* Dee Caruso, Gerald Gardner, *Cin* Frank Phillips, *Ed* Cotton Warburton, *Art* John B. Mansbridge, Walter Tyler, *Cos* Chuck Keehne, Emily Sundby, *Mus* Marvin Hamlisch, *Prod* Bill Walsh, A Walt Disney Production.

Cast: John Amos, *Coach Archer*, Jan-Michael Vincent, *Nanu*, Tim Conway, *Milo*, Roscoe Lee Browne, *Gazenga*, Dayle Haddon, *Jane*, Nancy Walker, *Landlady*, Billy DeWolfe, *Maxwell*, Danny Goldman, *Leopold*, Howard Cosell, Bud Palmer, Frank Gifford, Jim McKay, *Themselves*, Joe Kapp, *Cosell's Assistant*. G. $12,060,000.

Above-average Disney slapstick comedy. A college athletic coach (John Amos) and his assistant (Tim Conway) discover a jungle boy (Jan-Michael Vincent), while in Africa. Out of desperation, due to a terrible record, they bring him back to their college and turn him into a track star. *The World's Greatest Athlete* nicely satirizes college athletics and has some good sight gags, but it succeeds primarily because of its fine cast of comic performers.

930 **The World's Greatest Lover** (1977) *** 20th Century–Fox, 89 min. *Dir* Gene Wilder, *Scr* Gene Wilder, *Cin* Gerald Hirschfeld, *Ed* Chris Greenbury, Anthony A. Pellegrino, *Des* Terence Marsh, *Art* Steve Sardanis, *Cos* Darryl Athons, Carolina Ewart, Phyllis Garr, Ruth Myers, *Ed* Wynigear, *Mus* John Morris, *Prod* Gene Wilder, *Co-Prod* Terence Marsh.

Cast: Gene Wilder, *Rudy Valentine*, Carol Kane, *Annie*, Dom DeLuise, *Zitz*, Fritz Feld, *Hotel Manager*, Hannah Dean, *Maid*, Candice Azzara, *Anne Calassandro*, Carl Ballantine, *Uncle Harry*, Matt Collins, *Rudolph Valentino*, Lou Cutell, *Mr. Kipper*, James Gleason, *Room Clerk*, Ronny Graham, *Director*, Michael Huddleston, *Barber*, Florence Sundstrom, *Aunt Tillie*. PG. $10,645,000.

Uneven period satire of old Hollywood. A studio mogul devises a contest to find "the world's greatest lover", an actor to compete with Rudolph Valentino. Gene Wilder stars as the unlikely winner of the contest. Wilder mixes the slapstick style he learned from Mel Brooks with the visual style of Federico Fellini in an unusual comedy that works only in parts.

931 **The Wrath of God** (1972) ** MGM, 111 min. *Dir* Ralph Nelson, *Scr* Ralph Nelson, based on novel by James Graham, *Cin* Alex Phillips, Jr., *Ed* Richard Bracken, Terry Williams, Albert Wilson, *Des* John S. Poplin, Jr., *Mus* Lalo Schifrin, *Prod* Ralph Nelson, *Exec Prod* Peter Katz.

Cast: Robert Mitchum, *Van Horne*, Ken Hutchinson, *Emmet*, Victor Buono, *Jennings*, Paula Pritchett, *Chela*, Frank Langella, *De La Plata*, Rita Hayworth, *Senora De La Plata*, John Colicos, *Col. Santilla*, Gregory Sierra, *One-Eyed Rebel*, Enrique Lucero, *Indian Girl's Father*, Jose Luis Paredes, *Little Boy*, Frank Ramirez, *Cantina Operator*, Aurora Clavel, *Cantina Operator's Wife*, Jorge Russek, Victor Eberg, *Santilla's Aides*, Chano Urueta, *Old Man*, Panco Cordove, *Bartender*. PG.

Dismal action western starring Robert Mitchum as a renegade priest, who becomes involved in a Latin-American revolution during the 1920's. Mitchum, along with the help of two mercenaries (Victor Buono, Ken Hutchinson), is to assassinate a reclusive rebel (Frank Langella). *The Wrath of God* defies credibility and tends to be pretentious, despite its tongue-in-cheek treatment.

932 **WUSA** (1970) ** Paramount, 115 min. *Dir* Stuart Rosenberg, *Scr* Robert Stone, based on his novel *A Hall of Mirrors*, *Cin* Richard Moore, *Ed* Bob Wyman, *Art* Philip Jeffries, *Cos* Travilla, *Mus* Lalo Schifrin, *Prod* John Foreman, *Assoc Prod* Hank Moonjean.

Cast: Paul Newman, *Rheinhardt*, Joanne Woodward, *Geraldine*, Anthony Perkins, *Rainey*, Laurence Harvey, *Farley*, Pat Hingle, *Bingamon*, Cloris Leachman, *Philomeane*, Don Gordon, *Bogdanovich*, Michael Anderson, Jr., *Marvin*, Leigh French, *Girl*, Moses Gunn, *Clotho*, Bruce Cabot, *King Wolyoe*, B.J. Mason, *Roosevelt Berry*, Robert Quarry, *Noonan*, Wayne Rogers, *Calvin Minter*, Hal Baylor, *Shorty*, Jim Boles, *Hot Dog Vender*, Diane Ladd, *Barmaid*, Sahdji, *Hollywood*, Skip Young, *Jimmy Snipe*. PG.

Unusual drama about a neo-fascist radio station in the American South that preaches a right-wing takeover in the name of Americanism. Paul Newman stars as a disc jockey, who becomes a pawn for the station's obsessive owner (Pat Hingle). *WUSA* is certainly a film with good intentions, but it not well executed or convincing. The plot is a bit of a mess, and it simply falls apart.

933 **X Y & Zee** (1972) ** Britain, Columbia, 110 min. *Dir* Brian G. Hutton, *Scr* Edna O'Brien, *Cin* Billy Williams, *Ed* Jim Clark, *Art* Peter Mullins, *Cos* Beatrice Dawson, *Mus* Stanley Myers, *Prod* Jay Kanter, Alan Ladd, Jr., *Exec Prod* Elliott Kastner.

Cast: Elizabeth Taylor, *Zee*, Michael Caine, *Robert*, Susannah York, *Stella*, Margaret Leighton, *Gladys*, John Standing, *Gordon*, Mary Larkin, *Rita*, Michael Cashman, *Gavin*, Gino Melvazzi, *Head Waiter*. R.

Dismal menage a trois love story focusing on a married couple (Elizabeth Taylor, Michael Caine) and a woman (Susannah York), who has relations with both. *X Y & Zee* at times resembles an updating of *Who's Afraid of Virginia Woolf?* in its depiction of a bad marriage, but its attempt at the same savage humor simply falls flat, partially due to Taylor's bombastic performance.

934 **The Yakuza** (1975) *** Warner Bros., 112 min. *Dir* Sydney Pollack, *Scr* Paul Schrader, Robert Towne, *Story*, Leonard Schrader, *Cin* Duke Callaghan, Okazaki Kozo, *Ed* Don Guidice, Thomas Stanford, Fredric Steinkamp, *Des* Stephen Grimes, *Cos* Dorothy Jeakins, *Mus* Dave Grusin, *Prod* Sydney Pollack, *Co-Prod* Michael Hamilburg, *Exec Prod* Shundo Koji.

Cast: Robert Mitchum, *Harry Kilmer*, Takakura Ken, *Tanaku Ken*, Brian Keith, *George Tanner*, Herb Edelman, *Wheat*, Richard Jordan, *Dusty*, Kishi Keiko, *Eiko*, Okoda Eiji, *Tono*, James Shigeta, *Goro*, Kyosuke Mashida, *Kato*, Christine Kokubo, *Hanako*, Go Eiji, *Spider*, Lee Chirillo, *Louise*, M. Hisaka, *Boyfriend*, William Ross, *Tanner's Guard*, Akiyama, *Tono's Guard*, Harada, *Goro's Guard*. R.

Odd action adventure about the Japanese underworld, known as the "Yakuza". A group of Japanese hoods kidnaps the daughter of a wealthy American businessman (Brian Keith), who had backed down on a business deal. He hires an old army buddy (Robert Mitchum) to get her back. *The Yakuza* is inconsistent. It tries to be a straight violent action film, and at the same time a glossy Hollywood drama, but unfortunately it is not enough of either.

935 **Yanks** (1979) ** Universal, 141 min. *Dir* John Schlesinger (NB), *Scr* Walter Bernstein, Colin Welland, *Cin* Dick Bush, *Ed* Jim Clark, *Des* Brian Morris, *Art* Milly Burns, *Cos* Shirley Russell (BFA), *Mus* Richard Rodney Bennett, *Chor* Eleanor Fazan, *Prod* Joseph Janni, Lester Persky.

Cast: Richard Gere, *Matt*, Lisa Eichhorn, *Jean*, Vanessa Redgrave, *Helen*, William Devane, *John*, Chick Vennera, *Danny*, Wendy Morgan, *Mollie*, Rachel Roberts (BFA), *Mrs. Moreton*, Tony Melody, *Mr. Moreton*, Martin Smith, *Geoff*, Philip Whileman, *Billy*, Derek Thompson, *Ken*, Simon Harrison, *Tim*. R.

Well-made but dull love story set in England during WWII, involving American soldiers and English women. *Yanks* focuses on three different couples, in particular Richard Gere and Lisa Eichhorn. The re-creation of England during the 1940's is superb, with much attention to details and the attitudes of the people, particularly the conflict between American and English cultures. Unfortunately the storyline is clichéd and uninvolving, and the film is far too long.

936 **You Light Up My Life** (1977) ** Columbia, 90 min. *Dir* Joe Brooks, *Scr* Joe Brooks, *Cin* Eric Saarinen, *Ed* Lynzee Klingman, *Des* Tom Rasmussen, *Cos* Nancy Chadwick, John Patton, *Mus* Joe Brooks, *Song* "You Light Up My Life", *Mus* Joe Brooks (A, G), sung by Kasey Ciszk, *Prod* Joe Brooks, *Assoc Prod* Nick Grippo, Edwin Morgan.

Cast: Didi Conn, *Laurie Robinson*, Joe Silver, *Si Robinson*, Michael Zaslow, *Cris Nolan*, Stephan Nathan, *Ken Rothenberg*, Melanie Mayron, *Annie Gerard*, Amy Letterman, *Laurie as Child*, Marty Zagon, *Nussbaum*, Jerry Keller, *Conductor*, Lisa Reeves, *Carla*, John Gowans, *Charley*, Simmy Bow, *Granek*, Bernice Nicholson, *Mrs. Granek*, Ed Morgan, *Account Executive*, Joe Brooks, *Creative Director*. PG. $8,400,000.

Sentimental film starring Didi Conn as the daughter of an entertainer (Joe Silver), who tries herself to succeed as a professional singer. Very little goes right in her life and the film tries desperately to be a tearjerker, with an obligatory uplifting ending. Unfortunately the film is a bigger mess than her life, filled with clichéd situations and stereotypes. The sappy title song was more responsible for the film's success than the film itself.

937 **Young Frankenstein** (1974) *** 20th Century–Fox, 108 min. *Dir* Mel Brooks, *Scr* Mel Brooks, Gene Wilder (AN), based on characters created by

Mary Shelley, *Cin* Gerald Hirschfeld, *Ed* John Howard, *Des* Dale Hennesy, *Cos* Dorothy Jeakins, *Mus* John Morris, *Prod* Michael Gruskoff.

Cast: Gene Wilder, *Dr. Frankenstein*, Peter Boyle, *Monster*, Marty Feldman, *Igor*, Madeline Kahn, *Elizabeth*, Cloris Leachman, *Frau Blucher*, Teri Garr, *Inga*, Kenneth Mars, *Insp. Kemp*, Richard Haydn, *Herr Falkstein*, Liam Dunn, *Mr. Hilltop*, Gene Hackman, *Blind Man*, Danny Goldman, *Medical Student*, Leon Askin, *Herr Waldman*, Oscar Beregi, *Sadistic Jailer*, Lou Cutell, *Frightened Villager*, Arthur Malet, *Village Elder*, Richard Roth, *Insp. Kemp's Aide*, Monte Landis, Rusty Blitz, *Gravediggers*, Anne Beesley, *Little Girl*. PG. $38,825,000.

Well-made spoof of *Frankenstein*. Gene Wilder stars as the grandson of Baron Victor Frankenstein, who is lured to his grandfather's old castle in Transylvania and successfully continues the experiments. *Young Frankenstein* visually resembles the horror films of the 1930's and contains many plot elements from both *Frankenstein* and *The Bride of Frankenstein*. Mel Brooks made a quantum leap from *Blazing Saddles*, with this film, his most consistently witty comedy.

938 Young Winston (1972) (G-English Language Foreign Film) ****
Britain, Columbia, 145 min. *Dir* Richard Attenborough, *Scr* Carl Foreman (AN), based on the book *My Early Life: A Roving Commission* by Winston Churchill, *Cin* Gerry Turpin, *Ed* Kevin Connor, *Des* Don Ashton, Geoffrey Drake (AN), *Art* John Graysmark, William Hutchinson (AN), *Cos* Anthony Mendleson (AN, BFA), *Mus* Alfred Ralston, *Prod* Carl Foreman, *Assoc Prod* Harold Buck.

Cast: Simon Ward, *Winston*, Peter Cellier, *Captain 35th Sikhs*, Ronald Hines, *Adjutant 35th Sikhs*, Dino Shafeek, *Sikh Soldier*, John Mills, *Gen. Kitchener*, Anne Bancroft, *Lady Randolph Churchill*, Russell Lewis, *Winston at 7*, Pat Heywood, *Mrs. Everest*, Robert Shaw, *Lord Randolph Churchill*, Laurence Naismith, *Lord Salisbury*, William Dexter, *Arthur Balfoar*, Basil Dignam, *Joseph Chamberlain*, Robert Hardy, *Prep School Headmaster*, Edward Burnham, *Labouchere*, John Stuart, *Speaker Peel*, Colin Blakely, *Butcher*, Noel Davis, *Interviewer*, Michael Audreson, *Winston at 13*, Jack Hawkins, *Mr. Weldon*, Ian Holm, *George Buckle*, Richard Leech, *Mr. Moor* Clive Morton, *Mr. Roose*, Robert Flemyng, *Dr. Buzzard*, Reginald Marsh, *Prince of Wales*, Patrick Magee, *Gen. Bindon Blood*, Sir Winston's voice by Simon Ward. PG.

Excellent biography of Winston Churchill, England's great Prime Minister, covering his early years up through age 27. *Young Winston* is an epic adventure, on par with *Lawrence of Arabia*, combining both spectacular battle scenes, of his campaigns in India and Sudan, with more intimate scenes examining all facets of his personality. Simon Ward is excellent in the title role.

939 Zabriskie Point (1970) ** 112 min. *Dir* Michelangelo Antonioni, *Scr* Michelangelo Antonioni, Fred Gardner, Tonino Guerra, Clare Peploe, Sam Shepard, *Story* Michelangelo Antonioni, *Cin* Alfio Contini, *Ed* Franco Arcalli, *Des* Dean Tavoularis, *Cos* Ray Summers, *Prod* Carlo Ponti, *Exec Prod* Harrison Starr.

Cast: Mark Frechette, *Mark*, Daria Halprin, *David*, Paul Fix, *Cafe Owner*,

G.D. Spradlin, *Lee Allen's Associate*, Bill Garaway, *Morty*, Kathleen Cleaver, *Kathleen*, Rod Taylor, *Lee Allen*, Open Theatre of Joe Chaikin. R.

Disappointing first American film from Italian cinematic genius Michelangelo Antonioni. A young college radical on the run from the police steals an airplane, with which he buzzes a lone car driven by a secretary on her way to her boss' desert home. He runs out of gas, and she gives him a ride, which leads to a brief interlude. The plot is skimpy, but Antonioni can generally do more with less. *Zabriskie Point* has many of Antonioni's characteristics, an examination of the anguish of the characters with a heavy emphasis on their environment, but the film is uninspired and resembles most of the other anti-establishment films of the time.

940 **Zachariah** (1971) ** Cinerama Releasing Corporation, 92 min. *Dir* George Englund, *Scr* Joe Massot, The Firesign Theatre (Philip Austin, Peter Bergman, David Ossman, Philip Proctor), *Cin* Jorge Shahl, *Ed* Gary Griffen, *Des* Assheton Gorton, *Cos* Nino Novarese, *Mus* Jimmie Haskell, *Songs* Joe McDonald, Barry Melton, The James Gang, Doug Kershaw, White Lightnin', *Prod* George Englund, *Co-Prod* Lawrence Kubik.

Cast: John Rubinstein, *Zachariah*, Pat Quinn, *Belle Starr*, Don Johnson, *Matthew*, Country Joe and The Fish, *The Cracker Band*, Elvin Jones, *Job Cain*, Doug Kershaw, *The Fiddler*, William Challee, *The Old Man*, Robert Ball, *Stage Manager*, Dick Van Patten, *The Dude*, The James Gang, *Job Cain's Band*, White Lightnin', *Old Man's Band*, The New York Rock Ensemble, *Belle Starr's Band*. PG.

Strange western rock musical that bills itself as the "first electric western". It was first only because other filmmakers had the sense to completely avoid this ridiculous idea. *Zachariah* is essentially a dull morality play with religious overtones, set to rock music, and with all the warmth and humanity of a spaghetti western. The satirical comedy troupe, The Firesign Theatre, originated the idea, but they disowned the film after it was rewritten.

941 **Zandy's Bride** (1974) *** Warner Bros., 116 min. *Dir* Jan Troell, *Scr* Marc Norman, based on novel *The Stranger* by Lillian Bos Ross, *Cin* Jordan Cronenweth, *Ed* Gordon Scott, *Des* Al Brenner, *Cos* Patricia Norris, *Mus* Fred Karlin, *Prod* Harvey Matofsky.

Cast: Gene Hackman, *Zandy Allan*, Liv Ullman, *Hannah Lund*, Eileen Heckart, *Ma Allan*, Harry Dean Stanton, *Songer*, Joe Santos, *Frank Gallo*, Frank Cady, *Pa Allan*, Sam Bottoms, *Mel Allan*, Susan Tyrrell, *Maria Cordova*, Bob Simpson, *Bill Pincus*, Fabian Gregory Cordova, *Paco*, Don Wilbanks, *Farraday*, Vivian Gordon, *Street Girl*. PG.

Unusual western drama about a California rancher (Gene Hackman) and his mail-order bride (Liv Ullman). Their marriage begins shakily, because he treats her literally as a slave and she fights back, but predictably things work out. *Zandy's Bride* is an interesting portrait of the hardships of a frontier marriage and Hackman and Ullman are excellent. The film is visually impressive, but it falls short of being an American version of *The Emigrants*.

942 **Zardoz** (1974) **** Britain, 20th Century–Fox, 104 min. *Dir* John Boorman, *Scr* John Boorman, *Cin* Geoffrey Unsworth, *Ed* John Merritt, *Des* Anthony Pratt, *Cos* Christel Kruse Boorman, *Mus* David Munrow, *Prod* John Boorman, *Assoc Prod* Charles Orme.

Cast: Sean Connery, *Zed*, Charlotte Rampling, *Consuella*, Sara Kestelman, *May*, John Alderton, *Friend*, Sally Ann Newton, *Avalow*, Niall Buggy, *Zardoz/Arthur*, Bosco Hogan, *George*, Jessica Swift, *Apathetic*, Bairbre Dowling, *Star*, Christopher Casson, *Scientist*, Reginald Jarman, *Death*. R.

Outlandish science-fiction thriller that nearly defies description. Sean Connery portrays a barbarian who infiltrates a society of people known as the Eternals by becoming a stowaway inside a giant floating stone head. From this point on *Zardoz* becomes weird. This film, one of John Boorman's finest achievements, was almost unanimously hated upon release, but has since developed a strong cult following.

Name Index

Citations are to serial numbers of entries. Names beginning with de, d', la, von, etc., have generally been alphabetized under these particles.

D

H

Index

Index

O

S

Y